Communications in Computer and Information Science 850

More information about this series at http://www.springer.com/series/7899

Constantine Stephanidis (Ed.)

HCI International 2018 – Posters' Extended Abstracts

20th International Conference, HCI International 2018
Las Vegas, NV, USA, July 15–20, 2018
Proceedings, Part I

Editor
Constantine Stephanidis
University of Crete
and Foundation for Research
and Technology – Hellas (FORTH)
Heraklion, Crete
Greece

ISSN 1865-0929 ISSN 1865-0937 (electronic)
Communications in Computer and Information Science
ISBN 978-3-319-92269-0 ISBN 978-3-319-92270-6 (eBook)
https://doi.org/10.1007/978-3-319-92270-6

Library of Congress Control Number: 2018944385

Printed on acid-free paper

This Springer imprint is published by the registered company Springer International Publishing AG
part of Springer Nature
The registered company address is: Gewerbestrasse 11, 6330 Cham, Switzerland

Foreword

The 20th International Conference on Human-Computer Interaction, HCI International 2018, was held in Las Vegas, NV, USA, during July 15–20, 2018. The event incorporated the 14 conferences/thematic areas listed on the following page.

A total of 4,373 individuals from academia, research institutes, industry, and governmental agencies from 76 countries submitted contributions, and 1,170 papers and 195 posters have been included in the proceedings. These contributions address the latest research and development efforts and highlight the human aspects of design and use of computing systems. The contributions thoroughly cover the entire field of human-computer interaction, addressing major advances in knowledge and effective use of computers in a variety of application areas. The volumes constituting the full set of the conference proceedings are listed in the following pages.

I would like to thank the program board chairs and the members of the program boards of all thematic areas and affiliated conferences for their contribution to the highest scientific quality and the overall success of the HCI International 2018 conference.

This conference would not have been possible without the continuous and unwavering support and advice of the founder, Conference General Chair Emeritus and Conference Scientific Advisor Prof. Gavriel Salvendy. For his outstanding efforts, I would like to express my appreciation to the communications chair and editor of *HCI International News*, Dr. Abbas Moallem.

July 2018 Constantine Stephanidis

HCI International 2018 Thematic Areas and Affiliated Conferences

Thematic areas:

- Human-Computer Interaction (HCI 2018)
- Human Interface and the Management of Information (HIMI 2018)

Affiliated conferences:

- 15th International Conference on Engineering Psychology and Cognitive Ergonomics (EPCE 2018)
- 12th International Conference on Universal Access in Human-Computer Interaction (UAHCI 2018)
- 10th International Conference on Virtual, Augmented, and Mixed Reality (VAMR 2018)
- 10th International Conference on Cross-Cultural Design (CCD 2018)
- 10th International Conference on Social Computing and Social Media (SCSM 2018)
- 12th International Conference on Augmented Cognition (AC 2018)
- 9th International Conference on Digital Human Modeling and Applications in Health, Safety, Ergonomics, and Risk Management (DHM 2018)
- 7th International Conference on Design, User Experience, and Usability (DUXU 2018)
- 6th International Conference on Distributed, Ambient, and Pervasive Interactions (DAPI 2018)
- 5th International Conference on HCI in Business, Government, and Organizations (HCIBGO)
- 5th International Conference on Learning and Collaboration Technologies (LCT 2018)
- 4th International Conference on Human Aspects of IT for the Aged Population (ITAP 2018)

Conference Proceedings Volumes Full List

1. LNCS 10901, Human-Computer Interaction: Theories, Methods, and Human Issues (Part I), edited by Masaaki Kurosu
2. LNCS 10902, Human-Computer Interaction: Interaction in Context (Part II), edited by Masaaki Kurosu
3. LNCS 10903, Human-Computer Interaction: Interaction Technologies (Part III), edited by Masaaki Kurosu
4. LNCS 10904, Human Interface and the Management of Information: Interaction, Visualization, and Analytics (Part I), edited by Sakae Yamamoto and Hirohiko Mori
5. LNCS 10905, Human Interface and the Management of Information: Information in Applications and Services (Part II), edited by Sakae Yamamoto and Hirohiko Mori
6. LNAI 10906, Engineering Psychology and Cognitive Ergonomics, edited by Don Harris
7. LNCS 10907, Universal Access in Human-Computer Interaction: Methods, Technologies, and Users (Part I), edited by Margherita Antona and Constantine Stephanidis
8. LNCS 10908, Universal Access in Human-Computer Interaction: Virtual, Augmented, and Intelligent Environments (Part II), edited by Margherita Antona and Constantine Stephanidis
9. LNCS 10909, Virtual, Augmented and Mixed Reality: Interaction, Navigation, Visualization, Embodiment, and Simulation (Part I), edited by Jessie Y. C. Chen and Gino Fragomeni
10. LNCS 10910, Virtual, Augmented and Mixed Reality: Applications in Health, Cultural Heritage, and Industry (Part II), edited by Jessie Y. C. Chen and Gino Fragomeni
11. LNCS 10911, Cross-Cultural Design: Methods, Tools, and Users (Part I), edited by Pei-Luen Patrick Rau
12. LNCS 10912, Cross-Cultural Design: Applications in Cultural Heritage, Creativity, and Social Development (Part II), edited by Pei-Luen Patrick Rau
13. LNCS 10913, Social Computing and Social Media: User Experience and Behavior (Part I), edited by Gabriele Meiselwitz
14. LNCS 10914, Social Computing and Social Media: Technologies and Analytics (Part II), edited by Gabriele Meiselwitz
15. LNAI 10915, Augmented Cognition: Intelligent Technologies (Part I), edited by Dylan D. Schmorrow and Cali M. Fidopiastis
16. LNAI 10916, Augmented Cognition: Users and Contexts (Part II), edited by Dylan D. Schmorrow and Cali M. Fidopiastis
17. LNCS 10917, Digital Human Modeling and Applications in Health, Safety, Ergonomics, and Risk Management, edited by Vincent G. Duffy
18. LNCS 10918, Design, User Experience, and Usability: Theory and Practice (Part I), edited by Aaron Marcus and Wentao Wang

19. LNCS 10919, Design, User Experience, and Usability: Designing Interactions (Part II), edited by Aaron Marcus and Wentao Wang
20. LNCS 10920, Design, User Experience, and Usability: Users, Contexts, and Case Studies (Part III), edited by Aaron Marcus and Wentao Wang
21. LNCS 10921, Distributed, Ambient, and Pervasive Interactions: Understanding Humans (Part I), edited by Norbert Streitz and Shin'ichi Konomi
22. LNCS 10922, Distributed, Ambient, and Pervasive Interactions: Technologies and Contexts (Part II), edited by Norbert Streitz and Shin'ichi Konomi
23. LNCS 10923, HCI in Business, Government, and Organizations, edited by Fiona Fui-Hoon Nah and Bo Sophia Xiao
24. LNCS 10924, Learning and Collaboration Technologies: Design, Development and Technological Innovation (Part I), edited by Panayiotis Zaphiris and Andri Ioannou
25. LNCS 10925, Learning and Collaboration Technologies: Learning and Teaching (Part II), edited by Panayiotis Zaphiris and Andri Ioannou
26. LNCS 10926, Human Aspects of IT for the Aged Population: Acceptance, Communication, and Participation (Part I), edited by Jia Zhou and Gavriel Salvendy
27. LNCS 10927, Human Aspects of IT for the Aged Population: Applications in Health, Assistance, and Entertainment (Part II), edited by Jia Zhou and Gavriel Salvendy
28. CCIS 850, HCI International 2018 Posters Extended Abstracts (Part I), edited by Constantine Stephanidis
29. CCIS 851, HCI International 2018 Posters Extended Abstracts (Part II), edited by Constantine Stephanidis
30. CCIS 852, HCI International 2018 Posters Extended Abstracts (Part III), edited by Constantine Stephanidis

http://2018.hci.international/proceedings

HCI International 2018 Conference

The full list with the Program Board Chairs and the members of the Program Boards of all thematic areas and affiliated conferences is available online at:

http://www.hci.international/board-members-2018.php

HCI International 2019

The 21st International Conference on Human-Computer Interaction, HCI International 2019, will be held jointly with the affiliated conferences in Orlando, FL, USA, at Walt Disney World Swan and Dolphin Resort, July 26–31, 2019. It will cover a broad spectrum of themes related to Human-Computer Interaction, including theoretical issues, methods, tools, processes, and case studies in HCI design, as well as novel interaction techniques, interfaces, and applications. The proceedings will be published by Springer. More information will be available on the conference website: http://2019.hci.international/.

General Chair
Prof. Constantine Stephanidis
University of Crete and ICS-FORTH
Heraklion, Crete, Greece
E-mail: general_chair@hcii2019.org

http://2019.hci.international/

Contents – Part I

Interaction and Information

Images and Visualizations

Design, Usability and User Experience

Psychological, Cognitive and Neurocognitive Issues in HCI

Social Media and Analytics

Contents – Part II

Contents – Part III

Learning and Interaction

Interacting with Cultural Heritage

HCI in Commerce and Business

Smart Cities and Smart Environments

Interaction and Information

Post-correction of OCR Errors Using PyEnchant Spelling Suggestions Selected Through a Modified Needleman–Wunsch Algorithm

Ewerton Cappelatti(✉), Regina De Oliveira Heidrich, Ricardo Oliveira, Cintia Monticelli, Ronaldo Rodrigues, Rodrigo Goulart, and Eduardo Velho

Feevale University, RS 239, 2755, Novo Hamburgo, RS, Brazil
ewertonac@feevale.br

Abstract. In this article, the efforts made by the Vocalizer project development team to correct errors from texts generated by OCR Tesseract are described. Vocalizer consists of a device that captures images from books, converts them into plain texts with the aid of an OCR (Optical Character Recognition) software. It also prepares the post-processing of the obtained text, and converts its textual content into voice. The whole process is performed autonomously. In the post-processing step, a modified Needleman-Wunsch algorithm was applied to select the suggestions made by the spellchecker PyEnchant. The results obtained were reasonable, which encourages further research.

Keywords: Optical character recognition software · Error correction
Character recognition

1 Introduction

Brazilian government made great efforts aiming at the inclusion of people with visual impairment in the Educational System. Since 2012, Brazilian government invested in voice scanners, which resulted in high costs, and did not fully satisfy the national requirements.

Hence, Brazilian government launched a public call for voice scanner projects that meet the national requirements. Feevale University (Novo Hamburgo city, Brazil) and Pináculo company (Taquara city, Brazil) participated and won the public bid for the development of a project called Vocalizer.

Vocalizer project aims to develop a device that provides autonomy for visually impaired people. The project proposal includes an equipment for capturing and the transforming images into a plain text using the Tesseract OCR software [1], a post-processing step, which handles errors, and a final step of speech synthesis, which uses a vocalization software. One of the goals which guide the development of the device is that must be economically affordable.

This article describes the post-processing module and the strategy used to correct common errors from the output of Tesseract OCR. The adopted error handling strategy

C. Stephanidis (Ed.): HCII Posters 2018, CCIS 850, pp. 3–10, 2018.
https://doi.org/10.1007/978-3-319-92270-6_1

uses a generic spell check library called PyEnchant [2]. This library provides a list of words as suggestions for misspellings, which combined with an algorithm selects the best word. This algorithm uses a heuristic selection based on the algorithm Needleman-Wunsch [3], which was adapted to consider the most frequent errors generated by the OCR. This article describes, also, technical difficulties encountered during the correction of errors, as well as the solutions adopted to reduce the error rate during the process of obtaining the plain text used as source for the vocalization software.

2 Related Work

Volk et al. [4] used a set of regular expressions which constituted substitution patterns. These expressions are constructed based on the analysis of an extensive corpus of literature. These standards are used under certain conditions to minimize false positives. This approach classifies substitutions into three categories: the first is if the substitution frequency is at least twice as high as the misspelled word in the corpus, then substitution can be made; the second considers the options gathered for the substitution in the corpus, hence the one with the highest frequency is chosen; and the third category is the unconditional substitution.

Kissos and Dershowitz [5] used a module designed to generate correction suggestions based on the modified Levenshtein distance, in which other primitive editing operations (merging and division of characters), also known as alignments of 2:1 and 1:2, are used. Such method inserts in the list of suggestions situations in which exchanges such as 'ln' for 'h', and 'm' for 'nn' occur.

Tong and Evans [6] used a bigram technique in statistical language models. The system gets information from multiple sources including letter n-grams, character confusion probabilities, and word bigram probabilities. Words with 4 or fewer letters are also indexed by their letter bigrams. For example, "that" produces the following bigrams {#th, tha, hat, at #, th, ha, t #}.

Nylander [7] used statistics to find unanticipated frequent trigrams and phonotactical rules. The author did not use lexicons. She aimed at identifying errors and not fixing them for later proofreading.

Bassil and Alwani [8] proposed the use of a post-processing context-based error correction algorithm for detecting and correcting OCR non-word and real-word errors. This algorithm was based on Google online spelling suggestions.

3 General Description

One of the project steps is the use of an OCR software to transform the images obtained by the image capturing equipment into plain texts. Tesseract is the OCR software adopted for this project. This is an open-source optical character recognition software under the Apache 2.0 License. There are many challenges to using OCR software for reading book pages. Thick and multi-page books can generate reading errors, in addition, different types of lighting can make it difficult to recognize certain regions of pages as well. Due to these factors, Tesseract cannot have 100% character recognition accuracy.

One of the recognition problems is the occasional swap between two letters, such as 'a' recognized as 'o', 'f' recognized as 't', 'c' recognized as 'e', and so on. Other errors involve replacing a group of letters with a single letter or replacing one group of letters with another group of letters. This can be exemplified by the swapping of 'r' and 'n' by 'm', 'f' and 'i' by 'h', 'm' and 'l' by 'n' and 'd'. Other recognition problems result in a diverse range of different characters. In these cases, recovery is very difficult or impossible.

The first effort to post-correct the OCR errors was to develop a simple routine which uses the PyEnchant spell checking software method. Such method provides a list of suggested words to repair a specific misspelling. However, two problems were found with this approach. Primarily, the first word suggestion is not usually correct, but in another position of the suggested words list. Thus, choosing the first word from the list has become out of question. Secondly, in others cases, the suggested words list did not even contain the correct word. Considering this, any word choice would be wrong. Therefore, two others problems had to be addressed: (1) identify which words in the list is most appropriate to replace the word mistakenly recognized by the OCR and (2) increase the chances of the correct word being present in the suggestions list.

3.1 Selecting the Best Word from the OCR Tesseract List of Suggestions

Each word recognized by the Tesseract OCR application was submitted to PyEnchant spell checking software. For each word that resulted in an error code by the software, a suggestion list was formed by the *suggest()* method of the checker object. Then it was necessary to choose which word from the list was the closest to the word identified as wrong by PyEnchant. Table 1 shows examples of lists suggested by PyEnchant for words identified as errors.

Table 1. Examples of word lists suggested by PyEnchant.

Wrong word	Correct word	List of suggested words
Deseubra	Descubra	'desabra', **'descubra'**, 'dessaibra', ...
Lmpõe	Impõe	'lampie', 'limpe', 'limpo', 'lumpo', 'limpou', 'limpei', 'empoe', **'impõe'**, ...

In order to establish the distance between each word in the list and the word with errors, the first hypothesis is the use of Levenshtein algorithm to calculate distances [9]. This algorithm defines 'distance' as the minimum number of unit operations required to transform one string into another. However, due to the high substitution frequency, such as 'c' by 'e' when compared to others such as 'c' by ':', and the high substitution frequency between groups of letters by a single letter, such as 'r' and 'n' by 'm', in addition to substituting groups of letters by other groups of letters, this algorithm was discarded.

The second hypothesis is Needleman-Wunsch algorithm [3]. It has weights for positive and negative identifications, as well as for gaps. Nevertheless, the algorithm had to be modified to accommodate different substitution probabilities, and to consider substituting groups of letters for one letter or groups of letters for other groups of letters. The issue of the substitution of letters groups had already been identified by Volk et al. [4]. A different approach which uses substitution patterns elaborated using regular expressions, was adopted by them.

The Needleman-Wunsch global alignment algorithm constructs a matrix of E scores using the dynamic programming technique for two sequences A and B. As the algorithm advances, the score matrix is filled with the optimal alignment score between the m first characters of A, and the n first of B. This score is determined as the largest value among the threefold calculated values: $E[i-1, j] + g$, $E[i-1, j-1] + p(i, j)$, and $E[i, j-1] + g$, where g is the punctuation for the insertion of a gap, and $p(i, j)$ is a function that returns a value, if the letters match, and a different value, if they mismatch [10]. A table of typical scores for the Needleman-Wunsch global alignment algorithm can be seen in Fig. 1.

match:	2
mismatch:	-2
gap:	-1

Fig. 1. Typical score table used in the Needleman-Wunsch algorithm

Thus, the alignment scores were elaborated considering the substitutions made, and taking into account the occurrence and frequency of the letter sets identified in the corpus analysis. Firstly, previous statistics of the most common substitutions were found. In order to do this, a set of pages from books was typed, so text files could be compared with the text returned by the OCR. A Python script for text comparison returned the words which differed from where the most common substitutions were extracted. The substitutions frequency determined the score value used in the algorithm. In addition, common substitutions among groups of letters were identified, and formed a scoring basis for these groups. Figure 2 shows an excerpt from the scoring table using the modified algorithm.

match (default)	128
mismatch (default)	-128
gap penalty	-64
mismatch (a, á)	48
....	
mismatch (b, l>)	31
...	
mismatch (d, cl)	54
...	
mismatch (fo, lb)	40
...	

Fig. 2. Scores used in the modified algorithm.

The alignment algorithm was modified to consider not only one letter but also 2-letter sequences in its score. As the algorithm advances the score matrix gets filled. It takes into account the current character, but in some cases the subsequent character as well. As in the original algorithm, once the scoring matrix is obtained, one moves from the lower right position towards the upper left position, inserting gaps when necessary. The score is obtained in accordance with three possible cases:

(1) if there is a match, the score for it is added to the total score of the alignment;
(2) if there is a gap, the score for it is added, however, if there are more than two gaps in a row, the scores from the second gap are considerably higher;
(3) if there is a match between a letter and a group of letters or a group of letters and another group of letters, the score is obtained from a scoring table, according to the occurrence frequency established for those letters.

The score for the word from the spell-checker suggestions list is then determined. The word with the highest score in the list is the one which will be chosen for the substitution.

For example, by applying the alignment in the word *'dinasua'* the following list is obtained:

[dina sua, dina-sua, dinas, Danúsa, dinasta, dinastia, dianas, dionas, donas, duinas, dunas, dionísia, donosa, násua, Dinís, danas, densa, densa-a, dinamia, dines, dinos, Dinísio, dônias, danesa, danosa, densai-a, diénias, duanas, Diana, danais, densai, diana, danasse, densou-a, dincas, dindas, dingas, disnas, diapausa, dinda-a, NASA, Nasa, densou, dienos, diense, dina, diniés, disa, difusa, rinusa, danasse-a, dinastas, disna, dissana, dana-as, dana-se, dassa, densada, densara, densava, dense-a, denso-a, diesa, diesa-a, diosa, disué, nassa, densa-o, dindou-a, danou-as, dana-a, dana-os, diesai-a, dindasse-a, danou-a, diesou-a, dinda-se, dane-as, dano-as]

In this case, word *'dinastia'* got the highest score and the correction is successful. However, this is not always the case. Sometimes the word poorly recognized by OCR also exists in Portuguese, hence the algorithm does not detect the need for correction. There are also cases in which a Portuguese word is more similar to the wrong one than the word in the original text. For instance, the word *'gorros'* recognized by the OCR as *'gurros'* achieves higher scoring in the element *'guarros'* of the list. This is because a gap scores less negatively than a mismatch.

3.2 Improving the List of Suggestions by PyEnchant

In some situations, the list of suggestions does not have the correct word. This is due to some reasons: the modified word recognized by Tesseract, or the initial letters word change, makes PyEnchant SpellChecker provides a set of suggestions far from the desired word. In order to solve this issue, a heuristic routine was implemented. First, it identifies sets of letters that can be unambiguously replaced by other word set from Tesseract identification. Then, the word identified by the modified Tesseract is submitted once more to PyEnchant, which results in a second list of suggestions. The first list of suggestions is then concatenated with the second and submitted to the modified Needleman-Wunsch algorithm. The highest scoring word is then chosen. Experiments performed revealed significant improvement in the OCR error correction rate. Figure 3 shows the Vocalizer post-processing steps.

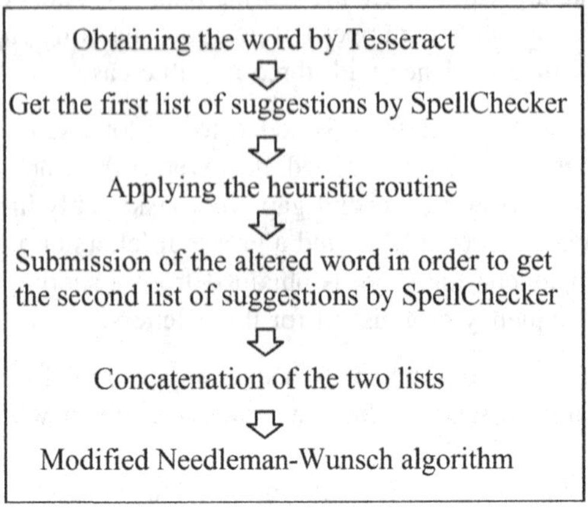

Obtaining the word by Tesseract
⇩
Get the first list of suggestions by SpellChecker
⇩
Applying the heuristic routine
⇩
Submission of the altered word in order to get the second list of suggestions by SpellChecker
⇩
Concatenation of the two lists
⇩
Modified Needleman-Wunsch algorithm

Fig. 3. Post-processing steps

The heuristic routine contains an identified set of likely modifications. These are usually at the beginning or at the end of the words and are performed to obtain a second list of the spelling checker. Examples of likely substitutions are 'gcnc' by 'gene' at the beginning of words, and 'enlo' by 'ento' at the end of words.

An example which illustrates the heuristic routine can be seen as follow. The word erroneously identified by OCR was 'Cncurrcgada'. The correct word should be '*encarregada*'. When submitted to the PyEnchant spellchecker the return is the following:

[Cancricida, Cancrocida, Cancericida, Concrecionada]

The correct word is not in the list and the reason is that both the beginning and the end of the word are incorrect. The heuristic routine changes *'rcgada'* by *'regada'* by supplying the spell-checker with a new word: *'Cncurregada'*. This resulted in a second list provided by PyEnchant:

[encarregada, encarregadão, encarregado, concretada, concurvada, encarregadas, encargada, encarregado-a, encarregadura, encarregar, encarrega-a, encarregara, encarregava, encorrugida, encarregai-a, encarregado-o]

The lists are concatenated, and the following list is obtained:

[encarregada, encarregadão, encarregado, concretada, concurvada, encarregadas, encargada, encarregado-a, encarregadura, encarregar, encarrega-a, encarregara, encarregava, encorrugida, encarregai-a, encarregado-o, Cancricida, Cancrocida, Cancericida, Concrecionada]

Once processed by the algorithm, it returns the word *'encarregada'*. In some cases, success is not achieved because words more similar syntactically may punctuate more, and its depends on how bad the word identified by OCR is damaged.

4 Results

Seven books were scanned, resulting in an initial set for testing algorithm. For each book a set of 20 pages was correctly typed so amount of errors could be evaluated. An evaluation of the text obtained by OCR was made comparing with the original text generating the number of different characters found. From these differences, the estimated difference was between 1.085% and 2.679% for texts in Portuguese and 4.77% for text with words in a foreign language.

Regarding the study, words separated by spaces or attached to each other were not considered because they were not treated by the algorithm. In addition, words which were so damaged that no recovery effort would be possible, such as '|:`lânicos' when the correct word would be 'britânicos', were not treated. Further evolution of the algorithm should be considered for these cases. Some tests results are shown in Table 2.

Table 2. Percentage of success in applying the algorithm.

Number of letters with error	Example Wrong word/correct word	Percentage of success
1	"deseubra'/'descubra'	48.96%
2	'dinasua'/'dinastia'	31.18%
3	'Cncurrcgada'/'Encarregada'	11.32%
>3	'biblioteca'/'biblimcca'	8.81%

If words considered extremely damaged were taken into account, the success percentages would decrease. Nevertheless, this issue must be addressed in a better reading and illumination images capturing. During the project, the reading improved considerably, nearly eliminating these situations.

5 Conclusions

Results obtained were reasonable, especially after inclusion of the heuristic routine in the algorithm to repair the words before a second submission to the spell checker. Considering the errors caused by the OCR were less than 3% for Brazilian literature texts, and 4.77% for texts with words in another language, the algorithm was capable of providing a text which was possible to be understood reasonably by visually impaired people. Further studies should be carried out aiming the treatment of words broken between spaces and words attached to others. The corpus used to create the substitution base should be expanded as more books are scanned and handled with the OCR tool.

References

1. Smith, R.: An overview of the Tesseract OCR engine. In: Proceedings of the Ninth International Conference on Document Analysis and Recognition, ICDAR 2007, vol. 2, pp. 629–633 (2007)
2. Ryan, K.: PyEnchant: a spellchecking library for Python. http://pythonhosted.org/pyenchant/faq.html. Accessed 05 Oct 2017
3. Needleman, S.B., Wunsch, C.D.: A general method applicable to the search for similarities in the amino acid sequence of two proteins. J. Mol. Biol. **48**(3), 443–453 (1970)
4. Volk, M., Furrer, L., Sennrich, R.: Strategies for reducing and correcting OCR error. In: Sporleder, C., van den Bosch, A., Zervanou, K. (eds.) Language Technology for Cultural Heritage, pp. 3–22. Springer, Berlin (2011). https://doi.org/10.1007/978-3-642-20227-8_1
5. Kissos, I., Dershowitz, N.: OCR error correction using character correction and feature-based word classification. In: Proceedings of the 12th IAPR Workshop on Document Analysis Systems, pp. 198–203 (2016)
6. Tong, X., Evans, D.A.: A statistical approach to automatic OCR error correction in context. In: Proceedings of the Fourth Workshop on Very Large Corpora, pp. 88–100 (1996)
7. Nylander, S.: Statistics and phonotactical rules in finding OCR errors. In: Proceedings of the NODALIDA, pp. 174–181 (1999)
8. Bassil, Y., Alwani, M.: OCR post-processing error correction algorithm using Google's online spelling suggestion. J. Emerg. Trends Comput. Inf. Sci. **3**(1), 90–99 (2012)
9. Levenshtein, V.I.: Binary codes capable of correcting deletions, insertions, and reversals. Sov. Phys. Dokl. **10**(8), 707–710 (1966)
10. Setúbal, J., Meidanis, J.: Introduction to Computational Molecular Biology. PWS Publishing Company, Boston (1997)

Whale Tracking: Software System for the Acquisition, Management and Processing of Data on the Blue Whale at Offshore

Blanca E. Carvajal-Gámez[1], Diane Gendron[2], and Manuel Alejandro Díaz-Casco[1](✉)

[1] Instituto Politécnico Nacional, Escuela Superior de Cómputo, Ciudad de México, Mexico
becarvajal@ipn.mx, maldiazc@gmail.com
[2] Instituto Politécnico Nacional, Centro Interdisciplinario de Ciencias Marinas, Baja California Sur, Mexico
dianegendroncicimar@gmail.com

Abstract. The acquisition of information in the field is one of the main activities in any type of research, advances in Information and Communication Technologies (ICTs) have allowed the development of hardware and software tools that researchers to acquire information from a more efficient and effective way; however, there are still situations in which it is not possible to apply these tools because they are not compatible with using them in the conditions of the environment or that do not adapt to the specific needs of users. In animal monitoring these difficulties are continually presented, this is due to the fact that this type of research is carried out in environments where the use of technologies is limited. In this paper we present a system to aid in the acquisition, management and processing of data in the field, in particular, the case of Blue Whale research is presented. Research on this species is conducted in the Gulf of Cortés, Mexico, under conditions where is not possible to use commercial technologies of data acquisition and processing. The proposed system allows researchers to acquire the necessary information from the Blue Whale during the monitoring process. It also offers the option to generate automated reports of the sightings done without needing to require another type of computing device or re-capture the information in another system.

Keywords: Animal monitoring · Process automation · Adaptability

1 Introduction

The acquisition of data in the field is one of the most important activities in any type of research; however, currently carrying out this procedure represents several difficulties because there are not adaptive technological tools that satisficed the specific needs of users and can be used in any type of environment [1, 2]. This paper presents the development and implementation of a system for the acquisition, management and processing of data in the field. The particular case that is addressed is the Blue Whale (*Balaenoptera musculus*) tracking at the coast of Baja California Sur, Mexico [3, 4].

C. Stephanidis (Ed.): HCII Posters 2018, CCIS 850, pp. 11–17, 2018.
https://doi.org/10.1007/978-3-319-92270-6_2

At present this species is in danger of extinction, so it is vital to acquire information on their behavior, migratory routes, food and health status, to identify possible threats and the factors that cause them. In order to obtain an optimum result it is necessary to capture the largest possible amount of information in the field accurately and as soon as possible [5].

This paper is structured as follows, in Sect. 2 describe the Blue Whale tracking process and the currently limitations, in Sect. 3 define the system proposal for the management of the information acquired in field, in Sect. 4 present the tests and the discussion of results obtained, and finally in Sect. 5 present the conclusions of the research and future work to be done.

2 Blue Whale Tracking

The lack of technological tools that can be used during the Blue Whale tracking forces the researchers to use methods of acquire information developed by them. In most cases tabular sheets are used where information is recorded manually as can be seen in Fig. 1, in other cases, improvised systems are developed that allow them to capture the information digitally, as shown in Fig. 2; however, in this type of systems once the data have been recorded there is no possibility to edit them, which forces the researcher to repeat the whole record in case of making a mistake; also may present inconsistencies in the communication between the devices, which prevents the record of new information, when this happens is necessary restart the computer and the system to proceed with the data capture. At present, for any of the cases, whether manual or electronic, data acquisition in the field represents a laborious and time-consuming task for the user, causing delays and setbacks in the development of the researches.

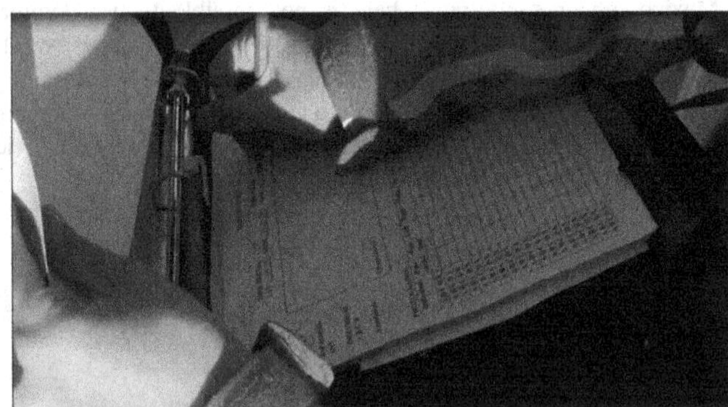

Fig. 1. Tabular sheet used to record information during Blue Whale tracking

Due to these difficulties, it was made an analysis of the acquire information process during Blue Whale tracking, in which the specific needs of the research, the profile of the users and the failures of the current electronic systems were considered. Thanks to this, it was possible to define the necessary requirements to develop a system that

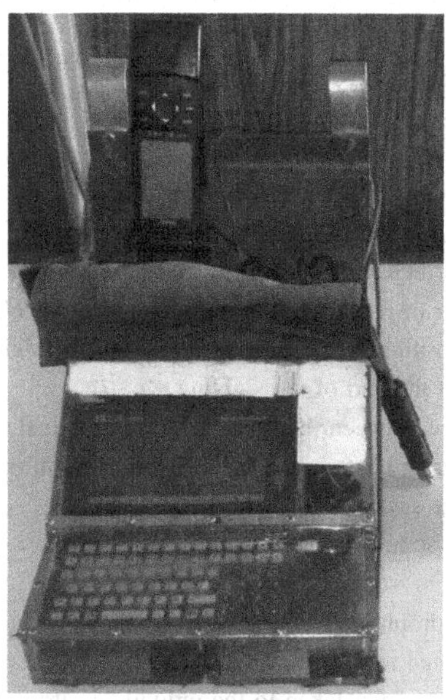

Fig. 2. System developed by researchers to acquire information during Blue Whale tracking

allows to acquire, manage and process the data in the field, and can be used in any type of environment with different computer equipment. As part of the requirements obtained were defined the functions that must be done by the system during the monitoring and the data necessary to perform an optimum analysis of the species. Table 1 presents the information that researchers need to record during the sighting of an individual.

Also, a protocol was established that must be done by the system during Blue Whale tracking. This establishes that when selecting the individual to observe should define the type to which it belongs, this could be "alone" or "mother and child", then must be assigned an alphanumeric identifier according to the type of the individual, after could be done the capture of the sightings. Each sighting begins when the individual emerges to the surface and ends when submerged, while the individual is on the surface are captured their descriptive data, and the geographical position and time of when a sighting begins and ends. The rest of the data can be captured during or after the sighting.

Table 1. Information needed to capture during a sighting

Information	Description
Initial position	GPS position of the boat at the start of the sighting
Initial time	Time at the start of the sighting
Initial distance	Distance between the boat and the individual at the start of the sighting
First breath	When the sighting was carried out, there was visual confirmation of the first breath of the individual

(*continued*)

Table 1. (*continued*)

Information	Description
Number of breaths	Number of breaths made by the individual during the sighting
Tail	At the time the sighting was performed, visual confirmation of the individual's tail out of the water
Superficial diving	During the sighting the individual performed surface diving
Behavior	Type of behavior performed by the individual
Count of specimens	Number of individuals in the vicinity of the observed individual
Final position	GPS position of the boat at the end of the sighting
Final time	Time at the end of the sighting
Final distance	Distance between the boat and the individual at the end of the sighting
Count of pangas	Number of boats in the vicinity when sighting
Pangas speed	Average speed of boats in the vicinity
Engine	Engine status during sighting
Visibility	Degree of visibility during sighting
Hydrophone	The hydrophone was used during the sighting
Observations	Additional information registered by the researcher
Photo id	Photo identifier taken to the individual during the sighting
Skin sample id	Skin sample identifier taken to the individual during the sighting
Feces sample id	Feces sample identifier taken to the individual during the sighting

3 Proposed System

The proposed system was developed using a model-view controller architecture (MVC) [6], thus programming for data and process management are independent of the user interface (GUI) [7], allowing the defined catch protocol can be carried out in a systematized manner. The information captured is stored in a local database, making it possible to edit and update the data at any time. The controls used in the interface present an automated behavior that depends on the events of the system and the restrictions of the protocol, which causes the system to act according to the information that is entered and adapted to the situation. The system interface is shown in Fig. 3, it consists of 8 main components: (1) Date: Shows the current date of the computer on which the system is running. (2) GPS panel: Displays the serial ports (COM) that are active on the computer. Selecting the GPS device port will give you updated position information. (3) Position panel: The position acquired by the GPS is displayed, it is divided into latitude and longitude. (4) Specimen Panel: Displays the identifier and the number of sightings of the specimen corresponding to the current tracking sheet. (5) New Tracking Sheet or New Specimen: Contains the controls to create a new tracking sheet according to the type of specimen selected: Single or Mother and child. (6) Sighting control panel: Encompass controls to add a new sighting (initial position) to the current sighting sheet and to end the sighting in which you are currently working (final position). These will be activated or deactivated according to the case that is needed in the tracking sheet. (7) Sample panel and photos: In this panel are the buttons to attach the identifiers of feces and skin samples, as well as the identifier of the photo corresponding to the sighting that is worked on the current tracking sheet. (8) Tracking Sheet Panel: Displays the created worksheets that are active. In this panel it is possible to interchange between the tracking sheets and work with each one according to how it is necessary.

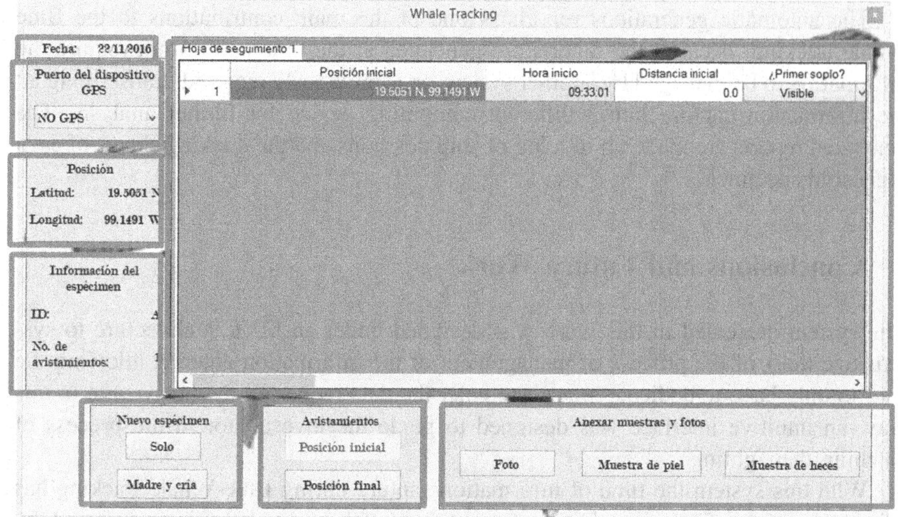

Fig. 3. Interface of the proposed system. (1) Date. (2) GPS panel. (3) Position panel. (4) Specimen panel. (5) New sheet of tracking sheet or new specimen. (6) Sighting control panel. (7) Sample panel and photos. (8) Tracking sheets panel.

4 Tests and Discussion of Results

The system was tested on a Toughbook CF-U1 which incorporates a GPS device. Thanks to the mobility of the Toughbook, it was possible to carry out tests in different environments. Each test consisted in capturing the data of a group of individuals in a random order. Some captures were made simultaneously in the same equipment with the objective of evaluating the capacity of the system to manage different amounts of information.

The average capture time of a sighting with the system is 3 min, during this period of time the first 12 fields of information mentioned in Table 1 are captured, this means that each field of information is filled in Approximately 15 s each. This represents a considerable improvement in the time and effort of capturing the information because the average capture time was usually 7 min, in addition to systematizing the capture of various fields the researcher can devote more attention to observing the actions of the Individual and make the corresponding observations in each system record. By using this system it was possible to register information of up to 5 specimens simultaneously while manually it was only possible to register the information of 2 specimens.

Thanks to the identification of the necessary data to be captured and the definition of the monitoring protocol, it was possible to include validation rules in the system, which confirm that the data entered have an appropriate format for the subsequent analysis. It was also possible to automate some activities such as the generation of identifiers for individuals according to their type and the capture of the navigation log. This log records the GPS positions of the device every 5 min when no active tracking sheet is found and every 2 min when monitoring an individual.

The automatic generations reports is one of the main contributions to the Blue Whale tracking, because the reports are generated at the time and do not require the information to be managed by another system or as previously required, transcribing all the information capture into a different computing device for further analysis. The generated reports are made up of a log of ship positions and the tracking sheets of each registered specimen.

5 Conclusions and Future Work

The system presented in this work was designed under an MVC architecture to systematize most of the process of management of the information entered, allowing the user to only have to dedicate himself to enter the data requested by the system. In this way, an intuitive interface was designed to guide the investigator in the process of catching the sighting.

With this system the time of information capture during Blue Whale tracking has been reduced by 50%, in addition to that the catch errors have been reduced by approximately 60%, mainly because many of the data are automatically registered and validated before making any changes. Thanks to this, the amount of work and time spent by researchers to validate, manage and acquire information has been considerably reduced.

This system is one of the first tools that adapts to the specific needs of users and also gives them the possibility of using it in any type of environment with any computer equipment.

As a future work, it is planned to adapt this system to share the information by various research groups in a general database, which allows a better comparison between the data collected, as well as the adequacy of the system to obtain automatic information regarding identification systems that are currently used, which will allow a better record of the evolution of Blue Whale specimens.

Acknowledgements. The team thanks the Instituto Politécnico Nacional for the facilities to develop this work, likewise thank CONACYT for the support provided to project 221284.

References

1. Mens, T., Demeyer, S.: Software Evolution, 1st edn. Springer Singapore Pte. Ltd., Singapore (2009)
2. Zhao, N., Wang, J., Li, T., Yu, Y., Dai, F., Xie, Z.: ESDDM: a software evolution process model based on evolution behavior interface. In: Chen, R. (ed.) ICICIS 2011. CCIS, vol. 135, pp. 562–567. Springer, Heidelberg (2011). https://doi.org/10.1007/978-3-642-18134-4_89

3. Robles Gil, P.: Los rituales del reencuentro. In: The human blue whale (2011). http://www.humanbluewhale.com/gallery/blue_whale_gallery1.html. Accessed 23 Mar 2017
4. Maxwell Braun, D.: Saving Baja blue whales for generations to come. In: Oceans Views (2016). http://voices.nationalgeographic.com/2016/01/14/saving-baja-blue-whales-for-generations-to-come/. Accessed 23 Mar 2017
5. Buckland, S.: Advanced Distance Sampling, 1st edn. Oxford University Press, Oxford (2010)
6. Maciel, A., Sankaranarayanan, G., Halic, T., Arikatla, V., Lu, Z., De, S.: Surgical model-view-controller simulation software framework for local and collaborative applications. Int. J. Comput. Assist. Radiol. Surg. **6**, 457–471 (2010)
7. Bittencourt, I., Baranauskas, M., Pereira, R., Dermeval, D., Isotani, S., Jaques, P.: A systematic review on multi-device inclusive environments. Univers. Access Inf. Soc. **15**, 737–772 (2015)

Is Web Navigation with Tablet More Difficult Than with Laptop?

Aline Chevalier(✉), Julien Rivière, Jean-Christophe Sakdavong, and Franck Amadieu

Université de Toulouse, Laboratoire Cognition, Langues, Langage, Ergonomie (CNRS UMR 5263), Maison de la recherche, 5 allées Antonio Machado, 31058 Toulouse cedex, France
aline.chevalier@univ-tlse2.fr

Abstract. Navigating websites is a common daily activity for many people. But websites may introduce usability problems that can disturb activity of web users, which may be more detrimental when users navigate tablet or smartphone (with small displays) and as the complexity of the navigation increases. To test this hypothesis, we carried out a study in which we manipulated the usability quality of the website, support used (tablet-10'1 inches *vs* laptop-17'3) and the complexity of navigational tasks to be performed. 79 students were divided into 4 independent groups: 20 with tablet and usable website, 19 with tablet and non-usable website, 20 with laptop and usable website and 20 with laptop and non-usable website. All the participants performed 3 simple tasks 3 difficult tasks and impossible tasks.

The main results showed that the complexity and the website visited impacted performances: simple tasks were solved easier than difficult and impossible ones, especially when participants performed usable website than non-usable website. But surprisingly, the use of tablet did not impair performances compared to laptop. These results may be due to the task to be performed. Navigating within a website with links is probably easier than to search information with search engine (which requires formulate queries, open many website, etc.).

Keywords: Navigation · Tablet · Usability · Search complexity

1 Introduction

Navigating websites is a common daily activity for many people with various devices such as desktop PC, laptop, smartphone or tablet.

Internet is mainly used for professional objectives, leisure, and education. But navigating the Web may be difficult when websites do not fit users' needs [1] and/or with the increase of complexity of navigational tasks to be performed [5]. Indeed, websites introducing usability problems may disturb activity of web users; for instance, if many irrelevant information elements are displayed, participants may experience difficulties in focusing attention on relevant ones, which may impact the selection of relevant links to be explored and so on. These usability problems may be more detrimental when users navigate tablet or smartphone (with small displays) [4]. Indeed,

C. Stephanidis (Ed.): HCII Posters 2018, CCIS 850, pp. 18–23, 2018.
https://doi.org/10.1007/978-3-319-92270-6_3

if the website is not responsive (e.g. adapted to the screen size), difficulties generated by usability violations may be more detrimental, because information may appear in small size and participants have to zoom on information and use touchscreens to move the zoom and see all information elements.

Because mobile devices like tablets or smartphones present particularities (small screen size, multitouch screen, fingers with lower accuracy than mouse devices) the issue of usability of websites and applications is crucial. A literature review conducted by Shitkova, Holler, Heide, Clever and Becker [7] led to a catalogue of usability guidelines for mobile websites and applications.

In a study on information searching task with tablets [3], it was showed that after an experience with using a tablet, participants stated advantages of tablet like portability and ease-of-use, but also disadvantages like the touch screen's ultra-sensitivity and the lack of participants' experience with a "non-tactile keyboard."

Therefore, usability violations and the complexity of the navigational tasks to be performed should impact negatively search performance of participants, especially when they used tablets. To test this hypothesis, we carried out a study in which we manipulated the usability quality of the website, support used (tablet-10'1 inches vs laptop-17'3) and the complexity of navigational tasks to be performed (simple vs difficult vs impossible tasks).

2 Method

2.1 Participants and Materiel

79 students (from 19 to 31 years old; M_{age} = 24, SD = 1.89), 40 males and 39 females, participated at this experiment. They were under-graduate students in psychology, language and management. They used Internet daily, several hours since many years.

Two versions of the same website were built:

- A usable website (UW) that complied with the usability guidelines for web interfaces (e.g., [6]) – see Fig. 1.
- A non-usable website (NUW) that included usability violations into all pages (each

Fig. 1. Home page of the usable website (UW).

Fig. 2. Home page of the non-usable website (NUW).

page included the same number of usability violations, i.e. colour of the link visited did not change, background/text contrast was low, etc.) – see Fig. 2.

This website presented products related to music (e.g. cds, tickets for concerts).

2.2 Procedure

The participants were divided into 4 independent groups: 20 navigated with tablet and usable website, 19 navigated with tablet and non-usable website, 20 with laptop and usable website and 20 with laptop and non-usable website.

All the participants performed 9 search tasks:

- 3 simples tasks for which the keywords provided matched with words in website.
- 3 difficult tasks for which inferential processes were required to find information.
- 3 impossible tasks for which no answer existed in website.

The same number of links to achieve to the target information was the same in the two websites for all tasks (except for impossible ones, since no answer existed into the websites).

The order of tasks was counterbalanced between participants.

All the actions they made were recorded with BAOBAB, ad-hoc software, which allows capturing traces of participants such as time required, links visited, etc.

3 Results

We computed the number of correct answers per complexity, task time (in sec.), clicks made (webpages opened up), and task statement rereading. These dependant variables were submitted to an analysis of variance (ANOVA) with support (laptop *versus* tablet) and website (UW *vs* NUW) as between-subject factors. Post-hoc analyses (Tukey-HSD) were performed to test significant interaction. The significance level was set at .05 for all statistical analyses. Partial η^2 was used as an index of the relative effect size.

All results are presented in Table 1.

3.1 Correct Answers Per Complexity (Simple *Vs* Difficult Tasks)

The participants provided more correct answers when navigated the UW than the NUW ($F(1,75) = 42{,}47$, $p < .0001$, $\eta_p^2 = .36$). The complexity also had a significant effect ($F(1,75) = 15{,}96$, $p < .001$, $\eta_p^2 = .17$) in favor of simple tasks. No significant effect of support (laptop *vs* tablet) appeared ($F(1,75) < 1$).

The complexity × website interaction was significant ($F(1,75) = 6{,}34$, $p < .05$, $\eta_p^2 = .08$). The post-hoc analyses only showed a significant difference between simple and difficult tasks when the participants performed the NUW ($p < .005$) and surprisingly they provided more correct answers for difficult than simple tasks.

Table 1. Means (and standard deviations) of correct answer, task time, pages visited (clicks made) and rereading of the task statement with regard to the website navigated, the support used and the task complexity.

	Usable website (UW)						Non-usable website (NUW)					
	Laptop			Tablet			Laptop			Tablet		
	Simple	Difficult	Impossible	Simple	Difficult	Impossible	Simple	Difficult	Impossible	Simple	Difficult	Impossible
Correct answers	.96 (.018)	.98 (.13)	–	.94 (.22)	.98 (.013)	–	.77 (.34)	.84(.36)	–	.67 (.44)	.91 (.28)	–
Task time	28.88 (15.01)	31.88 (15.07)	44.67 (31.15)	29.66 (16.03)	28.78 (17.92)	50.22 (58.39)	55.57 (45.82)	58.42 (42.52)	69.64 (75.27)	49.81 (4.35)	52.85 (38.09)	60.63 (48.68)
Pages visited	3.55 (3.56)	2.91 (1.7)	5.82 (4.24)	2.46 (2.24)	2.63 (1.98)	5.96 (5.56)	2.11 (.49)	5.28 (4.23)	11.49 (11.68)	2.33 (1.14)	5.17 (4.37)	10.11 (8.33)
Rereading of task statement	.2 (.43)	.2 (.39)	.1 (.3)	.14 (.32)	.26 (.43)	.22 (.42)	.27 (.87)	.32 (.62)	.18 (.39)	.12 (.36)	.18 (.38)	.23 (.46)

3.2 Task Time (in Sec.)

The participants needed lower time while navigating the UW than NUW ($F(1,75) = 26,73$, $p < .0001$, $\eta_p^2 = .26$). The complexity also had a significant effect ($F(1,75) = 7,02$, $p < .005$, $\eta_p^2 = .08$): the impossible tasks required longer time than simple and difficult ones (*ps* < .01).

The support had no significant effect on task time ($F(1,75) < 1$). None interaction was significant.

3.3 Number of Clicks (Webpages Visited)

As expected, the participants navigating the UW visited fewer webpages than participants navigating the NUW ($F(1,75) = 45,35$, $p < .0001$, $\eta_p^2 = .37$). The complexity of the tasks had a significant effect ($F(2,150) = 76,97$, $p < .0001$, $\eta_p^2 = .51$), since participants made more clicks to perform impossible tasks than difficult and simple ones (*ps* < .0001), and to perform difficult than simple tasks ($p < .0001$). The support did not impact significantly the number of webpages visited ($F(1,75) = 1.05$, n.s.).

The complexity × websites interaction was significant ($F(2,150) = 9,27$, $p < .0001$, $\eta_p^2 = .11$). More precisely, post-hoc analyses showed that the difficult tasks and impossible ones needed more webpages visited for the NUW than UW (*ps* < .005), whereas no significant difference appeared for the simple tasks between the two websites.

3.4 Rereading of Task Statement

Very few number of rereading was made. No significant effects were observed.

4 Conclusion

The main results showed that the complexity and the website visited impacted performance of participants. Indeed, simple tasks were solved easier than difficult and impossible ones, especially when participants performed usable website than non-usable website. These results corroborated previous studies we carried out [1, 2]: usable website generated higher performance than non-usable one for at both young and older web users.

But surprisingly, the use of tablet did not impair performances compared to laptop. These results may be due to the task to be performed. Navigating within a website with links is probably easier than to search information with search engine (which requires formulate queries, open many websites, etc.). The participants only had to choose the relevant links to be opened up and explored. Although that these actions are cognitively costly, the use of laptop or tablet did not impact, but the usability quality did as shown previously. So, based on these first results, tablets would be useful to navigate website and does not negatively impact users' performance.

Nevertheless, using the Web also involve search tasks with search engines. So, further studies are needed to determine if tablets may impact this activity.

Acknowledgments. This research is part of the project "Learning with Tablets: Acceptance and Cognitive Processes (LETACOP)" funded by the ANR (National Research Agency) – ANR-14-CE24-0032.

References

1. Chevalier, A., Kicka, M.: Web designers and Web users: influence of ergonomic quality of the Web site on information search. Int. J. Hum.-Comput. Stud. **64**, 1031–1048 (2006)
2. Chevalier, A., Dommes, A., Marquié, J.-C.: Strategy and accuracy during information search on the Web: Effects of age and complexity of the search questions. Comput. Hum. Behav. **53**, 305–315 (2015)
3. Jayroe, T.J., Wolfram, D.: Internet searching, tablet technology and older adults. Proc. Am. Soc. Inf. Sci. Technol. **49**, 1–3 (2012)
4. Liebe, U., Glenk, K., Oehlmann, M., Meyerhoff, J.: Does the use of mobile devices (tablets and smartphones) affect survey quality and choice behaviour in web surveys? J. Choice Model. **14**, 17–31 (2015)
5. Monchaux, S., Amadieu, F., Chevalier, A., Mariné, C.: Query strategies during information searching: effects of prior domain knowledge and complexity of the information problems to be solved. Inf. Process. Manag. **51**(5), 557–569 (2015)
6. Nielsen, J., Loranger, H.: Prioritizing Web Usability. New Riders Press, Berkeley (2006)
7. Shitkova, M., Holler, J., Heide, T., Clever, N., Becker, J.: Towards usability guidelines for mobile websites and applications. In: Proceedings of the 12th International Conference on Wirtschaftsinformatik, Osnabrück, Germany (2015)

Supporting Audiography: Design of a System for Sentimental Sound Recording, Classification and Playback

Tijs Duel(✉), David M. Frohlich, Christian Kroos, Yong Xu, Philip J. B. Jackson, and Mark D. Plumbley

University of Surrey, Guildford GU2 7XH, UK
t.duel@surrey.ac.uk

Abstract. It is now commonplace to capture and share images in photography as triggers for memory. In this paper we explore the possibility of using sound in the same sort of way, in a practice we call *audiography*. We report an initial design activity to create a system called *Audio Memories* comprising a ten second sound recorder, an intelligent archive for auto-classifying sound clips, and a multi-layered sound player for the social sharing of audio souvenirs around a table. The recorder and player components are essentially user experience probes that provide tangible interfaces for capturing and interacting with audio memory cues. We discuss our design decisions and process in creating these tools that harmonize user interaction and machine listening to evoke rich memories and conversations in an exploratory and open-ended way.

Keywords: Audiography · Sound souvenirs · Design · Machine listening

1 Introduction

We have all become familiar with capturing and sharing photographs as triggers for memory, reminiscing and storytelling. In fact, modern domestic photography is as much about communication as it is about imaging and memory [12]. The popularity of photography is evident if we look at the volume of photographs uploaded to social media sites every day. Facebook for example saw over 350 million pictures uploaded daily in 2013 [1]. However, this volume of photographs may be considered a problem for remembering as it becomes hard to retrieve photos relating to particular events, and easy to forget the photographs themselves [7, 13]. Furthermore photographs only relate to our visual memory for events.

In this paper we consider an alternative medium for the triggering and sharing of memories based on hearing rather than seeing, sound rather than image, and face-to-face sharing rather than online posting of media. We call this activity '*audiography*' to contrast it with photography and videography, and connect it with insights from our own prior work on audiophotography [6] and that of others exploring the sentimental properties of sound for memory and communication [2, 4, 10].

These studies show that audio recordings provide unique experiences and qualities for remembering compared to their visual counterparts, but that audio is more difficult

C. Stephanidis (Ed.): HCII Posters 2018, CCIS 850, pp. 24–31, 2018.
https://doi.org/10.1007/978-3-319-92270-6_4

to index and navigate in a non-visual way. For example, Bijsterveld and van Dijck [2] point out that professional music has always had nostalgic value for owners along with a variety of often accidental sound recordings made in the cassette tape era. Their collection of recordings show how these 'sound souvenirs' are captured and shared in different contexts. The same discovery was made in the first study of the domestic soundscape by Oleksik et al. [9] when asking families to record various sounds of family life. The families enjoyed this activity and asked to keep certain recordings which the authors termed 'sonic gems' because of their function in triggering precious memories. Dib et al. [4] supported this activity directly in a field trial of digital Dictaphones given to families for the purpose of remembering. This uncovered a host of values for sentimental sound recording, including the immersive nature of sound for transporting people back in time, its ambiguity in making space for imagination in recall and discussion in conversation, and its spontaneity and uncontrollability compared to images which can be more easily 'posed' than recordings.

These latter studies acknowledge the difficulty of organising and browsing digital sound recordings and suggest novel ways of making them tangible. Hence, Petrelli et al. [11] describe the design and use of a device called FM Radio (short for Family Memory Radio) through which families could 'tune in' to sound recordings clustered by time, type or favourites. Oleksik and Brown [10] describe the design and use of a system called Sonic Gems for recording and storing sentimental sound recordings in the form of pebble-like capsules in a bowl. Each device showed promise in supporting a new practice of sentimental sound recording and playback, but neither was designed to scale. Families had to classify recordings manually for playback through FM Radio and the unclassified Sonic gems would soon fill the bowl and become unmanageable. Linking sound recordings to photographs through 'audiophotography' provides a more sustainable solution to managing audio collections visually [5, 6]. However, the primacy of visual stimulation in an audiophoto may overpower some of the psychological properties of audio for remembering. So a requirement exists for a more manageable and scalable way of classifying and curating sentimental sound recordings.

In the rest of this paper we describe a design exploration to do this, drawing on machine hearing algorithms being developed on the *Making Sense of Sounds* project. This is a large multidisciplinary project at the Universities of Surrey and Salford in the UK, attempting to recognise and classify scenes from their sonic properties. Engineering work at Surrey and psychoacoustic work at Salford are being combined to deliver a method of automatically tagging naturalistic sound recordings with psychologically meaningful labels in a taxonomy of sound types. We believe this could be a critical enabling technology for sustainably managing sentimental sound collections and making them available for powerful new experiences of remembering and discussing the past.

2 Approach

To explore this design space we used a research-through-design approach to design a working prototype system called *Audio Memories.* This comprises separate audio recorder and playback devices operating as a pair. Rather than using standard consumer electronic platforms such as a smartphone and computer, custom appliances were created. This was done to rethink the design of such devices for this application and with sound as the dominant medium.

For example, we attempted to make the interfaces to the devices both tangible and screenless, excluding the conventional method of searching for media by text label input. This forced us to develop new methods of query using physical buttons and control knobs, with some level of unpredictability and serendipity of selection. We also wanted to make the devices attractive and accessible to young families with children as the target market, since they were shown in some of the previous studies above to be interested in sound souvenirs.

This paper is written as a design case study, culminating in the description of a working prototype. It essentially describes our design iterations over time for the recorder and player devices separately. In a future paper we will describe a full trial of the system with target families, to evaluate the effectiveness of the prototypes in meeting the design requirement for a scalable practice of audiography.

3 Recorder Evolution

3.1 Recorder I

Dibs' and Oleksik's, research participants requested tools to create short yet significant clips from their longer recordings, confirming the desire for an event-focused reminiscing. To answer this need we fixed the length of each recording to 10 s exactly. In this way the user would be encouraged to treat a recording at the onset actively as an (physically ephemeral) event instead of an indistinct variable-length documentation, but the disruption of any ongoing personal or environmental interaction would be minimized. Fixing the length of the clip also rendered pause and stop button superfluous; a single button would accomplish the entire process and it would not even be necessary to pay visual attention to it. A working mono-recorder was built as proof of concept (see Fig. 1(i)).

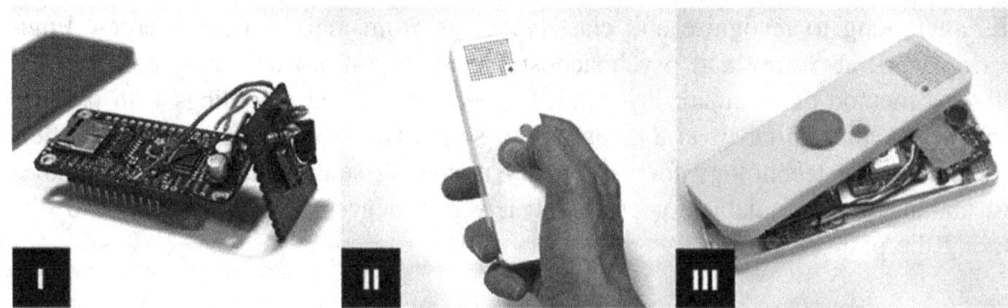

Fig. 1. Images of the main iterations of the recorder.

Besides investigating interaction and hardware we also started exploring the medium of ten second clips. We asked people linked to our group to start recording such clips and this resulted in a small library of audio recordings. We found that 10 s was largely sufficient to capture meaningful sound mementos.

3.2 Recorder II

The second design iteration introduced new core functionalities and explored design details of the casing (see Fig. 1(ii) and (iii)). The core hardware was upgraded to enable 16 bit 44.1 kHz stereo audio. The recordings were meant to capture the sonic experience of the original situation as closely as possible and using high-quality audio was deemed indispensable despite the larger processing and energy consumption footprint.

To give the user some instant control over the recorded content without compromising the overall idea of a minimal interfering device, a smaller 'delete' button was added next to the 'record' button. By triple-tapping this button the user is able to permanently remove the most recent recording.

We also took into consideration adding audio playback capabilities to the recorder, but after careful deliberation we decided against it. Firstly, the user's engagement in the ongoing situation should not be interrupted by the temptation to play back the recorded sound instantly. Secondly, the anticipation of listening to the recordings later on the playback device was considered to be a desirable quality on its own.

Finally, GPS localisation was implemented to add location meta-data to the recordings including also a time stamp. These meta-data provide initial means to index and navigate the accumulating audio collection.

3.3 Final Recorder Prototype

The final prototype for the recorder is shown in Fig. 3 below. The electronics were complimented with a vibration motor providing haptic feedback as to when a recording is started and completed. Furthermore, we improved the battery charger to reduce downtime. Most improvements were made on the case. The addition of a bright orange gave the design a friendlier and more playful nature. The sides are made using 3D printing improving its structural strength. The top and bottom required more accurate machining and are made through laser cutting Perspex. Using these rapid prototyping techniques, we improve reproducibility of the design. The intimate nature of audio recording raised issues of confidentiality. For the most secure data transfer to the player device we introduced a removable micro SD card at the bottom of the device. We also introduced an LED at the top of the device to publically signal recording activity to others.

4 Player Evolution

4.1 Early Conceptual Designs

To address the design challenges of digital archiving we adopted a more open-ended design approach; exploring multiple concepts through rapid prototyping. The resulting exploration can be classified in three categories: The first category is **GPS oriented**

searching (see Fig. 2(i)); moving the speaker cones the user could dowse for audio recordings. Finding sounds through this method could prove to be hard as the locations of recordings are not distributed evenly through space.

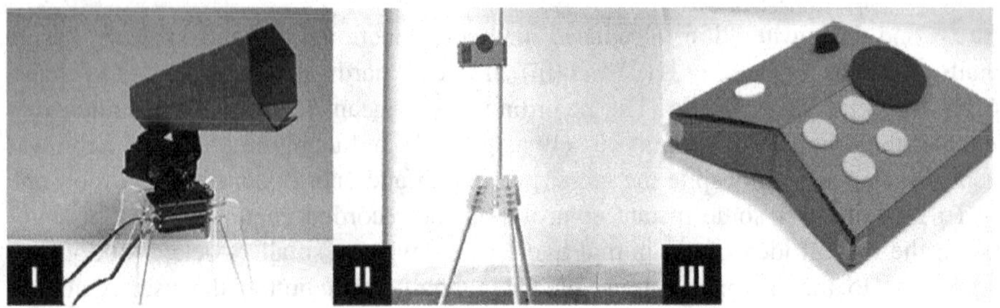

Fig. 2. Some examples of made concepts for the player. Each concept has its own way to navigate audio collections.

The second type of concept focusses on **chronological oriented searching** (see Fig. 2(ii)). The concept featured a vertical pole representing the stack of recordings in chronological order (newest on top). The speaker visualizes it relative position in time. While this way of browsing the collection definitely has its merits, the prototype was considered awkward to operate as it moved every ten seconds.

The final group of concepts explored the idea of **co-operative reminiscing** (see Fig. 2(iii)). Multisided interfaces enable multiple users to operate the device simultaneously, triggering a multitude of audio memories to create layered soundscapes. A technical demonstrator was realized using MAX/MSP and a surround sound system. The layering provided interesting reminiscing experiences, through introducing serendipity. One problem discovered in the audio experiments here was that some sound clips 'clashed' with each other. Typically sounds of the same type such as music or voiceover were difficult to listen to simultaneously. In addition, the short nature of the audio memories made it hard to effectively browse and layer sounds. Playback would move onto the next clip in the stack while users were deciding whether that was the clip they wanted to listen to.

4.2 Final Player Prototype

The final prototype blended features and functionalities of its prior explorations into a single design. It provides a tangible interface to browse one's digital audio mementos with up to two clips playing simultaneously (see Fig. 3).

The bottom left of the device features four tag buttons. These buttons can be used to select the content of the clips; mechanical sounds, nature sounds, speech and music. Combinations can be made as well. The categories are based on the audio taxonomy of everyday sounds by Bones et al. [3]. When the SD card of the recorder is inserted into the player it automatically downloads, analyses and labels the recordings. An audio classification method will label each clip with one (or more) of the four tags based on its dominant content.

Fig. 3. The final designed system

At the center of the interface is the Haptic Engine (H.E.). The H.E. is a dial that doubles as a loci of both input and output. While a clip plays the H.E. - similar to a record player – will slowly rotate, making a full revolution every ten seconds. Equipped with capacitive touch sensors it will disengage the motor and pause playback when held. Manual rotation enables users to browse their collection in time. Continuous rotation will make one jump through the collection in larger intervals. Users can keep track of their position within their collection through a 16 × 8 LED matrix depicting the date (in a MM-YY format). The LED matrix is situated behind the speaker cloth. When the LED's are off the matrix practically disappears.

At the back of the device is a rotary switch that enables the player to switch into layer mode. In this mode the player will analyse the track that is playing based on user input and layer it with a matching track played through a second speaker. This emulates a simplified spatial audio effect.

5 Discussion

Although we cannot present a tested solution for audiography, we have reported a design exploration culminating in a potential solution ready to test. This adopts a design approach based on tangible interaction with separate recording and playback devices that utilise time and GPS meta data inherited from the recorder. Further metadata in the form of sematic tags of sound type are added automatically by deep learning algorithms on the player. These allow searching for sounds by top level sound categories such as mechanical, nature, speech and music, together with chronological position in a 'clip stack' that has emerged as an important concept approximating time.

Various design issues surfaced in exploring options for the recorder and player which may be common to other audio recording and archiving domains. Regarding the recorder we found that the removal of a screen and speaker on a dedicated device leads to a simple one button interaction for recording. The lack of ability to review sounds on the recorder creates anticipation of the playback experience on the second device, and encourages batch transfer and playback in specific episodes. Ethical issues about the capture and control of sounds led us to incorporate LEDs signaling recording activity on the recorder, and removable storage which is physically moved to the player and cannot be accessed wirelessly.

Regarding the player, we quickly found that it was easier to use time and sound type metadata in comparison to GPS location. Without a screen it was not possible to use a map interface for sound clips, and alternative methods of pointing the device itself in various directions were not intuitively obvious. Therefore a static tabletop device for shared use was chosen for development, using a small number of buttons and dials for tangible control. The possibility of mixing or layering multiple sounds at playback was explored experientially with 10 s clips recorded on a smartphone to test the approach. This revealed the difficulty of listening to too many sounds at once and encouraged the design of a secondary layer as an option to a primary one. Many design discussions for the final player centred around the user experience of searching for specific sounds versus exploratory listening to sound sequences and combinations from approximate time points. Here we were inspired by studies showing the value of serendipitous interaction with media, to allow the system to play sound continuously with approximate user 'steering' [7, 8].

In general, we found ourselves moving between design of different types and levels in order to resolve the emerging design issues. Conceptual design was necessary at the top level to define a design trajectory for each device, which then led us into explorations of form, functionality and media. Because both devices were for handling sound, we found it necessary to record sound samples at various points and experiment with the experience of playback in different sequences and combinations.

A final dynamic for our player interaction, was the division of labour between human and machine intelligence and action. We found ourselves in unfamiliar territory of combining artificial intelligence and tangible interaction, through the sound type (tag) buttons which could retrieve a sub-set of sounds by type through a physical action. The complexity of manually selecting a secondary sound clip to play with a primary one also led us to leave this to the machine, based on a simple algorithm for ruling out 'clashes'. Whether users understand or enjoy the logic and experience of this kind of sound selection and playback remains to be seen in a user trial we plan to run next. For now we can say that machine listening and human listening can indeed be combined in a single device, to curate sounds from an archive in a scalable and interesting way.

Acknowledgements. This work was funded by a grant from the Engineering and Physical Sciences Research Council, as part of the Making Sense of Sounds Project (EP/N014111/1). We would like to thank our other colleagues on that project for their input to the design ideas in this paper.

References

1. Aslam S.: Facebook by the numbers: stats, demographics and fun facts. Omnicore online magazine (2018). https://www.omnicoreagency.com/facebook-statistics/
2. Bijsterveld, K., van Dijck, J. (eds.): Sound Souvenirs: Audio Technologies, Memory and Cultural Practices, vol. 2. Amsterdam University Press, Amsterdam (2009)

3. Bones, O.C., Cox, T.J., Davies, W.J.: Toward an evidence-based taxonomy of everyday sounds. J. Acoust. Soc. Am. **140**(4), 3266 (2016)
4. Dib, L., Petrelli, D., Whittaker, S.: Sonic souvenirs: exploring the paradoxes of recorded sound for family remembering. In: Proceedings of the 2010 ACM Conference on Computer Supported Cooperative Work, pp. 391–400. ACM (2010)
5. Frohlich, D.M.: Audiophotography: Bringing Photos to Life with Sounds. Springer, New York (2004). https://doi.org/10.1007/978-1-4020-2210-4
6. Frohlich, D.M.: Fast Design, Slow Innovation: Audiophotography Ten Years On. Springer, Cham (2015). https://doi.org/10.1007/978-3-319-21939-4
7. Frohlich, D.M., Wall, S., Kiddle, G.: Rediscovery of forgotten images in domestic photo collections. Pers. Ubiquit. Comput. **17**(4), 729–740 (2013)
8. Odom, W.T., Sellen, A.J., Banks, R., Kirk, D.S., Regan, T., Selby, M., Zimmerman, J.: Designing for slowness, anticipation and re-visitation: a long term field study of the photobox. In: Proceedings of the SIGCHI Conference on Human Factors in Computing Systems, pp. 1961–1970. ACM, April 2014
9. Oleksik, G., Frohlich, D., Brown, L.M., Sellen, A.: Sonic interventions: understanding and extending the domestic soundscape. In: Proceedings of the SIGCHI Conference on Human Factors in Computing Systems, pp. 1419–1428. ACM (2008)
10. Oleksik, G., Brown, L.M.: Sonic gems: exploring the potential of audio recording as a form of sentimental memory capture. In: Proceedings of the 22nd British HCI Group Annual Conference on People and Computers: Culture, Creativity, Interaction, vol. 1, pp. 163–172. British Computer Society (2008)
11. Petrelli, D., Villar, N., Kalnikaite, V., Dib, L., Whittaker, S.: FM radio: family interplay with sonic mementos. In: Proceedings of the SIGCHI Conference on Human Factors in Computing Systems, pp. 2371–2380. ACM, April 2010
12. Sarvas, R., Frohlich, D.M.: From Snapshots to Social Media-The Changing Picture of Domestic Photography. Springer, London (2011). https://doi.org/10.1007/978-0-85729-247-6
13. Whittaker, S., Bergman, O., Clough, P.: Easy on that trigger dad: a study of long term family photo retrieval. Pers. Ubiquit. Comput. **14**(1), 31–43 (2010)

Enhancing Itinerary Recommendation with Linked Open Data

Alessandro Fogli, Alessandro Micarelli, and Giuseppe Sansonetti(✉)

Department of Engineering, Roma Tre University,
Via della Vasca Navale 79, 00146 Rome, Italy
ale.fogli@stud.uniroma3.it, {micarel,gsansone}@dia.uniroma3.it

Abstract. This paper proposes a recommender system that exploits linked open data (LOD) to perform a social context-aware cross-domain recommendation of personalized itineraries integrated with multimedia and textual content. To this aim, the recommendation engine considers the user profile, the context of use, and the features of the points of interest (POIs) extracted from LOD sources. We describe how to extract data and process it to perform hybrid filtering. All recommendations are based on the user's features extracted implicitly and explicitly. These features are used to apply content-based filtering and collaborative filtering, weighing results based on similar users' experience. The preliminary results of an experimental evaluation on a sample of 20 real users show the effectiveness of the proposed system not only in terms of perceived accuracy, but also in terms of novelty, non-obviousness, and serendipity.

Keywords: Recommender systems · Points of interest
Linked open data

1 Introduction

Recommender systems (RSs) can play a fundamental role in improving the target user's experience [1,2]. The best-known companies oriented to the sale of items (i.e., products and/or services) have long realized that the personalization of the offer is a fundamental factor to remain competitive on the market. Consequently, great interest is given to the analysis and modeling of users' individual tastes, with the aim of suggesting new products of their possible interest. Nowadays, there are many types of recommender systems that differ based on the domain in which they are deployed or the strategies applied for their design. This article proposes to realize open recommender systems able to take advantage of linked open data to perform a social context-aware cross-domain recommendation of itineraries enriched with multimedia and textual content.

This paper is organized as follows. Section 2 presents some state-of-the-art systems sharing some aspects with our recommender. The architecture underlying the itinerary recommender is detailed in Sect. 3. Section 4 describes the performed experimental tests and the obtained findings. Finally, Sect. 5 reports our conclusions and plans for future work.

C. Stephanidis (Ed.): HCII Posters 2018, CCIS 850, pp. 32–39, 2018.
https://doi.org/10.1007/978-3-319-92270-6_5

2 Related Work

In this section, some RSs somehow related to the proposed one are described. Among the itinerary RSs, D'Agostino *et al.* [3] propose a personalized system able to suggest the target user itineraries satisfying not only her preferences and needs, but also her physical and social context. The recommendation process takes into account several aspects: in addition to the popularity of points of interest (POIs) (deducted considering, for example, the number of check-ins on social networking services such as Foursquare[1]), it includes the user profile, the current context of use, and the user's network of social links. The basic idea behind the work of Yoon *et al.* [4] is that planning trips to unknown regions is a difficult task for novice travelers. This burden can be alleviated if the residents of the area offer assistance to them [5]. This system carries out a recommendation of social itineraries realized by learning multiple digital paths generated by users, such as the GPS trajectories of residents and travel experts.

Regarding LOD-based RSs, the system proposed in [6] is a social recommender designed to analyze how data extracted from a user's activities on social networks can be enriched with the semantic knowledge provided by LOD [7]. In particular, such a RS is applied to the artistic and cultural heritage. The work by Heitmann and Hayes [8] demonstrates that LOD can be used to lower the barriers to access the information necessary for a RS. By reducing the data acquisition problem, LOD can indeed be used to fill the gaps of a collaborative filtering algorithm, in particular to mitigate the cold-start problem that occurs when it is needed to provide relevant recommendations for new users and new items [9].

3 Itinerary Recommender

In order to plan a personalized itinerary, the system exploits the interaction with the active user and provides her with targeted recommendations that increase her satisfaction with the results returned by the recommender. User data comes from explicit and implicit feedbacks. The first category includes responses collected through questionnaires submitted to the user. The second category includes implicitly collected data during the user's interaction with the application, for example, when choosing a specific route rather than another, or when making a new check-in. This data extends and refines the knowledge base of the user's preferences. Each user is characterized by a vector of weights whose values, between 0 and 1, linearly correspond to the user's interest in a certain category of venues.

Another crucial factor in the recommendation process is the current physical context [10, 11]. Almost all this information can be determined without the user's involvement. In fact, the position is detected by the GPS sensor of the mobile

[1] https://foursquare.com/.

device, just as the means of transport is detected by its accelerometer. Furthermore, the weather conditions are obtained by submitting queries to different meteorological services, based on the user's current location.

Each single point of interest that composes the final itinerary is created by extracting the data available in the LinkedGeoData project dataset[2]. To retrieve this data, it is necessary to construct a query in the SPARQL language. Query construction takes place dynamically based on the characteristics of the target user and the information extracted from the context. Subsequently, the system searches for the POIs with the greatest number of links inherent to the user's peculiarities in order to extract only the most similar venues and refine the recommendation. The extracted POIs are, then, filtered by means of a hybrid filtering process that takes into account both the collaborative and the content-based aspects. Representing users through a vector of numerical values makes it possible to cluster and classify them according to their preferences. This allows the system to evaluate the POIs that constitute the itineraries also based on the choices made by other users similar or connected to the target user. The results are, furthermore, filtered according to the context information by removing, for example, outdoor places in case of rain or those closed at that time.

The purpose of this work is to recommend itineraries, namely, paths that maximize the active user's satisfaction. For this reason, we modeled the whole problem as a directed graph $G = (V, E)$, where V is a set of vertices (or nodes) and E is a set of edges. Each node represents a venue, that is, one of the points of interest present in the LinkedGeoData triples. Each edge represents a direct connection between two nodes. Information about an edge includes the shortest path to move from one node to another and the travel time, taking into account the user's means of transport. This information is obtained through the Google Maps API[3]: for each pair of nodes (e_i, e_j) the system queries APIs for the travel time from e_i to e_j and the travel time from e_j to e_i, thus creating the edge. Once all the edges have been inferred, a complete graph is obtained from the initial node to the final node. Then, a routing algorithm is executed on it. More specifically, starting from the itinerary consisting of the only points of departure and arrival, further POIs are added gradually until all the time available has been spent. The insertion process is not random, but occurs during the sorting of POIs based on various factors, such as popularity and distance.

The routing algorithm returns many itineraries from the initial node to the final node. To obtain the first k that maximize the active user's satisfaction, a scoring function is used. Such a function takes into account: (i) the number of venues that constitute the path; (ii) the path popularity; (iii) the distance from the starting point to the destination point; (iv) the popularity of the itinerary between the user's friends; (v) the diversity of the venues in the itinerary according to their categories of membership. Once the score has been obtained, the routes are sorted according to it.

[2] http://linkedgeodata.org.

[3] https://developers.google.com/maps/.

Once the itinerary preferred by the user has been implicitly obtained, it can be exploited to realize cross-domain recommendations through the use of other LOD sources. Starting from such a route, SPARQL queries are submitted to infer the features related to the POIs that belong to it. Then, the system exploits the extracted features to search for items sharing the same features, through the use of different endpoints. Figure 1 shows an example of screenshot returned by the system, where the active user receives personalized recommendations concerning the itinerary to follow and the related contents (i.e., a book, a movie, and a music album) to enjoy for enhancing her experience.

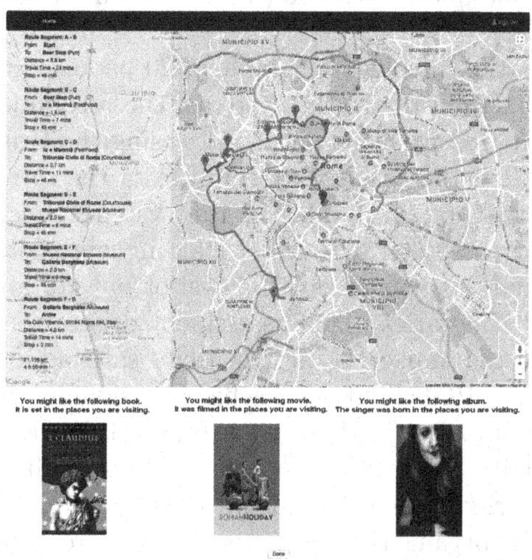

Fig. 1. Example of a system screenshot.

4 Experimental Evaluation

In this section, the results of preliminary tests are shown and discussed. The main objective of the performed tests was to evaluate the benefits of LOD in the implementation of recommender systems. In order to compare the advantages of LOD, it was necessary to use other data sources. Therefore, we decided to use the Foursquare API[4] to search for the venues inside the research area. Traditional evaluation approaches for recommender systems are based on offline testing. However, evaluating the perceived quality of an itinerary is an extremely subjective action. For this reason, we decided to use a sample of human testers in order to make the evaluations as impartial as possible. The direct involvement of users is aimed at establishing a qualitative estimation of the system based on user's perceptions. Testers were asked to try two different versions of the system, one enhanced with LOD and one with the Foursquare venues. Users were

[4] https://developer.foursquare.com/.

also asked to create a route within a city that they knew at least in part, so as to be able to assess the proposed final itineraries with full knowledge of the facts. For this reason the system has been deployed in different cities such as Rome, Amsterdam, and San Francisco. The different experimental steps were as follows. Through the registration form the user selects the categories she would like to visit in a hypothetical itinerary. Once the user profile has been created, the system prompts the insertion of some explicit data. Then, the user chooses among the returned itineraries the one that maximizes her level of satisfaction. Once the itinerary has been decided, the user fills in an evaluation form in order to evaluate the quality of the route returned by expressing her agreement or disagreement with some questions. The (dis)agreement scale is represented as a Likert five-point scale.

The system evaluation involved a sample of 20 people with different characteristics (see Table 1). To evaluate the systems, the recommendations obtained using LOD were compared with the ones made using the Foursquare APIs. The first evaluation made on the results extracted from the forms filled in by participants concerned the *precision* value of the system. Precision measures the ability of the system to return a route containing highly relevant POIs. The next evaluation carried out concerned the level of *novelty* and *non-obviousness* of the recommended itineraries. This assessment arises from the fact that an itinerary, in order to maximize the active user's satisfaction, has to not only include highly relevant POIs, but also achieve a significative level of novelty and a low level of obviousness in the routes returned. For assessing novelty and obviousness, we exploited data given by the user when filling in the evaluation form. The last test carried out concerned the *serendipity* metric, which measures how successful and surprising the recommendations are. The obtained experimental results are shown in Fig. 2. It can be noted that the results achieved by the system were encouraging for both versions tested. The graph in Fig. 2(a) shows that the system exploiting LOD has a slightly higher average precision

Table 1. Characteristics of testers.

	Item	Frequency	Percentage
Gender	Female	9	45%
	Male	11	55%
Age	18–30	13	65%
	31–50	4	20%
	51–70	3	15%
Profession	Student	10	50%
	Teacher	4	20%
	Employee	3	15%
	Freelancer	1	5%
	Unemployed	2	10%

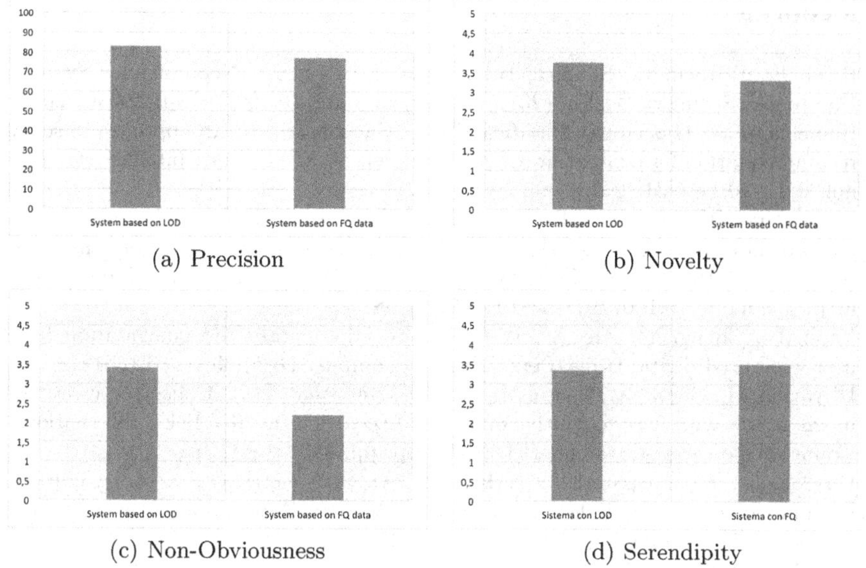

(a) Precision (b) Novelty

(c) Non-Obviousness (d) Serendipity

Fig. 2. Comparison analysis between the system based on LOD and the system based on Foursquare (FQ) data.

value than the system exploiting Foursquare (FQ) data. As for novelty and non-obviousness (see Fig. 2(b) and (c)), the LOD-based system still achieved better results than its variant. As for serendipity, the results reported in Fig. 2(d) show that the LOD-based system attained encouraging levels of serendipity, albeit slightly lower than the FQ-based system.

5 Conclusions

In this paper, we have described a personalized recommender system of itineraries that exploits linked open data (LOD) and takes into account the physical and social context of the target user. The preliminary experimental results show that LOD is indeed useful for realizing such systems.

Although such findings are encouraging, the possible future developments of this research work are various and can concern each of the modules of the proposed recommender. Moreover, it is certainly necessary to perform further experimental tests with more users and scenarios. Finally, further research activities are necessary for integrating the user profiles with additional information about their personality [12,13], as well as the temporal dynamics [14,15] and the actual nature [16–18] of their interests. Browsing activities on the Web are also rich of relevant information that can be considered in the user modeling process [19,20].

References

1. Ricci, F., Rokach, L., Shapira, B., Kantor, P.B. (eds.): Recommender Systems Handbook. Springer, Boston (2011). https://doi.org/10.1007/978-0-387-85820-3
2. Biancalana, C., Gasparetti, F., Micarelli, A., Sansonetti, G.: An approach to social recommendation for context-aware mobile services. ACM Trans. Intell. Syst. Technol. **4**(1), 10:1–10:31 (2013)
3. D'Agostino, D., Gasparetti, F., Micarelli, A., Sansonetti, G.: A social context-aware recommender of itineraries between relevant points of interest. In: Stephanidis, C. (ed.) HCI 2016, Part II. CCIS, vol. 618, pp. 354–359. Springer, Cham (2016). https://doi.org/10.1007/978-3-319-40542-1_58
4. Yoon, H., Zheng, Y., Xie, X., Woo, W.: Social itinerary recommendation from user-generated digital trails. Pers. Ubiquit. Comput. **16**(5), 469–484 (2012)
5. D'Aniello, G., Gaeta, A., Gaeta, M., Loia, V., Reformat, M.Z.: Collective awareness in smart city with fuzzy cognitive maps and fuzzy sets. In: 2016 IEEE International Conference on Fuzzy Systems (FUZZ-IEEE), pp. 1554–1561, July 2016
6. De Angelis, A., Gasparetti, F., Micarelli, A., Sansonetti, G.: A social cultural recommender based on linked open data. In: Adjunct Publication of the 25th Conference on User Modeling, Adaptation and Personalization. UMAP 20117. ACM, New York, pp. 329–332 (2017)
7. Biancalana, C., Gasparetti, F., Micarelli, A., Sansonetti, G.: Social semantic query expansion. ACM Trans. Intell. Syst. Technol. **4**(4), 60:1–60:43 (2013)
8. Heitmann, B., Hayes, C.: Using linked data to build open, collaborative recommender systems. In: Linked Data Meets Artificial Intelligence, Papers from the 2010 AAAI Spring Symposium, Technical report SS-10-07, Stanford, California, USA, 22–24 March 2010, Palo Alto, California, USA, pp. 76–81. AAAI Press (2010)
9. D'Aniello, G., Gaeta, M., Loia, V., Orciuoli, F., Tomasiello, S.: A dialogue-based approach enhanced with situation awareness and reinforcement learning for ubiquitous access to linked data. In: 2014 International Conference on Intelligent Networking and Collaborative Systems, pp. 249–256, September 2014
10. Biancalana, C., Flamini, A., Gasparetti, F., Micarelli, A., Millevolte, S., Sansonetti, G.: Enhancing traditional local search recommendations with context-awareness. In: Konstan, J.A., Conejo, R., Marzo, J.L., Oliver, N. (eds.) UMAP 2011. LNCS, vol. 6787, pp. 335–340. Springer, Heidelberg (2011). https://doi.org/10.1007/978-3-642-22362-4_29
11. Biancalana, C., Gasparetti, F., Micarelli, A., Miola, A., Sansonetti, G.: Context-aware movie recommendation based on signal processing and machine learning. In: Proceedings of the 2nd Challenge on Context-Aware Movie Recommendation. CAMRa 2011, pp. 5–10. ACM, New York (2011)
12. Bologna, C., De Rosa, A.C., De Vivo, A., Gaeta, M., Sansonetti, G., Viserta, V.: Personality-based recommendation in e-commerce. In: CEUR Workshop Proceedings, vol. 997. CEUR-WS.org, Aachen (2013)
13. Onori, M., Micarelli, A., Sansonetti, G.: A comparative analysis of personality-based music recommender systems. In: CEUR Workshop Proceedings, vol. 1680, pp. 55–59. CEUR-WS.org, Aachen (2016)
14. Arru, G., Gurini, D.F., Gasparetti, F., Micarelli, A., Sansonetti, G.: Signal-based user recommendation on Twitter. In: Proceedings of the 22nd International Conference on World Wide Web, WWW 2013 Companion, pp. 941–944. ACM, New York (2013)

15. Caldarelli, S., Gurini, D.F., Micarelli, A., Sansonetti, G.: A signal-based approach to news recommendation. In: CEUR Workshop Proceedings, vol. 1618. CEUR-WS.org, Aachen (2016)
16. Gurini, D.F., Gasparetti, F., Micarelli, A., Sansonetti, G.: A sentiment-based approach to twitter user recommendation. In: CEUR Workshop Proceedings, vol. 1066. CEUR-WS.org, Aachen (2013)
17. Gurini, D.F., Gasparetti, F., Micarelli, A., Sansonetti, G.: iSCUR: interest and sentiment-based community detection for user recommendation on Twitter. In: Dimitrova, V., Kuflik, T., Chin, D., Ricci, F., Dolog, P., Houben, G.-J. (eds.) UMAP 2014. LNCS, vol. 8538, pp. 314–319. Springer, Cham (2014). https://doi.org/10.1007/978-3-319-08786-3_27
18. Gurini, D.F., Gasparetti, F., Micarelli, A., Sansonetti, G.: Temporal people-to-people recommendation on social networks with sentiment-based matrix factorization. Future Gener. Comput. Syst. **78**, 430–439 (2018)
19. Gasparetti, F., Micarelli, A., Sansonetti, G.: Exploiting web browsing activities for user needs identification. In: 2014 International Conference on Computational Science and Computational Intelligence, vol. 2, pp. 86–89. IEEE Computer Society, Los Alamitos, March 2014
20. Bonifacio, A., Biancalana, C., Gasparetti, F., Micarelli, A., Sansonetti, G.: Implicit evaluation of user's expertise in scientific domains. In: Stephanidis, C. (ed.) HCI 2017. CCIS, vol. 713, pp. 420–427. Springer, Cham (2017). https://doi.org/10.1007/978-3-319-58750-9_58

Interface for a Better Tourist Experience, Bayesian Approach and Cox-Jaynes Support

Karim Elia Fraoua(✉) and Sylvain Michelin

Université Paris-Est Marne-La-Vallée, Equipe Dispositifs d'information et de Communication à l'Ere Numérique (DICEN IDF), Conservatoire National des Arts et Métiers, Université Paris-Nanterre, EA 7339, Champs-sur-Marne, France
{karim.fraoua, sylvain.michelin}@u-pem.fr

Abstract. This work presents a new way to enhance a tourism experience through an interface. Basically considering a Bayesian approach and introducing the Cox-Jaynes theorem, we can consider the improvement of this interface. We take in our approach how adding some features will ultimately create an interface that fit the needs of the tourist.

Keywords: Cox-Jaynes · Tourist behavior · Bayesian appraoch

1 Introduction

The quality of a tourist's visit becomes an important issue. In an unknown city or at least in asymmetric information, the experience can be felt [1] because the tourist does not know all the places to visit. Usually, the tourist uses social media, tourist guides, information sites or existing applications to know the interesting places to visit [2]. The interface is usually designed according to the existing offer proposed in a structured way the same approach considering that all users are identical, having the same culture, and the same beliefs. The observation is that often the tourist is not completely satisfied with his trip. He visits some places but others could escape him, because he did not have the necessary information to be able to reach it. More particularly when he misses some sites that are not far away from his trajectory, he maybe visit them as soon as he would have known their existences. This information gap is not always corrected by existing tools. We will analyze this visitor behavior, his mode of reasoning and propose a solution to improve his visit.

We will consider the use-centric approach incorporating a Bayesian approach [3]. This reflection can help to build a new interface, for better informations for the user and therefore for a better experience. The Bayesian approach is the first logical step to calculate or revise the probability of a hypothesis. Indeed, the tourist who visits a city makes assumptions relative to the choice of places to visit according to his degree of knowledge, or his beliefs. These beliefs are usually based on what he read on the websites, on social media or on word or mouth. In the Bayesian perspective, a probability is the numerical translation of this state of knowledge. Finally we will also integrate the new dimensions offered by so-called smart and connected cities based on sensors, open data, new ways of connectivity and exchange of informations [4]. In fact, We will allow the user to take advantage the free connections of cities.

C. Stephanidis (Ed.): HCII Posters 2018, CCIS 850, pp. 40–45, 2018.
https://doi.org/10.1007/978-3-319-92270-6_6

2 Tourist Behavior and Bayesian Modeling

A tourist visits a city with a priori behavior, that is he considers that if he visits for example Paris, he must visit museums, such as the Louvre, … He may not know that there are other sites to visit who often are on his move. It is sometimes a posteriori that he will know that there was a most interesting place he could have seen and it generates regrets. In addition, the tourist may also consider that one site is better than another, either on the basis of his beliefs or by consulting the evaluation sites. He then builds a utility related to this visit. The notion of utility U is an essential element in our decision making [5]. In this approach, a rational agent makes a calculation according to several components like profit due to this action, well-being, comfort… Trying to maximize this utility and for that we calculate the occurrence probability of each action, and so how we calculate this probability. Attributions of probabilities manifest the limits of our knowledge about a phenomenon. In fact, these measures only make sense in relation to our expectations. Frequentist interpretation defines probability assignments referring to frequencies in which certain events are repeated. Then the probability is defined as the relative frequency of occurrence of events over a long period [6]. In the case where the probability is based on a frequency of occurrence and we indicate all the knowledge we have to establish this probability of occurrence. No additional information will be able to modify our calculation. For example, no casino player would change his bet by seeing if it is raining outside. However this new element, this additional information, can be taken into account on the choice of a tourist visiting a city. In propensity probability, the measure of probabilities consists in considering them as measures of the possibilities of an event [7].

Thus the interest of the propensity approach is that no agent will use only a simple possibility to predict its eventual event. Moreover, the notion of possibility itself supposes that we can attribute to situations propensities, objective tendencies to the realization of these possibilities. In this model, the more informed the agent is, the more likely he can act according to a fact-based and frequency of occurrence. He must have information and a high level of knowledge. The notion of learning is very important in this propensity to act. This force of action can unfortunately not be identical for all agents and our tool will allow them to acquire necessary informations to calculate this probability, and consequently the best utility and the best experience.

2.1 Subjective Probabilities

In this approach the agent thinks to know the probability of appearance and does not try to calculate the true probability. The subjectivist conception of probability explains that the probabilistic results we calculate are solely linked to the limits of our knowledge of phenomena and especially of the ignorance of these limits [8]. Indeed, a subjective probability measures the degree of belief of an agent in the realization of an event, future or past. This hidden part of the reality is the cause of our subjective reasoning and we tend to simplify, to translate events according to our level of knowledge. For instance, if we suppose an agent does not know a place to visit, he builds his itinerary according to his beliefs and does not know the means to optimize his visits but will be sensitive to any information tending to improve the calculations and consequently to the actions improvement in order to enjoy his stay.

3 Bayesian Inference

This notion of subjective probability leads us to Bayes's work, which explains that we calculate a posteriori probabilities from a priori probabilities. Indeed, Bayesian inference is a simple mathematical theory that characterizes our "reasoning process" in a state of "uncertainty", our brain sometimes receives incomplete information and tend to supplement it according to our beliefs [3]. On this basis, we make decisions based on this calculation that allows us to obtain a probability only on the basis of estimation. We can think that going to a place believing that it is good to visit it. We will also consider the two ways we reason, the deductive and inductive approach. The deductive approach shows a mode of human reasoning where we say that all men are mortal and I am a man then I am mortal [9]. On the other hand in the inductive approach [10], we can lead to aberrant situations where we say that if all the cats are mortal and that I am mortal then I am a cat and that makes us lead to bad choices. We can begin to describe the idea that a tourist can end up in a disagreeable situation because he started from a bad reasoning. Bayes' formula makes it possible to put numerical values on the inductive reasoning. Classically, the agent will perform calculations that can enable him to evaluate a situation based on so-called subjective probabilities [11].

$$P(H|D) = \frac{P(D|H).P(H)}{P(D)} \tag{1}$$

$P(H)$ is the degree of belief that one has vis-à-vis the hypothesis H before taking into account the observations and it is called a priori probability. $P(H|D)$ is the degree of belief after taking into account observations, it is called a posteriori probability and $P(D|H)$ is the likelihood, and quantifies the degree of compatibility of hypothesis H and observations D. This formula makes it possible to revise our degrees of belief according to the observations and to make the inductive reasoning quantitative.

4 Cox-Jaynes Theorem and Error Corrections

This second aspect makes it possible to improve our application by giving a mathematical consideration of each of the functionalities. For Cox, an agent represents his degrees of belief by real numbers, he formulates a certain number of desiderata ensuring the consistency of his reasoning and deduces the properties necessarily verified by these real numbers [12]. Let's go back to the base of the beliefs of agents. One of the problems observed when choosing destinations is the degree of trust in the information issuer. Based on this fact, we must offer to the agent useful and reliable informations because we have indicated above, the agent is flexible and ethical i.e. he uses any pre-existing information to build his beliefs. According to Cox-Jaynes, this representation of the degrees of belief is done by real numbers, resulting in an internal consistency. If a conclusion can be obtained in many ways, each of these ways must lead to the same result, an intellectual honesty which means that the agent does not have to deliberately ignore the relevant information. Jaynes consistency of two identical mental states must be represented by two identical degrees of belief. For this reason, we can think about how agents acquire knowledge and on that basis we will design our interface.

5 Modality of Action of an Agent

An agent immersed in an environment is a person who acquires information through various sources, makes models and acts on what he considers useful. The agent is autonomous and possibly non-reactive, indeed he can ignore some of these perceptions and act or not. On the other hand, utility is a function which makes it possible to judge the value of an action, and is necessary for the decision-making process. The utility may vary over time, and depends on the type of agent and may be based on notions of survival, food, money. How to apply our model in the situation of an agent in asymmetric information, agent who has only low a priori probabilities about certain sites and who can miss opportunities to visit. In this situation, the most difficulty is to model this uncertainty or ignorance between a subjective uncertainty because of the insufficiency of our knowledge, and the real objective uncertainty that can exist because of the environment. Learning methods must answer these two main difficulties. First, we must note that an agent cannot learn if he does not have a minimum knowledge of the phenomenon he is studying. He must be able to give sense to the digital data received, specifically to understand that these data concern the same phenomenon. This notion of semantisation is important in our point of view, it is to be linked tç the informational and cultural level of the agent. It is obvious that our ability to understand remains limited to our ability to learn, unless we offer learning tools and the addition of wiki, video, route, map, presence of Guide-Speaker… to respond to needs of certain users. The tourism experience is therefore enriched. The agent then uses this model to integrate the new data and update its knowledge [13].

6 Features to Enhance the Tourist Experience

In this section, we consider that the functionalities that we will implement, based on the probabilistic theory of causality [14], have an effect on tourist decision. Indeed, we can consider that a cause have usually an effect, if an effect is observed after an action. This point of view is fundamental if we want to develop an interface with functionalities that makes possible, for an user, an increase of the information partition in the Bayesian sense, and as a consequence allow improvement of a priori probabilities. We will focus our research to determine the causes that can influence this probability, looking for active entities C_i that produce effects E_j, for example the places to visit. For each active cause C_i, a coefficient σ_i, representing its importance in the process, is measured [14]. The sign of σ_i measure the impact of the cause, the information acquired the effect observed and in our case if the decision of the tourist influenced by a new functionality. Our tool will constantly act in a positive way on the agent. We see clearly that by determining the causes C_i we can influence the propensity of a tourist to act. Moreover, we will integrate all specific forces, noted S_i, such as temporary exhibitions, the path to be accomplished given the geolocation of the tourist near the place to visit, amenities, kind of attraction forces on the tourist that have an impact on his decision. We aim to determine the transformation threshold of the a system states, represented by agent and the amount of informations available, i.e. to define the emergence of a new quality of agent and new decisions that would not have been taken specially if these informations were not available at first sight. By providing, the coefficients Ci related to the sites to visit and other factors that are provided by the city, that we have note Si, we see that the completeness of the information tends towards omniscience and can help tourist for a better way to enhance his experience (Fig. 1).

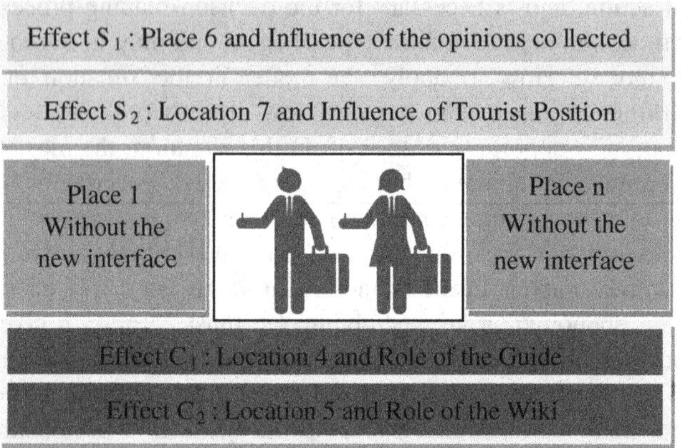

Fig. 1. Tourist in a different situations without our interface and with Causes C_i and/or Attraction S_i

7 Conclusion

In this work, we introduce a new approach for a new idea for functionalities, and we measure each contribution of each feature of this interface These characteristics have a weight and these causes may have an influence on the tourist, to make his visit easier and very pleasant. We considered the agent itself, using the Cox-Jaynes theorem, and we conclude an agent, if the information is accessible, to use this interface for his own well-being.

References

1. Maciocco, G., Serreli, S.: Enhancing the city: new perspectives for tourism and leisure. In: Maciocco, G., Serreli, S. (eds.) Enhancing the City, pp. 1–15. Springer, Dordrecht (2009). https://doi.org/10.1007/978-90-481-2419-0_1
2. Narangajavana, Y., Fiol, L.J.C., Tena, M.Á.M., Artola, R.M.R., García, J.S.: The influence of social media in creating expectations. An empirical study for a tourist destination. Ann. Tour. Res. **65**, 60–70 (2017)

3. Gilboa, I.: Rationality and the Bayesian paradigm. J. Econ. Methodol. **22**(3), 312–334 (2015)
4. Gretzel, U., Sigala, M., Xiang, Z., et al.: Electron Markets **25**, 179 (2015). https://doi.org/10.1007/s12525-015-0196-8
5. Lane, D.A.: Utility, decision, and quality of life. J. Chronic Dis. **40**(6), 585–591 (1987)
6. Ash, R.B.: Basic Probability Theory. Courier Corporation, North Chelmsford (2008)
7. Popper, K.R.: The propensity interpretation of probability. Br. J. Philos. Sci. **10**(37), 25–42 (1959)
8. Anscombe, F.J., Aumann, R.J.: A definition of subjective probability. Ann. Math. Stat. **34** (1), 199–205 (1963)
9. Johnson-Laird, P.N.: Mental models, deductive reasoning, and the brain. Cogn. Neurosci. **65**, 999–1008 (1995)
10. Perfors, A., Tenenbaum, J.B., Griffiths, T.L., Xu, F.: A tutorial introduction to Bayesian models of cognitive development. Cognition **120**(3), 302–321 (2011)
11. Ajzen, I., Fishbein, M.: A Bayesian analysis of attribution processes. Psychol. Bull. **82**(2), 261 (1975)
12. Clayton, A., Waddington, T.: Bridging the intuition gap in Cox's theorem: a Jaynesian argument for universality. Int. J. Approx. Reason. **80**, 36–51 (2017)
13. Furutani, T., Fujita, A.: A study on foreign tourists' behavior and consumer satisfaction in Kamakura. J. East. Asia Soc. Transp. Stud. **6**, 2154–2169 (2005)
14. Bellis, M.: Causalité, propension, probabilité. Intellectica **2**(21), 199–231 (1995)

Player Analytic Technologies in Tennis: An Investigation of Non-professional Players' Personal Values and Perceptual Orientations

Sebastian Guevara Martinez and Stephan Schlögl(✉)

Department of Management, Communication & IT,
MCI Management Center Innsbruck, 6020 Innsbruck, Austria
interaction@mci.edu

Abstract. The use of technology in sports has grown significantly in recent years. Analytic systems, in particular, have changed the way athletes train, execute and evaluate their performance. In tennis, however, the cost for installing, maintaining and operating such systems has so far prevented greater market penetration. While more affordable devices are emerging, their acceptance and consequent adoption remains low, although players and coaches understand their value and usefulness. Exploring hindering factors, the goal of the research presented in this paper was to better understand existing users, so as to identify those device features, which directly link to personal values and hence may be seen as most important for increasing adoption. Interviews with 20 amateur tennis players showed that the video feature seems to be most essential, as it helps players improve their game and consequently increase their competitiveness. Furthermore, they seem strongly interested in the systems' statistics and ranking functions.

Keywords: Player analytics technology · Means-end-chain theory
Value perception

1 Introduction

Throughout the last decade, the sports industry has experienced significant adaptations. The introduction of sport analytic systems has changed the way in which coaches and players analyze, understand and control performance growth. In tennis, however, this technological revolution has so far mainly focused on professionals and not so much on upcoming high performance junior or recreational players. In order to better understand potential success factors our research therefore focused on current users of such systems. That is, we used an interview study and consequent content analysis to identify personal values attributed to a distinct player analytic technology. From a hardware point of view, the focus

C. Stephanidis (Ed.): HCII Posters 2018, CCIS 850, pp. 46–53, 2018.
https://doi.org/10.1007/978-3-319-92270-6_7

was set on the *PlaySight SmartCourt*[1], as this seems to be the system with the largest number of features currently on the market. In order to identify users' personal values, we first identified relevant system attributes and then focused on understanding their consequences. Once attributes and consequence had been identified, the goal was to dig deeper and make users share their personal values, i.e. identify the goals motivating their system usage. These three elements, i.e. *attributes, consequences* and *values*, were identified using the Means-End Chains (MEC) theory [1].

2 Theory of Means-End Chains

MEC theory is based on the hypothesis that users/consumers of a product see the product and its attributes as a tool to accomplish a desired end-state. The theory states that consumers' product selections are linked to a hierarchical model composed of a product's *attributes*, the *consequences* of its use and the *personal values* attached to their product selection [2]. A chain is thus composed of three hierarchical levels linking *attributes* with *consequences* and *values*. The higher the level, the higher its abstraction [3]. The two lower levels (i.e. *attributes* and *consequences*) are concerned with the users' knowledge of a product's attributes and/or characteristics and the consequences linked to them. The highest, most abstract level (i.e. *values*) locates the personal values associated with using the system [4]. Thus, a ladder or chain reaching from *attributes* to *values* displays an individual's perceptual orientation towards a product, which helps identify the psychological consequences of product use and consequently relates to a user's personal values [5].

3 Research Methodology

We conducted a total of 20 interviews with amateur tennis players who use the *PlaySight SmartCourt* at least 2 times per week. The goal was to identify the relevant emotional triggers (i.e values) that motivate the utilization of this system. Following the above described MEC theory, the collected interview material was investigated using a laddering technique composed of the following five stages: (1) laddering, (2) coding, (3) development of an Implication Matrix, (4) development of a Hierarchical Value Map, and (5) identification of dominant perceptual orientations [2].

3.1 Laddering, Coding and Implication Matrix

We started with one-on-one interviews, aimed at understanding how users translate features into meaningful relations between themselves and the system. Here the focus was set on the *"Why is that so important for you?"* question. The goal

[1] https://www.playsight.com/.

was to identify a perceived link between the system's attributes and users' associated personal values. Next, these links were coded, i.e. categorized into *attributes*, *consequences* and *values*. The following Implication Matrix (IM) then composed a square matrix of these elements, listing codes in both rows and columns and forming interaction points between elements. Connections are illustrated in fractional form, where the left part of the decimal (the part preceding the comma) shows direct connections and the right part of the decimal (the part following the comma) shows indirect connections [6] (Note: A connection between elements is considered direct when they are next to each other, and indirect when the two elements are part of the same chain but not consecutively aligned [2]).

3.2 Hierarchical Value Map and Dominant Perceptual Orientations

The Hierarchical Value Map (HVM) seeks to visually represent the meaningful connections of the IM by focusing on those connections which fulfill a given cut-off criterion. In cases where the sample consists of 50 ore less participants a cut-off criterion of 3–5 connections is recommended [2]. The HVM further differentiates between five different types of relations:

- A → D: adjacent elements with a high number of direct connections.
- N → D: non-adjacent elements with a high number of direct connections.
- A → I: adjacent elements with a high number of indirect but low number of direct connections.
- N → I: non-adjacent elements with a low, non-zero number of direct but a high number of indirect connections.
- N → O: non-adjacent elements with a low (or zero) number of indirect connections.

The A → D relationships are the most important ones, signifying the base of the map. These relations are most common as they represent the strongest ties. The N → D relations are not very common, as most elements that have a lot of direct relations are mapped as adjacent. Nevertheless, in some cases an element may fit between two other elements and in doing so may even give a distinct meaning to this relation. The A → I relations appear usually when no dominant path is visible and two elements are mapped based on their indirect relation rather than their direct one. The N → I relations are also common as many of the elements which have indirect relations are found in chains that have a high number of repetitions. As a consequence, the strong ties or direct relations become dominant and are the ones mapped adjacently. Finally the N → O relation, which is the least common, refers to elements which are part of the same chain in the map but were never explicitly highlighted by a participant. This may occur when one consequence is associated with multiple attributes and every attribute is strongly linked to a particular personal value. So even if two elements have zero indirect relations they may be mapped as an N → O relation [2].

4 Discussion of Results

From the 20 interviews we extracted 109 chains; i.e. element relationships in the form of *attribute* → *consequence* → *value*, with a total of 35 unique elements (cf. Fig. 1), all of which were given a number so that they could be identified when building the consequent IM shown in Fig. 2. As already explained earlier, the IM displays the number of direct and indirect relations between different elements. For example, cell (1.12) shows that the attribute *Video* (1) and the consequence *Identify mistakes* (12) have a total of 22 relations of which 19 are direct and 3 are indirect.

Attributes	Consequences	Values
(1) Videos	(12) Identify mistakes	(25) Fun
(2) Statistics	(13) Improve game	(26) Independence
(3) User-friendly	(14) Coach feedback	(27) Efficiency
(4) Information Availability	(15) Save time	(28) Competitive
(5) Ranking	(16) Prepare next game/tournament	(29) Personal Fulfillment
(6) 3D Function	(17) Compare with other players	(30) Ambition
(7) Drill Function	(18) Better understanding	(31) Family
(8) Auto-tagging Function	(19) Better chances of winning	(32) Perfectionist
(9) Visualization Function	(20) Learn	(33) Responsibility
(10) Video Speed/Zoom Function	(21) No excuses	(34) Confidence
(11) Social Function	(22) Extra Motivation	(35) Health
	(23) See Your Progress	
	(24) Recognition	

Fig. 1. The 35 unique elements (i.e. attributes, consequences and values) extracted from 20 interviews.

In order to identify the most important element connections, the subsequent HVM includes only those relationships, which show at least tree links. It was further decided to only consider direct links, as such puts the focus on strong ties. Applying these two criteria the data was reduced by approximately one third. The resulting HVM is presented in Fig. 3.

4.1 General Findings

The first main conclusion that can be drawn from both the IM and the HVM is that the majority of attributes share the same consequence, i.e. they help *Identify mistakes* (12) in the game of players. The attributes *Auto-tagging* (8), *Video* (1), *Statistics* (2), *3D function* (6) and *Drill function* (7) are all A → D relations, with the consequence element *Identify mistakes* (12). Particularly dominant, given their high frequency, seem the row-column pairs 1 → 12, 2 → 12 and 1 → 10. The pair 1 → 12 alone shows a total number of 22 (19 direct and 3 indirect) links. Another important aspect highlighted by the HVM is the strong connection between the *Identify mistakes* element (12) and the *Improve game element* (13), with a total frequency of 51 connections (45 direct and 6 indirect).

	12	13	14	15	16	17	18	19	20	21	22	23	24	25	26	27	28	29	30	31	32	33	34	35
1	19.03	2.18	2.04		0.02			0.08	2.01	2.01				0.04			0.07	0.06	0.03		0.02	0.02	0.04	
2	7.01	6.05	0.01					0.08				1.00		0.01	0.01		0.10	0.02					0.01	
3	0.01	0.01		3.01			1.00								1.00	0.04				0.01				
4	2.04	0.06	3.00	4.00	0.02			0.03		1.00					0.01	0.01	0.03	0.02	0.01				0.03	
5						10.00								0.07			0.03		0.01					
6	5.00	2.05			0.01	1.00		0.02									0.05	0.01					0.02	
7	3.00	8.02						0.03			1.00			0.02			0.06	0.01	0.02				0.04	
8	6.01	4.09		2.01			1.01	0.03						0.04		0.01	0.07	0.02	0.02		0.01		0.03	
9	2.00	0.02					2.00	0.01						0.02			0.01	0.01						0.01
10	9.02	0.10	1.00				1.00	0.03	0.01								0.08	0.02	0.01				0.02	
11													1.00										0.01	
12		45.06	2.02		3.00		1.00	1.12	2.00	1.00				0.08	2.00	1.00	1.26	0.14	0.07		0.01		3.11	1.00
13	3.00		1.01					18.01						3.05		1.01	19.15	15.04	3.06		3.00		8.02	
14	2.00	3.02			1.00			0.01									1.01	0.02	1.00	0.02			1.01	
15	3.02	2.03					1.00	0.01							0.01	3.03	1.00	1.00	0.01	0.01	0.01		0.01	
16		2.00	1.00					1.02									0.02	0.01					1.01	
17					1.00									6.01			3.00		1.00				0.01	
18	2.01	2.03		2.00				1.00						0.01		0.01	0.03	0.01			0.01			
19														4.00			14.00	4.00					6.00	
20	1.00	2.02															0.02	0.01	0.01					
21		1.00																0.01				2.00	1.00	
22														1.00										
23																		1.00						
24																							1.00	
25																	1.00	1.00	1.00					
26																								
27																				1.00				
28														4.00					1.00					
29																1.00								
30																								
31																								
32																								
33																								
34																	2.00		3.00					
35																								

Fig. 2. The Implication Matrix built from found element connections.

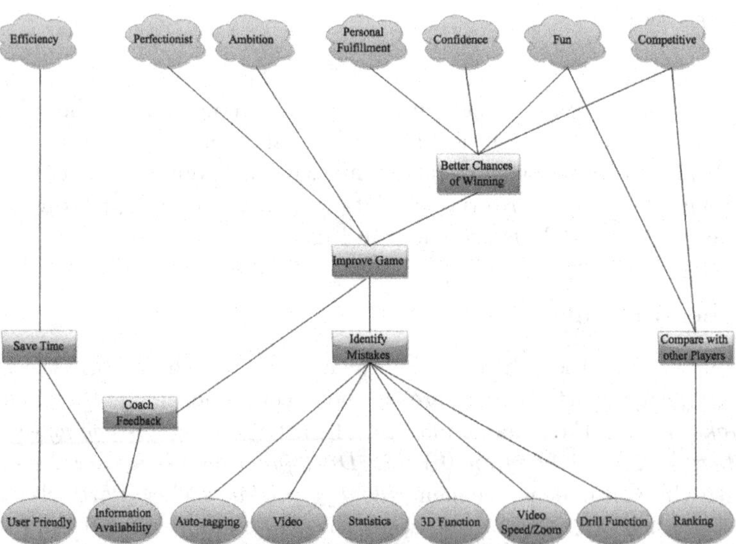

Fig. 3. The Hierarchical Value Map showing element relationships which met the defined threshold.

This shows a clear pattern, underlining that for most participants the consequence of identifying mistakes in their game means to work on them, and by doing so to ultimately improve their *Chances of winning* (19).

The pair 13 → 19 has a frequency of 19 relations, 18 of which are direct. Here it is important to highlight that the pair 13 → 28 is an N → D relation, for even though it shows a high number of direct relations they are mapped as indirect in the HVM (13 → 19 → 28). This is because the element *Better chance of winning* (19) fits between both of these elements and has furthermore a strong connection with the *Competitive* element (28). Also, the *Improve game* element (13), in addition to having an A → D link with the *Chance of winning* element (19), has also links to the elements *Ambition* (30) and *Perfectionist* (32).

Furthermore, is it important to inspect those three attributes which follow a different pathway in the HVM, i.e. *User friendly* (3), *Information availability* (4), and *Ranking* (5) (cf. Fig. 3). The *User friendly* attribute (3) is strongly connected to the *Save time* consequence (15) (although a frequency of 4 is significantly lower than those relation frequencies mentioned earlier). The only other attribute that shares this consequence is the *Information availability* attribute (4). Both of these chains are linked to the personal value *Efficiency* (27).

The *Information availability* element (4) is furthermore a part of the chain 4 → 14 → 13 → 19 → X, where X stands for a number of different elements (i.e. 32, 30, 29, 28, 25 or 34). The main difference between this chain and any of the chains leading to the *Improve game* element (13) is that this one includes the *Coach feedback* consequence (14) instead of the *Identify mistake* one (12). This means that here the link is not to the *Identify mistakes* element (12) but instead to the possibility of receiving feedback from the coach to reach the *Improvement in their game* consequence (13).

Furthermore interesting is that the *Ranking* function (5) is part of a unique chain, which is strongly connected to the *Compare with the other players* element (17). This attribute then conforms two different chains, one ending in *Fun* (25) and the other one ending in *Competitive* (28).

In order to extract more meaningful information from the HVM we will now focus on the most important *attributes*, *consequences* and *values*. Theses elements were determined by comparing the number of relations they were part of.

4.2 Dominant Perceptual Orientations

Any path from bottom (*attribute*) to top (*personal value*) is assumed to be a perceptual orientation [2]. The dominant perceptual orientations are the strongest and consequently most important chains in the HVM. In total we found 46 perceptual orientations. Referring to past studies (cf. [7,8]) we considered two rules in helping us determine the dominant ones. First, we defined a cut-off criterion by considering the mean number of relations (direct and indirect) depicted by all perceptual orientations. Second, such was separately applied to perceptual orientations with three, four and five elements. Doing this we found that in the group of perceptual orientations with three chain elements, only one of the chains seemed dominant. That is, the chain *Ranking* → *Compare with other players* → *Fun* was the only one whose value was above the mean. It had a total of 24 relations (16 direct and 8 indirect) which is 33% more than the average of all the other chains in this group.

Concerning the group of perceptual orientations with four elements, a small adaptation in the way those orientations were defined had to be performed so as to increase the accuracy of the results. That is, given that the *Identify mistake* and/or *Improve game* elements were part of more than 90% of all perceptual orientations mapped in the HVM, we decided to exclude their connections to *Information availability* → *Ambition* and *Information availability* → *Perfectionist*. Having applied this adaptation, the average number of relations for this group was 85.08, leading to five perceptual orientations regarded as being particularly strong, of which the one linking the *Video* and the *Ambition* elements (72 direct and 43 indirect relations) was the most dominant one. Important to note here is that four out of the five dominant perceptual orientations led to the *Ambition* value, highlighting its relevance for the user.

Finally, there were 28 perceptual orientations containing five elements. Even if this group had similar issues than the one before, the larger total minimized the effect the *Identify mistake* attribute (12) had on the mean, so that no adaptation was needed. On average a perceptual orientation in this group had 143 relations. A total of 13 of the chains were considered dominant. Here we see that all the chains that started from the *Video* attribute (1) are considered dominant. This is because video, being the core attribute of the system, is linked to more than one personal value. It is also important to highlight that the perceptual orientation *Video* → *Competitive* is the one with the largest number of relations (122 direct and 96 indirect). This is not surprising, considering that in this chain all the core elements are included. Another interesting point may be found in the fact that all the personal values involved in this group of perceptual orientations are in at least one of the dominant perceptual orientations. This speaks for the reliability of the result, as it shows that although the core value (i.e. *Competitive*) is the one which appears most, all of the others were represented in this group as well.

5 Conclusions

In summary, our results show that users perceive the *PlaySight SmartCourt*'s *Video* feature as the most essential one. Other relevant system features include the *Statistics* function, the *Auto-tagging* function, the *Drill* function, the *Video/speed* zoom function, *Information availability*, the *Ranking* function, and the system's overall *User-friendliness*. From a consequence perspective we found that two are perceived as particularly important. That is, the *Identify mistakes* and/or *Improve game* consequences appear in 94% of all identified perceptual orientations. Consequently it may be assumed that users who use an external aid in their tennis sessions do so in order to achieve better results in their game development. Such is also highlighted by the *Better chance of winning* consequence, following all the other core consequences identified in the HVM.

However, the personal values as to why users want to identify their mistakes and improve their game vary (although it is worth noting that a large number of them end in the *Competitive* value). We may therefore argue that the *PlaySight SmartCourt* system (and similar PAT devices) are predominantly used by competitive players who want to improve their game and consequently their performance in competitive events such tournaments. However, a large number of participants also associate the systems' features with values of *Personal fulfillment* and *Fun*. This means players do not only value pure competitive advances (i.e. win over others) but also aim at improving their game as a means of personal fulfillment. Finally, our analysis also showed that people use these systems to increase their *Confidence* - a potential marketing opportunity so far largely overlooked by system providers.

References

1. Gutman, J.: A means-end chain model based on consumer categorization processes. J. Mark. **46**, 60–72 (1982)
2. Reynolds, T.J., Gutman, J.: Laddering theory, method, analysis, and interpretation. J. Advert. Res. **28**, 11–31 (1988)
3. Gutman, J.: A means-end model for facilitating analysis of product markets based on consumer judgement. Adv. Consum. Res. **8**, 116–121 (1981)
4. Walker, B.A., Olson, J.C.: Means-end chains: connecting products with self. J. Bus. Res. **22**(2), 111–118 (1991)
5. Reynolds, T.J., Perkins, W.S.: Cognitive differentiation analysis: a new methodology for assessing the validity of means-end hierarchies. In: ACR North American Advances (1987)
6. Saaka, A., Sidon, C., Blake, B.F.: Laddering. a "how to do it" manual-with a note of caution. In: Research Reports in Consumer Behavior: How to Series. Cleveland State University, Ohio (2004)
7. Fotopoulos, C., Krystallis, A., Ness, M.: Consumers motivations in purchasing "new wines" in Greece with emphasis on wine produced by organic grapes1: a means-end chains approach. Zaragoza (Spain) **28**, 31 (2002)
8. Leão, A.L.M., Mello, S.C.: The means-end approach to understanding customer values of a on-line newspaper. BAR-Braz. Adm. Rev. **4**(1), 1–20 (2007)

ReMIS and ReMIS Cloud: Information Systems for Retrieving Disciplinary and Interdisciplinary Data

Daniel Kaltenthaler(✉), Johannes-Y. Lohrer, and Peer Kröger

Institut für Informatik, Ludwig-Maximilians-Universität München, Munich, Germany
{kaltenthaler,lohrer,kroeger}@dbs.ifi.lmu.de

Abstract. In this paper, we describe and compare the architectures of the two novel information systems ReMIS and ReMIS Cloud that were designed to retrieve interdisciplinary data. We deal with corresponding data often being spread over numerous, distributed, and heterogeneous data sources. This is a severe limitation for research since a comprehensive analysis can only be done when considering the entire context. Furthermore, analyses would additionally benefit from using interdisciplinary, but still coherent data. We describe the two different information systems and discuss the field of application. We highlight the differences and similarities of the architectures and show their benefit with an example from the archaeo-related sciences for which both information systems are reasonably applicable.

Keywords: Anonymous databases · Architecture · Content sharing
Data retrieval · Distributed data sources
Information management system · Interdisciplinary data · ReMIS
ReMIS cloud

1 Introduction

The retrieval of information is an important step in the process of increasing knowledge. Retrieving information from different sources on the same topic is essential to increase the base of information for analyses. But scientific analyses especially benefits from the consideration of distributed information of different disciplines to regard additional aspects. However, the retrieval of disciplinary and interdisciplinary data often is technically limited, has to be done manually by the scientists.

Methods to retrieve information from different data sources have been developed for many years and range from Data Warehouses [1] which gather all information in a single database, to Federated Information Systems [2,3] that allows interoperability and information sharing between decentrally organized information systems, and Mediator-based systems [4–6] that allow the retrieval of heterogeneous data from distributed sources.

C. Stephanidis (Ed.): HCII Posters 2018, CCIS 850, pp. 54–61, 2018.
https://doi.org/10.1007/978-3-319-92270-6_8

All these system have in common that the data sources have to be managed by a central managing instance that must know and is able to access the distributed data sources. These are suitable approaches for data sources within one corporation or institution. However, it is not a viable approach to grant access to the own data source to an administrator from a different company or institution, for example because of reasons of privacy.

Therefore, as a contribution to solve these problems, we introduce two different information systems:

1. The architecture *Reverse-Mediated Information System* (ReMIS) is motivated by the need to search distributed data together with further contexts from multiple heterogeneous sources. ReMIS uses dynamic joins of results from heterogeneous data formats. It is based on the concept of common Mediator-based systems, but was modified to grant data owners full control over their data and allow the provision of their data without the need of a central administrator. ReMIS is mainly designed to collate data from different sub-disciplines of one field.
2. The extended architecture ReMIS Cloud enables information retrieval by linking different distributed data sources together to find inter-domain knowledge with an intuitive search interface. The architecture utilizes a category-based data source registration to connect differently shaped data types and formats. This novel way of information retrieval enables scientists to cross-connect information with domain-extrinsic, but coherent knowledge. ReMIS Cloud is intended to provide a central platform where all disciplines can connect and contribute data to the network, considering the requirements of the ReMIS architecture.

In this paper, we first describe ReMIS in Sect. 2 and ReMIS Cloud in Sect. 3. Then, we discuss the field of application of the two mentioned information systems and highlight the differences and similarities of the architectures in Sect. 4. Finally, we show the benefit of the two systems with an example from the archaeo-related sciences, for which both information systems are reasonably applicable, in Sect. 5.

2 Reverse-Mediated Information System

In this section, we introduce the *Reverse-Mediated Information System* (ReMIS) [7,8] that is designed to connect heterogeneous information from distributed, anonymous databases.

Architecture: The basic concept of ReMIS is based upon the well-known Mediator-based system [4–6]. But opposed to the existing system, the configuration of the connected data sources is not done by a central managing instance. Instead, it is up to the administrators of the individual data sources to connect their data to the network. Therefore, they remain full control over their data, without a central administrator who has insight in both, the data structure and the data.

To connect a data source to the network, the data owners have to execute the Connector Application on their server. There, they have to assign a minimum set of parameters, called "Minimal Search Parameters" (MSP) that have to be mapped to the corresponding columns in the data source. The actual parameters of the MSP are different in each applied domain. The MSP is necessary for the search, to identify the different entries sets, and to guarantee that the connected database contains the searchable parameters. For example in Bavaria, Germany, the MSP in the archaeo-related domains consist of the excavation number and the find label number (a unique number for all objects found at the same location). These parameters are available in all archaeo-related databases, independent of the underlying sub-domain.

Furthermore, the Connector Application allows to set privacy settings, so that it is up to the data owners to decide which subsets of the data shall be searchable and which should remain private. There are two options: First, by defining columns that are returned and therefore which are not. Second, by specifying conditions which have to apply for a data set to be included in the result of a query. This allows to not consider columns with sensitive information as well as to hide data sets which shall not be made public.

Once all parameters of the MSP are assigned, the data source can be registered to the Server Application that is executed on a central platform. The Server Application stores all connections to the connected data sources, without storing any actual data. Then, the data source is configured and registered to the system.

Summarized, the main difference between the well-known Mediator-based system and ReMIS is, that Mediator-based systems require a central administrator to manage and connect the data sources and to mediate the requests from the users, as sketched in Fig. 1. The administrator has always to know each data source to be able to connect them. In contrast, ReMIS is designed to allow the data owners to register and manage their data to the system on their own, as sketched in Fig. 2. The required mediation set-up is executed by a wizard dialogue. The architecture forwards the user requests to the data sources where the request is mediated.

Data Retrieval: For the data retrieval, a form – either at a website or an embedded solution in an application – provides the possibility to the user to retrieve domain-specific information from all data sources that are connected to ReMIS. The domain-specific MSP is requested from the Server Application to enable displaying search fields for each parameter of the MSP. Then, the user enters the search term for each of the parameters of the MSP.

The search request of the user is first sent to the Server Application which forwards the user request to all connected data sources. There, the Connector Applications translate ("mediate") all parameters of the MSP to their local data scheme. Then, the local data source is queried for the data sets that matches with the user input – the definied privacy settings are also considered in this query. The result is then sent back to the user via the Server Application. The retrieved data is displayed in table view to the user which also can be exported to CSV or spreadsheet files.

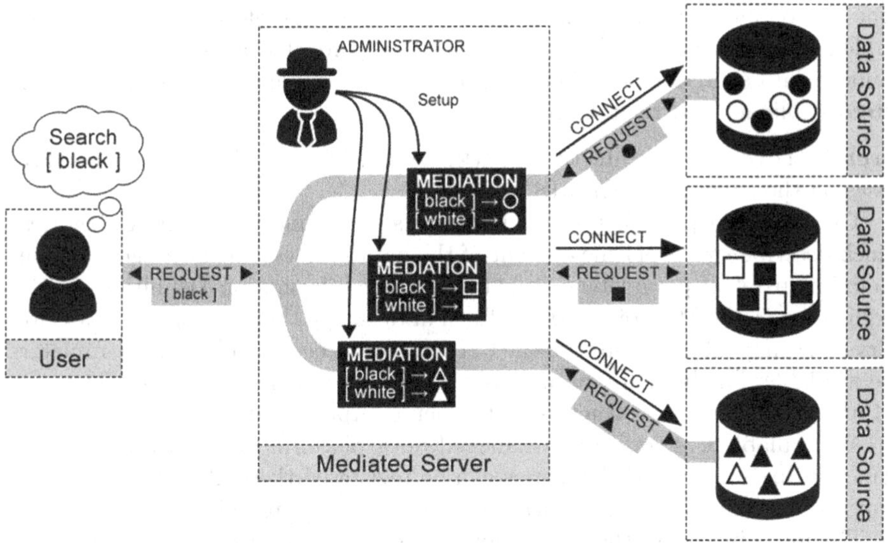

Fig. 1. Sketch of the well-known Mediator-based architecture [8].

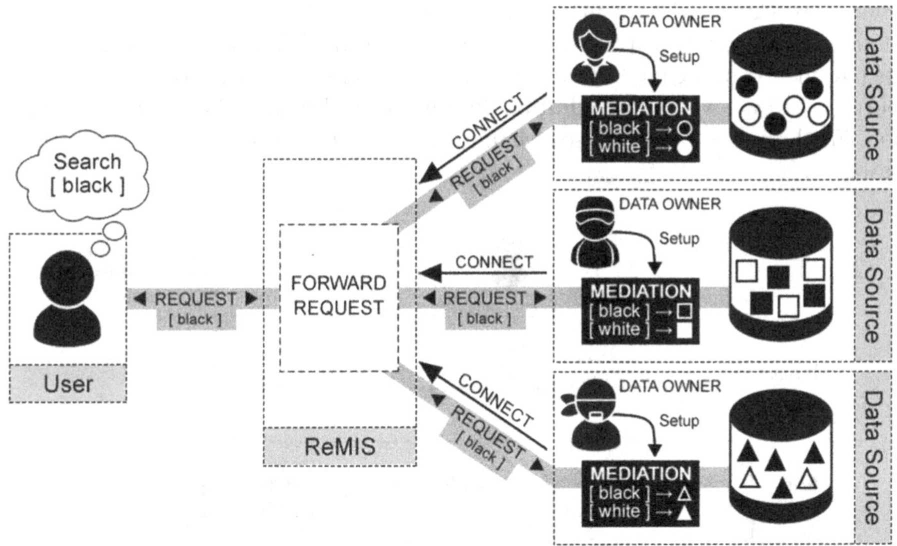

Fig. 2. Sketch of the *Reverse-Mediated Information System* (REMIS) [8].

3 REMIS-Cloud

The decentral architecture of REMIS is already a convincing approach for distributed, but similar structured data within one discipline. However, especially in sciences, the consideration of domain-extrinsic data is essential. Interdisciplinary data often exists for specific research areas but it is cumbersome and time-consuming to retrieve the coherent data sets. Therefore, we designed and implemented the ReMIS Cloud [9], an architecture that allows to register and connect data sources from different disciplines to enable the users to search for interdisciplinary, but related data sets.

Architecture: The architecture of ReMIS Cloud, that is sketched in Fig. 3, bases on the concepts of ReMIS.

The central aspect of the architecture is the management of "Categories" which describe (parts of) the content of the data sources. Each Category defines a minimum set of parameters, called "Category Information Definition" (CID) (equivalent to the MSP of ReMIS). Each data source that is assigned to a Category must map all parameters of the CID to guarantee that all search parameters are available. Furthermore, each Category can be assigned with tags. Basically, a Category equates the structure of the Server Application of ReMIS.

All available Categories are managed on a platform of a central server. In principle, any number of Categories can be registered there. A Category validation is reasonable to avoid duplicate or meaningless Categories.

The initialization of the connection between the data sources and the Categories is largely identical with the initialization of ReMIS between the Connector Application and the Server Application. However, there are two fundamental differences. First, a data source is not limited to one single Category. The connection to any number of Categories is possible provided that the assignment of the parameters of the CID to the data makes contextual sense. Second, each data source uses tags which can additionally be assigned in the Connector Application. Furthermore, each data source implicitly uses the tags of the corresponding Category.

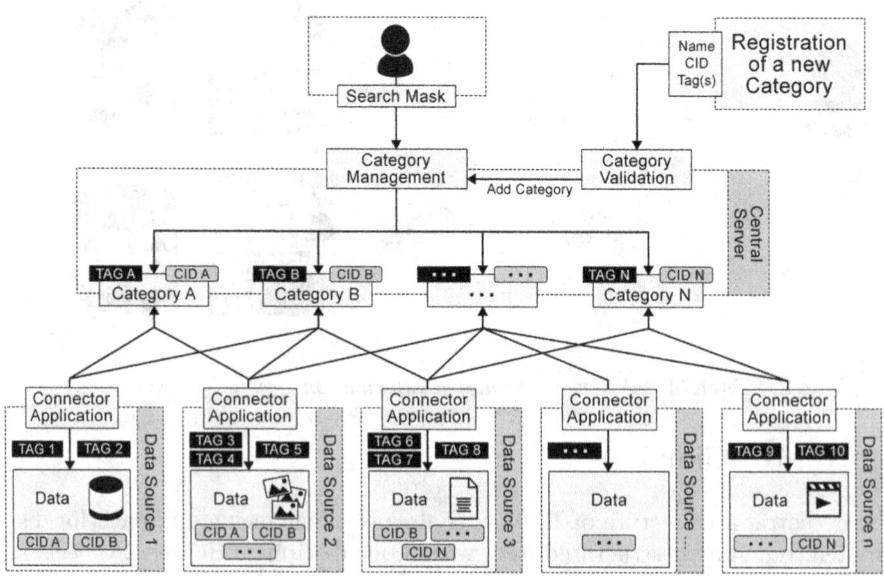

Fig. 3. An abstract sketch of the ReMIS Cloud architecture [9].

Data Retrieval: In step A of the data search, from a list of Categories C, the user can select all Categories $C^A \subseteq C$ that should be searched. For the selected Categories the corresponding CIDs are displayed in a search mask where the user can enter the search parameters P_{C^A} for the search request. Once the request is submitted, the central server forwards it to all data sources DS_{C^A} that are assigned to the selected Categories C^A. There, the Connector Applications translate all parameters of the query to their local data scheme. Considering the defined privacy settings, the result $R_{P_{C^A}}$ is retrieved from the data sources and is sent back via the central server to the user.

For step B, the user can select additional Categories $C^B \subseteq C \backslash C^A$ to achieve the retrieval of domain-extrinsic, but content-related information. The values P_{C^B} for the search parameters of the CIDs of the Categories C^B are read out of the result $R_{P_{C^A}}$. A further search request is executed over all data sources DS_{C^B} that are assigned to the selected Categories C^B. The result $R_{P_{C^B}}$ is then also sent back to the user.

Finally, the retrieved data $R := R_{P_{C^A}} \cup R_{P_{C^B}}$ is displayed in table view to the user. In step C, the users can filter the result R with the available tags to be able to only display the information of interest. The final result $R_{filtered} \subseteq R$ can be exported to CSV or spreadsheet files.

4 Comparison of ReMIS and ReMIS Cloud

While both presented information systems, ReMIS and ReMIS Cloud, have much in common, they still differ in some key elements. Basically, both systems enable the retrieval of heterogeneous data from distributed data sources. However, the most important difference is the scope of the systems. While ReMIS is only aimed for the retrieval of data from one well defined discipline, the ReMIS Cloud enables an interdisciplinary collation of data, including data from different scientific disciplines, knowledge information, inventory information, etc.

This requires a different infrastructure that is necessary for the systems. ReMIS is indended to be executed as single instances for each supported discipline. In comparison, the ReMIS Cloud is designed as a central platform where all Categories for the different disciplines can be added to enable interdisciplinary data retrieval. However, it is also conceivable to use an own instance of ReMIS Cloud for one field of application that has a large number of sub-disciplines.

In both systems, a central administrator, who manages all data sources, is not required in both systems. However, an administration of Categories is recommended for ReMIS Cloud to increase the quality of the available Categories. Data owners keep the full control about their data, the right management is administered in the Connector Applications, that means locally where the data sources are located. Only authorized data is transmitted to the information systems. It is the data owner who decides in the privacy settings which data can be searched and retrieved.

Briefly summarized, both systems, ReMIS and ReMIS Cloud, are designed for different scope of applications. However, it is not excluded that data sources can be connected to both systems, they are able to run in parallel on the same data source.

5 Use Case: Archaeo-Related Sciences

To demonstrate the application area in which ReMIS and ReMIS Cloud could prove useful, we want to present two use cases from the archaeo-related areas.

Retrieval of Distributed Information of an Excavation: After the excavation, the corpus of findings which were excavated (rest of buildings, artifacts, human burial remains, or faunal remains) are transfered to specialized (e.g. zooarchaeological, anthropological, archaeological, archaeobotanical, etc.) organisations where they are further analyzed and then archived or exhibited.

To analyze the find circumstances it can be important to also consider artifacts or remains of different categories which were found at the same location. For example in a grave, not only the human remains are interesting, but also which grave goods are found next to the human body to completely understand the historical context of the grave. However, since the data of the different types of findings are all distributely stored in databases of the different collections, retrieving this information requires the anthropologist to contact other scientists who have access to the different databases to get the information from them.

With ReMIS, all the different archaeo-related databases can be connected using the Minimal Find Sheet information for the MSP, that means the excavation number and the find sheet number. In Bavaria, Germany, these are assigned to the findings by the *Bavarian State Department of Monuments and Sites*[1] which are sent to the specialized collections, like the *Bavarian State Collection for Anthropology and Palaeoanatomy Munich*[2] or the *Bavarian State Archaeological Collection Munich*[3]. Therefore, it is guaranteed that the Minimal Find Sheet information is stored in all connected data sources. The scientist, who is interested in collating related information from the different disciplines, can use ReMIS to either query all connected data sources for a specific excavation (by searching a specific excavation number) or further restrict the findings with the find sheet number.

Retrieval of Excavation-Related, Interdisciplinary Information: With ReMIS distributed data from excavations can be collated. However, also the consideration of information from other disciplines is important. For example, other data sources contain climate information for different places which are registered to the Categories "Location" (for geographic coordinates) and "Climate" (for climate information). If the databases from the archaeo-related domain also contain geo data and therefore have also been registered to the Category "Location", this information could also easily be retrieved with ReMIS Cloud.

Therefore, first the Category "Archeao" is selected to retrieve the same data as in the first example of ReMIS. Then, in the second step, the selection of the additional Category "Location" enables retrieving related data from other

[1] www.blfd.bayern.de.
[2] www.sapm.mwn.de.
[3] www.archaeologie-bayern.de.

data sources that also have been subscribed to this Category. In this way, it is possible for the scientists to retrieve related (among others) climate information for their findings from the excavations.

References

1. Inmon, W.H.: Building the Data Warehouse. Wiley, New York (2005)
2. Sheth, A.P., Larson, J.A.: Federated database systems for managing distributed, heterogeneous, and autonomous databases. ACM Comput. Surv. **22**(3), 183–236 (1990)
3. Heimbigner, D., McLeod, D.: A federated architecture for information management. ACM Trans. Inf. Syst. **3**(3), 253–278 (1985)
4. Wiederhold, G.: Mediators in the architecture of future information systems. IEEE Comput. **25**(3), 38–49 (1992)
5. Wiederhold, G.: Interoperation, mediation, and ontologies. In: Proceeding of the International Symposium on 5th Generation Computer Systems (FGCS 1994), Workshop on Heterogeneous Cooperative Knowledge-Bases, pp. 33–48 (1994)
6. Wiederhold, G.: Mediators, concepts and practice. In: Özyer, T., Kianmehr, K., Tan, M., Zeng, J. (eds.) Information Reuse and Integration in Academia and Industry, pp. 1–27. Springer, Vienna (2013). https://doi.org/10.1007/978-3-7091-1538-1_1
7. Lohrer, J.-Y., Kaltenthaler, D., Kröger, P., Obermaier, H., van der Meijden, C.: Reverse mediated information system: web-based retrieval of distributed, anonymous information. In: 16th International Conference on WWW/Internet 2017, Vilamoura, Portugal, pp. 63–70 (2017)
8. Lohrer, J.-Y., Kaltenthaler, D., Richter, F., Sizova, T., Kröger, P., van der Meijden, C.: Retrieval of heterogeneous data from dynamic and anonymous sources. In: 8th IEEE International Conference Confluence 2018 on Cloud Computing, Data Science and Engineering, Noida, Uttar Pradesh, India, pp. 592–597 (2018)
9. Kaltenthaler, D., Lohrer, J.-Y., Richter, F., Kröger, P.: ReMIS cloud: a distributed information management system for interdisciplinary knowledge linkage. In: 8th International Conference on Internet Technologies and Society 2017, Sydney, Australia, pp. 107–114 (2017)

xBook, a Framework for Common Scientific Databases

Daniel Kaltenthaler[1(✉)], Johannes-Y. Lohrer[1], Peer Kröger[1], and Henriette Obermaier[2]

[1] Institut für Informatik, Ludwig-Maximilians-Universität München, Munich, Germany
{kaltenthaler,lohrer,kroeger}@dbs.ifi.lmu.de
[2] Bavarian State Collection for Anthropology and Palaeoanatomy, Munich, Germany
henriette.obermaier@palaeo.vetmed.uni-muenchen.de

Abstract. In this paper, we introduce xBook, an open-source framework that is designed for creating databases for heterogeneous scientific disciplines. Gathering and recording data is an essential part of scientific work. However, the challenges of the workflow are similar in the different fields. We want to support scientists in their work by offering a flexible and scalable framework that is intended to provide common functionalities to the inherited applications.

Keywords: Data analysis · Database · Features · Framework Launcher · Synchronization · xBook

1 Introduction

Collecting and sharing data is a frequent task in many scientific areas. Although each discipline has its own workflows and practices, the basic requirements are similar in many cases. Very often the gathered data has to be stored in a relational database, but an application to enter, search, exchange, analyze, and manage data, is also required to fulfill the scientific tasks. A common database framework solution, which is independent of the disciplinary field of work, could provide a general infrastructure to scientists that provides the widely used features.

Therefore, we implemented the xBook framework which provides built-in methods that follow the scientific workflow. Gathering and storing data to the database is enabled by dynamic input masks that can be composed by a wide range of predefined input fields. Custom input fields can also be integrated. The synchronization process, including a conflict management solution, allows the collaboration with colleagues, sharing of data with other users, and the possibility to work offline and synchronize data later. This process considers a flexible user and group rights management. The built-in Analysis Tool provides possibilities to execute analysis requests without special programming knowledge. Additionally, xBook also provides further features for data overview, filtering

C. Stephanidis (Ed.): HCII Posters 2018, CCIS 850, pp. 62–70, 2018.
https://doi.org/10.1007/978-3-319-92270-6_9

and search options, automatic application update processes, export and import possibilities, etc. Domain-specific features can also be implemented and added to any database. All features are integrated in a flexible, user-friendly graphical user interface that can be re-used and customized for each database application.

In this paper, we give an overview of the xBook framework and its features with four real examples of inherited applications from the archaeo-related domain.

2 Features

xBook is a generic open-source framework including the common and basic features for a database for scientific disciplines. Our main priority is to integrate – if possible – all features into the xBook framework to provide the available development to all "Books" (instances of xBook). Because each Book is built upon the xBook framework, all other Books also profit from this new feature. Each Book provides these common features: [1]

Collaboration Methods: For a database framework, which aims for the collaboration of different areas and scientists, it is important to offer different aspects that enable collaboration. The basis for the solution in xBook is the implementation of a synchronization which allows to share, to back-up, and to collaborate on specific data sets [2–4]. A synchronization method is especially required in sciences that gather their data directly in field work. Working on a global database is not always possible due to the lack of reliable Internet connections.

In xBook, data sets are organized as projects which each can be synchronized and shared. The users get displayed the list of projects in the synchronization panel that exist in the local database and the list of projects that exist on the server, as can be seen in Fig. 1 (left). From there, the projects to be synchronized can be chosen.

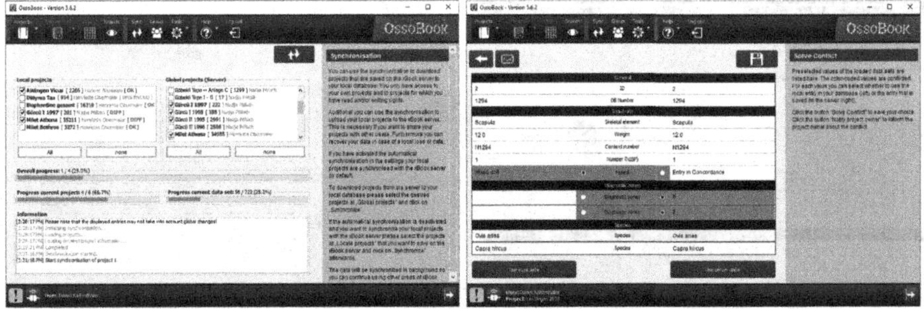

Fig. 1. Screenshots of the synchronization panel (left) and the conflict management panel (right) in OssoBook.

The synchronization uses timestamps on the global server to keep track of changes. Entries, that were edited on the clients, are marked with an indicator to keep track of entries that have to be synchronized. During the synchronization first all locally edited entries are sent to the server. Then, new or edited entries are synchronized back to the client in order of the timestamp of the entries on the server. A conflict might occur during the synchronization process if the timestamp of the synchronized entry is lower (older) than the timestamp on the server. Therefore, the user was not working on the most recent version of the entry as it has been edited on the server since the last execution of the synchronization. This conflict has to be solved by the user. The user can select whether to use the values that are saved on the client or the values that are saved in the local database in the conflict management screen, as can be seen in Fig. 1 (right). When the conflict of the entry is solved, the entry is updated on the server.

Additionally, a rights management is necessary to manage the access permissions to the data sets. The project owner authorizes other users to access or edit specific parts of the data. Since often the same work group of scientists (e.g. companies or within an institute) is working together, xBook also provides the definition of groups. This is necessary to avoid having to define and manage the rights for each single scientist of this group individually. The project owner can gain permissions to this group and the group owner can delegate the available rights within this group.

Analysis Methods: Analyzing data is usually the most important step of scientific work, regardless of the field of work. However, scientists may be specialized on other methods and may lack how to handle certain analysis tools or software which are necessary to create complex analyses. In addition, the export of data to spreadsheet or CSV files to use it in external applications can be aggravating, time-consuming, and error-prone.

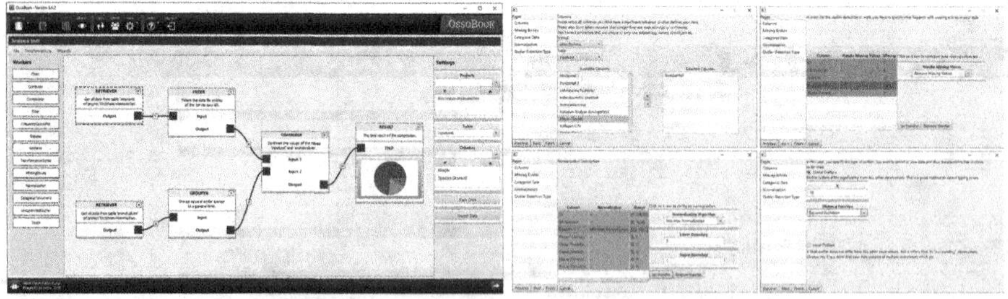

Fig. 2. Screenshots of the Analysis Tool which is embedded to OssoBook (left) and the Outlier Detection Wizard [7] (right).

Therefore, we developed the Analysis Tool [5,6] and embedded it into xBook (cf. Fig. 2 left) to provide analysis methods for the scientific data, without the requirement to first export and then import the data into another application. It is a flexible tool that provides a visual querying the data of the database scientists are used to work with. The tool is connected to the base application over a simple interface which defines the columns that can be used for the analyses. To composite an analysis the users can use independent modules called 'Workers' which each fulfill a specific task, e.g. retrieve, filter, sort, merge, or visualize data. Workers have inputs and outputs which can be connected to create the desired analyses.

By connecting the data output of one Worker with the data input of another Worker, a directed graph or multigraph is formed. The Workers in this graph are calculated, starting from the front Workers. The composition of the analysis can conclude in either an (exportable) table of data or a graphical representation in a diagram. This visual approach of the Analysis Tool enables the querying, analysis, and statistical evaluation of data, e.g. an outlier detection [7] (cf. Fig. 2 right), in the familiar user environment without the user having in-depth programming skills.

Graphical User Interface: xBook provides a flexible graphical user interface that consists of a basic, graphical structure which is used by each Book by default. These are necessary because all Books use the same logical structures, for example the login screen, the synchronization process, the settings, etc. However, these consist of dynamic elements that can individually be adjusted for each instance of xBook by override the abstract methods.

This way it is possible that each Book can have different input fields in the input mask, like indicated in Fig. 3. The xBook framework provides reusable input fields that contain the logic for handling and displaying the data. Each Book can integrate them into their input mask by defining their individual settings adjusted to the database, like the table or column where to store the data. Additionally, individual input fields can be implemented, the input masks are not limited to the predefined input fields. So each Book can have a complete different, individual structure of the input mask with diverse input fields that all consider the same program logic.

Similar to the input fields, it is also possible to customize the other elements of the graphical representation, for example to define the information displayed in the project overview screen, the general style of the Book (like the logo, the name of the Book, colors, etc.), the location where to save settings, the individual output for the export, etc. The navigation and sub navigation is also extendible to allow to integrate individual navigation elements for custom features.

This flexible structure has the advantage that all Books can reuse features and functions that have already been implemented before, either for the xBook framework or individual for another Book. This saves time and resources, so that necessary elements do not have to be implemented again and again for different applications.

xBook Launcher: The xBook Launcher (cf. Fig. 4) is the central application for the users to manage all Books. Since there are multiple instances of xBook we needed a stand-alone application that is independent of the Books, but allows to add each available Book.

This is done by entering the Book-specific URL in the xBook Launcher, then the Book will automatically be installed and can be executed. Existing Books are checked for updates and – if they are not up-to-date – be updated automatically to the current application version. Further update processes, to update the database scheme to the current version and to update the value tables used in the input fields of the Book, are integrated to xBook.

Further Features: Furthermore, the xBook framework provides several features that are required in scientific work. The stored data of the database is meaningfully displayed in a sortable data listing, considering that the values are human-readable. The framework provides an export method that saves the data in a CSV- or spreadsheet (XLS/XLSX) file on the local system. Both, the listing and the export, can be filtered by the user. The available projects can be searched for specific entries. A dynamic data importer is in development.

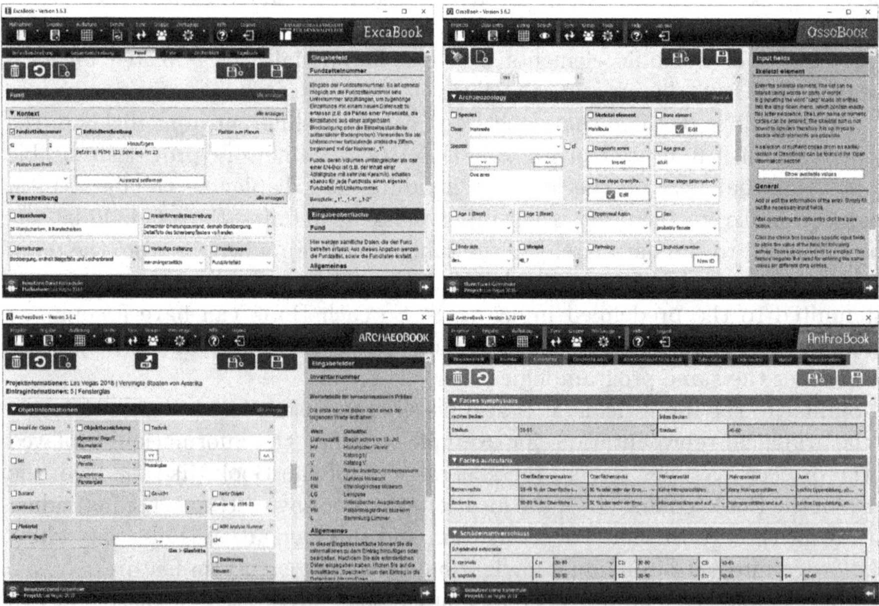

Fig. 3. Screenshots of the input masks of ExcaBook (top-left), OssoBook (top-right), ArchaeoBook (bottom-left), and AnthroBook (bottom-right).

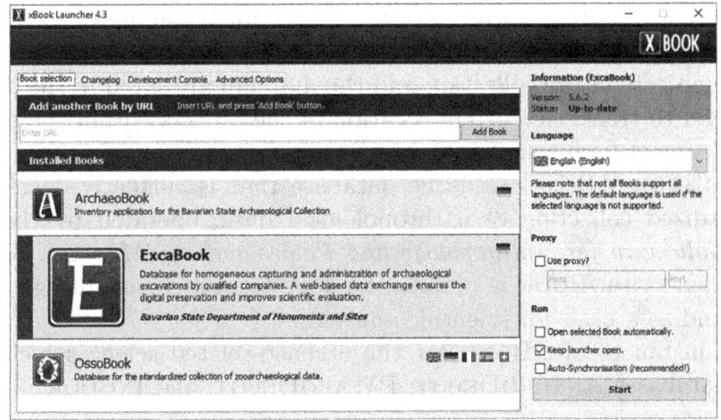

Fig. 4. Screenshot of the xBook Launcher.

3 Use Case: Databases in the Archaeo-Related Disciplines

In this section, we introduce four different databases from the archaeo-related domains that are based on the xBook framework. We first briefly describe each of the applications, then we describe the advantages that xBook provides them.

Archaeo-Related Databases: Examples of xBook Instances
Below, we introduce the available, archaeo-related instances of xBook.

ExcaBook [8] is an archaeological database for the documentation of excavations. It is used by the *Bavarian State Department of Monuments and Sites*[1] for the homogeneous capturing and administration of archaeological excavations by qualified companies. The state department creates new projects for the excavations and give the excavation companies access to the project. After the excavation is completed, they enter the excavation data into the database and transmit the data back to the state office by using the built-in synchronization method. Then, the state office continues internally administrating the data.

OssoBook [9] is a scientific database for the standardized collection of zooarchaeological data, for long-term archival storage, for data exchange, and serves as a basis for scientific analyses. It is currently used by approximately 350 users including scientists, Ph.D. students and students in institutes of universities, museums, and scientific collections with zooarchaeology as field of work as well as freelance zooarchaeologists. The synchronization method enables collaboration and the sharing of data. OssoBook is operated by the *Bavarian State Collection for Anthropology and Palaeoanatomy Munich*[2] and the *Institute of Palaeoanatomy, Domestication Research and History of Veterinary Medicine*[3] of the *Ludwig-Maximilians-Universität München*.

[1] www.blfd.bayern.de.
[2] www.sapm.mwn.de.
[3] www.palaeo.vetmed.uni-muenchen.de.

ArchaeoBook [10] is an inventory database for the archaeological findings of the *Bavarian State Archaeological Collection*[4]. The information and characteristics of the objects in the collection and the museum are saved in the database. It is also used to track the current location of the objects within the collection and to log loans of findings.

AnthroBook [11] is a scientific database that is currently developed for the standardized collection of anthropological data, operated by the *Bavarian State Collection for Anthropology and Palaeoanatomy Munich*[2]. Similar to OssoBook, AnthroBook is planned for long-term archival storage, for data exchange, and as a basis for scientific analyses.

Further instances of xBook for the archaeo-related sciences includes the inventory databases AnthroDepot, PalaeoDepot, and InBook.

Benefits for xBook Instances

The mentioned archaeo-related databases each focus on a different scenario: For administrating and retrieving homogeneous data (ExcaBook), for scientific usage (OssoBook and AnthroBook), and for inventory reasons (ArchaeoBook). However, they all benefit from the development of the xBook framework. xBook provides the features that were introduced in Sect. 2 that can be used by each database without having to implement an own solution.

The built-in synchronization method is flexible in use, each of the database use it for another purpose. While ExcaBook uses the synchronization to send and retrieve data to/from the excavation companies, OssoBook and AnthroBook requires the possibility to store data offline directly in the field and to synchronize the data later to share it with colleagues or other scientists, and ArchaeoBook use the method for house-internal collaboration.

Since xBook already provides the most basic structures, the developers of the databases could focus on the integration of the necessary input fields, without having to concern about how to save and load the data from the database and how to design the graphical representation. They benefit from a common graphical user interface and program logic which enables a fast development of a well-functioning application. Of course, customizations of the existing elements and the addition of new elements are still possible. Also the structure of the input masks are flexible for different uses. While OssoBook and ArchaeoBook each have one single input mask, ExcaBook uses several different input masks that are cross-linked among each other and AnthroBook manages one entry in several separates input masks.

Additionally, the workflow of a database application is comparable in the different archaeo-related disciplines – so the requirements for a database application are also similar. For example, all archaeo-related disciplines need a data export for long-term archiving or for standardized analysis tools. Since xBook provides an export feature the developers do not have to implement a new export method for each database. The same applies to the graphical user interface, user management methods, settings, etc.

[4] www.archaeologie-bayern.de.

Creating all these features individually for each single database application would take time and therefore could be expensive even if single features are small. Also bugs and errors have only to be fixed once in the framework instead of in each single application. Especially financially weak sciences benefit from saving money by using commonly developed frameworks like xBook.

4 Availability

The xBook Launcher is available from http://xbook.vetmed.uni-muenchen.de. From there, OssoBook, ArchaeoBook, and ExcaBook are publicly available.

References

1. Kaltenthaler, D., Lohrer, J.-Y.: The Historic Development of the Zooarchaeological Database OssoBook and the xBook Framework for Scientific Databases. ArXiv e-prints: arXiv:1801.08052 (2018)
2. Lohrer, J.-Y., Kaltenthaler, D., Kröger, P., van der Meijden, C., Obermaier, H.: A generic framework for synchronized distributed data management in archaeological related disciplines. In: 10th IEEE International Conference on e-Science, eScience 2014, São Paulo, Brazil, 20–24 October 2014, pp. 5–12 (2014)
3. Kaltenthaler, D., Lohrer, J.-Y., Kröger, P., van der Meijden, C., Obermaier, H.: Synchronized data management and its integration into a graphical user interface for archaeological related disciplines. In: Design, User Experience, and Usability: Users and Interactions–4th International Conference, DUXU 2015, Held as Part of HCI International 2015, Proceedings of Part II, Los Angeles, CA, USA, 2-7 August 2015, pp. 317–329 (2015)
4. Lohrer, J.-Y., Kaltenthaler, D., Kröger, P., van der Meijden, C., Obermaier, H.: A generic framework for synchronized distributed data management in archaeological related disciplines. Future Gener. Comput. Syst. **56**, 558–570 (2016)
5. Lohrer, J.-Y., Kaltenthaler, D., Kröger, P.: Leveraging data analysis for domain experts: an embeddable framework for basic data science tasks. In: 7th International Conference on Internet Technologies & Society 2016, Melbourne, Australia, pp. 51–58 (2016)
6. Kaltenthaler, D., Lohrer, J.-Y., Kröger, P.: Supporting domain experts understanding their data: a visual framework for assembling high-level analysis processes. In: 11th International Conference on Interfaces and Human Computer Interaction 2017, Lisbon, Portugal, pp. 217–221 (2017)
7. Blau, J.: Interactive outlier detection based on archaeological data. Bachelor thesis, Ludwig-Maximilians-Universität München, Germany (2018, to appear)
8. Kaltenthaler, D., Lohrer, J.-Y., Kröger, P; van der Meijden, Jantos, S., Rahm, A., Sassen, I., Wanke, T., Wanninger, R., Haberstroh, J., Sommer, S.: ExcaBook v5.6.2. [Computer Software], Munich, Germany (2018)
9. Kaltenthaler, D., Lohrer, J.-Y., Kröger, P; van der Meijden, C., Granado, E., Lamprecht, J., Nücke, F., Obermaier, H., Stopp, B., Baly, I., Callou, C., Gourichon, L., Peters, J., Pöllath, N., Schiebler, J.: OssoBook v5.6.2. [Computer Software], Munich, Germany; Basel, Switzerland (2018)

10. Kaltenthaler, D., Lohrer, J.-Y., Kröger, P; van der Meijden, Harrington, C., Claßen, E., Gebhard, R., Marzinzik, S., Schwarzberg, H.: ArchaeoBook v5.6.2. [Computer Software], Munich, Germany (2018)
11. Kaltenthaler, D., Lohrer, J.-Y., Kröger, P; van der Meijden, Mösch, A., Sizova, T., Harbeck, M., Toncala, A.: AnthroBook Development Version [Computer Software], Munich, Germany (2018)

Human Genome Data Protection Using PostgreSQL DBMS

Péter Lehotay-Kéry[1(✉)] and Attila Kiss[1,2]

[1] Department of Information Systems, Faculty of Informatics, ELTE Eötvös Loránd University, Budapest, Hungary
lkp@caesar.elte.hu
[2] J. Selye University, Komárno, Slovakia
kissae@ujs.sk

Abstract. There can be a data boom in the near future, due to cheaper methods make possible for everyone to keep their own DNA on their own device or on a central medical cloud. These are sensitive data. There are a lot of cases, when genomes are contained in text files. The size of these can even be 3 GB on every user. Secured data management is not solved in these files.

By using database managers, the levels of permissions can be managed, security and encryption is not the task of the user, because these are integrated into the database manager systems. In this paper, we would like to demonstrate, with the use of an open-source database manager system and with some typical bioinformatical algorithms, that bioinformatical methods can be solved with integrating them into the database manager systems. With efficiency measurements we would like to present, that the use of database manager systems can be efficient in more complex environments.

Keywords: Bioinformatics · Biology · Cryptography · Databases Genetics

1 Storing and Working with DNA

Deoxyribonucleic acid (DNA) is a complex molecule which contains the genetic information. These are built up by nucleotides. Each nucleotide is built up by 3 components: nucleobases (adenin - A, guanin - G, citozin - C, timin - T), a sugar called deoxyribose and a phosphate group.

In bioinformatics, we store DNA sequences as strings, which are composed by the 4 characters for the 4 nucleobases: 'C', 'G', 'A' and 'T'. Similarly, we can store RNA and protein sequence data too.

Typical function on these datasets is string matching, when we are looking for places, where a pattern occurs as a substring of a text, in our case a pattern of nucleotides in a DNA sequence. For example the Boyer-Moore algorithm, when we preprocess our pattern is a good choice on this task. But we can preprocess

C. Stephanidis (Ed.): HCII Posters 2018, CCIS 850, pp. 71–78, 2018.
https://doi.org/10.1007/978-3-319-92270-6_10

the genome too, using indexes: we can index with substrings, on suffix trees, on suffix arrays or FM indexes.

Due to sequencing errors and natural variations it's important when we work with DNAs to be able to let a certain number of mismatches when we do matching. For this case we must have approximate matching too. Sometimes it is not enough, so we use sequence alignment, which is a way of arranging the sequences of DNA, RNA, or protein to identify regions of similarity that may be a consequence of functional, structural, or evolutionary relationships between the sequences. For this, we can use dynamic programming.

Other typical function is the sequence assembly, when we align and merge fragments from a longer DNA sequence to reconstruct the original sequence. This is needed as DNA sequencing technology cannot read whole genomes in one go, but rather reads small pieces of between 20 and 30000 bases, depending on the technology used. We can use the shortest common superstring, overlap layout consensus assembly or De Bruijn Graphs for this task [1].

In this paper, we made measurements on naive matching and Hash table indexes.

2 Block Cyphers

PostgreSQL supports some block cypher algorithms. Block cyphers are working with a transformation specified with a symmetric key on fixed-length groups of bits, called block.

A block cipher consists of two paired algorithms, one for encryption E, the other for decryption D, which is the inverse of E. Both will accept 2 inputs: an input block of size n bits and a key of size k bits. Both will give a size n bit output block.

Feistel ciphers split the block of plain text to be encrypted into two equal-sized parts. The round function is applied to one half, then the output is XOR-ed with the other half. After that the two halves are swapped. From the examined ciphers, Blowfish, Triple DES and Cast-5 uses this method [2].

3 Related Works

There are some works already born on the topic of databases for bioinformatics. In [3] an efficient scheme have been presented in PostgreSQL, and compared with other scheme and with file based storage. In [4] measurements have been made on the effectiveness of PostgreSQL compared to Cassandra NoSQL database. In [5] where the authors used MySQL, presented scheme and queries. But none of these say anything about data protection or user hierarchies.

The used and tested bioinformatical algorithms are taken from [1].

When encrypting genomes, We must consider that cyphers with 64-bit blocks are vulnerable to birthday attacks because of the small block sizes [6]. However when attacking the AES, witch uses 128-bit blocks, the key can be recovered [7]. So perhaps there's no algorithm which gives 100% protection, but we should not just store these sensitive information without any encryption. For genome protection we also examined blockchain [8].

4 Results

We implemented the a library for bioinformatics, with processing methods working on encrypted genomes. It can easily be added and used in databases and queries and it can be used for matching, aligning nucleotides and indexing.

Permissions can be set to data accesses and to module accesses and also user hierarchy can be created.

We can crypt our genomes with chosen cipher algorithm.

5 Permissions

In PostgreSQL, we can use roles to manage access privileges. Roles can act as users, groups or both. Roles can own database objects and can manage the permissions on these objects.

Creating, dropping roles and can get the existing roles from the pg_roles catalog:

```
CREATE ROLE name
DROP ROLE name
SELECT rolname FROM pg_roles
```

A fresh system always contains a predefined role, which is always superuser and has the same name as the OS user, who initialized the cluster. Be careful, a superuser can bypass any permission checks. As a superuser, we can create more superusers. Being a superuser is a role attribute. The superuser has all these privileges.

Example attributes: superuser, permission to log in, to create databases, roles and setting the password:

```
CREATE ROLE name SUPERUSER
CREATE ROLE name LOGIN
CREATE ROLE name CREATEDB
CREATE ROLE name CREATEROLE
CREATE ROLE name PASSWORD 'string'
```

These attributes can be modified after the creation of the role using ALTER ROLE. Every object has an owner. Normally the owner is the role that has created the object. By default, only the owner or superuser can do anything with the object. Permissions must be set to change this. There are a lot of privileges: SELECT, INSERT, UPDATE, DELETE, TRUNCATE, REFERENCES, TRIGGER, CREATE, CONNECT, TEMPORARY, EXECUTE, USAGE and ALL for all privileges. Now we won't discuss all of these. The GRANT command can be used to set permissions. PUBLIC keyword can be used to give the permission to everyone on the system. We can revoke privileges using REVOKE.

Grant and revoke privileges:

```
GRANT privilege ON object TO role
REVOKE privilege ON object FROM role
```

If we want to use groups, we must first create a role. These usually don't have LOGIN role. Every member of the group can use SET ROLE to temporarily use the privileges of the group and objects created by the user role are considered to be owned by the group. Moreover roles that have the INHERIT attribute, automatically can use the privileges of their groups.

Add and remove roles to the group:

```
GRANT group_role TO role1, ...
REVOKE group_role FROM role1, ...
```

In our cases, superusers would be database engineers, and the genome of the users would be stored encrypted, to not let the superuser read them without the symmetric key: the password. The users would be the owners of their own genomes.

6 Genome Crypting

In PostgreSQL, we can use the pgcrypto extension to encrypt genomes. This module provides cryptographic functions, like digest() and encode() computing the binary hash of the given data, or hmac, which works only with a key. For password hashing we can use crypt() and gen_salt() (Fig. 1).

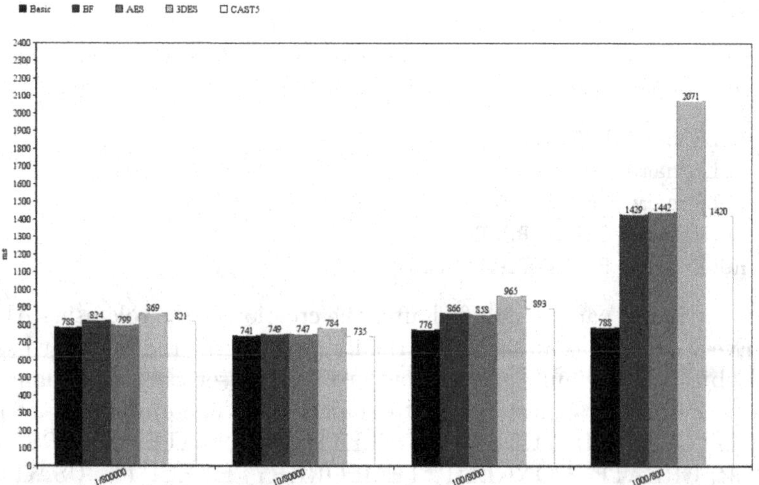

Fig. 1. Naive matching on 792 KB encrypted genome with different divisions into rows: x: number of rows/number of characters in each, y: time in ms

This module supports both symmetric-key and public-key encryption. We are using symmetric encryption, where the user will have a password and the user will store one's genome encrypted with that password. This encryption will be done by pgp_sym_encrypt(), decryption will be done by pgp_sym_decrypt().

When encrypting, we chose cipher algorithm, set it with 'cipher-algo' option, which provides bf, aes128, aes192, aes256, 3des, cast5. Based on the measurements, overall we can say, we will generally have slower algorithms with 3des. The others were similar. Moreover, based on the measurements, with the growing number of rows to decrypt, the distance between the basic and encrypted algorithms will grow. But on one row the encrypted version is not much slower. Usually we won't use much rows.

Blowfish (bf) is a 16-round Feistel network with a 64-bit block size and a variable key length from 32 bits up to 448 bits [9].

AES is based on the Rijndael encryption, used by some international organization like banks. Block size is 128-bit, key size 128-bit for AES128, 192 for AES192 and 256 for AES256 [10].

Although Triple DES (3des) is slower than the others, it gives good protection, used in the electronic payment industry too. It is not a completely new block cypher algorithm, it simple uses three DES keys, K1, K2 and K3, each of 56 bits on 64-bit blocks [11] (Fig. 2).

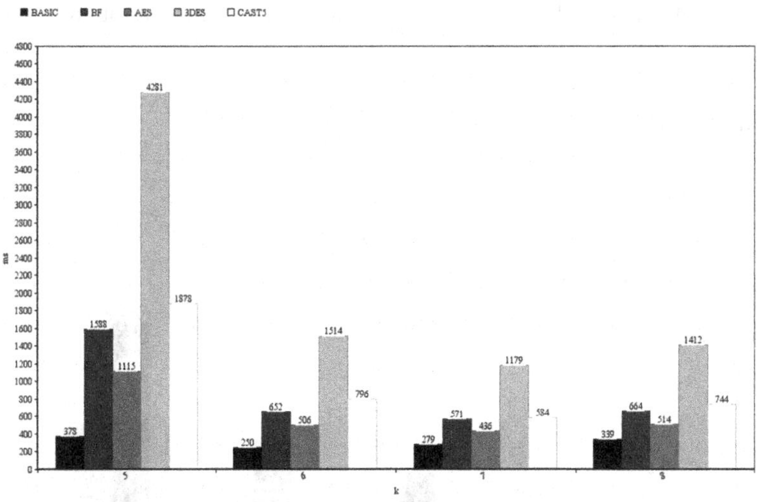

Fig. 2. Querying the index of a 792 KB encrypted genome with different stored kmer lengths: x: kmer, y: time in ms

Cast5 is a 12- or 16-round Feistel network with a 64-bit block size and a key size of between 40 and 128 bits. It is the default cipher in some versions of GPG and PGP [12].

Bad news about encrypted genomes that we tried some measurements using encrypted hash indexes too, in classical hash table style. But it was slower than the naive match because of the lot of rows and the lot of decryption.

We can solve this issue, if we put an index of a whole cell into a single cell. We convert the index into a json string and we encrypt that whole index into one cell.

In the hash index we store every kmer of the genome in sorted order and for every kmer the offsets.

Then when querying the index, we convert back, decrypt and process the index of the cell.

We can see that, our results are depend very much on how we chose k. Without encryption k = 6 is the best, but with encryption k = 7 is the best. Here 3Des is the slowest, too. But differences comes out much more on the cipher algorithms. Now we can clearly see that AES is the fastest, BF is the second, CAST5 is the third.

7 Genome Compression

We can use compression algorithms too, we can set the compress algorithm with 'compress-algo' option, which provides ZIP or ZLIP compressions. They usually have really similar compression result. We can also set the compression level with 'compress-level' option. PostgreSQL has some basic compression mechanisms (Fig. 3).

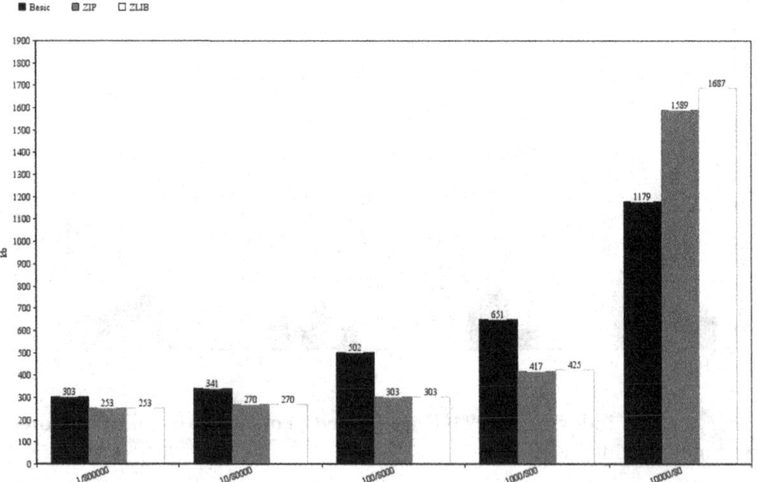

Fig. 3. Compression of 792 KB genome with different divisions into rows: x: number of rows/number of characters in each, y: overall table size in KB

What we can see here, we tried to store a 792 KB excerpt from the human genome in multiple ways. When we stored the whole in a single cell, the compression worked, but as we have divided the genome into more cells, and put smaller parts into the cells, the size grew, and in the end, became bigger than the source file. We can see that too, ZIP worked a little better on small parts, but ZLIB was a little faster in decompression.

With the basic compression mechanism we had the index table on 4,300 KB, but we could make it smaller with zip and zlib to 2,850 KB.

With the basic postresql compression, the whole 3,205,606 KB human genome has been stored on 1,181,802 KB, with ZLIB it has been decreased to 939,851 KB, with zip, it has further decreased to 939,835 KB.

8 Future Work

We are planning to extend the library with further functions, like faster up indexes, and will make it available it for free usage on more platforms. Moreover, we will compare the features of this PostgreSQL solution with solutions in other database manager systems. We will develop an online test user interface too. We will include the usage of blockchain on bioinformatical data.

Acknowledgment. The project was supported by the European Union, co-financed by the European Social Fund (EFOP-3.6.3-VEKOP-16-2017-00002).

References

1. Bockenhauer, H.-J., Bongartz, D.: Algorithmic Aspects of Bioinformatics. Springer, Heidelberg (2007). https://doi.org/10.1007/978-3-540-71913-7
2. Katz, J., Lindell, Y.: Introduction to Modern Cryptography. CRC Press, Boca Raton (2014)
3. Lichtenwalter, R.N., Zorina-Lichtenwalter, K., Diatchenko, L.: Genotypic data in relational databases: efficient storage and rapid retrieval. In: Kirikova, M., Nørvåg, K., Papadopoulos, G.A. (eds.) ADBIS 2017. LNCS, vol. 10509, pp. 408–421. Springer, Cham (2017). https://doi.org/10.1007/978-3-319-66917-5_27
4. Aniceto, R., Xavier, R., Guimarães, V., Hondo, F., Holanda, M., Walter, M.E., Lifschitz, S.: Evaluating the Cassandra NoSQL database approach for genomic data persistency. Int. J. Genomics **2015** (2015)
5. Rice, M., Gladstone, W., Weir, M.: Relational databases: a transparent framework for encouraging biology students to think informatically. Cell Biol. Educ. **3**(4), 241–252 (2004)
6. Bhargavan, K., Leurent, G.: On the practical (in-) security of 64-bit block ciphers: collision attacks on HTTP over TLS and OpenVPN. In: Proceedings of the 2016 ACM SIGSAC Conference on Computer and Communications Security, pp. 456–467. ACM (2016)
7. Bogdanov, A., Khovratovich, D., Rechberger, C.: Biclique cryptanalysis of the full AES. In: Lee, D.H., Wang, X. (eds.) ASIACRYPT 2011. LNCS, vol. 7073, pp. 344–371. Springer, Heidelberg (2011). https://doi.org/10.1007/978-3-642-25385-0_19

8. Mytis-Gkometh, P., Drosatos, G., Efraimidis, P.S., Kaldoudi, E.: Notarization of knowledge retrieval from biomedical repositories using blockchain technology. In: Maglaveras, N., Chouvarda, I., de Carvalho, P. (eds.) Precision Medicine Powered by pHealth and Connected Health. IP, vol. 66, pp. 69–73. Springer, Singapore (2018). https://doi.org/10.1007/978-981-10-7419-6_12
9. Schneier, B.: Description of a new variable-length key, 64-bit block cipher (Blowfish). In: Anderson, R. (ed.) FSE 1993. LNCS, vol. 809, pp. 191–204. Springer, Heidelberg (1994). https://doi.org/10.1007/3-540-58108-1_24
10. Daemen, J., Rijmen, V.: The Design of Rijndael: AES-the Advanced Encryption Standard. Springer, Heidelberg (2013). https://doi.org/10.1007/978-3-662-04722-4
11. Barker, E.: SP 800–67 Rev. 2, Recommendation for Triple Data Encryption Algorithm (TDEA) Block Cipher. NIST Special Publication 800:67 (2017)
12. Adams, C.: The cast-128 encryption algorithm (1997)

A Compliance Method for the Design and Airworthiness Certification of Civil Aircraft Flight Deck Human Factor

Haiyan Liu(✉), Dayong Dong, and Hua Meng

Shanghai Aircraft Design and Research Institute, Shanghai, China
liuhaiyan@comac.cc

Abstract. Detailed analyses of past incidents and accidents have shown that the majority of them are related to crew performance failures in the form of a series of errors, sometimes in combination with system failure, which led to severe safety consequences. Therefore, CS25.1302/FAR 25.1302 were issued in order to develop effective strategies for reducing flight crew error. But the methods of evaluating human error provided by the regulation are far less straightforward, and there are no absolute norms available to identify how good the human-system performance is.

This paper sets an integrated compliance method for the design progress and certification of Human factor of civil aircraft flight deck. In order to provide the pilots with more concise HMI and more friendly POP in the Human-centered cockpit, specialized attention should be paid on the human error risks related to the system integration level, complexity and novelty. Consideration on the Intended Function and Associated Flight Crew Tasks, Controls, Presentation of Information, System Behavior, Flight Crew Error Management were deeply discussed here in Validation and Verification of civil aircraft flight deck functions were adopted within the design process based on the System Engineering approach.

Recommendation on the means of compliance including statements of similarity, design description, calculations/analysis, evaluations and test were provided in terms of flight crew tasks. Researches and practice on the static evaluation, documental evaluation, sub-task evaluation as well as full-task evaluation were carried on in order to minimize the occurrence of human errors and the management of their effects. Documented matrix of MoC and a list of simulator/real aircraft test scenarios were planned for the verification of typical human errors relevant to flight deck performance.

The method is verified in the design progress of a china-designed type to produce a successful program.

Keywords: Flight deck · Human factor · Airworthiness certification

1 Introduction

Accidents most often result from a sequence or combination of errors and safety related events (e.g., equipment failure and weather conditions). Analyses show that the design of the flight deck and other systems can influence flight crew task performance and the occurrence and effects of some flight crew errors.

C. Stephanidis (Ed.): HCII Posters 2018, CCIS 850, pp. 79–84, 2018.
https://doi.org/10.1007/978-3-319-92270-6_11

Approval of flight deck systems with respect to design-related flight crew error has typically been addressed by referring to system specific or general applicability requirements, such as CS 25.1301(a), CS 25.771(a), and CS 25.1523. However, little or no guidance exists to show how the applicant may address potential crew limitations and errors. The regulation CS25.1302/FAR25.1302 is focus on human errors. The rule text is:

§25.1302 Installed systems and equipment for use by the flightcrew.

This section applies to installed equipment intended for flight-crew members' use in the operation of the aeroplane from their normally seated positions on the flight deck. This installed equipment must be shown, individually and in combination with other such equipment, to be designed so that qualified flight-crew members trained in its use can safely perform their tasks associated with its intended function by meeting the following requirements:

(a) *Flight deck controls must be installed to allow accomplishment of these tasks and information necessary to accomplish these tasks must be provided.*
(b) *Flight deck controls and information intended for flight crew use must:*
    (1) *Be presented in a clear and unambiguous form, at resolution and precision appropriate to the task.*
    (2) *Be accessible and usable by the flight crew in a manner consistent with the urgency, frequency, and duration of their tasks, and*
    (3) *Enable flight crew awareness, if awareness is required for safe operation, of the effects on the aeroplane or systems resulting from flight crew actions.*
(c) *Operationally-relevant behaviour of the installed equipment must be:*
    (1) *Predictable and unambiguous, and*
    (2) *Designed to enable the flight crew to intervene in a manner appropriate to the task.*
(d) *To the extent practicable, installed equipment must enable the flight crew to manage errors resulting from the kinds of flight crew interactions with the equipment that can be reasonably expected in service, assuming the flight crew is acting in good faith. This sub-paragraph (d) does not apply to skill-related errors associated with manual control of the aeroplane.*

Often, showing compliance with design requirements that relate to human abilities and limitations is subject to a great deal of interpretation. Findings may vary depending on the novelty, complexity, or degree of integration related to system design.

2 Certification Approach

The unique aspect of rule 25.1302 is that it considers the flight crew task as the guiding element for assuring safe operation of the aircraft. It is the task that defines what equipment needs to be used when, in what order, by whom and in what combination with other installed equipment. Note however that it is not the task that is being certificated, but the integrated combination of installed equipment that enables safe task execution in this particular flight deck design.

Flight crew high level task listing:

- Aviate - control the aircraft's path
  - Control aircraft to maintain flight (airspeed, altitude, attitude)
  - Monitor flight parameters (airspeed, altitude, attitude)
  - Configure aircraft flight surfaces
  - Configure flight guidance system (autopilot) for control of aircraft
  - Monitor flight guidance system (autopilot) control of aircraft
- Navigate - direct the aircraft from its origin to its destination
  - Control aircraft direction in flight in accordance with flight plan
  - Control aircraft direction on the ground
  - Configure flight guidance system and/or FMS for navigation of aircraft
  - Monitor flight guidance system and/or FMS navigation of aircraft
- Communicate - provide data and requests and receive instructions and information with ATC, company (dispatch, operations, maintenance, and ground crews), flight crew, and cabin crew
  - Configure communication system
  - Control (initiate and respond to) communications
  - Monitor communications
- Manage flight and systems - plan and monitor flight, manage and monitor systems and resources
  - Develop and modify flight plan
  - Monitor flight path, fuel consumption, and ATC clearance compliance
  - Configure systems
  - Monitor systems
  - Manage systems (including faults)
  - Monitor fuel
  - Manage fuel
  - Monitor weather
  - Monitor traffic, terrain, and obstacles
  - Monitor for hazardous atmospheric conditions
  - Manage flight (prioritise and integrate resources and systems; develop and modify flight plan).

Note that there are discrete types of tasks (with a clear start and finish) and continuous tasks like monitoring and manual flight control. Manual flight requires continuous attention and needs to be listed as such. Other monitoring activities are performed most often only when there is time left. Such tasks can be noted on a separate list for later analysis (the timeline will otherwise be contaminated with non-actual or assumed activities instead of real activities).

The certification approach proposed to demonstrate compliance with the requirements in CS 25.1302 also provides the basis for the demonstration of compliance with the Human Factors requirements.

2.1 Identify Systems Versus Flight Crew Tasks

Perform their tasks is an important part of the 25.1302 rule. The flight crew tasks therefore need to be specified first as required by the missions flown by the Aircrft. These tasks are sequenced on a timeline with the systems used, for both the Captain and First officer while flying nominal and non-nominal flights, including emergency handling, information, response and feedback (awareness) requirements will be specified for each task.

The results of the 25.1523 task analysis will be reused where possible and detailed according to 25.1302 requirements.

2.2 Analyse Characteristics of Intended Functions and Associated Crew Tasks

Task accomplishment requires the use of installed systems according to associated crew procedures. Flight crew tasks characteristics therefore have to be defined and analysed with respect to their:

- Urgency: urgent tasks need special access and simple actions
- Frequency: an often used system need easy access and feedback
- Duration: long tasks need protection against interruptions and errors.

2.3 Document Design Requirements and Human Performance Issues to Be Verified

AMC 25.1302 states that:

The applicant should identify design requirements applicable to each of the systems, components, and features for which means of demonstrating compliance must be selected. This can be accomplished in part by identifying design characteristics that can adversely affect flight crew performance, or that pertain to avoidance and management of flight crew errors……….

An initial list of requirements for each system will be drafted based on the earlier analysis of documents and information available. This list or matrix will, together with the flight crew task analysis timeline be used as input for a comprehensive flight deck review.

2.4 Perform Human Factors Flight Deck Audit

Initially a full human factors audit of the flight deck of the Aircraft will be undertaken. The objective of this audit will be to evaluate the basic ergonomic features of the system interfaces with respect to their stated intended function and their adequacy for addressing the high level crew tasks associated with operating a modern jet airliner. The tool used for the review will be CODEP (Cockpit Operability and Design Evaluation Procedure). This tool uses a task based approach that systematically addresses the accessibility of controls, the adequacy of presented information, the integration level of the flight deck etc.

The appropriate MOC for each system cannot be defined until the initial flight deck audit has been undertaken. The HF flight deck audit is, however, a key component in providing the scope and a framework for subsequently defining the appropriate certification MOC. The HF audit will be performed specifically to address the design issues within the scope of CS 25.1302.

For each system interface component, the degree of integration, complexity and novelty will also be assessed:

- The level of systems integration is concerned with the extent to which there are interactions and/or dependencies between systems which may affect the crew's operation of the aircraft.
- The complexity of the system refers to aspects such as the number of information elements the flight crew has to use to perform a given flight task or the number of control modes on a particular multifunction control.
- The novelty of systems on the flight deck may be based upon factors such as new methods of operation for established flight deck systems or unusual or additional operational procedures required as a result of the introduction of new technologies.

2.5 Produce Requirements Matrix with Proposed MOC List

The results of the flight deck audit will be used to produce the MOC list for the authority approval. to agree on the final insights and issues (if any) and approve the final test lists.

3 Means of Compliance Development

AMC 25.1302 requires that novel features may require extra scrutiny during the certification process whereas the process to approve less novel features may be somewhat less rigorous. However, until the formal human factors flight deck audit has been completed it will not be possible to specify a final list of the proposed method(s) to demonstrate the MOC applicable for each flight deck system/pilot interface.

Compliance may be established through by a combination of one or more generic methods: a statement of design similarity; the use of engineering drawings; calculation/formal analysis; evaluation and/or test.

- A 'statement of similarity' is a description of the system and a description of a previously certificated system detailing the physical, logical, and operational similarities. By such structured comparison with an existing flight deck function/feature it may be possible demonstrate its adequacy with respect to avoiding, detecting and/or recovering from errors without unnecessary effort.
- It may be possible to substantiate that a design meets the certification requirements simply by describing the design in the form of 'engineering drawings'. It is likely, though, that using drawings will be limited to describing the physical arrangement of equipment or demonstrating compliance with very simple presentational issues (e.g. the colour of warning functions).

- 'Calculations' or 'formal analyses' do not require interaction with an actual physical representation of the flight deck equipment. Formal error prediction techniques fall into this category.
- 'Evaluation' as a technique for demonstrating compliance may encompass a wide range of structured assessments involving rapid prototypes of interfaces, part prototypes or the real thing. 'Tests' as a means of demonstrating compliance are in many ways conducted the same manner as evaluations but are undertaken on a conforming product or system with a complete system interface (e.g. in an approved simulator) or in the aircraft itself. These may need to be conducted by, or in the presence of the certification authority.

4 Conclusion

Recommendation on the means of compliance including statements of similarity, design description, calculations/analysis, evaluations and test were provided in terms of flight crew tasks. Researches and practice on the static evaluation, documental evaluation, sub-task evaluation as well as full-task evaluation were carried on in order to minimize the occurrence of human errors and the management of their effects. Documented matrix of MoC and a list of simulator/real aircraft test scenarios were planned for the verification of typical human errors relevant to flight deck performance. The method is verified in the design progress of a china-designed type to produce a successful program.

References

Barnes, R.B., Adam, C.F.: Minimum crew certification human factors issues and approaches. World Aviation Congress & Exposition (1996)

Ahlstrom, V., Longo, K.: Human Factors Design Standard (HFDS) For Acquisition of Commercial Off-The-Shelf Subsystems, Non-Developmental Items, and Developmental Systems (DOT/FAA/CT-03/05 HF-STD-001). US DOT Federal Aviation Administration William J. Hughes Technical Center, Atlantic City, NJ (2003)

Xu, M., Jie, Y.: Research of airworthiness certification oriented scenario. Civ. Aircr. Des. Res. (2014)

Yeh, M., Jo, Y.J., Donovan, C., Gabree, S.: Human factors considerations in the design and evaluation of flight deck displays and controls. Flight Decks (2013)

Research on Information Architecture Based on Graphic Reasoning and Mental Model

Ren Long(✉) and Jiali Zhang

School of Mechanical Science and Engineering,
Huazhong University of Science and Technology, Wuhan, China
longren@hust.edu.cn

Abstract. The relationship between the formal structure of the graphical reasoning and the representation form of mental model is studied in this paper. Through comparative analysis of experimental samples, it is found that the layout, information classification and other elements of the mental model have a certain degree of commonality with the formal structure of graphical reasoning. Applying it to the interface design is the construction of information architecture. So that the user experience is optimal. And combining the formal structure of the graphical reasoning and the representation mode of mental model through usability testing is conductive to the establishment of the interface design prototype and improve user experience.

Keywords: Information architecture · Graph reasoning · Mental model

1 Research Background

With the rapid development of modern information technology and Internet technology, information product design has attracted more and more attention. As the important window of information product design and the important carrier of information presentation, UI design plays a more and more important role in communication of social culture. Graphic design language is an important component of interface design which can express various features of things and there is a change rule of expression pattern between them.

In interface design, abstract reasoning based on image reasoning is significant to reveal the essence of human intelligence and develop intelligence potential. The role of graphic reasoning in interface design has been gradually recognized. However, how to transmit information more quickly to users and make a better information structure of the interface, are worth to think about for researchers. At present, most of the research on interface uses mental model theory, and few people combine graphic reasoning with it. The purpose of this study is to research construction of interface design information architecture by exploring the construction of the interface design information architecture and the mental model representation. This provides more effective layout for the content of the interface design, making it more in line with the user's cognitive habits.

C. Stephanidis (Ed.): HCII Posters 2018, CCIS 850, pp. 85–92, 2018.
https://doi.org/10.1007/978-3-319-92270-6_12

2 Mental Model and Graphical Reasoning

2.1 Representation of Mental Model

The concept of "Mental Model" was originally proposed by Kenneth Craik. He believes that the mental model is used to explain the individual's cognitive process of the inner relations of things in the real world [1]. Later, many scholars refined and supplemented it from different perspectives. For example, Young thought that the mental model is used to interpret the purpose of people's behavior, the process of thinking, and the change of emotion and thinking in the course of carrying out the action [2].

The mental model is difficult to fully describe. With the different perception object, the expression method is different too. Therefore, there are variety of forms. For example, in the product design, people will determine the product's use method and function according to the product's shape, operation buttons, colors and other factors. In the interface design, designers guide user's operations based on the colors, graphics, and text, which are transmit to users through the interface [3]. We can study information architecture from the representation mode and behavioral mode of the mental model.

The representation mode belongs to the explicit element of the mental model. It conveys the interface to the user by vision, carries the input and output of information, and provides a window for the user to interact with it. Explicit elements clearly convey the information to the user, and it is also easily accessible for users. It includes the layout, colors, symbols, graphics, information classification, animation, copywriting, comparison, and background in the interface design.

The behavior mode belongs to the invisible element of the mental model and it is the interaction mode between interfaces. The recessive element is neither easily accessible for users, nor can it be shown in a concrete manner. It includes acceptance of behavior and response behavior. Accepted behaviors include single-clicks, double-clicks, etc.; responsive behaviors include tactile, auditory, and visual; common are vibrations, sounds, and morphological changes (Fig. 1).

The form of mental model consists of the interface system, and the user interface system can also as be composed of organization system, labeling system, navigation

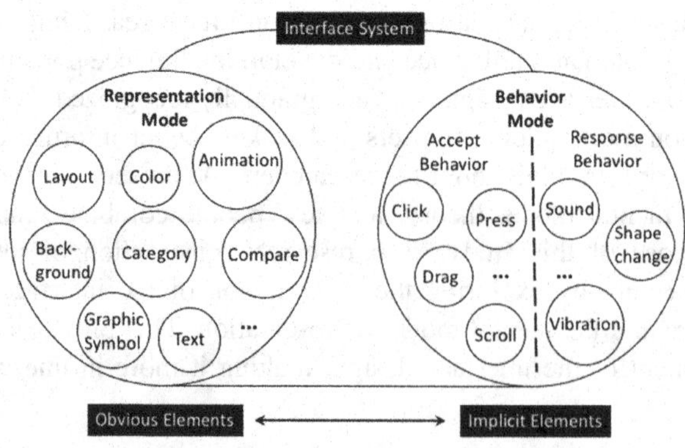

Fig. 1. Representation of mental model

system and search system. In these systems, patterns in various elements together constitute different sizes task flow, the task flow guide designers effectively to organize information, constitute the first dimension of information architecture.

2.2 Graphical Reasoning

Graphic reasoning is the thought process of infer other graphics or information from one or several known graphics. It is a comprehensive thinking process based on reasoning and other thinking modes; the validity of graphical reasoning considers not only the connection of the figure in the spatial structure, but also the connection between the graphics. Some conclusions of the graphical reasoning are certainly, and others may be uncertain. And graphical reasoning fosters divergent thinking [4].

In the process of figure reasoning, people seemingly complete the reasoning through objective carriers such as the flat composition of the graphic itself. In facts not only that, there is a very critical part that is the change of the structure between graphics [5]. People will first pay attention to the overall architecture, and then carefully analyze the changes in the internal details. After they find the relationship between the architecture of graphics, it will be very easy to do inferences. Thus, in graphic reasoning, it is an important part of reasoning activities that deducing the relationship of the formal structure between graphics, and it is the skeleton and architecture of graphic reasoning. Through the analysis of structure expression of graphic reasoning and information architecture, it is found that in the interface design, the structure form of graphic reasoning includes tree structure, matrix structure and linear structure, these structures can be used as another dimension of information architecture [6].

The relationship between the formal structure of the graphical reasoning and the representation form of mental model is studied in this paper. Through the analysis, it is found that the formal structure of graphic reasoning and the layout and information classification of the mental model in the form of expression have certain commonality, and the application of it in the interface design is the construction of information architecture (Fig. 2).

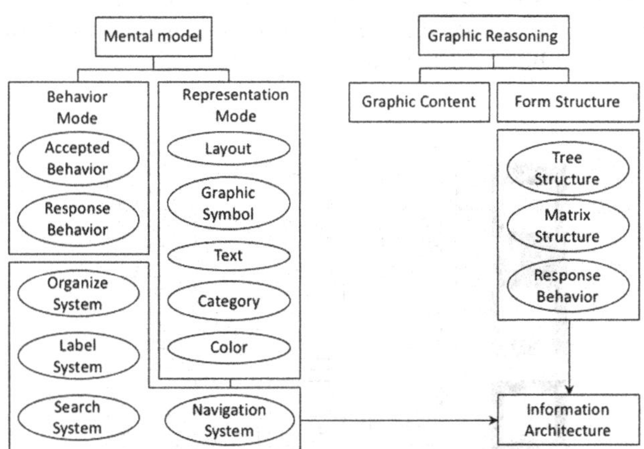

Fig. 2. Speculation of information architecture

Through research the reasoning mode and implementation process of the information architecture, combining the formal structure of the graphical reasoning and the performance model of the mental model, the two latitudes of the information architecture construction are obtained. Combining graphical reasoning with mental models to study information architecture, assume that in today's interface design, information architecture can be interpreted in the form of graphical reasoning. At the same time, this paper takes the Chinese largest social website-Qzone as an example to verify the conjecture.

3 Experimental Design

The experiment is based on the two dimensions of information architecture. First, extracting the product function of Qzone, and classifying the functions and analyzing the product architecture. From the Qzone architecture we can see that this product is mainly constructed by a tree structure (Fig. 3).

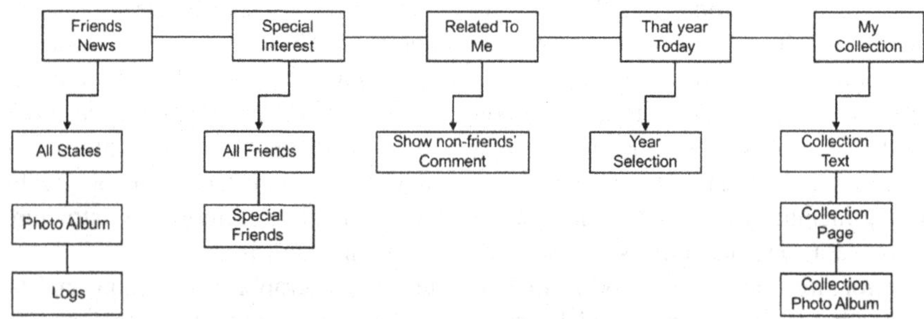

Fig. 3. Product functional architecture of Qzone

The structure of single graph transfer relations in tree structure and graphic reasoning is similar (Fig. 4). The establishment of a graphical reasoning proposition must satisfy three conditions, which are premise, reasoning requirements, and conclusions. It can be seen from the figure that the premise of reasoning is the pattern A → a1 → a2 → a10, B → b1 → b2 → b10, the reasoning requirement is C, and the conclusion is c1 → c2 → c10.

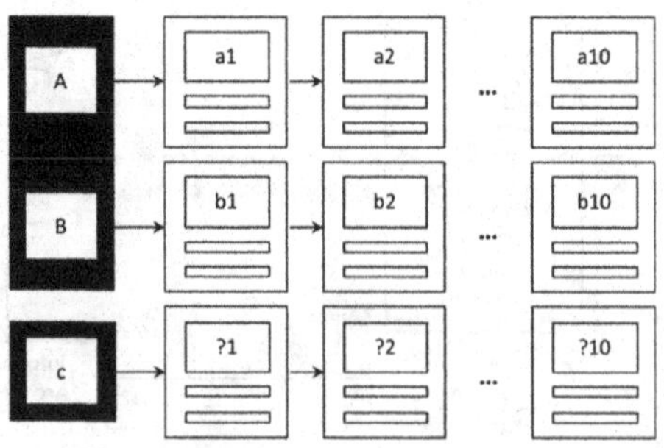

Fig. 4. Single graph transfer relation structure of graphic reasoning

Secondly, analyzing the page layout in Qzone, and the layout design of its organization system, navigation system, search systems and label systems can be explained by graphic reasoning, and It's really built through mental models.

The organizational structure of information is very important in the design of a website. Although users generally do not feel it exists, it defines the main way users browse. The functional structure in the Qzone is a tree structure. After subdivision, it was found that the organizational structure adopted by Qzone is a shallow and narrow architecture (Fig. 5).

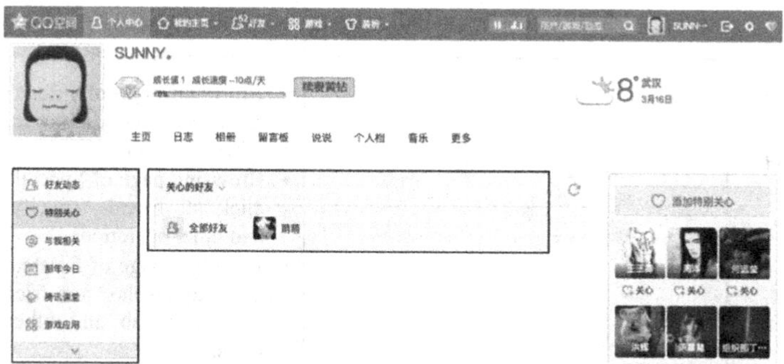

Fig. 5. Organization structure of Qzone

The navigation system is composed of several subsystems and is divided into global, local and situational navigation systems, which are embedded navigation. Qzone uses global navigation (Fig. 6). At the same time we found that the process of

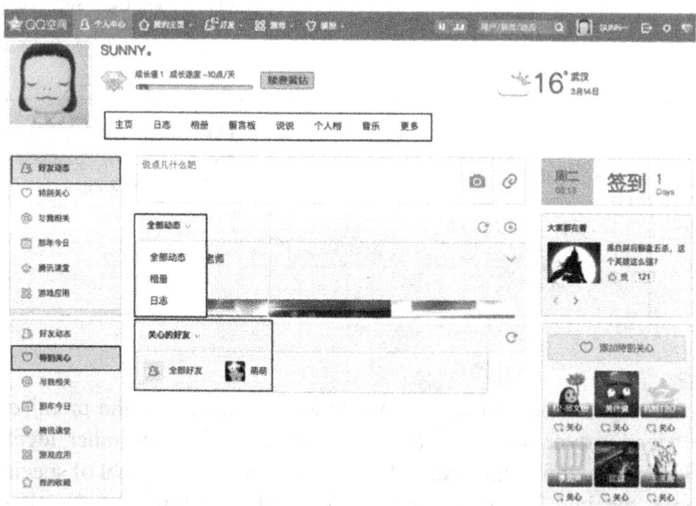

Fig. 6. Navigation system of Qzone

Table 1. Experiment task settings

Task	Material	Task Leader
Task1 The initial impression of the system, free to browse for 30s, can't click anything.		• Have you use this system before ? • If you just opened this interface and haven't clicked anything, what would you click first? • What do you think of the menu's classification? • Where do you think you are most concerned about? • Is this information useful to you?
Task2 Click Friend's News, Special Interest, and Related To Me.		• Browsing page of Friend's News, click on all news, albums, logs and other operations. • Browsing page of Special Interest, click all friends, specify friends and other operations. • Browsing page of Related To Me, click to display non-friend comments, refresh and other operations.
Task3 Click on That Year Today.		• Browsing page of That Year Today, Click different years, settings, etc.
Task4 Click on My Collection.		• Browsing page of My Collection, click on favorite pages, favorite photos, and right-side features.
Task5 Click on the sidebar.		• Go to the Visitors page to view recent visitors, blocked visitors, and visitor settings.

graphical reasoning can be verified on this system. Assume that the premise of inference is the friend's dynamic board and its secondary title. The other levels and its secondary title are becoming the result of reasoning. Taking the panel of special interest as an example, the interface of the second-level title conforms to the single-image transfer and the two-graph transfer relationship in graphical reasoning.

Finally, through usability testing, the Qzone is verified on the basis of the application of the theory. The interface design of Qzone meets the needs of users, and the usability is great.

The purpose of this stage is to verify whether Qzone's information architecture is well-available in the case of graphical reasoning and explanation. The satisfaction of user experience is the measurement result. The test material for this test was the Qzone website, and the same display was used as the carrier for testing. Thirty college students (18–24 years old) participated in this study. They are all from colleges and universities and are engaged in non-design industries.

Using user interviews and questionnaire surveys, users can complete typical tasks and evaluate the interactive design (ease of learning, efficiency, and task accuracy), interface design (content layout, menu style, etc.) and overall satisfaction after the operation, and give the assessment results. The task settings are as follows (Table 1).

After the user conducts the task test, the questionnaire is filled in again. The questionnaire uses a 7-point scale and divides each item from very poor to very good into 7 levels with scores ranging from low to high. After statistics the data, the histogram of the satisfaction of the user task operation is produced (Fig. 7).

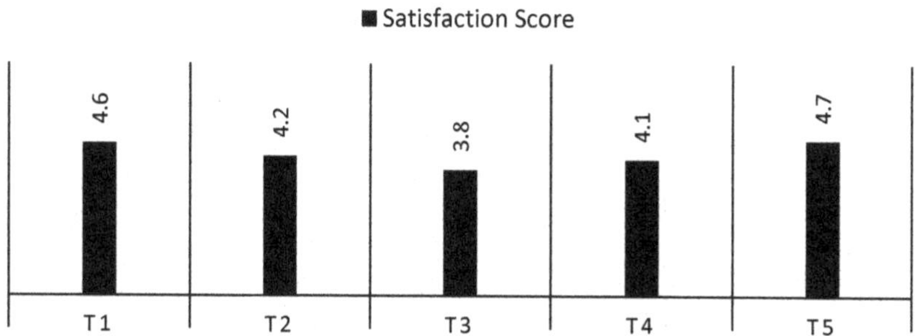

Fig. 7. User satisfaction mean of five tasks

From the results of user satisfaction analysis, the user satisfaction of the five tasks exceeded the average of the 7-point scale during the completion of the mobile operating system tasks, which basically achieved a better user experience.

4 Conclusion

The experimental results show that the combination of mental model representation and formal structure of graphic reasoning can facilitate the establishment of interface design prototype, and make the users experiences achieve the optimal. This paper through study and comparison of forms and graphic reasoning form structure of mental model, find the hidden behind the reasoning system for information architecture guidance is a perspective from the origins of usability design. In the future research, the relationship between graphic reasoning theory and interface design is still worth exploring.

References

1. Craik, K.: The Nature of Explanation. Cambridge University Press, Cambridge (1943)
2. Young, I.: Mental Models: Aligning Design Strategy with Human Behavior. Rosenfeld Media, New York (2008)
3. Johnson Laird, P.N.: Mental Models: Towards a Cognitive Science of Language, Inference and Consciousness. Harvard University Press, Cambridge (1983)
4. Chongyong, S.: Measurement of cognitive load & its application in multimedia learning. Ph.D. thesis. Soochow University, Suzhou (2012)
5. Long, R., Zhang, Y., Wang, Y.: Graphical logic paradigm and reasoning process research. In: 4th International Conference on Advanced Engineering Materials and Technology, AEMT 2014 (2014)
6. Long, R., Zhang, Y., Wang, Y.: Interface reasoning research based on manifestation pattern & cognitive load. In: 5th International Conference on Advanced Engineering Materials and Technology, AEMT 2015 (2015)

Information at Hand – Using Wearable Devices to Display Task Information in the Context of Industry 4.0

Sebastian Mach(✉), Almut Kastrau, and Franziska Schmalfuß

Chemnitz University of Technology,
Wilhelm-Raabe-Straße 43, 09120 Chemnitz, Germany
sebastian.mach@psychologie.tu-chemnitz.de

Abstract. In the context of Industry 4.0 and the extensive interconnection of every part of the production process, the industrial worker will still maintain a key role. It is important to support the workers by utilizing ongoing digitalization at work and also to provide suitable concepts for communication between human and automation. A possible solution could be the application of wearable devices such as smartwatches. They are able to automatically collect data about the state of the worker as well as provide relevant information for the worker about the status of machines. The aim of the present research is to investigate whether smartwatches are a suitable alternative to conventional methods of displaying information in an industrial environment - despite some limitations of smartwatches, like the small screen. Therefore, we conducted a laboratory study displaying different amount of information (a list of six tasks vs. only the next task) on different devices (monitor screen vs. smartwatch screen). We asked 32 participants to follow the displayed instructions and fulfill the tasks (crossword puzzles, Sudoku, number connection task). Afterwards, the participants rated the different types of information display with questionnaires (e.g., User Experience Questionnaire). Results show significant differences in some aspects of user experience supporting the advantage of utilizing smartwatches in an industrial context. However, information on a smartwatch should be as short and meaningful as possible.

Keywords: Industry 4.0 · User experience · Smartwatch · Task information

1 Introduction

In times of Industry 4.0, every part of the production process becomes interconnected and the digitalization of the factory processes is steadily ongoing to increase the potential to respond individually to customer demands, achieve more flexibility, and use given resources efficiently [1]. The factory floor worker will still maintain an important role as most of the working tasks might shift more towards higher complexity, flexibility, and abstract problem solving. Therefore, one of the objectives of the developments in context of Industry 4.0 is to successfully support the worker in this complex and flexible work environment [2]. The research project *Factory2Fit* (funded by the European Union's Horizon 2020 program, grant agreement No. 723277) aims at

C. Stephanidis (Ed.): HCII Posters 2018, CCIS 850, pp. 93–100, 2018.
https://doi.org/10.1007/978-3-319-92270-6_13

developing automation solutions for the factory of the future, by placing the worker in the center. One technical approach is using wearable devices. They combine different functionalities by providing the opportunity to collect physiological data for detecting, for instance, high workload at work [3, 4] and by serving as an interface between human and automation. In detail, some wrist-worn devices, like smartwatches, provide the possibility to receive and display information [5]. As one example, the worker, who is not in sight distance to all machines, could get a message on a smartwatch when a machine stopped due to technical problems or if tool switching is necessary. Sending individual instructions and information location-independent to the worker via wearable devices has already been tested [6, 7]. Hao and Helo [6] showed that supporting industrial workers with individual information via wearable devices could increase the performance and quality of the work. Although the potential of presenting machine status information or up-coming tasks via smartwatches is undeniable, it has not been fully investigated which possibilities and limitations exist regarding how and to which extend the information should be displayed on such a size-reduced smartwatch screen.

In the presented study, we examined how task relevant information should be displayed on a smartwatch. The small screen restricts the possibilities to capture a greater amount of information [8]. Therefore, to conceive information quickly, the small screen should only show essential information [9]. Additionally, users of small screens value good quality information and prefer rather more than less information [10]. Nevertheless, simplicity of an interface improves the user experience, in particular usability [11]. Usability describes "the extent to which a product can be used by specified users to achieve specified goals with effectiveness, efficiency, and satisfaction in a specified context of use" [12]. According to Schrepp and colleagues [13], user experience covers a broader range of facets describing the interaction with a product; including usability criteria (e.g., efficiency, controllability or learnability), and hedonic quality criteria [14] (e.g., stimulation, fun-of-use, novelty, emotions [15] and aesthetics [16]). A good user experience is essential for a successful implementation of new HMIs in work environments and research how to design interfaces of wearable devices to fulfill this criterion is rare.

One typical usage context for displaying information at work is, for example, displaying information about work tasks. This can be realized by supplying a list of tasks from which the worker can choose the next task, or by presenting only the next task, the worker should accomplish. The first option provides a better overview about the upcoming work and presenting a list of tasks provides a larger scope of action and makes use of a greater flexibility [17]. However, the latter option is corresponding with the demand of displaying sparse information on a smartwatch.

Following these results, we hypothesize that displaying information on a smartwatch provides better user experience compared to monitor screen (H1). However, for a task list, the literature review does not allow the formulation of a hypothesis. It needs to be explored if the user experience with a smartwatch exceeds the user experience with a monitor screen when information load is higher.

Furthermore, the presented research allows the assumption that presenting a list of tasks enhances user experience compared to only presenting the next task (H2). With this investigation, we aim at recommendations concerning information display on wearable devices in an industrial context.

2 Method

Thirty-two university students (17 female, 15 male) participated in a laboratory experiment. They were recruited via student mailing lists and received course credits for their participation. The average age was 24.7 years (*SD* = 4.16). Only three participants had experience with a smartwatch for more than one week, others had less or no experience (*n* = 29).

The experiment consisted of a 2 (information format) × 2 (display format) factorial within-subject design and involved three different stations where participants had to perform varying tasks. The designated tasks were presented as an action item list ('task list') or by showing the 'next task' (information format) via smartwatch or monitor screen (display format). The order in which the different conditions had to be accomplished as well as the order of the three different tasks were randomized using the Latin square. The actual tasks, the participants were asked to perform, were neither relevant for the evaluation of the information format nor the display format. The tasks included crossword puzzles, Sudoku, and a number connection task, which took 1–3 min to complete each.

The study procedure was submitted to the ethical committee of the Chemnitz University of Technology and no objections were expressed (no. V-240-15-SM-Smartwatch-27112017).

The facets of user experience were collected using the paper-pencil version of User Experience Questionnaire (UEQ) [18]. This questionnaire includes 26 items and consists of six subscales: attractiveness, perspicuity, efficiency, dependability, stimulation and novelty. The UEQ allows a quick assessment of the user experience and covers main aspects of usability (efficiency, perspicuity, and dependability) as well as user experience aspects (originality and stimulation). The participants rated their impressions on a seven-point semantic differential. All sub-scales showed satisfying internal reliabilities (.871 $\leq$ Cronbachs $\alpha_{\text{Attractiveness}} \leq$ .927; .690 $\leq$ Cronbachs $\alpha_{\text{Perspicuity}} \leq$ .895; .658 $\leq$ Cronbachs $\alpha_{\text{Efficiency}} \leq$ .758; .602 $\leq$ Cronbachs $\alpha_{\text{Dependability}} \leq$ .832; .704 $\leq$ Cronbachs $\alpha_{\text{Stimulation}} <$ .855; .727 $\leq$ Cronbachs $\alpha_{\text{Novelty}} \leq$ .882).

In the monitor condition, the list of tasks or the next task was displayed on a 22-inch Dell P2210 monitor screen. For presenting the list of tasks or the next task on the smartwatch, the Samsung Gear S3 Frontier was utilized. This device comes along with a self-developer kit, so that the possibility can be implemented to send messages via Bluetooth or WiFi independently from external, commercial services. Therefore, a special Universal Windows Platform application (UWP) as well as a Tizen application needed to be developed (see Fig. 1). Via the UWP application, the messages could be generated, and via the Tizen application, they could be received on the smartwatch.

The procedure was as follows. First, the participants read the participant information about the study and confirmed their consent. The three different tasks (crossword puzzles, Sudoku, and number connection task) were introduced by the experimenter. Afterwards, the smartwatch was put on the left arm by the participant. Depending on the condition, the participant was asked to either watch the monitor screen or the smartwatch for an instruction about the upcoming/actual task. If there were no more open questions, they passed through the four experimental conditions.

Fig. 1. List of tasks displayed on smartwatch (left, "To do: crossword puzzle D (station 3)…") or next task displayed on a smartwatch (right, "Next task: crossword puzzle A, (station 3)").

Within each condition, six tasks (each task twice) were processed. At the end of each condition, participants filled out the UEQ [18]. After all four conditions, they answered the demographic questionnaire. In the end, the participants could rate their favorite condition. In sum, the experiment lasted from 60 to 80 min.

3 Results

The data from the UEQ was digitalized in a data matrix following the analysis instruction provided [19]. According to the authors of the UEQ, mean scores were transformed (−3 to 3) [18]. The statistical description and calculations were done with RStudio [20]. For testing the hypotheses, an ANOVA with repeated measures was calculated [21] and assumptions were tested and fulfilled. The mean scores in each condition are shown in Fig. 2.

Results of the ANOVA with repeated measures regarding the display format supported partly hypothesis H1 (see Table 1). When comparing the display formats smartwatch and monitor screen, scores of the subscales attractiveness, stimulation, and novelty differed significantly. Compared to the monitor, participants rated the smartwatch as more attractive ($M_{\text{Smartwatch}} = 1.03$, $SD = 0.86$; $M_{\text{Monitor}} = 0.14$, $SD = 0.82$) and were more stimulated to use the product ($M_{\text{Smartwatch}} = 0.96$, $SD = 0.82$; $M_{\text{Monitor}} = -0.41$, $SD = 0.81$). They also rated the novelty of the smartwatch significantly higher ($M_{\text{Smartwatch}} = 1.07$, $SD = 0.86$) than the novelty of the monitor ($M_{\text{Monitor}} = -1.49$, $SD = 0.87$). According to Cohen [22], effects were large. Results displayed in Table 1 also show that the display format had no significant effects in perspicuity ($M_{\text{Smartwatch}} = 1.57$, $SD = 0.85$; $M_{\text{Monitor}} = 1.63$, $SD = 0.94$), efficiency ($M_{\text{Smartwatch}} = 1.25$, $SD = 0.83$; $M_{\text{Monitor}} = 1.04$, $SD = 0.85$) and dependability ($M_{\text{Smartwatch}} = 1.14$, $SD = 0.97$; $M_{\text{Monitor}} = 1.23$, $SD = 0.75$).

Hypothesis H2 was not supported by the data. Concerning the information format, the subscales attractiveness, perspicuity, efficiency, and stimulation differed highly significant (see Table 1), but the effect had the opposite direction. Contrary to our hypothesis, participants evaluated the information format, where only the next task was

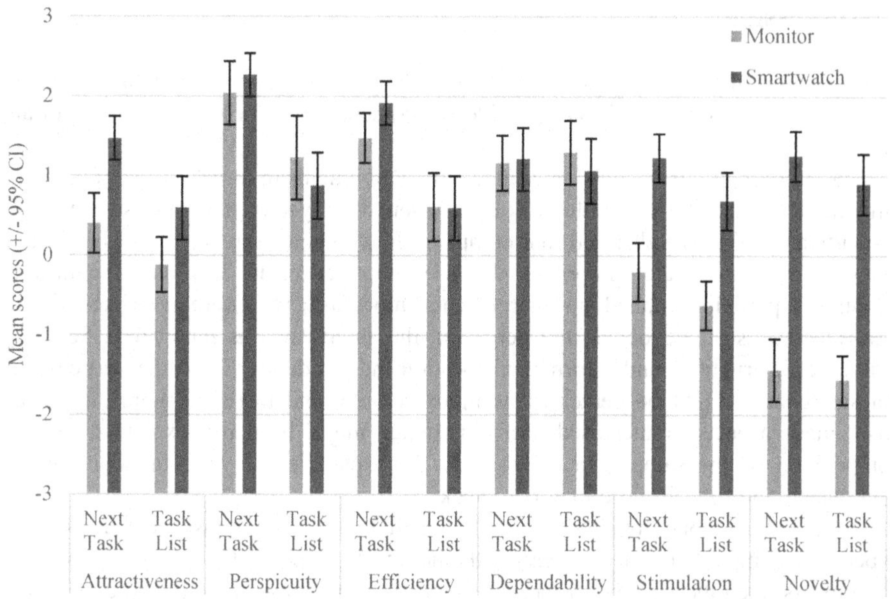

Fig. 2. Mean scores of UEQ subscales compared between the different experimental conditions.

Table 1. Results of ANOVAs with repeated measures for UEQ subscale scores.

Sub-scale	Display format			Information format			Interaction		
	F	*(df)*	η^2	*F*	*(df)*	η^2	*F*	*(df)*	η^2
Attractiveness	**38.83*****	**(1,31)**	**.17**	**24.83*****	**(1,31)**	**.11**	2.53	(1,31)	.01
Perspicuity	0.14	(1,31)	.00	**44.87*****	**(1,31)**	**.20**	**4.23***	**(1,31)**	**.02**
Efficiency	1.46	(1,31)	.01	**60.57*****	**(1,31)**	**.24**	3.33	(1,31)	.01
Dependability	0.50	(1,31)	.01	0.002	(1,31)	.00	1.46	(1,31)	.00
Stimulation	**55.13*****	**(1,31)**	**.36**	**14.17*****	**(1,31)**	**.06**	0.37	(1,31)	.00
Novelty	**132.5*****	**(1,31)**	**.64**	3.44	(1,31)	.02	1.73	(1,31)	.00

Note. ***$p < .001$, **$p < .01$, *$p < .05$, significant effects are bold written.

displayed, as more attractive (Attractiveness: $M_{\text{List}} = 0.24$, $SD = 0.88$; $M_{\text{Next}} = 0.93$, $SD = 0.77$), easier to get familiar with (Perspicuity: $M_{\text{List}} = 1.05$, $SD = 1.11$; $M_{\text{Next}} = 2.15$, $SD = 0.6$), more helping to solve the tasks (Efficiency: $M_{\text{List}} = 0.60$, $SD = 0.94$; $M_{\text{Next}} = 1.70$, $SD = 0.59$), and more exciting and higher motivating (Stimulation: $M_{\text{List}} = 0.03$, $SD = 0.71$; $M_{\text{Next}} = 0.51$, $SD = 0.74$). The findings showed medium to large effects.

The only significant interaction between display format and information format occurred within the subscale perspicuity; participants got easier used to the presentation of only the next task when using the smartwatch, though the effect size was rather small.

4 Discussion

The main aim of this study was to investigate the possibilities to display task relevant information on a smartwatch and provide recommendations for the application in an industrial environment.

Therefore, participants were presented with action items in form of a list of tasks or only the next task. The task or the list of tasks were displayed on a monitor screen or on a smartwatch. We hypothesized that compared to a monitor screen, displaying information on a smartwatch improves the user experience. In accordance with the hypothesis, participants rated the smartwatch as more attractive, were more excited and motivated to use the product, and perceived the smartwatch as innovative. Sending individual instructions and information location-independently [7] to the participants via smartwatch might be perceived as more flexible, and therefore more attractive. Also, these aspects of increased user experience might be partly explained by the composition of the sample, in which only three participants were familiar with a smartwatch and used it more than one week.

As for the second hypothesis, we assumed that a list of tasks enhances user experience compared to only presenting the next task. Opposite to our assumption, the participants rated the display format, where only the next task was displayed, as more attractive, easier to get familiar with, more helping to solve the tasks, and perceived the format as more exciting and motivating. This supports previous findings, that simplicity, especially the limited amount of information, enhances usability aspects like perspicuity and efficiency [11]. The increased information density that comes along with a task list seems to have not such a strong negative influence on the user experience as expected. This might be because of the experimental setting. Displaying other tasks, that have to be done in the future, did not provide important additional information. In another context, where the interconnection between the tasks and the sequence is important, displaying a list of tasks, from which the user can choose, might be more suitable.

The display format had no significant effects in perspicuity, efficiency, and dependability leading to the assumption, that these aspects are not as relevant for the evaluation of the devices. In addition, novelty might be not relevant for the information format.

In summary, untrained and novice persons see the new technology as exiting and supportive for displaying task relevant information. However, developers should aim at presenting information on a smartwatch as short and meaningful as possible. Future research should investigate the long-term effects of superiority concerning user experience of smartwatches. Therefore, industrial workers should be consulted, and the study should be replicated in an industrial context. In addition, a variation of display design and information format should be investigated.

In conclusion, the present study provided evidence that displaying information via a smartwatch can lead to increased user experience compared to a monitor. Additionally, the information should be as compact as possible but qualitatively adequate.

References

1. MacDougall, W.: Industrie 4.0: Smart Manufacturing for the Future. Germany Trade & Invest, Berlin (2014)
2. Kagermann, H., Wahlster, W., Helbig, J.: Securing the future of German manufacturing industry. In: Recommendations for Implementing the Strategic Initiative INDUSTRIE 4.0, Final Report of the Industrie 4.0 Working Group. Forschungsunion (2013)
3. Swan, M.: Sensor mania! The internet of things, wearable computing, objective metrics, and the quantified self 2.0. J. Sens. Actuator Netw. **1**, 217–253 (2012)
4. Schmalfuß, F., Mach, S., Klüber, K., Habelt, B., Beggiato, M., Körner, A., Krems, J.F.: Potential of wearable devices for mental workload detection in different physiological activity conditions. In: de Waard, D., Di Nocera, F., Coelho, D., Edworthy, J., Brookhuis, K., Ferlazzo, F., Franke, T., Toffetti, A.: (eds.), Proceedings of the Human Factors and Ergonomics Society Europe Chapter (2017). http://hfes-europe.org
5. Zhang, Y., Rau, P.L.P.: Playing with multiple wearable devices: exploring the influence of display, motion and gender. Comput. Hum. Behav. **50**, 148–158 (2015)
6. Hao, Y., Helo, P.: The role of wearable devices in meeting the needs of cloud manufacturing: a case study. Robot. Comput.-Integr. Manuf. **45**, 168–179 (2015)
7. Jo, H., Kang, S., Kwon, H.J., Lee, J.D.: In-door location-based smart factory cloud platform supporting device-to-device self-collaboration. In: 2017 IEEE International Conference Big Data and Smart Computing (BigComp), pp. 348–351 (2017)
8. Jones, M., Marsden, G., Mohd-Nasir, N., Boone, K., Buchanan, G.: Improving web interaction on small displays. Comput. Netw. **31**(11–16), 1129–1137 (1999)
9. Budiu, R.: The Apple Watch: User-Experience Appraisal. https://www.nngroup.com/articles/smartwatch/. Accessed 29 Mar 2018
10. Jones, M., Buchanan, G., Thimbleby, H.: Sorting out searching on small screen devices. In: Paternò, F. (ed.) Mobile HCI 2002. LNCS, vol. 2411, pp. 81–94. Springer, Heidelberg (2002). https://doi.org/10.1007/3-540-45756-9_8
11. Lee, D., Moon, J., Kim, Y.J., Mun, Y.Y.: Antecedents and consequences of mobile phone usability: linking simplicity and interactivity to satisfaction, trust, and brand loyalty. Inf. Manag. **52**(3), 295–304 (2015)
12. ISO: ISO 9241-210. Human-Centred Design for Interactive Systems. International Standard. International Organization for Standardization (2010)
13. Schrepp, M., Hinderks, A., Thomaschewski, J.: Applying the user experience questionnaire (UEQ) in different evaluation scenarios. In: Marcus, A. (ed.) DUXU 2014. LNCS, vol. 8517, pp. 383–392. Springer, Cham (2014). https://doi.org/10.1007/978-3-319-07668-3_37
14. Hassenzahl, M.: The effect of perceived hedonic quality on product appealingness. Int. J. Hum.-Comput. Interac. **13**, 479–497 (2001)
15. Norman, D.: Emotional Design: Why We Love (Or Hate) Everyday Things. Basic Books, Boulder (2003)
16. Tractinsky, N.: Aesthetics and apparent usability: empirical assessing cultural and methodological issues. In: CHI 1997 Electronic Publications (1997). http://www.acm.org/sigchi/chi97/proceedings/paper/nt.htm
17. Gustavsson, T.K., Jerbrant, A.: Task lists as infrastructure: an empirical study of multi-project work. Int. J. Proj. Organ. Manag. **4**(3), 272 (2012)
18. Laugwitz, B., Held, T., Schrepp, M.: Construction and evaluation of a user experience questionnaire. In: Holzinger, A. (ed.) USAB 2008. LNCS, vol. 5298, pp. 63–76. Springer, Heidelberg (2008). https://doi.org/10.1007/978-3-540-89350-9_6
19. UEQ-Online Homepage. http://www.ueq-online.org/. Accessed 29 Mar 2018

20. RStudio Team: RStudio: Integrated Development for R. RStudio Inc., Boston MA (2016). http://www.rstudio.com/
21. Lawrence, M.A.: ez: easy analysis and visualization of factorial experiments. R package version 4.4-0 (2016). https://CRAN.R-project.org/package=ez
22. Cohen, J.: Statistical Power Analysis for the Behavioral Sciences. Lawrence Earlbaum Associates, Hilsdale (1988)

Example Based Programming and Ontology Building: A Bioinformatic Application

Quentin Riché-Piotaix[1,2,3(✉)], Patrick Girard[1,3], Frédéric Bilan[1,2], and Ladjel Bellatreche[3]

[1] Université de Poitiers, Poitiers, France
quentin.riche.piotaix@univ-poitiers.fr
[2] CHU de Poitiers, Poitiers, France
[3] LIAS, ISAE-ENSMA, Poitiers, France

Abstract. To find ways to facilitate the querying process of heterogeneous databases reveals a critical research avenue, especially in biology. Making use of ontologies is considered one of the best solutions, which makes the activity of ontology design critical for biologists. However, such design process is not easily attainable by non-experts, issue sublimated by the constant evolution of the domain taxonomies [1]. Moreover, designing ontologies currently requires some expert knowledge of the domain as well as skills in database and ontology modelling. This fact was corroborated by our pilot study involving geneticists from the Poitiers hospital. The specialists did not possess any prior knowledge of conceptual data models. Nevertheless, they were able to build their own mental model of the situation that could later be correlated to the actual database models.

Compared to previous End-User Programming approaches, this experiment shows that End-User Programming techniques permit to build and use conceptual models without any need for specific training. In this poster, we describe the pilot study we conducted using geneticists during the dedicated ontologies design process that allows querying public databases. Several specific constraints were identified, along with their proposed solutions. A complete example of ontology design, built from the genetic field, is then described.

Keywords: Ontology · Database · Human-computer interaction
Genetic · Bioinformatic

1 Introduction

With the advent of new DNA sequencing techniques, a tremendous amount of data is constantly being generated in the field of genetics. They are distributed in many highly specialized databases that geneticists then interrogate successively. Researchers cross the results of their successive requests in order to make

C. Stephanidis (Ed.): HCII Posters 2018, CCIS 850, pp. 101–108, 2018.
https://doi.org/10.1007/978-3-319-92270-6_14

the diagnosis as reliable as possible. It would be very interesting for geneticists to be able to centralise the databases they use rather than to have to make requests on different bases as they currently do. Today's mapping of the field uses various databases containing concepts included in several databases, with semantic differences, and intra and inter-base relationships. This configuration illustrates the need for an ontology spanning the domain. Indeed, within the genetics field, some areas are fully covered, such as genes in Gene Ontology[1] or phenotypes in Human Phenotype Ontology[2], but there is no global ontology. Genetics is a constantly evolving wide and complex field. It is therefore impossible to consider creating and maintaining a complete ontology of the field without a considerable amount of human and material resources. As a rapidly expanding research field, a closed system would become very quickly out of date. Instead, we aim here to automatically build an ontology from the available data. Work already exists in this area, but most of it is aimed at extracting knowledge from unstructured information, such as sets of web pages, text and multimedia files. For genetics, databases already exist, and export files are available for download. However, the structure of the base is not available for perusal. Building an ad hoc tool for each database, if technically possible, is not a good solution due to the domain's constant evolutions. Here the design process will therefore be performed by reusing semi-structured data sources. Our interest is an approach capable of allowing end-users to build the systems that meet their needs. An End-User Programming approach was therefore selected, in line with geneticists' usual lack of expertise in computing. To perform this task, two options were available:

- To train geneticists to acquire the necessary computer skills (as it was done in [2])
- To create a system that disguises computer concepts to the novice user.

Most geneticists have neither the time nor the desire to learn how to code. Moreover, to train them would be as costly as using an expert database engineer, which is out of our scope and lacks adaptability to the domain's constant evolution. The only solution left was to use an approach that does not require any further apprenticeship. Partial answers to this problematic exist in different areas of research, including queries by example, but these systems focus heavily on queries rather than on building an interactive system. Our problematic of reconstruction was modified by this constraint and thus became: how to allow a computer science novice to create an ontology from genetic database exports only? We will present the particular context of this research study in Sect. 2. Our approach to system design will then be described in Sect. 3. To follow, a validation study of the approach will be presented in Sect. 4, and discussed in Sect. 5.

---

[1] http://geneontology.org.

[2] http://human-phenotype-ontology.github.io/.

2 Analysis

End-user programming (EUP) allows expert users (EU) with no or few programming skills to build programs related to their specific needs [3,4]. Most of the time, EUP is used to automate basic EU interactions, for example for repetitive tasks [5,6]. In our case, the needs to be elicited are situated on the conceptual level. Based on previous observations, our hypothesis is that by using EUP techniques, biology researchers - more specifically geneticists - could build ad-hoc ontologies in a more efficient manner for query generation that would render a quicker diagnosis. We observed common databases usage by geneticists and found that they create complex queries by making multiple simple queries across multiple databases. We concluded that they must already have their own mental model of the field. This allowed us to formulate our initial hypothesis: geneticists possess a mental model of the domain and it is possible to find semantic correlations between the way they represent it and the real model. We are not in a classic EUP case, which represents a computerized automation of repetitive EU tasks. We are at the conceptual level: we use EUP to allow the EU to create a structure that fits his/her mental model, also usable as a database schema. Applied to our situation, a classic EUP case is a system that allows the EU to query various database through their API. While this would work, the situation would not be resolved, as the EU would still have to create an ad hoc program for each API. That is why we focus on the conceptual model.

2.1 A Genetics Case Study

To support our approach statistically, we have defined an example by selecting three databases only: OMIM morbidmap[3] (contains mainly diseases associated with genes), dbSNP[4] (identifies point mutations), and finally a projection of HPO (contains mainly association phenotype-disease). These three bases were chosen because of their diversity in form and substance. Indeed, it presents slightly different structures at the header level, with a visible header (not necessarily formatted in the same way as the data), or without any header (replaced by textual explanations in another file). They were mostly selected due to their content, representing four essential notions within the world of genetics: genes, diseases, phenotypes and variations.

2.2 Case Study Constraints

Most current approaches use complex artificial intelligence to limit the role of the domain expert in the design process. This is a very consistent approach, since the data often come from corpus extracted from the Web, without direct link with such experts. In this project, our configuration elicited another set of constraints, as follow:

[3] https://www.omim.org.

[4] https://www.ncbi.nlm.nih.gov/projects/SNP.

- Accessibility to domain experts, all computer science novices.
- During the design process, these experts will be alone, they will not have access to ontologists or database specialists.
- The experts' confidence in the results must be total, which means that the EU must be able to check the automatic steps. Our goal is therefore to rely as much as possible on the available resources, which are the EU and the data, in order to free ourselves from the heavy approaches of machine learning, or the use of an external ontology engineer. We do not want to only make an ontology, we want to have it done expertly.

2.3 Difficulties Encountered

Current approaches to creating ontologies are facing several pitfalls, at different level of system actions:

Issue 1. Several important notions of databases must be known (such as tables, attributes or relations).

Issue 2. The interfaces are developed to be compatible with the target audience, that is to say engineers specialized in data management and ontologies. The solution often adopted is to rely on a standard domain such as SPARQL [7].

Issue 3. When the data comes from unstructured files, it is difficult to extract the relations [8].

Issue 4. When the data comes from semi-structured files, the format dependency is very important, and it is common to have errors and malformations making the machine interpretation process extremely complex [9].

Issue 5. Most tools are designed following machine learning approaches, they are very dependent on the size of the corpus, and the trust given to each source to avoid conflicts [10].

Issue 6. Since sources are often included iteratively, one after the other, this greatly increases the chances of duplicating an entity that comes from two different sources [11].

Issue 7. Finally, it is complicated to find a good way to evaluate the quality of the ontology produced, and therefore the system's reliability. The ideal solution would be a manual review of the ontology by domain experts able to validate or not the links between the entities. However this would also be too costly. Automation of this phase are under development [12], but will not be detailed here any further.

For the first issue, we may rely on the EU by asking them information, or request a verification of the data structure. The second is a classic EUP issue, we will probably face it, but we cannot use informatic standard, as they are not known by our EU. We must include these EU into the design phase and make sure that the interfaces are clear. We are not concerned with issue 3, but issue 4 will require an intelligent parsing step in order to overcome any potential file malformations. As the EU needs control choices, we cannot use a machine learning approach, so issue 5 is also discarded. Issue 6 can be solved because of the presence of identifiers in the data. This can be used to avoid duplicating entities. Finally, the last issue is moot here since our ontology was directly developed by the domain expert. However, we can evaluate the result according to a subjective criterion, by checking whether the ontology fits the provided data.

3 Domain Vocabulary

In order to create a system capable of answering our problematic, we must provide three answers. We first need to prove our initial hypothesis: there are relationships between the geneticist's mental representation model and the database concepts used in the model. If this hypothesis is validated, it should be possible to characterise these relations by investigating how EU express them: what vocabulary is used? Which grammatical structures? Finally, based on these results, we must deduce adapted solutions for the EU to inform the concepts that interest us.

3.1 Approach

We first wanted to check that geneticists are able to extract concepts and relationships from data sources by themselves. We also investigated whether other database concepts are described spontaneously by the EU. We then determined how these notions were described, and whether it was possible to find a correspondence between the EU's vocabulary and the database notions. We were particularly attentive at the possible apparition of homonyms or synonyms. To investigate this issue, the following domain vocabulary definition test was proposed to five domain experts: Each participant was asked to verbalise the content of export file from three domain databases. We recorded the think-aloud and searched for possible equivalences between these people's vocabulary choices and ontology notions. From the recordings, we were able to verify our initial hypothesis and note that the geneticists do indeed use databases notions. We then listed the vocabulary and syntactical structures in context and explored their usage:

- Concepts were generally easily isolated when belonging directly to the field of expertise only.
- Attributes were well distributed between well-defined concepts. The notion of identifier was very present, since each concept had at least one identifier per database. Participants found them without problems, even for concepts they did not understand.
- Attribute types were not requested from participants, and never were specified spontaneously. This is not critical, since they can be guessed or requested later from the EU.
- Regarding relations, we found 21 different descriptions to talk about three types of relations: 0:n, 1:n and concept-attribute. The three most frequent descriptions were "have multiple" and "associated with" that described a 0:n relationship, as well as "correspond to" to describe a Concept-Attribute relationship. EU therefore used many synonyms (use of several words to describe

a relationship). Only one EU could use up to 4 synonyms for a relationship. Several homonyms (use of a word to describe several types of relationship) have also been noted. They are related to the presence of several participants, but unlike the synonyms, each participant remained constant, using one word per type of relationship. The two identified homonyms were "associated with" and "have several", used to describe the three types of relations present, however traditionally chosen to describe 0:n relationship.
- Cardinalities were not always detectable orally. When they were specified, this involved the use of modal verbs such as "may" and "must", as well as the use of specific determinants such as "many". This enabled the building of structures such as "a disease must have one or more phenotypes".

4 Prototype Validation

This domain vocabulary definition test proved that it is possible to find a correspondence between the words used by geneticists and the ontological notions necessary for the construction of the system. We have thereafter imagined and developed a prototype that served as a translator between the geneticist and the ontology, to be confronted to our end-users. As previously mentioned, EU are usually highly connected to the data, so we made the data visible throughout the process, which consists of 4 steps:

- Import and parsing of data;
- Creation of the present concepts, with their attributes;
- Creation of relations between concepts, with their cardinalities;
- Visualization of the final ontology.

These different steps were performed using a classic web interface. The first step allowed the EU to load his/her data file and view it directly. He/She could then interact directly with a set of parsing parameters, which allowed him/her to easily find the most useful settings to perform his/her task. When the data display became clear, the EU could enter the concepts and their attributes. A verification step avoided inserting duplicated entries in the ontology, and forced the EU to define a primary key. If a concept already existed, it then ought to be entered as a synonym. Finally, the EU entered relations using a syntax close to the results of the domain vocabulary definition test, relying in particular on drop-down lists of modal such as "may" or "must". Finally, a visualization screen allowed EU to summarize easily concepts and relations present in the ontology. The main objective of this study was to evaluate the usability of the approach. Should the test be a success, even partial, the approach would then be feasible. On the opposite, no conclusion could be drawn as either the approach could be unreliable, or no solution could be computed. In case of favorable results, we would then evaluate the different steps to identify possible blocking point. Finally, we would collect the opinions of EU passing the test to improve the prototype. Four geneticists were recruited for this study. They were asked to create an ontology using the three aforementioned databases with our prototype.

4.1 Results

None of the ontologies created were perfect, because of optimization problems, missing concepts and/or relations. All of them were however fully usable. An example of optimization problem lied in a concept being artificially split into two concepts linked by a 1:1 relation. In addition, several issues concerning the resulting ontologies and the EU's behavior during the tests drew our attention:

- Several synonyms were used at the concept level, such as "phenotypes", sometimes called "symptoms".
- One of the EU created foreign keys before creating any relation. This anticipation can probably be attributed to his personal Access 8 database creation experience.
- Even though some of the attributes were very close semantically, none were misallocated.

5 Discussion

As shown in the previous section, EU have generally managed to provide an implementable result, with no help from the data. However, we can imagine situations that would require more help, asking for clarification from the EU and helping him rely on the provided data. For example, an automatic detection of 1:1 relations could enquire whether it would not be more relevant to group concepts in a single entity. On the one hand, we can imagine the opposite case, where a concept initially included in another must be extracted in the light of new data, in order to create an independent entity. On the other hand, it would be impossible to detect the creation of false concepts, such as the one called "transcript" in our case. However, we can hope the EU would be aware of the problem and seek a more adaptable solution. This issue for example could have been resolved by deleting the concept and adding an attribute to another. Conceptual omissions can traditionally be detected if none of the columns of a database are loaded. However these can also be on purpose, as it was the case with one of the EU. Whilst relational omissions are difficult to detect, except in some special cases. However, one can rely on the presence of concepts in the same file to deduce a probable relationship between the two: the presence of genes and SNP in a single base generally indicates a link between SNP and genes. Relationships can be reflected, and missing cardinalities can be requested from the EU. Cardinality errors would have to be checked in the data itself. It would be impossible to find a definite answer in all cases: impossible for example to contradict a relation 0:n, but a relation 0:1 can be easily verified.

The first issue we had seen in the analysis section can easily be handled. The second has been verified by this validation study, and the debriefing of the test. EU who have passed the study may now be fully involved in future development so we can keep clear interfaces. Our parsing phase shown that file's minor malformations can be handled, we must continue to test it with bigger malformations. Finally, we have not faced the sixth issue yet, we might encounter it with more databases.

6 Conclusion

With this case study, we shown that it is possible for a domain expert, novice in computer science, to build an ontology from existing data. We have evoked the problems faced by users and proposed several solutions. The construction of such as system, however, is not completely solved, since many semantic problems will have to be solved at the data level. Finally, the creation of an adapted query system could allow end-users to find a concrete interest in its use.

References

1. Petasis, G., Karkaletsis, V., Paliouras, G., Krithara, A., Zavitsanos, E.: Ontology population and enrichment: state of the art. In: Paliouras, G., Spyropoulos, C.D., Tsatsaronis, G. (eds.) Knowledge-Driven Multimedia Information Extraction and Ontology Evolution. LNCS (LNAI), vol. 6050, pp. 134–166. Springer, Heidelberg (2011). https://doi.org/10.1007/978-3-642-20795-2_6
2. Letondal, C.: Interaction and programming. Ph.D. thesis, Université Paris Sud - Paris XI (2001)
3. Cypher, A., Halbert, D.C.: Watch What I Do: Programming by Demonstration. MIT press, Cambridge (1993)
4. Lieberman, H.: Your Wish is My Command: Programming by Example. Morgan Kaufmann, Burlington (2001)
5. Girard, P.: Bringing programming by demonstration to cad users. In: Your Wish is My Command, pp. 135–VII. Elsevier (2001)
6. Goubali, O., Girard, P., Guittet, L., Bignon, A., Kesraoui, D., Berruet, P., Bouillon, J.-F.: Designing functional specifications for complex systems. In: Kurosu, M. (ed.) HCI 2016. LNCS, vol. 9731, pp. 166–177. Springer, Cham (2016). https://doi.org/10.1007/978-3-319-39510-4_16
7. Lefrançois, M., Zimmermann, A., Bakerally, N.: Génération de RDF à partir de sources de données aux formats hétérogènes (2017)
8. Kim, S., Alani, H., Hall, W., Lewis, P., Millard, D., Shadbolt, N., Weal, M.: Artequakt: generating tailored biographies from automatically annotated fragments from the web (2002)
9. O'Connor, M.J., Halaschek-Wiener, C., Musen, M.A.: Mapping master: a flexible approach for mapping spreadsheets to OWL. In: Patel-Schneider, P.F., Pan, Y., Hitzler, P., Mika, P., Zhang, L., Pan, J.Z., Horrocks, I., Glimm, B. (eds.) ISWC 2010. LNCS, vol. 6497, pp. 194–208. Springer, Heidelberg (2010). https://doi.org/10.1007/978-3-642-17749-1_13
10. Brewster, C., Iria, J., Zhang, Z., Ciravegna, F., Guthrie, L., Wilks, Y.: Dynamic iterative ontology learning. In: 6th International Conference on Recent Advances in Natural Language Processing (2007)
11. Dimou, A., Sande, M.V., Colpaert, P., Mannens, E., Van De Walle, R.: Extending R2RML to a source-independent mapping language for RDF. In: Proceedings of the 2013th International Conference on Posters & #38; Demonstrations Track, Aachen, Germany, ISWC-PD 2013, vol. 1035, pp. 237–240. CEUR-WS.org (2013)
12. Drumond, L., Girardi, R.: A survey of ontology learning procedures. In: de Freitas, F.L.G., Stuckenschmidt, H., Pinto, H.S., Malucelli, A., Corcho, O. (eds.) CEUR Workshop Proceedings of WONTO, vol. 427. CEUR-WS.org (2008)

Visual Analysis for Overcoming Population Decline and Vitalizing Local Economy in Japan

Ryosuke Saga(✉)

Graduate School of Humanities and Sustainable System Sciences,
Osaka Prefecture University, 1-1 Gakuen-Cho, Sakai, Osaka, Japan
saga@cs.osakafu-u.ac.jp

Abstract. This study describes visual analysis to understand and comprehend the strategies in local governments. The Japanese government established Headquarters for Overcoming Population Decline and Vitalizing Local Economy to solve population and economic decline. On the basis of the comprehensive strategy from the headquarters, each local government also formulates original strategies. This study analyzes two networks, namely, word and government networks, generated by their strategic statements. By analyzing these networks, we understand that each local government adopts a similar strategy based on marriage, emigration, health, medical care, and so on.

Keywords: Visualization · Graph integration · Graph drawing
Co-occurrence network

1 Introduction

The Japanese population tends to decrease after the peak in 2008 [1]. The population is predicted at 97 million in 2050 and 50 million at the beginning of the 22nd century. The population concentration in Tokyo is accelerating. Tokyo area (Tokyo, Saitama, Chiba, and Kanagawa prefectures) has overturned 119,000 people for 20 consecutive years, whereas Osaka and Nagoya areas recorded over delivery for three consecutive years starting 2015. The majority of population movements to Tokyo area are young people; and 90,000 people are aged of 15–24 years. In 2015, Tokyo area had a population of 36,126,000 people, which was more than a quarter of the total population.

Rural areas are facing the problem of population decline, which results in the shrinking of the regional economies and consequently accelerates the population decline. The declining population has caused a serious manpower shortage, leading to the decline in businesses and rural areas.

The cabinet established the Headquarters for Overcoming Population Decline and Vitalizing Local Economy in Japan. The goal of the institution is for each region to create an autonomous and sustainable society that utilizes its respective features [2]. To eliminate the harmful effects of traditional policies, to overcome the population decline, and to ensure the regional creation, the headquarters launched the five principles of policy toward "creation of towns, people, and workers."

On the basis of these five principles, the headquarters formulated the "Comprehensive Strategy for Town, People, and Creation" to overcome the population decline

C. Stephanidis (Ed.): HCII Posters 2018, CCIS 850, pp. 109–114, 2018.
https://doi.org/10.1007/978-3-319-92270-6_15

and a five-year plan to realize a vibrant Japanese society in the future. This strategy is a summary of the five-year targets and the basic direction and details of policies from FY 2015. The local governments also formulated their own comprehensive strategies based on this comprehensive strategy.

The unique comprehensive strategies have the same tendency because they are based on the "Comprehensive Strategy for Town, People, and Creation". However, each local government environment is different, and strategies are also different and specialized for each government. For example, the population vision and strategy of each district in the 23 districts of Tokyo are similar, but the strategy differs between the 23 districts and the local governments. Implementing the PDCA (Plan, Do, Check, Action) cycle is also mandatory in executing this strategy so that local governments should evaluate the results obtained from their strategies and plan new strategies for improvement.

When a local government is successful, the possibility that another government succeeds equally increases by sharing ideas. A successful local government becomes a role model for other local governments, and the possibility of the success of the strategy increases. However, the reference relationships, that is, similarities among the strategies, are unclear. Hence, finding related governments as role models is difficult.

This study visualizes the relationships among local governments by comparing the strategies with each other. We utilize network visualization to comprehend the relationships and global causality hidden in communities. We also consider the reasons and find information from different viewpoints.

2 Analysis Process

The comprehensive strategy basically is shown in document (that is, sentences and figures). We collect the texts from the strategy statements. To find the cores and keys of strategy, we extract keywords by using TF-IDF. Based on the keywords, we generate two networks and perform clustering for analysis.

2.1 Keyword Extraction

Keyword extraction is a basic process in text mining. Morphological analysis is conducted for text data before keyword extraction. We identify parts of speech and filter the unnecessary POS set. We adopt words that belong to a verb, noun, adjective, adverb, and interjection. We remove stop words that have no meaning. We extract the keywords after preprocessing. To extract the keywords, we use the TF-IDF algorithm as follows:

$$TFIDF_{ij} = TF_{ij} * IDF_i, \tag{1}$$

$$TF_{ij} = \frac{v_{ij}}{n_j}, \text{ and} \tag{2}$$

$$IDF_i = log\frac{N}{df_i} + 1, \tag{3}$$

where v_{ij} is the frequency of the appearance of word i in document j ($j \in D, D$: document set), n_j is the sum of words in document j, N is the number of documents in a document set, and df_i is the number of documents word i appears in.

Finally, we extract the keywords for a document set using Eq. (4):

$$TFIDF_i = \sum\nolimits_{j \epsilon D} TFIDF_{ij}. \tag{4}$$

We extract the important keywords for document sets by using Eq. (4) and ranking the keywords based on the value of $TFIDF_i$. In this study, the top 100 words (including same-ranked words) are regarded as keywords and are utilized as nodes in the network.

2.2 Generating Networks

A network is often called a *graph*, which is a representation of a set of objects called nodes, where some pairs of objects are connected by links. We generate two networks using the extracted keywords. One consists of government names as nodes and tendency of keywords as links. We call this network *government network* for convenience. Another network consists of keywords as nodes and co-occurrence degree as links. We call this network *word network* for convenience. We can understand the positions of each government by analyzing the former network. We can understand key concepts and important topics by analyzing the latter network.

These links in both networks are essentially equal to similarities. We utilize cosine similarity, which is calculated using Eq. (5):

$$cos(A, B) = \frac{\vec{A} \cdot \vec{B}}{|\vec{A}||\vec{B}|}, \tag{5}$$

where $\vec{A} \cdot \vec{B}$ is an inner product and $|\vec{A}|$, $|\vec{B}|$ is the norm of each vector that expresses node attributes.

2.3 Clustering

Clustering is a method used to understand the causality and topics hidden in the data and to summarize, classify, and separate data. Several clustering methods, also known as community detection methods, are used for graph mining. We can understand easily the positions and key concepts as described above by clustering. This study uses the method proposed by Newman [3]; the method aggregates the nodes based on modularity, which has a value close to 1. Modularity is defined as follows:

$$Q = \sum\nolimits_i \left(e_{ii} - a_i^2\right), \tag{6}$$

where e_{ij} is the percentage of the number of edges from cluster i to cluster j to the total edges, e_{ii} is the percentage of the number of internal edges in cluster i to the total number of edges, and a_i is the percentage of the number of edges connected to cluster

i to the total number of edges. The Newman method focuses on ΔQ, as shown in Eq. (7):

$$\Delta Q = 2(e_{ij} - a_i a_j). \tag{7}$$

The process of the Newman method is as follows:

1. All nodes are allocated as clusters.
2. ΔQ is calculated for all pairs of clusters.
3. Two clusters with the highest ΔQ are aggregated.
4. Steps 2–4 are repeated until $\Delta Q < 0$.

3 Analysis

We collected texts from 1609 local governments by hand. Morphological analysis and POS tagger were performed using MeCab. The government network was generated using the top 200 keywords and the thresholds of links over 0.7. The word network was generated using 500 keywords and the thresholds of links over 0.7.

Figures 1 and 2 are the word network and the government network, respectively, visualized using Graphviz [4]. The colors in these networks except white mean cluster information. The cluster with more than five nodes is labeled manually because it can be labeled easily.

The word network looks sparse and is divided into seven clusters, namely, health, sightseeing, disaster prevention, medical care, traffic, road, welfare, and enterprise. Also, the government network is a dense network; each government takes similar strategies to others. However, after clustering, the clusters are categorized into "married, education," "health, education," "project, health," "facility equipment, security," "attraction of enterprise, emigration," "married, emigration," and "emigration, married, health, and medical," which are the keywords about population increment that appear as common elements beyond several clusters. These elements attach importance to the comprehensive strategy. Promoting emigration, development of faculty equipment for marriage, education for children, and healthy living are important and basic strategies for rebuilding health.

Next, we verify these results by referring to several governments. In the emigration strategy, Kitakyushu City approaches 20–34-year-old women for city promotion to handle the needs of emigration and sightseeing and promote and generate information for women based on the known needs. Kitakyushu City also supports living fee, especially, housing fee for young people. Kitakyushu City also provides avenues to meet a new partner. For young people to desire marriage, Kitakyushu City supports the foundation and management of meeting chance providers and holds a seminar about communication skills, marriage, and birth consciousness. Higashi Yoshino Village supports the rebuilding and reform of houses and operates shared offices for immigrants [5]. This village manages a databases of single persons. The database is used to facilitate introductions between singles. Shimanto City in Kochi Prefecture invites satellite offices, call centers, and next-generation farming companies and prepares the shared offices in the same way as Higashi Yoshino Village [6]. For the health strategy, Higashi Yoshino Village provides a watching system service for elder people and supports sports. Kudo Village in Iwate Prefecture supports consultancy for special health advice and cancer diagnosis. For education, Miyoshi City in Tokushima Prefecture and surrounding cities promote education systems specialized on the area and support the travel fee for foreign cities [7].

Each local government implements similar strategies but manages their young people based on a specialized strategy in each area.

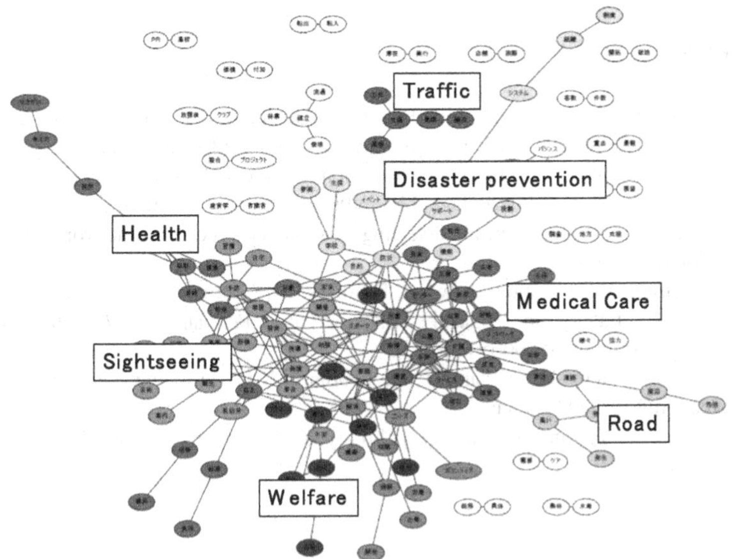

Fig. 1. Word network with label (Color figure online)

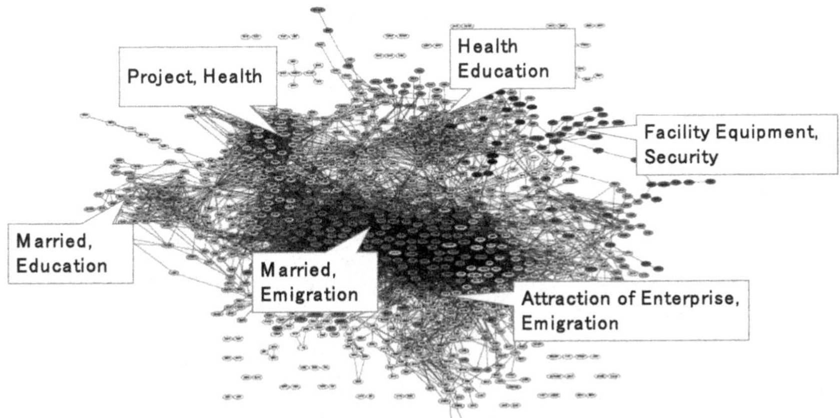

Fig. 2. Local government network attached with features keywords (Color figure online)

4 Conclusion

This study described network visualization to understand and comprehend the strategies of local governments. We analyzed two networks, namely, word and government networks. Results showed that the local governments adopt similar strategies but maintain their originality by using their strengths.

Acknowledgment. This work was supported by JSPS KAKENHI (grant nos. 16K01250 and 25420448).

References

1. Comprehensive Strategy of Overcoming Population Decline and Vitalizing Local Economy in Japan, March 2017. http://www.kantei.go.jp/jp/singi/sousei/info/pdf/20141227siryou5.pdf
2. Meeting of the Council on Overcoming Population Decline and Vitalizing Local Economy in Japan, February 2017. http://japan.kantei.go.jp/96_abe/actions/201410/10article2.html
3. Newman, M.E.J.: Fast algorithm for detecting community structure in networks. Phys. Rev. E **69**(6), 066133 (2004)
4. Graphviz – Graph Visualization Software, February 2017. http://www.graphviz.org/
5. Comprehensive strategy in Higashi Yoshino City, February 2017. http://www.city.kitakyushu.lg.jp/soumu/28500005.html
6. Comprehensive strategy in Shimanto City, February 2017. http://www.city.shimanto.lg.jp/gyosei/creation/doc/file02-03.pdf
7. Comprehensive strategy in Miyoshi City, February 2017. https://www.miyoshi.i-tokushma.jp/docs/4885.html

User Interface for Managing and Refining Related Patent Terms

Girish Showkatramani, Arthi Krishna(✉), Ye Jin, Aaron Pepe, Naresh Nula, and Greg Gabel

United States Patent and Trademark Office, Alexandria, VA, USA
{Girish.Showkatramani,Arthi.Krishna,Ye.Jin, Aaron.Pepe,Naresh.Nula,Greg.Gabel}@uspto.gov

Abstract. One of the crucial aspects of the patent examination process is assessing the patentability of an invention by performing extensive keyword-based searches to identify related existing inventions (or lack thereof). The expertise of identifying the most effective keywords is a critical skill and time-intensive step in the examination process. Recently, word embedding [1] techniques have demonstrated value in identifying related words. In word embedding, the vector representation of an individual word is computed based on its context, and so words with similar meaning exhibit similar vector representation. Using a number of alternate data sources and word embedding techniques we are able to generate a variety of word embedding models. For example, we initially clustered patent data based on the different areas of interests such as Computer Architecture or Biology, and used this data to train Word2Vec [2] and fastText [3] models. Even though the generated word embedding models were reliable and scalable, none of the models by itself was sophisticated enough to match an experts choice of keywords.

In this study, we have developed a user interface (Fig. 1) that allows domain experts to quickly evaluate several word embedding models and curate a more sophisticated set of related patent terms by combining results from several models or in some cases even augmenting to them by hand. Our application thereby seeks to provide a functional and usable centralized interface towards searching and identifying related terms in the patent domain.

Keywords: Human-computer interaction · Natural language processing Patent · Synonyms · Word embedding · Patent search · Word similarity Clustering

1 Introduction

Searching prior art to determine whether or not a patent can be granted for a claimed invention is one of the most crucial and time intensive aspect of the patent examination. This is owing to the fact that a comprehensive prior art search is involved in deciding whether any previous publication discloses the claimed invention or not. Currently, patent examiners perform extensive keyword based searches in existing patents and other published documents (non-patent literature) using a variety of sources such as technical documents, computer databases etc. to identify terms that are related to the

C. Stephanidis (Ed.): HCII Posters 2018, CCIS 850, pp. 115–120, 2018.
https://doi.org/10.1007/978-3-319-92270-6_16

filed patent application. This process of manually searching and evaluating results is very laborious and time consuming and the length of search time depends on the complexity of the invention. Furthermore, the overall efficiency in identifying related patent terms in existing patents and publications heavily relies on the expertise of the patent examiner.

In recent years, word embeddings have been shown to provide representation of words in a meaningful way and thus have become popular in Natural Language Processing applications [4–6]. In word embedding techniques, each word is represented as a vector in an n-dimension space, learned from very large dataset, in a way such that the semantic relationship between the words is captured. Mostly, word embedding techniques are based on Harris distributional hypothesis [7], which states that words that occur in the same contexts tend to have similar meanings. Individual words are represented as vectors of real numbers using their context such that similar words tend to have similar vector representations. Furthermore, over the years, numerous algorithms have been developed to generate word embedding models [8–12]. More recently, shallow neural networks based methods that can learn phrases vector representations have been introduced and have found to be very effective on word similarity and analogy tasks [2, 3].

The purpose of this study is to develop a centralized user interface that can be help patent examiners identify related patent terms and thus aid in making decisions regarding prior art.

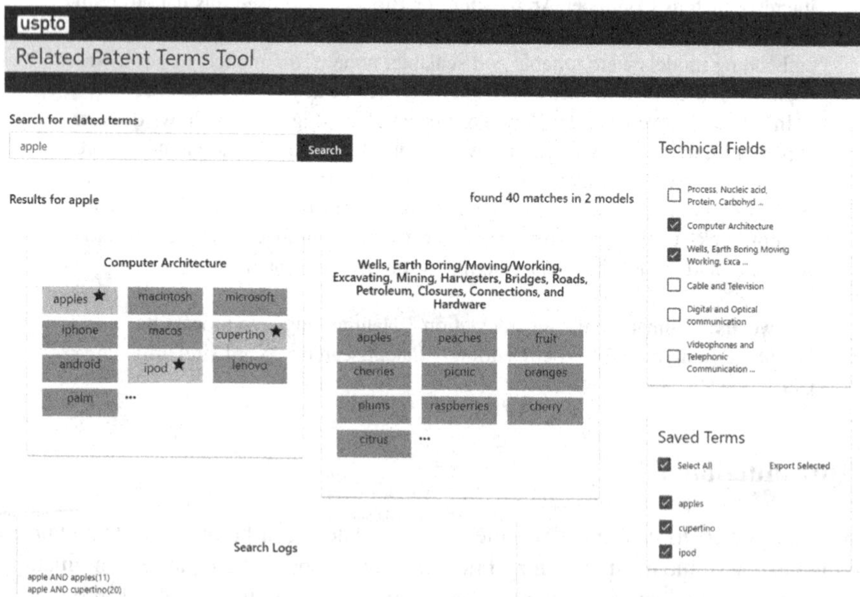

Fig. 1. Related patent terms.

2 Related Terms Search

We have built a search system that will allow patent examiners and other domain experts to evaluate the quality of related patent terms returned by the different models. In our study, we initially created clusters of patent data depending on the areas of interests such as Computer Architecture, Biology, Surface Transportation, Plants, Optics etc. to name a few. These clustered groups of patent data were then trained to generate word embedding models. The word embedding models were then utilized to query and identify related patent terms in the patent corpus. For example, when "*apple*" is entered as an input key term, all the terms related to apple are displayed in the Computer Architecture group and the oil wells group (see Fig. 1). Our application thereby seeks to provide a centralized interface that will act as a knowledge management and curation tool to patent examiners in identifying related patent terms.

The "Technical Fields" menu allows users to choose the different models to compare. For each chosen model, the corresponding tile with top 10 closest words appears in the results. Clicking on the ellipsis expands the result set can and shows more terms. User is able to choose, by clicking on the star icons, multiple terms across several models. As shown in "Saved Terms" menu on the right side, these selected terms can then be exported. The following sections describe the data set variations and alternate word embedding technologies used to create these models.

3 Dataset

The patent text for the granted United States patents and pre grant published patent applications, available publically on the (http://patents.reedtech.com/), serves as the primary data source. All of the patent text including the full text describing the invention and tables, mathematical expressions etc. are used to train the word embedding models.

The patent dataset is first clustered in to different areas of interests such as Computer Architecture, Biology, Surface Transportation, Plants, Optics etc. This clustered raw data is pre-processed, for example, stop words and non-alphanumeric characters are removed. The processed text acts as input for generating word embedding models (see Fig. 2).

4 Methods

Two state-of-the-art methods are used for generating word embeddings: Word2Vec [2] and fastText [3].

4.1 Word2Vec

The processed clustered data is trained using the Word2Vec neural network model. Word2vec is a group of related models that learn word embeddings in an unsupervised manner. These models are shallow neural networks that are trained to capture the semantic relationship between words. Word2vec models take large corpus of text as input and encode each unique tokens as N dimensional vectors. The mapping of words to vectors allows words with similar context to be placed proximally closer to one another in the vector space. The following hyperparameters were set for training the skip-gram model: minimum count of words, size of negative samples, embedding size and epochs to train.

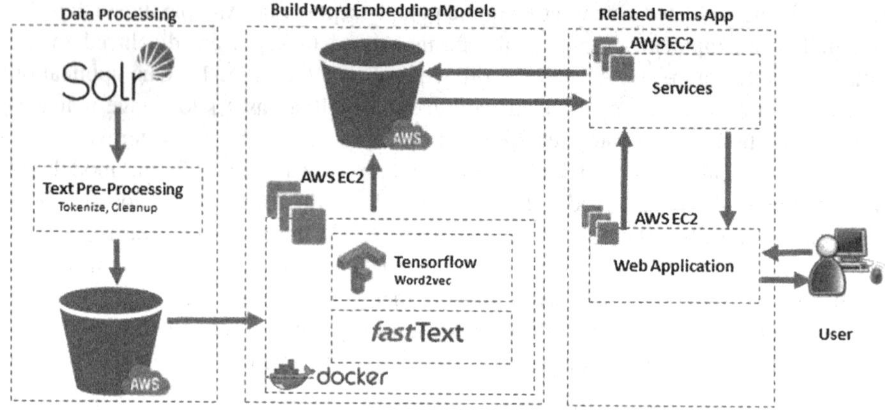

Fig. 2. System architecture.

4.2 fastText

We also trained the processed clustered data using fastText word embedding method. In the process of computing embedding, fastText enhances word vectors with subword information using additional character N-gram of variable length. This allows the algorithm to identify prefixes, suffixes, morphological nuances and syntactic structure and makes them useful for morphologically rich languages. The following hyperparameters were set for training the fastText word vector model: window size, learning rate, wordNgrams, minimum count of words, dimensions and epochs to train.

5 Infrastructure

Amazon Web Services (AWS) cloud infrastructure and Docker [13] were utilized for identifying related patent terms. AWS m4.16xlarge (64 Core Intel Xeon E5-2676 v3 Haswell processor and 256 GB DDR3 RAM) spot instance was utilized for generating word embeddings. AWS EC2 spot instances were chosen since they have an advantage of providing surplus of computing resource at a lower price compared to the on-demand instance price. In addition, Docker light-weight containers were configured to ease the configuration and setup of the TensorFlow framework [14].

6 Explanation – Search Logs

Word embedding models are flexible and a general way to capture co-occurrence relations between words. However, these models do not offer explanations or reasons for the answers. Often when users spot an unexpected word in the related terms, the users often want to know why. Our use case, patent search, lends itself to explaining the occurrence. By mining patent search logs shared by examiners, we are able to show instances of patent examiners having used the two terms together in a search query. These examples offer insights into why and how the related term is used (Fig. 3).

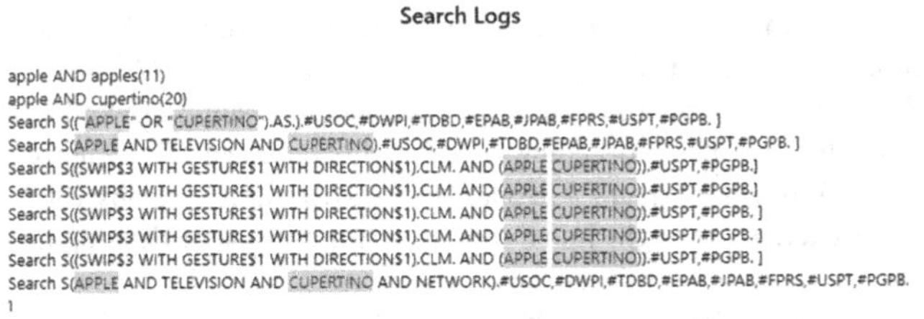

Search Logs

```
apple AND apples(11)
apple AND cupertino(20)
Search S(("APPLE" OR "CUPERTINO").AS.).#USOC,#DWPI,#TDBD,#EPAB,#JPAB,#FPRS,#USPT,#PGPB. ]
Search S(APPLE AND TELEVISION AND CUPERTINO).#USOC,#DWPI,#TDBD,#EPAB,#JPAB,#FPRS,#USPT,#PGPB. ]
Search S((SWIP$3 WITH GESTURE$1 WITH DIRECTION$1).CLM. AND (APPLE CUPERTINO)).#USPT,#PGPB.]
Search S((SWIP$3 WITH GESTURE$1 WITH DIRECTION$1).CLM. AND (APPLE CUPERTINO)).#USPT,#PGPB.]
Search S((SWIP$3 WITH GESTURE$1 WITH DIRECTION$1).CLM. AND (APPLE CUPERTINO)).#USPT,#PGPB. ]
Search S((SWIP$3 WITH GESTURE$1 WITH DIRECTION$1).CLM. AND (APPLE CUPERTINO)).#USPT,#PGPB. ]
Search S((SWIP$3 WITH GESTURE$1 WITH DIRECTION$1).CLM. AND (APPLE CUPERTINO)).#USPT,#PGPB. ]
Search S(APPLE AND TELEVISION AND CUPERTINO AND NETWORK).#USOC,#DWPI,#TDBD,#EPAB,#JPAB,#FPRS,#USPT,#PGPB.
]
```

Fig. 3. Explanation from search logs.

7 Conclusion

Using recent advances in word embedding [1] techniques we have been able to produce several models for identifying patent terms related to a keyword. However, none of the models by itself was sophisticated enough to match an experts choice of keyword expansion. In this effort, we have designed and implemented a centralized user interface that allows users to consolidate and curate related terms across different models. In addition, the interface offers explanation and insight into why the related term was suggested. In future work, we would like to explore crowd sourcing of the curated patent terms.

Acknowledgments. The authors would like to thank David Chiles, David Landrith and Thomas Beach for their support of this effort.

References

1. Yitan, L., Linli, X.: Word embedding revisited: a new representation learning and explicit matrix factorization perspective (PDF). In: International Joint Conference on Artificial Intelligence (2015)
2. Mikolov, T., Sutskever, I., Chen, K., Corrado, G., Dean, J.: Distributed representation of words and phrases and their compositionality. In: NIPS: Proceedings of Neural Information Processing Systems Nevada, USA, pp. 3111–3119 (2013)
3. Joulin, A., Grave, E., Bojanowski, P., Mikolov, T.: Bag of tricks for efficient text classification (2016)

4. Bojanowski, P., Joulin, A., Mikolov, T.: Alternative structures for character-level RNNs (2015)
5. Zhang, X., Zhao, J., Lecun, Y.: Character-level convolutional networks for text classification. In: Neural Information Processing Systems (2015)
6. Yoon, K., Jernite, Y., Sontag, D., Rush, A.M.: Character-aware neural language models (2015)
7. Bengio, Y., Ducharme, R., Vincent, P., Jauvin, C.: A neural probabilistic language model. J. Mach. Learn. Res. **3**, 1137–1155 (2003)
8. Harris, Z.: Distributional structure. Word **10**(23), 146–162 (1954)
9. Turney, P.D., Pantel, P.: From frequency to meaning: vector space models of semantics. J. Artif. Intell. Res. **37**, 141–188 (2010)
10. Baroni, M., Lenci, A.: Distributional memory: a general framework for corpus-based semantics. Comput. Linguist. **36**(4), 673–721 (2010)
11. Collobert, R., Weston, J., Bottou, L., Karlen, M., Kavukcuoglu, K., Kuksa, P.: Natural language processing (almost) from scratch. J. Mach. Learn. Res. **12**, 2493–2537 (2011)
12. Mikolov, T., Chen, K., Corrado, G., Dean, J.: Efficient estimation of word representations in vector space. In: ICLR: Proceeding of the International Conference on Learning Representations Workshop Track, Arizona, USA (2013). arxiv.org/abs/1301.3781
13. Merkel, D.: Docker: lightweight linux containers for consistent development and deployment (2014)
14. Abadi, M., Agarwal, A., Barham, P., Brevdo, E., Chen, Z., Citro, C., Corrado, G.S., Davis, A., Dean, J., Devin, M., et al.: TensorFlow: large-scale machine learning on heterogeneous systems (2015)

Development of an Interactive Evolutionary Computation Catalog Interface with User Gaze Information

Hiroshi Takenouchi[1(✉)] and Masataka Tokumaru[2]

[1] Fukuoka Institute of Technology, Fukuoka 811-0295, Japan
h-takenouchi@fit.ac.jp
[2] Kansai University, Osaka 564-8680, Japan

Abstract. We propose a catalog interface for the Interactive Evolutionary Computation (IEC) system. When a user views a product catalog, the system obtains the user's gaze information and implements evolutionary computation. We verify the effectiveness of the proposed system using evaluation experiments with real users. The experimental results show that the proposed system can generate solutions that offer results equivalent to comparable systems and reduce the evaluation load of the users.

Keywords: Gaze information
Interactive Evolutionary Computation · Catalog interface

1 Introduction

Internet users often purchase products from online product catalog. Users search for their favorite products with keyword retrieval or product feature searches. However, they must input information related their preferences and may not always search for their favorite products.

In this study, we built a system with an Interactive Evolutionary Computation (IEC) method using a user's gaze information to generate or recommend a product that satisfies the user. This method creates products based on the user's subjective evaluations and the Evolutionary Computation (EC) technique [1]. Previously proposed systems that have applied IEC include various image retrieval [2] and music generation [3] systems. However, in such systems, the user evaluation loads of candidate solutions are large.

To address this problem, IEC researchers have proposed a system with biometric information using methods that utilize a user's biometric information, such as heartbeats or brainwaves to evaluate products [4,5]. The system can obtain a user's evaluation information as the user is viewing the candidate solutions. User evaluation is achieved without the system evaluating the candidate solutions expressly. However, the user must wear special devices such as a heart rate meter or an electroencephalograph, for the system to monitor biometric information. Such IEC systems have been difficult to popularize.

C. Stephanidis (Ed.): HCII Posters 2018, CCIS 850, pp. 121–128, 2018.
https://doi.org/10.1007/978-3-319-92270-6_17

To provide an alternative systems, we applied user gaze information to the evaluation of products. Such information includes the potential preferences of the users [6]. To apply a user's gaze information to the evaluation of candidate solutions, IEC systems can obtain the user's evaluation information by merely having the user view multiple candidate solutions. Such a technique is effective for marketing applications that require a good understanding of a user's potential preferences. Moreover, when a user views a product catalog, the system learns the user's preferences and recommends various goods that are likely to satisfy the user.

Previous IEC systems using user gaze information have been proposed [7,8]. Although, while their results achieved a certain level of effectiveness, such studies have failed to clearly verify the overall effectiveness of a user gaze information-based method. Moreover, user motivation is thought to be an issue in the evaluation of the objects used in these systems. In a previous study, we verified the effectiveness of one method in terms of the evolutionary performance of candidate solutions but using a conventional IEC system that utilized a 10-stage evaluation method as a comparison method [9]. However, our study performed only a basic investigation and did not build a system to be applied in real situations.

Hence, we propose an IEC system that applies catalog-type interfaces and evaluates product designs using user gaze information. The user views product designs with the catalog interface and turns pages to view other products. The proposed system performs EC operations while the user turns the pages. Moreover, the proposed system uses the Genetic Algorithm (GA) method as an EC method in the IEC. According to the user's gaze information, product designs that fit the user's preferences are displayed on the right-hand pages of the catalog, and various recommended product designs are displayed on the left-hand pages.

We perform the evaluation experiment with real users to verify the effectiveness of the proposed system with regard to the performance of its EC of candidate solutions and the degree of usability of the system. The experiment uses three systems. The first system is the proposed system, and the second one is the manual evaluation system, in which users evaluate candidate solutions usign a 5-stage evaluation method. The manual system had the same interfaces as the proposed one. The last system is our previous system [9]. After the experiment, we distribute questionnaires to users in order to investigate the satisfaction level of generated designs as well as the user's evaluation load and the appearance of the interfaces.

2 Proposed System

2.1 Schematic of the Proposed System

Figure 1 shows the schematic of the proposed system. A user creates a design of their favorite running shoes. First, the system generates the initial gene-type candidate solutions, which consist of bit patterns. Next, the system presents the product designs corresponding to the gene-type candidate solutions. Then, the user views all candidate solutions as if viewing a product catalog while the system measures the user's gaze information. The user turns the pages to view other products. As the user views some of the products, the proposed system evaluates candidate solutions with the user's gaze information and creates new candidate solutions by GA processing.

Each candidate solution is evaluated using the user's gaze information. To obtain the user gaze information, we use a Tobii Pro X2-30 eye tracker, which measured the user's gaze information at a rate of 30 [Hz].

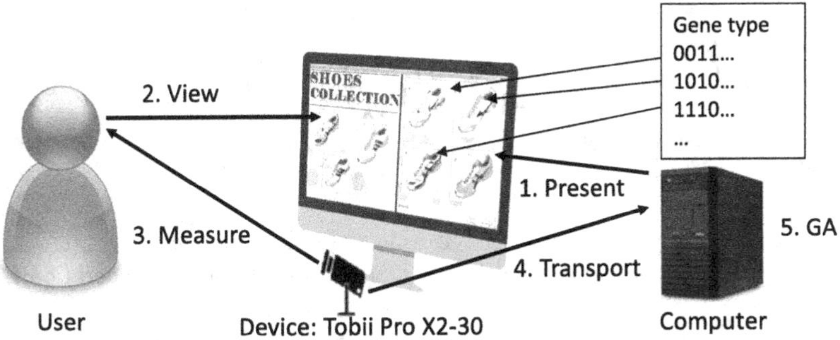

Fig. 1. Outline of the proposed system

2.2 Evaluation Interface

Generally, a product catalog has various layout interfaces for presenting the various product designs. Therefore, the proposed system changes the interface at every generation.

Figure 2 shows the interfaces of the proposed system. After the system has started, it presents initial candidate solutions on the interface (Fig. 2(a)). The user views the presented designs freely. If the user clicks the allow button (bottom right of the interface) to turn the pages, the system randomly chooses from the interfaces (Fig. 2(b)–(c)) and presents the new designs. The interfaces include seven to eight designs. The proposed system generates eight candidate solutions for every generation. If the proposed system uses an interface that has only seven presented designs, the design that is not presented is assigned an evaluation value of 0.

2.3 Evaluation of Candidate Solutions

Figure 3 shows the candidate evaluation of the proposed system. First, the proposed system measures the user gaze positions for each sampling (black circles in Fig. 3) and then counts the number of user gaze positions for each candidate solution. If the gaze position is away from the interface, the system does not

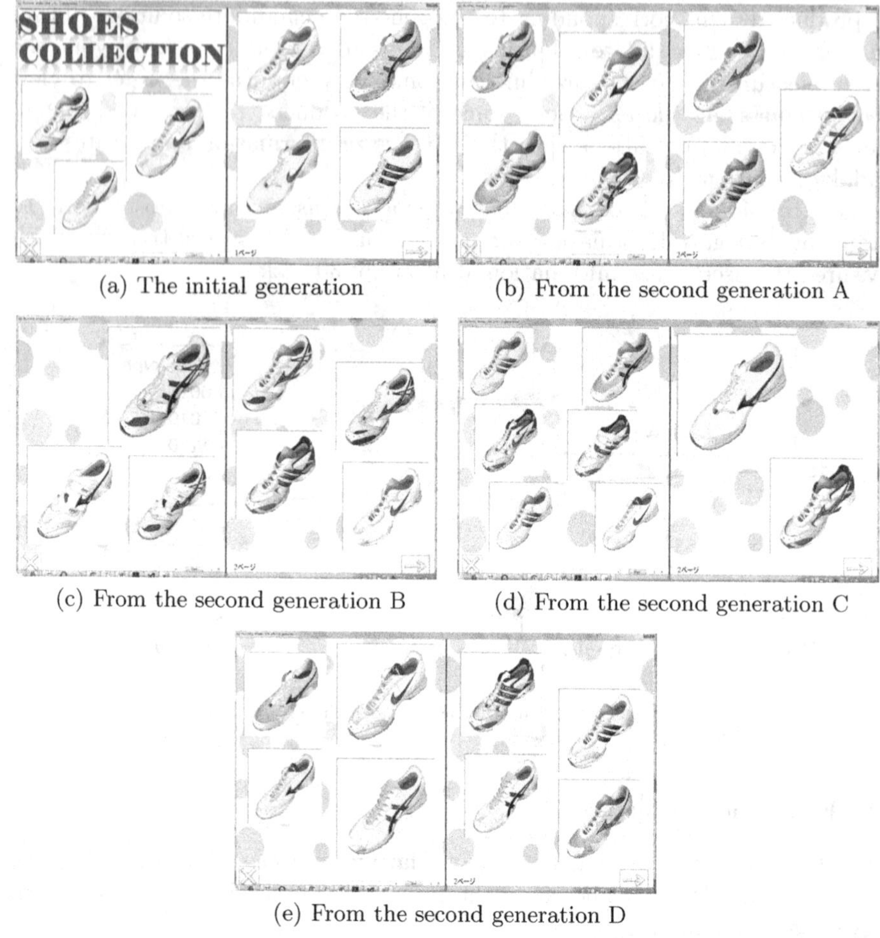

(a) The initial generation

(b) From the second generation A

(c) From the second generation B

(d) From the second generation C

(e) From the second generation D

Fig. 2. Evaluation interfaces of the proposed system

measure or count the number of user gaze positions. For example, when the number of user gaze position samples of each candidate solution p_1–p_8 is s_1–s_8, each s_i equals 3, 2, 2, 1, 3, 3, 2, and 2. Next, the proposed system normalizes these values in a range from 0 to 100. Then, the evaluation values of each candidate solution v_i are 100, 50, 50, 0, 100, 100, 50, and 50. The system uses these evaluation values v_i for GA processing.

3 Evaluation Experiments

3.1 Outline of the Experiment

Here, we investigate the effectiveness of the proposed system with real users. Twenty subjects (ten men and ten women) in their twenties participate in the

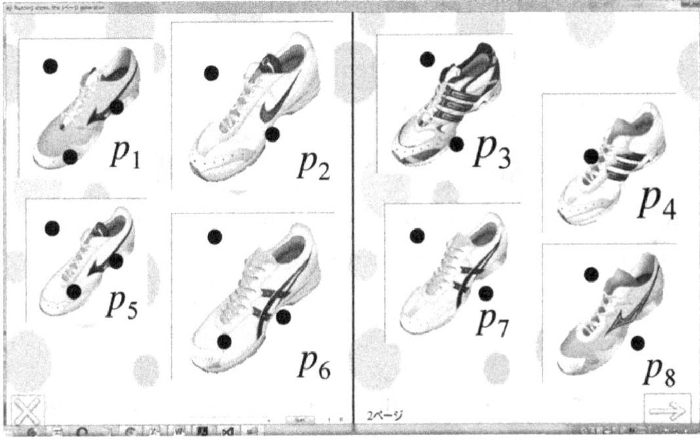

Fig. 3. Evaluation method of candidate solutions of the proposed system

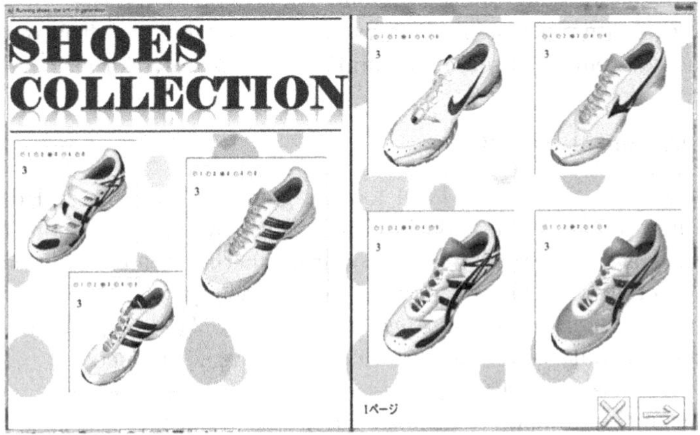

Fig. 4. Interface of the manual evaluation system

experiment, which uses three systems: the proposed system, the manual evaluation system, and our previous system.

Figure 4 shows the interaface of the manual evaluation system. The subject inputs the evaluation values using radio buttons beside each design. These evaluation values are normalized within a range of 0–100 for GA processing. Whenever the user turns the pages, the system changes the interface and presents new designs as well as the proposed system. The candidate solutions of our previous system are evaluated the same manner as is the proposed system.

Table 1 shows the experimental parameters. All the systems uses the same experimental parameters. We use running shoes designs [9]. Each design consists of five parts. Each part has eight designs expressed by 3 bits (gene length: 15 bits). The system can generate 32,768 running shoe designs. The subjects used

Table 1. Experimental parameters

Gene row	Bit pattern
Gene length	15 bits
Generations	10
Candidate solutions	7 or 8
Selection	Roulette selection + elite preservation
Crossover	Uniform crossover
Mutation rate	20%

each system to view freely, evaluate, and select designs for shoes that they would want to wear for running.

We distribute questionnaires to survey the satisfaction levels of the generated candidate solutions as well as the usability (i.e., the level of evaluation load) and appearance of the interface of each system. We also measured the time taken by the users to evaluate the designs. Moreover, we considered the effect of the order in which each system was used and randomly set the order for each subject.

3.2 Experimental Results

Figure 5 shows the satisfaction level for the generated designs and degrees of usability. The average satisfaction level for all the systems was more than 3.5. We performed the statistical test to confirm whether there were statistically significant differences in the satisfaction levels of each system. However, we made no confirmations when the significance level was 5%. We demonstrated that the proposed system could create designs that satisfied the subjects.

The average usability of the proposed and previous systems was more than 3.5, and that of the manual evaluation system was about 2.7. With the results of the statistical test at a 5% of significance level, we confirmed statistically significant differences between the proposed and manual evaluatiuon systems as well as between the previous and the manual evaluation systems. When using the manual evaluation system, the subjects manually evaluated the designs. However, in the proposed and previous systems, they evaluated the designs more easily, because they only viewed the designs. The operation loads of the proposed and previous systems were smaller than that of the manual evaluation system.

In an IEC system, the time spent evaluating designs is a significant factor in reducing the evaluation loads of users. Figure 6 shows the time spent evaluating the designs for each system. The subjects used ten generations with each system. The evaluation time was measured from the point of the initial presentation of the designs to the completion of the evaluations in the final generation. The evaluation times required for all systems were less than 240 [s]. The evaluation times required for the proposed and previous systems were shorter than that for the manual one. With the results of the statistical test with the 5% of the significance level, we confirmed significant differences among all the systems.

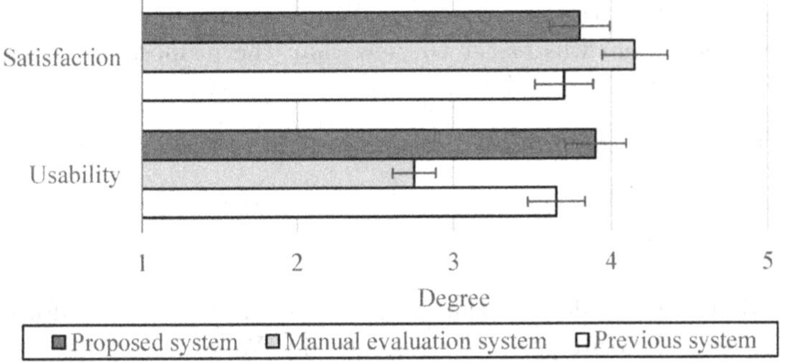

Fig. 5. Satisfaction level for the generated designs and usability degree

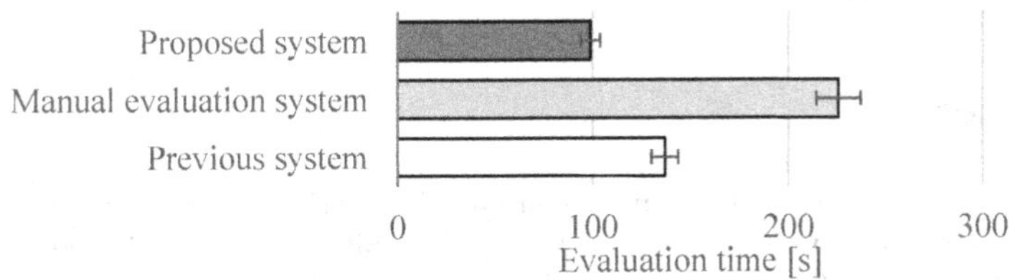

Fig. 6. Evaluation time for the proposed system

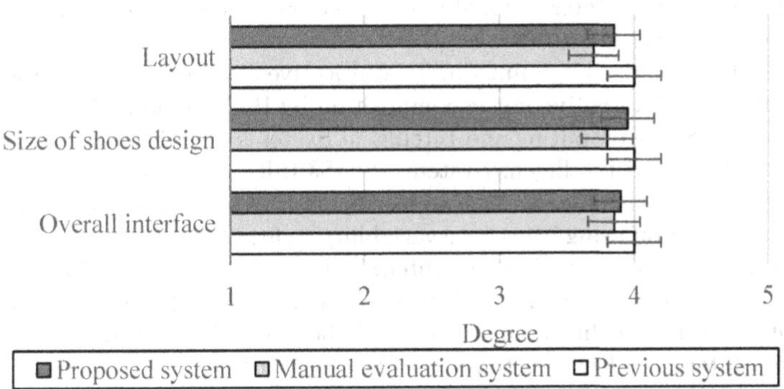

Fig. 7. Appearance of the interfaces

These differences were due to the subjects having only viewed the presented designs or their favorite ones using the proposed and previous systems.

Figure 7 shows the results of the questionnaires given to the users for evaluating the interfaces of the proposed system. We assumed the use of the proposed system in real situations, as the appearance of the interface was important for this system. The average of all the questionnaire items was the same. Therefore, we did not confirm the advantage of the appearances of the interface of the proposed system. Some subjects made the following comments:

- It is interesting that the proposed system has various interfaces.
- The previous system was easier to view than the proposed system because the former arranged the designs in a row.

We intend to improve the proposed system in light of these comments.

4 Conclusions

We proposed an IEC catalog interface system using a user's gaze information to generate the user's favorite product automatically. We evaluated the usability of the proposed system by conducting an experiment with real users. In the future, we will improve the evolutionary algorithm to make more effective searches for a user's favorite products.

References

1. Takagi, H.: Interactive evolutionary computation: fusion of the capabilities of EC optimization and human evaluation. Proc. IEEE **89**(9), 1275–1296 (2001)
2. Lai, C.C., Chen, Y.C.: A user-oriented image retrieval system based on interactive genetic algorithm. IEEE Trans. Instrum. Meas. **60**(10), 3318–3325 (2011)
3. Marques, V.M., Reis, C., Machado, J.A.T.: Interactive evolutionary computation in music. In: 2010 IEEE International Conference on Systems Man and Cybernetics, SMC, pp. 3501–3507 (2010)
4. Unehara, M., Yamada, K., Shimada, T.: Subjective evaluation of music with brain wave analysis for interactive music composition by IEC. In: Joint 7th International Conference on Soft Computing and Intelligent Systems and 15th International Symposium on Advanced Intelligent Systems, SCIS&ISIS 2014, pp. 66–70 (2014)
5. Fukumoto, M., Nakashima, S., Ogawa, S., Imai, J.: An extended interactive evolutionary computation using heart rate variability as fitness value for composing music chord progression. J. Adv. Comput. Intell. Intell. Inf. **15**(9), 1329–1336 (2011)
6. Moniri, M.M., Valcarcel, F.A.E., Merkel, D., Sonntag, D.: Human gaze and focus-of-attention in dual reality human-robot collaboration. In: 12th International Conference on Intelligent Environments, pp. 238–241 (2016)
7. Pallez, D., Collard, P., Baccino, T., Dumercy, L.: Eye-tracking evolutionary algorithm to minimize user's fatigue in IEC applied to interactive one-max problem. In: Proceedings of the 10th Annual Conference on Genetic and Evolutionary Computation, GECCO 2007, pp. 2883–2886 (2007)
8. Holmes, T., Zanker, J.: Eye on the prize: using overt visual attention to drive fitness for interactive evolutionary computation. In: Proceedings of the 10th Annual Conference on Genetic and Evolutionary Computation, GECCO 2008, pp. 1531–1538 (2008)
9. Takenouchi, H., Tokumaru, M.: Applying gaze information to interactive evolutionary computation. In: The 33rd Fuzzy System Symposium, TF1-3, pp. 357–360 (2017). (in Japanese)

Research on User-Centered Information Design in SVOD Service

Wonseok Yang[1(✉)], Satoshi Yahiro[1], and Keitaro Sato[2]

[1] Engineering and Design, Shibaura Institute of Technology, 3-9-14, Shibaura, Minato-ku, Tokyo, Japan
yang@shibaura-it.ac.jp

[2] Graduate School of Engineering and Science, Shibaura Institute of Technology, 3-7-5, Toyo-su, Koto-ku, Tokyo, Japan

Abstract. SVOD services distribute a huge amount of video content and the UI is designed such that the user chooses what he/she wishes to view from the available content. For this reason, it is important to make it easy for the user to choose the content. However, the UI at present does not provide sufficient information for the user to conveniently search for content provided by the service. This could adversely affect the satisfaction experienced by users. In this research, we aimed to verify that information design incorporating the concept of user-centered design is effective for SVOD service and will improve the usability of these services. We compared the UI each service on the TV and similarities and differences between each service's UI. From these results, we can show that usability at the time of using the service improves by using various methods for user-centered information design. This leads to improved user satisfaction.

Keywords: SVOD service · User centered design · Information architecture

1 Introduction

There are a lot of services in Japan (2015) with a monthly fixed rate service. These services are collectively known as SVOD. Netflix and Amazon Prime are examples of these services. These services distribute a huge amount of video content and the UI is designed such that the user chooses what he/she wishes to view from the available content [1, 2]. For this reason, it is important to make it easy for the user to choose the content. However, the UI at present does not provide sufficient information for the user to conveniently search for content provided by the service [3]. This could adversely affect the satisfaction experienced by users. Therefore, in order to investigate the usability when the user uses the SVOD service, some experiments were conducted. First, a questionnaire was used to evaluate the number and type of contents of the SVOD service, the number of contents displayed on the screen, the position of the category/genre in the site, the structure of the category/genre, and other related categories [4]. Based on the results, we grasp the current state of service structure and clarified the difference between each service. In addition, we investigated the UI of PCs, iPhones, and TVs and observed the difference of how to divide content and how to display [5].

C. Stephanidis (Ed.): HCII Posters 2018, CCIS 850, pp. 129–135, 2018.
https://doi.org/10.1007/978-3-319-92270-6_18

2 UCD for Content Distribution Service

Given that a content distribution service has many types of content, it is necessary to design services, sites, and information so that users can use them. Also, due to diversification of usage environments, it is assumed to be used in various devices and situations [6, 7]. Based on the characteristics of such services, we think that it is necessary to incorporate the concept of user-centric design (UCD) and to consider organizing services centrally on the user side in order to make the service easier to use and enjoy [8] (Fig. 1).

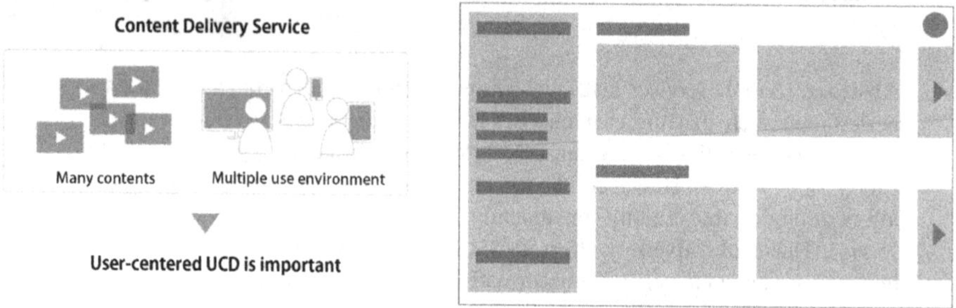

Fig. 1. UI of content delivery service and UCD & SVOD service

2.1 Organizing and Structuring Information in the SVOD Service

As the SVOD service has many types of content as described above, information design to structure them becomes important. Information services in the video service are meant to categorize works by category or genre and link them for cross referencing. Because users search for content based on information such as categorization and genre division, it is considered important that a UCD that can be understood by the user is made.

2.2 Influence of UI on Usability of Service

The UI of the SVOD service connects the user and the content, and even if the user can understand the displayed information, usability is low if it is not easy to use, and we risk a decline in the satisfaction level for the service [9]. Conversely, if the information displayed by the UI is closer to the user, we believe that we can improve usability and the satisfaction level of the service [10, 11].

3 Investigation of the Current Situation of SVOD Service

A current-status survey was conducted for 10 services: Hulu, Netflix, Amazon Prime Video, U-NEXT, dTV, Video Path, Premium GYAO!, Rakuten SHOWTIME, TSUTAYA TV, and Geo Channel, which provide SVOD services in Japan. Survey items mainly include the count and type of content, the context on the screen, the number of tips displayed, the position of the category/genre section in the site, and the type and structure of the category/genre section.

Table 1. SVOD service current status survey result

	Position of category / Genre List	Number of contents/screen	Number of out-of-view contents	Feature	Recommend	Genre	Similar Movie	Ranking	Popular content
hulu	The bottom of the site	2 Feature 16 Contents	1 Feature 4 Contents	○	○	○	×	×	○
netflix	In the menu displayed at the top	3 Feature 15 Contents	3 Feature 3 Contents	○	○	○	×	×	×
U-NEXT	Inside the site	3 Feature 15 Contents	3 Feature 3 Contents	○	○	○	×	○	×
dTV	The bottom of the site	4 Feature 20 Contents	-	×	×	○	×	○	×
Amazon Prime Video	Same place and layout as site contents	4 Feature 20 Contents	1 Feature 8Contents	○	×	○	×	×	○
TSUTAYA TV	Right side of search bar	2 Feature 10 Contents	1 Feature 5 Contents	○	○	○	×	○	×
Rakuten Showtime	Top of the site	3 Feature 29 Contents	2 Feature 2 Contents	○	○	○	×	○	○
Prime GYAO!	Top of the site	3Feature 28 Contents	3Feature 4 Contents	○	○	○	○	○	△
videopass	The bottom of the site	3 Feature 15 Contents	-	○	○	○	×	○	○
Geochannel	Inside the site	3 Feature 15 Contents	-	○	○	○	×	○	×

The result is as presented in Table 1, obtaining the current status of the service structure and clarifying the difference between each service. Regarding the number and structure of categories and genres in particular, a wide range of genres and categories ranging from 49 to 223 were seen. Next, a UI survey was conducted for Netflix with several compatible devices. The devices used for the survey are iPhone, a PC, Apple TV, and Amazon Fire Stick.

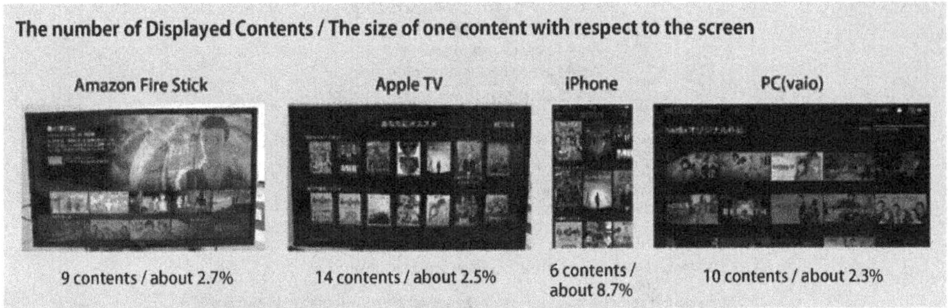

Fig. 2. Number of displayed contents/size of one content with respect to the screen

Regarding content display, the differences shown in Fig. 2 were seen. The UI was designed in a unified manner, but there were slight differences in the number of content divisions: 15 for iPhones while Apple TV was at 154, and the trend leans toward TVs.

The number of content divisions was abundant. In addition, among the above 10 services, Hulu, Netflix, Amazon Prime Video, U-NEXT, dTV, and GYAO! were displayed on a TV using Amazon Fire Stick and the UI was compared. The tendencies and features as shown in Fig. 3 were seen, and it was possible to grasp the common features of the TV UI.

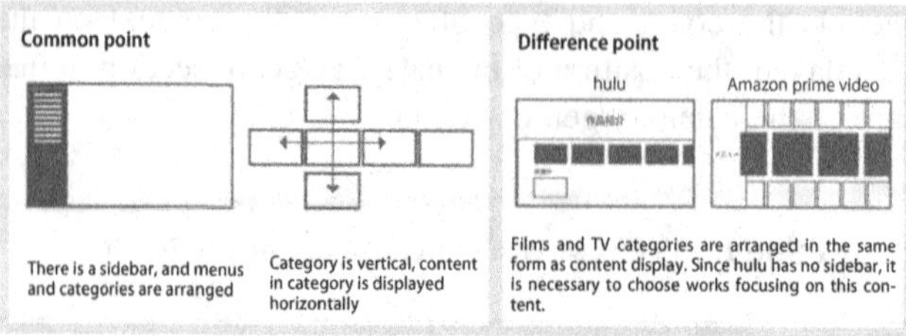

Fig. 3. Characteristics obtained from TV UI survey

3.1 Analysis of Upper and Lower Relationships for Grasping High-Level Needs

In order to grasp the high-level needs of users, 10 people provided good points and bad points about the SVOD service and we analyzed the top-bottom relationship based on it. Figure 4 summarizes the results. The SVOD service user is not bound by time and place, he wants to see the things that interest him when he wants to see it, and he wants a payment structure where money is paid even if he is not looking at any content, rather than paying per view. Two top needs have been revealed. In particular, user-centric information design is considered to be important, as comfort-related needs relate to usability of services, such as whether they can find what they want to see [12].

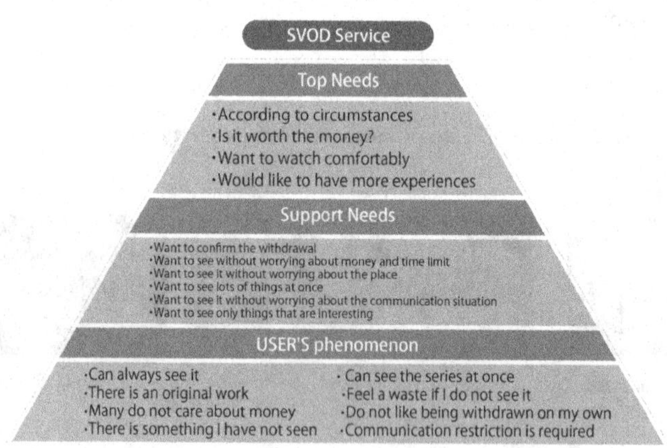

Fig. 4. Result of upper and lower relation analysis

3.2 Card Sorting for Grasping the Mental Model

From the keywords related to categories and genres of each service confirmed in the current survey, we omitted the ones with the same or similar meaning and narrowed down the keywords to 100. These keywords were used to create cards, and participants were asked to group the cards as they liked into 10 categories.

A tendency of this classification, as shown in Fig. 5, is that the menu group is divided into other groups to create a higher hierarchy, separated by "movie" or

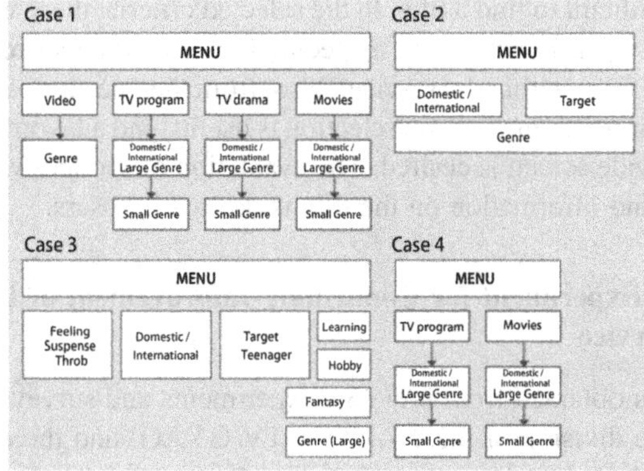

Fig. 5. Example of grouping

"television", genre keywords are also divided into large genres and small genres, and "domestic" and "international" were lower in the hierarchy than "movie" and "television". In addition, we were able to find the average number of cards per group and keywords that we do not know or need.

4 Observation Experiment and Questionnaire Survey

In order to clarify the selection criteria of the work, the features requested by the users, and the issues with the TV UI, we conducted experiments to actually use the service. In the experiment, we made each of the five subjects to ask for one specific title of their choosing and one title we wanted to see out of the titles in the service. For the experiments, we used Amazon Fire Stick, targeting five services: Hulu, Netflix, U-NEXT, dTV, and GYAO! Also, we asked a questionnaire about the impressions of/suggestion for service experience after completion of the experiment. Figure 6 shows a part of the survey results. From experiments and questionnaires, it turned out that depending on the

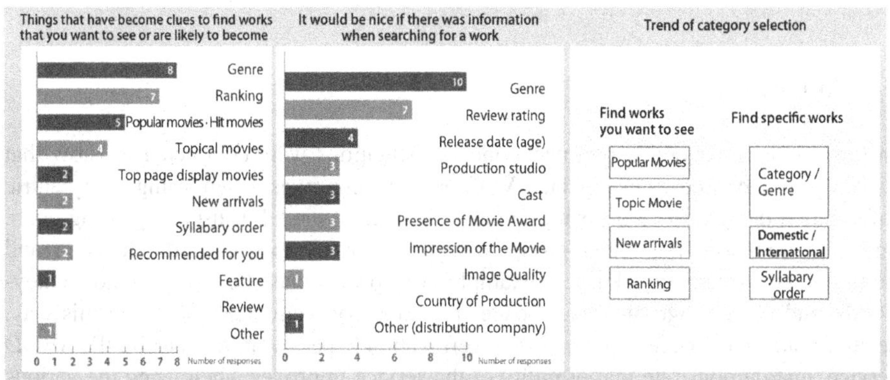

Fig. 6. Sample of the survey results

service, it may be difficult to find a title. In the selected criteria, there were differences in the categories used when searching for a specific title and when searching for what the viewer wants to see from within the service. Also, from the questionnaire, we can clarify that there is a sidebar preference, menu selection is useful, and a layout that displays a lot of content using a wide screen is desired. The evaluation of services with about 12 titles displayed is high, and information on the title is desired by users.

4.1 Verification Experiment for Confirming Improvement of Usability of SVOD Service

Based on the results obtained from previous experiments and surveys, we changed the categorization/genre division of the TV UI for TV GYAO! and the display method of the titles; we added 10 UI elements before the change and 10 after the change and compared them. Experimental results are as shown in Table 2, and compared with the before-change evaluation, the score was high for items such as appearance and actual ease of use, experience when looking for titles, and the manner of displaying titles. However, items with low evaluation such as genre/category categorization were also seen. UI elements other than the changed items and the influence of the operation method were considered.

Table 2. Evaluation result of verification experiment

	Q2)Easy ease of use	Q6)Ease of actual use	Q7) Ease of searching for CONTENTS	Q7(2) CONTENTS indication	Q7(3) Genre / Categorization
UI before change	4.8	4.6	5	4.3	5.3
UI after the change	5.7	4.9	4.9	5.3	4.9
Numerical difference (old UI standard)	(+)0.9	(+)0.3	(-)0.1	(+)1.0	(-)0.4

	Q2)Easy ease of use	Q6)Ease of actual use	Q7) Ease of searching for CONTENTS	Q7(2) CONTENTS indication	Q7(3) Genre / Categorization
UI before change	5.2	4.4	5	4.6	4.8
UI after the change	6.2	6	5.8	6	5.8
Numerical difference (old UI standard)	(+)1.0	(+)1.6	(+)0.8	(+)1.4	(+)1.0

5 Conclusion

In this research, several experiments and investigations were conducted to show that usability at the time of using an SVOD service improves when using user-centric information design. In card sorting to grasp the mental model of users regarding genre and categorization, the menu group, categorization by movies and television and domestic and international titles, examples of special classification, unknown keywords, and the average number of pages per category were clear points. In this way, several issues have been revealed in the verification experiment, and also in the SVOD service, that demonstrate that usability of the service improves when using the various methods of user-centric information design we made. Through this research, when designing an SVOD service, we see that it is important to design with the user in mind, but at the same time, we found that it is not easy to appreciate the ease of providing services, like the ease of content management. In future, we would like to consider SVOD services in terms of ease of operation. In addition, in an SVOD service, since the type of content to be handled is different for each service, it is necessary to flexibly adapt the information design to each target. Therefore, it is important to understand the content of the target service, and in terms of information design, both the user and the service-management side can be considered to use or operate the service. We will also consider information design based on the characteristics of the contents of the service. Also, as for the verification experiment, since it was an experiment in a situation somewhat different from the actual-use environment, we think that some bias has been introduced in the experimental results. For this reason, the necessity of a prototyping television tool that can easily display created prototypes on a television needs to be used to verify service use on the television. It is necessary to consider this verification method while the Internet service diversifies.

References

1. Namatame, M., Kitajima, M.: Exploring hyperlink representations for attaining usability and accessibility of web pages: an eye-tracking study on web design (1). Bull. Jpn. Soc. Sci. Des. **58**(2), 105 (2011)
2. Sakaiosamu: Expanding television advertisement, video and content. Future of business. Sendenkaigi (2016)
3. Yoshitsubaki, K., Watanabe, T.: User-centered web design-mental model gaps between elderly users and developers. IEICE Technical report WIT2010-74(2011-2) (2011)
4. Kim, J., Miyazaki, M., Tamagaki, Y., Ohara, Y.: Point of web navigation with easy search: the case study of online bookstore. Bull. JSSD **53**(5), 43–52 (2006)
5. Doi, M.: Web design in view of human interface (< Special feature > Usability). J. Inf. Sci. Technol. Assoc. **54**(8), 407–412 (2004)
6. Toda, H., Tanabe, H., Hitaka, T., Hoshi, T.: Situation - adaptive retrieval system for interactive TV service. IPSJ (FI) 2002(41(2002-FI-067)), 21 May 2002, pp. 121–128 (2002)
7. Hatano, J.: Proposal of content recommendation and filtering technology with user metadata for cooperative broadcasting and communication. NTT Cyber Solution Laboratories. ISSN 13426893
8. Yamazaki, K., Yoshitake, R.: Design for ease of use - user centered design. IBM JAPAN, Maruzen (2004)
9. Kurosu, M.: Fundamentals of human-centered design. Kindaikagakusha (2013)
10. Hasegawa, A.: IA 100 - Information architecture design for user experience design. BMM (2009)
11. Ministry of Internal Affairs and Communications, Japan: Communications Usage Trend Survey (2016)
12. http://www.soumu.go.jp/johotsusintokei/whitepaper/ja/h28/html/nc252110.html
13. Ando, M.: Dynamic change of long term usability: change of context of use and influence of it. Sokendai Rev. Cult. Soc. Stud. **3**, 27–45 (2007)
14. Camara, C.: The UX Learner's Guide Book. MdN (2016)
15. Inoue, N.: How has the information and communication technology developed (2016). beret.co

Research on Filter Naming Mechanism Based on Emotional Expression and Cognitive Integration

Ke Zhong, Chen Tang, and Liqun Zhang(✉)

Institute of Design Management, Shanghai Jiao Tong University, Shanghai, China
zhanglliqun@gmail.com

Abstract. With the development of information technology especially the mobile Internet, more people are using the camera in mobile phone and using apps in it to process the pictures, meanwhile a variety of filters are used of a high frequency. However, strange filter naming mechanisms bring users a bad experience and make them confused. How to establish a new filter naming mechanism that can improve the cognitive efficiency of users and verify it by experiments are the focus of this paper. Firstly, research the motivations of using filters, then extract and sort out the existing main filter naming mechanisms. Then use the analysis of text or questionnaire to extract the emotional expression of imagery words of using filters, sort out the words by cluster analysis. Through a research of correlation analysis, the emotional expression of imagery word closest to the filter are obtained, and a new filter naming mechanism is gotten. Finally, through a comparative experiment we can see that the new filter naming mechanism can greatly improve the users' cognitive efficiency and their experience. This study not only fills the blanks in the field of filter naming research, but provides a new research idea for deeper research on user's emotional expression and its stimulating factors. It can be foreseen that the research methods and results can be applied to product and visual design, sociology research and other specific areas, playing a guiding and testing role.

Keywords: Filter naming mechanism · Emotional experience
Cognitive integration

1 Introduction

With the development of information technology especially the rapid development of mobile Internet, more people are using the mobile phones' camera to take photos and post-processing the photos at the same time using the apps at mobile phones [1]. At the same time, a variety of filters are used of high frequency, Instagram, Snapseed, Meitu Xiu Xiu, VSCO and other apps almost become a necessary software of mobile terminal for everyone.

However, strange filter naming mechanisms of those apps bring users a bad experience and make them confused.

This research aims to purpose a new filter naming mechanism based on emotional expression and cognitive integration. The new filter naming mechanism not only

C. Stephanidis (Ed.): HCII Posters 2018, CCIS 850, pp. 136–143, 2018.
https://doi.org/10.1007/978-3-319-92270-6_19

analyzes from the view of the actual work of the filter, but also fully combines the user's emotional expression when using the filter. The final contrast test also shows that such a new filter naming mechanism does greatly improve the users' cognitive efficiency when using the filters.

This research creatively proposes a mechanism for the filter naming. The mechanism has the following advantages,

- Replace the original confusing way of filter naming, it greatly improves user's cognitive efficiency and experience when using the apps about filter. And users can have a preliminary cognition of the effect of filters when they see the new filters' names.
- The existing filters can be optimized according to the emotions that users want to express when using filters. At the same time, other new filters can also be designed from this perspective.
- It can be targeted to rename the same filters for users in different countries or regions by this new mechanism, in this way that we can make user's cognitive efficiency and experience better when using filters.

The rest of the paper is organized as follows. The motivations for users to use the filter of mobile terminal and current main types of filter naming methods are sorted out in Sect. 2. Section 3 presented a new filter naming mechanism. To verify the rationality of the proposed mechanism, experiments with small sample size have been done. The process and analyses are presented in Sect. 4. Section 5 is the summary and prospect.

2 Desktop Research

2.1 Motivations

A Variety of Emotional Expression Needs. Each filter software has a variety of filter effects for users to try and switch, and users can use different filters to express users' different emotions. Emotion refers to the subjective feelings or experiences of the individual [2]. Emotional experience refers to the individual subjective experience of emotion [3]. Emotion is a part of attitude. It is in harmony with the introverted feelings and intentions in attitude. It is a more complex and stable physiological evaluation and experience of physiology [4, 5].

Easy to Use. Traditional image post-processed software, such as Photoshop and Lightroom, all involve various professional vocabularies and knowledge such as curve, color balance, saturation and so on [6]. Users don't need to consider these parameters when they use these filter software of mobile terminal, it is easy to access and easy to use.

Efficient. Users only need to switch filters when they are using these filters, and choose a filter that they like. The whole process is usually less than 1 min.

Nice Effect. These filters are generated by professionals after repeated debugging according to the professional knowledge of psychology and photography. The effect is undoubtedly better than that produced by nonprofessional users.

2.2 Existing Filter Naming Methods

By the Effect. This kind of filters is named with the actual effect of the filter. There is a certain correlation between the name of the filter and the actual effect of the filter. For example, Instagram's filter [Rise]: there are warm colors, a little bit of sunrise yellow, and also let the images soft, so named [Rise]; VSCO's filter [New Modern]: fashion is the main sensation to users, the color is bright and full of impact, with new modern, so it is named it. The [Bright] of Snapseed improves the brightness, contrast and saturation of the picture, giving people a sense of [Bright]. [A Picnic in The Woods] of the Meitu Xiu Xiu is green with high contrast and strong color. It gives people a sense of we are take a picnic in the woods, so it is called [A Picnic in The Woods].

By the Technology and Form. This kind of filters is named by the technology and form of the filters. The number of this part of the filters is small, but classic. They are to reproduce some classic forms of the picture effect in the history of the development of photography. For example, Instagram [X-Pro] is a kind of washing technique's abbreviation, [Cross-Processing] (cross flushing), which can achieve different film effect with different chemical solvents, and this is precisely reproducing the filter to reach the flushing technique effect; VSCO [K] is the abbreviation of Kodachrome: Inspiration from the classic Kodak color slides Kodachrome, K series of filters that follow its predecessor. Snapseed [Faded Glow] is the simulation of photography in the dark corner of a filter; Meitu Xiu Xiu [LOMO] is a kind of color reproduction in 1950s production of a special camera out of the bright effect.

No Connection. There is no connection between this kind of filter naming and the actual effect of the filter. Most of them are named by the names of the designers, or the place names related to the designers, or the names of their pets and so on. A lot of filters of Instagram's name was derived from this, for example, [Juno] was named by the designer Krieger, who had a pet called Juno. Amaro is an Italy wine, there were a lot of underground bars at that time, and Systrom and Mike Krieger, the filter's designers were obsessed with Amaro. When they drunk Amoro in a bar, the filter was born out, so the filter's name also came into being.

Through the research, we can find that the filters are lack of standardization in naming, mostly are random, just in accordance with the designers' personal willingness, which brings users bad experience, let the users very confused during using them. Therefore, it is very important to establish a set of filter naming rules which can improve the users' cognitive efficiency and improve the users' use experience.

At the same time, through the analysis of the above three types of filter naming rules we can find that the first type of naming rule has the strongest correlation between the filters' names and their effect, and can be suitable for the majority of filters, but its lack of unity and certain norms, and the name of many filters are too subtle and restrained, for example Meitu Xiu Xiu's [37.2], [After The Youth] [Yogurt], and so on, and filters of VSCO using the first letter of the name to display, which will make the user more confused when in use. Therefore, the focus of this paper is to propose a more standardized and direct filter naming mechanism which is more conducive to improving user cognitive efficiency and user experience, and verify it through a comparative experiment.

3 A New Filter Naming Mechanism

The original motivation of using the filter is to express one of the emotions at this time. Different pictures record different scenes, express different mood of users, so do filters. With the same scene and the same picture, users will use different filters to express different emotions.

On the other hand, the filter is a kind of one button to make an automatic post-processing tool for pictures, while referring to the post-processing of pictures, the main parameters involved are exposure, contrast, saturation, hue and color temperature, highlight, shadow and so on.

Therefore, this paper innovatively proposes the filter naming mechanism of "adjectives + nouns". Using the first letters of "adjectives" and "nouns", "A" and "N", so this mechanism is called "AN" (Fig. 1):

$\text{Name}_i = \text{adj}_i + \text{noun}_i$

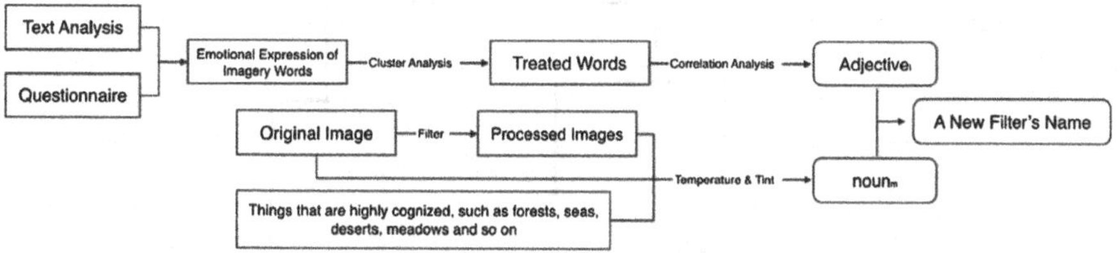

Fig. 1. Filter naming mechanism

Among them, adjectives mainly express the relationship between the filter and the emotion that the user wants to express, and the nouns mainly show the parameter information of the color temperature and color of the filter.

3.1 Adjective

First, through text analysis and questionnaire, the emotional expression of imagery words while the users are using filters are collected. Then carry out the clustering analysis of the emotional expression of imagery words collected.

Clustering Analysis. Clustering is a common data analysis tool and a basic algorithm for data mining. The essence of clustering analysis is to divide data into several clusters according to the relevance. Therefore, it has high similarity within clusters and big difference between clusters [7] (Fig. 2).

Based on the semantic relevance coefficient in the matrix to build N-dimensional space, the Euclidean distance formula (1) can be used to calculate the spatial distance of two tags. The closer, the more similar tags can be considered.

$$\text{Euclid}(1, 2) = \sqrt[2]{(x_1 - x_2)^2 + (y_1 - y_2)^2 + (z_1 - z_2)^2} \tag{1}$$

Word \ Word	W_1	W_2	W_3	…	W_n
W_1	1	6	9	…	3
W_2	2	1	4	…	6
W_3	4	2	1	…	7
…	…	…	…	1	…
W_n	3	8	5	…	1

Fig. 2. Semantic correlation matrix of emotional expression of imagery words

The shortest two clusters are merged into a large cluster until all small clusters are merged into a large cluster. The whole process can be shown in a form of a tree structure. Any number of semantic groups can be got through hierarchical clustering analysis [8–10] (Fig. 3).

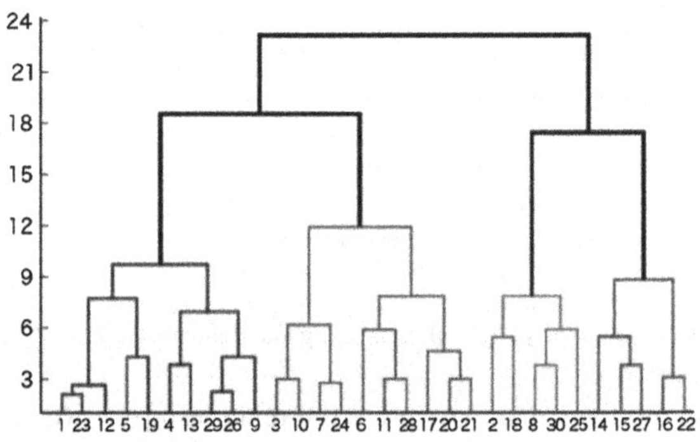

Fig. 3. Hierarchical clustering

Through clustering analysis, we can get the emotional expression of imagery words m after screening. Then, we randomly select high resolution l images from the Internet. The selected categories include portrait, scenery, still life and documentary. When choosing, avoid obvious emotional bias. At the same time, the scope of the selection is from the global scope, to ensure that the selection of pictures is comprehensive, rich and random. The l images are all processed by filter i, and the images of the l group are obtained (two pictures before and after processing are a group). Then, find a certain number of ordinary users to score the correlation between the filter and the emotional expression of imagery words [11, 12] (Fig. 4).

Image \ Word	W_1	W_2	W_3	…	W_m
I_1	C_{11}	C_{12}	C_{13}	…	C_{1m}
I_2	C_{21}	C_{22}	C_{23}	…	C_{2m}
I_3	C_{31}	C_{32}	C_{33}	…	C_{3m}
…	…	…	…	…	…
I_l	C_{l1}	C_{l2}	C_{l3}	…	C_{lm}

Fig. 4. A word-image matrix

Average the scores of all users and a correlation matrix is obtained. Then select the minimum of the average value of every column. The emotional expression of imagery word in that column is taken as the adjective we want.

3.2 Noun

The effect of each filter is with a unique tint or color temperature, or to make the image brighter or darker. In a word, they adjust the parameters of the pictures, such as color temperature, hue, high light, shadow, saturation and so on.

These changes in color temperature or tint are apparent, can let us think of something in daily life. For example, blue will let us think of the sea and the sky; Green will let us think of grassland, forest; Yellow will let us think of the desert, the sun, gold and so on [13].

Therefore, from the perspective of parameters related to post processing, combining with the effect of the filters, choose the corresponding items from things that are highly cognized, such as forests, seas, deserts, meadows and so on as the noun we want [14].

4 Experimental Verification

According to the filter naming mechanism "AN" mentioned above, we firstly got 44 emotional expression of imagery words of 105 users (48 male and 57 female) by questionnaires. Then, 10 emotional expression of imagery words were obtained by clustering analysis. We randomly selected 20 images through the Internet to analyze the correlation between the filter effect and 10 emotional expression of imagery words. Finally, the [RISE] and [Gingham] of Instagram were renamed as [Relaxing Wood] and [Cool Stone]. Twenty images are shown in Fig. 5. And part screen shot of correlation score is shown in Fig. 6.

Fig. 5. Random 20 images

Then, we randomly selected other 30 images through the Internet, processed them with two filters, the 60 sets of images were obtained. And then we found out 30 ordinary users (14 male and 16 female), let them associate the images with the names, the names in A group were [RISE] and [Gingham], B group were [Rise Wood] and [Cool Stone]. The results of the experiment showed that the correct rate of the A group was 63.7% and the B group was 86.1%.

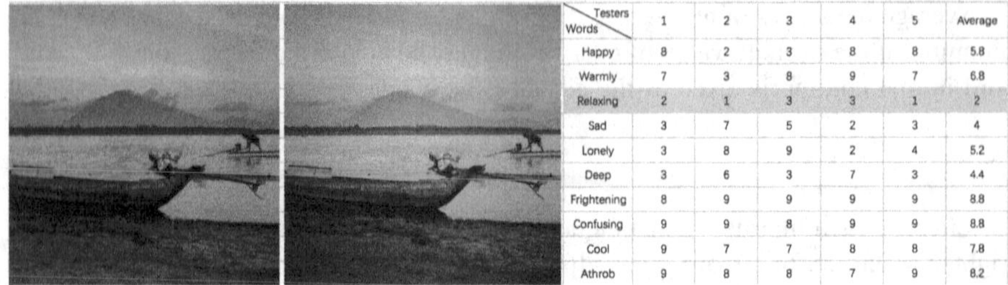

Testers / Words	1	2	3	4	5	Average
Happy	8	2	3	8	8	5.8
Warmly	7	3	8	9	7	6.8
Relaxing	2	1	3	3	1	2
Sad	3	7	5	2	3	4
Lonely	3	8	9	2	4	5.2
Deep	3	6	3	7	3	4.4
Frightening	8	9	9	9	9	8.8
Confusing	9	9	8	9	9	8.8
Cool	9	7	7	8	8	7.8
Athrob	9	8	8	7	9	8.2

Fig. 6. Part screen shot of correlation score

The experimental results showed that the new filter naming mechanism did greatly improve the users' cognitive efficiency in the filters' name when using the filters.

5 Conclusion

This paper initially envisages a new filter naming mechanism based on emotional expression and cognitive integration. Its core idea is to construct a model by using the association between the effect of the filter and the emotional expression of imagery words of the user, and the integration of the user's cognition.

The new filter naming mechanism proposed in this paper is finally verified by a preliminary experiment, which is of great help to improve user's cognitive efficiency when using filters. Meanwhile, the new filter naming mechanism makes the current messy filter naming rules more unified and standardized.

However, because of the differences in culture, language and semantic expression of each country, the model proposed in this paper can be targeted to improve closer to the cultural and linguistic environment of every country, and make the model more representative.

It can be foreseen that the research methods and results can be applied to product and visual design, sociology research and other specific areas, playing a guiding and testing role.

References

1. Ahonen, T.: Mobile as 7th of the Mass Media: Cellphone, Cameraphone, Iphone, Smartphone. Futuretext, Summit (2008)
2. Fox, E.: Emotion Science Cognitive and Neuroscientific Approaches to Understanding Human Emotions. Palgrave Macmillan, Basingstoke (2008)
3. Carstensen, L.L., Pasupathi, M., Mayr, U., Nesselroade, J.R.: Emotional experience in everyday life across the adult life span. J. Pers. Soc. Psychol. **79**(4), 644 (2000)
4. Scherer, K.R.: What are emotions? And how can they be measured? Soc. Sci. Inf. **44**(4), 695–729 (2005)
5. Norman, D.A.: Emotional design: why we love (or hate) everyday things (2004)

6. Liang, T., Zhang, L., Xie, M.: Research on image emotional semantic retrieval mechanism based on cognitive quantification model. In: Marcus, A., Wang, W. (eds.) DUXU 2017. LNCS, vol. 10290, pp. 115–128. Springer, Cham (2017). https://doi.org/10.1007/978-3-319-58640-3_10
7. Caruso, R.D., Postel, G.C.: Image editing with Adobe Photoshop 6.0. Radiograph. Rev. Publ. Radiol. Soc. N. Am. Inc. **22**(4), 993 (2002)
8. Johnson, R.A., Wichern, D.W.: Applied multivariate statistical analysis. Technometrics **25** (4), 385–386 (1982). 3rd edn
9. Plume, M.L.: SPSS (statistical package for the social sciences). Encycl. Inf. Syst. **38**(4), 187–196 (2003)
10. Green, S.B., Salkind, N.J., Jones, T.M.: Using SPSS for Windows; Analyzing and Understanding Data. Prentice Hall PTR, Upper Saddle River (1996)
11. Liu, T., Liu, S., Chen, Z., Ma, W.Y.: An evaluation on feature selection for text clustering. In: ICML, pp. 488–495 (2003)
12. Berry, M.W., Castellanos, M.: Survey of Text Mining II: Clustering, Classification, and Retrieval. Springer, London (2008). https://doi.org/10.1007/978-1-84800-046-9
13. Elliot, A.J., Maier, M.A.: Color psychology: effects of perceiving color on psychological functioning in humans. Ann. Rev. Psychol. **65**(65), 95 (2014)
14. Frijda, N.H.: Emotion, cognitive structure, and action tendency. Cognit. Emot. **1**(2), 115–143 (1987)

Images and Visualizations

Study on Comprehensibility and Influencing Factors of Universal Safety Signs

Yongquan Chen[1], Xuefei Long[3], and Chuan-yu Zou[2](✉)

[1] Research Centre of Way Guidance, China National Institute of Standardization, Beijing, China

[2] AQSIQ Key Laboratory of Human Factors and Ergonomics (CNIS), Beijing, China
zouchy@cnis.gov.cn

[3] Department of Psychology, Tsinghua University, Beijing, China

Abstract. Safety signs have been widely used as a non-verbal, visually perceptible way to convey critical situation-specific information to intended users.

In this study, eight safety signs were tested. Over 330 respondents were involved. To explore statistically significant relationships between symbol comprehension and influencing factors, Pearson's Chi-square tests, logistic regression analysis, and correspondence analysis were conducted.

Six out of eight safety signs have comprehensibility scores higher than the level recommended by ISO standard.

In this test, "age" is considered as an important factor affecting comprehensibility. Pearson's Chi-square test is adopted in order to test the relationships between symbol comprehensibility and age. Since more than 20% expected values are less than 5, Fisher exact test is introduced to improve reliability.

Keywords: Safety sign · Comprehensibility test · Graphical symbol

1 Introduction

Hazards are everywhere in our daily life: slippery ground may cause accidental fractures; falling objects from construction sites may cause personal injuries; improper use of electricity, unsupervised playing toys, emergency may cause personal injuries and property damage. In Albert et al. study, alarming workplace incident rates, especially in the construction sector, continue to be of global concern [1]. The casualties and property damage of the emergency are mainly caused by two factors: one is caused by the emergency itself; another is caused by human negligence, such as inadequate early warning, inadequate emergency shelter, delayed evacuation, and poor choice of emergency path [2]. Standardization of safety signs with consistent pictograms is an effective way to speed up and aid the cognitive thought process in detecting signage and determining meaning [3].

Safety sign is defined as "sign giving a general safety message, obtained by a combination of a colour and geometric shape and which, by the addition of a graphical symbol, gives a particular safety message" in ISO 17724:2003 [5] developed by International Organization for Standardization.

C. Stephanidis (Ed.): HCII Posters 2018, CCIS 850, pp. 147–153, 2018.
https://doi.org/10.1007/978-3-319-92270-6_20

Safety signs are categorized into five kinds according to their function, each functions and relative colours and geometric shapes are show in Table 1.

Table 1. Categorization of safety signs

Safety signs	Colours and geometric shapes	Function
Safe condition signs		Indicate an evacuation route, the location of safety equipment or a safety facility, or a safety action.
Fire equipment signs		Indicate the location of fire equipment.
Mandatory action signs		Indicate that a specific course of action is to be taken.
Prohibition signs		Indicate that a specific behaviour is forbidden.
Warning signs		Indicate a specific source of potential harm

2 Methods

2.1 Respondents

386 respondents were recruited and paid to participate in the test. All had normal or corrected-to-normal visual acuities and healthy physical conditions, without ophthalmic diseases. They did not have any history of neurological and mental diseases. All took part in the experiment with personal computers.

2.2 Questionnaires

Computer screen presentation is applied while carrying out the comprehensibility test. The test material includes four parts: an instruction page of test procedure, a respondent self-report page, an example page of a commonly known graphical symbol, and 9 screen test pages.

On the instruction page, the encoding information of safety signs was provided, which included the particular shape, colour of border, colour of background, and the relative safety information, for example "a symbol on a yellow background indicates a specific source of potential harm".

2.3 Safety Signs to Be Tested

In this study, 9 safety signs were tested, including: No campfire, No camping, No pets allowed, No photography, No hanger, No selfie sticks, No eating, Warning: Uneven access (up), Warning: Uneven access (down) (See in Fig. 1).

Fig. 1. 9 Safety signs in comprehensibility test

2.4 Procedure

The comprehensibility test of 9 safety signs was conducted in the Institute of Human Factors and Ergonomics lab in China National Institute of Standardization. After arriving at the laboratory, respondents signed the informed consent and completed self-report page about their demographic information. Show an example page of a commonly known safety signs and confirm that all respondents say that they understand their task. All respondents were required to complete the test independently by reading and filling the test pages one by one.

On each screen test page show in the centre of the page one of the 9 safety signs to be tested and below it a line for the respondent's answer. Each sign was set in 50 mm × 50 mm square. Each sign was accompanied by a short description to inform the respondents the place that the sign is likely to be seen. The respondents were asked to write down their answers to the question:" What do you think this sign means?" If the respondent was unable to assign a meaning to the symbol, they should wrote down the response "Don't know" on the line. All the test pages were presented in random order for each respondent. Respondents were indicated how many pages there were left. If they forgot to fill the response, they would be reminded and couldn't move to the next page.

2.5 Categorizing the Results

For each safety signs, a list of all responses was generated. Three response-categorizers were appointed to work separately and assign each response on the list to the four standard categories (1, 2a, 2b, or 3) shown in Table 2.

Table 2. Categorization of responses

Category	Meaning
1	Correct
2a	Wrong
2b	Wrong and the response given is the opposite of the intended meaning
3	The response given is "Don't know"

If the categorizers did not agree on the category to which a specific response should be assigned, they should discuss and reach an agreed judgment. Convert the frequencies in category "1" into percentage values and then multiply by 100, thus the data of each safety signs' comprehensibility was obtained.

3 Test Results and Analysis

The data of each safety signs' comprehensibility and respondents' demographic information were analyzed by Matlab (shown in Table 3). To explore statistically significant relationships between comprehension and influencing factors, Pearson's Chi-square tests, logistic regression analysis, and correspondence analysis were conducted.

Table 3. Test results for 9 safety signs comprehensibility test

	No campfire	No camping	No pets allowed	No photography	No hanger
Score	93.8%	49.9%	88.6%	97.2%	90.4%
χ^2	12.844	11.888	7.943	6.949	6.895
p	0.046	0.065	0.242	0.326	0.142
Fisher	13.395	11.927	8.336	6.091	5.377
p	**0.029**	**0.042**	0.169	0.327	0.200
	No selfie sticks	No eating	Warning: uneven access (up)	Warning: uneven access (down)	
Score	62.1%	75.6%	75.6%	64.5%	
χ^2	13.683	21.226	22.034	22.034	
p	0.033	0.002	0.001	0.001	
Fisher	13.550	20.676	20.267	20.267	
p	**0.034**	**0.003**	**0.003**	**0.000**	

4 Discussion

ISO/TC 145 determined 67% as the acceptable score for comprehensibility test of a graphical symbol. 6 signs with 67% or more of the correct response were as follows: No campfire, No pets allowed, No photography, No hanger, No eating, Warning: Uneven access (up). 3 symbols with low comprehensibility were: No camping, No selfie sticks, and Warning: Uneven access (down).

4.1 Relationship of Age and Comprehensibility

In the test conducted in China, age is considered as an important factor affecting comprehensibility. Results of the relationships between age and sign comprehension are shown in cross tables (See Table 3). Pearson's Chi-square test is adopted in order to test the relationships between symbol comprehensibility and age. Since more than 20% expected values are less than 5, Fisher exact test is introduced to improve reliability.

The results in Table 3 indicate that safety symbol comprehension is statistically correlated with age overall, for two-thirds of symbols have p-values smaller than the significance level 0.05.

Furthermore, we use logistic regression to explore which age ranges influence comprehension significantly. We discover that for most safety signs that have significant relationships with comprehension, the coefficients of age ranges 1&2 both have p-values less than 0.05 and coefficients below zero. This indicates that compared with age range 3 (>51years old), participants in age ranges 1&2 are more likely to comprehend safety signs correctly.

Correspondence analysis is conducted for further analysis. Take symbol 'No eating' as an example.

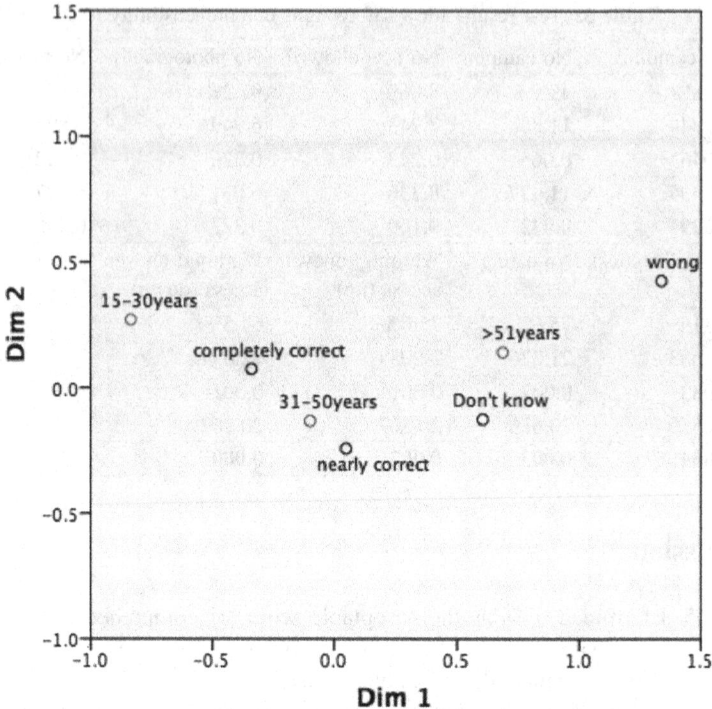

Fig. 2. Correspondence plot for 'No eating'

As shown in Fig. 2, Dim 1 explains 98.1% of the relationship between age and comprehensibility. People aged 13–30 turn out to give correct answers, those aged 31–50 are more likely to comprehend 'No eating' symbol nearly correctly, and those aged 51 and above tend to give wrong answers about the meaning of the symbol.

5 Conclusion

The test results showed that when developing a new safety sign, designers should paid more attention to the comprehensibility capacity of different people. It was found that 6 signs among 9 tested have significant relationship with age. The younger respondents have less difficulty than elders in comprehending safety signs.

Results of this study demonstrate that symbol comprehensibility can be influenced significantly by t respondents' age.

Acknowledgments. This research was supported by National Quality Infrastructure (NQI) Program (2016YFF0201700, 2016YFF0202806).

References

1. Albert, A., Hallowell, M.R., Kleiner, B., et al.: Enhancing construction hazard recognition with high-fidelity augmented virtuality. J. Constr. Eng. Manag. **140**(7), 615–621 (2014)
2. Dianye, Z., Rao, Z.: The passenger ship of inland waterway is choosing the simulation study for the emergency evacuation route. Comput. Simul. **2018**(01), 151–154 (2018). 内河客船人员遇险应急疏散路径选择仿真研究
3. Rousek, J.B., Hallbeck, M.S.: Improving and analyzing signage within a healthcare setting. Appl. Ergon. **42**(6), 771–784 (2011)
4. ISO 7010:2011: Graphical symbols—safety colours and safety signs—registered safety signs. 2011. International Organization for Standardization (ISO) (2011). 01.080.10
5. ISO 17724:2003: Graphical symbols – Vocabulary. International Organization for Standardization (ISO) (2003). 01.080.10

Activity Based Mobile User Interface Visualization for Geo-Applications

Tekeste Demesie Dagne[1], Elefelious G. Belay[2(✉)], and Stefano Valtolina[2]

[1] Faculty of Computing, Bahir Dar University, Bahir Dar, Ethiopia
lolteke@gmail.com
[2] Department of Computer Science, University of Milan, Celoria 20, 20133 Milan, Italy
elefelious.belay@unimi.it, valtolin@di.unimi.it

Abstract. Mobile interface design covers wide range of issues, ranging from user type to user activity. Considering mobile interaction in spatial context of use, we propose activity based UI configuration for mobile geo-applications. The proposed approach were evaluated using point-of-interests application on three common human activities. The results showed that our approach ensures good context detection performance and enhances usability.

Keywords: Mobile interaction design · User activity · UI visualization User experience

1 Introduction

The diversified environment in which mobile device is used has become a critical challenge for the development of mobile apps [1]. As mobile apps become more complex and versatile, specific development tools as well as efficient UI design frameworks have paramount importance. This eventually facilitates development of usable, interactive and high-quality mobile applications.

Nowadays, mobile apps are being used in various situations, user types, and context of use. These applications need to adjust their behavior and interface to respond as per the current contextual factors and user preference. Usability of the applications also depend on different contextual factors, these factors include user, task, environment and device [2]. It is therefore important to analyze and define the various contexts and context of use to design and develop applications, which will know when and what to adapt to improve usability.

Mobile apps that can change user interface at runtime based on the context (such as activity) will enhance user satisfaction, efficiency, and effectiveness, it will also foster good user experience. Adaption provide a way to adjust various display options during the context change. The change includes layout item, size, color, ways of displaying interface, presentation of menus and lists.

This paper presents some evaluation results of our model in providing suitable mobile (geo-app) UI based on user's activity and provide a visual adjustment.

C. Stephanidis (Ed.): HCII Posters 2018, CCIS 850, pp. 154–158, 2018.
https://doi.org/10.1007/978-3-319-92270-6_21

2 Related Work

Mobile interaction design is about shaping the experience of using a mobile apps [3]. In recent years, a number of efforts has been devoted in designing mobile interfaces considered various aspect of the users and user groups. These features includes the user skill, knowledge, experience, and their context of use [4–6].

Adaptive mobile applications can adapt itself at runtime automatically based on the dynamic user profile and contextual data gained from the end user or the environment [7]. An experiment were conducted using smartphone (AdaptiveCalc) to measure the performance and acceptance of the adaptive UI with the non-adaptive one. And the overall result showed has better acceptance and performance rate [7]. Other efforts include: ArcheoApp which is an adaptive application developed to support various user groups who have different needs [8]. Other author also consider comprehensive user profiles (such as visual, cognitive and emotional-processing parameters) to improve performance of adaptions [8]. Other research also presents some concepts (like hiding unused fields, pre-selection) and challenges (like determining which variables to use for developing adaptions) of context-based adaptions [9].

3 Methodology

First, we analyzed existing literatures and develop model that addresses activity based visual adjustment. Following that we develop application that respond to contextual change.

The application, Tour BD is adaptive mobile geo-app developed based on our model. Interaction log files were recorded to analyze the accuracy of visualized adaptation implemented in our application. The application were installed in 15 research participants for evaluation and log files were captured. The experiment is performed on three human activities: sitting (standing), walking and running for 30 min. As a result, adaptation performance is evaluated on the basis of synthetic metrics indicators.

A standard user satisfaction measurement also applied to measure the usability of the application. The following section will briefly discuss the silent findings of the evaluation.

4 Findings and Discussions

In our model, the UI adaptation is performed based on the contextual data collected at runtime. This process is carried out in asynchronous manner where tasks are not altered during the process of UI adaptation. The UI will automatically load after the contextual information is collected and modified. For example, if users' activity mode changed from sitting/standing to walking, the runtime execution object informs the context interpreter to re-adjust the UI, thus the UI adjustment will effect.

The application developed for this evaluation is Tour BD (which is also found in Google Play Store). The primary aim of this geo app is to explore and validate the benefits of context adaptation in order to achieve the usability metrics.

The context detection performance and user satisfaction were measured using synthetic metrics indicators and standard user satisfaction measurement tools. For adaptation performance log files were analyzed to validate the accuracy of visualized adaptation implemented by our application.

Table 1 shows the average results of activity detection for each activity modes tested per 10 min. The continuity of detection ranged from 284–290. This indicates that the adaptation were smooth in different activity modes. The columns indicates the number of correctly and incorrectly identified tasks executed for each modes/levels of context detection, while rows indicates the number of relevant tasks that are retrieved for each modes/levels of context detection in a column.

Table 1. Average results of activity detection/10 min logged from 15 participants.

	Sitting/standing	Walking	Running
Sitting/standing	284	11	5
Walking	2	270	13
Running	0	9	266
Total	286	290	284

The accuracy of activity detection results are affected by differences in mobile phone. Table 2 illustrates the average precision, recall, F-score, and accuracy results of activity detection. The average accuracy results for all three metrics where above 92%. It is interesting to note that the detection achieved high level of accuracy in sitting (or standing) mode. In all, the average accuracy rate ranged from 89% to 94%.

Table 2. Average precision (P), recall (R), F-score (F) and accuracy (A) of detection.

		Activity modes		
		Sitting/standing	Walking	Running
Accuracy measures	P	0.99	0.93	0.94
	R	0.95	0.95	0.97
	F	0.97	0.94	0.95
	A	0.94	0.89	0.91

As shown in Fig. 1, 94.07%, 100% and 92.89% detection attempts was correct in running, sitting (or standing) and walking activity modes respectively. The average detection accuracy is 95.66%. The continuity of task execution in adaptation ranged from 211–248 per 10 min indicates the smoothness of activity detection. Additionally, the accuracy (92%) indicates the quality of adaptation.

It is important to note that the succession of tasks in activity detection can highly affect the smoothness of adaptation. The rise of the gap between detected tasks implies that detection was interrupted due to some reason. One of the reason is the capability of mobile devices in order to perform continuous tasks effectively. Tracing the execution of sensors task helps to analyze the succession of tasks execution during context detection. The highest and lowest number of tasks executed in three modes of activity detection were ranged from 284–290, indicates that it were smooth. Figure 2 describes the results of task execution patterns of each activity modes.

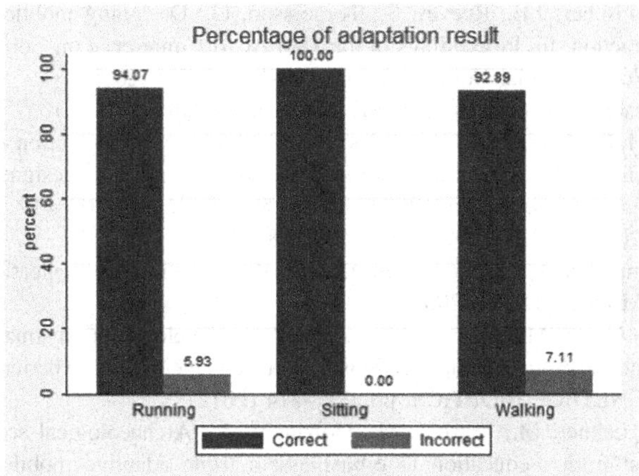

Fig. 1. Percentage of adaptation result for each activity mode.

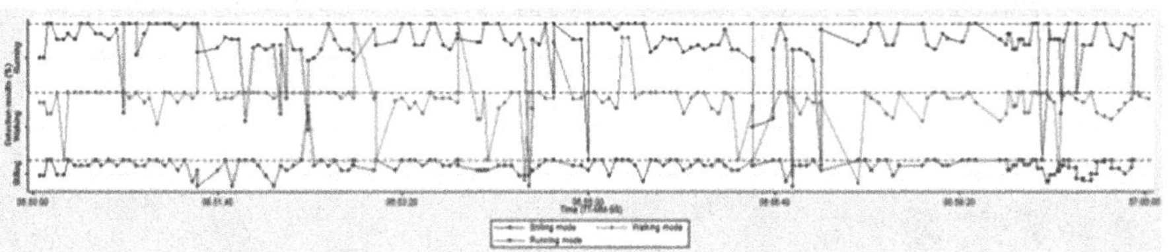

Fig. 2. Task execution patterns of each mode.

5 Conclusion

In this paper, we designed a new approach for automatic user's physical activity recognition using a smartphone. This is mainly used for visualization adjustment which work based on user context. The data used in this paper were obtained from sensors integrated into smartphones. For evaluating the proposed approach, the study develops mobile application. We used different measurement techniques to analyze the accuracy of activity detection. The activity based UI configuration were employed on three common activities and achieved a promising results.

References

1. Dhar, S., Varshney, U.: Challenges and business models for mobile location-based services and advertising. Commun. ACM **54**(5), 121–128 (2011)
2. ISO: ISO/DIS 9241-9 Ergonomic Requirements for office Work with Visual Display Terminals, Non-keyboard Input Device Requirements. International Standard, International Organization for Standardization (1998)

3. Lundgren, S., Fischer, J.E., Reeves, S., Torgersson, O.: Designing mobile experiences for collocated interaction. In: Proceedings of the 18th ACM Conference on Computer Supported Cooperative Work & Social Computing, pp. 496–507. ACM (2015)
4. Tidwell, J.: Designing Interfaces. O'Reilly Media Inc., Newton (2010)
5. Belay, E.G., McCrickard, D.S., Besufekad, S.A.: Mobile user interaction development for low-literacy trends and recurrent design problems: a perspective from designers in developing country. In: Rau, P.L. (ed.) CCD 2016. LNCS, vol. 9741, pp. 409–417. Springer, Cham (2016). https://doi.org/10.1007/978-3-319-40093-8_41
6. Kangas, E., Kinnunen, T.: Applying user-centered design to mobile application development. Commun. ACM **48**(7), 55–59 (2005)
7. Holzinger, A., Geier, M., Germanakos, P.: On the development of smart adaptive user interfaces for mobile e-business applications-towards enhancing user experience-some lessons learned. In: DCNET/ICE-B/OPTICS, pp. 205–214 (2012)
8. Holzinger, K., Lehner, M., Fassold, M., Holzinger, A.: Archaeological scavenger hunt on mobile devices: from e-education to e-business: a triple adaptive mobile application for supporting experts, tourists and children. In: ICETE 2011 8th International Joint Conference on e-Business and Telecommunications. SciTec., Sevilla (2011)
9. Germanakos, P., Tsianos, N., Lekkas, Z., Mourlas, C., Samaras, G.: Realizing comprehensive user profile as the core element of adaptive and personalized communication environments and systems. Comput. J. **52**(7), 749–770 (2009)

On Gaze Estimation Using Integral Projection of Eye Images

Lan-Rong Dung[1(✉)], Yu-Cheng Lee[1], and Yin-Yi Wu[2]

[1] National Chiao Tung University, Hsinchu 30010, Taiwan
lennon@nctu.edu.tw
[2] National Chung-Shan Institute of Science and Technology, Taoyuan, Taiwan

Abstract. This paper presents a gaze estimation algorithm using integral projection of eye images with advantage of low additional hardware requirement and low computational power. The algorithm needs only a webcam under nature light source and captured eye images in a non-intrusive way. Before integral projection, we used binarization process to eliminate the non-related image information to gaze position. Projected on binary eye images with projection adjustment method to avoid eye tilt makes projection error and defined the accurate integral range of eye ROI images to achieve robust gaze estimation. We analyzed the projection diagram with skewness to describe the variation of different gaze position. In skewness calculation, the pixel coordinate of eye ROI images has been normalized to avoid head moved back and forth makes the size of ROI changed. In horizontal direction, the error angle of our algorithm is 2.29°, maximum error angle is 4.8° and the resolution we defined is 7.5. Because our algorithm is inaccurate in vertical, we could only estimate gaze direction, but to estimate precise angle. The computational power of our algorithm is low, the average execution time of each frame is only 0.01652 s, only 24% of opponent.

Keywords: Gaze estimation · Integral projection · Skewness

1 Introduction

Gaze estimation is an important technique in human-computer interaction area. The gaze information reveals what we are paying attention to and our mental state. This technique could apply in several areas in our daily life such as assistive techniques, automotive, learning ability research and advertisement research.

The gaze estimation and eye tracking techniques have developed several decades. It could divide into four categories, Electro-Oculography, Scleral Search Coils, Infrared-Oculography and Video-Oculography [8]. In these four categories, video-based method is the most widely used method, because it could get and develop easier than other three categories and it won't causes potential danger to our eye. The method we proposed is also video-based method, so we will focus on this method in the following introduction. The video-based method can subdivided into two categories, feature-based method and appearance-based method. Feature-based method using characteristics on our eyes like iris, pupil, corneal reflections and eye corner to estimates eye

C. Stephanidis (Ed.): HCII Posters 2018, CCIS 850, pp. 159–167, 2018.
https://doi.org/10.1007/978-3-319-92270-6_22

movement. In Yang's [1] paper, they proposed a gaze estimation algorithm with near-infrared light sources. With precise detecting the pupil center and using the position between pupil center and corneal reflections, it could estimate the eye gaze on the screen. Appearance-based method using template matching and training large samples to estimate eye gaze directions. In Raudonis's [2] paper, they proposed an algorithm using PCA method to find the six components of eye images first and using ANN (Artificial Neural Network) to classify the position of pupil, when calibration procedure they could get the training samples to matching the gaze direction.

No matter feature-based method or appearance-based method have some defects. Feature-based method needs additional hardware like special camera and near-infrared light sources. Precise detecting pupil center costs lots of computational power. Appearance-based method needs lots of samples to training. Because of these problems this paper proposed a gaze estimation algorithm using integral projection of eye images. With advantages of low additional hardware requirement and computational power, estimating eye gaze in a non-intrusive way. The horizontal direction average error angle of our algorithm is 2.29°, the maximum error angle is 4.8°. The resolution we defined is 7.5, it means in the case of zero error angel, the horizontal direction of screen could divided into 7.5 sections. Because of the limitation of our algorithm, in the vertical direction the algorithm we proposed could only estimate directions but to estimate precise gaze angle. We will introduce the algorithm details in the following sections. Video object tracking is an important topic within the field of computer vision. It has a wide range of applications such as human-vehicle navigation, computer interaction, etc. Various approaches for object tracking have been proposed. [1] proposed a tracking method based on mean shift. It maximizes the similarity iteratively by comparing the color histogram of the object. The advantage is the elimination of a brute force search and low computation. [2] extended to 3D domain, combines color and spatial information to solve the problems of orientation changing and small scale changing. [3] used stochastic meta-descent optimization method. It can track fast moving objects with significant scale change in a low-frame-rate video.

2 Related Work

The face and eye detection are using the haar-cascade classifiers. Because the eye position on face will not change, we use this characteristic to set the ROI of eye images and don't need to re-detect eye position every frame.

In mathematics and statistics, moment is a kind of indicator to measure the morphological characteristics of a point set, includes first moment, second moment, third moment and fourth moment [3]. The first moment means mean of distribution, second moment means standard deviation, third moment means skewness and fourth moment means kurtosis. In our algorithm, we will use skewness to estimating eye gaze.

Skewness is a measurement of asymmetry of the probability distribution. According to Pearson's moment coefficient of skewness, the skewness γ defines in (1).

$$\gamma = E\left[\left(\frac{X-\mu}{\sigma}\right)^3\right] = \frac{E[X^3] - 3\mu\sigma^2 - \mu^3}{\sigma^3} \tag{1}$$

σ is standard deviation, X is a random variable, E is the expect value operator and μ is mean.

3 Proposed Method

In this paper, we proposed a gaze estimation algorithm using integral projection of eye images. In Fig. 1, it shows the structure of our algorithm. It could divided into three main processing stages, pre-processing and integral projection, integral projection adjustment and projection diagram analysis.

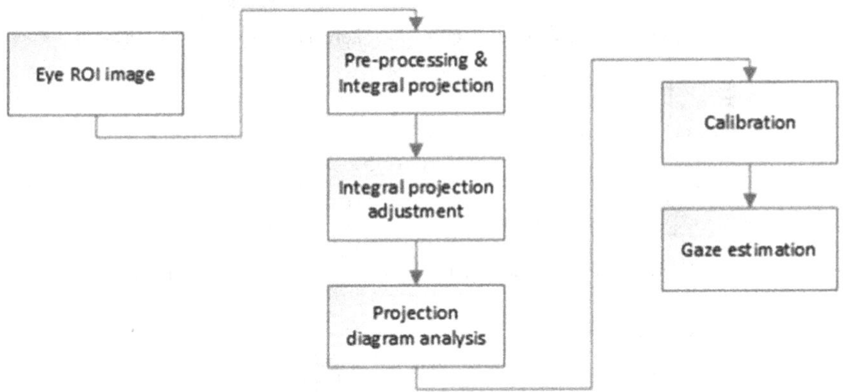

Fig. 1. The flow chart of proposed algorithm.

Integral projection function is proposed by Zhou [4], the mathematic function shows in (2) and (3).

$$IPF_v = \int_{y1}^{y2} I(x,y)dy \tag{2}$$

$$IPF_{\mathrm{h}} = \int_{x1}^{x2} I(x,y)dx \tag{3}$$

IPF_v is vertical projection function and IPF_h is horizontal projection funtion.$I(x,y)$ is the gray scale value on image coordinate (x,y).

Figure 2 shows the horizontal and vertical projection of eye image. In pre-processing stage, we will use binarization process. We found that using integral projection based on gray scale image may have some problems. There is some image information which is not related to eye gaze like skin. If we projected using gray scale image, it may causes error in gaze estimation stage. So before integral projection, we binarized the image by Otsu's thresholding [5] method and projecting only black pixels, the following projection diagram analysis will focused on binary image. The projection result shows in Fig. 3.

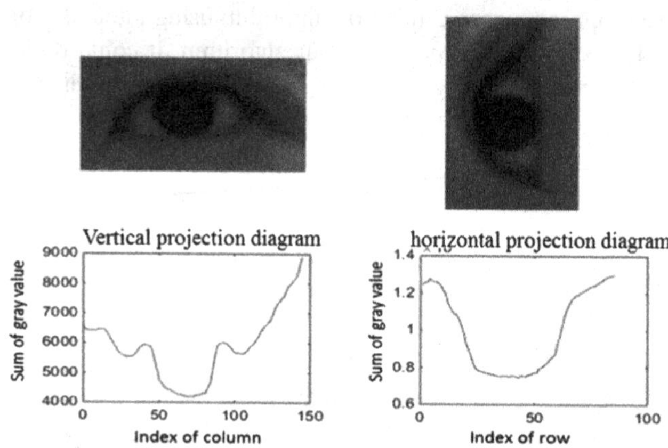

Fig. 2. The horizontal and vertical projection on gray scale image.

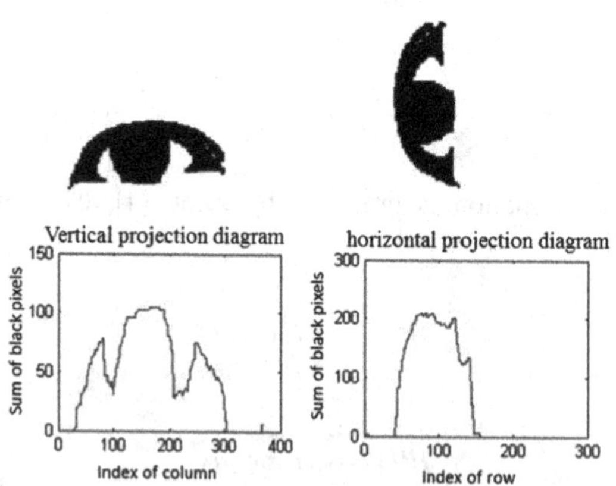

Fig. 3. The horizontal and vertical projection on binary image.

The projection is still on whole ROI image of eye now, but the head's slightly movement may cause eye tilting and makes projection error. Because of these problems we will need to adjust projection surface by using features on our eyes.

In integral projection adjustment stage, we proposed two adjustment methods, one is ellipse fitting method. Human's eye could approach to an ellipse, using ellipse fitting [9] to fit the best ellipse of eye. After get the ellipse, we could reset the ROI image size of eye, the long axis and short axis of ellipse becomes the integral projection surface and integral range of horizontal and vertical direction. We calculate the angle θ between ellipse long axis and horizontal plane and the pixel coordinate (x, y) on original ROI image could transform to the new coordinate (x′, y′). The relationship between (x, y) and (x′, y′) shows in (4).

$$\begin{bmatrix} x' \\ y' \end{bmatrix} = \begin{bmatrix} \cos\theta & -\sin\theta \\ \sin\theta & \cos\theta \end{bmatrix} \begin{bmatrix} x \\ y \end{bmatrix} \tag{4}$$

After pixel coordinate transformation, we could do the integral projection on the eye ROI image. Another adjustment method is canthus line, human's canthus is a good reference point, so we detecting canthus by FAST-corner [6] detection. It used a 7 × 7 mask scanning on image by comparing the gray scale value of center pixel and other sixteen pixels around it.

The detection result shows in Fig. 4(a), the green points are possible canthus position. Because our canthus may locate on the furthest position of eye, it means it will locate on the endpoints of ellipse long axis. So, we using the ellipse fitting result shows in Fig. 4(b) to get the final canthus points, it shows in Fig. 4(c). After we get the canthus, the canthus line and its orthogonal line becomes horizontal and vertical projection range and reset the ROI of eye image size. We calculated the angle θ between canthus line and horizontal plane, and do the pixels coordinate transformation which we have mentioned in ellipse fitting method. In the following sections we will compare two different projection adjustment methods and choose the better one to become a part of our algorithm.

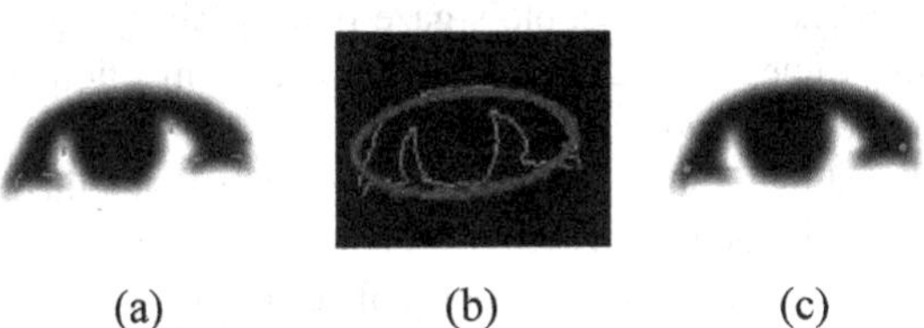

(a) (b) (c)

Fig. 4. The corner detection by FAST algorithm and the canthus point selection by ellipse fitting.

After projection adjustment, we could get the projection diagram. The projection diagram reveals the gaze information, Fig. 5 shows horizontal and vertical projection diagram when gaze direction is changed. In the projection diagram analysis stage we used skewness to describe the projection diagram.

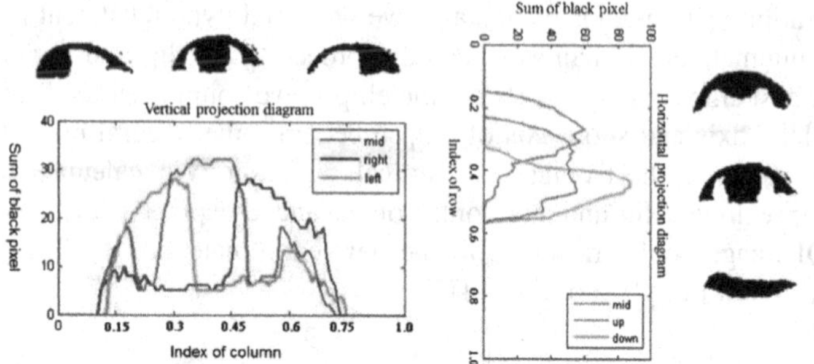

Fig. 5. The horizontal and vertical projection diagram under different gaze direction.

Before calculating skewness, we need to calculate the mean position of the projection diagram first. One important thing is, when head moved back and forth in front of camera, the width and height of eye ROI images will changed, it may cause error if we calculated mean of projection diagram by exact index value. To avoid this problem, the pixel coordinate of eye ROI images have been normalized. According to the formula we mentioned above, (5) and (6) show the calculation of mean values.

$$\mu_v = E[x] = \sum xP(x) = \frac{\sum (x_i/width) \cdot y_i}{\sum y_i} \tag{5}$$

$$\mu_h = E[y] = \sum yP(y) = \frac{\sum (y_i/height) \cdot x_i}{\sum x_i} \tag{6}$$

μ_v is the mean of vertical projection diagram, μ_h is the mean of horizontal projection diagram, width is the width of eye ROI image, height is the height of eye ROI image. After we have mean, we could calculated the skewness of projection diagram to describe the degree of skew when people's gaze point is changing and estimated gaze position by skewness value. According to the formula we mentioned above, (2) shows the calculation formula of skewness γ.

We have introduced integral projection and two projection adjustment methods. To evaluate which adjustment method is better, we conducted an experiment. There are ten volunteers, each person measured three times, collected total thirty samples to evaluate the result. The distance between screen to volunteers' eye is 40 cm, every gaze points on screen shows in Fig. 6, the angle between each gaze point is 3°. The red calibration point is used to normalized the data set, we will discussed how does the mean and skewness we measured under the regular gaze angle and evaluated the effect of pre-processing method and projection adjustment methods.

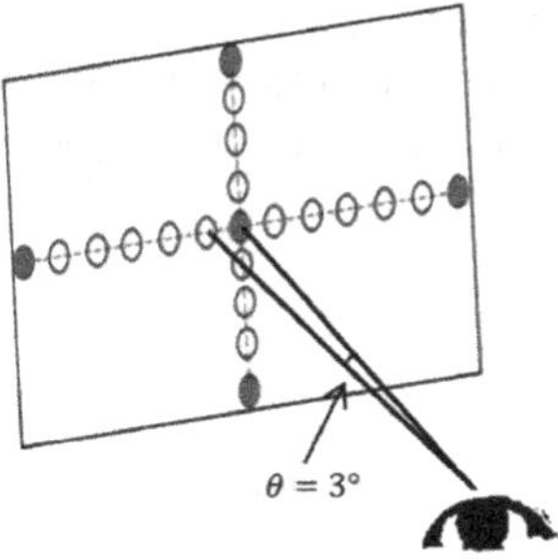

Fig. 6. The schematic diagram of gaze points on screen (red points are calibration points) (Color figure online)

Figures 7 and 8 show the results of skewness analysis. The horizontal axis of plot is gaze angle, positive is left direction gaze points, negative is right direction gaze points and zero is midpoint. The vertical axis of plot is normalized mean and the black line is the ideal standard line.

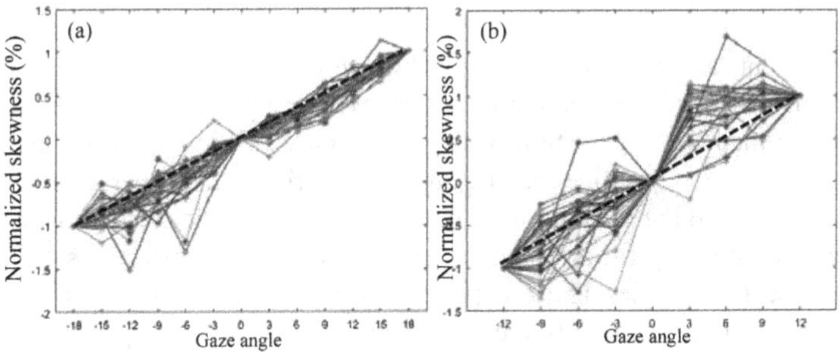

Fig. 7. The skewness analysis of (a) horizontal (b) vertical direction with projection adjustment of ellipse fitting method.

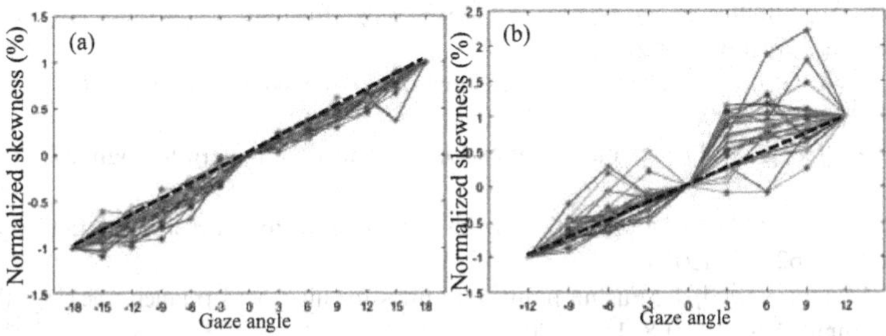

Fig. 8. The skewness analysis of (a) horizontal (b) vertical direction with projection adjustment of canthus line methods.

We estimated the execution time every frame and compared to another eye tracker proposed by Ferhat [7], under the same hardware and environment, CPU: Intel Core i5-4570; Ram: 8 GB; OS: Ubuntu 12.04. The comparison of execution time shows in Fig. 9.

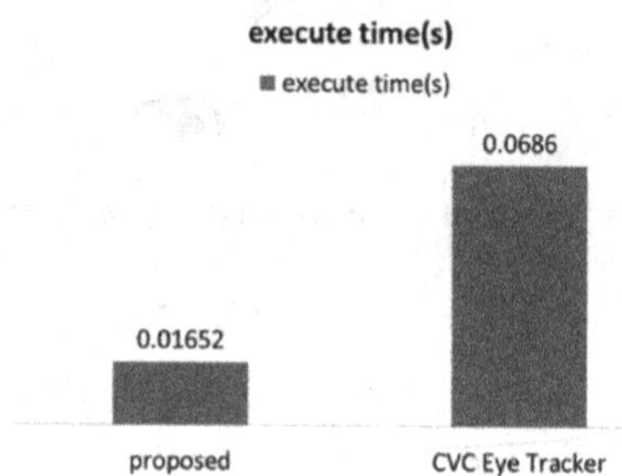

Fig. 9. Comparison of execute time.

4 Conclusion

This paper presents a gaze estimation algorithm with only a webcam under nature light sources and using integral projection of binary eye images with projection adjustment by canthus line method to achieve robust gaze estimation. We analyzed the projection diagram by skewness to describe the diagram characteristics. The average error angle in horizontal is 2.29° and the resolution we defined is 7.5. In vertical direction, because of the limitation of our algorithm, it could only estimate gaze directions but couldn't estimate precise gaze angle. The computational power of our algorithm is low, the average execution time of each frame is 0.01652 s, only 24% of opponent.

References

1. Yang, X., Sun, J., Liu, J., Chu, J., Liu, W., Gao, Y.: Agaze tracking scheme for eye-based intelligent control. In: 8th WCICA, pp. 50–55 (2010)
2. Raudonis, V., Simutis, R., Narvydas, G.: Discrete eye tracking for medical applications. In: 2nd ISABEL, pp. 1–6 (2009)
3. Joanes, D.N., Gill, C.A.: Comparing measures of sample skewness and kurtosis. J. R. Stat. Soc. **47**, 183–189 (1998)
4. Zhou, Z.H., Geng, X.: Projection functions for eye detection. Pattern Recogn. **37**, 1049–1056 (2004)
5. Otsu, N.: A threshold selection method from gray-level histograms. IEEE Trans. Syst. Man Cybern. **9**(1), 62–66 (1979)
6. Rosten, E., Drummond, T.: Fusing points and lines for high performance tracking. IEEE Int. Conf. Comput. Vis. **2**, 1508–1515 (2005)

7. Ferhat, O., Vilariño, F.: Low cost eye tracking: the current panorama. Comput. Intell. Neurosci. (2016)
8. Chennamma, O.H.R., Yuan, X.H.: A survey on eye-gaze tracking techniques. Indian J. Comput. Sci. Eng. **4**(5), 388–393 (2013)
9. Fitzgibbon, A.W., Fisher, R.B.: A buyer's guide to conic fitting. In: Proceedings of the 6th British Conference on Machine Vision, vol. 2, pp. 513–522 (1995)

Proposal of Remote Face-to-Face Communication System with Line of Sight Matching Based on Pupil Detection

Kiyotaka Fukumoto(✉), Yoshiyuki Yamamoto, and Yoshinobu Ebisawa

Graduate School of Integrated Science and Technology, Shizuoka University, Hamamatsu 432-8561, Japan
{fukumoto.kiyotaka, ebisawa.yoshinobu}@shizuoka.ac.jp

Abstract. In general, remote face-to-face communication systems via the Internet, it is impossible to match the eyes of a user and a communication partner with each other because their face positions displayed in PC screens, at which they look, are different from the positions of the cameras for shooting their faces. To solve this problem, we proposed a remote head-free system which was based on the combination of a wide-angle color camera located behind a 45-deg inclined magic mirror, our pupil detection technique, image deformation techniques, and so on. The same two systems were assigned to the user and the partner. The narrow region image including a whole of the user's face image was cut out from the image obtained from the wide-angle color camera in the user's system, was displayed in the partner's system so that the midpoint of the detected right and left pupils of the user's face image virtually located at the position of the color camera in the partner's system, and vice versa. In addition, to deal with large back and forth or lateral head movements, the displayed face image of the user was adjusted in its size and distorted by using the projection transformation so that it always looked like the same size as the user's face and looked like the front face as seen from the partner, and vice versa. The questionnaire results obtained from experiment showed the tendency that the subjects' lines of sight matched each other, and the other questionnaire items about the system showed high evaluation.

Keywords: Remote communication · Pupil detection
Projection transformation

1 Introduction

Recently, remote face-to-face communication systems via the Internet (e.g., Skype) has spread. In such a system, it is impossible to match users' lines of sight with each other because a position on a PC screen, at which the user looking, is different from the position of a camera for capturing the face image of the user. To solve this problem, a communication system with lines of sight matching by using a magic mirror was proposed [1]. By installing the camera behind the 45-deg inclined mirror, the system matched the position of the camera and the gaze position on the screen. However, the system did not allow large head movements of the users.

C. Stephanidis (Ed.): HCII Posters 2018, CCIS 850, pp. 168–175, 2018.
https://doi.org/10.1007/978-3-319-92270-6_23

The present paper proposes a novel head-free remote communication system based on the combination of our pupil detection technique [2], a color wide-angle camera behind an 45-deg inclined magic mirror, which captures the user's face image, the image deformation technique, and so on. In the system, the face image is cut out from the wide-angle color image, resized, and deformed according to the user's pupil positions. Hence, even when a large back and forth or lateral head movement occurs, the face image of each other's looks like the same size as the actual face and looks like the front face image seen from the other user.

2 Method

2.1 Overview of the Proposed System and Pupil Detection Method

Figure 1 shows the overview of the proposed system. The display was installed horizontally and its screen image was reflected by the 45-inclined magic mirror (transmission; approximately 10%, reflection; approximately 50%). A user looked the virtual screen of the display screen by the mirror. A wide-angle color camera for capturing the image including the user's face was installed behind the magic mirror. Here, the optical axis of the camera was perpendicular to the virtual screen and passed through the center of the screen. By displaying the partner's face image so that the midpoint of both pupils in the partner's face image coincides with the camera position, it was possible to match each user's line of sight.

In order to detect the pupils, three optical systems, each of which was composed of a black-and-white video camera, near-infrared LED light sources, near-infrared pass optical filter, and so on, were installed at the gap between the display and the magic mirror. The pupils were detected from the difference image created by subtracting a dark pupil image from a successive bright pupil image [2]. 3D pupil coordinates were obtained by stereo matching using detected pupil coordinates.

When the user wore eyeglasses, frames and lens of the glasses produced reflection images in the camera image (glass reflections). If the glass reflections overlapped the pupil image, the pupil detection and stereo matching were impossible. By using the

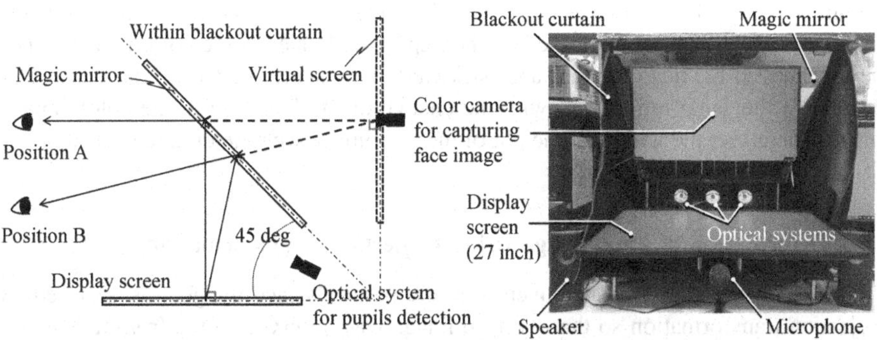

Fig. 1. Overview of the proposed head-free remote communication system.

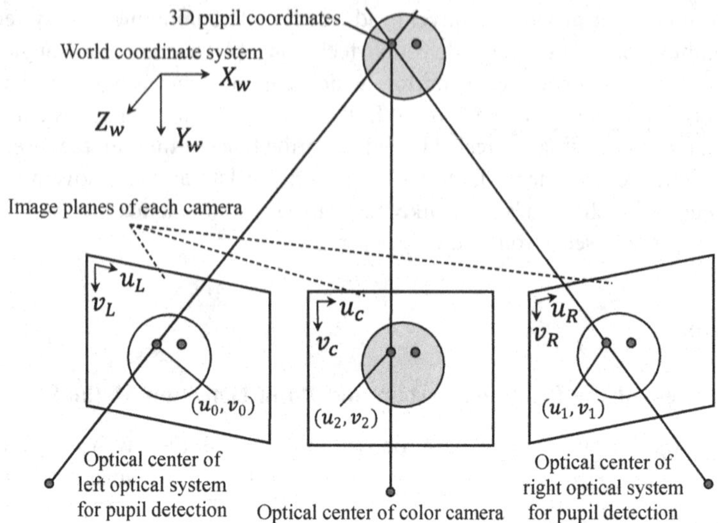

Fig. 2. Estimation method of pupil coordinates in color camera image using our pupil detection technique.

three (more than two) optical systems, stereo matching was performed using the detected pupils from the two camera images even if the pupils were not able to be detected from other one camera image.

The three optical systems and the color camera were calibrated simultaneously by Zhang's camera calibration method [3]. Therefore, pupil coordinates in the color camera image were able to estimate by projecting the 3D pupil coordinates to the color camera image (Fig. 2).

2.2 Cutting Out Face Image from Color Camera Image

As shown in Fig. 3, the color camera images, 3D pupil coordinates, pupil coordinates in color images, and voices obtained from microphones, were mutually transmitted and received between the two systems via TCP communication. A partner's face region within the received color image was cut out into a rectangle of a certain range using the distance between both pupils based on the pupil coordinates in the color image. When the user moved the head forward and backward, the distance between both pupils also changes at the same ratio along with the change of the face size in the color camera image. Therefore, the width and height of the face image were determined based on the distance between both pupils.

2.3 Deformation of Face Image Using Projection Transformation

To deal with the user's head movements, the partner's face image was distorted by projection transformation so that the face image was observed as the front face image as seen from the user. In Fig. 4, the quadrangle $A'B'C'D'$ on the display screen plane

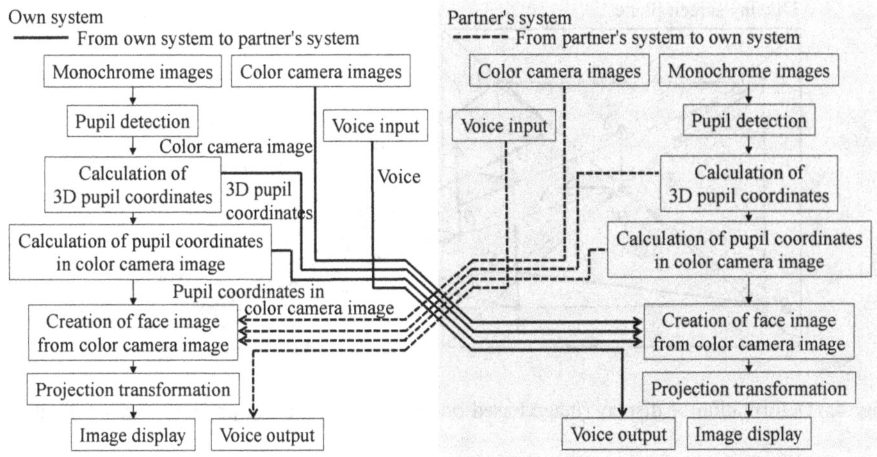

Fig. 3. Data transmission/reception between systems via TCP communication.

indicates the deformed face image-displayed area observed by the user, which was created based on the face image obtained from the color camera image of the partner. This image was distorted by projection transformation so that it can be seen as the original rectangular image without distortion (front face) as seen from the user position where was expressed by the midpoint M between both pupils. Specifically, the rectangle $ABCD$ was defined as the front face image plane, which was perpendicular to the line $O'M$ connecting the reference point O' (corresponding to the camera position) on the quadrangle $A'B'C'D'$ and the point M. It was assumed that the pixels of the partner's face image were aligned in this image plane. In the front face image plane, the point O was the position of the midpoint between both pupils of the partner. The distance OM was a constant value. Here, xyz and XYZ coordinate systems with the origin O and O' were defined, respectively. In the XYZ coordinate system, the intersection $P(X_i, Y_i, Z_i)$ between the image plane and the line connecting arbitrary pixel $P'(X_i, Y_i, 0)$ and the point M was obtained while scanning within the display screen plane. The point P was transformed into a point $p(x_i, y_i, 0)$ in the xyz coordinate system. When the point p existed within the $ABCD$, the pixel value of $P'(X_i, Y_i, 0)$ in the display screen plane was calculated from the values of the pixels near $p(x_i, y_i, 0)$ using the bilinear interpolation method. Thus, even when the user's head moved laterally from the front of the display screen or when the distance between the head and display screen plane changed, the user was able to look the partner's front face image with a certain size. Furthermore, the xyz coordinate system was rotated around the z-axis so that the intersections where the perpendicular lines were drawn from the left and right pupils to the image plane existed on the x-axis of the xyz coordinate system. Even if the user rolled the head, the partner's face image on the display screen rotates along with the user's head rotation, the retinal image hardly rotated.

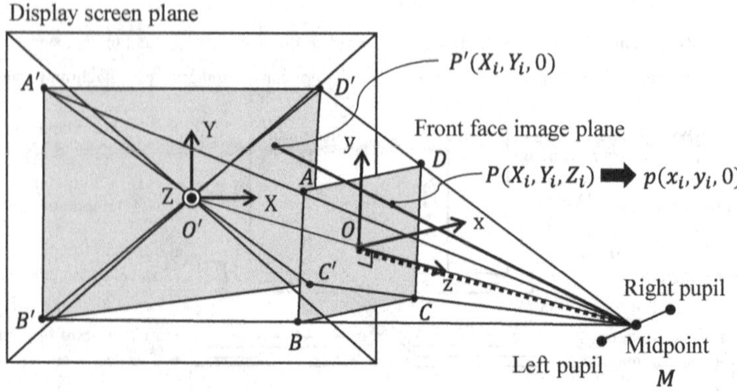

Fig. 4. Deformation of display image based on pupil position using projective transformation.

(a) Subject moved his head to left

(b) Subject moved his head upward

(c) Subject moved his head forward

(d) Subject rolled his head to left

Fig. 5. Each camera image and displayed face images without proposed methods.

3 Experiments

3.1 System Evaluation Using Camera Images

Subjects A and B were asked to be seated approximately 70 cm from the display screen and to move the head to left, right, upward, downward, forward, and backward and to roll to left and right. An eye camera for capturing the PC screen was attached to the middle of the eyebrows of the subject A.

Figure 5 shows the examples of the images when the original color camera images were displayed (without the proposed methods). The subject moved the head to left, upward, and forward and rotated to left, respectively. In each of (a)–(d), the upper left shows the image of the eye camera, the upper right is the image captured from behind each subject, and the lower two images show the face images presented to each subject. The eye camera images showed the partner's face images which had the various size and slope corresponding to the head position and rotation of the subject.

Figure 6 shows the examples of the images with the proposed methods when the subject moved the head to left, upward, and forward and rotated to left, respectively. In

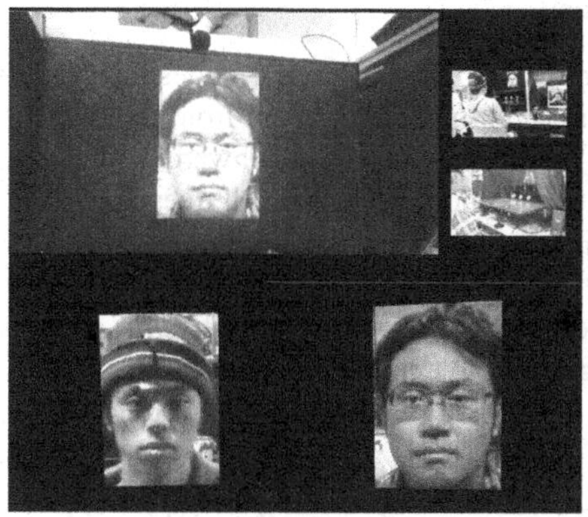

(a) Subject moved his head to left

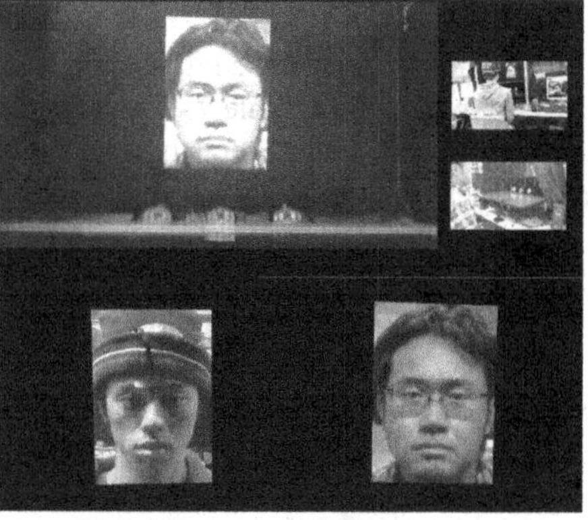

(b) Subject moved his head upward

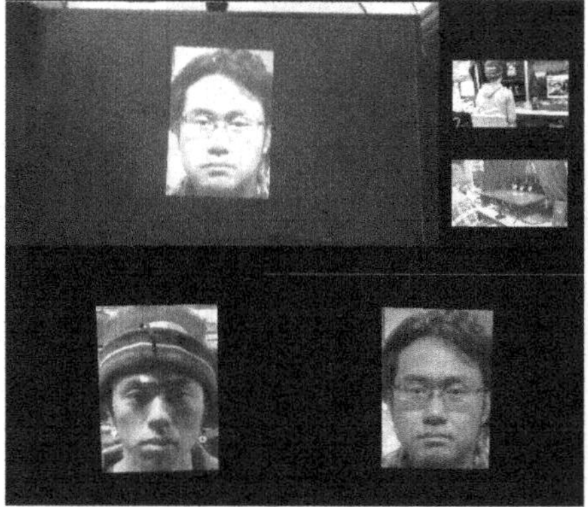

(c) Subject moved his head forward

(d) Subject rolled his head to left

Fig. 6. Each camera image and displayed face images with proposed methods.

Table 1. Questionnaire concerning the proposed system.

No.	Questions
1	Did you match the line of sight with partner? (without deformation by projection transformation)
2	Did you match the line of sight with partner? (with deformation by projective transformation)
3	Did you observe the front face image? (without deformation)
4	Did you observe the front face image? (with deformation)
5	Did you observe the bigger or smaller face compared to the actual face?
6	Did you feel the appropriate face size?
7	Did you feel that partner's face did not rotate when you rotated your head?

these conditions, the similar face images were captured from the eye camera. When the head was rotated, the presented face image also rotated, therefore, the subject A was able to observe the standing face image of the subject B.

3.2 Questionnaire About Proposed System

Twelve subjects were asked to use the system and to answer the seven questions about the system shown in Table 1. The subjects sat approximately 70 cm from the display and moved the head several times to left, right, upward, and downward within the range where both pupils were able to be detected (about ±15 cm). All questions were evaluated in five grades. For questions except questions 5 and 6, "Yes" is set to 5, "No" to 1, and "Neither" to 3. In question 5, "Bigger" is set to 5, "Smaller" to 1, and "Neither" to 3. In question 6, "Big" is set to 5, "Small" to 1, and "Just right" to 3.

Figure 7 shows the results of the questionnaire. When the deformation of the face image by the projection transformation was performed, the high scores were obtained

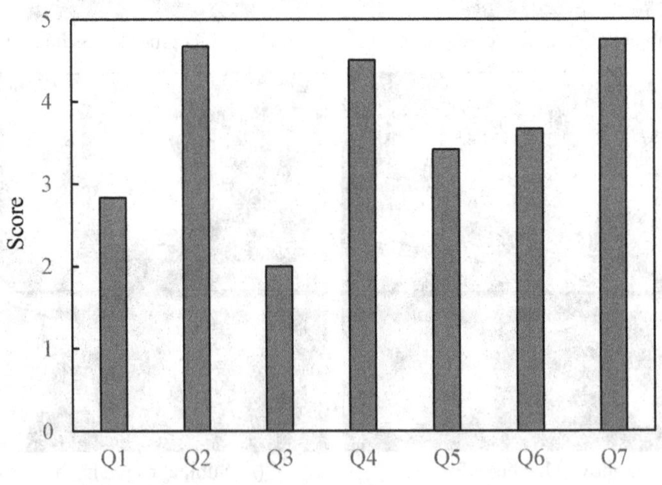

Fig. 7. Results of questionnaire.

in the questions 2 and 4 about matching the line of sight and looking like the front face image compared to the condition without the deformation. Therefore, these results suggest that the proposed system improved realistic feeling compared to the conventional communication system.

4 Conclusions

In the present paper, we proposed the head-free face-to-face remote communication system with line-of-sight matching based on our pupil detection technique [2], a wide-angle color camera located behind a 45-deg inclined magic mirror, the image deformation techniques, and so on. In the experiment, we confirmed the realistic displayed partner's face images obtained from the eye camera images attached to the middle of the eyebrows. The results of the questionnaire suggested the improvements of usability and reality compared to the conventional system.

References

1. Yaskawa information systems: NetSHAKER TalkEye. https://www.ysknet.co.jp/
2. Ebisawa, Y., Fukumoto, K.: Head-free remote eye-gaze detection system based on pupil-corneal reflection method with easy calibration using two stereo-calibrated video cameras. IEEE Trans. Biomed. Eng. **60**(10), 2952–2960 (2013)
3. Zhang, Z.: A flexible new technique for camera calibration. IEEE Trans. Pattern Anal. Mach. Intell. **22**(11), 1330–1334 (2000)

Ergonomic Design of Target Symbols for Fighter Aircraft Cockpit Displays Based on Usability Evaluation

Sung-Ho Kim[1], Woo-Seok Jang[1], Heung-Seob Kim[1], Hyoung-Seog Chung[2], Yong-Duk Kim[3], Woo-Jin Lee[3], and Hyeon-Ju Seol[4(✉)]

[1] Department of Systems Engineering, Air Force Academy, Cheongju, South Korea
{dilemma37,himono0219,afrotc02}@naver.com

[2] Department of Aerospace Engineering, Air Force Academy, Cheongju, South Korea
kafachung@gmail.com

[3] Agency for Defense Development, Daejeon, South Korea
{yd.kim,lwjx4f4}@add.re.kr

[4] School of Integrated National Security, Chungnam National University, Daejeon, South Korea
hyeonju.seol@gmail.com

Abstract. Ergonomic design of target symbol is required for fighter pilots to recognize and interpret target infromation effectively since the latest cockpit display provides huge amount of information. The purpose of this study is to analyze the structure of target symbol, establish coding design guidelines, and design ergonomic target symbol based on the results of usability evaluation for fighter pilots. A structure of target symbol and coding design guidelines analyzed in terms of information dimension (e.g., target type, identification friend or foe, acquisition status, maneuvering status, Data source) and coding dimension (e.g., shape, color, line, alphanumeric character) through literature review. Design alternatives for a target symbol were devised by extracting optimal combination of the information and coding dimension. A usability evaluation was conducted by 19 fighter pilots in their 20 s and 30 s using a relative preference rankings on design alternatives for a target symbol. As a result of conjoint analysis based on usability evaluation data, optimal combination of attributes in terms of target type was only shape coding, that in terms of identification friend or foe was shape, color, and alphanumeric character coding, that in terms of acquisition status was shape, color, and line coding, that in terms of maneuvering status was line and alphanumeric character coding, that in terms of data source was color and line coding. This study suggested that an improved target symbol based on the usability evaluation and design method of target symbol which can be applied to a variety of symbol designs such as public signs.

Keywords: Symbol design · Usability evaluation · Conjoint analysis

C. Stephanidis (Ed.): HCII Posters 2018, CCIS 850, pp. 176–182, 2018.
https://doi.org/10.1007/978-3-319-92270-6_24

1 Introduction

A target symbol on cockpit display is a crucial factor for fighter pilots to achieve air operations successfully. Warfighting symbology has been used for delivering standardized information about military objects to a large number of stakeholder groups in joint operations quickly and accurately [1]. Especially, Ergonomic design of target symbol is required for fighter pilots to reduce learning time and prevent human errors in interpretating target infromation since the latest cockpit display provides huge amount of information.

Analysis and evaluation for the effects of symbol coding techniques are needed to design ergonomic target symbol. The objective of the coding techniques is for users to distinguish between individual information, discover functionally related information, realize the relationship between information, and identify important information within a visual display [2]. The coding techniques requires to use cosistent and meaningful coding, guarantee the legibility or transmission time of information, and establish standards for all coding within the system. Meanwhile, optimal combination of symbol information structure and coding techniques can be derived from usability evaluation that reflects acutal users' needs.

The purpose of this study is to establish design criteria and alternatives of the target symbol and propose ergonomic target symbol based on the result of usability evaluation. The design criteria and alternatives of the target symbol were set up by analyzing target information structure and coding techniques through literature review. The usability evaluation was performed by measuring pilots' preference rankings of alternatives of the target symbol. Finally, relatively suitable coding techniques for each target information structure were found by applying conjoint analysis (CA) technique to usability evaluation data.

2 Target Symbol Design

2.1 Design Criteria

Design criteria were defined in the information dimension and the coding dimension through literature review such as military standard, technical order, and journal paper. The information dimension is meaning elements that structure of the target symbol represents, including target type, identification friend or foe, acquisition status, maneuvering status, and data source. Target type refers to the main mission area where the military objects are active and is classified into air, ground, and sea surface. Identification friend or foe means the threat level represented by the military objects and is divided into friendly, neutral, unknown, suspect, and hostile standard identity. Acquisition status defines the condition that an aircraft is tracking the military objects and is classified into air to air next to shoot and air to ground next to shoot status. Maneuvering status is detailed information about motion of the military objects under operation environment and is divided into altitude and airspeed. Data source stands for the main subject that detects the military objects and ownship sensor, offboard sensor, and ownship correlation sensor with offboard.

On the other hand, the coding dimension is expression elements that meaning elements of the target symbol represent, including shape, color, line style, and alphanumeric character coding. Shape coding is classified into circle, triangle, square, diamond, and trapezoid shape. Color coding is divided into red, blue, green, yellow, purple, and white color. Line style coding is associated with solid line, dotted line, double line, vertex line, line direction, and line length. Alphanumeric character coding consists of letters and numbers.

2.2 Design Alternatives

This study examined symbol design guidelines considering human cognitive characteristics in order to create alternatives of the target symbol. For instance, affordance design is necessary for users to understand the symbol meaning and take proper action quickly. Also, two or more multi-dimensional coding design is required to improve human cognitive accuracy.

The alternatives of the target symbol were suggested by prioritizing design for coding dimension in terms of information dimension considering the examined design guidelines. Alternatives for target type were designed with shape coding as the primary means and color, line style, and alphanumeric character coding as the secondary. Alternatives for identification friend or foe were invented by shape and color coding as the primary means and line style and alphanumeric character coding as the secondary. Alternatives for acquisition status were produced by line style and color coding as the primary means and shape and alphanumeric character coding as the secondary. Alternatives for maneuvering status were devised by shape, line style, and alphanumeric character coding as the primary means except color coding. Alternatives for data source were made with shape coding as the primary means and line style and alphanumeric character coding as the secondary except color coding. Table 1 shows an example of the alternatives of the target symbol for identification friend or foe.

Table 1. Alternatives of target symbols for identification of friend or foe

Identification of friend or foe	Alternatives							
	#1	#2	#3	#4	#5	#6	#7	#8
Friend								F
Neutral								N
Unknown								U
Suspect								S
Enemy								H

3 Usability Evaluation

3.1 Method

Usability evaluation data was obtained using questionnaires for each alternatives, and these alternatives were analyzed to identify the best configuration of coding dimensions. To conduct the usability evaluation, a total of 19 fighter pilots at Republic of Korea Air Force in their 20 s to 30 s were asked to take part in the study. The participants determined the relative preference ranking of the designed alternatives of target symbol by coding dimension in terms of information dimension. Then, the best configuration of coding dimension was identified by CA technique.

CA technique is used to predict the users' decision-making through the relative preference of different characteristics and functions of products or service [3]. CA technique defines the different characteristics and functions of products or services as 'attributes' and the several sub-options of each attribute as 'levels' [4]. Researchers can easily identify the reason why users prefer alternatives of target symbols based on pre-defined attributes and the improving direction of alternatives of target symbols based on newly defined attributes which shows potential alternatives for users by using CA technique [5]. In this study, five CA model were established for covering five information dimensions including the attributes and levels of target symbols to conduct CA technique. In CA models, Primary coding dimensions were defined as independent attributes and each coding dimension was divided into specific levels. Meanwhile, secondary coding dimensions were integrated as one attribute (Additional mark) and each coding dimension was defined as each level. Table 2 represents the attributes and levels for target symbols.

Table 2. Attributes and levels for target symbols

Information dimension	Attributes	Levels
Target type	Shape	5 (Shape combination #1 – #5)
	Additional mark	4 (None, color, line style, alphanumeric character)
Identification of friend or foe	Shape	3 (Shape combination #1 – #3)
	Color	3 (Color combination #1 – #3)
	Additional mark	3 (None, line style, alphanumeric character)
Acquisition status	Line style	3 (Solid line, dotted line, vertex line)
	Color	2 (Red, Yellow)
	Additional mark	4 (Shape combination #1 – #3, alphanumeric character)
Maneuvering status	Altitude	3 (Shape, line style, alphanumeric character)
	Airspeed	3 (Shape, line style, alphanumeric character)
Data source	Shape	3 (Shape combination #1 – #3)
	Additional mark	3 (None, line style, alphanumeric character)

3.2 Results

As a result of CA based on usability evaluation data, the different configurations of coding dimension was preferred for each information dimension as shown in Table 3. In this table, weight means the importance of each attributes, while part-worth means the contribution of a level to the total utility and most preferred levels of each attributes are highlighted. Part-worth can be considered as the proxy parameter of relative users' preference score, thus, if a certain level had the highest part-worth, this level was most preferred level for the users.

Table 3. Result of conjoint analysis (part-worth and importance weight)

Information Dimension	Attributes	Level (part-worth)					Weight
Target type	Shape	#1 (3.347)	#2 (0.979)	#3 (-1.232)	#4 (-2.442)	#5 (-0.653)	0.574
	Additional mark	None (1.842)	Color (-0.368)	Line style (-1)	Alpha numeric character (-0.474)	-	0.426
Identification of friend or foe	Shape	#1 (0.86)	#2 (0.649)	#3 (-1.509)	-	-	0.382
	Color	#1 (1.018)	#2 (-0.414)	#3 (-0.614)	-	-	0.328
	Additional mark	None (-0.14)	Line style (-0.982)	Alpha numeric character (1.123)	-	-	0.290
Acquisition status	Line style	Solid (0.667)	Dotted (0.298)	Vertex (-0.965)	-	-	0.366
	Color	Red (-0.842)	Yellow (0.842)	-	-	-	0.209
	Additional mark	Shape #1 (0.671)	Shape #2 (1.461)	Shape #3 (-0.013)	Alpha numeric character (-2.118)	-	0.435
Maneuvering status	Altitude	Alpha numeric character (0.596)	Line (-0.614)	Shape (0.018)	-	-	0.608
	Airspeed	Alpha numeric character (0.667)	Line (-0.386)	Shape (-0.281)	-	-	0.392
Data source	Shape	#1 (-0.678)	#2 (2.83)	#3 (-2.152)	-	-	0.625
	Additional mark	None (1.638)	Line style (0)	Alpha numeric character (-1.638)	-	-	0.375

Before identifying the optimal configuration for each information dimension, used code dimensions were analyzed. In Target type dimension, only shape coding was preferred for users. In attributes in terms of Identification friend or foe, Shape, Color and Alphanumeric character coding were most preferable. In attributes in terms of Acquisition status, most preferred target symbol was determined by shape, color and line style coding. In attributes in terms of Maneuvering statue, Alphanumeric character coding was mainly used to identify the altitude and airspeed. Lastly, in attributes in terms of Data source, shape coding was mainly changed depending on data source of other information.

The optimal configurations could be extracted from the utility which was highest in each information dimension. The utility of all possible configurations was calculated by multiplying weight and part-worth of corresponding levels. Table 4 represented the best configurations and actual designed symbols of each information dimension.

Table 4. Best designed target symbols of each information dimension

Information dimension	Designed Symbols				
Target type	Air	Ground	Sea		
				-	-
Identification of friend or foe	Friend	Neutral	Unknown	Suspect	Enemy
	F	N	U	S	H
Acquisition status	Air/Air	Air/Ground			
			-	-	-
Maneuvering status	Altitude	Airspeed			
	22 300	22 300	-	-	-
Data source	Ownship	Offboard	Correlation		
				-	-

4 Conclusion

The present study suggested ergonomically improved design of target symbols on cockpit display based on usability evaluation. In order to design target symbol in systematic and quantitative manner, the information structure and coding techniques of the target symbol were analyzed and the usability evaluation was conducted by pilots on the alternatives of the target symbol. The improved design of target symbols was finally derived from identifying the optimal combination of coding dimension about each information dimension by CA of usability values. The target symbol design method based on usability evaluation in this study can be applied to design various symbols such as public signs.

A usability evaluation with more pilots in the actual flight environment and various ergonomic evaluation measures are needed for further research. This study evaluated the usability through the questionnaires of 19 pilots. However, to verify the utility of improved design of target symbol, a usability evaluation for a larger number of pilots is required to be conducted in the actual flight environment. In addition, this study conducted usability evaluation using relative preference ranking, but using an ergonomic evaluation measures is necessary to analyze users' cognitive characteristics such as recognizability, learnability, memorability.

References

1. MIL-STD-2525C: Common Warfighting Symbology. U.S. Government Printing Office, Washington (2008)
2. MIL-STD-1472G: Human Engineering Design Criteria for Military Systems, Equipment and Facilities. U.S. Government Printing Office, Washington (2011)
3. Green, P.E., Srinivasan, V.: Conjoint analysis in marketing: new developments with implications for research and practice. J. Mark. **54**(4), 3–19 (1990)
4. Silayoi, P., Speece, M.: The importance of packaging attributes: a conjoint analysis approach. Eur. J. Mark. **41**(11/12), 1495–1517 (2007)
5. Yoon, B., Park, Y.: Development of new technology forecasting algorithm: hybrid approach for morphology analysis and conjoint analysis of patent information. IEEE Trans. Eng. Manag. **54**(3), 588–599 (2007)

Research on Information Interfaces Visual Search Efficiency and Matching Mechanism Based on Similarity Theory

Ya-jun Li and Ruiting Yang(✉)

Nanjing University of Science and Technology, Nanjing 210094, Jiangsu, China
453909824@qq.com

Abstract. Based on the similarity theory of visual search, this paper mainly studies the relationship between the characteristics of mobile phone interactive interface and the efficiency of visual search. Summing up the pictures' background information and layout regularity from existing cases as the experimental variables, this paper conducts eye-tracking experiment. It studies the influence of the pictures' background information and layout regularity on the efficiency of visual search through multifactor analysis of variance and average value comparing analysis on search time and fixation counts. The experimental results show that users' visual search efficiency varies significantly with two variables, e.g., whether the pictures contain background information and whether the layout is regular.

Keywords: Similarity theory · Information interfaces · Search efficiency Matching

1 Introduction

Visual search is the cognitive process of searching for a specific target object under a certain background [1]. It is not only an important method of daily learning and obtaining outside information but also a significant part of various professional tasks, for example, map reading, the X-ray luggage inspection, medical image analysis, driving and web searching [2]. As the dominant status of mobile internet is strengthened gradually, the user communities of various mobile phone applications are expanding and users' visual search efficiency has been an important subject for improving user experience in mobile phone interactive interface design.

2 Research Status

According to *The 40th Statistical Report on Internet Development in China*, during the first half of 2017, applications on business transaction keep growing rapidly on China Mobile Internet and the characteristics of upgraded consumption in the online shopping market are more conspicuous, while user preferences are gradually shifting to quality, intelligence and new product consumption. Studies by people such as Aurora showed

C. Stephanidis (Ed.): HCII Posters 2018, CCIS 850, pp. 183–190, 2018.
https://doi.org/10.1007/978-3-319-92270-6_25

that image navigation can deliver more information to users, and abundant information can enhance the attractiveness to users as well as promoting users' search behaviors [3]. Lulu took the WeChat platform as the research object. By analyzing its interface layout, images and visual performance, she found that images are more intuitive and easier to understand, besides, rich icon interfaces tend to be more attractive to users [4]. From the perspectives of visual search and visual browsing regularities, Ting Liu and others analyzed the influence of mobile phone news apps' graphic and textual layouts on users' reading efficiency, and studied eye-tracking regularities of visual browsing and visual search under different layout schemes [5]. In conclusion, most of the existing researches analyze users' visual behaviors from the perspective of interface characteristics, which tend to analyze the cognition results, but seldom study users' behavior regularities and behavior mechanisms. Based on the similarity theory of visual search processing, taking the shopping APP interface as an experimental sample and through the eye-tracking experiment, this study mainly researches users' visual search efficiency and mechanism in different types of interfaces.

3 Similarity Theory and Interaction Design

In interactive interface design, the efficiency of visual search is related to the characteristics of the interface. In cognitive psychology, the efficiency of visual search is closely related to the way of human cognitive processing. Duncan and Humphreys put forward the similarity theory of visual search in 1989. In this theory, visual search is divided into two processes: perceptual description and reaction judgment. It emphasizes that efficiency of search task is determined by the difference between target stimulus and interference item and the similarity among the interference items [6]. Based on the similarity theory of visual search, taking the efficiency of visual search in mobile phone interactive interface as the experimental sample, this study mainly discuss the characteristics of visual search efficiency in different types of interfaces and analyze the forming system (Fig. 1).

In this study, we take shopping App interface as the example. During the process of interaction between the user and the mobile phone interface, the process of looking for a target product by a user can be regarded as a process of visual search and matching. We know from the similarity theory that visual search efficiency is closely related to target items and interference items, therefore, by comparing and analyzing the interface elements of the mainstream shopping Apps, this study sums up following 2 group of variables at first stage: whether the product pictures contain background information (including shooting background, accessories and text labels, without them is a single product picture); whether the layout is regular (regularity means the same picture arrangement shows repeatedly, unregular layout means no picture arrangements are the same). By designing and conducting eye-tracking experiment, this study collects users' eye movement and behaviors' data to observe users' visual search efficiency. Combining with the existing work, this paper made the following assumption: visual search efficiency is higher when users browsing pages with pictures that has no background information and with regular layout, otherwise, visual search efficiency becomes lower.

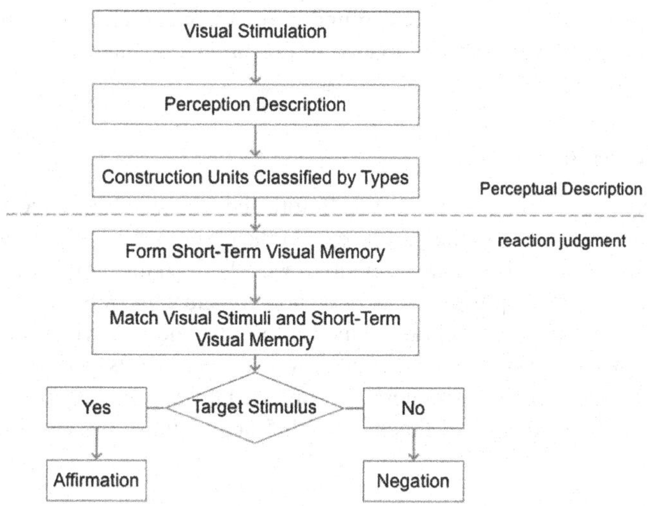

Fig. 1. Visual search process under the similarity theory

4 App Interface Search Eye-Tracking Experiment

4.1 Tested Objects

The experiment recruited 10 undergraduates which include 5 males and 5 females. Their ages are among 22–26 and all of them have experience with using shopping apps. They all have normal or corrected vision, no one has color blindness or color weakness.

4.2 Experiment Devices

Experiment devices include Tobii Glasses eye-tracking instrument, desktops (with 19 in. 1920 * 1080 resolution screen) and Tobii Studio 3.2 eye-tracking data analysis software. Before the experiment starting, every subject is calibrated. Sample pictures are of the same size to the mobile phone screens and shown on the 19 in. screen. Subjects sit keeping their eyes level with the screen and the distance between their eyes to the screen is 40 cm, close to the distance between their eyes to their mobile phone screens.

The environment of mobile interface is different from computer interface. Limited by equipment conditions, the mobile phone interface cannot be evaluated directly in this experiment. But previous research shows: user performance tests prove that availability assessment conducted by the computer simulated mobile phone prototype interface is effective [7].

4.3 Test Design and Material

This test is designed for the factors of 2 pictures' background information (with or without) $\times$ 2 pictures' layout regularity (with or without), and test material is analog shopping interface. By combining the variables, it formed 4 different kinds of test interfaces: interface of pictures without background information but with regular layout, interface of pictures with background information and regular layout, interface of pictures without background information or regular layout, interface of pictures with background information but without regular layout.

4.4 Test Procedure

The test is carried out in a quiet room. Before the test starting, subjects carry out nine-point calibration and learning test, keep their heads motionless after calibration and conducted learning test, then start migration test. The learning process is as follows: present the targets for 2s—present the fixation point on the upper left for 2s—present the test interface with 1 pictures—click the mouse to finish the task when find the target; The migration test process is as below: present the targets for 2s—present the fixation point 2s—present a migration test interface—find the target, click the mouse to finish the task and turn to the next page (4 times)—finish 5 tasks—finish the test (Fig. 2).

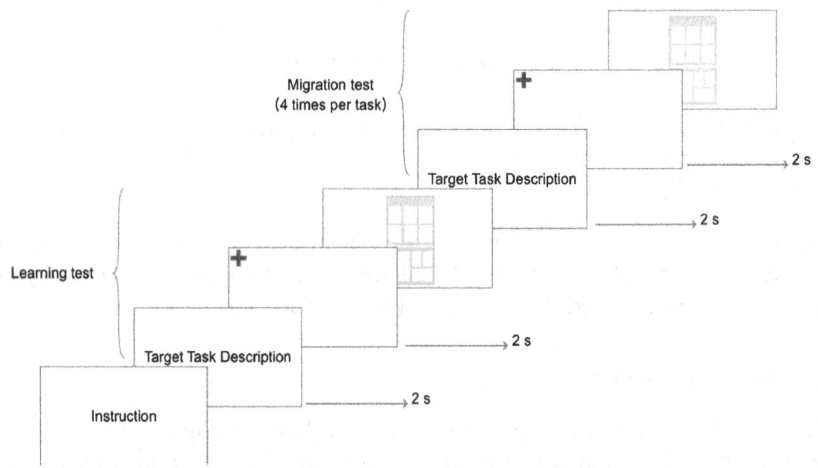

Fig. 2. Example of experimental process

4.5 Data Processing

The 10 groups of data are all effective. Eye movement data is recorded by eye-tracking instrument, behavior data is counted by stopwatch, they are used to record the search time and fixation counts for studying. Test data are analyzed and processed by spss 23.0.

5 Data Analysis

5.1 Time Spent for Searching Targets

Through the statistics of time spent on turning the test pages, we get the descriptive statistics (Table 1) and results of multifactor analysis of variance for the search time on the test interface (Table 2).

Table 1. Descriptive statistics of search time on the test interface

	Pictures without background information		Pictures with background information	
	M	SD	M	SD
Regular layout	3482	789	4590	840
Unregular layout	3838	1042	4650	784

Table 2. MANOVA for search time on the test interface

	df	F	Sig
Background information	1	31.837	.000
Layout regularity	1	40.935	.001
Background information * layout regularity	2	11.837	.164

From the multifactor analysis of variance, we drew the following conclusion: pictures' background information has an obvious main effect ($F = 31.837$, $p < 0.05$), which indicates subjects' search efficiency is higher in interface of pictures without background information than in interface of pictures with background information. Layout regularity also have an obvious main effect ($F = 40.935$, $p < 0.05$), which indicates subjects' search efficiency is higher in interface with regular layout than in interface without regular layout. Picture background information and layout regularity have significant interactive effects ($F = 11.837$, $p < 0.05$). Influenced by both factors, the search time subjects spent on different types of interface is significantly different.

According to the descriptive statistics of search time, pages of which pictures without background information and have regular layout take a shorter average search time than of those pictures with background information and have unregular layout. The independent t-test result is $F = 68.802$, $p < 0.05$, which indicates that the original assumption is incorrect. Therefore, pages of which pictures without background information and have regular layout take an obviously shorter average search time than of those pictures with background information and have unregular layout.

5.2 Total Fixations

By extraction and analysis on eye movement data through Tobii Studio and spss23.0, we get the descriptive statistics (Table 3) and multifactor analysis of variance for total fixations on test interface (Table 4).

Table 3. Descriptive statistics for total fixations on test interface (/times)

	Pictures without background information		Pictures with background information	
	Accuracy (%)	SD	Accuracy (%)	SD
Regular layout	78.7	10.92	66.2	31.03
Unregular layout	73.2	23.94	45.3	29.32

Table 4. MANOVA for total fixations on test interface

	df	F	Sig
Background information	1	14.862	.000
Layout regularity	1	4.809	.031
Background information * layout regularity	1	1.837	.153

From the multifactor analysis of variance, we draw the following conclusion: pictures' background information has an obvious main effect ($F = 29.297$, $p < 0.05$), which indicates subjects' fixations on interface of pictures without background information are less than on interface of pictures with background information. Layout regularity also have an obvious main effect ($F = 56.658$, $p < 0.05$), which indicates subjects' fixations on interface with regular layout are less than on interface without regular layout. Pictures' background information and layout regularity have significant interactive effects ($F = 11.604$, $p < 0.05$). Influenced by both factors, subjects' fixations on different types of interface is significantly different.

According to the descriptive statistics, interfaces of which pictures with background information and have unregular layout get more average fixations than of those pictures without background information and have regular layout. The independent t-test result is $F = 15.202$, $p < 0.05$, which indicates that the original assumption is incorrect. Therefore, pages of which pictures with background information and have unregular layout obviously get more total fixations than of those pictures without background information and have regular layout.

6 Experiment Analysis

In this study, visual search efficiency of mobile phone interface under different variable conditions is studied through eye-tracking test analysis and based on experimental data analysis. Below conclusion is drawn: affected by the variables of whether the pictures contain background information and whether the layout has regularity, subjects' visual search efficiency varies significantly. Therefore, discussions in this paper are based on the two variables.

6.1 Visual Search Time

According to the experimental data, subjects obviously spent less time in interfaces of pictures without background information and have regular layout than in those of pictures with background information and have unregular layout. In previous studies, people like Scharroo considered that visual search efficiency goes down as pictures' complexity level rises [7]; Jing Li and other found from studies that the type, adjacency state and connection mode of shape coding are important factors for whether it can be fast captured. Above findings are all in conformity with the experimental results of this study. In view of similarity theory, with pictures' background information as interference item, the content for subjects to compare in visual search process is increased. Besides, pictures appear at a random position in interfaces with unregular layout, which decreases the similarity among interference items. Therefore, it takes more search time in interfaces containing pictures with background information and have unregular layout. In interfaces with regular layout, pictures are in the same position and without background information, which enables subjects to seize the content of pictures and then compare and judge quickly. That is to say, it decreases the similarity between targets and interference items, so interfaces without background information and with regular layout takes less search time.

6.2 Counts of Fixations

According to the test results, fixations on interfaces containing pictures without background information and regular layout is obviously less than on interfaces containing pictures with background information and unregular layout. As pictures without background information are easy to focus and regular layout interfaces guide users' vision path regularly, which help to improve visual search efficiency, thus interfaces containing pictures without background information and regular layout get less fixations. Background information in pictures increases the information of targets, which makes the increased fixations in pictures with background information. Besides, unregular layout interfaces have disordered and possibly repeated vision path, which makes the relatively more fixations in interfaces of pictures with background information and unregular layout.

6.3 Deficiencies

After analysis of the results and profound consideration in the later stage, we find below problems: control variables are not clearly classified, which may affect the test results. Instead of motion environment, subjects are in static state when simulating the mobile phone operation in front of the computer screen, which may affect the test results. During the process of data analysis, we only discussed the two extremes of variables' combined effect and need further simple effect analysis on the specific relations between the factors of dual effects.

6.4 Conclusion

Similarity theory is one of the visual search and processing theories based on external characteristics guidance. This paper is based on the theory and studied the visual search efficiency and its mechanism in interfaces with different characteristics. According to the results, we draw the following conclusions:

1. In interactive interface design of mobile phone, the effect of pictures' background information and layout regularity need to be considered. Users' visual search efficiency and cognitive performance can be improved by simplifying pictures' background information and adding regularity of pictures' layout.
2. Visual search efficiency is relatively higher in interfaces where pictures are without background information. Pictures' background information would decrease visual search efficiency. In interactive interface design of mobile phone, pictures with

background information of different complexity are needed according to different designs.

3. Visual search efficiency is relatively higher in interfaces with regular layout and would decrease in interfaces with unregular layout. Thus in interactive interface design of mobile phone, we should focus on interfaces in regular layout to reducing users' cognitive cost and improve cognitive performance.
4. As users' visual search efficiency takes the dual effect of picture background information and layout regularity, we should set users' visual search efficiency according to different interface functions in interactive interface design of mobile phones. To enrich users' operation performance, we can guide different visual search efficiency by changing the complexity of pictures' background information and the regularity level of layout.

7 Epilogue

Based on the similarity theory of visual search, this paper mainly studies users' visual search efficiency in different types of mobile phone interactive interfaces, and draw the conclusion that the factors of picture background information and layout regularity would obviously affect visual search efficiency. It also discussed the matching mechanism under the effect of the two factors. However, this study only discussed the combined effect of the factors, and our next study should include detailed analysis in specific situations of the factors.

Acknowledgement. This study is supported by the Project supported by the National Social Science Foundation of China (Project No. 16BSH127).

References

1. Wickens, C.D., et al.: Engineering Psychology and Human Performance, pp. 34–60. China Machine Press, Beijing (2014)
2. Gong, Y., Zhang, S., Liu, Z., Shen, F.: Eye movement study on color effects to icon visual search efficiency. J. Zhejiang Univ. (Eng. Sci.) (10), 1987–1994 (2016)
3. Aurora, B.: Icon usability, New York (2014)
4. Lulu, Y.: Visual integration research of sharing graphics based on WeChat platform. Packag. Eng. (22), 123–127 (2015)
5. Liu, T., Hou, W.: Graphic layout design study of mobile news APP based on visual behavior. J. Beijing Univ. Posts Telecommun. (Soc. Sci. Ed.) **18**(3), 6–13 (2016)
6. Iwai, Y., Shimizu, H., Yachida, M.: Real-time context-based gesture recognition using HMM and automaton. In: Proceedings of International Workshop on the Recognition, Analysis, and Tracking of Faces and Gestures in Real-Time Systems, pp. 127–134. IEEE Computer Society Press, Los Alamitos (1999)
7. Dai, J., Ge, L.: Usability evaluation of mobile phone prototype interfaces. Chin. J. Ergon. (02), 13–15+37 (2007)

Knowde: A Visual Search Interface

Maurice Schleußinger[1(✉)] and Maria Henkel[2]

[1] Center of Information and Media Technology, Heinrich Heine University, Universitätsstr. 1, 40225 Düsseldorf, Germany
maurice.schleussinger@hhu.de

[2] Heinrich Heine University, Universitätsstr. 1, 40225 Düsseldorf, Germany

Abstract. Information Visualizations are well established to represent high density information in an intuitive and interactive way. There are no popular general retrieval systems, however, which utilize the power of information visualizations for search result representation. This paper describes Knowde, a search interface with purely visual result representation. It employs a powerful information retrieval system and works in a common web browser in real-time. This working prototype, with three different variations of network graphs will assist us in exploring current issues in visualization research, such as the challenge of system evaluation.

Keywords: Visualization · Information retrieval
Information system · Visual search interface

1 Introduction

In the digital age, the quantity and complexity of information we have to deal with in everyday life, has reached a whole new level. And while there is an abundance of services that help us with the retrieval and processing of needed information, the drive for more efficiency and an competitive advantage leads us to innovate systems, processes and services endlessly. Especially businesses recognize "the need for more effective tools for extracting knowledge from the data warehouses they are gathering" [11] and are implementing information visualization in their work flows. When it comes to human understanding of information, the visual approach is a very powerful one. "Visual displays provide the highest bandwidth channel from the computer to the human", which helps us to understand "large-scale and small-scale features of the data" observed and supports us in gaining new insight, for example, by recognizing properties of and also problems with the data, that were not anticipated before [24]. As a great quantity of information can be processed more quickly with the help of visualization, it is not only helpful for "scientists and analysts", but also for "commercial and personal use" [11]. And yet, current search engines and interfaces work with text-based lists as means of result representation. And while information visualization is a research focus of growing interest over the recent years, little to none systems that utilize interactive visualizations for information retrieval purposes have established themselves as major player in the information systems

C. Stephanidis (Ed.): HCII Posters 2018, CCIS 850, pp. 191–198, 2018.
https://doi.org/10.1007/978-3-319-92270-6_26

and services market. Earlier approaches in combining information search and visualization in one system exist, but yielded mixed results in mostly modest evaluation attempts [6] and were sometimes limited by bulky and slow hardware. Nowadays, we can say that we possess the required technology to enable better and more appealing design for retrieval and visual representation of information - not only on the web, but also in three-dimensional environments. To evaluate how visualization can optimize and enhance the information seeking and understanding process, we designed a visual search engine called Knowde. Additionally, we aim to tackle the several challenges and difficulties in evaluation of visual search interfaces. Knowde (**Know**ledge No**de**), is an information retrieval system that employs elements of information visualization as integral part of the result presentation. It adapts network graphs into a web search interface, using them as the sole means of search result representation and main focus for user interaction.

The purpose of this work is to introduce the Knowde system in its design and function. For which we briefly review related work and continue to present the system itself. Followed by a quick overview over issues and challenges such as evaluation methodology and cognitive load.

2 Related Work

The idea of combining search and visualization in one system is not new. Earlier approaches, the information space prototype by Rohrer and Swing [17], SENTINEL and NIRVE [5], attempted 3D visualizations, requiring the user to navigate a 3-dimensional space, using mouse and keyboard input and a 2-dimensional computer monitor. User evaluation yielded mixed results. [25] developed Jigsaw, a system which already focused on the interactive exploration of relationships between entities (e.g. humans) in reports. It features a variety of user interfaces combined in one system. However search query functionality is limited and not focus of the research. The *SIZL* (Searching for Information in a Zoom Landscape) system [8] features multiple search filters which can be combined to limit the result set in a 2.5D interface (an interface with 3D elements in a fixed 2D perspective). They create a specialized system which can accumulate the result sets of multiple searches for later review, but do not aim to provide a visual search interface for broad document search. [10] developed an interactive User Interface called *Vizster* for browsing social networks. Its visualization is realized by a graph which centers around the user and displays their friends and their connectedness (via nodes and lines) as well as possible clusters of friends. It also features a list of details for a selected user and allows a simple keyword search. We want to employ a similar system for multimedia documents and emphasize the search functionality. FacetMap [21] features a search and filter system which puts emphasis on the navigation of hierarchical categories like date and type. Their visualization focuses on labeled bubbles in a grid system organized into categories. The system utilized data sets with rich metadata, contrary to many real world databases. Their evaluation showed users did not clearly prefer their system over an traditional interface (nor did performance improve significantly).

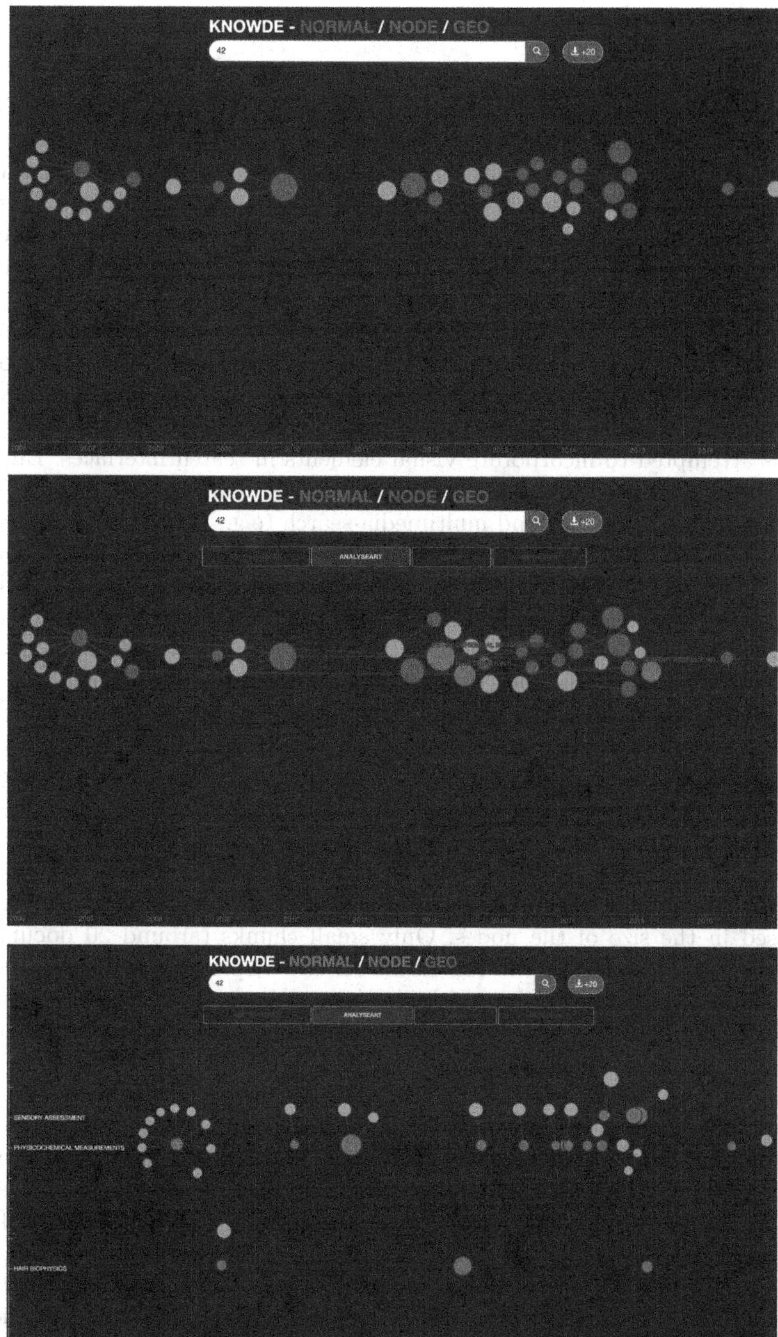

Fig. 1. Screenshots of the Knowde system's three modes (top to bottom) (Color figure online)

3 System and Data Set

Knowdes' core design principle is the Visual Information Seeking Mantra by [19]: A viable visual design provides "overview first, zoom and filter, then details-on-demand.", a step which is repeated multiple times during the data exploration process. Additionally, we classify our data set with the Task by Data Type Taxonomy by Shneiderman [19] and Keim's classification of Information Visualization [12], a simplified and modernized variation. The given dataset is a combination of multidimensional data, including temporal and text data. Concluding from this classification, our visual representation should feature a temporal visualization, a representation of document entities as well as their relation and visualization of the multidimensional categorical information. To incorporate this, the system features different variations of node-link diagrams, or network graphs, enhanced by a time line. As mentioned before, some previously developed systems attempted to incorporate visual elements in search interfaces. But few of them actually focus on a powerful search, with state-of-the-art retrieval performance, term completion and multimedia-search (e.g., Office files) in junction with simple, intuitive visualizations on a temporal scale with a clear & modern design. The concrete visual design incorporates graphical codes from the visual grammar by Ware [24]. Entities are closed contours (circular nodes), relationships are lines between entities. Proximity between entities suggests a similarity (grouping). The visual system features three different modes as shown in Fig. 1. They consist of a fixed search bar at the top and, depending on the mode, buttons for category selection. The entirety of the screen is dominated by the actual visualization of search results as network graphs. Resulting from the specific structure of the company's data set used in this example, there are two connected node types: reports (blue) and their attachments (green). The search function features a powerful search index which enables access to all textual information provided in the many file formats of the provided data set. Result relevance is expressed in the size of the nodes. Only small chunks (around 20 documents with their attachments) of the full result set are displayed initially, to reduce visual clutter, but more results can be loaded on demand. The user can fluidly zoom and drag in the visualization at any point using the computer's mouse. All resulting reports are sorted on a time axis based on their creation date.

This interface, *mode 1* is the basis for all other modes (Fig. 1, top). It allows us to evaluate the core idea of Knowde, interactive network graphs for result representation as well as more complex variations, in direct comparison. The point of having different modes or variations of the same interface is to gain more out of the evaluation results. Simply said, we want to find out which if any of our ideas perform well with users. In *mode 2*, categorical information is displayed in the form of a third type of nodes (orange). These additional nodes are sized by absolute occurrences in the result set and are connected to all report nodes with the corresponding category (Fig. 1, middle). In *mode 3*, the same categorical information is displayed on the y-Axis of the window. The white stripes on the axis represent the total amount of values for the selected category, but only matching values are labeled. The value labels are sorted alphabetically and scale on zooming and panning together with the nodes (Fig. 1, bottom). Therefore, at any point the category information for visible nodes can be retrieved and never changes its relative position. While *modes 2* and *3* transport the same additional information (categorical information), the means of displaying it differ. Evaluation will indicate if there is a user favorite and why.

As Knowde was developed in cooperation with a large, internationally operating company, a real data set was used. It consisted of 4571 reports, which linked to 7350 attachments. This sums up to a total of 4.3 GB of text files, images, office documents & videos. The prototyped system aims to be easily accessible. To allow all this, the final prototype only requires a modern web-browser running Javascript. The user simply visits a website and starts searching and exploring. The search index itself is implemented with Elasticsearch[1], it provides a highly configurable search index for a variety of input data, and scales well for even larger data sets. Since the data set also contains a variety of office files, much of it is only accessible if the search index can cover such files as well. Elasticsearch provides a plugin which extracts text information from common formats (PPT, XLS, PDF and more. It can also recognize text in images and make them searchable too. The system contains an inverted index of all existing documents and processes keyword queries by splitting into separate keywords at whitespaces and joining them with the logical OR operator. Since Elasticsearch boosts documents matching multiple keywords we still get the most relevant results first. For relevance ranking, a variation of the Vector Space Model with TF/IDF calculations [7] is applied. Most of the extensive configuration possibilities remain at their default values and result in an acceptable (basic) IR system at this point [1,2,20]. Data transfer for the interface and the visualization data is handled with the Meteor web framework, which provides web pages to the client's browser and keeps data between the server and the browser continuously synchronized. The user interface itself is implemented in styled HTML. For any user interactivity and styling of dynamic content (the visualization), the Javascript library D3[2] is used. It provides basic building blocks and paradigms for data visualization of any kind, ranging from a simple bar chart to complex force layouts. In summary, we designed an Information System based on established paradigms (Visual Information Seeking Mantra, Ware's design grammar). The prototype features three modes with different variations of the design to allow meaningful evaluation. It uses using modern and powerful technologies for all components (Backend, User Interface, IR system). However, there are important issues to address as we step forward in the development and the evaluation of Knowde.

4 Conclusion and Current Issues

4.1 Addressing the Issue of Scale

Even before the development of the prototype began, the limit of scale for basically any visual representation of data entities became apparent. Using the web

[1] https://www.elastic.co/products/elasticsearch.
[2] https://d3js.org/.

browser and D3 JavaScript library, more than 1000 data points render the interface unusable [3]. Using significantly better performing technologies (e.g., with programming languages like C(++) or Java) would decrease both prototyping efficiency and user accessibility. There are, however, other possible solutions: [23] claim there are use cases or technical limitations which make an grand overview of a data set impractical. They suggest a focus on user-relevant subgraphs and to enable continued browsing of subgraphs (loaded from a server as needed) to simulate an uninterrupted user-experience. [13] system displays nodes (search results) on a 2D plane aligned by their closeness to the entered search terms. The user can re-rank the results by tapping on the area between these search terms. *Mode 2* of Knowde is similar. The user can filter by clicking a category node to only show results of that category. [13] evaluation suggests an improvement in retrieval precision for complex tasks. Both [13,23] offer solutions for a real limitation of Knowde. Scale. While the performance of Knowde is very good for even hundreds of items, the UI would become unresponsive if there was not a cut-off for the number of search results at some point. A future version could feature a real "overview first" [19] showing an aggregated overview (e.g. documents grouped by year) of the entire data set, followed by specific sub-graphs determined by user input queries and implemented in a way as suggested by [23] or [13] ("details-on-demand").

4.2 Evaluating Visual Search Systems

To prove and improve the value of visual search interfaces, they have to be thoroughly evaluated and compared to conservative information systems. This kind of evaluation, however, is a very challenging task. Ellis and Dix [6] reviewed "65 papers describing new visualization application or techniques" and found that only 12 described any evaluation and only two of them were deemed successful by the authors. They list several challenges and difficulties in visualization evaluation but also offer advice. To summarize: A good evaluation of for visualization systems should be based on real data, with relevant test subjects. It should not be limited to improve a system in small steps, but instead focus heavily on the exploration of truly novel insight regarding the research question(s). It should feature an iterative approach similar to the *user-centered design* introduced by [16]. With its "holistic and comprehensive approach" the ISE Model qualifies as a general guideline for evaluating an information service [18]. It provides a number of evaluation techniques which are grouped in five dimensions, and allow extensive evaluation of key areas of any information system. It was not explicitly designed for visual information services but can still be adapted for such systems. Wares' guidelines for evaluation techniques of visual systems mentions many of the methods proposed by ISE as well [24]. The evaluation of Knowde employs and emphasizes the techniques of ISE which are useful for the evaluation of the visual interface component of such services. The first evaluation was conducted with 24 participants, employees of the company which provided the data set. Interviews consisted of an introduction where the system was explained, followed by a questionnaire regarding the dimensions of ISE. Most users found Knowde to be easy to use, useful and fun. It was ranked to be significantly better than the previously used system at the company. We also found a high overall system acceptance among the test users. Additionally, as part of the critical incident technique and as a thinking-aloud task, test subjects were asked to comment on anything extraordinary or unusual (positive or negative) and mention anything which comes into their minds. This allowed us to collect user interface improvements as well as some qualitative statements about the system. More details about the evaluation results and their implications will be discussed in a separate article.

4.3 Advances in Design vs. System Acceptance

Whether a system is accepted by users is influenced by different aspects. Many models divide system acceptance into the sub-dimensions "ease of use", "usefulness", "trust" and "fun" [22]. A visual search interface like Knowde promises to be enjoyable and useful but may not be accepted due to other reasons. Although it has, to us, become a usual and casual activity, searching for information "is a mentally intensive task" [9]. In some cases, even a "spartan presentation" may be "too complex for some people." [9]. Hence, greater functionality or a higher density of information are no improvements if the resulting system is too hard to use. While there might be the risk of cognitive overload there is also the simple issue of habit. A visual approach may be unusual for users who are used to a certain design when it comes to information retrieval, for example the text-based lists that are common in web search. [16] explains, that today's users have a firm mental model of how a (web) search should look. "Deviating from this expected design almost always causes usability problems." We still believe that todays user-habits will change. Many of the design guidelines that are good practice now, might be obsolete for the next generation of knowledge systems. Until then, a hybrid approach may be the solution [4,14,15].

References

1. Baeza-Yates, R., Ribeiro-Neto, B.: Modern Information Retrieval. Addison-Wesley Longman Publishing Co, Boston (1999)
2. Belkin, N.J., Croft, W.B.: Retrieval techniques. In: Williams, M.E. (ed.) Annual Review of Information Science and Technology, vol. 22, pp. 109–145. Elsevier Science Inc., New York (1987)
3. Bostock, M., Ogievetsky, V., Heer, J.: D3 data-driven documents. IEEE Trans. Vis. Comput. Graph. **17**, 2301–2309 (2011)
4. Clarkson, E.C., Desai, K., Foley, J.D.: ResultMaps: visualization for search interfaces. IEEE Trans. Vis. Comput. Graph. **15**, 1057–1064 (2009)
5. Cugini, J., Laskowski, S., Sebrechts, M.: Design of 3D visualization of search results: evolution and evaluation. In: 12th Annual International Symposium: Electronic Imaging 2000: Visual Data Exploration and Analysis, vol. 3960, pp. 198–210 (2000)
6. Ellis, G., Dix, A.: An explorative analysis of user evaluation studies in information visualisation. In: Proceedings of the 2006 AVI Workshop on BEyond Time and Errors: Novel Evaluation Methods for Information Visualization - BELIV 2006, p. 1 (2006)

7. Gormley, C., Tong, Z.: Elasticsearch the Definite Guide. O'Reilly Media, Sebastopol (2010)
8. Grierson, H.J., Corney, J.R., Hatcher, G.D.: Using visual representations for the searching and browsing of large, complex, multimedia data sets. Int. J. Inf. Manag. **35**, 244–252 (2015)
9. Hearst, M.: The design of search user interfaces. In: Search User Interfaces (2009)
10. Heer, J., Boyd, D.: Vizster: visualizing online social networks. In: Proceedings - IEEE Symposium on Information Visualization, INFO VIS, pp. 33–40 (2005)
11. Heer, J., van Ham, F., Carpendale, S., Weaver, C., Isenberg, P.: Creation and collaboration: engaging new audiences for information visualization. In: Kerren, A., Stasko, J.T., Fekete, J.-D., North, C. (eds.) Information Visualization. LNCS, vol. 4950, pp. 92–133. Springer, Heidelberg (2008). https://doi.org/10.1007/978-3-540-70956-5_5
12. Keim, D.A.: Information visualization and visual data mining. IEEE Trans. Vis. Comput. Graph. **8**, 1–8 (2002)
13. Klouche, K., Ruotsalo, T., Micallef, L., Andolina, S., Jacucci, G.: Visual re-ranking for multi-aspect information retrieval. In: Proceedings of CHIIR 2017. pp. 57–66 (2017)
14. Kraker, P., Kittel, C., Enkhbayar, A.: Open knowledge maps: creating a visual interface to the world's scientific knowledge based on natural language processing. 027.7. J Libr. Cult. **4**, 98–103 (2016)
15. Nguyen, T.N., Zhang, J.: A novel visualization model for web search results. IEEE Trans. Vis. Comput. Graph. **12**, 981–988 (2006)
16. Nielsen, J.: Usability Engineering. Morgan Kaufmann Publishers Inc., San Francisco (1993)
17. Rohrer, R.M., Swing, E.: Web-based information visualization. IEEE Comput. Graph. Appl. **17**, 52–59 (1997)
18. Schumann, L., Stock, W.G.: The Information Service Evaluation (ISE) model. Webology **11**(1) (2014). Article no. 115
19. Shneiderman, B.: The eyes have it: a task by data type taxonomy for information visualizations. In: The Craft of Information Visualization, pp. 364–371 (2003)
20. Shneiderman, B., Byrd, D., Croft, W.B.: Clarifying search: a user-interface framework for text searches. D-Lib Mag. **3**(1), 18–20 (1997)
21. Smith, G., Czerwinski, M., Meyers, B., Robbins, D., Robertson, G., Tan, D.S.: FacetMap: a scalable search and browse visualization. IEEE Trans. Vis. Comput. Graph. **12**, 797–804 (2006)
22. Stock, W.G., Stock, M.: Handbook of Information Science. De Gruyter Saur, Berlin (2013)
23. van Ham, F., Perer, A.: Search, show context, expand on demand: supporting large graph exploration with degree-of-interest. IEEE Trans. Vis. Comput. Graph. **15**, 953–960 (2009)
24. Ware, C.: Information Vizualization: Perception for Design. Elsevier, Amsterdam (2004)
25. Yi, J.S., ah Kang, Y., Stasko, J.T., Jacko, J.A.: Toward a deeper understanding of the role of interaction in information visualization. IEEE Trans. Vis. Comput. Graph. **13**, 1224–1231 (2007)

Trademark Image Similarity Search

Girish Showkatramani, Sashi Nareddi, Chris Doninger, Greg Gabel, and Arthi Krishna(✉)

United States Patent and Trademark Office, Alexandria, VA, USA
{Girish.Showkatramani,Sashi.Nareddi,Chris.Doninger, Greg.Gabel,Arthi.Krishna}@uspto.gov

Abstract. A trademark may be a word, phrase, symbol, sound, color, scent or design, or a combination of these, that identifies and distinguishes the products or services of a particular source from those of others. One of the crucial steps both prior to filing of the trademark applications as well as during the review of these applications is conducting a thorough trademark search to determine whether the proposed mark is likely to cause confusion with prior registered trademarks and pending trademark applications. Currently, the trademark applicants or their representatives and examining attorneys manually search the United States Patent and Trademark Office (USPTO) database that contains all of the active and inactive trademark registrations and applications. This search process relies on words and Trademark Design codes (which are hand annotated labels of design features) to search for images, thereby limiting the overall search process to primarily text-based search. For marks having image characteristics, users visually look at the image and other design characteristics and compare it with existing registered or pending trademarks to determine its uniqueness. Overall, the process of exhaustively looking at all the images that are categorized using a specific design code, while comprehensive, may take a substantial amount of time.

Recently, Convolutional Networks (CNNs) have revolutionized the field of computer vision and demonstrated excellent performance in image classification and feature extraction. In this study, we utilize CNN to address the problem of searching trademarks similar to a chosen mark based on the image characteristics. A corpus of trademark images are pre-processed and then passed through a trained neural network to extract the image features. We then use these features to perform image search using the approximate nearest neighbor (ANN) variant of the nearest neighbor search (NNS) algorithm as depicted in Fig. 2. NNS is a form of proximity search that aims to find closest (or most similar) data points/items from a collection of data points/items.

This system thereby seeks to provide an efficient image-based search alternate to the current keyword and category of design code combination of searching.

Keywords: Approximate nearest neighbors · CBIR · Deep learning LIRE · Solr · Trademark image search

C. Stephanidis (Ed.): HCII Posters 2018, CCIS 850, pp. 199–205, 2018.
https://doi.org/10.1007/978-3-319-92270-6_27

1 Introduction

A trademark may be a recognizable word, phrase, symbol, sound, color, scent or design, or a combination of these, that identifies products or services of an individual, an organization or a particular source from those of others. The two primary purposes of a trademark are to: (1) protect brand names and logos used on goods and services and give the trademark owner the exclusive right to use the mark; and (2) act as a source indicator for consumers to ensure that the products and services they utilize under particular brands emanate from the sources that they expect [1]. Selecting a mark is the first step in the overall trademark application/registration process. One of the key factors in choosing a mark and filing it for registration is determining whether a "likelihood of confusion" [2] exists with the mark that is being filed or anything that has already been registered or filed. USPTO examines every trademark application for compliance with federal rules and laws and grants registrations when, among a host of other factors, no likelihood of confusion exists. In fact, "likelihood of confusion" between the mark that is being filed and a mark already registered or in a pending application, is the most common reason for refusal of a trademark application. Therefore, before the trademark filing process, each trademark applicant is strongly encouraged, though not required, to conduct a thorough trademark search to determine whether the proposed mark is likely to cause confusion with any existing registered trademarks or pending trademark applications [1].

Currently, the trademark applicants, and/or their attorneys and representatives, manually search the USPTO's database of active and inactive trademark registrations and applications using the Trademark Electronic Search System (TESS) search engine. This search engine provides access to crucial information such as text and images of registered marks, and marks in pending and abandoned applications. During this search phase, trademark applicants, or their attorneys or representatives, visually identify and determine whether there are any same or similar marks for related goods and/or services that have already registered or are pending. Furthermore, a thorough study of each mark is required to determine that the goods and services are not related [1]. In addition, once the trademark application has been filed, it is forwarded to a trademark-examining attorney for legal review. During the review phase, the USPTO examining attorneys also manually search existing USPTO records of registered trademarks and prior pending applications to determine potential likelihood of confusion using the USPTO search system (known as X-search, which utilizes the same database as TESS, though the interface differs). Overall, the process of manually researching and identifying marks with similar text and image characteristics is a complex task that often takes a substantial amount of time.

Recently, Content-Based Image Retrieval (CBIR) systems have led to advancement in image retrieval and recognition methods by finding and retrieving images independent from the metadata. In CBIR, image global and local low-level features are extracted by their visual content such as shape, texture, and color or any other information that can be derived from the image itself. Similarly, Convolutional Networks (CNNs) [3] have achieved great success in the field of computer vision and demonstrated excellent performance in large-scale image classification [4] and object detection [5]. Moreover, in the last few years, CNNs have emerged as a methodology in extracting features [6, 7] such as basic shapes, textures, and colors etc. from the unlabeled data. Most notably, a significant advancement in the deep learning-based methods has been seen after Krizhevsky et al. [8] achieved the first place on the ILSVRC 2012 challenge using a CNN model that achieved top 1 and top 5 error rates of 37.5% and 17.5%. This has been made possible due to the rapid growth in the amount of annotated data [9], powerful graphic processing units (GPUs) [10] and advancements in computing architecture. Additionally, in the last few years, the depth of CNNs has advanced greatly from 8 layers (AlexNet) [8] to 19 layers (VGGNet) [4], 22 layers (GoogleNet) [11], and even 152 layers (ResNet) [12], improving the overall classification accuracy. Furthermore, numerous deep learning libraries and platforms such as TensorFlow [13], Theano [14], Caffe [15], Torch [16], Computational Network Toolkit [17] etc. have been developed and made available in the open source platform, enabling further research in simplifying the complexity of deep neural networks.

In this paper, we address the problem of searching trademarks similar to a chosen mark using a neural network pre-trained on the trademark dataset. TensorFlow-Slim high level neural network API library was firstly used to extract the image features from the pre-trained Inception-ResNet-v2 [18] neural network. The approximate nearest neighbor algorithm was then used to identify the "nearest neighbors", that is, trademarks similar to the input mark.

Fig. 1. Example images from USPTO trademark dataset.

2 Approaches

2.1 Content Based Image Retrieval Approach

Lucene Image Retrieval (LIRE) [21], an open source Java library was used for extracting the global and local features of the downloaded trademark images. The global features that were extracted include: Joint Color Descriptor (JCD), Pyramid Histogram of Oriented Gradients (PHOG), MPEG-7 descriptors scalable color, Color and edge directivity descriptor (CEDD) and Fuzzy color and texture histogram (FCTH). Besides this, local features were extracted based on the OpenCV implementations of SIFT and SURF. The extracted global and local image features were then stored in a Lucene index for later retrieval. For identifying similar images, LIRE either took the input query feature or extracted the feature from the input image. A linear search is then performed by reading the images from the stored Lucene index sequentially and comparing them with the input image to return a ranked order list of the best matching n candidates.

2.2 CNN Based Image Search

A total of 100,000 trademark images in Fig. 1 were downloaded from the USPTO database. The image features were then extracted by passing the images through the neural network that was pre-trained on the trademark dataset. These extracted features were used to perform image searching using the approximate nearest neighbor (ANN) variant of the nearest neighbor search (NNS) algorithm. Nearest neighbor search (NNS) is a form of proximity search that computes the distances from the query point to every single point in the target dataset and returns the data points that are closest to the query point. This technique has been successfully applied in numerous fields of applications, such as computer vision, pattern recognition, and content-based image retrieval, to name a few.

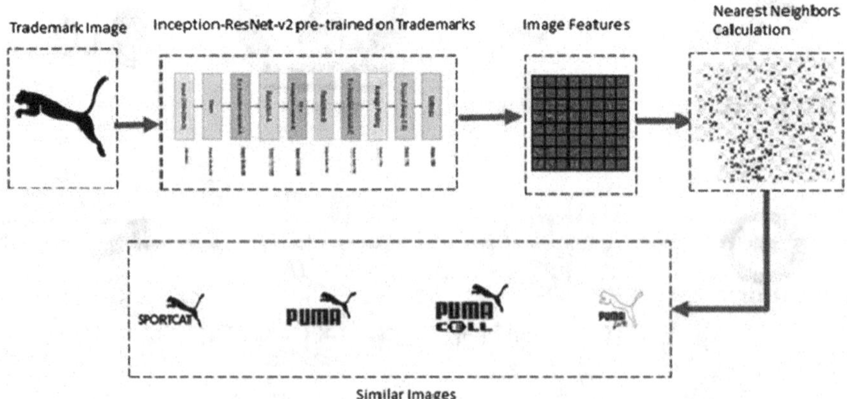

Fig. 2. Image search using CNN and NNS.

For image search feature, Approximate Nearest Neighbor Oh Yeah (ANNOY) [19] and NearPy [20] libraries, were used for identifying the nearest neighbors. Each image of the trademark dataset was passed through the trained ResNet-v2 neural network as depicted in Fig. 2 to extract the intermediate representation (feature vector) of the image. These image vectors were then saved in a binary format and used to search and identify the nearest neighbors. Finally, the cosine distance between the image and the nearest neighbors was computed and then the nearest neighbors were sorted by distance to return the top K nearest neighbors.

3 Infrastructure

Amazon Web Services (AWS) cloud infrastructure and Docker [22] were utilized for performing trademark image search. AWS m4.16xlarge (64 Core Intel Xeon E5-2676 v3 Haswell processor and 256 GB DDR3 RAM) spot instance was utilized for extracting image features and then identifying the nearest neighbors of the input mark. For the machine learning approach, AWS EC2 spot instances were chosen since they have an advantage of providing surplus of computing resource at a lower price compared to the on-demand instance price. Also, Docker light weight containers were configured to ease the configuration and setup of the TensorFlow framework.

4 Results

Using a simplistic test data set (trademark variation of images from the same owner), we were able to validate the results of CNN image search approach. The test proved Mean Average Precision (MAP) score of 0.69. This sample set of comparing variations of say Puma® variations though a good starting point is not close to the complexity of the test case faced by a trademark examining attorney. We are currently in the process of obtaining a more realistic test data set curated by Trademark experts, and plan to pursue testing those (Fig. 3).

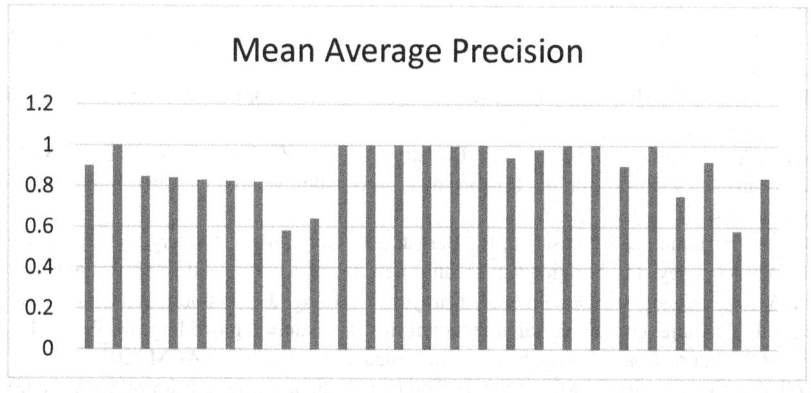

Fig. 3. MAP scores of CNN image search.

5 Conclusion

The current mechanism of searching Trademarks that depends on meta-tags such as trademark design codes, while still being the more comprehensive method of searching for likelihood of confusion in trademark images, is time consuming. By taking advantage of recent advances in Convolutional Networks (CNNs), we have been able to provide an alternate way to search for Trademarks based on image.

References

1. Patent Office Department of Commerce: Trademark Manual of Examining Procedure (TMEP). Department of Commerce, Patent and Trademark Office, Washington, D.C. (1974)
2. Bartow, A.: Likelihood of confusion. San Diego Law Rev. **41** (2004)
3. LeCun, Y., Bengio, Y., Hinton, G.: Deep learning. Nature **521**, 436–444 (2015)
4. Simonyan, K., Zisserman, A.: Very deep convolutional networks for large-scale image recognition (2014)
5. Girshick, R., Donahue, J., Darrell, T., Malik, J.: Rich feature hierarchies for accurate object detection and semantic segmentation. In: Proceedings of the Conference on Computer Vision and Pattern Recognition, pp. 580–587 (2014)
6. Zeiler, M.D., Fergus, R.: Visualizing and understanding convolutional networks. In: Fleet, D., Pajdla, T., Schiele, B., Tuytelaars, T. (eds.) ECCV 2014. LNCS, vol. 8689, pp. 818–833. Springer, Cham (2014). https://doi.org/10.1007/978-3-319-10590-1_53
7. Donahue, J., Jia, Y., Vinyals, O., Hoffman, J., Zhang, N., Tzeng, E., Darrell, T.: DeCAF: a deep convolutional activation feature for generic visual recognition. In: International Conference in Machine Learning (2014)
8. Krizhevsky, A., Sutskever, I., Hinton, G.: Imagenet classification with deep convolutional neural networks. In: Advances in Neural Information Processing Systems, vol. 25, pp. 1106–1114 (2012)
9. Deng, J., Dong, W., Socher, R., Li, L.J., Li, K., Fei-Fei, L.: ImageNet: a large-scale hierarchical image database. In: IEEE Conference on Computer Vision and Pattern Recognition, pp. 248–255. IEEE (2009)
10. Dean, J., Corrado, G., Monga, R., Chen, K., Devin, M., Mao, M., Ranzato, M., Senior, A., Tucker, P., Yang, K., Le, Q.V., Ng, A.Y.: Large scale distributed deep networks. In: NIPS, pp. 1232–1240 (2012)
11. Szegedy, C., Liu, W., Jia, Y., Sermanet, P.: Going deeper with convolutions. In: CVPR, pp. 1–9 (2015)
12. He, K., Zhang, X., Ren, S., Sun, J.: Deep residual learning for image recognition. In: CVPR, pp. 770–778 (2016)
13. Abadi, M., Agarwal, A., Barham, P., Brevdo, E., Chen, Z., Citro, C., Corrado, G.S., Davis, A., Dean, J., Devin, M., et al.: TensorFlow: large-scale machine learning on heterogeneous systems (2015)
14. Bastien, F., Lamblin, P., Pascanu, R., Bergstra, J., Goodfellow, I., Bergeron, A., Bouchard, N., Warde-Farley, D., Bengio, Y.: Theano: new features and speed improvements (2012)
15. Jia, Y., Shelhamer, E., Donahue, J., Karayev, S., Long, J., Girshick, R., Guadarrama, S., Darrell, T.: Caffe: convolutional architecture for fast feature embedding. In: Proceedings of the ACM International Conference on Multimedia, pp. 675–678. ACM (2014)
16. Collobert, R., Bengio, S., Mariéthoz, J.: Torch: a modular machine learning software library. Technical report IDIAP-RR 02-46, IDIAP (2002)

17. Agarwal, A., Akchurin, E., Basoglu, C., Chen, G., Cyphers, S., Droppo, J., Eversole, A., Guenter, B., Hillebrand, M., Hoens, R., Huang, X., Huang, Z., Ivanov, V., Kamenev, A., Kranen, P., Kuchaiev, O., Manousek, W., May, A., Mitra, B., Nano, O., Navarro, G., Orlov, A., Padmilac, M., Parthasarathi, H., Peng, B., Reznichenko, A., Seide, F., Seltzer, M.L., Slaney, M., Stolcke, A., Wang, Y., Wang, H., Yao, K., Yu, D., Zhang, Y., Zweig, G.: An introduction to computational networks and the computational network toolkit. Technical report MSR-TR-2014-112, August 2014. https://github.com/Microsoft/CNTK
18. Szegedy, C., et al.: Inception-v4, Inception-ResNet and the impact of residual connections on learning (2016)
19. Spotify, Annoy. https://github.com/spotify/annoy
20. NearPy. https://github.com/pixelogik/NearPy
21. Lux, M., Chatzichristofis, S.A.: LIRE: lucene image retrieval: an extensible Java CBIR library. In: ACM Multimedia (2008)
22. Merkel, D.: Docker: lightweight linux containers for consistent development and deployment. Linux J. **2014**(239), 2 (2014)

User-Based Error Verification Method of Laser Beam Homogenizer

Jee Ho Song[1], Han Sol Shin[1], Tae Jun Yu[2], and Kun Lee[3(✉)]

[1] Department of Information and Communication, Handong Global University, Pohang, Republic of Korea

[2] Department of Advanced Green Energy and Environment, Handong Global University, Pohang, Republic of Korea

[3] School of Computer Science and Electronic Engineering, Handong Global University, Pohang, Republic of Korea

kunlee@handong.edu

Abstract. In the laser homogenization experiment, there is a difference between the output from the pre-design and the output from the actual experiment. This is because, apart from the design mistake, the mistake of some lens placement during the lens assembly process greatly affects the final result. Unless there is a way to automate the alignment of all the lenses from the beginning, the only way to find and fix these errors is to re-arrange all the lenses. In this paper, we propose a new error verification method. To accomplish this, we first store all the output that can occur due to the change of the lens arrangement during the simulation process, and then use the machine learning to connect the relationship between the output images obtained from the actual experiment and the previously obtained data.

Keywords: Laser physics · Laser intensity · Data analysis · Contour Machine learning

1 Introduction

The laser is amplified by inductive emission and is used in various applications such as energy, new materials, semiconductors, and medical care required in the 21st century. In order to obtain a high output laser, Handong Intense Laser Lab (HILL) is studying to make the beam bundle into a rectangular parallelepiped shape (Fig. 1) for even energy distribution of the medium [1–3].

For Laser Beam Homogenizing experiment, several mirrors and lenses are used. However, unlike the mathematical approach, the results obtained through actual experiments are often different from those expected. The reason is that the laser, also referred to as the light, has the property which allows it to easily interfere with the surrounding environment. In this study, we propose a method to help the error verification and adjustment of experimental setup based on the case when the adjustment of each module (mirror, lens, etc.) is wrong. To do this, we try to learn the output images based on the parameters of the module through the deep learning algorithm and find out which output image of the experiment matches with the image using the parameters.

C. Stephanidis (Ed.): HCII Posters 2018, CCIS 850, pp. 206–210, 2018.
https://doi.org/10.1007/978-3-319-92270-6_28

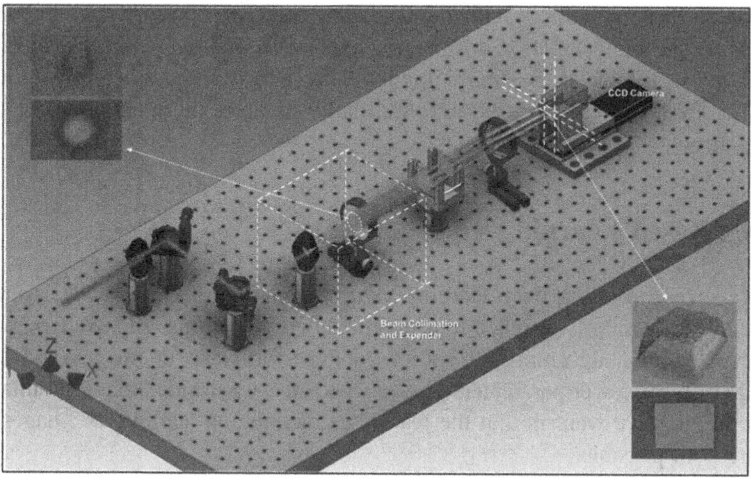

Fig. 1. Experimental setup for Laser Beam Homogenizing (HILL, 2017, used with permission).

2 Problem Description

As mentioned above, there are several parameters (focal length, mirror angle and so on) that are required for experimental setup for homogenizing. Figure 2(a) and (c) show the result when the focal length of the lens is different, and the remaining parameters are the same. And, (a) and (b) use the same focal length (F_C) lens but different position of CCD camera for image sensing.

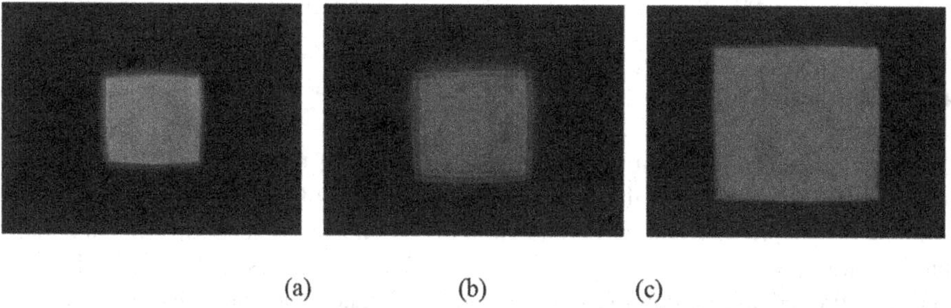

(a) (b) (c)

Fig. 2. Outputs with different parameters: (a) F_C = 32 mm, CCD = 0 mm, (b) F_C = 32 mm, CCD = −20 mm, (c) F_C = 60 mm, CCD = 0 mm

As can be seen from the results, some of the changes in some parameters result in different overall results. In particular, the parameters used in the experiments are the position and angle values of each module (two mirrors and four lenses, one lens array, and CCD) as shown again in Fig. 1. However, in order to adjust a total of 16 parameters, it must pass through the human hand. There are other ways to tune through the machine, but the installation cost is very expensive, and the possibility of machine failure is not negligible. It is almost impossible to adjust 16 parameters without mistakes. Therefore, we will study how to find faulty modules on the contrary, assuming there are errors.

3 CNN-Based Learning

There are several existing deep learning algorithms. Among them, CNN is the most widely known algorithm, designed to use minimal preprocessing (Fig. 3). Compared to other deep learning algorithms, it shows good performance in images and has the advantage of using fewer parameters [4–9]. Especially, we decided that it is suitable for the direction that we want in that the feature extraction and learning of images in the image are both possible.

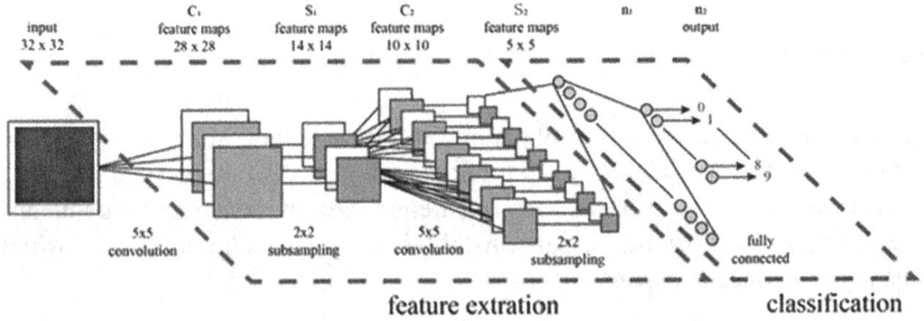

Fig. 3. Convolution neural network architecture model.

4 Proposed System

Using the advantage of identifying the partial features of CNN, we want to learn the output image to which the value applies in various cases of the parameters used in the simulation. The proposed system is shown in Fig. 4. Images to be learned include those that are not properly homogenized. Classification of images will be possible by characterizing edges and color (energy magnitude) related parts as shown in Fig. 5. At the end of the learning, we use the images obtained from the actual experiment as a training data set and derive the parameters of the matched learned image. Based on this parameter, we can expect the current state of the parameters of the modules used in the actual experiment. 1-layer and 2-layer of neural network for Laser Beam Homogenizer are shown in Figs. 6 and 7, respectively.

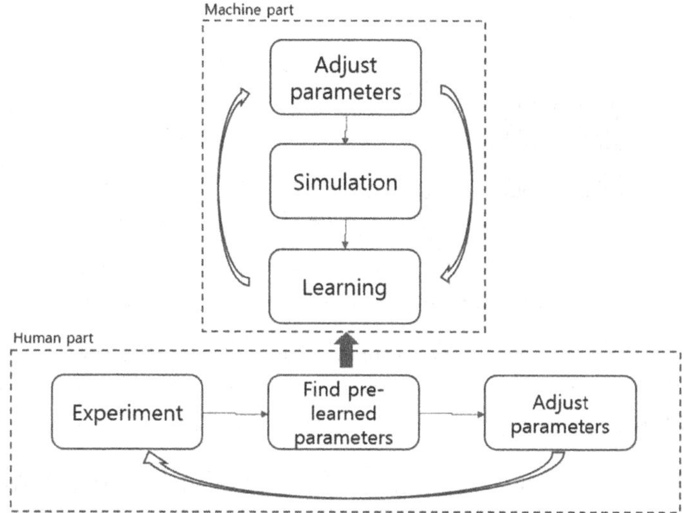

Fig. 4. Proposed method.

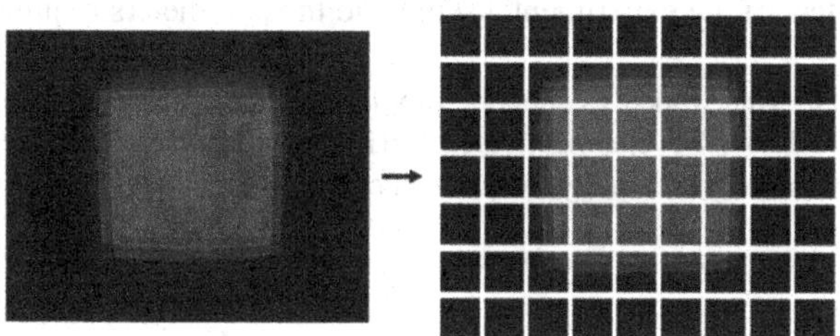

Fig. 5. Partial features of the image. (Color figure online)

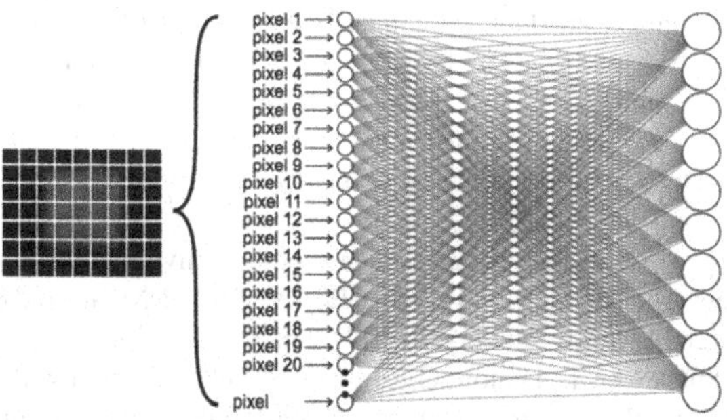

Fig. 6. 1-layer neural network for Laser Beam Homogenizer

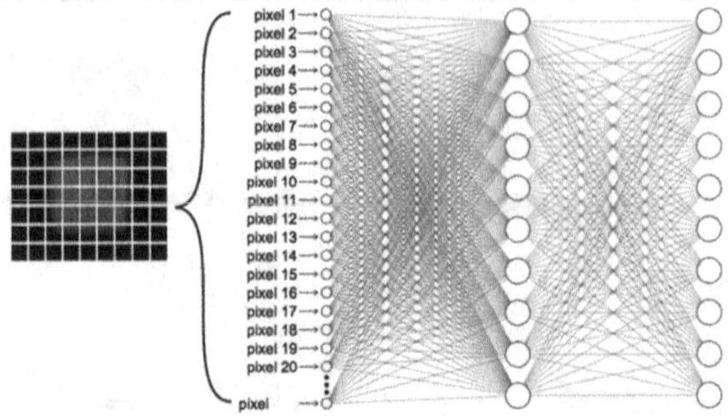

Fig. 7. 2-layer neural network for Laser Beam Homogenizer

5 Conclusion

In experiments involving human beings, the existence of errors is natural. We consider these errors as one piece of information and want to learn human error through CNN. Based on the proposed method, we use simulation images including errors as test data, and try to find error modules by seeding the images obtained through actual experiments. In future work, we will implement this method and provide a guide for the interaction between parameters of the experimental setup and the parameters required by the users.

Acknowledgments. This work was supported by the Industrial Strategic technology development program, 10048964, Development of 125 J•Hz laser system for laser peering funded by Ministry of Trade, Industry & Energy (MI, republic of Korea).

References

1. Hwang, S., et al.: Design of square-shaped beam homogenizer for petawatt-class Ti: sapphire amplifier. Opt. Express **25**(9), 9511–9520 (2017)
2. Kim, T., et al.: Numerical analysis of working distance of square-shaped beam homogenizer for laser shock peening. Curr. Opt. Photonics **1**(3), 221–227 (2017)
3. Kim, T., et al.: Analysis of the square beam energy efficiency of a homogenizer near the target for laser shock peening. J. Opt. Soc. Korea **20**(3), 407–412 (2016)
4. LeCun, Y., Bengio, Y., Hinton, G.: Deep learning. Nature **521**(7553), 436 (2015)
5. Schmidhuber, J.: Deep learning in neural networks: an overview. Neural Netw. **61**, 85–117 (2015)
6. Zeiler, M.D., Fergus, R.: Visualizing and understanding convolutional networks. In: Fleet, D., Pajdla, T., Schiele, B., Tuytelaars, T. (eds.) ECCV 2014. LNCS, vol. 8689, pp. 818–833. Springer, Cham (2014). https://doi.org/10.1007/978-3-319-10590-1_53
7. Krizhevsky, A., Sutskever, I., Hinton, G.E.: ImageNet classification with deep convolutional neural networks. In: Advances in Neural Information Processing Systems (2012)
8. Oquab, M., et al.: Learning and transferring mid-level image representations using convolutional neural networks. In: 2014 IEEE Conference on Computer Vision and Pattern Recognition, CVPR. IEEE (2014)
9. Provost, F.: Machine learning from imbalanced data sets 101. In: Proceedings of the AAAI 2000 Workshop on Imbalanced Data Sets (2000)

Conversion of Player Locations from Football Goal Scene Videos to a 2D Top View

Kazuma Tomikawa and Ryosuke Saga(✉)

Graduate School of Humanities and Sustainable System Sciences, Osaka Prefecture University, 1-1, Gakuencho, Naka-ku Sakai-shi, Osaka, Japan
sya01178@edu.osakafu-u.ac.jp, saga@cs.osakafu-u.ac.jp

Abstract. This paper describes a new process of generating a top view figure from football game videos that shows the positions of players to facilitate an efficient game analysis. At present, the top view figure is often created manually at the practical level and requires much time, thereby highlighting the need to automate the creation of this figure. In the proposed process, the top view figure is created in four steps. First, lines are detected from binarized images to recognize the area in front of the goal. Second, by using the recognized area and the predefined image of the football field, a projective transformation matrix is calculated to transform the point of view. Third, the players are extracted from the image by using the selective search method, while the sides of these players is determined based on their color information. The camera movement must also be detected in each frame and its influence must be ignored by tracking the feature points of the audiences' seats. Fourth, considering the player information, the projective transformation matrix, and the camera movement, the top view figures are created by calculating the actual positions of players. Although the experiment results show few problems, we have successfully created top view figures for all frames in the selected football game video.

Keywords: Video content analysis · Football videos · Field line detection Object detection

1 Introduction

Data analysis has become very important in sports over the recent years. In any sport, top-level teams collect information about their opponents and analyze their tactics.

In football, a relatively large amount of information needs to be handled. Meanwhile, in baseball and volleyball, the position of players needs to be determined. Although determining the position of players may also be necessary in other sports such as football, basketball, and hockey, the players in these sports often move away from their original positions. Player arrangement is more important in sports with fluid player arrangements, such as basketball and football, than in sports with non-fluid player arrangements, such as baseball and volleyball. Among these sports, given that football has the largest number of players playing at the same time, this sport contains plenty of information available for analysis. Therefore, football is suitable for the data analysis.

C. Stephanidis (Ed.): HCII Posters 2018, CCIS 850, pp. 211–218, 2018.
https://doi.org/10.1007/978-3-319-92270-6_29

Fig. 1. Comparing an image and top view figure of a football game

Table 1. Comparison of related works

	Mackowiak et al. [1]	Zhang [2]	Xu et al. [3]	Our method
Field detection	○	○	×	○
Player detection	○	×	○	○
Number of cameras	1	1	8	1
Line detection method	Hough transformation	Hough transformation	Hough transformation	Own method

However, the data for analysis are usually collected manually at the practical level. Football managers often spend much time watching videos of their opponent's previous matches. Given that football contains a large amount of information, this sport has a high demand for automated data collection.

Player arrangement is among the most important elements in football videos, but one cannot easily determine the accurate placement of each player from a video that is recorded diagonally from above as shown in the left side of Fig. 1. Therefore, by creating a top view figure as shown in the right side of Fig. 1, we can clearly study player arrangement and subsequently facilitate the data analysis. However, given the difficulty of creating such top view figure manually from the video, automating the top view figure creation process is important.

Given that the goal is the most important factor in a football game, this research uses a football video, especially a video of players scoring a goal, as its target.

2 Related Work

Football video analysis has been examined in several studies as summarized in Table 1. Maćkowiak et al. [1] proposed a method for detecting the field and the players from a football video. Zhang [2] conducted a field detection procedure yet failed to recognize the players. Xu et al. [3] proposed a method for tracking players in a video by using multiple cameras. The efficiency of the analysis can be improved by detecting the players in a video by using a single camera.

Similar to the aforementioned works, this study applies Hough transformation [4] for line detection. Although Hough transformation is generally applied for line segment detection, this method can detect many short line segments, thereby necessitating an additional clustering procedure. However, such additional procedure may reduce the accuracy of the entire line detection process.

3 Process Overview

The process of creating a top view figure from a football video is illustrated in Fig. 2. The main operations involved in this process include field detection, player detection, and camera movement detection.

An image that shows the penalty area (the area in front of the goal) must be used as a frame for field detection. Given that a video with a scoring scene always presents a view of the penalty area in its end, the last frame of this video is extracted as a processing image.

3.1 Field Detection

Detecting the field location is necessary to find the actual position of players. The field location is usually detected based on field lines, which are often located by using a binarized image that presents a view of the field (in white) and the field lines (in black). Instead of using Hough transformation, this work proposes a new line detection process for the same reasons stated above. First, two points on the edge of the image are chosen and connected to make a line. If many black pixels are present, then we deduce a field line on this line. Afterward, we detect the end point of this line by cutting out the portion with a large amount of black pixels, and then we create a line segment. This process of combining all possible two points can detect all line segments in an image. Based on their inclination, we can classify these lines into those lines parallel to (under the goal) and vertical to the goal line. The noises in these lines are ignored.

Four line segments constitute the penalty area even though other line segments are also detected. Another area, labelled as goal area, is located inside the penalty area, and the other detected line segments are considered part of this area. Therefore, we can choose four line segments for the penalty area by considering their attributes, such as their segments. By calculating the intersection of each line segment, four vertices of the penalty area are detected and used for the projective transformation matrix. The location of each area and line is shown in Fig. 2.

3.2 Creating a Projective Transformation Matrix

Projective transformation is a technique of transforming a certain point (x, y) to another point (u, v) based on the formula (1). A projective transformation matrix is included in this equation as a transformation coefficient. Given that this matrix contains eight unknown variables, these unknown variables are obtained by defining four couples of points and substituting them into the equation as well as by solving an eight-dimensional simultaneous linear equation. By determining the four vertices of the penalty area in football image as the four points before the conversion and by determining the four vertices of the penalty area in the predefined field image (the yellow points in Fig. 2) as the four points after the conversion, a matrix for transforming the coordinates on the image into the coordinates in the football field is acquired.

$$\begin{pmatrix} u \\ v \\ 1 \end{pmatrix} = \begin{pmatrix} a & b & c \\ d & e & f \\ g & h & 1 \end{pmatrix} \begin{pmatrix} x \\ y \\ 1 \end{pmatrix} \tag{1}$$

3.3 Camera Movement Detection

To recognize camera work, the movement of the audience seat's feature points is tracked. We use good features to track and extract these feature points [5], and then we use optical flow to track the motion of the input feature points based on the color information between two images and return the coordinates of these points after movement. The concept of optical flow was introduced by Gibson in the 1940s [6]. Through this procedure, we can determine how much the camera has moved from the beginning in each frame.

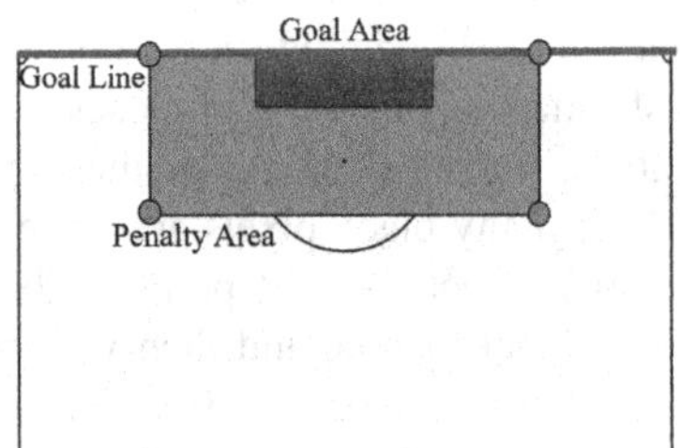

Fig. 2. Predefined simple football field image (Color figure online)

3.4 Player Detection

Our player detection module is based on selective search [7]. We output rectangular player regions by applying this module on every frame of the video. We set the middle point of the lower edge of the rectangle as the position coordinate of the region.

3.5 Top View Figure Creation

By considering the coordinate of players in an image, the projective transformation matrix, and the camera movement, the real position of each player is calculated in each frame. We treat two players that are located in the same position in two consecutive frames as the same player. However, some players were left undetected in this process. Therefore, when comparing three consecutive frames, if a player takes the same position in the first and third frames yet moves to another position in the second frame, then we treat this player as a missing player and complement it in the second frame.

The color of the pixel at the center of the object region of each player is saved as the kit color of each player and used to identify the team of each player. We calculate the kit color value of two same players by averaging their color values. Afterward, we treat two different players with similar kit colors as belonging to the same team. For each team, we average the RGB values of the belonging players and calculate the team color. We draw circles on the position of each player in his/her team color to create the top view figures.

4 Experiment and Evaluation

This experiment used part of a footage taken during the UEFA Champions League 2016/2017 final match between Juventus and Real Madrid. We specifically used the scene where Real Madrid scored the first goal 20 min into the game. The video contained 148 frames within 4 s and 15 players, including 7 Juventus players (in white kit), 6 Real Madrid players (purple), 1 Juventus goalie (yellow), and 1 referee (blue).

We created top view figures following the process described in Sect. 3 and measured accuracy based on three points. The first point is the player detection rate. We counted the detected players in the created figures and the players that were shown in each frame of the video before calculating the overall detection rate. The second point is the accuracy of camera work correction, which we measured by creating images that are shifted by the value of camera work correction for each frame. We chose one feature point in the audience seat and manually examined its movement. If the camera work correction is completely accurate, then the movement must be zero in all frames. Third, we checked whether the side of players was identified correctly. We set the answer data as shown in Table 2 and judged the team of each player comparing with this.

Table 2. Each team's kit color

Team	Kit color (value of RGB)
Juventus	(255, 255, 255)
Real Madrid	(93, 0, 255)
Juventus (goalie)	(255, 255, 0)
Referee	(0, 60, 255)

We eventually created top view figures in all 148 frames of the video. Figure 3 shows the last frame of the video and the corresponding figure, Fig. 4 shows the player detection results for each frame, and Fig. 5 shows the error value of camera movement correction for each frame. Table 3 shows the identification results for the teams of each player. Numbers 0 to 147 are assigned to all frames to distinguish them from one another.

Fig. 3. Frame no. 147 and the top view figure

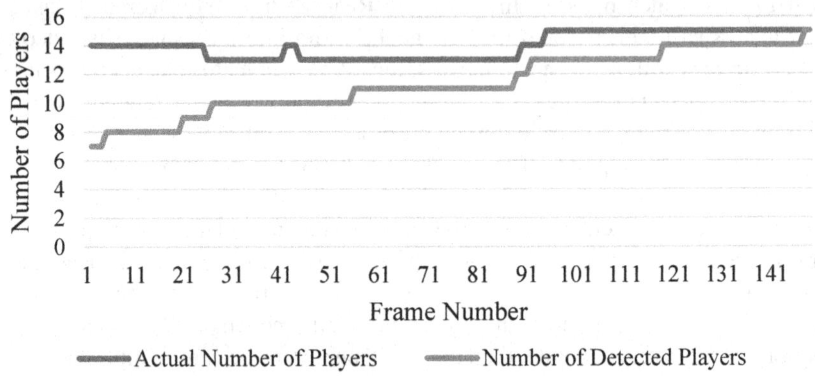

Fig. 4. Result of player detection for each frame

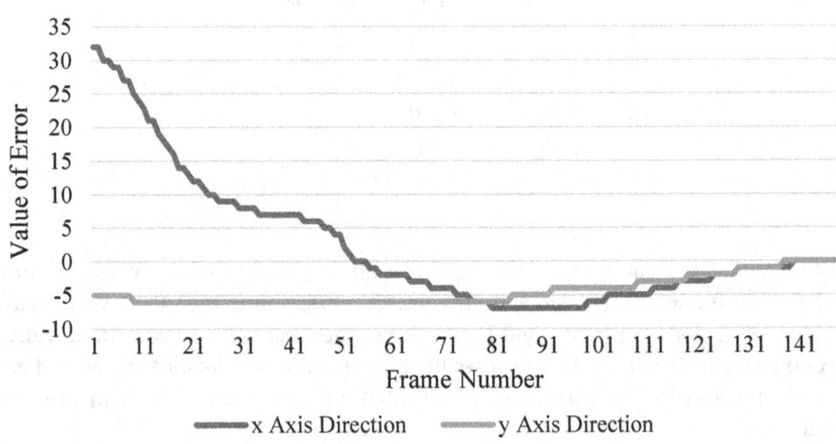

Fig. 5. Error of camera movement correction for each frame

Table 3. Result of identification of each player's team

Player no.	Actual team	Result of identification
1	Real Madrid	Real Madrid
2	Juventus	Juventus
3	Juventus	Juventus
4	Juventus goalie	Juventus goalie
5	Referee	Referee
6	Real Madrid	Real Madrid
7	Juventus	Juventus
8	Juventus	Referee
9	Juventus	Real Madrid
10	Real Madrid	Real Madrid
11	Real Madrid	Real Madrid
12	Real Madrid	Real Madrid
13	Real Madrid	Real Madrid
14	Juventus	Juventus
15	Juventus	Juventus

All frames had a total of 2066 players, among which 1643 were detected correctly. The player detection rate was approximately 79.5%. The detection failure was mainly attributed to two factors. First, two or more players were counted as one when they overlapped in the screen. In our method, a single player was treated as one player in all subsequent frames, thereby reducing the detection failure rate. Second, we tried to complement an undetected player but failed to do so in all cases. If a player could not be detected at the time of using selective search in a certain frame and if this player was not detected in any preceding or succeeding frames, then we could not complement this player.

For the camera work correction, we found errors of 6 and 32 pixels in the x and y axes at maximum. If the camera movement speed increases, then distortion occurs in the feature points and its color and shape might change, thereby increasing the difficulty of tracking these points.

As shown in Table 3, 2 out of the 15 teams in the video were misidentified. The average RGB value approaches gray, thereby reducing the clear color difference. We also used the color of the center point of each object area as the kit color of each player even though this color is uncertain. To improve accuracy, a highly reliable information must be obtained.

5 Conclusion

The efficiency of the football data collection must be enhanced. In this paper, we aimed to automate the procedure of generating top view figures from a football video to clearly detect the arrangement of players. First, we recognized the players and the field from the frame images. Second, we detected lines from the binarized image by considering color information and used selective search as our player detection method. Third, we calculated the actual position of players based on the camera movement. Fourth, we recognized the camera movement by tracking the feature points in the audience's seats. To calculate the actual position of players, we used a projective transformation matrix. Although some accuracy problems were found in our results, the experiment successfully generated top view figures in each frame.

References

1. Maćkowiak, S., Konieczny, J., Kurc, M., Maćkowiak, P.: Football player detection in video broadcast. In: Bolc, L., Tadeusiewicz, R., Chmielewski, L.J., Wojciechowski, K. (eds.) ICCVG 2010. LNCS, vol. 6375, pp. 118–125. Springer, Heidelberg (2010). https://doi.org/10.1007/978-3-642-15907-7_15
2. Zhang, S.: Research on detection of field lines in soccer videos. Adv. Sci. Technol. Lett. **75** (SIP 2014), 45–49 (2014)
3. Xu, M., Orwell, J., Jones, G.: Tracking football players with multiple cameras. In: Image Processing ICIP 2004, pp. 1–4 (2004)
4. Duda, R.O., Hart, P.E.: Use of the hough transformation to detect lines and curves in pictures. Commun. ACM **15**(1), 11–15 (1972)
5. Shi, J., Tomasi, C.: Good features to track. In: IEEE Conference on Computer Vision and Pattern Recognition (CVPR 1994), pp. 1–8 (1994)
6. Gibson, J.J.: The Perception of the Visual World. Houghton Mifflin Company, Boston (1950)
7. Uijlings, J.R.R., van de Sande, K.E.A., Gevers, T., Smeulders, A.W.M.: Selective search for object recognition. Int. J. Comput. Vis. **104**(2), 154–171 (2013)

Flux Extraction Based on General Regression Neural Network for Two-Dimensional Spectral Image

Zhen Wang, Qian Yin(✉), Ping Guo, and Xin Zheng

Image Processing and Pattern Recognition Laboratory,
Beijing Normal University, Beijing, China
wang_zhen@mail.bnu.edu.cn,
{yinqian, zhengxin}@bnu.edu.cn, pguo@ieee.org

Abstract. In this paper, one novel method to extract flux from two dimensional spectral images which we observed through LAMOST (Large Area Multi-Object Fiber Spectroscopic Telescope) is proposed. First of all, the spectral images are preprocessed. Then, in the flux extraction algorithm, the GRNN (General Regression Neural Network) and double Gaussian function are employed to simulate the profile of each spectrum in spatial orientation. We perform our experiment, with same radial basis function, by GRNN and RBFNN (Radial Basis Function Neural Network) method. The experimental results show that our method performs higher SNR (Signal Noise Ration) and lower time-consuming that is more applicable in such massive spectral data.

Keywords: LAMOST · GRNN · Flux extraction · Spectral data

1 Introduction

LAMOST, the abbreviation of Large Area Multi-Object Fiber Spectroscopic Telescope, has the ability to obtain 4000 targets data simultaneously in one observation. More about LAMOST has been described in references [1, 2]. The energy of the celestial targets transmitted through two different cameras [3] and then imaging onto the slit of each spectrograph, finally we obtain the spectra through shooting by CCD cameras.

There are a lot of processes while dealing with two-dimensional spectral images [4]. Flux extraction is one of the most essential procedures that highly affect the subsequent processing steps. The energy of each spectrum diffused not only in spatial direction but also diffused a little bit in wavelength one. Flux extraction is mainly to extract flux of different spectra at each pixel along these two directions.

Methods we now utilized in flux extraction are mainly divided into two kinds. They are flux extraction in one-dimensional (1D) and in two-dimensional (2D). Methods based on 2D [5, 6], such as profile fitting methods, that is to choose an appropriate function to simulate the profile of each spectrum in both spatial and wavelength direction. However, due to the changes of spectrum energy in the wavelength direction reflects the spectra information of the target objects. Therefore, flux extraction in the wavelength direction may break the structure and data integrity of spectrum information. Therefore, methods we applied in LAMOST now are still based on 1D data.

C. Stephanidis (Ed.): HCII Posters 2018, CCIS 850, pp. 219–226, 2018.
https://doi.org/10.1007/978-3-319-92270-6_30

The original method based on 1D is the aperture extraction method [7] that is to choose an appropriate aperture around each fiber center and then counts up all flux within the aperture along spatial direction. The method is simple and cost less time. However, the disadvantage is that it is strongly depends on the aperture size and it cannot solve cross-talk [8] with adjacent fibers. An optimal aperture method [9] then appeared to give different pixel a different weight. The method can improve the SNR (signal noise ration). However, it is also highly depending on the aperture parameter setting.

Another method is the profile fitting method [10], which is to choose an appropriate function, usually we choose Gaussian function to approximate the profile in spatial direction and then obtain each pixel corresponding flux through the function. The method can overcome the cross-talk problem. However, it also has a disadvantage. There are 250 spectra data in each spectra image, as for such massive spectra data, each fiber has a different profile function in different wavelength. Therefore, profile fitting method is time-consuming and it is not appropriate for LAMOST spectra data.

An improved approach is using RBF neural network [11] which is to choose Gaussian function as radial basis function to fit profiles. The method works well, however it cannot possess both a higher SNR and lower time consuming simultaneously.

In this paper, an improved method is proposed to extract spectra flux through GRNN (General Regression Neural Network), a frequent method to fit various non-linear functions. GRNN neural network is an improved RBF network with four layers. We compare our method with RBF one with same radial basis function and same parameters. The results show that the method we proposed in this paper not only possesses higher precision with higher signal-to-noise ratio but also cost less time.

The rest of the paper is organized as follows. The principle and architecture of GRNN is detailed in Sect. 2. The flux extraction algorithm is presented in Sect. 3. Experimental results and comparison are revealed in Sect. 4 and finally following a conclusion in Sect. 5.

2 The Principle and Architecture of GRNN

2.1 The Principle of GRNN

General Regression Neural Network is a commonly used method to do nonlinear fitting in recent years which is based on non-linear regression analysis [12]. GRNN has a strongly nonlinear mapping ability and fast learning speed. It does not need a weight training process, so it is faster than RBFNN which has a layer decision and a time-consuming training phase. In addition, GRNN has the ability to deal with unstable data.

We assume there are two randomly variables x and y, $f(x, y)$ represents the known joint continuous probability density function. The observed value of x is x_0. The probability density of y is given by the following:

$$E(y|x_0) = \frac{\int_{-\infty}^{+\infty} y f(x_0, y) dy}{\int_{-\infty}^{+\infty} f(x_0, y) dy} \tag{1}$$

$y(x_0)$ is the predicted output, however, the density function $f(x_0, y)$ usually is uncertain. According to non-parametric estimation, we estimate $f(x_0, y)$ with the sample sets $\{x_i, y_i\}_{i=1}^{n}$ through the following:

$$f(x_0, y) = \frac{1}{n(2\pi)^{\frac{p+1}{2}}\sigma^{p+1}} \sum_{i=1}^{n} e^{-d(x_{0,x_i})} e^{-d(y, y_i)} \tag{2}$$

$$d(x_{0,x_i}) = \sum_{j=1}^{p} [(x_{0j} - x_{ij})/\sigma]^2, d(y, y_i) = [y - y_i]^2 \tag{3}$$

Where p is the dimension of the variable x and n is the number of the observation samples, the final output is able to be calculated by:

$$y(x_0) = \frac{\sum_{i=1}^{n}(e^{-d(x_{0,x_i})} \int_{-\infty}^{+\infty} y_i e^{-d(y,y_i)} dy)}{\sum_{i=1}^{n}(e^{-d(x_{0,x_i})} \int_{-\infty}^{+\infty} e^{-d(y,y_i)} dy)} \tag{4}$$

$$y(x_0) = \frac{\sum_{i=1}^{n} y_i e^{-d(y,y_i)}}{\sum_{i=1}^{n} e^{-d(y,y_i)}} \tag{5}$$

2.2 The Architecture of GRNN

GRNN is a transformation of RBFNN [13] with four layers. The first one is an input layer, which represent the input spectra signal in this paper. The second one is the hidden layer, we also call radial basic layer, which is to choose an appropriate transfer function. There are lots of transfer functions and the commonly used one is Gaussian basis function. The third one is a summation layer and finally an output layer. The architecture of the network is shown in Fig. 1.

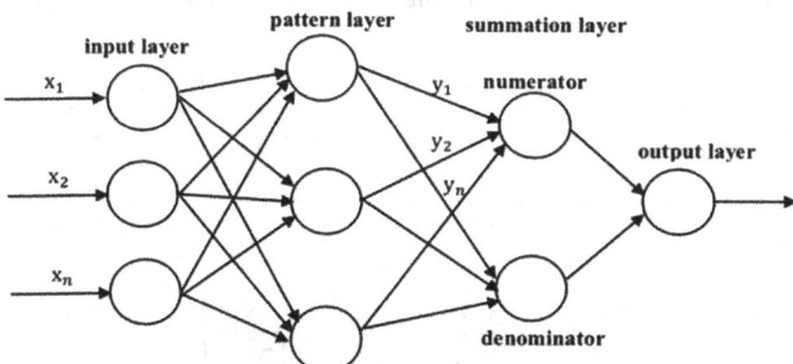

Fig. 1. The network architecture of GRNN.

3 Flux Extraction Algorithm

3.1 Preprocessing the Spectra

The spectral images we processed in this paper are flat field spectra images, as shown in Fig. 2. The vertical and the horizontal direction are the wavelength and spatial direction respectively. The spatial one is also the flux extraction direction. The flat images are preprocessed including bias subtraction and tracing fiber center [14].

Fig. 2. Part of an integrity flat image.

3.2 The Network Structure and Training Algorithm

As introduced above, there are 250 fiber spectra on each CCD image, so the 250 spectra data are the input data. The second step is to choose an appropriate radial basic function. In this paper, we use double Gaussian function [15] to extract flux and verify the feasibility of the algorithm. The double Gaussian function (DGF) is as follows:

$$G(x) = \frac{A}{\sqrt{2\pi}\sigma}\exp\left\{\frac{-(x - x_c - \Delta x)^2}{2\sigma^2}\right\} + \frac{A}{\sqrt{2\pi}\sigma}\exp\left\{\frac{-(x - x_c + \Delta x)^2}{2\sigma^2}\right\} \tag{6}$$

where

$$A = F_{peak} \cdot \frac{\sqrt{2\pi}\sigma}{2} \cdot \exp\left\{\frac{-(\Delta x)^2}{2\sigma^2}\right\}^{-1} \tag{7}$$

The two single Gaussian functions have the same amplitude A, x_c is the center of each fiber, Δx is the distance to the center x_c, σ is the variance of each fiber. F_{peak} represents the peak value of each spectra profile.

There are three parameters we need to determine which are x_c, Δx and σ. As mentioned above, x_c is a constant value for each profile. Therefore, the crucial step is to determine Δx and σ. Since in the single Gaussian function, the initial σ is 3.5 (depends on the FWHM). In this paper, we choose the initial value of Δx and σ both as 1.7. We use the following formula to adjust Δx and σ:

$$\mathrm{error}_{\mathrm{cen}} = \frac{F_{\mathrm{cen}} - G_{\mathrm{cen}}}{F_{\mathrm{cen}}} \mathrm{error}_{\mathrm{wing}} = \frac{F_{\mathrm{wing}} - G_{\mathrm{wing}}}{F_{\mathrm{wing}}} \tag{8}$$

$$\Delta x = \Delta x \cdot (1 + \mathrm{error}_{\mathrm{cen}}) \quad \sigma = \sigma \cdot \left(1 + \mathrm{error}_{\mathrm{wing}}\right) \tag{9}$$

where F_{cen} and G_{cen} are the actual flux around the center and the approximation, respectively. The two errors are used to adjust Δx and σ.

4 The Experimental Results and Analysis

In this section, we compare our method with aperture and RBFNN method, some of the flux extraction results are as shown in Figs. 3 and 4.

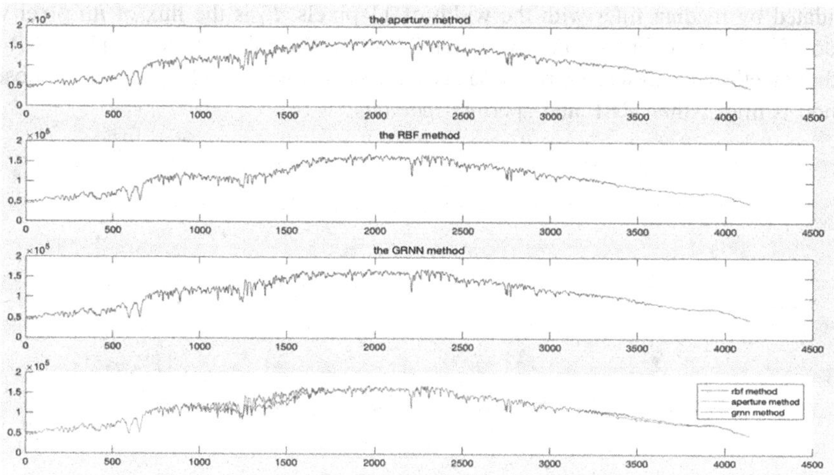

Fig. 3. The aperture, RBF and GRNN methods of results.

In order to verify the accuracy of our proposed method, we evaluate it through two different aspects: the signal noise ratio (SNR) and the time consumption. We first use the same method as [15] to calculate SNR:

$$\mathrm{SNR} = \frac{1}{N}\sum_{i=1}^{N} \frac{F_M^i}{|F_i - F_M^i|}$$

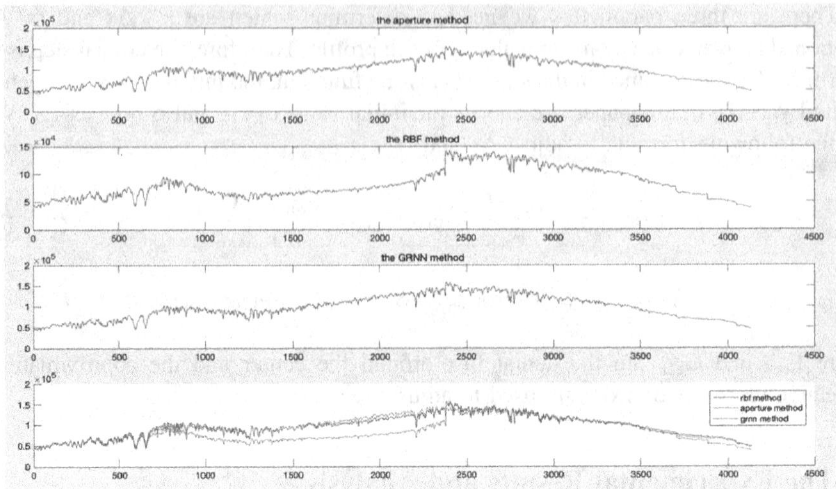

Fig. 4. The aperture, RBF and GRNN methods of results.

where N is the selected pixels, F_M^i is the corresponding flux of the continuum which is calculated by median filter with the width of 11 pixels. F_i is the flux of ith pixel we extract. The experimental results are shown in Fig. 5. We calculate the average SNR of the three methods in different pixel area, as shown in Table 1, the SNR of our proposed method is higher than RBF and aperture methods.

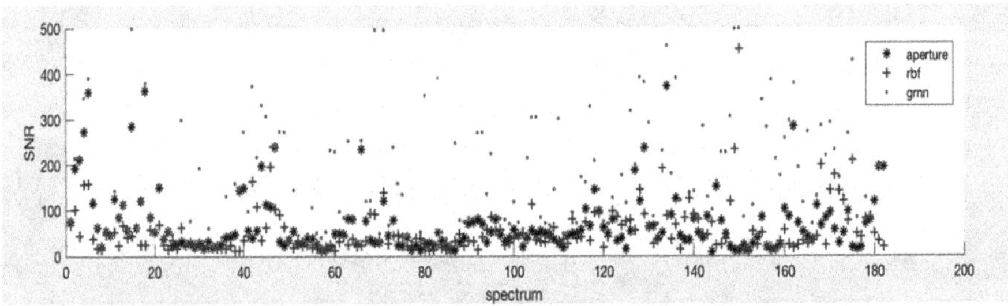

Fig. 5. The SNR of three methods for some of the spectra.

Moreover, we also compare the time consumption of the three methods, as shown in Table 2. Although the aperture method possesses lower time consumption, it cannot improve the SNR of flux extraction. GRNN method cost less time than RBF method which also has a higher SNR.

Table 1. The average SNR of aperture, RBF and GRNN methods

Pixel area	Aperture method	RBFNN method	GRNN method
[1, 1000]	251.738	233.724	263.318
[1500, 2000]	257.934	246.726	418.321
[3500, 4000]	387.809	326.208	449.504

Table 2. The time consumption of three methods

	Aperture method	RBFNN method	GRNN method
Time consumption	35.96	668.940	499.280

5 Conclusion

In this paper, we proposed a novel method which utilizing GRNN to extract flux of the LAMOST spectra data. We use double Gaussian basis function to approximate the profile of the spectra in spatial orientation. Some contrast experiments are implemented on the same spectra data. The experimental results show that the GRNN method we presented in this paper possess both a higher SNR and lower time consuming than aperture and RBFNN methods. This is more suitable for LAMOST which has such massive data.

Acknowledgements. The research work described in this paper was fully supported by the grants from the National Key Research and Development Program (Project No. 2017YFC1502505), the National Natural Science Foundation of China (Project No. 61472043), the Joint Research Fund in Astronomy (U1531242) under cooperative agreement between the NSFC and CAS. Prof. Qian Yin is the author to whom all correspondence should be addressed.

References

1. Cui, X.: Progress and prospect of LAMOST project. In: Proceedings of the SPIE 626703, pp. 1–8 (2006)
2. Zhao, G., Zhao, Y.H., Chu, Y.Q., et al.: LAMOST spectral survey—an overview. Res. Astron. Astrophys. **12**(7), 723–734 (2012)
3. Su, D., Zou, W.Y., Zhang, Z., et al.: Experimental system of segmented-mirror active optics. In: Astronomical Telescopes and Instrumentation. International Society for Optics and Photonics (2000)
4. Zhu, J., Zhu, Z., Wang, C., et al.: Cosmic-ray detection based on gray-scale morphology of spectroscopic CCD images. Publ. Astron. Soc. Aust. **26**(1), 69–74 (2009)
5. Zhang, B., Zhu, J., Ye, Z.: Fiber spectrum extraction for LAMOST based on 2-D exponential polynomial model. Exp. Astron. **33**(1), 211–223 (2012)
6. Yin, Q., Guo, P., Liu, H., et al.: Blind deconvolution for astronomical spectrum extraction from two-dimensional multifiber spectrum images. Opt. Express **25**(5), 5133–5145 (2017)
7. Horne, K.: An optimal extraction algorithm for CCD spectroscopy. Publ. Astron. Soc. Pac. **98**, 609–617 (1986)

8. Bolton, A.S., Schlegel, D.J.: Spectro-perfectionism: an algorithmic framework for photon noise-limited extraction of optical fiber spectroscopy. Publ. Astron. Soc. Pac. **122**, 248–257 (2010)
9. Robertson, J.G.: Optimal extraction of single-object spectra from observations with two-dimensional detectors. Publ. Astron. Soc. Pac. **98**, 1220–1231 (1986)
10. Sharp, R., Birchall, M.N.: Optimal extraction of fibreoptic spectroscopy. Publ. Astron. Soc. Aust. **27**(01), 91–103 (2010)
11. Qin, H., Ye, Z., Luo, A., et al.: An adaptive algorithm based on RBF for extracting the flux of fiber spectrum. Proc. SPIE – Int. Soc. Opt. Eng. **7019**, 701934.1–701934.11 (2008)
12. Specht, D.F.: A general regression neural network. IEEE Trans. Neural Netw. **2**(6), 568 (1991)
13. Wu, Y., Wang, H., Zhang, B., et al.: Using radial basis function networks for function approximation and classification. ISRN Appl. Math. **2012**(2012), 1089–1122 (2012)
14. Murray, G.J., Allington-Smith, J.R., Dodsworth, G.N., et al.: TEIFU: a high-resolution integral field unit for the William Herschel Telescope. In: Astronomical Telescopes and Instrumentation, pp. 611–622. International Society for Optics and Photonics (2000)
15. Qin, H., Ye, Z., Luo, A.L.: Flux extraction based on radial basic function for LAMOST. Publ. Astron. Soc. Pac. **121**(878), 408–413 (2009)

Design, Usability and User Experience

Complex System HCI as a Triangle of Interface, Content, and Person Interaction

Michael J. Albers(✉)

Department of English, East Carolina University, Greenville, NC 27858, USA
albersm@ecu.edu

Abstract. For complex systems, the human-system interaction alone should not be the focus of the design problem. Complex system HCI needs to move well beyond human-interface concerns and consider how the triangle formed by interface, content, and person interact within the situational context. Complicating the design of the triangle is that reality implies not a single person, but many people (different audiences) each with varying information needs, which implies dynamic content and may require varying interactions.

Keywords: Complex information · Information creation · Content HCI

1 Introduction

Traditionally, both design teams and researchers relied on a reductionist approach to problem solving. Break the situation into simpler and simpler parts until each one is understandable. This might be a good goal, but applied to complex problems it risks failing to consider interactions or information relationships. Back in 2007, Redish pointed out that the usability of complex systems is not the same as usability of simple systems, but a fundamentally different beast. Assuming a complex system is a sum of its parts at best redefines it as a complicated system. But worse, it typically redefines it as a collection of simple systems that can be completely described. Unfortunately, this redefinition ignores the deeper interactions between the parts; the user interactions with the system and the content yield a final result that is more than the sum of the parts. [Very brief definition: I define simple systems as those that have a correct answer and which can be fully described. However, complex systems have no single or correct answer and the full information needs cannot be described (Albers 2004)].

A fundamental design disconnect is that the backend operates according to clean physical laws. Complex IT systems are assembled from smaller systems. With the reductionist nature of software, it works to break any problem into individual components. But between the screen and the human, the reductionist logic gets replaced with human psychology. The interaction of essentially all non-trivial programs and informational websites becomes complex. So, we need to consider the cognitive complexity of the interaction and presentation (Endsley and Jones 2012).

Information complexity comes into play when the user needs involve complex information and when the user has open-ended questions. HCI answers these needs

C. Stephanidis (Ed.): HCII Posters 2018, CCIS 850, pp. 229–235, 2018.
https://doi.org/10.1007/978-3-319-92270-6_31

requires addressing the complexity of the entire contextual situation. Therefore, as Mirel (2002) states, "people's actual approaches to complex tasks and problems.... are contextually conditioned, emergent, opportunistic, and contingent. Therefore, complex work cannot be formalized into formulaic, rule-driven, context-free procedures" (p. 259). A basic question that often gets lost in the reduction process is "How much can the problem be reduced before the problem itself starts to be changed?" I'm previously addressed the inherent problems in taking a complex situation and transforming it into a simple one (Albers 2004).

Textbooks state a technical communicator translates information for an audience. However, complex information requires more than simply translation, but requires a fundamental transformation to form an integrated synthesis of information that fits the situational context. All of the information flowing into the content must be reshaped (transformed) into a form that supports a person's strategies for comprehension and decision making.

Developing complex information requires considerations of the interactions of audience with the information and the information flow. As such, the complexities of developing the information and ensuring (testing) it communicates effectively is a much bigger problem than the sum of the parts—with parts defined here as context, content, person, and interface. An interesting question that often does not seem to be explicitly mentioned with regards to information analysis is "What should be communicated?" With open-ended, complex texts, this becomes a much deeper question than one of directly moving information from the source to the reader.

Fundamental design issues with complex information stem from the dynamic interactions of content and situation (context); they are tightly coupled in a non-linear relationship. As a result, changing situations mean that good information and decisions today may be bad information and decisions tomorrow. Human psychology and the socio-technical issues/processes inherent within the situation interact non-linearly with the information. How well the content gets communicated depends on how well those issues are handled within the information development process.

One factor contributing to the complexity is that the writer and/or usability tester must ensure a dynamic combination of information merges into a coherence flow. But more than just merging together, the information must be transformed to fit the reader's needs.

2 Triangle Formed by Interface, Content, and Person

At a high level, the HCI of complex systems can be considered as a triangle with the sides formed by: interface, content, and person, with all three embedded in the situation (Fig. 1). Considering complex situation HCI as a triangle embedded within the situation can help emphasize the design issues.

When interacting with complex information, people strive to use the available information and make good decisions. The real problem is often not the information availability, but that it is poorly presented. In other words, the person could not effectively use the relevant information to reduce their uncertainty of the situation (Albers 2012).

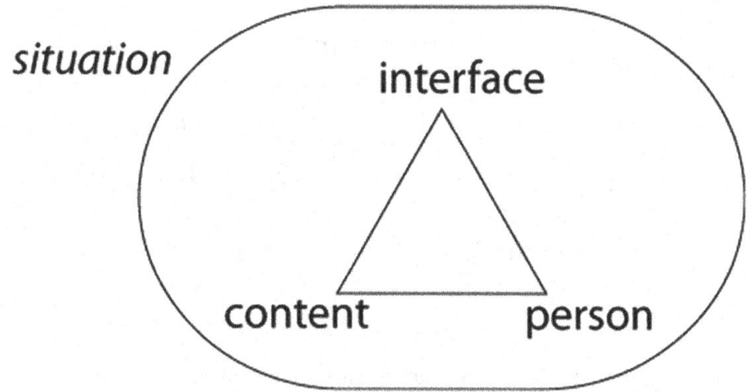

Fig. 1. Triangle for communicating complex information.

Writers and/or usability testers must ensure a dynamic combination of different information elements merge into a coherence flow. But more than just merging together, the information must be transformed to fit the reader's needs. The transformation aspect complicates the issues of content strategy by bringing to the forefront issues of the dynamic natures of information and situations, changing information needs, and different audience needs. Designing complex information that meets these multiple needs requires considerations of the interactions of audience with the information and the information flow.

As a workable model, the triangle in Fig. 1 fails to convey the dynamic nature needed to visualize communication issues. Converting the triangle to a Venn diagram helps with the visualization (Fig. 2). The maximum communication occurs when the overlap of the content, person needs, and interaction are maximized.

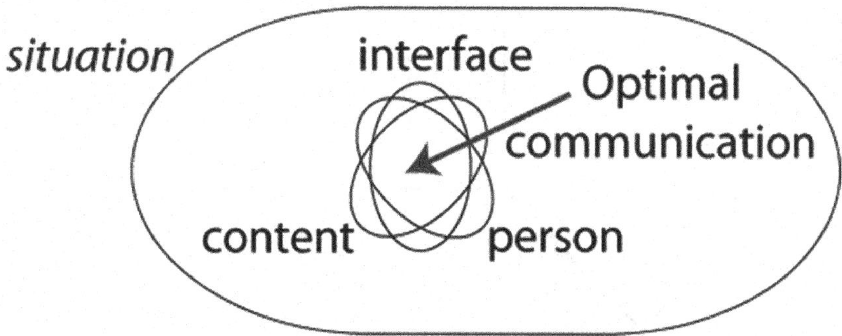

Fig. 2. Forming the area of optimal communication.

The overlapping nature of the three factors helps to visualize communication successes or failures. If effective communication only happens within the overlapping area, communication problems occur with any one factor gets shifted out of the mix

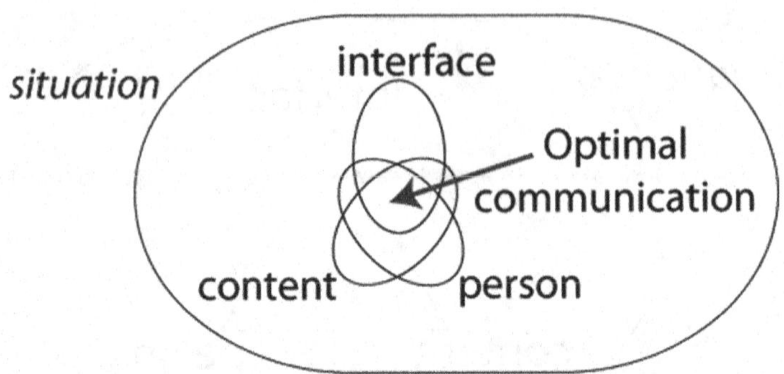

Fig. 3. Mismatched areas impair communication.

(Fig. 3). A poor interface impairs the ability of a person to access and interact with the content. Perhaps it was too complicated or too simplistic to provide the information in an effective manner. Likewise, superficial audience analysis can pull the person oval out since the content/interface fail to fit the audience needs. Or content that is technically correct but not relevant to the situation pulls the content oval away from optimal positioning.

The system of ovals work well for understanding simple systems, but it still lacks a good visualization of the dynamic nature of a complex system. I earlier explored this idea with determining content needs (Albers 2003), but now look at it within the overall situation. The changing natures of the content and information needs are difficult to convey with ovals. A graph structure works better (Fig. 4).

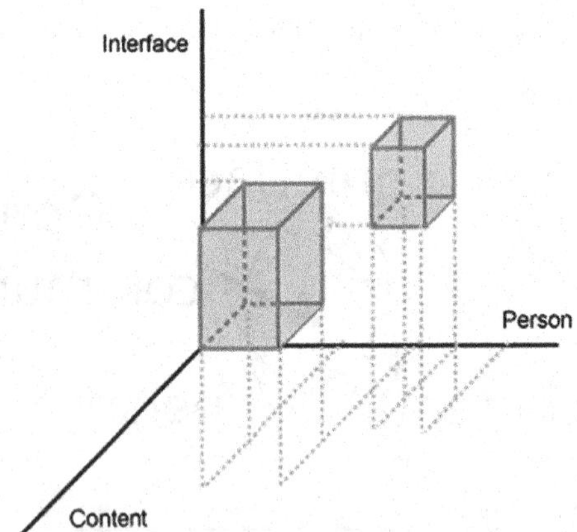

Fig. 4. Areas to design to support communication. The communication requirements for the situation focus on the shaded areas. Areas outside of the shaded areas are irrelevant to the current situation. In reality, the area edges would show a gradient as it spreads outward.

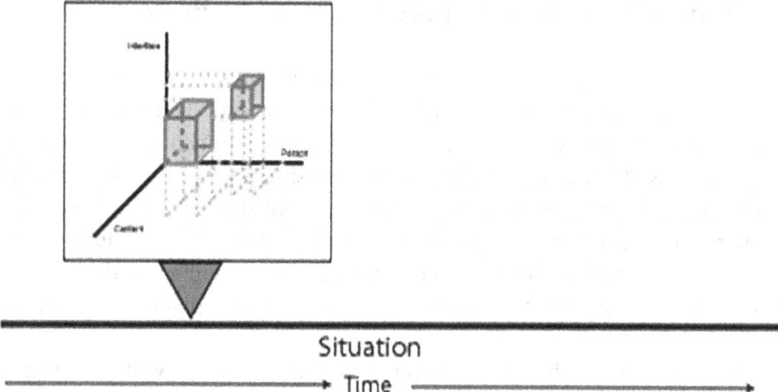

Fig. 5. Optimal communication graph embedded within a dynamic situation. A situation evolves over time and the graph moves/evolves with it.

Unfortunately, with the four variables—situation, content, person, and interface—a better method of capturing the idea requires a 4 dimensional graph (Fig. 5). Something that is impossible to create on paper or solid model. However, we can consider the idea of a 3 dimensional graph embedded within the higher dimensional situation space.

The situation evolves over time and the shape of the 3D graph changes along with that evolution (Fig. 6). Just like a slider changes sound or light intensity, moving the graph along the situation axis imparts changes to all three dimensions making it up.

Because of the non-linear aspects of complex information systems, the situation must always move forward. It cannot move backwards, and even if it could, the changes could not be undone. Moving from A to B and back to A would not result in the same graph at A both times.

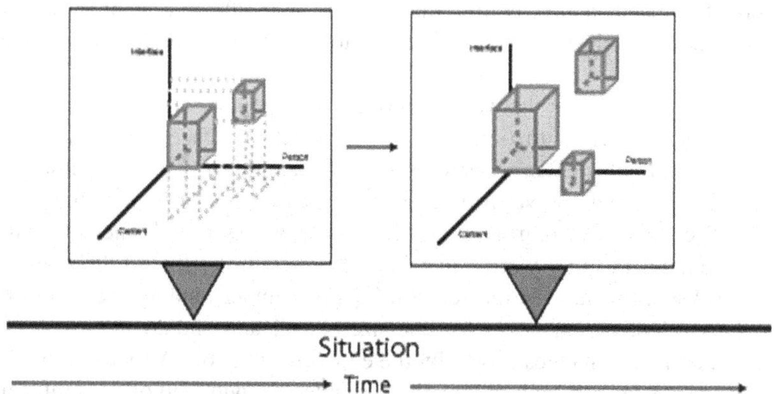

Fig. 6. Changes to the interface-content-person graph as the situation changes. As the situation evolves the information needs change. In this example, a new area has appeared and the size/position of the initial two areas has changed.

3 HCI Implications for Complex Information Presentation

A fundamental design issue with complex information stems from its dynamic aspects; changing situations means that high quality information and decisions today may be low quality information and poor decisions tomorrow. Human psychology and the socio-technical issues/processes inherent within the situation interact non-linearly with the information. How well the content gets communicated depends on how well those issues are handled within the information development process. The situation changes, which changes the relevant content, which changes the person's priorities for content and the relationships within that content, which has the potential to change the interface.

The design analysis's job is to understand how the situation will change and how the three factors change relevant to the situation change. Once those factors are understood, then the individual factors of content and interface can be defined to fit the changing person's information needs.

Previously, I pointed out that the interesting question that often does not seem to be explicitly mentioned with regards to information analysis is "What should be communicated?" In a traditional task analysis, this question doesn't make sense since it's the correct steps that are being communicated. With open-ended text, this becomes a much deeper and vital question. Audience analysis as normally practiced, if actually practiced at all, doesn't help since demographics don't explain information needs.

Another design issue to avoid is HCI that focuses too much on the button pushing, ignoring the socio-technical issues, and trying to achieve a no-fail at a trivial level. The result is an "accurate" system that no one wants to use because it doesn't really meet their needs.

4 Conclusion

Effective communication within complex situations requires understanding the audience information needs and providing that content in an effective manner. This paper looked a four part model for understanding how to define and mentally connect the four parts.

Situation The interactions between interface and person are the standard HCI approach. The situation (context) in which interface, person and content interact is too often ignored as a significant player. Complex situations are dynamic and evolve over time and/or based on user interactions.

Interface The interface controls how the person accesses and interacts with the content. In other words, that interaction controls (filters) the content and subsequent information relationships and understanding they form of the situation. It can never by one-size-fits all and should change to fit the interaction changes driven by the evolving situation. A focus on buttons or screens fails to capture how the user interacts with and obtains information relevant to the situation.

Content Content presentation cannot be ignored for complex information. Content is often discounted with claims of "we can't control that." Yet, understanding a complex situation depends on both the content presentation and how effectively relationships are formed within the information (Albers 2010). When those relationships are not formed, the person does not understand the situation and can make poor decisions.

Person A "user" or "reader" is too often a made-up audience constructed in the writer/designer/tester's head to conform to how she views the reader. With such a reader, their comprehension and decision strategies play a minimal part. Yet, understanding the strategies used by different parts of the audience as they use the information form the foundation for creating high quality complex information. All of the information flowing into the content must be reshaped (transformed) into a form that supports those strategies for comprehension and decision making.

Together the four factors can be considered as interacting as part of a 4-dimensional graph with the areas of information needs being plotted on that graph.

References

Albers, M.: Multidimensional audience analysis for dynamic information. J. Tech. Writ. Commun. **33**(3), 263–279 (2003)

Albers, M.: Communication of Complex Information: User Goals and Information Needs for Dynamic Web Information. Erlbaum, Mahwah (2004)

Albers, M.: Usability and information relationships: considering content relationships when testing complex information. In: Albers, M.J., Still, B. (eds.) Usability of Complex Information Systems: Evaluation of User Interaction. CRC Press (2010)

Albers, M.: Communication as reducing uncertainty. In: 31st Annual International Conference on Computer Documentation, Seattle, WA, 4–5 October 2012 (2012)

Endsley, M., Jones, D.: Designing for Situation Awareness: An Approach to Human-Centered Design, 2nd edn. Taylor and Francis, London (2012)

Mirel, B.: Design strategies for complex problem-solving software. In: Albers, M., Mazur, B. (eds.) Content and Complexity: Information Design in Software Development and Documentation, pp. 255–284. Earlbaum, Hillsdale (2002)

Redish, J.: Expanding usability testing to evaluate complex systems. J. Usab. Stud. **2**(3), 102–111 (2007)

Cross-Cultural Empathy: Learning About Diverse Users in Design Thinking Process

Ewa Callahan(✉)

Quinnipiac University, Hamden, CT 06158, USA
Ewa.Callahan@Quinnipiac.edu

Abstract. This poster explores the concept of cognitive and emotional empathy in the context of *Design Thinking* process when players come from different cultural backgrounds. It discusses the challenges facing the design teams and addresses differences in visual representations in tools that center on empathy with the user. In the light of cultural theories, especially Geert Hofstede's dimensions of culture [1, 2], the poster proposes a framework based on cultural theories that facilitate understanding of the design thinking process in cross-cultural context. The emphasis is placed on the creation of the visual tools that facilitate interactions among the members of the design teams, as well as interactions between the design team and the user.

Keywords: Empathy · Design Thinking · Cross-cultural

1 Introduction

The term *Design Thinking* relates to the set of strategies designers use in the process of creating new interfaces and systems. This solution-based system sees innovation as an intersection of human, technical and business factors. The first step in the process is empathy with users. Empathy in the design process is understood in the broad context of perspective taking [3] both as emotional and cognitive empathy, bridging the concepts of feelings and knowledge [4]. The emotional intelligence can be shared with other project team members through sets of visual tools (e.g., journey mapping, storytelling and metaphors [5], storyboards and mood boards). At this stage of the process, designers gather information about the user and can do so using visual aids.

Since the emotional and cognitive empathy is based on the experience, the cultural differences in experience provide a challenge for the research teams that design products for diverse markets. While current research concentrates on cultural differences in the problem solving, the area focused on empathy and user insight from the perspective of cross-cultural understanding remains largely unexplored, although the results of most recent studies [6, 7] show the importance of cross-cultural studies of the Design Thinking process. Considering that empathy provides the first step that connects the designer and the user, who might come from two different cultural backgrounds, analysis of this part of the process requires special attention.

C. Stephanidis (Ed.): HCII Posters 2018, CCIS 850, pp. 236–240, 2018.
https://doi.org/10.1007/978-3-319-92270-6_32

2 Design Thinking

The term *Design Thinking* was popularized in a title of a book by Rowe [8], a professor of architecture at Harvard, who used it to describe methods used by architects and urban planners in their design processes. While initial use of the term was confined to architecture, it also found its use in business environment, in a somewhat modified understanding. Its popularity in the current usage is attributed to the consulting firm IDEO [5], and especially its leadership, founder David Kelly [9] and chief executive officer Brown [10]. The process of Design Thinking helps provide a solution to a number of design problems (often wicked problems) and is solution oriented (as opposed to problem oriented approaches).

Commonly distinguished phases of the process are defined as: empathize, define, ideate, prototype and test. Empathy therefore is a starting point of the process (although in some models described as understanding/point of view) [11]. In each of those phases a variety of tools are used to facilitate interactions and design specific artifacts. Common Design Thinking Tools include, among others [5]: visualization techniques (charts, graphs, storytelling), ethnography research, structured collaborative, sense-making techniques (mind mapping, ideation, brainstorming, concept development), assumption identification, prototyping, co-creation and filed experiments). The design of visualization tools is a process in itself.

3 Empathy

Empathy with the user is an important step in a design process. Empathy can be defined in a variety of ways. In layman's terms it might be presented as "walking in someone else's shoes" but the concept of empathy is much more complex, especially in the context of Design Thinking process. Gasparini [4], in her analysis of empathy explains empathy from the perspective of two different dimensions: emotional, when a person instinctively feels experiences of others, and cognitive, when one can through understanding analyze situations of others. Both of those types play a role in design, depending on the function of the process. Emotional empathy will play a greater role when we view Design Thinking as the Creation of Artifacts or a Reflective Practice, while cognitive empathy will play a greater role, when we view Design Thinking as a Problem–Solving activity, Practice Based Activity, and Creation of Meaning. In the latter cases the designers will not have to feel the experiences of users in order to understand them. Cognitive empathy also influences the way the design team works and interacts. The differences are equalized through mutual understanding [4].

Learning about the users' needs through empathy can be done using Empathic Design Research Strategies [12], that include a variety of methods that require empathizing with the user, either on the emotional or cognitive level. Those include informal interviews and conversations, ethnographic type observations, as well as collaborations focused on a shared goal. In this process life-expert-users, with different personal capital, become co-creators, generating real life solutions [12]. The different personal capital, understood as personal and behavioral traits will include culture that might be not shared between the designer and user.

4 Culture and Design Thinking

Just like empathy, culture can be defined in multiple ways. In 1952 Kroeber and Kluckhohn [13] gathered examples of over 160 different definitions of culture, separating them into three categories: definitions based on shared values, definitions based on problem solving and third category that encompassed other definitions. The definitions that present cultures from the perspective of common behaviors and problem solving allow to seek the role of empathy in the *Design Thinking* process, as problem solving provides a common ground. In the crossroads of culture and empathy stands the concept of *cultural intelligence* [14], an ability to function in culturally diverse settings and represents adjustments a person can make to fit into different cultures.

The definitions that describe cultural difference and similarities from the perspective of difference and similarities in the problem solving approaches are especially useful to consider when analyzing design process and its players. Other approaches utilize cultural theories, like, for example dimensions of culture postulated by Hofstede [1, 2]. Hofstede identified initially four, later five different dimensions, in which national cultures vary: power distance, individualism and collectivism, masculinity and femininity, uncertainty avoidance and short vs long term orientation. Power distance relates to the level of acceptance of differences in power, individualism measures the level of collective vs, individualistic approaches, masculinity focuses on achievement and assertiveness, while more feminine cultures focus on cooperation and quality of life. Uncertainty avoidance measures how comfortable cultures are with uncertain situations. Short vs, Long term orientation relates to seeking rewards immediately or working for future gain. Hofstede theory gained popularity in various areas of research, and recently has also been used to examine *Design Thinking*. Thoring et al. [11] in their study examined each dimension in relation to the design process, people, space and mindset attempting to identify which cultures utilize the Design Thinking the best. The authors do not provide any practical solutions and conclude that each dimension has some positive and negative effects on Design Thinking process. The authors' approach is very broad and considering a number of possible variables difficult to test in its entirety.

However, Hofstede's dimensions can be utilized in a smaller capacity. As stated before, empathy and learning about the user relies on a number of tools, many with a visual component. While those tools themselves have not been inspected, the preferences for visual aesthetics with connection to Hofstede's dimensions have already been studied [15–17] and identified markers for the model (Table 1).

The design of visual aids to facilitate empathy is one of the areas where the tools are in itself artifacts of culture. For example, the design of personas, used commonly in USA, and in the majority showing individuals as the typical user, can be modified for the more collectivist cultures to present not only the individuals but also their relations to others. Metaphors could be adjusted to fit a country's preferences. Journey mapping could include limited or multiple choices and different amounts of data depending on culture. Testing Hofstede's theory on a small scale in the countries/cultures on the opposite sides of each dimension could help recognize differences in the approaches to learning about the user in different cultures.

Table 1. Visual cues and Hofstede's dimensions of culture [15–17]

Dimension	High	Low
Power distance	• Symmetry	• Asymmetry
	• Tall hierarchies	• Shallow hierarchies
	• Images of leaders	• Images of both genders
Individualism	• Images of individuals	• Images of groups
	• Images of young	• Images of aged and experienced
	• Emphasis on action	• Emphasis on state of being
Masculinity	• Limited choices	• Multiple choices
	• Orientation toward goals	• Orientation toward relationships
	• Graphics used for utilitarian purposes	• Graphics used for visual appeal
Uncertainty avoidance	• Limited choices	• Variety of choices
	• Restricted amounts of data	• Unrestricted amounts of data

References

1. Hofstede, G.: Culture's Consequences: International Differences in Work-Related Values. Sage Publications, Beverly Hills (1980)
2. Hofstede, G.: Culture and Organisations: Software of the Mind. HarperCollins, London (1994)
3. Köppen, E., Meinel, C.: Empathy via design thinking: creation of sense and knowledge. In: Plattner, H., Meinel, C., Leifer, L. (eds.) Design Thinking Research. UI, pp. 15–28. Springer, Cham (2015). https://doi.org/10.1007/978-3-319-06823-7_2
4. Gasparini, A.: Perspective and use of empathy in design thinking. In: The Eight International Conference on Advances in Computer-Human Interactions, ACHI, pp. 49–54 (2015)
5. Liedtka, J.: Perspective: linking design thinking with innovation outcomes through cognitive bias reduction. J. Prod. Innov. Manag. **32**(6), 925–938 (2015)
6. Christensen, B.T., Ball, L.J., Halskov, K.: Analysing Design Thinking: Studies of Cross-Cultural Co-Creation. CRC Press, Boca Raton (2017)
7. Clemmensen, T., Ranjan, A., Bødker, M.: How cultural knowledge shapes core design thinking—A situation specific analysis. CoDesign, pp. 1–18 (2017)
8. Rowe, P.: Design Thinking. The MIT Press, Cambridge (1987)
9. Kelley, T., Littman, J.: The Ten Faces of Innovation: IDEO's Strategies for Beating the Devil's Advocate and Driving Creativity Throughout Your Organization. Doubleday, New York (2005)
10. Brown, T.: Change by Design: How Design Thinking Transforms Organizations and Inspires Innovation. Harper-Collins, New York (2009)
11. Thoring, K., Luippold, C., Mueller, R.: The impact of cultural differences in design thinking education. In: Design Research Society's Conference (2014)
12. McDonagh, D., Thomas, J.: Rethinking design thinking: empathy supporting innovation. Aust. Med. J. - Health Des. 1 **3**(8), 458–464 (2010)
13. Kroeber, A.L., Kluckhohn, C.: Culture: a critical review of concepts and definitions. Harvard University Peabody Museum of American Archeology and Ethnology Papers 47 (1952)
14. Ang, S., Van Dyne, L.: Handbook of Cultural Intelligence: Theory, Measurements, and Applications. Sharpe, London (2008)

15. Marcus, A., Gould, E.W.: Cultural dimensions and global Web user-interface design: What? So what? Now what? In: Proceedings of the 6th Conference on Human Factors and the Web, 19 June 2000. http://www.amanda.com/resources/hfweb2000/hfweb00.marcus.html. Accessed 15 June 2001
16. Ackerman, S.K.: Mapping user interface design to culture dimensions. In: Paper Presented at International Workshop on Internationalization of Products and Systems, Austin, TX, USA (2002). http://www.iwips2002.org/downloads/AMA_XCult_13Jul02.ppt. Accessed 20 May 2002
17. Callahan, E.: Cultural similarities and differences in the design of university web sites. J. Comput.-Med. Commun. **11**(1), 239–273 (2005)

Redesign of Cartesian Diver for Underwater Expression Combining Dynamic Fabrication with Non-contact Manipulation

Amy Koike(✉), Kazuki Takazawa, Satoshi Hashizume, Mose Sakashita, Daitetsu Sato, and Yoichi Ochiai

University of Tsukuba, Tsukuba, Japan
amy23kik@gmail.com

Abstract. In this study, we aim to combine dynamic fabrication with non-contact manipulation system applying the mechanism of Cartesian Diver. To achieve this, we propose the design method for underwater objects and non-contact manipulation technique using water pressure with PID control. We successfully designed and manipulate the object by our method. We discussed the principles and methods to create a digitally designed and fabricated the diver and to stabilize it in the middle of water.

Keywords: Dynamic fabrication · PIDcontrol · Cartesian Diver Underwater

1 Introduction

Cartesian Diver is known as a toy which swims up and down underwater. The diver is often used as demonstration of Pascal's law and Archimedes's principle. It uses the change of water pressure and specific structure to swim objects underwater situation. In this paper, we computationally design the diver in the context of dynamic fabrication and non-contact manipulation. Thus, this work expands the expressions of underwater entertainment situation such as aquarium or theme park.

Dynamic fabrication is one of the widely spreading research topics among Human Computer Interaction (HCI) communities. Some dynamic fabrication studies, for example, balanced models [8], spinnable objects [1] and floating objects [13], are proposed. More recently, Prévost et al. presented a bistable balanced object using movable embedded masses [7]. This study is one of example which enhance the degree of freedom in dynamic fabrication. Moreover, there are some methods adding controllability to fabricated objects using non-contact manipulation systems; controlling magnetic field [5], acoustic field [6] or air jets [4].

In this work, we aim to combine dynamic fabrication with non-contact manipulation system applying the mechanism of the diver. Our contributions are

C. Stephanidis (Ed.): HCII Posters 2018, CCIS 850, pp. 241–246, 2018.
https://doi.org/10.1007/978-3-319-92270-6_33

- to propose the design method for underwater objects,
- to propose the non-contact underwater object manipulation method and implementation and
- to conduct quantitative evaluation about relationship between parameter of fabrication and stability of manipulation.

2 Related Work

2.1 Fabrication

In HCI communities, optimization algorithms and digital fabrication techniques are frequently used for adding controllable physical properties to the real-world objects. These methods are applied to various targets, such as musical instruments [11,12], mechanical toys [2,14,15], and toys-redesigning [9,10].

Prévost et al., Bächer et al., and Wang et al. applied voxel carving for controling the center of mass to balancing objects [8], spinnable objects [1] and floating objects [13]. Moreover, Prévost et al. presents a bistable balanced objects using embedded movable masses [7]. In this study, we combined underwater non-contact manipulation system with dynamic fabrication for adding spatial controllability to underwater objects.

2.2 Manipulation

The methods to control the real-world objects are categorized into two types. Putting actuators inside the objects or actuating their surroundings such as air or water. The latter method is also divided to two ways; contact or non-contact.

Follmer et al. proposed contact manipulation system using shape-changing display [3]. Examples of non-contact manipulation include magnetic field [5], acoustic field [6], and air jets [4].

In this study, we introduce underwater non-contact manipulation technique using water pressure with PID control.

3 Design Method

To design a 3D model to function as the diver, we define four fundamental requirements. To swim up and down underwater situation, the diver

1. has to float when you put it into a water tank and
2. is necessary to have a hole which water enters into it when water pressure is applied to the water tank.
   To make the diver swim with the correct orientation which defined by the designer,
3. the hole is located on the same vertical line with center of gravity and
4. rotation moments should not be occurred.

We formulated these requirements for applying them to digital fabrication system. Requirements 1. and 2. are formulated as:

$$\boldsymbol{F_G} + \rho_w V_{max} \boldsymbol{g} > \boldsymbol{F_B} > \boldsymbol{F_G} \tag{1}$$

where $\boldsymbol{F_G}$ is the gravitational force on the object and $\boldsymbol{F_B}$ is the upward buoyancy force. V_{max} is maximum volume of water that our setup can apply to the diver, ρ_w is water density and g is gravitational acceleration. Also, requirements 3. and 4. are formulated as:

$$\boldsymbol{C_B} \times \boldsymbol{F_B} = \boldsymbol{C_G} \times \boldsymbol{F_G} \tag{2}$$

where $\boldsymbol{C_G}$ is the center of gravity and $\boldsymbol{C_B}$ is the center of buoyancy. Figure 1 shows our design method overview.

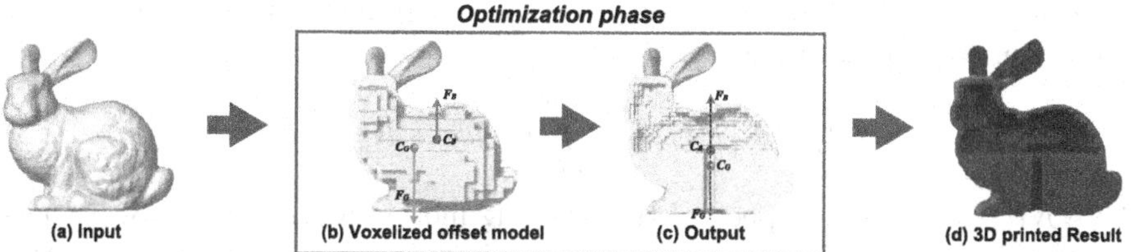

Fig. 1. Overview of our design method to create the Cartesian Diver. (a) First, we prepare a solid model as input. (b) Second, offset the model and voxelize it. (c) Then, apply voxel carving algorithm and (d) the model is 3D printed as the diver.

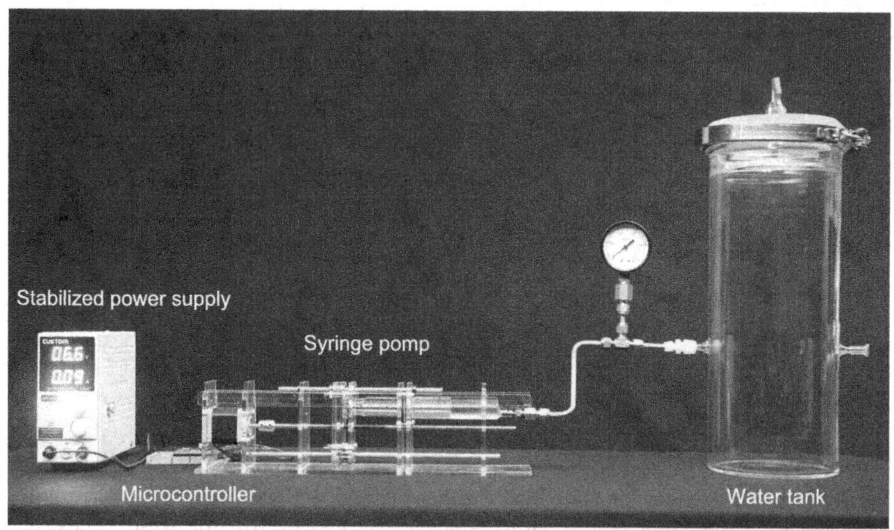

Fig. 2. System setup.

4 Manipulation Method and System Setup

To manipulate the position of the diver, we adopt PID control and implement the system setup (Fig. 2).

Our system consists of a water tank which is connected to a syringe pomp by a tube. The syringe pomp moves forward or backward by a stepping motor. The motor is controlled by a microcontroller. When it works, water pressure inside the tank is changed and it comes to decrease or increase the buoyant force applied to the diver. We installed a camera to track the position of the diver and send the value to the microcontroller.

Besides changing the water pressure, there are several ways to manipulate the diver; changing the temperature of the liquid or using two kinds of liquid each density is different. However, these methods have disadvantages of responsiveness and interactivity.

In this study, therefore, we adopt PID control to manipulate the diver. PID control can be expressed mathematically as:

$$N(t) = K_p e(t) + K_i \int_0^t e(\tau) d\tau + K_d \frac{de(t)}{dt} \tag{3}$$

where $N(t)$ is rotational speed of the stepping motor, K_p is a factor of proportionality, K_i is integration constant and K_d is differential constant. Also, $e(t)$ indicates difference between a target position and the present position of the diver. Figure 3 shows pipeline of PID control.

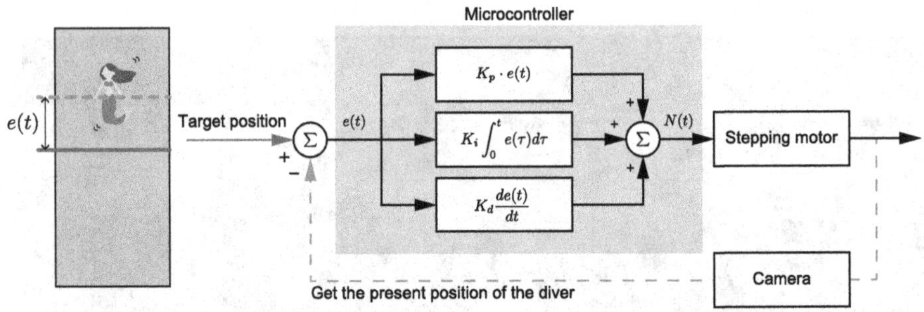

Fig. 3. Block diagram of PID control.

5 Result

5.1 Fabrication

We fabricated a variety of the divers and attained a result that they swim up and down in the correct orientation. However, it has limitation about material properties; water solubility and density.

Due to manipulate the diver underwater, we cannot use water soluble materials as 3D printing material. In this study, we do not consider a material which density lighter than water because it is rarely used in 3D printing.

5.2 Manipulation

We observed the position deviation of the diver under applying PID control. Gravity, buoyancy, and fluid resistance are applied to the diver while the diver is moving. Fluid resistance F_D is defined by the properties of the fluid, the shape, and the speed of the object:

$$F_D = \frac{1}{2}\rho v^2 C_D S \tag{4}$$

where ρ is the density of the fluid, v is the speed of the object relative to the fluid, C_D is the drag coefficient and S is the cross sectional area. The cross sectional area is defined as orthographic projection toward direction of movement of the object. Therefore we examined effectiveness of the cross sectional area of the diver to stability under the control (Fig. 4).

Under the control, the object oscillate near the target position. It is caused by two system setup factors; frictional force applied to the syringe pomp and image processing delay. We need to improve the system setup to decrease these factors in the future work.

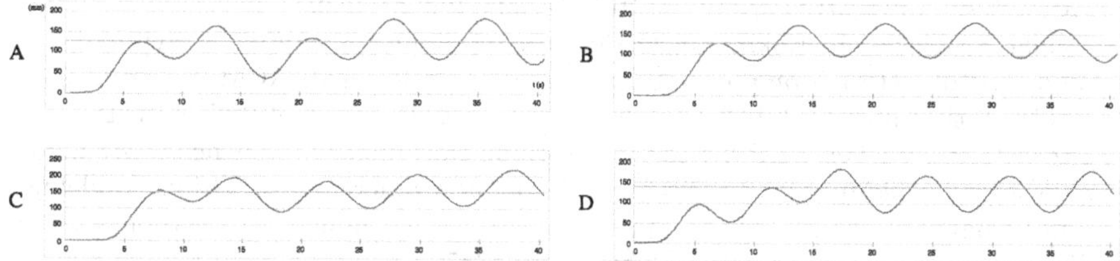

Fig. 4. These graphs show behavior of four Cartesian Divers under PID control. Those cross sectional area are different; A is 425π, B is 400π, C is 350π and D is 300π. Those volume (62800mm^3) and and the material (3D printed PLA) are same. Red line is the target position. (Color figure online)

6 Conclusion

In this study, we aim to combine dynamic fabrication with non-contact manipulation system. To achieve this, we proposed the design methods applying the mechanism of Cartesian Diver.

We successfully design and manipulate the diver and discussed limitations.We observed the motion of the diver under applying PID control. Then we discussed about limitation about material properties and system setup. We believe this study extends the possibilities of new underwater expressions.

References

1. Bächer, M., Whiting, E., Bickel, B., Sorkine-Hornung, O.: Spin-it: optimizing moment of inertia for spinnable objects. ACM Trans. Graph. **33**(4), Article no. 96 (2014), 10 p. https://doi.org/10.1145/2601097.2601157
2. Coros, S., Thomaszewski, B., Noris, G., Sueda, S., Forberg, M., Sumner, R.W., Matusik, W., Bickel, B.: Computational design of mechanical characters. ACM Trans. Graph. **32**(4), Article no. 83 (2013), 12 p. https://doi.org/10.1145/2461912.2461953
3. Follmer, S., Leithinger, D., Olwal, A., Hogge, A., Ishii, H.: inFORM: dynamic physical affordances and constraints through shape and object actuation. In: Proceedings of the 26th Annual ACM Symposium on User Interface Software and Technology (UIST 2013), pp. 417–426. ACM, New York (2013). https://doi.org/10.1145/2501988.2502032
4. Hiroshi, M., Yoshihiro, Y., Satoshi, I., Motoki, S., Toshiro, N., Yuriko, S., Minoru, K., Masanori, Y.: Contactless active force closure manipulation using multiple air jets. In: 2010 IEEE International Conference on Systems, Man and Cybernetics, pp. 4154–4160 (2010). https://doi.org/10.1109/ICSMC.2010.5642402
5. Lee, J., Post, R., Ishii, H.: ZeroN: mid-air tangible interaction enabled by computer controlled magnetic levitation. In: Proceedings of the 24th Annual ACM Symposium on User Interface Software and Technology (UIST 2011), pp. 327–336 (2011). ACM, New York. https://doi.org/10.1145/2047196.2047239
6. Ochiai, Y., Hoshi, T., Rekimoto, J.: Pixie dust: graphics generated by levitated and animated objects in computational acoustic-potential field. ACM Trans. Graph. **33**(4), Article no. 85 (2014), 13 p. https://doi.org/10.1145/2601097.2601118.
7. Prévost, R., Bächer, M., Jarosz, W., Sorkine-Hornung, O.: Balancing 3D models with movable masses. In: Proceedings of the Conference on Vision, Modeling and Visualization (VMV 2016), pp. 9–16 (2016). Eurographics Association, Goslar Germany. https://doi.org/10.2312/vmv.20161337
8. Prévost, R., Whiting, E., Lefebvre, S., Sorkine-Hornung, O.: Make it stand: balancing shapes for 3D fabrication. ACM Trans. Graph. **32**(4), Article no. 81 (2013), 10 p. https://doi.org/10.1145/2461912.2461957.
9. Sun, T., Zheng, C.: Computational design of twisty joints and puzzles. ACM Trans. Graph. **34**(4), Article no. 101 (2015), 11 p. https://doi.org/10.1145/2766961.
10. Umetani, N., Koyama, Y., Schmidt, R., Igarashi, T.: Pteromys: interactive design and optimization of free-formed free-flight model airplanes. ACM Trans. Graph. **33**(4), Article no. 65 (2014), 10 p. https://doi.org/10.1145/2601097.2601129
11. Umetani, N., Mitani, J., Igarashi, T.: Designing custom-made metallophone with concurrent eigenanalysis. In: NIME (2010)
12. Umetani, N., Panotopoulou, A., Schmidt, R., Whiting, E.: Printone: interactive resonance simulation for free-form print-wind instrument design. ACM Trans. Graph. **35**(6), Article no. 184 (2016), 14 p. https://doi.org/10.1145/2980179.2980250
13. Wang, L., Whiting, E.: Buoyancy optimization for computational fabrication. Comput. Graph. Forum **35**(2), 49–58 (2016). https://doi.org/10.1111/cgf.12810
14. Zhang, R., Auzinger, T., Ceylan, D., Li, W., Bickel, B.: Functionality-aware retargeting of mechanisms to 3D shapes. ACM Trans. Graph. **36**(4), Article no. 81 (2017), 13 p. https://doi.org/10.1145/3072959.3073710
15. Zhu, L., Xu, W., Snyder, J., Liu, Y., Wang, G., Guo, B.: Motion-guided mechanical toy modeling. ACM Trans. Graph. **31**(6), Article no. 127 (2012), 10 p. https://doi.org/10.1145/2366145.2366146

Understanding the Acceptance of Health Management Mobile Services: Integrating Theory of Planned Behavior and Health Belief Model

Wen-Tsung Ku[1] and Pi-Jung Hsieh[2(✉)]

[1] Department of Physical Medicine and Rehabilitation, St. Martin De Porres Hospital, Chia-Yi, Taiwan, R.O.C.
kib56265@gmail.com

[2] Department of Hospital and Health Care Administration, Chia Nan University of Pharmacy and Science, Tainan, Taiwan, R.O.C.
beerun@seed.net.tw

Abstract. With the increasingly aging population and health information technology (IT) advances, self-health management has become an important topic. In particular, middle-aged and elderly people are considered to have higher risks of contracting multiple chronic diseases and complications, thus increasing the need for healthcare. For this reason, the Taiwan Health Promotion Administration (HPA) intends to build the health management mobile service (HMMS) whereby everyone's health records will be stored in the health promotion platform. The HMMS improves transmission of personalized preventive health information to those most in need. Although several prior researches have focused on the factors that impact on the adoption or use of health information management and electronic medical record, however, the literature directly related to people' self-health management behavior toward HMMS is scant. Thus, this study proposes a theoretical model to explain citizen's intention to use a personal health information system in self-health management. A field survey was conducted in Taiwan to collect data from citizens. A total of 105 valid responses were obtained, constituting a response rate of 97.88%. The results indicate that attitude, subjective norm, and perceived susceptibility have positive effects on usage intention. However, perceived behavioral control and perceived severity do not significantly affect behavioral intention. The study has implications on the development of strategies to improve personal health IT acceptance.

Keywords: Self-health management · Health management mobile service Health belief

1 Introduction

With Taiwan now considered an aging society, middle-aged and elderly people are considered to have higher risks of contracting multiple chronic diseases and complications, thus increasing the need for healthcare. Thus, the Taiwan HPA must meet a

C. Stephanidis (Ed.): HCII Posters 2018, CCIS 850, pp. 247–252, 2018.
https://doi.org/10.1007/978-3-319-92270-6_34

growing demand for chronic illness and geriatric care. To promote self-health management, the HPA established the mobile-based health promotion platform. This platform acts as a foundation for holistic health management mobile cloud services, enabling citizens to input health-related data and check preventive health records. Thus, the HMMS improves transmission of personalized preventive health information to those most in need. Despite its tremendous potential, about 0.09% of the citizens in Taiwan were using the HMMS to access personal health records. Although several prior researches have focused on the factors that impact on the adoption or use of health information management and electronic medical record [1–3], however, the literature directly related to citizen' self-health management behavior toward health management mobile service is scant. However, the self-management is not a simple activity, but a social and economic, interactive process between citizens and medical institutions. Thus, the existing variables of technology acceptance models do not fully reflect the motives of use. Previous research has suggested the need for incorporating additional health behavior factors to improve the predictive capacity and explanatory power of these dimensions. A variety of health behavior theories can be used to explain the health technology acceptance phenomenon. Among these theories, two theoretical models that have been extensively used to predict patient involvement in health-related behaviors are the health belief model (HBM) [4] and the theory of planned behavior (TPB) [5]. According the TPB and HBM perspective, this study proposes a theoretical model to explain citizens' intention to use of health management mobile service in self-health management.

2 Literature Review

The theory of reasoned action (TRA) [6] suggests that a person's behavior is determined by his or her intention to perform the behavior and that this intention is consequently a function of the person's attitude and his or her subjective norm toward that behavior. Although the TRA has been evaluated and supported in numerous contexts, it offers a weak explanation of the essence of behavior. Ajzen [5] asserted that the TPB eliminated the TRA's limitations regarding managing behavior over which people have incomplete volitional control. Ajzen [5] showed that attitude and subjective norm determine a person's intention to use, and he further proposed that the person's perceived behavioral control (PBC) reflects the degree to which he or she feels that successfully engaging in that behavior is completely under his or her control. Behavioral intention measures the strength of a person's willingness to exert effort when performing certain behavioral activities. Attitude (A) explains the assessment of favorable behavior for the person, which directly influences the strength of the behavior and beliefs regarding the likely outcome. Accordingly, attitude is equated with attitudinal beliefs that link a behavior to a certain outcome weighted by the desirability evaluation of that outcome. Subjective norm (SN) expresses the perceived social pressure of a person who intends to perform a behavior, and is related to normative beliefs regarding the expectations of other people. PBC is composed of human beliefs concerning capability and the controllability of performing the behavior. There are several examples of using the TPB to explain users' behavior, and a number of studies have applied the TPB to guideline implementations [7, 8]. The HBM tries to explain people's preventive health behaviors and considers health behavior a function of two basic mechanisms: threat perception and behavioral evaluation [9]. Perception of disease threat depends on two beliefs, i.e., the perceived susceptibility to the disease and perceived severity of the disease [9]. Behavioral evaluation is based on the perceived benefits and perceived barriers. Perceived benefits refer to an individual's assessment of the positive consequences of adopting a health behavior, including the extent to which it reduces the risk of the disease or the severity of its consequences. Perceived barriers refer to an individual's assessment of the influences that discourage the adoption of the health action. Prior studies have also shown that the HBM has good explanatory power in predicting users' health IT acceptance [10, 11]. Therefore, this study applies the HMMS to explain citizen's intention to use the HMMS for self-health management. HBM proposes two factors similar to the TPB to explain health behavior. For example, the concepts of perceived benefits and perceived barriers are very similar in notion to attitude and PBC respectively [12, 13]. Meanwhile, the two models are complementary in some aspects. If we combine TPB and HBM to explore influencing factors of behavior, more variance of outcome variables could be explained.

3 Research Model

According the TPB and HBM perspective, we linked the three TPB constructs (i.e., attitude, SN, and PBC) and two HBM constructs (i.e., perceived susceptibility and perceived severity) to behavior intentions. Figure 1 shows the proposed research model.

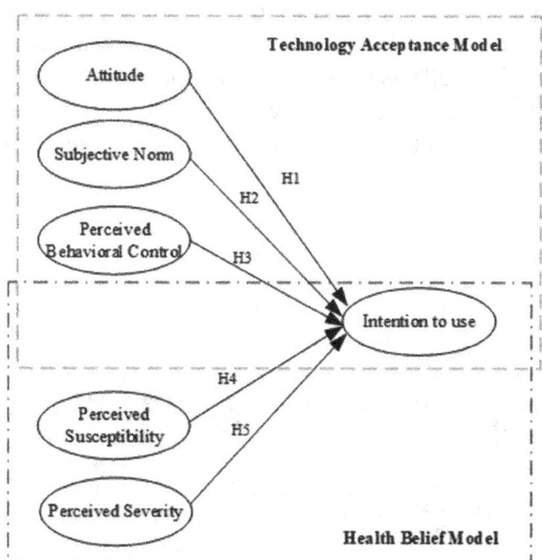

Fig. 1. Research framework

4 Research Methodology

This study employed an online survey for data collection because online surveys provide researchers with various benefits such as saving time and reducing expenses by overcoming geographic distance [14]. We conducted structural equation modeling using partial least squares (PLS) estimations for the data analysis. We tested the reliability and validity of the proposed model. The model was deemed reliable if the construct reliability was greater than 0.8. Convergent validity was assessed based on the following criteria: (a) statistically significant item loading greater than 0.7, (b) composite construct reliability greater than 0.8, and (c) average variance extracted (AVE) greater than 0.5. The discriminant validity of the constructs was assessed based on the criterion that the square root of the AVE for each construct should be greater than the corresponding correlations with all the other constructs [15].

5 Results and Analysis

The 105 valid responses we obtained constitute a response rate of 97.88%. Slightly more than half (53.8%) of the respondents were females. The majority of respondents (62.9%) were between the ages of 20 and 29 years. The education level for 50.8% of the respondents was university. 52.1% of the respondents had more than three years of mobile device usage experience. The construct reliabilities are all greater than 0.9. For the convergent validity, the item loadings are all greater than 0.7, and the AVEs range from 0.63 to 0.89. For the discriminant validity, the square root of the AVE for each construct is greater than its corresponding correlations with the other constructs. These results indicate acceptable reliability and validity. Figure 2 presents the test results for the structural model. The results indicate that attitude, subjective norm, and perceived susceptibility have positive effects on usage intention. However, in our research, perceived behavioral control and perceived severity did not significantly affect behavior intention. These variables together explained 67% of the variance of intention to use.

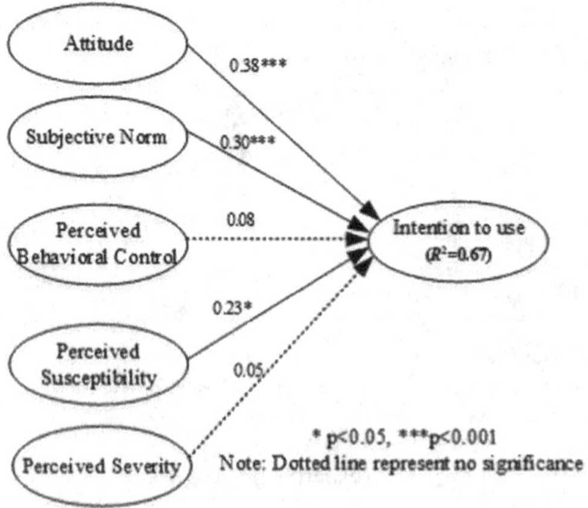

Fig. 2. Results of the structural model

6 Conclusion and Discussion

The effects of these usage intention variables were significant in explaining citizens' usage behavior because they are consistent with Rosenstock [9], who maintained the relative importance of perceived susceptibility, in predicting usage intention varies across behaviors and situations. Thus, individuals who perceive a higher degree of susceptibility are more likely to know their health records so that they can manage and confirm their own health status. This finding is consistent with the result obtained by in Nundy et al. [16]. Furthermore, the results showed that of all the main determinants, subjective norm had the strongest effect on behavioral intention. This result coincides with the findings of previous studies on technology adoption [3]. When a user had a greater perception that most people who are important to them think that they should use a new technology, they are more likely to commit to this perceived pressure and are more willing to use the health management mobile services. Attitude was an influential factor in the elderly peoples' intention to use the HMMS, although its effect was smaller than the subjective norm. This implication coincides with the findings of previous studies on heath IT adoption [17]. This highlights the critical role of attitude in health technology acceptance decision-making by individual users and therefore singles out the importance of attitude cultivation and management to successful health IT implementation. In summary, the main contribution of this study is that it is the first to explore citizen's usage behavior by extant technology acceptance and health behavior theories. The integration approach adopted as the basis of the proposed model provides a more complete set of antecedents that offers a better explanation of citizen's intention to adopt technologies such as the HMMS; thus, enhancing the practical contributions of this study. The results indicate that the research model provides a good understanding of the factors that influence the intention to use the HMMS. We offer implications regarding medical practice and academic research that are based on our findings. We hope that this study will stimulate future interest in the big heath data acceptance phenomena and motivate researchers to examine in greater depth this unexplored yet potentially fertile area of research.

References

1. Lai, J.Y., Wang, J.: Switching attitudes of taiwanese middle-aged and elderly patients toward cloud healthcare services: an exploratory study. Technol. Forecast. Soc. Chang. **92**, 155–167 (2015)
2. Sun, Y., Wang, N., Guo, X., Peng, Z.: Understanding the acceptance of mobile health services: a comparison and integration of alternative models. J. Electron. Commer. Res. **14** (2), 183–200 (2013)
3. Nur, F.N., Moon, N.N.: Health care system based on cloud computing. Asian Trans. Comput. **2**(5), 9–11 (2012)
4. Rosenstock, I.M.: What research in motivation suggests for public health. Am. J. Public Health Nations Health **50**, 295–301 (1960)
5. Ajzen, I.: From intentions to actions: a theory of planned behavior. In: Kuhl, J., Beckmann, J. (eds.) Action Control. SSSSP, pp. 11–39. Springer, Heidelberg (1985). https://doi.org/10.1007/978-3-642-69746-3_2

6. Fishbein, M., Ajzen, I.: Belief, Attitude, Intention, and Behavior: An Introduction to Theory and Research. Addison-Wesley, Reading (1975)
7. Chapman, K.M., Ham, J.O., Liesen, P., Winter, L.: Applying behavioral models to dietary education of elderly diabetic patients. J. Nutr. Educ. **27**(2), 75–79 (1995)
8. Gupchup, G.V., Abhyankar, U.L., Worley, M.M., Raisch, D.W., Marfatia, A.A., Namdar, R.: Relationships between hispanic ethnicity and attitudes and beliefs toward herbal medicine use among older adults. Res. Soc. Adm. Pharm. **2**(2), 266–279 (2006)
9. Rosenstock, I.M.: Why people use health services. Milbank Mem. Fund Q. **44**(3), 94–127 (1966)
10. Melzner, J., Heinze, J., Fritsch, T.: Mobile health applications in workplace health promotion: an integrated conceptual adoption framework. Proc. Technol. **16**, 1374–1382 (2014)
11. Huang, J.C.: Remote health monitoring adoption model based on artificial neural networks. Expert Syst. Appl. **37**, 307–314 (2010)
12. Sun, X., Guo, P.Y., Wang, S., Sun, J.: Predicting iron-fortified soy sauce consumption intention: application of the theory of planned behavior and health belief model. J. Nutr. Educ. Behav. **38**(5), 31–40 (2006)
13. Alharbi, S., Drew, S.: Using the technology acceptance model in understanding academics' behavioural intention to use learning management systems. Int. J. Adv. Comput. Sci. Appl. **5** (1), 143–155 (2014)
14. Chin, W.W.: Issues and opinion on structural equation modelling. MIS Q. **22**(1), 7–16 (1998)
15. Chin, W.W., Marcolin, B.L., Newsted, P.R.: A partial least squares latent variable modeling approach for measuring interaction effects: results from a Monte Carlo simulation study and an electronic-mail emotion/adoption study. Inf. Syst. Res. **14**(2), 189–217 (2003)
16. Nundy, S., Dick, J.J., Solomon, M.C., Peek, M.E.: Developing a behavioral model for mobile phone-based diabetes interventions. Patient Educ. Couns. **90**, 125–132 (2013)
17. Hsieh, P.J.: Physicians' acceptance of electronic medical records exchange: an extension of the decomposed TPB model with institutional trust and perceived risk. Int. J. Med. Inform. **84**(1), 1–14 (2015)

A Review of the Current Intelligent Personal Agents

Sean Li[1(✉)] and Xiaojun (Jenny) Yuan[2]

[1] Rosa International Middle School, Cherry Hill, NJ 08003, USA
seanhaoranli@gmail.com
[2] College of Emergency Preparedness, Homeland Security and Cybersecurity
University at Albany, State University of New York, Albany, NY 12222, USA
xyuan@albany.edu

Abstract. In artificial intelligence, an intelligent personal agent (IPA) is a software designed to use online resources to help people complete simple tasks and respond to questions with natural language. In the market, people wonder if there is a best IPA and have done preliminary testing on them [4]. In this study, we aim at investigating the use of IPAs in people's daily lives. We are also interested in identifying factors that may have an impact on the usability of IPAs. The IPAs we select are Apple Siri, Amazon Alexa, Google Assistant and Microsoft Cortana. We first compare the natural language user interfaces of the above mentioned four IPAs. Next, we examine how researchers have evaluated the use of the four IPAs with the focus on identifying factors affecting the usability of the IPAs. At the end, future research directions are discussed.

Keywords: Intelligent personal agents · Usability · User interface

1 Introduction

According to [1], an intelligent personal agent (IPA) is "software that has been designed to assist people with basic tasks, usually providing information using natural language". In [7], an IPA is "an application that uses inputs such as the user's voice, vision (images), and contextual information to provide assistance by answering questions in natural language, making recommendations, and performing actions". With the rapid technical development of natural language processing and artificial intelligence, IPAs are becoming an important assistant in people's professional work and daily lives [2]. IPAs respond to questions from users through using online resources. Users' questions vary depending on what they need at that specific moment, for example, weather, restaurant or driving directions. Most importantly, an IPA employs voice commands via a natural language user interface to assist users by answering their voice queries and carrying out tasks.

In a study comparing the use of four popularly used IPAs, including Apple Siri, Amazon Alexa, Google Assistant and Microsoft Cortana, Dunn [4] took an initiative to find out if there is a best IPA in the market. In this paper, we carried out a review on studies investigating the use of IPAs. In the following, we first introduce the user

C. Stephanidis (Ed.): HCII Posters 2018, CCIS 850, pp. 253–257, 2018.
https://doi.org/10.1007/978-3-319-92270-6_35

interfaces of the four IPAs, and then review existing research on the use of IPAs with the focus on factors affecting the usability of IPAs. At the end, future research directions are discussed.

2 Four Intelligent Personal Agents (IPAs)

In the market, Apple Siri, Amazon Alexa, Google Assistant and Microsoft Cortana have been widely used by the public. When people talk to IPAs, a user-friendly interface is critical. The interfaces of the above-mentioned four IPAs are shown as below in Fig. 1. As shown in Fig. 1, Alexa is the only one that has no textual interaction with the users. The other three IPAs look similar at the interface level by providing a textual dialogue and recommendations to the users. All the four IPAs have voice input.

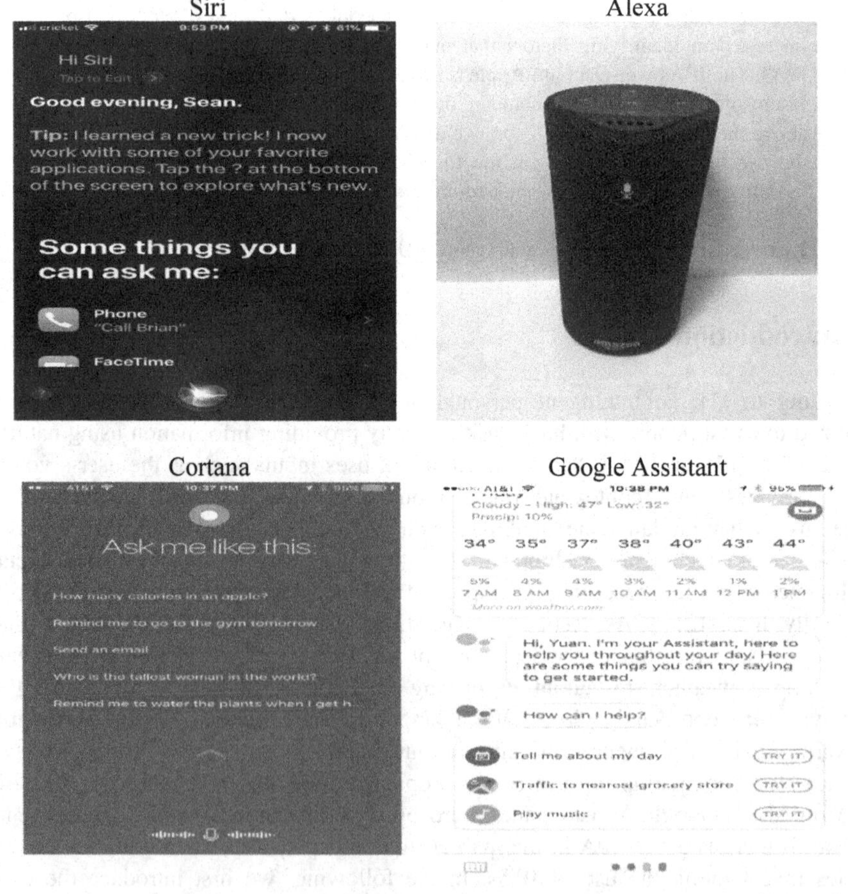

Fig. 1. The user interfaces of the four IPAs.

3 Comparison of the Four IPAs

Research has been done to compare the four IPAs. A study conducted by Dunn [4] highlighted the advantages and disadvantages each IPA had over the other in terms of categories including travel, email, messaging, sports, music, weather, calendar, social, translation, basic tasks, general knowledge and personality. Dunn reported that Google Assistant did very well in assisting with direction and sending emails. Siri came out on top in the areas related to phone call, text, and checking emails. Cortana was also quite good when sending texts, therefore tying with Google Assistant and Siri in this area. Alexa was efficient at reading tweets.

Each IPA has its pros and cons. Schultz [11] found that Cortana can analyze data at an efficient speed with accuracy, and correct pronunciation. However, at times, Cortana pulls up Bing when the answer is very simple, and it is unnecessary to input the query into Bing. As described by [10], Siri is useful when accessing settings, finding emails, doing mathematics, and transforming measurements. The few problems that Siri has are, at times, Siri has trouble comprehending what one is trying to say even though the level of speech is very basic. Also, if Wi-Fi dies then Siri goes along with it. Brandon [3] reported that Alexa understands complex speech and can come up with a reasonable if not accurate response. The main problem that Alexa has is that it crashes. In his article, Moore [9] indicated that Google Home, which runs Google Assistant, provides factual responses to questions asked, with efficiency also. Google Assistant can also understand follow up questions. The problem with Google Assistant is that it lags behind compared to other assistants when it comes to third party support.

With the growing demand of IPAs in the world, how to design a usable IPA that can satisfy users' professional and daily needs is becoming an important research topic. In the following, we discuss some factors that may have an impact on the usability of IPAs.

4 Factors Affecting the Use of IPAs

Research has shown that voice can affect the usability of interactive voice response systems that provide ubiquitous user interfaces to enable customers to collect information and perform tasks [5]. Specifically, [5] found out that voice personality and speaker gender have an impact on the perceived usability of the system. For example, male voices can lead to higher usability metrics than female voices.

The tasks an IPA performs include professional and personal tasks, and an IPA was designed to help users in doing his professional tasks while taking care of the personal tasks [2]. Users' personal tasks may change frequently based on their immediate needs. For different tasks, their complexity can vary. Dunn [4] indicated the potential impact of task type and task complexity on the usability of IPAs. In completing tasks, voice-based interactions may cause increased cognitive workload for users. Stayer et al. [12] tested the effect of voice-based interactions using 3 different IPAs (e.g., Apple's Siri, Google's Google Now for Android phones, and Microsoft's Cortana) on the cognitive workload of the driver. It seems that systematic differences exist between the smartphones. The Google system placed lower cognitive workload on the driver than the other two systems. Further analysis demonstrated that such differences were associated with the number of system errors, the time to complete tasks, and the complexity and intuitiveness of the devices.

Miangah and Nezarat [8] claimed that "the speech aspect of mobile learning is as significant as textual aspect of it, since it enables learners to comfortably speak with a system recording their voice and allowing them to listen back to themselves (p. 314)".

Based on this claim, the way users interact or communicate with the IPAs could motivate users' learning [6]. For example, Goksel-Canbek and Mutlu [6] found out that the speech/language dialogues between users and Siri may help users improve language skills on speaking (pronunciation) and listening. Therefore, the design of the dialogue structure of the user interface is one of the factors that may influence the usability of IPAs.

In sum, factors such as voice personality, speaker gender, task types, the complexity and intuitiveness of the devices, as well as the design of the dialogue structure of the user interface could have an impact on the usability of IPAs.

5 Conclusion and Future Work

We conducted a review on studies investigating the use of IPAs. Four IPAs, that is, Apple Siri, Amazon Alexa, Google Assistant and Microsoft Cortana, were selected and compared. Factors that may have an impact on the usability of IPAs were identified.

As [2] claimed, "IPA will play a very important role in the near future". It is time for researchers and developers to catch the opportunities and also confront the challenges of the development of IPA. With the advance of artificial intelligence and natural language processing technologies, the future application of IPAs would be able to take into account users' emotion, personal characteristics, and their personal needs, and to deal with complex tasks in various settings, including education, health, and entertainment, etc.

In the field of human computer interaction, how to make IPAs more usable and make users feel pleasing and satisfactory is becoming a very important topic. As can be seen from Fig. 1, there exist differences between the interfaces of the four IPAs. We need to answer the question if and how the various interface features affect the usability of IPAs. In addition, it would be interesting to explore the relationship between different tasks (including task complexity and task types) and the usability of IPAs. Besides gender, other user characteristics such as domain knowledge may be considered. For example, we can examine if users' domain knowledge have an impact on the interaction between users and IPAs, in particular when dealing with complicated tasks in the medical field.

In the near future, we plan to do a crowdsourcing study to explore if and how the level of task complexity, the types of tasks, and users' domain knowledge can have an impact on the usability and user experience of IPAs.

References

1. Beal, V.: IPA - intelligent personal assistant. https://www.webopedia.com/TERM/I/intelligent-personal-assistant.html. Accessed 2 Jan 2018
2. Bhinderwala, A., Shukla, N., Cherarajan, V.: Intelligent personal agent. Int. J. Comput. Appl. 9–12 (2014). (0975 – 8887) National Conference on Role of Engineers in Nation Building 2014 (NCRENB-14)
3. Brandon, J.: The pros and cons of using Amazon Alexa as a model for chatbots. https://venturebeat.com/2016/07/30/the-pros-and-cons-of-using-amazon-alexa-as-a-model-for-chatbots/. Accessed 3 Dec 2018
4. Dunn, J.: We put Siri, Alexa, Google Assistant, and Cortana through a marathon of tests to see who's winning the virtual assistant race—here's what we found. Business Insider. http://www.businessinsider.com/siri-vs-google-assistant-cortana-alexa-2016-11. Accessed 2 Jan 2018
5. Edwards, R., Kortum, P.: He says, she says: does voice affect usability? In: Proceedings of the Human Factors and Ergonomics Society Annual Meeting, vol. 56, no. 1, pp. 1486–1490. SAGE Publications, Los Angeles (2012)
6. Goksel-Canbek, N., Mutlu, M.E.: On the track of artificial intelligence: learning with intelligent personal assistants. Int. J. Hum. Sci. **13**(1), 592–601 (2016)
7. Hauswald, J., Laurenzano, M.A., Zhang, Y., Li, C., Rovinski, A., Khurana, A., Dreslinski, R.G., Mudge, T., Petrucci, V., Tang, L., Mars, J.: Sirius: an open end-to-end voice and vision personal assistant and its implications for future warehouse scale computers. In: Proceedings of the Twentieth International Conference on Architectural Support for Programming Languages and Operating Systems, pp. 223–238. ACM (2015)
8. Miangah, T.M., Nezarat, A.: Mobile-assisted language learning. Int. J. Distrib. Parallel Syst. **3**(1), 309–319 (2012)
9. Moore, Q.: Google home pros and cons review: advantages and disadvantages. https://techranker.net/google-home-pros-cons-review-advantages-disadvantages/. Accessed 3 Dec 2018
10. Norton team: hey Siri: the pros and cons of voice commands. https://uk.norton.com/norton-blog/2016/02/hey_siri_the_prosa.html. Accessed 3 Dec 2018
11. Shultz, G.: The pros and cons of Cortana in build 9926 of Windows 10, 30 Jan 2015. https://www.techrepublic.com/article/the-pros-and-cons-of-cortana-in-build-9926-of-windows-10/. Accessed 3 Dec 2018
12. Strayer, D.L., et al.: The smartphone and the driver's cognitive workload: a comparison of Apple, Google, and Microsoft's intelligent personal assistants. Can. J. Exp. Psychol. **71**(2), 93–110 (2017)

Digi-Craft: A Creative Process in Form-Finding Beyond the Accuracy of 3D Printing

Chor-Kheng Lim(✉)

Department of Art and Design, Yuan Ze University, Taoyuan, Taiwan
kheng@saturn.yzu.edu.tw

Abstract. This study aims to explore the creative way in using 3D printer during form-finding process. We found a creative process blurring the accuracy of 3D printing. We use the "Stringing" effect as the modelling method and enhance the abstraction of 3D printing, which called Digi-Craft. Finally, we successfully fabricate the coral-like, hanging lines, meshing surface 3D printed models. These models' shapes are not fully created in 3D model; some parts are "Stringing" parts which we controlled by 3D printing factors. We hope this method will improve the creativity of form-finding design process in using 3D printing.

Keywords: Form-finding · 3D printing · Stringing · Accuracy Abstraction

1 Introduction

3D printing was known as "rapid prototyping". Its official nomenclature of "Additive Manufacturing" (AM) is defined as "a process of joining materials to make objects from 3D model data, usually layer upon layer, as opposed to subtractive manufacturing methodologies" (ASTM 2012). There are different methods of AM, including the most widely adopted technologies, fused deposition modelling (FDM), stereolithography (SLA), selective laser sintering (SLS) and 3D printing (3DP), but new additive processes continue to be developed and commercialized (Petrovic et al. 2011).

In the late 20th century, 3D printers were extremely expensive and could only be used to print a limited number of products. Consequently, the development of open source hardware and low-cost 3D printers induce the 3D printing began to lead a worldwide manufacturing revolution. It expands the freedom of complex forms/shapes manufacture, and gives a great impact to design field too.

2 Problem and Objective

If we reviewing the traditional additive manufacturing process, it actually began from the ancient period, around 2500 BC. The Traditional additive fabrication began with clay coiling pottery, by making a long snake of clay and coiling it up into a pot shape.

C. Stephanidis (Ed.): HCII Posters 2018, CCIS 850, pp. 258–262, 2018.
https://doi.org/10.1007/978-3-319-92270-6_36

The clay coiling process is a handmade process and it performs the hand-craft inaccuracy and abstraction. In the manufacturing process, artist have the opportunity to modify the shapes of pottery at any time by hand (Fig. 1).

Fig. 1. Clay coiling pottery (around 2500 BC)

However, 3D printing showing the accuracy of the digital manufacture process. The 3D model was first created and then export to .STL format CAD file. As the CAD file is not machine readable and thus needs an intermediate software, Slicer. The intermediate software such as Kisslicer, CURA, etc., enable slice the geometries into layers, and deals with extruder heating, layer thickness, speed, and calculates the toolpath to creates a Gcode file, which is machine readable. The whole process is very accuracy and the model manufacture in layers digitally.

As the 3D printing has the advantage in complex and freeform model making, designers or artists enable to utilize this technique to represent their design forms. However, the accuracy operation while manufacture prompt to the limitation of the creativity in conceptual design process. As the tools in aiding design thinking of form finding in the conceptual design stage, does the 3D printing process have its characteristics of abstraction?

In order to enhance the usage of 3D printing in the form making process, especially to aid in the early conceptual process, furthermore to blurring the accuracy process and beyond the establish operation, this study attempts to combine the characteristic of inaccuracy and abstraction like the hand-craft clay coiling process to digital 3D printing process. The aim of this study is to find out the creative way of using 3D printing and to propose a new model making method: Digi-Craft, a form finding process beyond the accuracy of 3D printing.

3 Methodology

From questionnaires by designers and data analysis, we conclude the design factors which can affect the accuracy and abstraction in form-finding design process. The following shows the factors concluded as Table 1.

Table 1. Design factors of accuracy and abstraction.

	Accuracy factors	Abstraction factors
Stiffness	Rigid	Soft, flexible
Form	Geometric shape, math form	Freeform shape, natural form
Material	Metal, plywood	Fabric, clay
Structure	Compression	Tension

Then we conducted the 3D printing experiment based on the analyzed factors. In order to find out the abstraction and inaccuracy in 3D printing manufacture operations, we test the freeform, natural shapes, and tried to test the fabric-like, flexible-like models. To control the machine parameters, we adjust the four main 3D printing control factors:

a. Temperature (extruder heating, bed heating)
b. Speed (travel speed, extruder speed)
c. Retraction
d. Cooling (fans).

4 Unexpected Discovery

3D prints sometimes show small strands of plastic on places where the 3d printers shouldn't print and the print head must only travel from one place to another. These unwanted strands of plastic is called Stringing (Fig. 2). We found that the Stringing effect in 3D printing is very interesting, normally it's a drawback of 3D printing. If we create the fine CAD 3D model to slice and send to print normally, it will not appear in the model fabrication process. But if we set the wrong temperature, speed or other issues, it will appear and damage the model in the result. As this effect appear unexpectedly, and also inaccuracy, we decided to use it in form finding process to represent the fabric-like and flexible-like characteristic. After testing the parameters of the five control factors, we success to create the stringing effect according to our desire, but still keep the abstraction (Fig. 2).

Fig. 2. Stringing effect in 3D printing

We used the same 3D model CAD file (simple modeling) to print out slightly different 3D printing models, which integrate the rigid parts (3D model) and flexible parts (3D printing factors). Finally, we successfully fabricate the coral-like, hanging lines, meshing surface 3D printed models (Fig. 3). These models' shapes are not fully created in 3D model; some parts are "stringing" parts which we controlled by 3D printing factors.

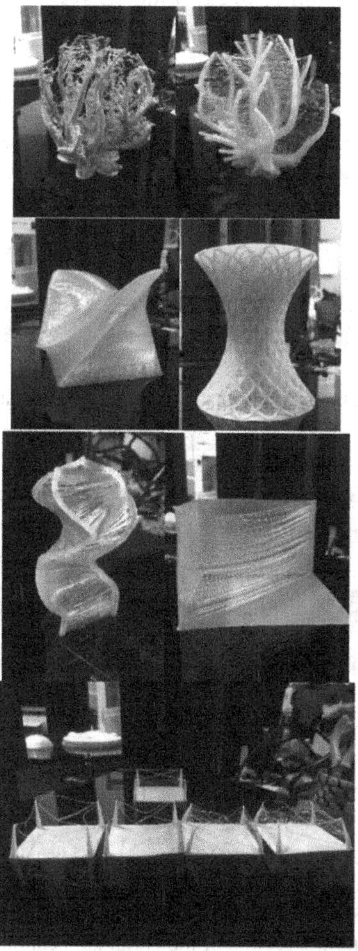

Fig. 3. Model making: integration of rigid parts (3D model) and flexible parts (stringing)

As we need to create the Stringing parts, we tried to figure out the toolpaths generated by the Slicer software in the beginning (Fig. 4), however we cannot modify the toolpaths in the existing software. As we need to create our own toolpath so that we can generate the stringing shape which we desire. Therefore, we try to use the "lines modelling" or "toolpath modelling" method in creating design forms to generate the toolpath directly from coding tools (Processing, Grasshopper). Then controlled the 3D print factors to print the forms (Fig. 5). The models are printed very fast and province materials.

Consequently, we propose a new 3D printing modelling method that can generate the fabric-like, hanging-lines and thinnest surface models. We tried to turn the disadvantages to advantages by creative thinking. We find out the creative way of using 3D printing and conclude a new model making method which called Digi-Craft, a form finding process beyond the accuracy of 3D printing. We hope this method will improve the creativity of form-finding design process in using 3D printing.

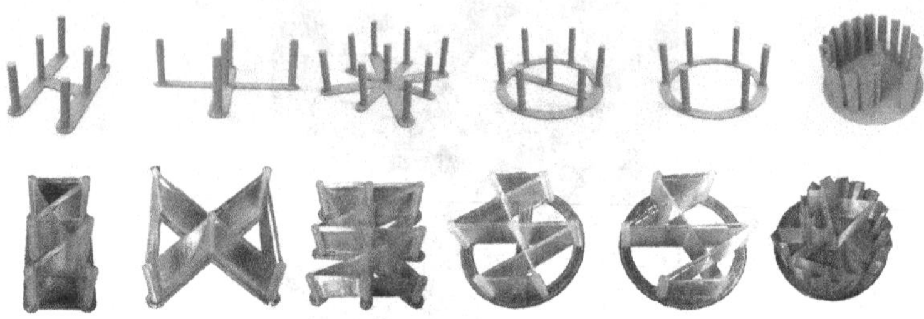

Fig. 4. Analysis process of the toolpaths (stringing) generated by Slicer software

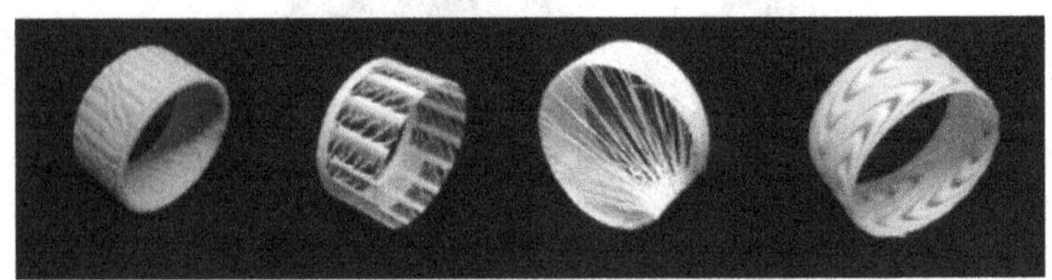

Fig. 5. 3D printed model making from Digit-Craft method

References

ASTM: ASTM F2792-12a: Standard Terminology for Additive Manufacturing Technologies. ASTM International, West Conshohocken (2012)

Petrovic, V., Gonzalez, J.V.H., Ferrando, O.J., Gordillo, J.D., Puchades, J.R.B., Grinan, L.P.: Additive layered manufacturing: sectors of industrial application shown through case studies. Int. J. Prod. Res. **49**(4), 1061–1079 (2011)

A Generalizable Method for Validating the Utility of Process Analytics with Usability Assessments

Ryan Mullins(✉), Chad Weiss, Brent D. Fegley, and Ben Ford

Aptima, Inc., Woburn, MA 01801, USA
rmullins@aptima.com

Abstract. Crowdsourcing systems rely on assessments of individual performance over time to assign tasking that improves aggregate performance. We call these combinations of performance assessment and task allocation *process analytics*. As crowdsourcing advances to include greater levels of task complexity, validating *process analytics*, which requires replicable behaviors across crowds, becomes more challenging and urgent. Here, we present a work-in-progress design for validating *process analytics* using integrated usability assessments, which we view as a sufficient proxy for crowdsourced problem-solving. Using the process of developing a crowdsourcing system itself as a use case, we begin by distributing usability assessments to two independent, equally-sized, and otherwise comparable subgroups of a crowd. The first subgroup (control) uses a conventional method of usability assessment; the second (treatment), a distributed method. Differences in subgroup performance determine the degree to which the *process analytics* for the distributed method vary about the conventional method.

Keywords: Crowdsourcing · Usability assessment · Process analytics Performance assessment

1 Introduction

In recent years, crowdsourcing, specifically the act of leveraging collective intelligence via computer-supported systems, has exploded in popularity. Research has shown the value of crowdsourcing approaches in a variety of domains, from word processing [1] to dataset development [10] to geopolitical event forecasting [9]. The value of these systems comes from their ability to assess individual performance over time and tailor tasking assignments to improve aggregate performance (see [5,11,13,14], among others). We call these combinations of performance assessment and task allocation capabilities *process analytics*; and our goal is to validate the utility of *process analytics* relative to some baseline.

Recent research has tried to apply crowdsourcing approaches to increasingly complex problems, for example argumentation [6] and composable teaming [13].

C. Stephanidis (Ed.): HCII Posters 2018, CCIS 850, pp. 263–267, 2018.
https://doi.org/10.1007/978-3-319-92270-6_37

As such work continues, we expect to encounter sufficiently complex, defeasible, incendiary, and latent problems that require more adaptive and abstracted *process analytics*, which is to say problems where the process is more important than the individual in the workflow. Some examples include organizational change management, strategic corporate decision-making, and cultural change management (see [2,7,8], among others). We refer to these collectively as organizational problem-solving challenges.

We hypothesize that *process analytics* may be replicable validated via a proxy process that (a) presents participants with a repeatable task of meaningful complexity and (b) is not dependent on the behavioral characteristics of the crowds used for assessing system performance. Below, we present a work-in-progress design for validating the utility of *process analytics* designed to enable crowd-sourced organizational problem-solving using usability assessments as the proxy process.

2 Validation of Utility Through Usability Assessment

Our primary obstacles in validating *process analytics* are (a) the limited ability to replicate organizational state and participant behaviors to support rigorous performance comparison (see [3], among others), and (b) the latency between the decision to implement a solution and the manifestation of its repercussions (see [4], among others). The following subsections discuss the suitability of usability assessment as a proxy process, the method by which usability assessment will be implemented, and initial performance measures used for comparison.

2.1 Assessing the Suitability of Usability

Fidelity and timeliness are our primary suitability measures. Regarding fidelity, sufficient proxy processes must capture the complexities and nuances of debating organizational problems and their solutions. Ideal proxies will also capture the sequenced and dependent nature of solutions to complex organizational problems. Modern, agile product management—the utilization of end-user feedback to drive future development—is an equally complex, nuanced, and interdependent process. Solutions and their prioritization must address and/or align with three critical perspectives: functionality required by end-users, technical feasibility of implementation, and the vision of various stakeholder groups. These perspectives are also proxies for perspectives found in organizational restructuring problems.

Regarding timeliness, the validation method we use must produce results at a much more rapid pace than organizational change. Modern product management and development practices are trending towards week- and month-long iteration cycles, if not faster, which is an order of magnitude increase, at minimum, compared to the latency of organizational problem-solving. Similarly, we can directly assess the impact of a change (i.e., the utility and usability of a feature) across product iterations, a process that would require orders-of-magnitude differences in level of effort to model and validate in organizational change problems.

Given measures of fidelity and timeliness, usability assessment supporting product management objectives has sufficient character as a proxy for organizational problem-solving, particularly for validating *process analytics*.

2.2 A Method of Implementation

Our method is an extension of common practices in the product development, Agile software development, and user experience engineering communities. We assume that the crowdsourcing tool being evaluated uses some form of issue management tool (e.g., Jira[1] or GitHub[2]) to independently track the status of features, bug fixes, etc. being considered for future releases. Our method requires that knowledge elicitation mechanisms germane to usability assessment and product enhancement have been integrated into the crowdsourcing system. The goal is to have participants generate a ranked list of items (i.e., features and bugs) that should be addressed in the next release. Our generalized process for achieving this goal has three phases, derived from guerilla UX methods [12]:

1. An *elicitation phase*, where pain-points, bugs, and new feature ideas are solicited and refined;
2. An *assessment phase*, where technical cost and end-user value are calculated; and
3. A *debate phase*, where ideas are selected for inclusion in the next release of the system based on the aforementioned assessments.

Assessments are distributed to two independent and comparable subgroups of the crowd. The first group (control) uses the "conventional" method, where product owners and stakeholders engage face-to-face with participants only during the *elicitation phase* of the process. The second group (treatment) uses the "distributed" method, where participants engage in all phases (excepting the technical cost component of the assessment phase, which we assume to require significant expertise). Decisions regarding when and how to engage participants in the treatment group are made using the tool's *process analytics*. Data collected from these interactions are manually or automatically recorded, respectively, in the issue management system for life-cycle tracking and other uses discussed below. The membership of each group can and should be varied between versions of the tool in order to counteract biases.

2.3 Performance Measurement and Comparison

Process analytic validation occurs by comparing the outputs of the control and treatment groups. We expect that, over time, performance of the treatment group will exceed the performance of the control group along the following measures:

[1] https://www.atlassian.com/software/jira/features.
[2] https://github.com/features/project-management/.

- Time to complete a task, where "task" may be defined as brainstorming in service of feature idea elicitation, debate about competing ideas, or the use of various voting mechanisms to develop the final list of features, among other examples.
- Volume of ideas generated. While we anticipate that the total volume will reduce over time, we expect that the amount of time required to produce the same volume of ideas will be consistently lower for the treatment group.
- Reduced problem recurrence, measurement of which is enabled through the analysis of the items that have been stored in the issue management system of choice.
- Scoped scale, where ideas (i.e., problems, solutions, feedback) become more atomic and well-defined over time.
- Frequency of interaction (i.e., how often the group uses the tool).
- Degree of participation (i.e., how many tasks are being engaged).

3 Future Work

We have presented a novel method for validating the utility of *process analytics* used in crowdsourcing tools using an adapted version of usability assessments. This method provides a replicable and timely alternative to other analytic validation methods used in crowdsourcing research, while preserving the fidelity of complex problem-solving challenges. We are currently pilot-testing this method with our tool for organizational crowdsourced problem-solving and plan to publish our findings regarding the ecological validity of this method in the future. If successful, we expect to see improvements in task completion time and problem scoping, increased idea generation, and decreased problem recurrence in the treatment group when compared to the control group. This method should generalize to a broad spectrum of complex crowdsourcing tasks.

Acknowledgements. This research was performed in connection with contract N68335-18-C-0040 with the U.S. Office of Naval Research. We would like to thank Dr. Yiling Chen, Dr. Predrag Neskovic, Dr. James Intriligator, Mr. Roger Barry, Mr. Vilmos Csizmadia, and Ms. Kelsey Loanes for their contributions to this work as thought partners.

References

1. Bernstein, M.S., Little, G., Miller, R.C., Hartmann, B., Ackerman, M.S., Karger, D.R., Crowell, D., Panovich, K.: Soylent: a word processor with a crowd inside. Commun. ACM **58**(8), 85–94 (2015). https://doi.org/10.1145/2791285
2. Burns, T.E., Stalker, G.M.: The Management of Innovation. Oxford University Press, Oxford (1961)
3. Camerer, C.F., Dreber, A., Forsell, E., Ho, T.H., Huber, J., Johannesson, M., Kirchler, M., Almenberg, J., Altmejd, A., Chan, T., et al.: Evaluating replicability of laboratory experiments in economics. Science **351**(6280), 1433–1436 (2016)

4. Dahl, M.S.: Organizational change and employee stress. Manag. Sci. **57**(2), 240–256 (2011)
5. Dawid, A.P., Skene, A.M.: Maximum likelihood estimation of observer error-rates using the EM algorithm. Appl. Stat. **28**, 20–28 (1979)
6. Drapeau, R., Chilton, L.B., Bragg, J., Weld, D.S.: Microtalk: using argumentation to improve crowdsourcing accuracy. In: Fourth AAAI Conference on Human Computation and Crowdsourcing (2016)
7. Jimmieson, N.L., Peach, M., White, K.M.: Utilizing the theory of planned behavior to inform change management: an investigation of employee intentions to support organizational change. J. Appl. Behav. Sci. **44**(2), 237–262 (2008)
8. Kerber, K., Buono, A.F.: Rethinking organizational change: reframing the challenge of change management. Organ. Dev. J. **23**(3), 23 (2005)
9. Mellers, B., Stone, E., Murray, T., Minster, A., Rohrbaugh, N., Bishop, M., Chen, E., Baker, J., Hou, Y., Horowitz, M., Ungar, L., Tetlock, P.: Identifying and cultivating superforecasters as a method of improving probabilistic predictions. Perspect. Psychol. Sci. **10**(3), 267–281 (2015). https://doi.org/10.1177/1745691615577794
10. Post, M., Callison-Burch, C., Osborne, M.: Constructing parallel corpora for six Indian languages via crowdsourcing. In: Proceedings of the Seventh Workshop on Statistical Machine Translation, pp. 401–409. Association for Computational Linguistics, Montréal, Canada, June 2012. http://www.aclweb.org/anthology/W12-3152
11. Tetlock, P.E., Gardner, D.: Superforecasting: The Art and Science of Prediction. Random House, New York City (2016)
12. Unger, R., Warfel, T.Z.: Guerilla UX Research Methods: Thrifty, Fast, and Effective User Experience Research Techniques. Morgan Kaufmann, Burlington (2012)
13. Valentine, M.A., Retelny, D., To, A., Rahmati, N., Doshi, T., Bernstein, M.S.: Flash organizations: crowdsourcing complex work by structuring crowds as organizations. In: Proceedings of the 2017 CHI Conference on Human Factors in Computing Systems, pp. 3523–3537. ACM (2017)
14. Yin, M., Chen, Y.: Predicting crowd work quality under monetary interventions. In: Fourth AAAI Conference on Human Computation and Crowdsourcing. The Association for the Advancement of Artificial Intelligence (2016)

Designer's Personal Fabrication: Understand the Designers Who Learn 3D Printing Design in China

Jue Ren[1(✉)] and Leirah Wang[2]

[1] Harbin Institution of Technology, Shenzhen, China
2284164@qq.com
[2] Xubrance, Shanghai, China
leirah.wang@xuberance.com

Abstract. The main area of 3D printing is about material science, STEM education for kids, industrial engineering and applications in medical science in China. And a new wave of customized 3D printing application raises up in fashion, jewelry, food and furniture industry recently. More and more students who major in architecture and art want to turn their career into 3D printing design. Taking Xuberance's professional 3D printing designer workshop as a case study this paper presents the role of 3D printing designers to the massive change in the pattern of interactive computing. We find that designers who learning 3D printing design skill are taking it for personal development and success in career and startup. This self-driven learning purpose make designers as one kind of end user for 3D printing material, printers, software and training courses. At the meanwhile, these 3D printing designers are making new products for their own customers. It is 3D printing designer, not 3D printers, connecting the industry and the customers, and introduce new domain knowledge from end users into industry with customized 3D printing products, such as untrained end users can get one haute couture with design only could be seen in architecture before.

Keywords: 3D printing designer · Personal fabrication

1 Introduction

Although 3D printing is a technology with a history more than 30 years, the 3D printing technology is introduced into mainland China initiated by the new discourses of Chinese government for maker and innovation recently, mostly reported by media to be used in maker space as a makers' tool to create new products for users industrial and engineer-based prototyping. For this reason, first wave of users of 3D printing technology in China seem to be technical and professional users, such as grassroots maker, manufacturing factories and new technology company in China.

With the popularization of the Additive Manufacturing and the upgrading of the 3D printing materials, China government has taken 3D printing as one of national strategy [1]. According to media reports, in the new 2020 plan, it is hoped that the sales volume of the 3D printing industry would get a booming market of 2 billion RMB [2] will be reached.

C. Stephanidis (Ed.): HCII Posters 2018, CCIS 850, pp. 268–272, 2018.
https://doi.org/10.1007/978-3-319-92270-6_38

More and more consumers accept the 3D printing products with strong demand for fashion, fan-entertainment, customized clothing, jewelry, food and other new computation. At the same time, personal manufacturing is also rising in China, and designers who are artists, architects and art designers start to move into 3D printing design industry bring the multi discipline dome knowledge into this area [3, 4].

China's manufacturing industry needs for 3D printing talents are more than 8 million [5]. With the upgrade of digital economy and new consuming industry, it is provides a great deal of space for the needs of 3D printing design talents.

This means that the design education needs to integrate into 3D printing design education as soon as possible, so that students in the design field can adapt to the needs of prospective employers in the future [6].

But the current 3D printing design education is mainly in primary and secondary schools' stem education [7] and hardware, additive manufacture industry, health, material and engineering area.

There are many studies on industrial and emerging-based design education, but the corresponding 3D printing education is less.

With the rise of customized design, 3D printing designers have become a hub for personal manufacture, without good 3D printing designers, customers could get introduced to new products printed by 3D printing technology [8].

This study was initiated in 2014–2015, where there was few professional 3D printing educational courses, and 3D printing designers has to learn 3D printing design technology mostly by themselves online. By the end of 2014, Xuberance, which is the first professional 3D printing company in China has made 13 workshops around the world.

This study hopes to provide a preliminary exploration to 1. Where does the designers come from when there's no enough academic training in this area? 2. What the motivation for these designers to learn 3D printing design? 3. Learning the 3D printing design has an impact on their careers. 4. 3D printing design education how to respond to talent needs.

What are the main features of the 3D printing designer in China? Chinese 3D printing designers have entered the industry for a number of opportunities, Chinese 3D printing designers, understanding of the industry.

2 Research Approach

This research uses mix-method, such as online questionnaire, multi-site ethnography in Wuhan and Shenzhen [9]. Researchers take part in 2 workshop with the designers in two cities [10]. 53 informants, most are young university students and new designers under the age of 25 (see Fig. 1), and 30 males and 23 females (see Fig. 2), who are interviewed with a semi-structure online questionnaire.

3 The Findings

This research found that 94.3% of the interviewees have a bachelor's degree, and they are from different disciplines, including art design, architecture, urban planning, electronics, mechanical engineering, sculpture, psychology and business management.

44 of them have taken Xubrance's 3D printing design workshop. 35 of them are willing to take 3D printing design as a part-time job.

There were 39 of them, 22 males and 17 females, who were not engaged in 3D industry before the training, but after the training 31 of them were very interested in taking the job 3D printing designers, most of them also are architecture.

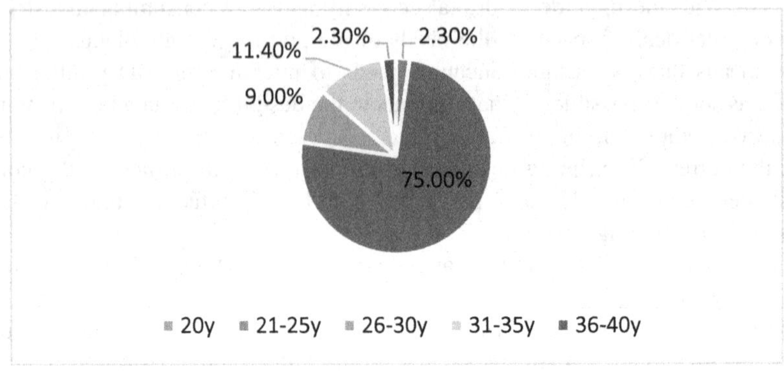

Fig. 1. Age riot of informants (n = 53)

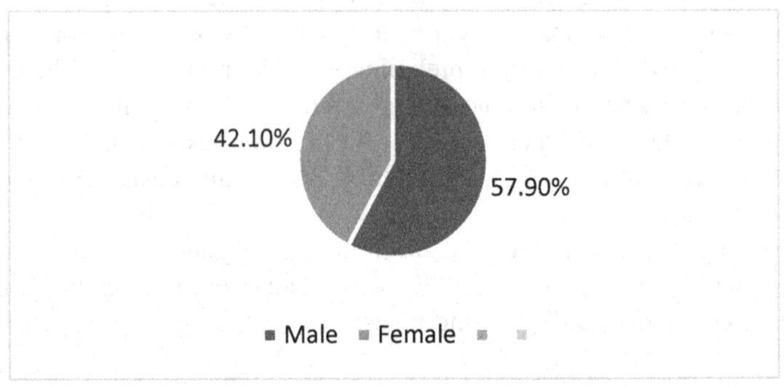

Fig. 2. Gender riot of informants (n = 53)

They are primarily interested in learning a 3D printing design to achieve "personal development". They want to be able to build personal brands, increase revenue, or start their own business.

They mainly come from private companies and schools, and average annual income is less than 50,000 RMB, so most of them expect part-time jobs to work in 3D printing designs or build their own personal brand, and most of them want to increase annual income to full-time salary of 160,000–300,000 RMB, and part-time salary of 60,000–100,000 RMB.

The most important factors that influence the participant's selection of training courses are form of workshop, mentors' skill, cities, training fees, etc. Because they already have some basic design courses in their major area, most young designers want to be able to learn the full-process curriculum and master level classes.

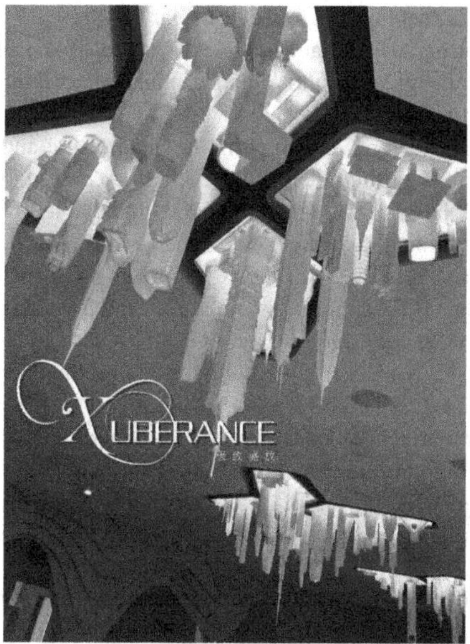

Fig. 3. Drop ceiling in a coffee shop in Shanghai, which is 3D printing designed with image of most famous buildings in the world (Designed by Steven Ma)

4 Conclusion

In this exploratory case studies, we found that:

1. Motivation for designers who learn 3D printing design is mainly related to their personal development need, such as ego trip and build their own brands.
2. Most of designers join this new 3D printing design industry is very young, and take their own domain knowledge [11] into this area, which take a domain knowledge flow from other discipline into 3D printing design, such as Steven Ma is trained as an architect, and then he brings architect's perspective into his 3D printing design works (see Fig. 3).
3. There is a need to increase interdisciplinary content across 3D printing design education curriculum.
4. It is designers who want to make their company and brands to do their personal fabrication, connecting the material industry and engineering-based products to the ending consumers.

Acknowledgements. We would like to thank all the informants who are interviewed.

References

1. MIIT: Interpretation of the plan of action for the development of the timber manufacturing industry (2017–2020). http://www.miit.gov.cn/n1146285/n1146352/n3054355/n3057585/n3057591/c5956821/content.html. Accessed 10 Mar 2018
2. Chinese.com: 12 departments: the annual sales revenue of the 3D printing industry will exceed RMB 20 billion by 2020. http://finance.china.com.cn/industry/20171213/4470584.shtml. Accessed 10 Mar 2018
3. Newatlas.com: How 3D printing is disrupting the architecture and design industry. https://newatlas.com/3d-printing-housing-architecture/53083/. Accessed 10 Mar 2018
4. Hipolite, W.: China's Nanjing Arts Institute Debuts Incredible 3D Printed Fashion. https://3dprint.com/67832/3d-printed-fashion-show/. Accessed 10 Mar 2018
5. Lu, B., Wang, Y., Zhao, Y.: Review of the development of 3D printing industry during the Twelfth Five-Year Plan Period. http://gjss.ndrc.gov.cn/zttp/xyqzlxxhg/201712/t20171221_871245.html. Accessed 10 Mar 2018
6. Kwon, Y.M., Lee, Y.-A., Kim, S.J.: Case study on 3D printing education in fashion design coursework. Fashion Text. **4**(1), 26 (2017)
7. Zhaochen, D.T.: Alternative 3D education for children: course design of 3D printing interactivity for Beijing's primary schools. In: Proceedings of the Fifth International Symposium of Chinese CHI, pp. 30–35. ACM (2017)
8. Ma, S.: Mass customisation: designed in China, produced globally. Architectural Des. **87**(6), 58–63 (2017)
9. Marcus, G.E.: Ethnography in/of the world system: the emergence of multi-sited ethnography. Ann. Rev. Anthropol. **1**, 95–117 (1995)
10. Xambó, A., Jewitt, C., Price, S.: Towards an integrated methodological framework for understanding embodiment in HCI. In: CHI 2014 Extended Abstracts on Human Factors in Computing Systems, pp. 1411–1416 (2014)
11. Baudisch, P.: Personal fabrication in HCI: trends and challenges. In: Proceedings of the International Working Conference on Advanced Visual Interfaces, pp. 1–2. ACM (2016)

A Preliminary Usability Assessment of a 3D Printable Orthosis Design System

Michaela Servi[1], Yary Volpe[1(✉)], Francesca Uccheddu[1], Rocco Furferi[1], Lapo Governi[1], and Simone Lazzeri[2]

[1] Department of Industrial Engineering, University of Florence, Via Di Santa Marta 3, 50139 Florence, Italy
{michaela.servi,yary.volpe,francesca.uccheddu, rocco.furferi,lapo.governi}@unifi.it

[2] Children's Hospital A. Meyer of Florence, Viale Gaetano Pieraccini 24, 50139 Florence, Italy
simone.lazzeri@meyer.it

Abstract. The standard treatment for bones fractures entails the use of a tailor-made plaster cast which has several disadvantages: its weight generally causes discomfort, it cannot be taken off without breaking it, it can cause skin rashes and prevents ventilation of the treated area. Therefore, the application of traditional casts to orthopaedics patients does not represent, to date, the best option. To overcome the above-mentioned drawbacks, many strategies based on reverse engineering and additive manufacturing techniques have been proposed and proved to be a valid alternative for producing custom orthoses. Encouraged by the aforementioned results, the authors have developed a low-cost system (called *Oplà*), specifically dedicated to the hand-wrist-arm district of paediatric patients and capable of creating a 3D CAD model of the orthosis ready to be printed by using additive manufacturing techniques. Such a system comprises a 3D scanner, a control software and a semi-automatic CAD procedure to easily model the orthopaedic device on each patient, without the need of CAD modelling professionals. To evaluate if *Oplà* can be effectively used by the medical staff to design patient specific 3D printable orthoses in the clinical practice, a preliminary usability assessment has been performed. Five professional nurses from the Meyer Children's Hospital of Florence (Italy) have been selected and trained in the use of the system. Subsequently, each of them has been asked to perform the whole process for the same patient. Effectiveness, efficiency and satisfaction have been measured in accordance to ISO 9241-11. Results proved that the *Oplà* system is characterized by a good usability allowing the user to easily and intuitively perform all the tasks in a reasonable time.

Keywords: Usability · CAD · Reverse engineering · Cast modelling

1 Introduction

The present research has been carried out in the framework of a multidisciplinary collaboration between the Meyer's Children Hospital and the Department of Industrial Engineering in Florence (Italy) by relying on the basic idea that 3D technologies,

C. Stephanidis (Ed.): HCII Posters 2018, CCIS 850, pp. 273–280, 2018.
https://doi.org/10.1007/978-3-319-92270-6_39

thanks to the possibility of delivering novel patient tailored solutions, enable more effective approaches in the medical scene. This study addresses the problem of building custom-sized plastic made arm orthoses for children with the aim of improving the traditional arm plaster cast performances by increasing the lightness and the ventilation of the device, while reducing most of the actual risks, such as compartment syndrome, ischemia, heat injury, pressure sores and skin breakdown [1]. Several solutions for personalized casts have been technically investigated, examples can be found in [2, 3]; nevertheless, the literature is still lacking a complete clinic-ready infrastructure which could be fully exploited by the medical staff not needing the presence of an expert CAD modeller. The proposed infrastructure (called *Oplà*) consists in both an ad hoc paediatric hand-wrist-arm 3D scanner and a control software to ease both the acquisition and the modelling process, that entirely eliminates the need of experts to construct the orthopaedic device. In fact, to convey a custom-made orthosis the two critical phases are the patient's anatomy acquisition and the device modelling, followed by a 3D printing process. The *Oplà* designing process is completely user-oriented and based on two principal objectives: (i) to hide from the medical staff the underlying technical schemes of both anatomy acquisition and orthosis modelling; (ii) to build a reliable instrument which could be used within a paediatric clinical facility. For these reasons, *Oplà* enables a rapid acquisition process, differently from state of the art scanners which are either very expensive or need to immobilize the patient for at least 30 s to reproduce the correct anatomy. The control software, instead, has been designed to be intuitive and user-friendly, and to facilitate the modelling process which is indeed a non-trivial procedure since it must be adapted to different paediatric anatomies varying in shape and size. In this work, the preliminary usability of the proposed software is tested with objective metrics on a sample of 5 professional nurses from the Meyer Children's Hospital of Florence (Italy). In Sect. 2 the proposed approach is presented; Sect. 3 describe the used metrics; finally, in Sect. 4, the obtained results are presented, and conclusions are drafted.

2 Proposed Framework

With the aim of designing a user oriented paediatric framework for patient specific plastic cast manufacturing, a fast, reconfigurable, robust and accurate 3D hand-wrist-arm scanner has been designed. The scanner is coupled with a comprehensive user-friendly software conveying all the algorithms needed to build the 360° 3D model of the arm and to extract important features of the CAD model of the related orthosis. The realization of the final model will be performed in a different environment with a CAD procedure guided by the extracted features. This model, see Fig. 1, is composed of two halves, to ease the application, locked through a zip tie-based mechanism.

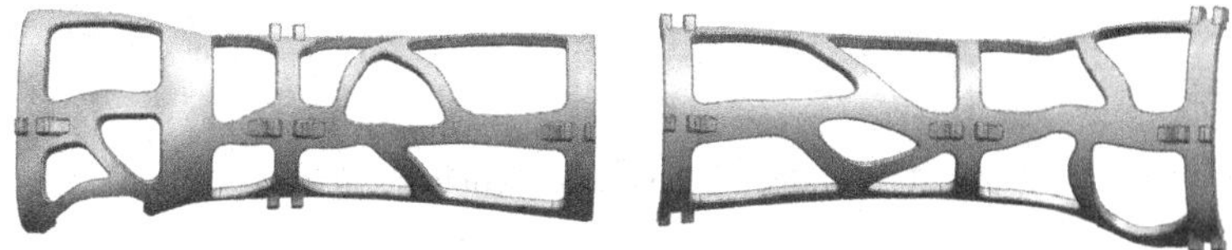

Fig. 1. Example of final orthosis model

2.1 Harm-Wrist-Hand 3D Scanner

The paediatric setting imposes compelling requirements to be used in the clinical practice [4]. With the aim of covering the full range of sizes variation of growing children, the arm scanner is composed of two rings hosting several close-range depth cameras [5] and a moving support for the elbow (Fig. 2).

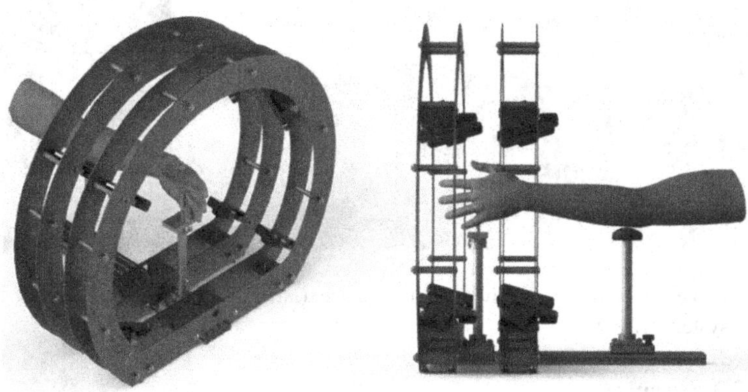

Fig. 2. The designed HWA 3D scanner

Each ring structure has a diameter of 720 mm, the support for the hand is positioned between the two rings and each camera is placed at approximately 245–255 mm from it. This allows to acquire anatomies with length varying from 200 mm up to 410 mm (covering in average the age size 3 yo–18 yo). The scanner is provided with a software developed to calculate the 360° model of the arm, envisage the alignment, cleaning and fusion of the depth camera images.

The control software has been designed to allow the medical staff to easily acquire the patient anatomy and define key features of the 3D printed orthosis (e.g. boundaries, length etc.). The possible operations are collected in a toolbar as shown in Fig. 3. The main steps to be performed by the users have been grouped in five tasks and are described in the following paragraphs.

Fig. 3. Toolbar of the devised control software

Task 1: Patient Preparation and Arm Positioning

During this step the clinical professionals oversee the positioning of a white gauze on the patient's arm and the drawing of some visual references; specifically, they are asked to draw the knuckles line, the thumb finger base, the main orthosis boundaries, and the ulnar styloid process perimeter to next help the correct reconstruction of the orthosis model (Fig. 3 on the left). Once ready, the patient is asked to place the arm into the 3D scanner, to assume the resting configuration (with the hand defining an angle of 10°–20° with the arm, Fig. 4) [1] and keep it during the scanning phase.

Fig. 4. Example of landmarks drawn on the gauze (left); positioning of the arm into the acquisition system (right)

Task 2: 3D Scanning

Once the arm is positioned, the clinical specialist is ready to press the *3D Scan* button. The program launches a notification sound when the images are stored (within ~2.5 s), after which the patient can remove the arm from the scanner. In background the software processes the acquired raw data to obtain the point cloud of the wrist-hand-arm district.

Task 3: 3D Data Selection and Cut

When the 360° 3D image of the arm is ready the user must press the button *Select Area* to select and cut all those portions of points which will not be part of the orthosis (see Fig. 5). During this phase and the following, the user will take advantage of the lines previously drawn on the gauze. At the end of this step, the user must press the *Smooth* button to let the software perform the smoothing step in background.

Fig. 5. Workflow of the third task

Task 4: Thumb Finger Opening

During this phase, the user must remove the thumb finger to create the correct opening to allow the patient to freely move such finger. To perform this task, the user must navigate the 3D model to identify the right point of view to cut, by using a rectangular selection, the thumb. Also, the user must select the area defining the opening space for the thumb finger. These operations are shown in Fig. 6.

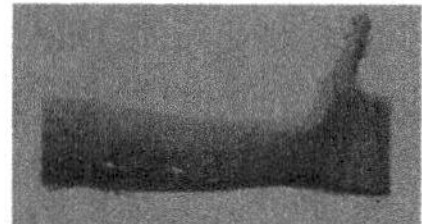

Fig. 6. Workflow of the fourth task

Task 5: Zip Ties Positioning

The last task consists in pressing the *Triangulate* button to let the software perform, in background, the Poisson surface reconstruction which is a smooth and detailed mesh, and which automatically close the hole produced by removing the thumb finger.

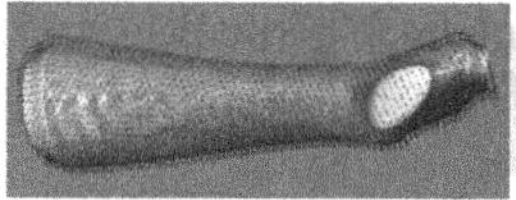

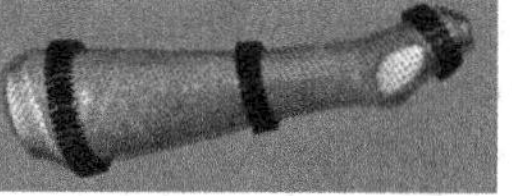

Fig. 7. Workflow of the fifth task

Once the mesh has been computed the user has to press the button *Sections*: the program will automatically extract and visualize sectional profile of the mesh necessary to generate the CAD model of the orthosis. Finally, pressing the button *Insert zip-ties* the user can define the zip-ties housing locations (see Fig. 7). This task is the final step of the user-guided procedure since the final CAD model of the orthosis, including optimized shape to reduce weight and to allow breathability, is automatically generated into a CAD environment (e.g. Siemens NX®).

3 Usability Analysis

According to the ISO 9126 series of standards, the most extensive software quality model developed to date [6], usability is interpreted as "the extent to which a product can be used by specified users to achieve specified goals with *effectiveness*, *efficiency* and *satisfaction* in a specified context of use". Usability can be expressed as the capability of the software product to be understood, learned, used and be attractive to the user, and is a combination of factors including: intuitive design, ease of learning, efficiency of use, memorability, error frequency and severity, subjective satisfaction. To evaluate the usability is a key step for User-Centered Design (UCD) framework for software development, defined in the ISO-13407 standard [7]. Accordingly, usability evaluation must occur within the design life-cycle, with the results of the evaluation feeding back into modifications to the design.

3.1 Participants

Five participants have been chosen among the Meyer Children's Hospital orthopedic nurses; specifically, orthopedic nurses have been chosen over doctors since they oversee the typical casting procedure for bone fractures. Despite studies have demonstrated that the identification of flaws in the software remarkably increases with a higher number of participants, the common practice is to test the usability on five users [8, 9]. Accordingly, five participants are considered to be enough for this preliminary study. The usability sessions have been conducted in a quiet and private room reserved for this task accommodating the scanning system. Institutional Review Board approval has been obtained from the study organization to conduct this research.

3.2 Methods

A preliminary meeting has been held to explain to participants each single task, and to give the possibility to familiarize with the procedure. After this preliminary phase, participants' tests have been scheduled individually and the test has been performed by participants without any help by observers. Each participant has been asked to perform the whole process for the same patient. The evaluation of each metric has been carried out as follow:

Effectiveness is calculated measuring the completion rate, by assigning a binary value of '1' if the test participant manages to complete a task and '0' otherwise.

$$Effectiveness = \frac{number\ of\ tasks\ completed\ successfully}{total\ number\ of\ tasks\ undertaken} \tag{1}$$

Efficiency is measured in terms of task time, i.e. the time spent by the users to achieve the goals

$$Time\ Based\ Efficiency = \frac{\sum_{j=1}^{R}\sum_{i=1}^{N}\frac{n_{ij}}{t_{ij}}}{NR} \tag{2}$$

$$Overall\ Relative\ Efficiency = \frac{\sum_{j=1}^{R}\sum_{i=1}^{N} n_{ij} * t_{ij}}{\sum_{j=1}^{R}\sum_{i=1}^{N} t_{ij}} \tag{3}$$

Where: N = total number of tasks, R = number of users, n_{ij} = result of task i by user j, t_{ij} = time spent by user j to complete task i.

Satisfaction is measured through standardized satisfaction questionnaires: the SEQ (Single Ease Question) questionnaire, which is reliable, sensitive, valid and easy to respond [10], has been administered after each task; the SUS (System Usability Scale) questionnaire [11], which has been found to give very accurate results, has been administered after the usability test session.

4 Results and Conclusions

The tables below illustrate the results of the usability metrics described above. Generally speaking, the tests score is positive, highlighting both the general good impact of the software and some major flaws. As it can be noted from Table 1 all effectiveness scores exceed the 78% value, which is considered to be the average value for this metric [12].

Table 1. Effectiveness results scored by each user

	User #1	User #2	User #3	User #4	User #5
Effectiveness	80%	100%	80%	100%	100%

Efficiency, which is the speed of work with the product, is typically compared with the Expert Efficiency, the highest possible speed of work. As it is shown in Table 2, the efficiency obtained with non-trained users (i.e. the one measured immediately after the introductory presentation) is equal to ~0.3 goal/min, and it is only twice as the reported expert efficiency. The Overall Relative Efficiency, i.e. the ratio of the time taken by the users who successfully completed all the tasks in relation to the total time taken by all users, is higher than 90%, thus proving a good efficiency of the system.

Table 2. Time-based and overall relative efficiency results

Time-based efficiency	Expert efficiency	Overall relative efficiency
0.309 goal/min	0.6 goal/min	91.3%

SEQ results are reported as the average SEQ value obtained by each user (see Table 3). Considering that satisfaction results typically range between 4.8 and 5.1 [13], results demonstrate a general high score of satisfaction by single users. The most challenging task for users with no 3D modelling expertise has been task 4 (Thumb finger opening). Future work will be oriented to the simplification of this step to be performed within a medical facility.

Table 3. SEQ score averaged over each user

	User #1	User #2	User #3	User #4	User #5
AVG SEQ score	5.6	6	3.6	5.4	5.2
Task with lower score	Task 4	Task 4	Task 4	Task 4	Task 4

Results of the SUS questionnaire are reported in Fig. 8, where values below the red dashed line are to be considered as strongly insufficient, the orange line states the sufficiency threshold, and results above the green line are to be considered optimal. The tested software obtained an average result of 85, and all scores are above the sufficiency line, stating a general high level of satisfaction of the users.

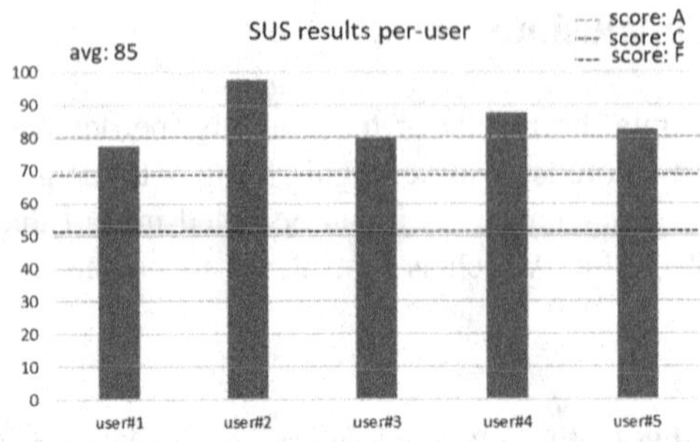

Fig. 8. SUS questionnaire results (in blue) and reference thresholds

References

1. Chudnofsky, C.R., Byers, S.: Splinting techniques. In: Roberts, J.R., Hedges, J.R., Chanmugam, A.S. (eds.) Clinical Procedures in Emergency Medicine, 4th edn., p. 989. Saunders, Philadelphia (2004)
2. CORTEX. http://www.evilldesign.com/cortex. Accessed 05 Mar 2018
3. Lin, H., Shi, L., Wang, D.: A rapid and intelligent designing technique for patient-specific and 3D-printed orthopedic cast. 3D Printing Med. **2**(1), 4 (2015)
4. Carfagni, M., Furferi, R., Governi, L., Servi, M., Uccheddu, F., Volpe, Y., Mcgreevy, K.: Fast and low cost acquisition and reconstruction system for human hand-wrist-arm anatomy. Procedia Manuf. **11**, 1600–1608 (2017)
5. Carfagni, M., Furferi, R., Governi, L., Servi, M., Uccheddu, F., Volpe, Y.: On the performance of the Intel SR300 depth camera: metrological and critical characterization. IEEE Sens. J. **17**(14), 4508–4519 (2017)
6. Abran, A., Khelifi, A., Suryn, W., Seffah, A.: Usability meanings and interpretations in ISO standards. Softw. Qual. J. **11**(4), 325–338 (2003)
7. Jokela, T., Iivari, N., Matero, J., Karukka, M.: The standard of user-centered design and the standard definition of usability: analyzing ISO 13407 against ISO 9241-11. In: Proceedings of the Latin American Conference on Human-Computer Interaction. ACM (2003)
8. Nielsen, J., Landauer, T. K.: A mathematical model of the finding of usability problems. In: Proceedings of the INTERACT 1993 and CHI 1993 Conference on Human Factors in Computing Systems. ACM (1993)
9. Faulkner, L.: Beyond the five-user assumption: benefits of increased sample sizes in usability testing. Behav. Res. Methods Instrum. Comput. **35**(3), 379–383 (2003)
10. Sauro, J., Lewis, J.R.: Quantifying the User Experience: Practical Statistics for User Research. Morgan Kaufmann, Burlington (2016)
11. Brooke, J.: SUS-a quick and dirty usability scale. Usability Eval. Ind. **189**(194), 4–7 (1996)
12. Jeff Sauros blog entry: What Is A Good Task-Completion Rate? 21 March 2011. http://www.measuringusability.com/sus.php. Accessed 05 Mar 2018
13. Jeff Sauros blog entry: 10 Things To Know About The Single Ease Question (SEQ), 30 October 2012. http://www.measuringusability.com/sus.php. Accessed 05 Mar 2018

Optimal Keyboard Design by Using Particle Swarm Optimization

Ricardo Soto, Broderick Crawford, and José Toro(✉)

Pontificia Universidad Católica de Valparaíso, Valparaíso, Chile
{ricardo.soto,broderick.crawford}@ucv.cl, jose.toro.p@mail.pucv.cl

Abstract. The use of appropriate keyboards clearly improves the typing activity, making the task faster and the workstation more comfortable. On the contrary, intensive use of inappropriate/unergonomic keyboards may lead to musculoskeletal injuries. During the last years the design of optimal keyboards as appeared as an interesting problem from UI design. The idea is to arrange the letters on a keyboard according to a given ergonomic criteria in order to maximize typing speed, and reduce fatigue as well as typing errors. In this paper, we focus on the letter assignment problem, whose goal is to minimize the cost of the keyboard which is computed according to the Fitts law and the movement time among keys. In particular, we employ particle swarm optimization (PSO), which is one of the pioneers metaheuristics that has been largely used to solve different problems from multiple application domains.

Keywords: Letter assignment problem · Keyboard optimization Metaheuristics

1 Introduction

The letter assignment problem (LAP) is an optimization problem from UI design devoted to find optimal keyboards configurations. The goal is to arrange a set of letters according to ergonomic criterion in order to maximize typing speed, while reducing typing errors and tiredness. The problem is relevant as many repetitive stress injuries are caused by the inappropriate use of keyboards. The LAP is based on the Fitts law, which can be seen as an estimation of typing performance involving distance of keys and their width. In the optimization sphere, it is well-known that linear objective functions with linear constraints can definitely be solved with exact methods such as the simplex one. However, the LAP is an instance of the quadratic assignment problem (QAP) which is NP-Hard whose mathematical formulation involves a quadratic objective function. As a consequence, today there is no polynomial-time algorithm able to guarantee the global optimum. Then, to tackle this problem, we propose the use of metaheuristics, which are multi-purpose problem solvers devoted to particularly tackle large instances of complex optimization problems. They are commonly able to provide near-optimal solutions in a limited amount of time when the use of exact

C. Stephanidis (Ed.): HCII Posters 2018, CCIS 850, pp. 281–284, 2018.
https://doi.org/10.1007/978-3-319-92270-6_40

methods is too expensive. In particular, we employ particle swarm optimization (PSO), which is one of the pioneers metaheuristics that has been largely used to solve different problems from multiple application domains. Interesting results are provided where PSO is able to rapidly find optimal designs for different keyboard configurations.

2 The Letter Assignment Problem

The letter assignment problem (LAP) derives from the well-known quadratic assignment problem (QAP) which belongs to the NP-hard class of problems, no existing then evidence of a polynomial-time algorithm able to guarantee the global optimum. To this end, the use of metaheuristics appear as a suitable candidate for conveniently tackling this problem. The LAP is the defined as follows: given n letters and n keyslots, the goal is to minimize an average cost c_{kl} of pressing the letter l after the letter k. The average cost is weighted by a bigram probability denoted as p_{kl}, as depicted in Eq. 1.

$$min \sum_{k} \sum_{l} p_{kl} \dot{c}_{kl} \tag{1}$$

The p_{kl} probabilities are computed by a bigram distribution of representative corpus of text as explained in [1], while the cost is calculated by Eq. 2

$$c_{kl} = \sum_{i=1}^{n} \sum_{j=1}^{n} t_{ij} x_{ki} x_{lj} \tag{2}$$

where $x_{lj} = 1$ if letter l is assigned to keyslot j and $x_{lj} = 0$ otherwise. t_{ij} is the movement time (MT) from key i to key j, normally computed by Fitts' law [5], as depicted in Eq. 3.

$$MT = a + b \log_2(\frac{D_{kl}}{W_l} + 1) \tag{3}$$

where D_{kl} is the distance between letters k and l and W_l represents the width of the keyslot holding l, a and b are constants that depend on the choice of input device. This function provides an estimation of the capable performance of a experience user. The LAP also involves the following constraints.

$$\sum_{l=1}^{n} x_{lj=1} \qquad \forall j \in \{1, \ldots, n\} \tag{4}$$

$$\sum_{j=1} x_{lj} \qquad \forall l \in \{1, \ldots, n\} \tag{5}$$

$$x_{lj} \in \{0, 1\} \qquad \forall l, j \in \{1, \ldots, n\} \tag{6}$$

Constraint 4 is responsible for that each slot contains only one letter. Equation 5 ensures that each letter is assigned to only one slot and finally Eq. 6 guarantees the binary solutions. The technique employed to solve this problem is presented in the next section.

3 Particle Swarm Optimization

Particle swarm optimization (PSO) is one the pioneer and more tested metaheuristics [3]. It belongs to the class of population-based metaheuristics, where the population is composed of a set of agents called particles that explore promising regions of the search space in order to find optimal solutions. The classic PSO algorithm is depicted in Fig. 1

```
For each particle
  Initialize particle
End

While maximum iterations or stop criteria is not reached
  For each particle
    Calculate fitness value
    If the fitness value is better than the best fitness value
      (pBest) in history
      set current value as the new pBest
    End
  End

Choose the particle with the best fitness value of
all the particles as the gBest
    For each particle
      Calculate particle velocity according Eq 7.
      Update particle position according Eq 8.
    End
End
```

Fig. 1. PSO algorithm

$$V_p^d = V_p^d + c_1 * rand * (pbest_p^d - present_p^d) + c_2 * rand * (gbest^d - present_p^d) \quad (7)$$

$$present_p^d = present_p^d + V_p^d \quad (8)$$

where V_p^d is the velocity of the dimension d of the particle p, $present_p^d$ is the current dimension d of the particle p, $pbest_p^d$ is the dimension d of the best position that p has had, $gbest^d$ is the dimension d of the best global position of the swarm, $rand$ is an evenly distributed random number between 0 and 1, $c1$ and $c2$ are learning factors.

3.1 Discretization

Given that LAP is a binary problem we must adapt the PSO algorithm to fit the model properly. To this end, we employ a method based on a transfer and a discretization function as detailed in [4] in which we take the probability p_{mutj} of mutating the jth column of the solution in the particle p to the actual speed. In this particular case we use the S-shape transfer function, as shown below.

$$pmut_n^j = \frac{1}{1 + e^{2v_n^j}} \tag{9}$$

Next, we generate the new binary value, based on the $pmut_n^j$, from the discretization function as shown in Eq. 10.

$$n_j^{'} = \begin{cases} best_j \ if \ \alpha \leq pmut_n^j \\ n_j \ otherwise \end{cases} \tag{10}$$

where α is an evenly distributed random number between 0 and 1.

4 Results and Conclusions

The PSO algorithm was tested with the 26 Letter Trapezoid Layout for touch-screens and the Zhai-Hunter-Smith's variant of the Fitts-Bigram ($a = 0.0, b = 0.084, c = 0.127$), proposed in [2]. This keyboard has a search space of $4 * 10^{26}$ and we assumed that the space bar is fixed at the bottom. The algorithm was able to get a fitness of 297.57437 in 5 h. Considering that the QWERTY layout has a score of 356.546251 based on the LAP metric and the known optimum found in previous research is 278.381124 [2], this is a promising result.

In this paper, we have presented ongoing work about PSO algorithms for solving the LAP. The problem is interesting as many repetitive stress injuries are caused by the inappropriate use of keyboards. As future work we expect to solve more instances of the LAP, and improve the performance of the proposed PSO. Analogous UI problems could also be solved with different metaheuristics.

Acknowledgments. Ricardo Soto is supported by Grant CONICYT/FONDECYT/REGULAR/1160455 and Broderick Crawford is supported by Grant CONICYT/FONDECYT/REGULAR/1171243.

References

1. Bi, X., Smith, B.A., Zhai, S.: Multilingual touchscreen keyboard design and optimization. Hum.-Comput. Interact. **27**(4), 352–382 (2012)
2. Karrenbauer, A., Oulasvirta, A.: Improvements to keyboard optimization with integer programming. In: Proceedings of the 27th Annual ACM Symposium on User Interface Software and Technology, UIST 2014, pp. 621–626. ACM, New York (2014)
3. Kennedy, J., Eberhart, R.: Particle swarm optimization. In: Proceedings of the IEEE International Conference on Neural Networks, vol. 4, pp. 1942–1948, November 1995
4. Lanza-Gutierrez, J.M., Crawford, B., Soto, R., Berrios, N., Gomez-Pulido, J.A., Paredes, F.: Analyzing the effects of binarization techniques when solving the set covering problem through swarm optimization. Expert Syst. Appl. **70**, 67–82 (2017)
5. MacKenzie, I.S., Zhang, S.X.: The design and evaluation of a high-performance soft keyboard. In: Proceeding of the CHI 1999 Conference on Human Factors in Computing Systems: The CHI is the Limit, pp. 25–31. ACM (1999)

Differences in Consumers' Evaluation of Product Design Values by Thinking Style

Jaehye Suk and Kee Ok Kim(✉)

Sungkyunkwan University, Seoul, South Korea
kokim@skku.edu

Abstract. This study examined the effects of consumers' purchase thinking style on their evaluation of product design values in relation to two product types, refrigerators and dining tables. Data were collected from 300 Korean consumers aged in their 30s to 50s from December 7th to December 15th in 2017. SPSS 22.0 was used to conduct repeated measures ANOVA and regression analyses on the data. Consumer thinking styles were classified into rational and experiential, and product design values were classified into rational, kinesthetic, and emotional through exploratory factor analysis. The results were as follows. First, consumers' concern for rational design value was slightly higher for refrigerators than for dining tables, while emotional design value was evaluated in the opposite direction. Second, adjusted R^2s indicated that socioeconomic background and product design value explained consumers' experiential thinking styles better than rational thinking styles. We found that consumers' evaluations of product design values differed by their thinking style and product type. Understanding consumers' thinking styles could enhance product designers' knowledge on consumer purchasing preferences.

Keywords: Dual-process theory · Rational thinking style
Experiential thinking style · Situation Specific Thinking Style

1 Introduction

Novak and Hoffman [1] developed the Situation Specific Thinking Style (SSTS) by applying Dual Process Theory [2] to the two qualitatively different systems of consumer information processing in purchase situations. This study examined consumers' purchase thinking style relating to two product types, refrigerators and dining tables, and the effect of their thinking styles on their evaluation of the product design values.

2 Methods

2.1 Participants

Data were collected from 300 Korean consumers aged in their 20s to 40s from December 7th to December 15th in 2017. Quota sampling was applied by gender and age. Participants all registered through a professional market research organization.

C. Stephanidis (Ed.): HCII Posters 2018, CCIS 850, pp. 285–289, 2018.
https://doi.org/10.1007/978-3-319-92270-6_41

Table 1. Description of the respondents

(N=300)

		Frequency (%)
Gender	Male	150 (50.0)
	Female	150 (50.0)
Age	20-29	100 (33.3)
	30-39	100 (33.3)
	40-49	100 (33.3)
Household income per month (KRW)[a]	Less than 4 million	113 (37.7)
	4-7 million	109 (36.3)
	Over 7 million	78 (26.0)
Education	High school or less	31 (10.3)
	College/University	235 (78.3)
	Graduate school or higher	34 (11.3)

Note. a KRW 1 million = USD 926.18

The sample characteristics are presented in Table 1. SPSS 22.0 was used to analyze the data, specifically, to conduct repeated ANOVA and regression analyses.

2.2 Measurements

Consumer thinking style was measured using the 12 items generated by Novak and Hoffman [1]. These 12 items were divided into two hypothetical constructs: rational

Table 2. Exploratory factor analysis: consumer thinking style

	Rational	Emotional	Explained variance (%)	α
I used my gut feelings	.840		32.153	.872
I used my instincts	.834			
I relied on my sense of intuition	.832			
I used my heart as a guide for my actions	.799			
I trusted my hunches	.762			
I went by what felt good to me	.584			
I reasoned things out carefully		.810	26.487	.833
I was very aware of my thinking process		.791		
I tackled this task systematically		.768		
I applied precise rules to deduce the answers		.727		
I approached this task analytically		.686		
I figure things out logically		.632		
Cumulative explained variance (%)	58.641			
KMO	.855			

and emotional thinking styles. Rational and emotional thinking styles were measured with six items each.

On the basis of previous studies by Ravasi and Stiglian [3], and Homburg et al. [4], eleven items for measuring product design values were constructed. These were classified into three hypothetical constructs: rational, kinesthetic, and emotional design values. Rational design value was measured by three items while kinesthetic design value by four items, and emotional design value also by four items. To validate the scales and test their reliabilities, exploratory factor analyses (EFAs) and Cronbach's α tests were performed as shown in Tables 2 and 3.

Table 3. Exploratory factor analysis: design values

	Refrigerator			Dining table		
	Factor loading	Explained variance (%)	α	Factor loading	Explained variance (%)	α
Rational						
Reliability	.758	39.233	.805	.776	40.256	.812
Quality/function	.721			.730		
Durability	.730			.748		
Kinesthetic						
Convenience	.801	11.187	.799	.789	11.301	.803
Ease of use	.701			.727		
Simplicity	.698			.673		
Harmony of space	.739			.743		
Emotional						
The latest	.824	10.257	.829	.853	10.378	.831
Discrimination	.753			.726		
Design	.761			.798		
Feeling	.735			.704		
Cumulative explained variance (%)	60.677			61.935		
KMO	.853			.892		

3 Results

3.1 Consumer Thinking Style and Product Design Value: EFAs

To investigate consumer thinking style and product design value of the two different products, EFAs using varimax rotation were conducted, as shown in Tables 2, 3, and 4. For consumer thinking style, two factors were extracted, namely, rational and emotional, which cumulatively explained 58.64% of data variation. For product design

Table 4. Repeated measures ANOVA

	Group		Source	SS	*df*	*F*	Bonferroni
	Refrigerator[a]	Dining table[a]					
Rational	4.198 (.590)	4.056 (.602)	Treatment	3.034	1	34.789***	A > B
			Error	26.077	299		
Kinesthetic	3.902 (.531)	3.863 (.557)	Treatment	.220	1	2.764	
			Error	23.842	299		
Emotional	3.493 (.614)	3.573 (.613)	Treatment	.960	1	11.463**	A < B
			Error	25.040	299		

* $p < .05$, ** $p < .01$, *** $p < .001$
Note. [a]Mean (SD)

value, three factors were extracted, namely rational, kinesthetic, and emotional, which cumulatively explained 60.68%, and 61.94% of the variance for refrigerator and dining table, respectively.

3.2 Product Design Values by Product Type

As shown in Table 4, repeated ANOVA was conducted to analyze the differences in product design values of the two different product types. Consumers viewed rational design value more highly for refrigerator than for dining table (p < . 001), while emotional design value was evaluated in the opposite direction (p < .01). Kinesthetic value of product design was not significantly different between the two product types.

3.3 Consumers' SSTS Toward Refrigerator and Dining Table

Consumers' SSTS toward refrigerator and dining table were analyzed using regression models, as shown in Table 5. Four regression models were statistically significant and the variance inflation factor for each independent variable was less than 1, indicating multicollinearity was not present.

Adjusted R^2s indicated that socioeconomic background and product design value explained consumers' experiential thinking styles (adjusted $R^2 = 42.0, 38.0$, respectively) better than rational thinking styles (adjusted $R^2 = 28.5, 29.9$, respectively). Men were more likely adopt rational thinking styles than women, while experiential thinking styles did not differ by sex. Rational product design values were significant for all thinking styles regardless of the product type, while emotional product design values were only significant for experiential thinking styles. Kinesthetic product design values were significant for both thinking styles for refrigerator, while they were only significant for rational thinking styles for dining table.

Table 5. Consumers' SSTS toward refrigerator and dining table

	Refrigerator				Dining table			
	Rational SSTS		Experiential SSTS		Rational SSTS		Experiential SSTS	
	B	β	B	β	B	β	B	β
Sociodemographic variables								
Female	−.178	−.161**	−.024	−.018	−.150	−.054**	.043	.032
Age	.005	.064	−.007	−.083	.002	.004	−.008	−.093
Education[a]								
University	.090	.067	−.061	−.037	.069	.093	.027	.017
Graduate	.129	.074	−.163	−.076	.190	.120	−.141	−.066
Household income[b]								
Middle	−.014	−.013	−.028	−.021	.190	.072	−.036	−.026
High	.120	.095	−.025	−.016	.144	.083	.028	.018
Design values								
Rational	.314	.335***	−.166	−.144*	.384	.059**	−.147	−.130*
Kinesthetic	.242	.232**	.195	.152*	.142	.069*	.139	.114
Emotional	.047	.076	.659	.595**	.042	.052	.656	.592***
F	14.267***		25.093***		15.196***		21.345**	
R^2	.307		.438		.320		.398	
Adj. R^2	.285		.420		.299		.380	
Durbin-Watson	1.926		1.959		1.927		2.042	

* $p < .05$, ** $p < .01$, *** $p < .001$

Notes. [a]Reference group: High school or less

[b]Reference group: Low income (less than KRW 3 million)

4 Conclusion

In conclusion, consumers' evaluations of product design values differ by their thinking styles and by product types. This implies that understanding consumers' thinking styles could enhance product designers' knowledge on consumer preferences and, therefore, could enhance consumer satisfaction by fulfilling appropriate product design values.

References

1. Novak, T.P., Hoffman, D.L.: The fit of thinking style and situation: new measures of situation-specific experiential and rational cognition. J. Consum. Res. **36**(1), 56–72 (2008)
2. Epstein, S., Pacini, R.: Some Basic Issues Regarding Dual-Process Theories from the Perspective of Cognitive-Experiential Self-theory. Dual-Process Theories in Social Psychology. Guilford Press, New York City (1999)
3. Ravasi, D., Stigliani, I.: Product design: a review and research agenda for management studies. Int. J. Manag. Rev. **14**(4), 464–488 (2012)
4. Homburg, C., Schwemmle, M., Kuehnl, D.: New product design: concept, measurement, and consequences. J. Mark. **79**(3), 41–56 (2015)

Interaction Design Process Oriented by Metrics

Jessica Suzuki(✉) and Edna Dias Canedo

Computer Science Department, University of Brasília (UnB),
Brasília, DF 70910-900, Brazil
suzukijessicaa@gmail.com, ednacanedo@unb.br

Abstract. Software quality is more than code, it expands beyond the code, the noticeable aspects for the user must be considered. In order to capture these aspects one can look towards the area of Interaction Design, which is studied within the discipline of Human-Computer Interaction (HCI). To apply the concepts of this discipline, procedures must be respected, thus forming a process. When considering software quality, one must consider processes it is the use of metrics. In this context, this paper explores a process of design interaction oriented by metrics. Supported by a literature review and methodology, the process is defined supporting this underlying argument. A questionnaire targeted with knowing in the field will reveal results aimed at validating and improving the proposed process.

Keywords: Interaction design · Human-Computer Interaction
Process oriented by metrics · Interaction design process · Usability process

1 Introduction

Every day we are in contact with some product/software that requires some form of human interaction. Alarm clocks, mobile devices and remote controls all depend on our interaction. It is important to assess how easy it is to use these daily products. We must look at the process of Interaction Design, which is defined as "creating experiences that improve and understand the way of people work, communicate and interact" (Preece et al. 2015).

Interaction Design has been studied through the subject Human-Computer Interaction (HCI). This subject is "worried about evaluation and implementation of interactive computer systems for human use and with the study of the main phenomena around them" (Rocha and Baranauskas 2003).

This process tries to increase quality of software in regards to human interaction with and perception of said software. Unfortunately, many products are not necessarily designed with the user in mind (Preece et al. 2015).

In other words, whoever designed the product did not think about the end user that would use it, often making it difficult for the user to interact with the product.

In order to improve user interaction with the system, HCI attempts to redirect user concern, bringing usability, the degree to which a product or system can be used by specific users to achieve specific goals such as effectiveness, efficiency and satisfaction

C. Stephanidis (Ed.): HCII Posters 2018, CCIS 850, pp. 290–297, 2018.
https://doi.org/10.1007/978-3-319-92270-6_42

in a specific usage context (SQuaRE 2011). For the user, the software is the interface, so your design should adapt to it, not the other way around. In his book, Norman (2013) says:

To create a technology that suits the human being, it is necessary to study it. However, today we have a tendency to study only technology. Therefore, people are required to adapt to technology. The time has come to reverse the trend, the time to make technology fit for people.

The interface is a system item that can affect the quality of the product, so it is important to analyse and adapt it according to the user need. According to Crosby (1992) "Quality is conformity to requirements", what means, if a product is fulfilling all its requirements, it has quality. However, the concern with software quality goes beyond the quality of the code. Quality aspects perceivable by the user should also be considered. In order to establish standards in the quality aspect of the software product, the International Organization for Standardization (ISO) has created a set of standards, which have been called Systems and software Quality Requirements and Evaluation (SQuaRE). This standard defines characteristics and sub-characteristics of quality.

It is necessary to define the quality characteristics to be achieved in the software. SQuaRE can help with this definition, as a great difficulty is to be able to evaluate these characteristics once they are defined. For this purpose, software measurement, which is "a quantitative evaluation of any aspect of Software Engineering processes and products", can be used (Bass et al. 1999). The Goal Questions Metrics (GQM) method, which starts from a top-down approach, is widely used for measurement. The GQM starts from the measurement objective, following to the questions from which metrics are derived.

With the aim to capture the user aspects and improve the system interface quality, this paper proposes an interaction design process oriented by metrics using as a base an existed process in the literature.

The remainder of this paper is organized as follows: Sect. 2 presents the project methodology. Section 3 addresses the literature review. Section 4 details the interaction design process oriented by metrics defined, and the Sect. 5 the validation of it. The conclusion and future works are presented in Sect. 6.

2 Methodology

In order to define an interaction design process oriented by metrics to measure quality aspects during the process and not only in the final product, this work was divided into four stages:

- The first stage is a literary review based on the principles of a systematic review in Software Engineering, following a protocol, to identify the existing interaction design processes;
- The third stage was defining the process;
- The last stage was the process validation using questionnaire.

3 Literature Review

This section shows a resume of the literature review made, based on a systematic review in Software Engineering area. Its purpose was to achieve the specific goal of identifying a detailed interaction design process. The review was divided into three phases: planning, research execution and results analysis.

3.1 A Subsection Sample

In the planning phase, the objectives, the research questions and the search strategy were defined.

I - **Objective** – The literary review goal is to identify an already existing interaction design process with a high detailed level, so then, to reach the research general objective.

II - **Research execution** - To reach the literary review specific objective, a research execution was defined.

Q1 – Which are the existing interaction design processes, considering a high detailed level?

III - **Search strategy for task selection** – The search string was defined in Portuguese and also used in English, using logical operator 'and' and 'or'. The following search strings have been defined:

- (("process") and (usability" or "HCI" or "interface design" or "interaction design" or "centred user"))
- or (("software engineering process") and ("HCI"))
- or ("interaction design") or ("HCI").

In order to identify relevant primary studies in the existing creation of the interaction design process oriented by metrics research, we defined the following selection criteria:

Inclusion criteria:

- Studies written in English, Portuguese and Spanish with any aspect of interaction design process oriented by metrics as main focus.
- Papers and books starting from 1989.

Exclusion criteria:

- Studies outside the scope of this research;
- Studies that do not provide enough evidence for this research;
- Duplicate studies. When a study has been published in more than one conference, workshop or journal, the most complete version will be used, i.e., the one which explains it in more detail.

3.2 Execution

Initially, 160 articles and 8 books were identified, resulting in 168 works. First, there was an elimination of works that were not possible from finding any process reference.

Later, there was a selection of works, which referee to HCI process or Usability Interaction Design, integrated or not to other applications, methodologies or processes. Lastly, eleven (11) remained to get data collect.

3.3 Result Analysis

In the final literary review, it was noticed that the most HCI process study is connected to make a relation from HCI process integration to the software development process. The works were analyzed according to their level of detail, where this level refers to contain activities, description of activities, tasks to be performed within each activity, inputs and outputs of the activity, and artefacts. After these analyses, the Deborah Mayhew book "The usability engineering lifecycle" (1999), was selected to assist as a basis for the definition of the interaction design process oriented by metrics.

4 Interaction Design Process Oriented by Metrics

For the development of the interaction, design process oriented by metrics proposed in this work, the Mayhew (1999) process was used as the basis. Thus, it is worth mentioning that because it was based on an already existing process, some specifications of the activities are similar to those defined by Mayhew (1999).

For the development of the interaction, design process oriented by metrics proposed in this work, the Mayhew (1999) process was used as the basis. Thus, it is worth mentioning that because it was based on an already existing process, some specifications of the activities are similar to those defined by Mayhew (1999).

4.1 Process Objective

Late identification of poor software quality can lead to costs for the customer, not to mention end-user dissatisfaction. That is why the development of software comes every day more being carried out with the help of HCI, which aims at user centralization. Even with the process facing the user, it is difficult to measure the quality of the product. Therefore, a process oriented to metrics was proposed so that, throughout the process, this quality is measured qualitatively or quantitatively. The process is divided into two phases: requirements analysis; Design, evaluation and development. Within each phase are the activities, which follow the template of objective, description, input, output, technique, task, role involve.

4.2 Requirements Analysis

The requirements analysis phase, as the name says, is responsible for identifying the requirements, seeking to understand the whole scenario in which the system will be inserted. It is at this stage that the GQM is planned and the objective and the questions regarding product quality are defined, as can be seen in the upper part of the process in Fig. 1. Currently, in the literature there are templates to assist in the definition of the objective.

4.3 Design, Evaluation and Development

The second range of the process is the design, evaluation, and development phase that is where the system builds along with its design and is divided into three levels. At the first level the conceptual model is carried out, at the second level the screen design standards, and lastly the detailed design of the user interface. All levels are followed by evaluations, and level 2define the metrics for the level.

4.4 Details of Role Involved

The roles for the process oriented by metrics were defined following the RACI responsibilities matrix as defined by COBIT (2012). RACI in English means, responsible, accountable, consulted, informed, which means:

'R' (Responsible): Is the one who performs the task; 'A' (Accountable): Is who is responsible for the correct execution of the task, is often the owner of the project; 'C' (Consulted): Are the people who provide information for the project; 'I' (Informed): Is the one who receives information about the progress of the task.

4.5 Details of Role Involve

Team Manager - is responsible for IT (Information Technology) for the project under development; Project Manager - is responsible for the project, as well as its progress; Requirements Analyst - is responsible for identifying system requirements; Usability Analyst - is responsible for the usability of the system; Metrics Analyst - is responsible for defining and analysing metrics; Developer - is responsible for developing the system; User - is the end user of the system.

5 Process Validation

A search is often a retrospective investigation, when, for example, a tool or technique has been used for a while. The main ways of collecting qualitative or quantitative data are interviews or questionnaires. These are done by taking a sample that is representative of the population being studied. The results of the research are then analysed to derive descriptive and explanatory conclusions (Wohlin et al, 2012). The method chosen to validate this work was the questionnaire.

5.1 Target Audience

The first group to answer the questionnaire was students of a postgraduate class in Information Technology Management at the Faculty of Technology of the University of Brasília; these students cursed the discipline of Software Processes.

The second group was students of the graduate in Software Engineering at the University of Brasilia that had already cursed the discipline HCI.

5.2 The Questionnaire

The questionnaire was made in the TYPEFORM and contains 25 questions, which are type: multiple choice, yes or no, classification, scale and text. The questions are to define the user profile and the process quality.

5.3 Data Collected

The questionnaire was answered by 29 students of the postgraduate in Information Technology Management and 18 students of the graduate in Software Engineering and had already coursed HCI. It is important to cite that some students continued the questionnaire without answer some questions.

5.4 Analysis of Data Collected

According to the data collected was possible to verify the following information about the knowledge in HCI: 42% none, 36% little, 11% moderate, 11% good and 0% very good as shows the Graph 1. The Graph 2 represents the percentage of the knowledge in Software Process, which 4% has none, 24% little, 20% moderate, 39% good and 13% very good. So, their answers about process can really contribute to improve the process.

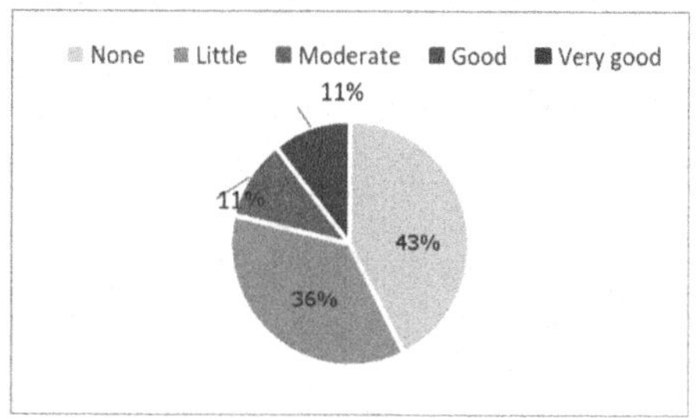

Graph 1. Knowledge in HCI.

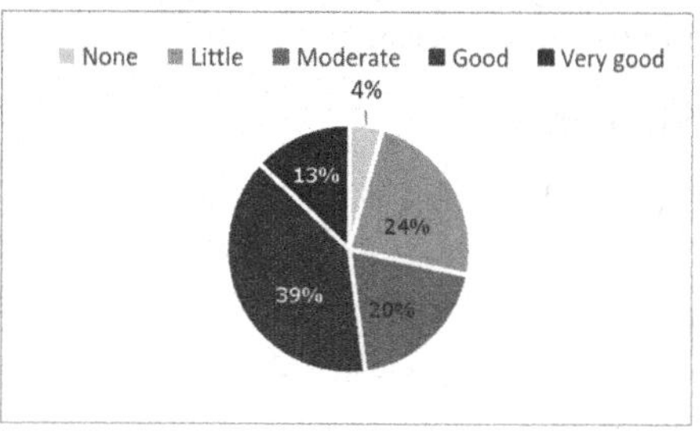

Graph 2. Knowledge in software process.

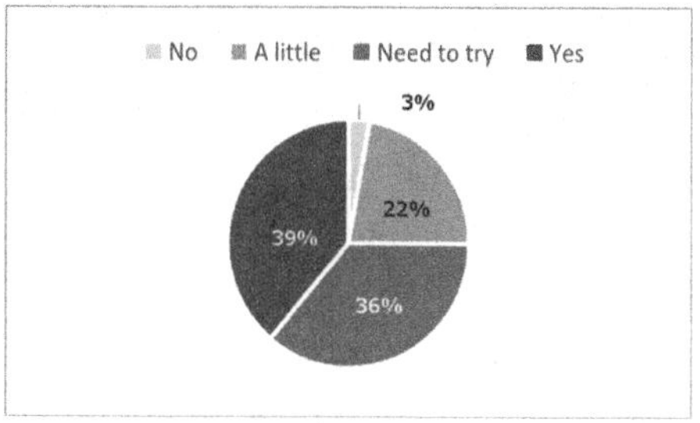

Graph 3. Is it possible to measure the interface quality using the process?

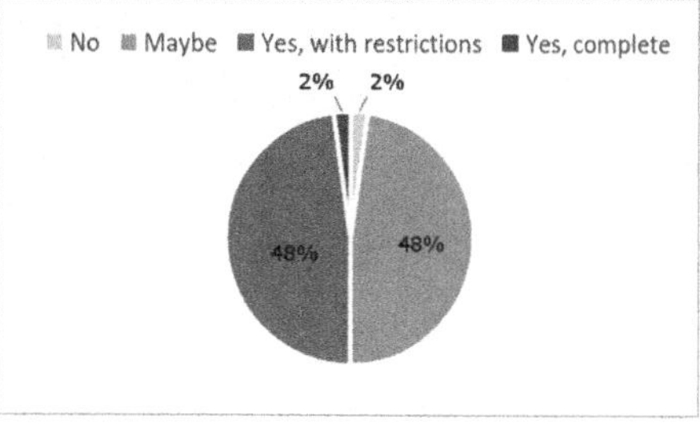

Graph 4. Would you adopt the proposed process?

The Graph 3 represents the students' opinion about the possibility to measure the interface quality using the process proposed, and the answers are: 3% no, 22% a little, 36% need to try and 39% yes. The Graph 4 shows that the most students would use the proposed process, 48% with restrictions and 48% would use complete.

These evaluations were made with the first version of the process, according to the feedback, the process was modified to the version 2. The Fig. 1 represents the version 2, and this new version will be validated with a new group through the questionnaire.

The biggest difference between the version 1 and version 2 is the number of activities. The process was divided into 3 phases and now there are only 2.

6 Conclusion

There are many studies currently attempting to relate software development to the HCI area. In this way, most of these integrate activities related to interaction design, in a software development process.

The interaction design process oriented by metrics aims to improve the interface quality of software products, facilitating the analysis of this quality through the metrics defined during the process. Based on the selected Mayhew (1999) process, the proposed process was adapted, adding GQM activities throughout the process, and detailing each activity according to the items: objective, description, input, output, technique, task, role involved.

In a future work, with the objective of validating the new version of the process oriented by metrics proposed, a questionnaire will be applied, with a different group to improve the process.

Appendix

See Fig. 1.

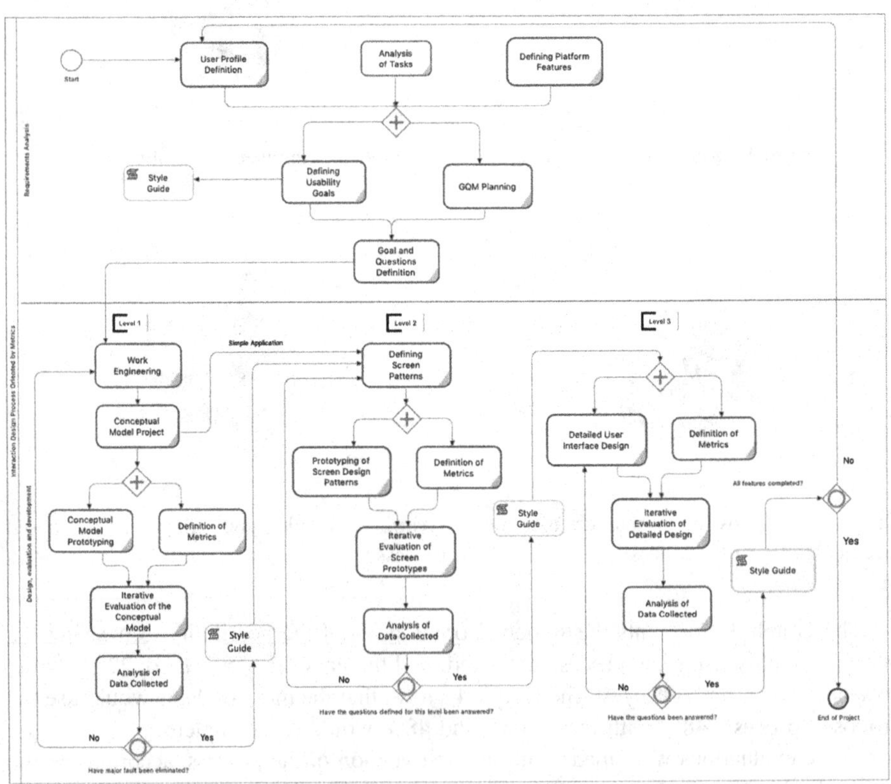

Fig. 1. Interaction design process oriented by metrics.

References

Barbosa, S., Silva, B.: Interação Humano-Computador. Elsevier, Rio de Janeiro (2010)
Bass, L., et al.: Constructing Superior Software (1999)
BonitaSoft. http://www.bonitasoft.com/
Crosby, P.B.: Quality is Free: The Art of Making Quality Certain (1992)
Hewett, T.T., et al.: ACM SIGCHI Curricula for Human-Computer Interaction. ACM, New York City (1992)
ISACA: COBIT 5: A Business Framework for the Governance and Management (2012)
ISO12207: Systems and software engineering - Software life cycle processes (2008)
ISO25010: Software Engineering – Software Product Quality Requirements and Evaluation (SQuaRE) (2011)
Mayhew, D.: The usability engineering lifecycle (1999)
Norman, D.: Design of Everyday Things: Revised and Expanded. Basic Books, New York (2013)
Pfleeger, L.: Software Engineering: Theory and Practice. Pearson, New York (2009)
Pressman, R.S.: Software Engineering: A Practitioner's Approach. McGraw-Hill Education, New York (2009)
Rocha, H.V., Baranauskas, M.C.: Design e Avaliação de Interfaces Humano-Computador. UNICAMP, Campinas (2003)
Preece, J., Sharp, H., Rogers, Y.: Interaction Design – Beyond Human-Computer Interaction, 4th edn. Wiley, Chichester (2015)
Solingen, V., Bergout, E.: The Goal/Question/Metric Method: A Practical Guide for Quality Improvement of Software Development. McGraw-Hill, New York City (1999)
Sommerville, I.: Software Engineering. Addison-Wesley, New York (2010)
Wohlin, C., et al.: Experimentation in Software Engineering. Springer, Heidelberg (2012)

Women, Gender Equality, and Digital Technology

Rojin Vishkaie(✉)

Ball State University, Muncie, IN 47306, USA
vishkaie@bsu.edu

Abstract. This exploratory study investigates the subject of the gender equality and women's empowerment and their engagement in smart development, with a primary focus on ICT and wearable technologies, such as small-scale intelligent devices and interactive sensor elements. Although a growing body of academic research on the topic is increasing, there is a gap in envisioning how aspects of the wearable technologies can optimally engage with the context of the development field and women's empowerment in developing countries. The main contributions of this study combine both empirical and conceptual design components to support the design and evaluation of a smart development that enhances gender equality and women's empowerment in developing countries. The first step towards this study was to con-duct a pilot study that involved five newly arrived African women in the USA. Participants were asked to discuss their experience with the role that current digital technology plays in women's empowerment and gender equality.

Keywords: Women's empowerment · Digital technology
Empirical and conceptual design studies · Human-computer interaction
Interaction design

1 Introduction

In the field of development, gender equality and women's empowerment are still key challenges to overcome in many developing countries with complex social and cultural factors. In this context, development interventions can be made more effective when factors such as gender inequality and the marginalization of the needs and roles of women, are reduced. Employing Information Communication Technology (ICT) as a means to increase gender equality and empowerment of women, can potentially contribute to greater health, development, and economic outcomes in developing countries. In many developed countries, small scale, intelligent devices and interactive sensor elements are being incorporated into clothing, fashion, and other types of wearables, significantly impacting the modern lifestyle. More recently, there has been a rapid growth in both interest and use of these technologies that are quickly becoming mainstream. However, despite this rapid growth, there is limited exploration into the influence of these technologies, particularly in the context of the development field and women's empowerment in developing countries [1–10].

C. Stephanidis (Ed.): HCII Posters 2018, CCIS 850, pp. 298–303, 2018.
https://doi.org/10.1007/978-3-319-92270-6_43

Building upon existing academic research, as well as an initial exploration into enhancing women's empowerment using digital tools, the results aim to better inform the explorations into gender equality and women's empowerment. This study presents a step towards integrating the use of digital tools and enhancing women's empowerment. A preliminary pilot study in a focus group format was conducted. The overall results of the discussion with women showed that they believe current digital tools and wearable and sensor technologies maybe inadequate to educate facilitate behavior change among women in developing countries. The following sections expand on the scope of the study and the preliminary study conducted.

2 Study Scope

This study proposes to explore the role of ICT in creating a smart development to enhance gender equality and women's empowerment in developing countries. Specifically, this study explores the role of current digital technologies and the untapped potential for wearable technologies, to enable and empower women in developing countries. This empowerment can have a positive effect on confidence and decision-making in households and society, as well as a sense of increased safety from violence, which are all issues that must be addressed to enhance gender equality. This study is multidisciplinary, focusing on social science, design, technology, and human-computer interaction Human Computer Interaction (HCI) aspects of gender equality and women's empowerment in developing countries. In this study, empirical and design research study will be employed to investigate the current use of wearable technologies to determine their impact for educating and empowering women via health, nutrition, family planning, and economic information. Ultimately, this study introduces an unconventional attempt to create low-cost interactive tools using wearable technologies to examine the influence of smart development and measure the impact of different aspects of smart development, such as health and development programs (e.g., contraceptive prevalence rate), access to digital financial services, equitable decision-making power, and shared control over assets and income. As a result, this study would allow for monitoring and real-time feedback of gender equality and women's empowerment in developing countries [1–10]. For example, the low-cost interactive tools will be used as a bracelet, necklace, or button to measure women's body temperature, heart rate, or perspiration activity. This data will be collected and fed back to medical professionals for monitoring and improving women's health. Button cells will be used to power the low-cost interactive tools.

2.1 Objectives

This study will have the following objectives:

- To investigate the role that current digital technologies play in enhancing gender equality and women's empowerment. This objective aims to explore the way mobile phones are used to educate women via providing information.

- To examine the role that available digital technologies play in communicating the health, development, and economic information to enhance education of women in the developing countries. This objective aims to investigate the way mobile phones are used in developing countries to educate women via providing health, nutrition, family planning, and economic information.
- To understand the influence of wearable technologies in educating women in developing countries. This objective aims to explore strengths and weaknesses that wearable and current digital technologies have, thus defining a user centered design process for the creation of low-cost interactive tools which can help enhance gender equality and women's empowerment in developing countries.
- To design and evaluate low-cost interactive tools to enhance gender equality and women's empowerment in developing countries. This objective attempts to determine the effectiveness of health, nutrition, family planning, and economic information in gender equality, women's empowerment, as well as educating women in developing countries.

2.2 Method and Study Design

This study will employ the qualitative methodology of ethnography and contextual design, as well as semi-structured interviews, participant and non-participant observations, structured survey-based methods, as well as walkthroughs of experimental prototypes. Focus groups and think-aloud methods will also be used in this study. In this study, a generalizable experience sampling system will be developed via a wearable technology platform for the real-time collection and delivery of information on health, nutrition, family planning, and economic aspects of development while influencing gender equality and women's empowerment. In a series of small trials, information will be fed back to women about their experience in a number of innovative ways. These experiences will then be examined to determine whether and how the information influences women's interactions and behavior. These user-informed experiences can encourage empowerment and equality influences, thus potentially providing positive evidence to be drawn from the experience of women within smart development. This study aims to encourage women to reflect on how they feel and where and when they have positive experiences towards empowerment and equality, while using digital wearable technologies [11–15]. Moreover, the low-cost interactive tools will be evaluated by USA-based, female participants for usability and acceptability. While USA-based, female participants may have different needs and demands to those in developing countries, testing in the USA will be cheaper than testing overseas, which would take place in Phase II if the study outcome was successful.

3 Study To-Date

3.1 Pilot Study

Initially, a pilot study was conducted as a small-scale, focus group exploration designed to gather information prior to a larger study. The results of the pilot study will be used to improve the quality of efficiency of a further, larger study. Furthermore, in the pilot study, a total of five participants including African women - two Liberians, two Madagascans, and one Guinean - who recently arrived in the USA were recruited by using a purposeful sampling technique, and via an email distribution list sent to African community association in the USA. Participants had the freedom to explain their background, existing knowledge, and prior experience. The discussion in the focus group was led by the researcher. The focus group was held to identify potential conflicts in terminology arising out of the influence of digital technologies to enhance education of women in the developing countries or expectations from different individuals participating in the discussion. To enable participants to put forward their own opinions in a supportive environment, they were allowed to give their opinions and discuss their ideas about the role of digital technology in women's empowerment and gender equality with the other participants in the focus group.

3.2 Procedure

In the pilot study, extensive, manual note taking and audio recording were used to document the discussion. The discussion notes and audio recordings were written up and transcribed verbatim. The discussion within the focus group lasted approximately for two hours. Moreover, affinity-diagramming technique was then used to analyze the data.

3.3 Findings

Though time was limited during the preliminary pilot study, the focus group discussion informed a better understanding of role that current digital technologies including wearables that play in educating women in developing countries.

All Participants noted that current digital and wearable technologies do not facilitate women's empowerment and gender equality. All participants mentioned that new wearable and sensor technologies should be incorporated into the social and economic norms of target communities within the low-income settings of developing countries. As one participant noted, (P3): "Women in low-income countries have limited knowledge of the benefits of digital [and wearable] technologies. And, there is a lack of social support, often women who don't reach these facilities are left out."

Participants also believed that the barriers for women's behavior change are numerous and span motivation, ability, skills, knowledge, and environment. Participants were particularly interested in obtaining health-related information which could potentially improve maternal, newborn, and child health. Furthermore, some of the participants' suggestions involve the following: sensors for an expectant mother and newborn that measure blood pressure, heart rate, respiratory rate, temperature, sleep state, and activity; sensors to facilitate hand washing or other infection prevention measures; wearables that reinforce positive behavior in the mother in language interaction. As one participant said, (P5): "It would be very helpful to be alerted when the baby sleeps and wakes up, also to have patches that measures the baby's metabolites such as glucose."

4 Future Work

If the study in Phase I demonstrates promising results, hence a study Phase II will be conducted in developing countries (e.g., an African country). Study Phase II will be focusing on the planning of a business model for the manufacture, distribution, marketing, and retailing of the low-cost interactive tools which could potentially enhance gender equality and women's empowerment.

5 Conclusion

This study attempts to contribute to a deeper understanding of the role that current digital technologies play in improving gender equality and women's empowerment in developing countries. This study will succeed in further contributing to exploring the role that wearable technologies could potentially play in investigating the influence of smart development as well as gender equality and empowerment of women. On the design and empirical level, this study will contribute to the creation and evaluation of future, low-cost interactive tools that help create enabling environments and educate women via accessible health, development, and economic information.

References

1. Gates, M.: Putting women and girls at the center of development. Science **345**(6202), 1273–1275 (2014)
2. World Bank: World Development Report 2012: Gender Equality and Development. World Bank, Washington, DC, USA (2011)
3. Grameen Foundation: Women, Mobile Phones, and Savings: A Grameen Foundation Case Study. Grameen Foundation, Washington, DC, USA (2012)
4. World Bank: Voice and Agency: Empowering Women and Girls for Shares Prosperity. World Bank, Washington, DC, USA (2014)
5. Haddad, L., Hoddinott, J., Alderman, H.: Intrahousehold Resource Allocation in Developing Countries - Model, Methods, and Policy. The John Hopkins University Press, Baltimore (1997)
6. Miner, C., Chen, D., Campbell, C.: Digital jewelry: wearable technology for everyday life. In: CHI 2001 Extended Abstracts on Human Factors in Computing Systems (CHI EA 2001), pp. 45–46. ACM, USA (2011)
7. Cherie Blair Foundation for Women: Women and Mobile: A Global Opportunity. GSMA Association and Cherie Blair Foundation, London, UK (2010)
8. Everts, S.: Gender and Technology: Empowering Women, Engendering Development. Zed Books, London (1998)
9. Leonardo, M.: Gender at the Crossroads of Knowledge: Feminist Anthropology in the Postmodern Era. University of California Press, Berkeley (1991)
10. Cohoon, J., Aspray, W.: Women and Information Technology: Research on Underrepresentation. The MIT Press, Cambridge (2006)
11. Beyer, H., Holtzblatt, K.: Contextual Design - Defining Customer-Centered Systems. Morgan Kaufmann Publisher, San Francisco (1998)

12. Creswell, J.: Qualitative Inquiry and Research Design: Choosing Among Five Approaches. SAGE Publishing, California (2007)
13. Rogers, Y., Sharp, H., Preece, J.: Interaction Design: Beyond Human-Computer Interaction. Wiley, Sussex (2011)
14. Schuler, D., Namioka, A.: Participatory Design: Principles and Practices. Lawrence Erlbaum Associates, Hillsdale (1993)
15. Larson, R., Csikszentmihalyi, M.: The experience sampling method. In: New Directions for Methodology of Social and Behavioral Science, vol. 15, pp. 41–56 (1983)

A User-Centered Terminology for Existing and Upcoming ICT Devices, Services and Applications

Bruno von Niman[1], Martin Böcker[2], and Angel Bóveda[3](✉)

[1] Vonniman Consulting, Dalen 13, 13245 Saltsjö-Boo, Sweden
bruno@vonniman.com
[2] Dr. Böcker & Dr. Schneider GbR, Konstanz, Germany
boecker@humanfactors.de
[3] Wireless Partners SLL, Sangenjo 5, 28034 Madrid, Spain
angel.boveda@wirelesspartners.es

Abstract. Users who are unfamiliar with the terms used in ICT devices, services, or applications may be reluctant to use those features, thereby missing out on the potential benefits of those features and preventing manufacturers and service providers from making revenue from the uptake of those features. The Human Factors Technical Committee (TC HF) of the European Telecommunication Standards Institute (ETSI) has initiated work, co-funded by the European Commission, to develop the freely available ETSI Guide EG 203 499 [2] addressing this need.

Keywords: User-centered · Terminology · Human factors · User interface ICT devices · Accessibility

1 The Problem of Diverse Terminologies

The terms (words, labels) used in the user interface (UI) of a device, service or application may present an obstacle for users if the users are not familiar with those terms or if the users are unsure as to their meaning. While some terms are introduced by manufacturers to denote a new class of feature or to distinguish own features from those offered by competitors, most other terms denoting device or service features are not necessarily intended for differentiation. However, in the absence of a harmonized or recommended terminology, the use of those terms may differ considerably among manufacturers and service providers.

The alternative to a wide and confusing plethora of terms encountered by end users is a minimum degree of harmonization among devices, services, and application, i.e. in those areas that are not intended by manufacturers to convey a certain brand feature or image, a harmonized terminology can be employed that helps preventing the following negative effects of an uncontrolled growth of terms:

- Increased user difficulties in understanding complex, ambiguous and inconstantly-used terms, leading to unnecessary confusion
- Increased efforts in user education (user guides)

C. Stephanidis (Ed.): HCII Posters 2018, CCIS 850, pp. 304–308, 2018.
https://doi.org/10.1007/978-3-319-92270-6_44

- Increased costs for user support (hotline calls and call agent training)
- Limited feature discovery and unclear user expectations (customers who do not understand certain features may not use them, hence revenue may be missed)
- Limited uptake (users may be reluctant to use a feature as they are not sure whether it has the expected effect)
- Increase of cognitive complexity and subsequent learning effort
- Abuse in the use of proprietary terms and lack of consistent use of terms.

The need for a harmonized terminology of device and service features increases as new features and services are being introduced and marketed every year and as new device and service providers continue to enter a dynamic market. Applications, services, and applications are frequently updated, often without providing an update of the user documentation to the users. In addition, as network operators' business models change (e.g. fewer subsidized devices linked to fixed service plans), end-user loyalty to network operators and device manufacturers decreases.

2 An Approach for Harmonizing ICT Terms

2.1 Prior ETSI Work in the Field

The ETSI Guide EG 202 132 [1] identified the lack of a standardized terminology for device and service features as one of the main obstacles that users, and in particular older users and users with impairments, struggle with. Currently, terms are being employed that use specialist and/or foreign-language terms and abbreviations and one and the same feature is labelled differently across manufacturers and service providers. EG 202 132 [1] specified the terms for a number of areas, mostly focused on telephony, including voice mail, e-mail, MMS, SMS WAP, call features, and terminal functionality. EG 202 132 [1] was limited to English-language.

2.2 The ETSI STF 540

ETSI STF (Special Task Force) 540 is a group of experts set by ETSI, under the direction of the ETSI Technical Committee Human Factors (TC HF) and co-funded by the European Commission, with the objective of investigating the problem of diverse terminologies in modern ICT devices. STF 540 is tasked to produce a new ETSI Guide, EG 203 499 [2], addressing and providing solutions to this need. EG 203 499 will be published by ETSI as an open, freely available document.

2.3 The ETSI Guide EG 203 499

Based on the previous ETSI Guide [1] that was limited to telephony terms and to terms in English, the new document will address new areas and will provide terminology recommendations in five languages English, French, German, Italian, and Spanish. The recommended terminology will be applicable to product UI and user documentation design, also easing knowledge and learning transfer. For this work, a Design-for-All approach was chosen that takes functional limitations of elderly users and those with cognitive, physical or sensory variations into account.

Intended users of EG 203 499 are those designing, developing, implementing and deploying user interfaces for and interaction with mobile ICT devices, services, and applications.

Intended end users of the terminology recommended by the ETSI Guide will be the people who use mobile ICT devices, services, and applications ranging from first time users to experienced users.

2.4 Methodology

The method employed for developing harmonized terminologies consisted of three phases (see Fig. 1):

- Phase 1: Identification of objects and activities from a range of functional areas such as telephony and photography
- Phase 2: Collection of terms used by major stakeholders
- Phase 3: Analysis of terms collected and selection of recommended terms.

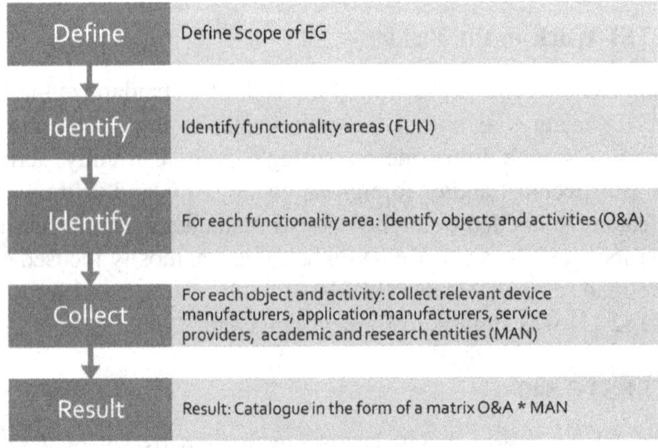

Fig. 1. Overview of methodology

2.5 Phase 1: Identification of Objects and Activities

In this first phase, functional areas such as telephony and photography were identified that define the range of functionalities covered by the present document. Those functional areas cover those functionalities that are most frequently used by many or most users of mobile ICT devices.

For each functional area, relevant objects and activities (i.e. those that are frequently used and used by many users) were identified and defined. The following principles were applied in this process:

Objects and activities were selected if they help users

- Identifying the functionality (i.e. help the user understand what it does)
- Accessing the functionality

- Understanding the available options related to a functionality
- Understanding messages displayed in the context of using a functionality (e.g. error feedback).

Objects and activities were not selected if they cover:

- The content of an application (e.g. "photo", "take the first exit at the roundabout") or the style of the interaction
- Common terms easily found in a dictionary (e.g. "hotel")
- Common verbal expressions indicating an action taken on an object (e.g. "take a photo")
- Words, acronyms, or abbreviations used in a specific technical sense (e.g. "CCNR").

Those objects and activities that are relevant for several or all functional areas are treated as basic terms, dealt with in a separate section of the EG.

2.6 Phase 2: Collection of Terms

For each functional area, relevant providers (device manufacturers, service providers, and application vendors) are identified and the terms used by them for the objects and activities of the respective functional area are collected in the five languages covered by this document (e.g. providers included in the analysis for the functional area "photography" are Apple, Samsung, Huawei, Motorola, and LG, based on their market share in Europe for the product category smart phone).

In most cases, the number of providers had to be limited to five in order to keep the effort for the analysis manageable. The preliminary analysis showed that not all functionalities were offered by all (five) providers. Functionalities offered by one provider only are not included in the analysis.

2.7 Phase 3: Analysis and Selection

In the final phase of the work, the terms collected in Phase 2 are reviewed and the terms to be recommended are selected. This included

- Check for consistency between manufacturers (i.e. prevalence of certain terms)
- Preference of terms that reflect the language of the users as opposed to the language of developers
- Compliance with linguistic requirements from the five languages covered.

Most importantly, localization experts and/or specialists in the linguistics of the respective languages are consulted to support the selection process.

3 Scope of the Harmonized Terminologies

The selection of the functional areas and, within them, objects and activities, is one of the phases of the project. According to current status of the work, the recommended terms to be published in the EG are divided into the following domains or categories:

1. Basic terms
2. Telephony

3. Media
4. Messaging
5. Navigation and maps
6. Banking and payments
7. Health
8. Travel
9. Searching and browsing
10. Social media
11. Photography
12. Games
13. Tools/Miscellaneous

Each of those domains includes relevant subcategories that support the readers in finding the terms they are looking for (e.g. in the case of the domain "Photography", the subcategories are "Taking Photos", "Handling Photos", and "Taking and Handling Videos").

4 Status of the Work

Currently, the expert's team has defined the scope of the EG and is in the phase of identifying functionality areas, objects and activities candidate for inclusion in the guide. Preliminary lists of items have already been prepared for discussion with relevant stakeholders. The systematic investigation on the terminology used by the major players in each area (device manufacturers, service providers, and application vendors) has already been initiated and will continue during 2018. Finally, a list of recommended terms will be prepared taking into account the several criteria described for phase 3. Localization experts and/or specialists in the linguistics of the respective languages will be consulted to support the selection process for each of the five languages.

The ETSI TB (Technical Body) approval of the final document (ETSI guide) is scheduled for April 2019. The document will be publicly available (free of charge) after ETSI publication scheduled for July 2019.

References

1. ETSI EG 202 132 v1.1.1: Human Factors (HF); User Interfaces; Guidelines for generic user interface elements for mobile terminals and services (2004–2008). This reference contains harmonized, English-language terms for areas including UI hardware and software, configuration of services, call features and terminal functionality. Finalized in 2004, it needs updating and expansion to cover features, services and applications not available at that time and other important language
2. ETSI EG 203 499: Human Factors (HF); User-centered terminology for existing and upcoming ICT devices, services and applications. Draft under development, for publication in July 2019

Research on Dishwasher with User Experience Evaluation

Zhongting Wang, Ling Luo(✉), and Chaoyi Zhao

AQSIQ Key Laboratory of Human Factors and Ergonomics (CNIS), Beijing, China
{wangzht, luoling, zhaochy}@cnis.gov.cn

Abstract. Dishwasher was introduced into China at the end of 80s, but was rarely known or used by Chinese families. In the past, there are rarely few user experience researches about dishwashers. This study developed a user experience evaluation based on task scenarios for three types of dishwashers, aimed at exploiting some suitable design ideas and suggestions in the evaluation for dishwasher localization.

Keywords: User experience evaluation · Task scenario · Dishwashers Design

1 Introduction

Dishwasher originated in Europe and was introduced into China at the end of 80s. However, at present, dishwasher coverage hasn't reached 3% in cities of China after decades. Washing dishes and tableware is a tedious, time-consuming and costly work due to the different types of greasy dirt according to the Chinese eating habits. Dishwasher can reduce lots of washing work in kitchens but why can't it be widely accepted by domestic consumers with such good help?

Sun et al. [1], Yue [2], Long [3] et al., studied the development of dishwasher in China, and pointed out that the reasons restricting the popularization of dishwasher in Chinese family various in high price, power consumption, water consumption, mismatching with Chinese tableware and Chinese habits etc. How can dishwasher really solve the pain point of Chinese users' demand and be accepted by Chinese consumers, is the main difficulty of localization design of dishwasher in China. At present, the research on dishwasher abroad mainly focuses on the energy consumption, cleaning and detergent safety. And there is not much academic research on dishwashers in China, mostly focused on three aspects on washing mode, structure and energy consumption. Localization of dishwasher needs to study the Chinese consumer's habits and cognitive logics and also the various types of greasy dirt and tableware in Chinese kitchens. Therefore, according to the dishwasher application and development at home, we developed the user experience evaluation on three dishwashers on China market.

User Experience reflects the perception and subjective feeling when using a product. User experience can be quantified and illustrated with examples base on usability [4]. While user experience refers to the specify feeling a person in the specify

C. Stephanidis (Ed.): HCII Posters 2018, CCIS 850, pp. 309–315, 2018.
https://doi.org/10.1007/978-3-319-92270-6_45

circumstance, the evaluation should be implemented in specify scenarios. The sequential task scenarios were launched including locating plate and bowls, operating dishwashers' interface, washing, fetching plate and bowls, and cleaning the dishwashers and so on. We concerned three aspects of the dishwashers, structure and component design, user interaction interface design, and cleaning and maintain design. And we observed and recoded the effectiveness, efficiency, satisfaction complied to ISO 9241 through all task scenarios. Besides, a post-Test interview was applied after the evaluation. This study aimed at exploiting some suitable design ideas and suggestions in the evaluation for dishwasher localization.

2 User Experience Evaluation Based on Task Scenarios

To explore the factors that affect the comfort of the dishwashers and the potential problems in the design of the current dishwasher products, three types of dishwashers were chosen, with different brands but same capacity. The sequential task scenarios were carried out, which are shown in the following table (see Table 1).

Table 1. The sequential of the task scenarios

Serials number	Task scenarios	Usability design concerned	Observed and recoded contents
a	Open the dishwasher	Structure and component design	Usability (effectiveness, efficiency, satisfaction)
b	Locate plates and bowls		
c	Fill in detergents and slats		
d	Detergents' gear setting		
e	Close the dishwasher		
f	Choose suitable functions and operate	User interaction interface design	
g	Dishes and bowls washing		
h	Open dishwasher while finished	Structure and component design	
i	Fetch the dishes and bowls		
j	Clean the dishwasher	Cleaning and maintain design	

2.1 Evaluation Environment

The evaluation was carried out in a kitchen-similar environment with basin. The three types of dishwashers were installed on the same surface. To avoid the experimental bias, the brand identity of the products was covered. The pollution be brushed on each plate and bowl was the same quantity with fixed proportion of cooking oils, soy sauce, salt, sugar, vinegar etc. which simulated the cooking habits of ordinary Chinese families. And the polluted dishes were boiled and stayed cool for a same time before being brushed (Fig. 1).

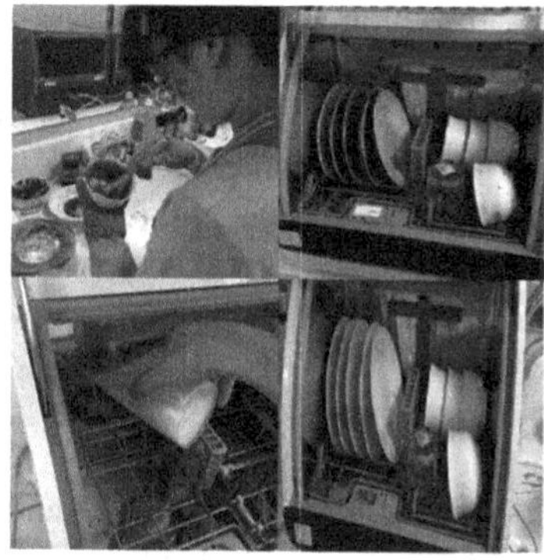

Fig. 1. The environment of the evaluation

2.2 Target Users and Procedures

A total of 12 participants (6 females, 6 males) involved in the evaluation. To cover the broader population characteristics, the participants were of three types, users who already have a dishwasher and use it regularly, users who have known about and want to buy a dishwasher, users who have non-knowledge of dishwashers.

Before the evaluation, users were told about the whole procedure. And 6 sets of tableware were polluted. The users were asked to complete the sequential of the tasks of usability test. Three contents were recorded including effectiveness, efficiency, satisfaction, and a post-Test interview was applied to each user after the evaluation, respectively.

2.3 Data Analysis

Through the evaluation, effectiveness, efficiency and satisfaction were recorded. A repeated ANOVA were used for statistical analysis. SPSS (16.0 J, SPSS Inc.) was used for calculation.

3 Results

The following is the result of subjective and objective measurement we obtained in the evaluation. We will dissect the evaluation results in three parts to explore the potential problems of dishwasher design of the dishwashers: structure and component design, user interaction interface design and cleaning and maintain design.

3.1 The Result of the Structure and Component Design of the Three Types of Dishwashers

The usability for structure and component design will be shown in two task scenarios, one is the tableware placing and fetching (scenario b and i, see Table 1), the other is detergents and slats filling and gear setting (scenario c and d, see Table 1). The effectiveness, efficiency and satisfaction were recorded and analyzed, the typical tasks' results which can indicate the main problems of the design are shown in Figs. 2 and 3. It can be inferred from the figures that the average typical tasks' data are various of different dishwasher types. The repeated measure ANOVA shows significant main effects of different dishwasher type (F placing (2,22) = 3.586, P = 0.045 < 0.05, Fdetergents' gear (2,22) = 5.296, P = 0.013 < 0.05) on the three task scenarios specifying in tableware placing, detergents' gear setting, but no significant main effects on tableware fetching and detergents filling.

Further, the LSD post hoc test results (see Tables 2 and 3) showed that the tableware placing in dishwasher B is more convenient than dishwasher A and C, detergents' gear setting in dishwasher C is much simpler and easier understanding than dishwasher A and B.

In the post interview, participants pointed out that dishwasher A and C are foreign brand, and the internal structure is designed by European style. 66.67% users feedback the interior space design is not reasonable (such as the lack of specialized support), low utilization rate, and does not comply with the use of Chinese kitchen utensils. But dishwasher C's detergents' gear set is designed well for easy known, while the design on dishwasher A and B is concealed on the user interaction interface which is hard to find and learn.

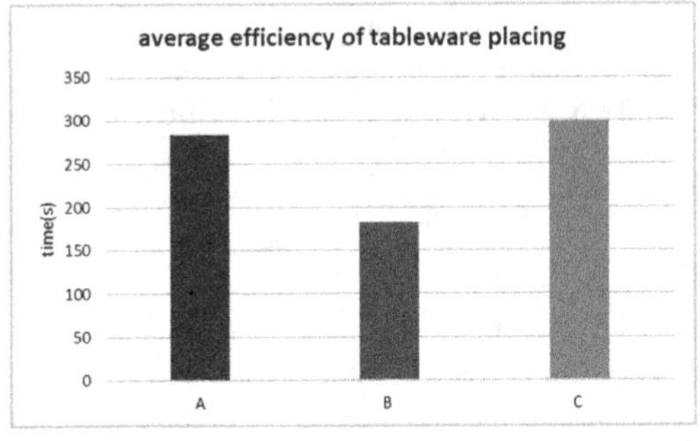

Fig. 2. The average efficiency of tableware placing of the three dishwashers

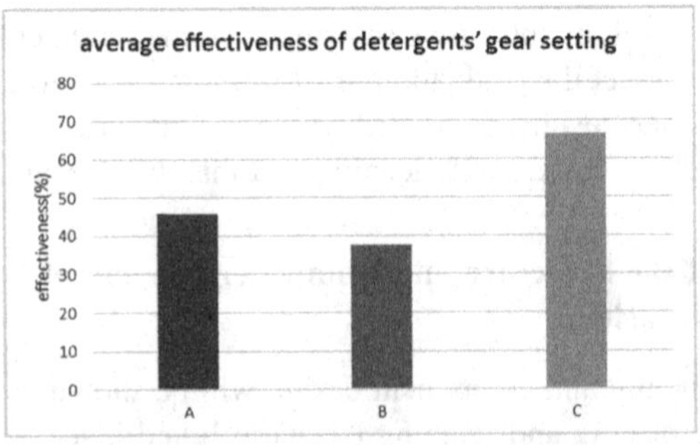

Fig. 3. The average effectiveness of detergents' gear setting of the three dishwashers

Table 2. Results of the LSD post hoc test on the average efficiency of tableware placing

Dishwasher type	LSD post hoc test result (placing)	
	Std. error	Sig.
A vs. B	36.111	.017*
C vs. B	45.645	.026*
A vs. C	58.187	.794

Table 3. Results of the LSD post hoc test on the average effectiveness of detergents' gear setting

Dishwasher type	LSD post hoc test result	
	Std. error	Sig.
A vs. B	.083	.339
C vs. B	.074	.017*
A vs. C	.114	.027*

3.2 The Result of the User Interaction Interface Design for Three Dishwashers

The usability for user interaction interface design will be shown in the program setting (scenario f, see Table 1). The effectiveness, efficiency and satisfaction were recorded and analyzed, the results which can indicate the main problems of the design are shown in Fig. 4. It can be inferred from the figures that the program setting task's data are various of different dishwasher types. The repeated measure ANOVA shows significant main effects of different dishwasher types ($F(2,22) = 3.878$, $P = 0.036 < 0.05$). Further, the LSD post hoc test results (see Table 4) showed that program setting in dishwasher C is much simpler and easier understanding than dishwasher A and B.

In the post interview, participants pointed out that the terminology of interaction interface on dishwasher A which is foreign brand uses literal translation cause highly misunderstanding and maloperation. And the operation logic is not consistent with Chinese cognitive habits due to unsatisfactory and dislike.

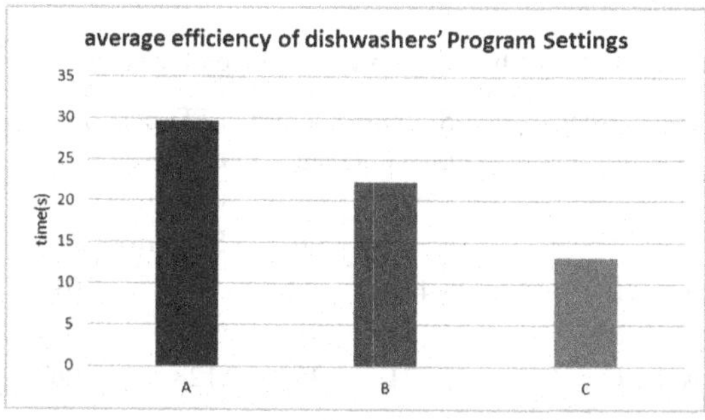

Fig. 4. The average efficiency of dishwashers' program settings

Table 4. Results of the LSD post hoc test on the average efficiency of dishwashers' program settings

Dishwasher type	LSD post hoc test result	
	Std. error	Sig.
A vs. B	7.342	.345
C vs. B	6.159	.021*
A vs. C	3.738	.031*

3.3 The Result of the Cleaning and Maintain Design for Three Dishwashers

The usability for cleaning and maintain design will be shown in cleaning the dishwasher (scenario j, see Table 1). The effectiveness, efficiency and satisfaction were recorded and analyzed, the results which can indicate the main problems of the design are shown in Fig. 5. It can be inferred from the figures that the average data are various of different dishwasher types. The repeated measure ANOVA shows significant main effects of different dishwasher types ($F_{cleaning\ efficiency}$ (2,22) = 7.301, P = 0.004 < 0.05, $F_{cleaning\ satisfaction}$ (2,22) = 6.049, P = 0.008 < 0.05). Further, the LSD post hoc test results (see Table 5) showed that cleaning and maintain of dishwasher B is more difficult than dishwasher A and C, and dishwasher B causes more unsatisfaction.

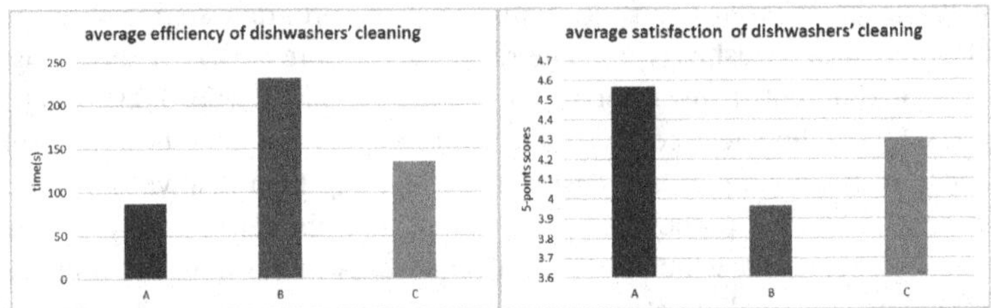

Fig. 5. The average efficiency and satisfaction scores of the three dishwashers cleaning

Table 5. Results of the LSD post hoc test on the average efficiency of dishwashers' cleaning

Dishwasher type	LSD post hoc test result (efficiency)		LSD post hoc test result (satisfaction)	
	Std. error	Sig.	Std. error	Sig.
A vs. B	28.407	.000**	.201	.012*
C vs. B	44.342	.054*	.183	.088
A vs. C	40.721	.257	.128	.067

In the post interview, participants pointed out that the spray arm in dishwasher B is installed in a special way, which requires the user to use the force disassembly cause all users' complaint.

4 Discussion and Conclusion

The present study was concerned with user's objective response and subjective satisfaction on dishwashers through a sequential of the task scenarios. The results of this evaluation shows that, as a kind of exotic, the dishwasher products on the Chinese market have some typical problems more or less. The dishwashers of foreign brand appear more understanding problems and mismatching of Chinese tableware but better structure to clean and maintain than domestic dishwashers.

We can sum up the following contents from this evaluation. Firstly, the structure and component design of the current dishwashers on China markets doesn't match with the Chinese family tableware. Secondly, operation mode design is not consistent with users' using habits. Thirdly, the mode of interface operation is not consistent with the user's cognition. Fourthly, the identification and description is not consistent with the user's cognition. Slightly change on appearance or literal translation into Chinese, cannot really touch the Chinese user pain points.

In future, the development of dishwasher products should concentrate more energies on the contents mentioned above. Dishwasher enterprises should do more research on Chinese consumers' physiology characteristic and cognitive and habits, and strive to meet the consumers' true demands.

Acknowledgement. Our work is supported by the scientific research foundation of China National Institute of Standardization, Beijing, China (Grant No. 242016Y-4700).

References

1. Sun, J., Li, B., Wang, S.: Present situation of dishwasher and new exploration to realize the dishwasher popularization of China. Mod. Sci. Instrum. **2012**(1), 137–141 (2012)
2. Yue, J.: The general situation of the development and the industry of the household dishwasher products. China Appliance Technol. **2014**(12) (2014)
3. Hua, L.: Study on countermeasures and problems of household dishwasher. Value Eng. **35** (15), 248–249 (2016)
4. Bill, A., Tullis, T.: Quantifying the User Experience (2009)

Quantitative Usability Testing Based on Eye Fixation-Related Potentials

Kimihiro Yamanaka(✉)

Intelligence and Informatics, Konan University, Kobe, Japan
kiyamana@konan-u.ac.jp

Abstract. To propose a quantitative usability testing index for each step of information processing, we measured eye fixation-related potentials (EFRPs) under the condition simulating touch panel operation. A characteristic of EFRPs is that conventional usability testing or other special testing is unnecessary because eye fixation can be used as a trigger. In this study, there were two kinds of tasks such as visual cognition and search. In visual cognition tasks, after addition and subtraction, the participant input the answer by selecting orderly number corresponding to the numerical answer displayed on the monitor. In visual search tasks, a number selected randomly was displayed on the monitor, and the participant answered the question by searching the same number out of numbers arranged randomly on the monitor. And then, EFRPs were measured to estimate cognitive load for task-related information processing. EFRP data were compared with data from a usability questionnaire, revealing that EFRPs enable the quantification of cognitive load.

Keywords: Quantitative usability testing index · Physiological signal
Eye movement · Eye Fixation-Related Potentials (EFRPs)

1 Introduction

In conventional usability testing, a questionnaire survey is commonly used to obtain users' subjective views. By additionally evaluating quantitative factors such as operation time and a N/E ratio, it is possible to show whether the entire system is good or bad, but not where or how improvements should be made. In addition, a large amount of data is required for proper subjective evaluation, and its reproducibility is generally low [1].

To overcome drawbacks specific to subjective testing, the utility of usability testing based on biological information closely related to human cognition was investigated in this study. To design a practical improvement plan, we focused on cognitive processing involved in the handling of a target system or product to reveal which steps impose a heavy cognitive load. To quantify cognitive loads, electroencephalography (EEG) was performed to measure event-related potentials (ERPs) [2, 3]. As shown in Fig. 1, ERPs are represented by a wave that contains information on the cognitive function of information processing. However, because ERPs are triggered at the time of information acquisition, it cannot be used for accurate measurements in situations where the trigger cannot be specified. In this study, we therefore investigated the utility and

C. Stephanidis (Ed.): HCII Posters 2018, CCIS 850, pp. 316–321, 2018.
https://doi.org/10.1007/978-3-319-92270-6_46

validity of eye fixation-related potentials (EFRPs) [4], with eye fixation as the onset of information acquisition, in the measurement of cognitive load.

To reveal quantitative usability testing indices that enable the extraction of problems from the perspective of information processing, we evaluated EFRPs and ERPs under the same task environment to clarify whether they serve as comparable testing indices.

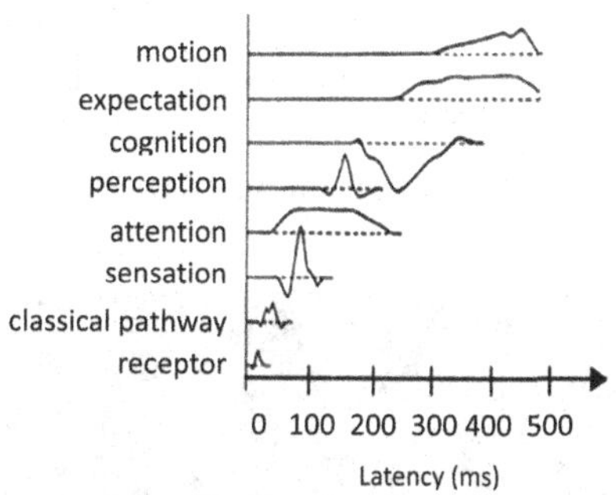

Fig. 1. ERPs wave

2 Experimental Methods

In a study analyzing the movement of fingers on a touch panel, we extracted movements involved in thinking and searching, showing that it is possible to test usability based on the movement of users. These thinking and searching movements correspond to the two basic motions Plan and Search in Therblig motion analysis. They are also represented by the ERP P300 component, which reflects the task difficulty. As in the study by Ando, the present study was conducted with 9 healthy male and female undergraduate/graduate students.

Experiments are summarized in Fig. 2. In a shielded room, each participant sat in front of a desk and performed visual cognition and visual search tasks (Fig. 3) in a random order. Each task consisting of 10 questions was repeated 3 times in a row to give a total of 30 questions. In visual cognition tasks, after addition and subtraction, the participant input the answer by selecting a number corresponding to the numerical answer from numbers 1–50 displayed on the monitor. In visual search tasks, a number selected randomly from 1–50 was displayed on the monitor, and the participant answered the question by searching the same number out of numbers arranged randomly on the monitor. The participants rested for 3 min between tasks.

A data recorder was used to concurrently record eye movement monitored by an eye tracking device (EyeLink II; SR Research) mounted on the head and electrocardiogram and EEG monitored using a multi-telemeter system (WEB-5000; Nihon Kohden). EEG was performed in accordance with the International 10–20 system [5] with the electrode placed at Fz (frontal lobe) and Cz and Pz (parietal lobe). In addition, an original questionnaire was developed to subjectively evaluate loss of interest, amount of load, difficulty, and stress (on a scale of 1–7) after each task.

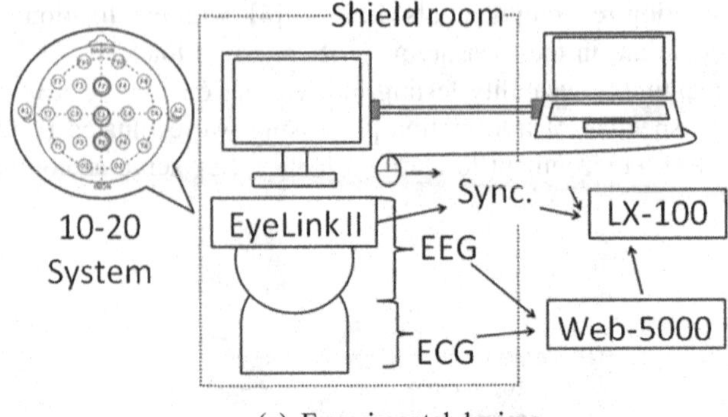

(a) Experimental devices

(b) Snapshot of experiment

Fig. 2. Experimental setup

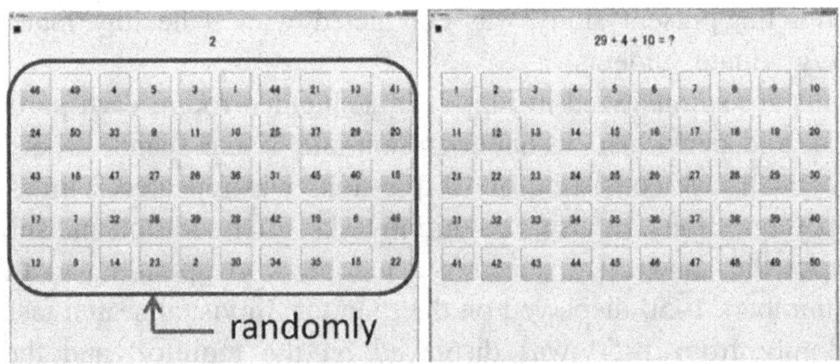

Fig. 3. Visual cognition and visual search tasks

3 Experimental Results and Discussion

No significant difference in scores was observed between the two tasks. In addition, no intergroup difference was observed in electrocardiograms (low/high frequency), although load tended to be higher in visual search tasks.

Using the display of each question or eye fixation as a trigger in ERP or EFRP measurement, respectively, EEG data were recorded from Fz, Cz, and Pz between 100 ms before and 1000 ms after trigger onset and were averaged to obtain representative ERP and EFRP waveforms (Fig. 4). As shown in the figure, the cognitive component N2 and the attention and processing component P300 were clearly present, indicating that EEG was measured properly. Therefore, to identify each component, we performed principal component analysis [6] of spatial and temporal information using 30 ERP or EFRP waveforms (30 = 2 tasks × 3 recording sites × 5 subjects). For analysis, 51 potentials were extracted from the graph at a 20-ms interval. Five principal components covering 93.54% were extracted in ERPs, whereas four principal components covering 94.87% was extracted in EFRPs. We measured the peak value of the principal component that increased the loading in the 300-ms latency which is associated with cognition, and the area between 300–124 ms to 300 + 124 ms (176–424 ms) was defined as a characteristic value and was subjected to analysis of variance. A significant difference was observed between Fz and Cz ($p < 0.05$) in ERPs and between Fz and Cz ($p < 0.05$) and between Cz and Pz ($p < 0.05$) in EFRPs (Fig. 5).

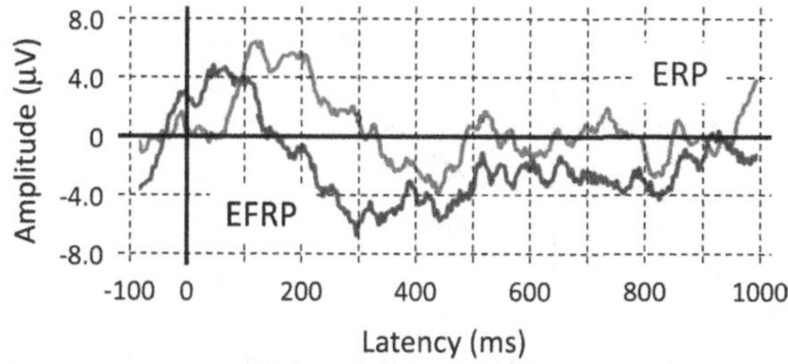

Fig. 4. ERP and EFRP waveforms

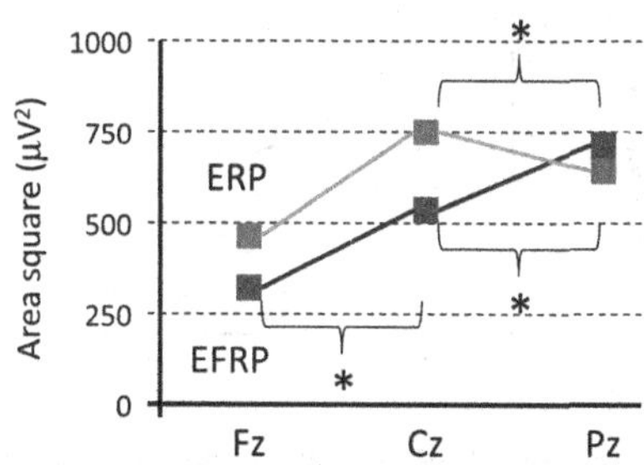

Fig. 5. Results of principal component analysis

Electrocardiographic findings and ERPs showed loading tended to increase in visual cognition tasks compared with visual search tasks ($p < 0.05$) (Fig. 6). In addition, loading was higher at Cz and Pz in the parietal region than at Fz in the frontal region in both ERPs and EFRPs (Fig. 5). Cz and Pz correspond to the somatosensory area and parietal association area in the parietal lobe. The parietal association area is known to reflect visuospatial load in information processing. Our findings suggest that both ERPs and EFRPs increase as the level of difficulty in visual information processing increases, as the processing happens when the target number is found from among the randomly placed numbers. In other words, the present visual search task can be used to evaluate loads associated with searching. However, we were unable to reveal parameters useful for the evaluation of loads involved in thinking. Because mental calculation was involved in the visual cognition tasks, additional cognitive loads might have been needed to calculate and memorize numbers. Because memory generally plays an important role in thinking, ERP and EFRP measurements were performed in the occipitotemporal region (T5, T6, O1, and O2) which reflects information processing involving memory [7].

Figure 7 shows results of an analysis conducted in the same way as the analysis of Fig. 6. The horizontal axis indicates the brain area. One of the systems is for the visual cognition task, and the other system is for the visual search task. In visual cognition tasks, the amplitude of waves tended to be larger at T6 and O2 as expected, indicating that cognitive load involved in visual cognition tasks can be quantified by recording ERPs through the electrodes placed in the occipitotemporal area.

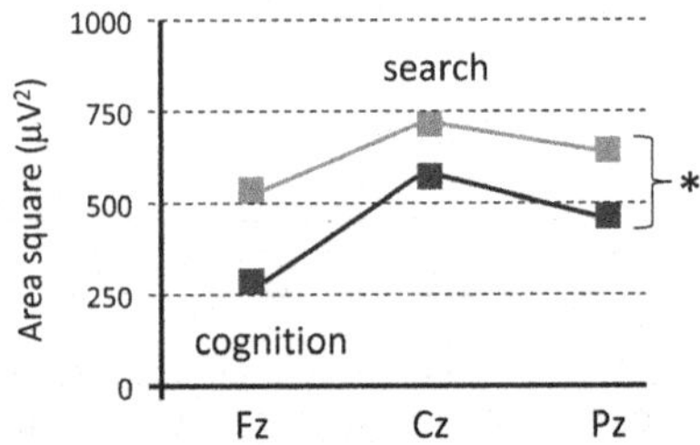

Fig. 6. Visual search task and frontal, parietal lobe (*: $p < 0.05$)

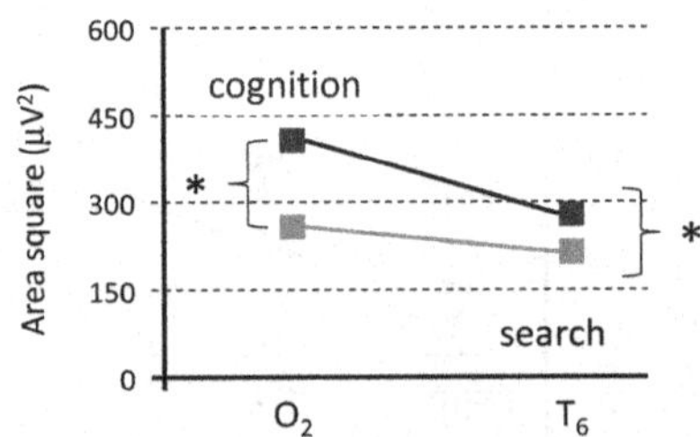

Fig. 7. Visual cognition task and occipitotemporal area (*: $p < 0.05$)

4 Conclusions

In summary, three major findings in this study are as follows:

(1) In visual search tasks, which involve visuospatial information processing, cognitive loads can be quantified by recording ERPs in the parietal region.

(2) In visual cognition tasks, which are greatly associated with memory in information processing, cognitive loads can be quantified by recording ERPs in the occipitotemporal region.
(3) Similar results between EFRPs and ERPs indicate that EFRPs are a practical index for use in usability testing.

References

1. Rubin, J., Chisnell, D.: Handbook of Usability Testing, p. 348. Wiley Publishing Inc., Boston (2008)
2. Johnson, Jr., R. (ed.): Event-Related Brain Potentials and Cognition (Oxford Psychology Series), p. 237. Oxford University Press, New York (1995)
3. Papanicolaou, A.C. (ed.): The Oxford Handbook of Functional Brain Imaging in Neuropsychology and Cognitive Neurosciences (Oxford Library of Psychology), p. 397. Oxford University Press, Oxford (2017)
4. Devillez, H., Guyader, N., Guérin-Dugué, A.: An eye fixation–related potentials analysis of the P300 potential for fixations onto a target object when exploring natural scenes. J. Vis. **15** (3), 20 (2015). https://doi.org/10.1167/15.13.20
5. Libenson, M.H.: Practical Approach to Electroencephalography, p. 464. Saunders, Philadelphia (2009)
6. Bollen, J., Van de Sompel, H., Hagberg, A., Chute, R.: A principal component analysis of 39 scientific impact measures. PLoS ONE **4**(6), e6022 (2009). https://doi.org/10.1371/journal.pone.0006022
7. Lara, V., Marcuse, M.D., Madeline, C., Fields, M.D., Yoo, J.J.: Rowan's Primer of EEG, p. 216. Elsevier, Edinburgh (2015)

Appropriateness of User Experience Design

Wei Yu, Yun Yang(✉), and Yanan Ni

School of Art, Design and Media,
East China University of Science and Technology,
M. Box 286, No. 130, Meilong Road, Xuhui District, Shanghai 200237, China
weiyu@ecust.edu.cn, Yyun66681@qq.com, 695097575@qq.com

Abstract. In the Internet era, though the user-centered design discipline plays a promoting role in modern design, the significance of user experience design is greatly overstated. It concerns the feeling of people carefully and tries to meet the physiological and psychological need of users. How can we keep the appropriateness of "people oriented"? Today we find ourselves in an ever more globalized world in economy and culture. Designers encounter the puzzle brought about by over-commercialization and over people oriented as well as human being's evolution safety and the challenge of global ecological environment deterioration. As driven by commercial interests, over design is made to meet users' demand without a bottom line, which makes users overindulges in and depends on the so-called people-oriented design in the depth of commercial interest first, over use of ecological resources and other design ethics questions. This paper tries to cooperate the appropriateness rule of the "people oriented" idea of design activities with the idea of Chinese traditional "harmony between the universe and humanity", absorb nutrients from oriental culture and rethink professional ethics, social responsibility and environmental protection mission of designers, which has practical significance and theoretical value to help designers to handle the harmonious and sustainable development relation between humanity and true self, humanity and society system as well as humanity and nature.

Keywords: Design ethics · Oriental culture · People oriented

1 Brief Review on the Status of "People Oriented"

1.1 Design and Technology

According to Martin Heidegge (2004), modern science and technology has changed the moral relationship between people. Negative effects brought about to human civilization by technology have been realized by ethicists very early. Industrialization brings us the development of technology. The development of science and technology at the beginning tries to increase productivity for social production, and each device is with more functions to simplify our life. Nowadays, the development of virtual experience, artificial intelligence, big data cloud storage and other technologies makes technology either provide convenience for our life, or even give more capacities other than the instinct to us. We are in an intellectualized system net consisting of the computer

C. Stephanidis (Ed.): HCII Posters 2018, CCIS 850, pp. 322–330, 2018.
https://doi.org/10.1007/978-3-319-92270-6_47

system, and instead of being controlled by people, the system "reacts upon us and layouts the natural world again in a big way" (2015). Technology influences our life style and way of thinking.

Questions brought about by technical improvement are also multidimensional. In the "Internet+" era, take-out will be delivered to our home and we only need to click the mobile phone screen slightly, which is obviously a typical service mode of "from cradle to tomb". Such consumerism culture has no other meaning except accelerating the social rhythm and dispelling the funny of (eating) life. Another example is the "flow" concept (2017) advocated by today's game design and virtual experience design, namely a kind of immersive experience, makes people indulge in the virtual world, prevent people from finding the entrance of true life and harm the body and heart.

We should think about the ethical relationship between design and technology, and we need to realize that human being cannot avoid the destiny to the technology world; while such technology force is still in further development, and nobody can avoid it. Technology can give empower design; as a designer, we should reflect on and think about the original design point and rethink and criticize design. We cannot let the force expansion of technology dispels the value of true life finally. We will not only provide what users want, but also provide an objective thinking environment based on their values and help users treat the world again by introducing a new angle of view through the article designed and take a new look at their own role and location around the application of the article designed (2012).

1.2 Excessive "People Oriented" Design

In the Internet era, the significance of user experience design is elevated to an all-time high. It concerns the feeling of people and tries to meet the physiological and psychological need of users. It stresses the ease of use, optimization and efficiency more in the human-computer interaction (HCI) to try to reduce the cognitive work of users when they face equipment. Such seemingly "people oriented" design thought has indeed increased the overall production efficiency during the application of users ostensibly, while it also causes immoderate reliance of users on technology. Thus, it weakens users' cognitive and question solving capacity owned by them (2017). Today's map navigation function is extremely convenient, the system will plan an optimal path for you, and you can arrive at your destination easily without taking your bearings and checking the guideboard during the whole process only by inputting the start point and end point. However, such accurate, specific and step-by-step assistance reduces the situational awareness of drivers greatly, namely, orientation cognition owned by people naturally and the capacity of mastering the road condition and instructions and remembering the route. It causes that more and more young people become obsessed with road, and they even can get lost without the help of navigation software on their way to work or back home.

Similarly, people's calculative ability, ability to remember things and ability of listening, speaking, reading and writing are weaker and weaker due to the more and more considerable user experience. Scientific calculator software helps us calculate each bill in our life whenever and wherever possible; memorandum and reminder software informs us of the plan of a day, a week even a whole year and reminds us at the time point set; spell check and automatic error correction software automatically correct our errors when we are tapping the keyboard. All these things make our memory of words be more and more indistinct.

Technology should take improving but not weakening the ability of people as the target because all of us do not want to be replaced by machines someday just as described in science fiction films. Therefore, instead of meeting people's greedy demands unconditionally, designers should clearly realize the finiteness and appropriateness of people oriented, concern negative effects (mainly immoderate reliance) of software caused to users during a long-term application and provide sustainable appropriate design responsibility with their boundless sense of design ethics when designing good user experience.

2 Reflection on the Status of Design Ethics and Focus on Chinese "Harmony Between the Universe and Humanity" Thought

2.1 Reflection on the Status of Design Ethics

As the growing global concern on irrational design, environmental pollution, resources waste brought by over design and other questions, how to lead rational consumption, green consumption of the whole society and regulate design rules through design becomes more and more appealing.

In traditional product design, taking mobile phone as an example, designers make the product be used for a long period by designing changeable modules, ruggedized shells, standardization of modules, extensible devices and other means. At this stage, the design mainly devotes itself to ensure the durability of products. As the increase of the product complexity, the design starts to concentrate on identifying and eliminating adverse factors that hinder the durable application of the product to ensure the reliability and the performance of easy to maintain of the product (2011). However, the product can still be discarded due to the "planned abolishment system" of manufacturers and the seeking new thought of consumers when the product has owned good characteristics and durability. Finally, it will cause high-entropy and high-carbon destroys to resources and ecology.

Moreover, in today's service economy age, products and services are basically binding consumption, and the concept of "product design" has also been expanded to "product service system design". For "materialized products", it commits itself to promote the usability and ease of use of products and make users of products acquire good experience. For the non-materialization trend of products, service and experience becomes a major issue. Therefore, to meet the experience satisfaction of users is throughout the whole process as the corresponding design strategy, while the design ethics is basically neglected or desalted.

The Internet thinking comes into being in the Internet era, which makes people attach importance to service and experience from design and manufacturing materialized products. Nevertheless, in the field of interface and interactive design, the cognitive pattern changes rapidly as the advance in science and technology and the proposal of new views. It easily causes user fatigue even cognitive dissonance. Merchants and designers often regard in-depth entertainment and interest reveling as the potential pain spots of users and develop that continuously, the consequence of which is to cause that users, especially teenagers, enjoy it and cannot help themselves. It not only harms the physical and psychological health of teenagers extremely, but also causes more and more social and family questions.

2.2 Design Ethics in "Harmony Between the Universe and Humanity" Thought

Use experience design means to promote the use experience of users on products, and it puts more emphasis on the thing that products or services should promote the spiritual satisfaction in non-material ways and display the design principle of "people oriented". Today we find ourselves in an ever more globalized world in economy and culture. Designers face the challenge of multiple values conflict, and it cannot meet the design ethics questions of over design, business interest trap and others faced by design today to stick to the guidance of traditional western philosophy thought continuously. The paper indicates that the people oriented design implication and design method need to change along with the technology promotion and era development and master the development process of the people oriented design idea under the new trend. Therefore, the paper tries to combine modern design with traditional Chinese philosophical thought, absorb nutrients from oriental culture and rethink professional ethics and social responsibility, find the design "supreme good" target and regard the ethics value and property as one of the inherent characteristics of design, which has important practical significance to help designers to handle the harmonious and sustainable development relation between people and true self, people and society as well as people and nature.

2.2.1 Implication of "Harmony Between the Universe and Humanity" Thought

"Harmony between the universe and humanity is a "nature – ethics" sense integrating the universe, human being and earth formed by ancient Chinese during the process for survival; it is one of the elementary propositions in Chinese traditional philosophy. As a kind of simple systematic perspective, this thought has very far-reaching influence on the handling of the Chinese traditional relation between humanity and true self, humanity and society as well as humanity and nature.

The universe-humanity thought is a significant thought that guides the most initiative element – "humanity" in the system consisting of humanity, nature and society to handle internal and external relationships. In the system, "universe" includes natural universe, social universe and transcendent universe; "harmony" expresses not only the accessibility between "humanity" and "universe", but also the intimacy and integration between "humanity" and "universe". Instead of meaning individual "persons", "humanity" means a community with shared future for humanity and ecological fate that is restrained by natural law, social regulation and material basis and cooperates with "universe". Thus, the display of "harmony between the universe and humanity" implication should include:

(1) On the plane of handling the relationship with nature: humanity is harmonious with nature through the rational cognition of natural law.
(2) On the plane of handling the relationship with society: humanity should abide by social ethics standards to be close to natural law.
(3) On the plane of handling true self: be simple and integrate harmony of soul through strengthening self-cultivation.

2.2.2 Rational Human-Based View in "Harmony Between the Universe and Humanity" Thought

The people oriented or people-centered thought in the "harmony between the universe and humanity" thought is its quintessence. Man is the intelligent part of the universe, and people are valued in the universe. Though the Chinese universe-humanity thought admits the dominant role of people, it does not equal to the condition that people is in an absolute leading position. Behaviors of people are restrained by natural law, and people should achieve "following their hearts' desire without overstepping the line", namely, the quintessence – degree in the doctrine of the mean. It is absolutely not that people are the external subject in western culture, and the "universe" is an article that is conquered and transformed by people. Furthermore, instead of the exquisite egoists' alienation human-based view of selfish, self-indulgence and desires for material welfare showed by western consumerism, the essence of "people oriented" thought is a kind of multi-win and intergrowth harmonious and moderate play of "mutual benefit between the universe and humanity" under the precondition of conforming to natural and social ethics. In case of conflicts between local interests and public interests, instead of resolving them in the destroy method of conflicts, we should communicate and coordinate actively and take the realization of life harmony and happiness of majority people to the hilt as the vision.

2.2.3 Natural Intergrowth in "Harmony Between the Universe and Humanity" Thought

Xici states that "lead the natural changes in the nature of heaven and earth but not overdo, and carry all things but not be with missing"; Zhu Xi deems that "objects are animals and plants; love means proper use of resources. The "lead" and "use" has properly described the requirement of the universe-humanity thought on the role of people. "Lead" requires people to take the heaven and earth as the model and people as a natural ecological species, which actually takes the organic component links in the nature as the precondition and abides by natural law; "use" stresses that people should fulfill people's creativity and fetch from the natural abstemiously based on climate and other natural phenomena and by using natural law fully.

In terms of handling the relationship between people and nature and how to fulfill the main body role of people in such relationship, the traditional Chinese universe-humanity through contains unique intelligence: we should realize the "intergrowth" between people and nature, and make them interact with each other and rely on each other in such thought. It emphasizes that people and environment is a unity of opposite. People should follow the law and not violate human nature. Furthermore, it includes "kiss and Jen, Jen and the love of things". Those propositions have the same goal with the sustainable design principle advocated by the current international society.

3 Life-Cycle Assessment Theory of User Experience Design Based on Oriental "Harmony Between the Universe and Humanity" Cultural View

3.1 Basic Thinking of Life-Cycle Assessment Theory of User Experience Design Based on Oriental Culture

(1) Concern actual demands of users, and display the universal love human-centered spirit of "harmony between the universe and humanity".

The paper reflects how to define the reasonable boundaries of the "people oriented" design through in use experience design and what its bottom line. The target pursued by design has turned to meet everlasting spirit consumption from meeting the basic function and moderate spiritual needs. The original "interest of the entire human race oriented" is gradually replaced by "self-centered". The "people oriented" design should not be the supreme business rule that designers separate the common destiny of people and nature, society and ecology by designers, handle all things separately by taking people's greed as the center, neglect or avoid ecological responsibility and social justice, take consumption stimulation as the kingly way and meet consumers excessively. Xunzi has said: "Fire and water possess a spirit but no life, grass and trees possess a life but no awareness, birds and animals possess awareness but no sense of morality, only humans possess spirit, life, awareness as well as the sense of morality, hence the noblest beings in the world". Xunzi affirms the value of people from the evolution rule of natural universe and reveals the difference between people and nature. In the universe and people intergrowth and heaven and human mutual connection in the "harmony between the universe and humanity", the position of the universe and people is not absolutely opposite. People has subjectivity in the process of changing the material universe, but they are no the dominant power. Designers should recognize their responsibility, understand users' actual demands when researching and developing products and provide an objective thinking environment based on their values:

A. Designers should research users' psychology, value preference, functional requirement, cultural background and others and understand their actual demands.
B. They should show the long-term influence of the product and service on users, instead of increasing users' feeling of dependency and deteriorating their cognitive ability, which is helpful for designers to pay more attention to enhancing the cognitive ability of users with the product or service except considering the ease of use, probation and other elements.

(2) Follow natural law, balance "take" and "use", and establish a wisdom of ecological ethics.

The innovation point of this paper is to dig the relationship between people and nature and how we can play the main body role of people in such relationship: we should establish the idea of "intergrowth" of people and nature, mutual interaction and interdependency and stress that people and environment is a unity of opposite. People should follow natural law, protect and make for all things, develop and use resources and technologies properly and adequately, place ecological protection factors and basic function realization at the same position from the angle of the life-cycle of products during the design process, consider the retrievability, low carbon, reutilization, detachability, ease of maintenance of materials and structures and conduct sustainable assessment of products and services.

3.2 Explore New Life-Cycle Life System of Product Design

3.2.1 LCA Life-Cycle Assessment Standard System

In domestic, a perfect life-cycle assessment standard is still lacked. This paper proposes a new life-cycle assessment system of user experience design based on the famous "LCA (Life-cycle Assessment)" standard. LCA is a programmatic report proposed by SETAC according to the major conclusion in an academic conference of Portugal in 1993 (2003). It is a method that can make quantitative analysis on the environmental influence of the whole process from raw material extraction, manufacturing, consumption, application, recycle to final abandoning of a product. LCA includes the following 4 steps (see Fig. 1):

(1) Confirm the target and scope: define the target, life-cycle scope and system boundary of research.
(2) List analysis: count the input quantity of raw materials, accessories and energy and the output quantity that is discharged to atmosphere, water body, soil and other external environments during the process in each life process, and form a process list.
(3) Influence assessment: conduct quantitative calculation and assessment based on the process list.
(4) Result interpretation and suggestion: find out the distance between the current situation and the target confirmed through the comparison between the list and influence assessment, and give the difference and rectification opinion.

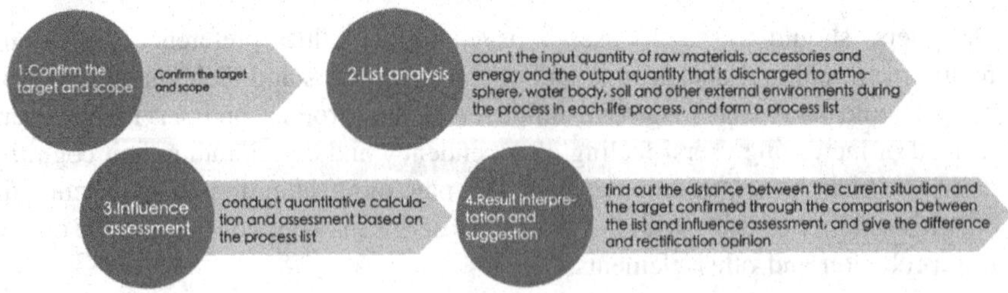

Fig. 1. Life-cycle assessment

The assessment method can not only be used in the life cycle rating of actual products, but also be used in the comparison of the ecological influence of design schemes, which is beneficial for reducing ecological influences caused during the research and development of products as well as the later period from the source.

3.2.2 Explore New Life-Cycle Life System of Product Design

The paper supplements the qualitative analysis that should be owned in the service system on non-quantitative assessments lacked in LCA based on LCA and proposes WLCA (the Whole Life-cycle Assessment) (see Fig. 2). Its specific steps include:

(1) Position the design target and scope accurately: it requires defining design target, life-cycle scope and system boundary for users' psychology, value preference, functional requirement, prediction on product or service, educational and cultural background, exploitativeness and implementation of design.
(2) System analysis: dismantle the output quantity at each stage from research & development to product or service production, application, feedback (material design also includes waste recycle) and others, and form a list.
(3) Influence assessment: Conduct quantitative (product design) or qualitative (service design) assessments based on the list, and consider the influence on environment, economy and society.
(4) Result interpretation and suggestion: find out the distance between the current situation and the target confirmed through the comparison between the list and influence assessment, and give the difference and rectification opinion.

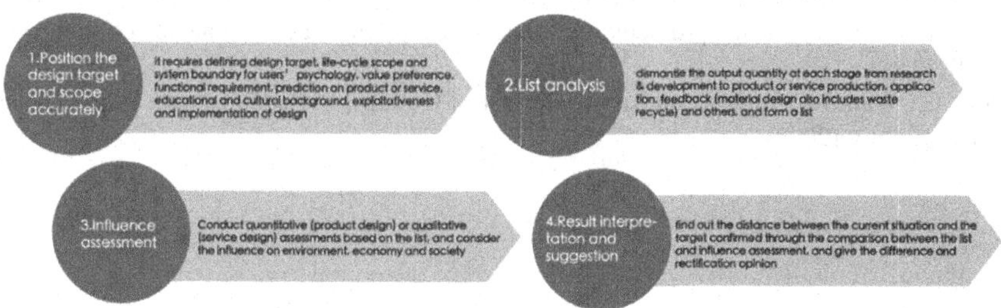

Fig. 2. The whole life-cycle assessment

Characteristics of the design life-cycle assessment in the paper is reflected in the promotion of attentions on users, which stresses the trace of post feedback of products or services, can propose qualitative analysis aiming at the current interactive design and virtual experience design, and perfects the assessment scope of LCA.

4 Conclusion

In this paper, it firstly introduces the Chinese "harmony between the universe and humanity" thought; the human-based view and the wisdom of ecological ethics contained in the thought have significant practical and far-reaching significance for designers to handle the relationship between "humanity and true self, humanity and society system as well as humanity and nature". On the basis, the paper develops the description of the current situation and thinking of "people oriented" design, expands to the wider experience design and service design from the narrow interactive design field and discusses the relationship of design, technology and sustainability as well as responsibilities that the society and designers should bear for design. Finally, in terms of the appropriateness principle of user experience design, it discusses a new life-cycle assessment system creatively, under the framework of which, it conducts quantitative or qualitative analysis on the attention on users and the trace and feedback of products and service, perfects or expands the existing assessment system of the user experience design.

References

1. Heidegger, M.: Question concerning technology. In: Kaplan, D.M. (ed.) Readings in the Philosophy of Technology, pp. 35–51. Rowman & Littlefield Publishers, New York (2004)
2. Anthony Townsend (America), Smart Cities. China CITIC J. (2015)
3. Blevis, E., Preist, C., Schien, D., Ho, P.: Further connecting sustainable interaction design with sustainable digital infrastructure design. In: LIMITS 2017, Santa Barbara (2017)
4. Jiayu, W.: Reflective Design Though in Social Interaction Research (2012)
5. Balasubramanian, G., Lee, H., Poon, K.W., Lim, W.-K., Yong, W.K.: Towards establishing design principles for balancing usability and maintaining cognitive abilities. In: Marcus, A., Wang, W. (eds.) DUXU 2017. LNCS, vol. 10288, pp. 3–18. Springer, Cham (2017). https://doi.org/10.1007/978-3-319-58634-2_1
6. Shedroff, N.: Design is the problem: the future of design must be sustainable. Tsinghua Univ. J. (2011)
7. Tang, C., Wan, R.: Analysis on Life-cycle List of Cotton Textiles. Shanghai Textile Science & Technology (2003)

Psychological, Cognitive and Neurocognitive Issues in HCI

An Unsafe Act Autodetection Methodology in Nuclear Power Plant Operations

Jeeyea Ahn, Jae Min Kim, and Seung Jun Lee(✉)

Ulsan National Institute of Science and Technology, 50, UNIST-gil, Ulsan 44919, Republic of Korea
{jeeya, jaemink, sjlee420}@unist.ac.kr

Abstract. Nowadays, automation has been generalized with artificial intelligences in many areas. In nuclear power plants, some features which have simple logics in nuclear power plants such as reactor trip and engineered safety features (ESFs) actuation have been automated, whereas, other components have not been automated yet, so human operators are still necessary to control the reactor in emergency or abnormal situations. However, there exists a risk of human errors since human operators are involved in nuclear power operations. That is because, human error may contribute to the risk of severe accidents. To reduce those human errors, moreover, to draw to extend the portion of automation in nuclear power plants, a framework which automatically detects Unsafe Acts (UAs) which are occurred in advanced main control rooms of nuclear power plants has been introduced. Human operators are supposed to operate nuclear power plants by following operating procedures. However, in real operational situation, they violate operating procedures sometimes to achieve the goal (to keep the plant integrity) based on their own experiences and their know-hows. Critical safety functions (CSFs) can disentangle whether an operator's action will adversely affect plant integrity. Thus, the UA autodetection system considers both procedure violation and CSFs violation to find out errors made by human operator.

Keywords: Unsafe act · Autodetection · Nuclear power plant operation

1 Instruction

As modern technology enters the Fourth Industrial Revolution, Modern artificial intelligence techniques are very pervasive. In some cases, artificial intelligence replaces human tasks (i.e. autonomous vehicle) or supports human performances (i.e. online assistants such as Siri and Bixby). As technologies support human, human workload may decrease, so that human performance and efficiency would be increased, and the probability of human error would be decreased.

Nuclear power has the limelight since it generates clean and economic energy. However, the severe accident in nuclear power plant might bring terrible consequences. The risk of nuclear power plant must manage strictly. Because of that characteristics, technologies which apply to the nuclear industry are appraised very precisely and conservatively.

C. Stephanidis (Ed.): HCII Posters 2018, CCIS 850, pp. 333–339, 2018.
https://doi.org/10.1007/978-3-319-92270-6_48

Nuclear industry is one of the fields which human-factor may significantly affect the risk of severe disaster. In fact, the most of severe accidents (e.g. Three Miles Island, Chernobyl Accidents) in nuclear power plants have been occurred on account of human-factor failures, namely human errors. Thus, a lot of researchers who are involved in this nuclear area have been trying to eliminate those human errors entirely. Thanks to the efforts, in nuclear power plants, some features which have simple logics such as reactor trip and engineered safety features (ESFs) actuation have been automated. However, other components have not been automated yet, so human operators are still necessary to control the reactor in emergency or abnormal situations. Since human operators are still involved in nuclear power operations, there remains a risk of human errors.

In advanced main control rooms of nuclear power plants, computerized procedures are implemented instead of paper procedures which used to be employed in conventional main control rooms. Applying computer-based procedures in the main control room allows to reduce mental workload, enhance situation awareness, and produce lower errors of omission than paper-based procedures [1]. The number of human errors in nuclear power plant operation may decrease thanks to the computerized procedure system (CPS). However, new types of human errors are being considered which may occur [2].

In this paper, we propose a framework which automatically detects Unsafe Acts (UAs) which are occurred in advanced main control rooms in nuclear power plant to reduce those human errors, moreover, to draw to extend the portion of automation in nuclear power plants.

2 Background Information

2.1 Unsafe Acts

Unsafe actions are actions inappropriately taken by plant personnel, or not taken when needed, that result in a degraded plant safety condition [3]. Nuclear power plant operation is proceduralized to reduce mental workload of human operators. Human operators basically follow operating procedures. An action which does not follow the operating procedure, the action may adversely affect nuclear power plant integrity. In this case, the action will be a candidate of UAs. Human operators of nuclear power plants work for a plant for a long time by its nature. Some operators who have a lot of experiences and know-hows in nuclear power plant operation. Sometimes, the seasoned operators decide what they will do in different way than operating procedures. They perform the steps which they believe more important earlier, they run different devices than what procedures instruct to control the system. Not all these violations negatively affect integrity of the nuclear power plant. Another mean or criterion is required to distinct UAs that would harm the plant integrity among the candidates of UAs.

2.2 Critical Safety Functions

Critical safety functions are a group of actions that prevent core melt or minimize radiation releases to the general public. They can be used to provide a hierarchy of practical plant protection that an operator should use [4]. The functions designed to protect against core melt, preserve containment integrity, and maintain vital auxiliaries needed to support the other safety functions are identified (Table 1). These safety functions show plant safety statements, so parameters included in the functions will indicate if the plant integrity is adversely affected in practice.

Table 1. Classification of critical safety functions

Anti-core melt
– Reactivity control – Reactor cooling system (RCS) inventory control – RCS pressure control – RCS heat removal – Core heat removal
Containment integrity
– Containment isolation – Containment pressure control – Containment temperature control – Combustible gas control
Maintain vital auxiliaries
– Vital power maintenance

2.3 Nuclear Simulator

After Three Mile Island and Chernobyl accidents, it has come out into the open that operator errors contribute to extend and progress of severe accidents in nuclear power plants. The importance of training using simulators has increased sharply [5].

Generally, training simulators for nuclear power plants are classified into three categories: compact or basic principle simulator, full-scope simulator, part-task simulator. Compact or basic-principle simulator is intended to illustrate general concepts and demonstrate and display of the fundamental physical processes of a plant. Full-scope simulator is more complete and accurate simulator describing the whole plant and system. Part-task simulator is designed for a single specific system functionally divided from a whole plant [6]. The UA autodetecting system can be developed by using nuclear simulator to generating AI training data sets and verify the system. We used CNS which is a compact nuclear simulator developed by Korea Atomic Energy Research Institute (KAERI). The CNS modeled a three loop Westinghouse Pressurizer Water Reactor (PWR), 993 MWe, mostly referred to as the Kori Unit 3&4 in Korea (Fig. 1).

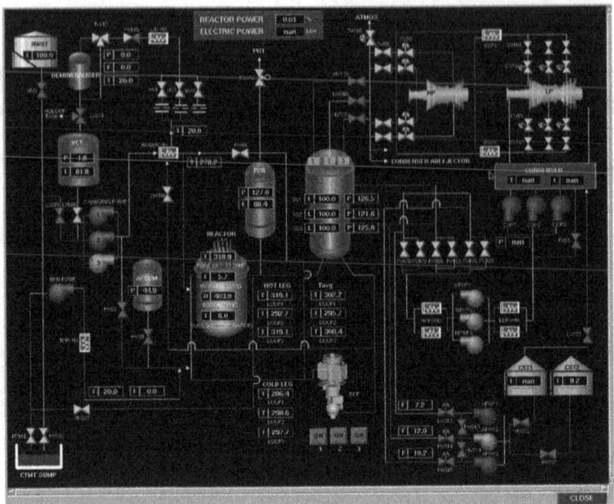

Fig. 1. The compact nuclear simulator (CNS), 993 MWe PWR

3 Unsafe Acts Autodetection Framework

The UA auto-detecting process basically has three steps (Fig. 2).

I. Procedure Violation Check
II. Evaluation of the Effect on Critical Safety Functions
III. Recovery Operation Suggestion

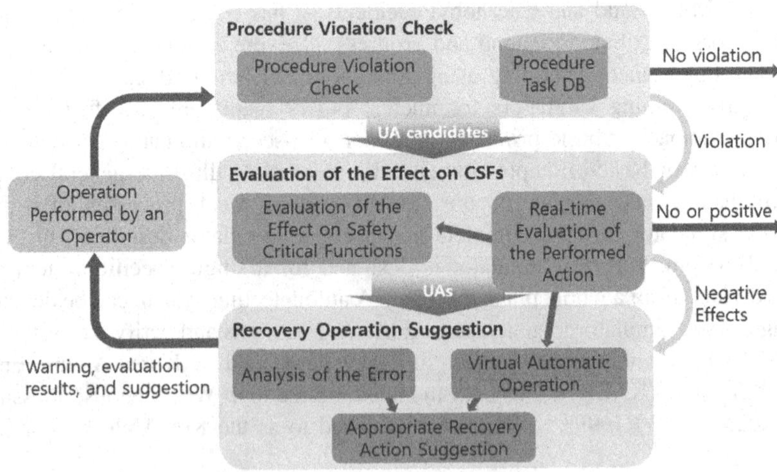

Fig. 2. Unsafe acts autodetection framework

In the first step, the system checks procedure compliance. It judges which tasks in an instruction are required to be performed or not, and whether an action performed by an operator complies the operating procedure. If not, the action will be classified as a UA candidate. In the next step, the effect on critical safety functions of the UA candidate is evaluated. When negative effects are expected, the UA candidate is set to be a UA. Then, the system gives a warning to the operator with evaluation results and suggests a recovery operation. The operator can recognize his/her mistake and restore it quickly with the information given by the system.

3.1 Procedure Violation Check

To check procedure compliance, procedure task database is needed. The procedure task database includes all tasks prescribed in operating procedures corresponding to each state. The tasks in procedures can be categorized into four types, Information verification, procedure transfer, situation evaluation and execution [7] (Table 2).

Table 2. The classification scheme of erroneous behaviors

Category	Proceduralized task	Description examples in EOPs
Information verification	Verifying alarm occurrence	Determine a turbine trip alarm
	Verifying state of indicator	Verify that one reactor coolant pump is running
	Synthetically verifying information	Verify if safety injection completion conditions are satisfied
	Reading simple value	Read the charging pump flow rate
	Comparing parameter	Verify if the pressurizer level is within 25–35%
	Comparing using graph constraint	Check if the reactor coolant system subcooling margin is within the subcooling operation area on the attached graph
	Comparing for abnormality	Check if the containment vessel is in an adverse state
	Evaluating trend	Check if the pressurizer level is stable
Procedure transfer	Transferring procedure	Perform the diagnostic procedure
	Transferring step in procedure	Go to step 22.0
Situation evaluation	Diagnosing	Investigate the cause of a pressurizer relief valve abnormality
	Identifying overall status	Evaluate the necessity of plant cooling
	Predicting	Evaluate the long-term plant status

(*continued*)

Table 2. (*continued*)

Category	Proceduralized task	Description examples in EOPs
Execution	Manipulating simple (discrete) control	Close the steam bypass control valve
	Manipulating simple (continuous) control	Establish the set point of the steam generator power operated relief valve at 81.5 kg/cm^2
	Manipulating dynamically	Discharge steam to the condenser using the turbine bypass valve
	Notifying/requesting to MCR outside	Stop the reactor coolant pump using a field breaker

3.2 Evaluation of the Effects on Critical Safety Functions

To evaluate the effect on safety critical functions, waiting for change in parameters related to the functions takes time, so it would be too late to cope with the situation. Artificial intelligent training can be a solution. A trained artificial intelligence with operating history can predict trends of the changes derived by operators' actions. However, the states which require to use emergency operating procedures are rarely happened in real nuclear power plant operation, so operators practice emergency operations using simulators. Training data from operating history can be generated based on plenty of operating scenarios by using a nuclear simulator.

3.3 Recovery Operation Suggestion

When UAs are detected, recovery operation guide will be provided. In this step, the trained AI suggests the best option to cope with the UA. In the virtual plant, an optimize operation is running automatically, and the operation will be shown to the human operator who made the UA. Before showing, error analysis should be conducted.

4 Discussion and Conclusions

In this work, a framework which identifies unsafe acts of plant personnel in nuclear power plant is suggested. To begin with, actions which violate operating procedures are classified as UA candidates. Then, the expected trends of parameters related to critical safety functions sort out UA from the candidates. If the identified UAs are noticed to the human operator in nuclear power plants, he/she will be able to cope with the errors made by themselves speedily. To expect the trends, a AI algorithm and database should be built. If training data corresponding to various operating actions for different operating circumstances are collected based on the framework, plenty of data can be produced which are required to analyze human errors for the new digitalized system in nuclear power plants. Furthermore, this framework and database can be a base to control all safety critical functions simultaneously using an automated system. It would us to take a step toward making the operating system be fully digitalized and automated.

References

1. Yang, C.-W., Yang, L.-C., Cheng, T.-C., Jou, Y.-T., Chiou, S.-W.: Assessing mental workload and situation awareness in the evaluation of computerized procedures in the main control room. Nuclear Eng. Des. **250**, 713–719 (2012)
2. Min, D., Chun, Y.-H., Kim, B.: An evaluation of computerized procedure system in nuclear power plant. IFAC Proc. **34**(16), 519–524 (2001)
3. U.S. NRC: Technical Basis and Implementation Guidelines for a Technique for Human Event Analysis (ATHEANA), NUREG-1624 (2000)
4. William, R.C., Nancy, J.P., James, F.C., Michael, T.C., Walter, M.G.: The critical safety functions and plant operation. Nuclear Technol. **55**(3), 690–712 (1981). https://doi.org/10.13182/nt81-a32814
5. U.S. NRC: TMI-2 Lessons Learned Task Force Final Report, NUREG-0585 (1979)
6. Kwqn, K.-C., Park, J.-C., Jung, C.-H., Lee, J.-S., Kim, J.-Y.: Compact nuclear simulator and its upgrade plan. Training simulators in nuclear power plants: experience, programme design and assessment methodology. In: Proceedings of a specialists' meeting, p. 227. International Atomic Energy Agency (1997)
7. Kim, Y., Park, J., Jung, W.: A classification scheme of erroneous behaviors for human error probability estimations based on simulator data. Reliabil. Eng. Syst. Safety **163**, 1–13 (2017)

Interactive Narratives, Counterfactual Thinking and Personality in Video Games

Catherine A. Bacos(✉), Michael P. McCreery, and Jeffrey R. Laferriere

University of Nevada, Las Vegas, NV 89154, USA
catherine.bacos@unlv.edu

Abstract. Interactive narratives in video games allow players to experience a variety of storyline pathways, inviting players to think about alternative choices that might lead to different outcomes. These branching story structures can induce counterfactual thinking, the process of forming mental representations of past events to imagine alternative outcomes. Video games can be used to track and analyze behaviors during gameplay that are indicative of cognitive processes. As a gameplay analytics approach to assessing such behaviors, video games afford the measurement of factors that may influence those behaviors. Little is known about how personality influences the use of counterfactuals. As such, the focus of the present study was to investigate the effect of the Big Five personality traits (i.e., agreeableness, conscientiousness, emotional stability, extraversion, and intellect) on in-game behaviors indicative of counterfactual thinking (CFT). Participants ($N = 132$) played an interactive, narrative-based video game twice. In-game behaviors indicative of CFT (i.e., changes in answer choices across gameplays) were coded and analyzed to determine whether they were dependent on participants' in-game experiences (i.e., outcomes and valence of answer choices) and individual differences (i.e., personality dimensions). The outcome of failure and the valence of answer choices in the first gameplay had significant effects on CFT. The results also indicated a significant interaction between the outcome of the first gameplay and conscientiousness in their effect on CFT. Implications for these findings are discussed.

Keywords: Interactive narratives · Counterfactual thinking · Personality Video games · Behavior regulation · Assessment

1 Introduction

Games provide a venue for enacting mental simulations that may not be possible in the real world. Not only can alternative pathways be imagined, but in a game, the player can carry out and experience the imagined alternative path. Primed by in-game experiences, mental simulations of alternative pathways in a game are cognitive processes players rely on to inform their in-game decisions. Such internal cognitive processes, though unobservable, may be inferred from behaviors [1]. Games can be used to analyze such behaviors, and through behaviors, mental processes [2].

C. Stephanidis (Ed.): HCII Posters 2018, CCIS 850, pp. 340–347, 2018.
https://doi.org/10.1007/978-3-319-92270-6_49

1.1 Personality

To better understand how thinking influences behavior, one should begin to examine underlying individual differences. A significant factor known to influence a person's behavior is personality [3]. According to trait theory, individual differences exist along a set of dispositional traits that make up a person's personality. Relatively stable and enduring, these traits may predict whether an individual is more likely to exhibit certain behaviors. Trait dimensions can be identified using personality scales and statistical analysis. The most well-known model for describing personality is the Big Five, which identifies five major dimensions of personality: agreeableness, conscientiousness, emotional stability, extraversion, and intellect [4]. Genes and the environment appear to influence Big Five traits [4]; and despite differences in levels across cultures, Big Five traits seem to be universal [5].

1.2 Counterfactual Thinking

Another individual difference that can influence behavior is the tendency of some individuals to engage in cognitive processes such as counterfactual thinking. Current theory proposes that counterfactual thinking is strongly connected to course correction, goal cognition, and behavior regulation [6]. Counterfactual thinking, the process of forming mental representations of past events to imagine alternative outcomes, involves thoughts about how things could have been better (i.e., upward counterfactual thinking) or how things could have been worse (i.e., downward counterfactual thinking). Negative outcomes are known to influence the production of counterfactuals [7]. For example, in situations where one experiences a failed goal, counterfactual thinking is used to consider another way to achieve that goal [6].

In a study highlighting the importance of taking both individual differences and contextual factors into account when predicting counterfactual thinking, the use of counterfactuals was compared between participants who read versus acted out scenarios designed to induce counterfactual thinking [8]. The results showed that readers focused more on the choice options and actors focused more on the problem features of the scenario, indicating that the role (i.e., passive versus active) and the context in which the individual acquires information matters in terms of the function of counterfactual thinking [8]. These findings demonstrate the need to assess counterfactual thinking in various roles and environments.

1.3 Video Games as Behavioral and Cognitive Assessments

As an alternative to research procedures that explicitly and obtrusively ask participants through experimental prompts or self-report measures to engage in counterfactual thinking, the use of video games can serve as a game analytic approach to collect data on participants' spontaneous use of counterfactual thinking. This natural approach allows researchers to draw more definite conclusions about the antecedents and consequences of counterfactual thinking as it occurs spontaneously [9]. Since cognitive processes can be inferred from behavior [1], behaviors that indicate the use of counterfactual thinking can be observed in video games. The ability to track and analyze player performance and behaviors indicative of cognitive processes in a controlled and replicable setting is an affordance of video games that make them an ideal medium for assessing how individuals regulate their behavior to reach a goal (e.g., problem solving) [2]. Using games, researchers can assess in-game behaviors such as decision-making and problem-solving and compare them to other measures related to the player and their environment.

1.4 Interactive Narratives and Counterfactual Thinking

Interactive narratives such as those found in nonlinear video games are especially ideal for assessing players' regulation of behavior because interactive narratives are essentially an exercise in counterfactual thinking [10]. Branching narrative structures allow players to experience a variety of storyline pathways and require course correction, goal cognition, and behavior regulation as the players plot and re-plot their decisions. Such in-game behaviors, indicative of cognitive processes, may be attributed to an individual's in-game experiences. For example, players will learn to adjust or "tune" their behaviors in response to in-game experiences such as failed outcomes [11]. The theory of counterfactual thinking may also serve as an explanation for the player's motivation to engage in such choice behavior changes. Additionally, individual differences associated with personality traits may also contribute to these behaviors as they have been shown to impact how behavior manifests in vivo [12] and in video games [13].

While there have been several studies on the tendency of individuals with certain narrow traits to use counterfactual thinking (e.g., optimism and self-esteem) [14, 15], there have been very few published studies on the effect of broader dimensions of personality on counterfactual thinking (CFT). To address this gap, the present study investigated the effect of personality traits (i.e. Big Five personality dimensions) on in-game behaviors indicative of CFT (i.e., changes in answer choices across gameplays). Since these measures were taken in the context of an interactive narrative-based video game, the in-game experiences (i.e., outcome and valence of answer choices) were also considered as potential factors. To explore these variables, the following research questions framed the study:

1. **Effect of Game Experiences on CFT.** Do in-game experiences (i.e., outcome of the first gameplay and valence of answer choices in the first gameplay) predict behavioral choices indicative of counterfactual thinking (i.e., changes in answer choices across gameplays)?
2. **Effect of Personality on CFT Depending on Outcome.** Depending on the outcome of the first gameplay, do Big Five personality dimensions predict behavioral choices indicative of counterfactual thinking (i.e., changes in answer choices across gameplays)?

2 Method

2.1 Participants

Participants were recruited through a subject pool from a college of education in the southwestern United States. A power analysis was conducted to determine sample size for the largest model. Results (f2 = .15; level = .8; p = .05; Cohen, 1992) indicated that a minimum of 67 subjects was needed to analyze the largest model. One hundred and forty-seven completed the present study, however only 132 participants were included in the data analysis due to incomplete data sets. Gender demographics for the sample consisted of 36 males and 96 females. A gender breakdown such as this is consistent with colleges of education [16]. The racial makeup of the sample was: 45.5% White, 7.6% Black or African-American, 17.4% Hispanic or Latino, 16.7% Asian, 2.3% Native Hawaiian or Pacific Islander, and 10.6% who reported two or more races. The average age of the sample was approximately 25 (sd = ~7) years old.

2.2 Materials and Procedures

Instruments. For this study only two sets of instrumentation data were collected. The first set was personality dimension scales (i.e., agreeableness, conscientiousness, emotional stability, extraversion, and intellect) from the IPIP Big 5 Personality Scales [17]. Each of these scales is a 10-Item, 5-point, Likert-type questionnaire. Psychometric data provided by the author [17] showed good reliability with internal consistency coefficients of .79 and .84 respectively. The second set of data collected consisted of a questionnaire collecting demographic and gameplay feedback data.

The Deed Video Game. The Deed [18] is a single-player roleplaying video game with a branching storyline known as an interactive narrative. In games with branching narratives, players are forced to make choices that will lead to several possible outcomes. The Deed is a murder mystery in reverse as the objective is to plot a crime rather than solve it. A combination of player choices leads to seven possible outcomes in the game, which can be broken into three outcome categories: (1) failure (i.e., conviction of murder), (2) partial success (i.e., unsolved murder, no conviction), and (3) complete success (i.e., a non-player character is found guilty for the murder). The Deed begins with the choice to play the introduction during which players learn about the character they will play, a young man who returns home after discovering his father's plans to disinherit him in favor of his sister, and receive instructions related to plotting the murder of the sister. Players are instructed to converse with the relatives and search the house for useful objects (i.e., items of evidence and weapons). Two objects must be selected before the narrative can advance to the second part of the game, the dinner celebrating the father's birthday. The third part is committing the murder, and the final part is the interview with the crime investigator. The interview is followed by the game outcome.

Procedures. This study was part of a larger study examining video games as stealth assessments. For brevity, only the procedures of the current study are reported. The procedures included two plays of the video game The Deed [18] followed by the completion of a questionnaire collecting demographic and gameplay feedback data, and the completion of personality dimension scales (IPIP Big 5 Personality Scales) [17]. All participants provided informed consent to participate in the study in line with the Institutional Review Board (IRB) requirements at the data collection site.

Gameplay Analytics. The game elements of The Deed [18] were deconstructed to identify the multiple narrative pathways in the game. In the first part of the game, players can choose to interact with up to five non-player characters (NPCs): maid, butler, father, mother, and sister. Players can choose to respond to several possible questions from NPCs; six of the questions are mandatory. That is, those same six questions appear in each gameplay and players must respond to them to advance the narrative. For this study, only those six questions were measured to score participants' changes in response choices across gameplays. Video gameplays of each subject were recorded using Fraps [19]. Subjects' first and second gameplays were coded for outcomes. The following behavioral choices were coded and analyzed: (1) total number of changes to answer choices in response to non-player characters across gameplays and (2) the total valence (i.e. positive or negative value) of answer choices in the first gameplay.

3 Results

3.1 Data Normalcy

Prior to answering the research questions, data normalcy was assessed for skewness and kurtosis. Although disagreement exists related to absolute values (i.e., 2 or 3) associated with skewness and kurtosis [20], for the current study the absolute value of 2 was applied. Results of the analysis indicated that all variables fell with within acceptable limits.

3.2 Effect of Game Experiences on CFT

To answer question one, dummy coding was used to code the categorical variables for the three outcomes of the first gameplay (i.e., failed, partially failed, and successful) so that the variables of interest (i.e., failed outcomes, which are associated with counterfactual thinking) could be analyzed in multiple regression. Table 1 shows the two dummy coded variables. A simultaneous regression analysis was conducted to predict the number of changes in response choices across gameplays (i.e., CFT) from the two dummy variables and the valence of answer choices in the first gameplay (Valence A). A significant regression equation was found, $F(3,128) = 11.844$, $p < .001$, $R2 = .217$ (see Table 2). The Fully Failed outcome was a statistically significant predictor of CFT ($b = 1.119$, $SE = .432$, $p = .006$, 95% CI = .344, 2.055; $\beta = .337$). The Partially Failed outcome was a statistically significant predictor of CFT ($b = 1.109$, $SE = .503$, $p = .029$, 95% CI = .114, 2.104; $\beta = .268$). Valence A was a statistically significant predictor of CFT ($b = -.475$, $SE = .088$, $p = .000$, 95% CI = −.650, −.301; $\beta = -.422$).

Table 1. Conversion of three categorical variables into two dummy variables.

Group	Fully Failed Outcome A	Partially Failed Outcome A
1. Fully Failed	1	0
2. Partially Failed	0	1
3. Successful	0	0

Table 2. Effect of game experiences on CFT.

Variable	*B*	β	*t*	*p*
Fully Failed	1.199	.337	2.775	.006
Partially Failed	1.109	.268	2.205	.029
Valence A	−.475	−.422	−5.397	.000
R^2	.217			
F	11.844			.000

3.3 Effect of Interaction on CFT

To answer question two, whether the effect of personality dimensions on CFT (i.e., changes in answer choices across games) depend on the outcome of the game, simultaneous linear regression analyses were conducted to test the interaction between Outcome A (i.e., the outcome of the first gameplay) and each of the Big Five dimensions of personality (i.e., agreeableness, conscientiousness, emotional stability, extraversion, and intellect). To analyze the interaction varialbe in multiple regression, a dummy variable was created for Outcome A (i.e., no win and win), the values for each of the personality dimensions were centered, and cross-products between those variables were created (e.g., Interaction OutA_Con means the interaction between Outcome A and Conscientiousness). A significant interaction was found for Outcome A and the personality dimension of conscientiousness (see Fig. 1 and Table 3). For subjects with successful outcomes (i.e., win), conscientiousness had a negative effect on CFT, but little effect on the subjects with failed outcomes (i.e., no win).

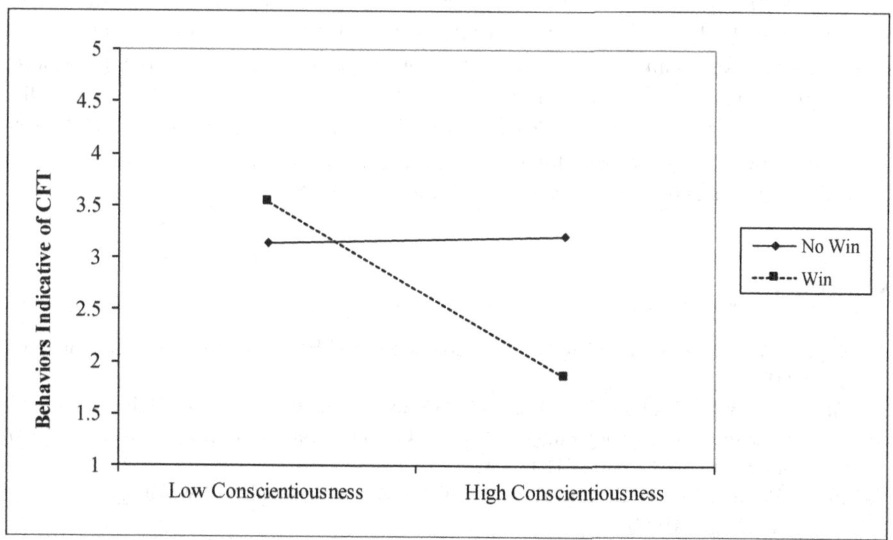

Fig. 1. Regression lines illustrating the interaction of Outcome A (i.e., no win and win) and the personality dimension conscientiousness in their effects on behaviors indicative of CFT (i.e., changes in answer choices across games).

Table 3. Effect of interaction between Outcome A and conscientiousness on CFT.

Variable	*B*	β	*t*	*p*
Outcome A	−.486	−.137	−1.631	.105
Conscientiousness	.006	.020	.193	.847
Interaction OutA_Con	−.167	−.310	−3.055	.003
R^2	.104			
F	4.952			.003

4 Discussion

The present study employed a gameplay analytics approach to determine whether in-game behaviors indicative of counterfactual thinking, CFT (i.e., changes in answer choices across gameplays), were dependent on participants' individual differences (i.e., personality traits) and in-game experiences (i.e., failed outcome and answer choice valence of first gameplay). The outcome of failure and the valence of answer choices in the first gameplay both had significant effects on CFT. As failed outcomes increased, CFT was predicted to increase. As valence (i.e., positive or negative value of answer choices) increased, CFT was predicted to decrease. In addition, the results indicated a significant interaction between the outcome of the first gameplay and conscientiousness in their effect on CFT. These findings suggest that for subjects with successful outcomes, higher levels of conscientiousness will result in a decrease in behaviors indicative of counterfactual thinking. For subjects with failed outcomes, however, it appears that conscientiousness has little effect on behaviors indicative of counterfactual thinking. While conscientiousness, depending on gameplay outcomes, influences counterfactual thinking, the game environment (i.e., interactive narrative) serves as a natural catalyst for counterfactual thinking because the interactive narrative, by design, is an exercise in counterfactual thinking. Altogether, the results of the study suggest the game environment, game experiences, and individual differences should all be considered to understand how these interrelated variables contribute to the overall effect on the use of counterfactual thinking for behavior regulation.

References

1. Mayer, R.E.: Thinking, Problem Solving, Cognition. WH Freeman/Times Books/Henry Holt & Co. (1992)
2. Shute, V.J., Wang, L., Greiff, S., Zhao, W., Moore, G.: Measuring problem solving skills via stealth assessment in an engaging video game. Comput. Hum. Behav. **63**, 106–117 (2016). https://doi.org/10.1016/j.chb.2016.05.047
3. Hogan, R., Johnson, J., Briggs, S. (eds.): Handbook of Personality Psychology. Academic Press, San Diego (1997)
4. McCrae, R.R., Costa, P.T.: Personality in Adulthood: A Five-Factor Theory Perspective. The Guilford Press, New York (2003)

5. Heine, S.J., Buchtel, E.E.: Personality: the universal and the culturally specific. Annu. Rev. Psychol. **60**, 369–394 (2009). https://doi.org/10.1146/annurev.psych.60.110707.163655
6. Epstude, K., Roese, N.J.: The functional theory of counterfactual thinking. Personal. Soc. Psychol. Rev. **12**, 168–192 (2008). https://doi.org/10.1177/1088868308316091
7. Roese, N.J.: The functional basis of counterfactual thinking. J. Personal. Soc. Psychol. **1994** (66), 805–818 (1994). https://doi.org/10.1037/0022-3514.66.5.805
8. Girotto, V., Ferrante, D., Pighin, S., Gonzalez, M.: Postdecisional counterfactual thinking by actors and readers **18**, 510–515 (2007). https://doi.org/10.1111/j.1467-9280.2007.01931.x
9. Sanna, L.J., Turley, K.J.: Antecedents to spontaneous counterfactual thinking: effects of expectancy violation and outcome valence. Personal. Soc. Psychol. Bull. **22**, 906–919 (1996). https://doi.org/10.1177/0146167296229005
10. Green, M.C., Jenkins, K.M.: Interactive narratives: processes and outcomes in user-directed stories. J. Commun. **64**, 479–500 (2014). https://doi.org/10.1177/0146167296229005
11. Schrader, P.G., McCreery, M.P., Vallett, D.: Performance in situ. In: Baek, Y. (ed.) Game-Based Learning: Theory, Strategies and Performance Outcomes. Nova Science Publishers, Hauppauge (2017)
12. John, O.P., Robins, R.W., Pervin, L.A. (eds.): Handbook of Personality. The Guilford Press, New York (2010)
13. McCreery, M.P., Kathleen Krach, S., Schrader, P.G., Boone, R.: Defining the virtual self: personality, behavior, and the psychology of embodiment. Comput. Human Behav. **28**, 976–983 (2012). https://doi.org/10.1016/j.chb.2011.12.019
14. Kasimatis, M., Wells, G.L.: Individual differences in counterfactual thinking. In: Roese, N. J. (eds.) What Might Have Been: The Social Psychology of Counterfactual Thinking, pp. 81–101. Lawrence Erlbaum Associates, Mahwah (1995)
15. Sanna, L.J., Carter, S.E., Small, E.M.: The road not taken: counterfactual thinking over time. In: Press, O.U. (ed.) Judgments Over Time: The Interplay of Thoughts, Feelings, and Behaviors, New York, NY, pp. 163–181 (2006)
16. Snyder, T.D., de Brey, C., Dillow, S.A.: Digest of Education Statistics 2014, Washington, DC (2016)
17. Goldberg, L.R.: A broad-bandwidth, public domain, personality inventory measuring the lower-level facets of several five-factor models (1999). http://projects.ori.org/lrg/PDFs_papers/Abroad-bandwidthinventory.pdf
18. Grab the Games: The Deed [Computer Software] (2015)
19. Beepa Pty Ltd.: Fraps [Computer Software] (2013)
20. Tabachnick, B.G., Fidell, L.S.: Using Multivariate Statistics (1996)

A Fundamental Study Toward Development of a New Brain Computer Interface Using a Checker-Board Pattern Reversal Stimulation

Ingon Chanpornpakdi[1(✉)], Junya Enjoji[1], Tatsuhiro Kimura[2], Hiroshi Ohshima[1], and Kiyoyuki Yamazaki[1(✉)]

[1] Tokai University, Isehara, Kanagawa Prefecture, Japan
c.ingon.mint@gmail.com, ymzkkyyk@gmail.com
[2] Tokai University, Kumamoto, Kumamoto Prefecture, Japan

Abstract. The purpose of this study is to investigate the spectral changes of electroencephalogram (EEG) toward development of a new Brain Computer Interface (BCI) for disabled people with verbal communication disorders such as Amyotrophic Lateral Sclerosis (ALS). In this study, an experiment using EEG recordings was carried out in nine healthy adult volunteers. Periodically reversing checker-board stimuli with two kinds of frequencies (5, 15 Hz) were used to observe users' selective attention from EEG spectral changes. The stimuli were displayed in two different ways, independently displayed and simultaneously displayed, on the LCD of a personal computer. Volunteers were instructed to attend either 5, 15 Hz or neither of the reversing stimulus during EEG recordings. Obtained EEG data were analyzed by FFT and those power spectra were calculated. As a result, two different frequencies reversal stimuli generated peak of EEG spectrum with attended stimulus frequency. However, the peak generated by 5 Hz stimulus was somehow bigger than that of 15 Hz stimulus due to individual differences. To obtain the comparable height of EEG spectral peaks, the compensate procedure to reduce the sensitivity difference between the two frequencies for each person is required. From a comparison of the EEG power spectral structures, subjective binary decision (5 or 15 Hz reversal stimuli) could be discriminated objectively. Utilizing this phenomenon, EEG based BCI for subjective selection extraction can be constructed. Some problems of feasibility of this method as a BCI were also discussed.

Keywords: Electroencephalogram (EEG) · Brain Computer Interface (BCI) Checker board pattern stimuli · Welfare technology

1 Introduction

There were a lot of researches using BCI to improve the quality of life (QOL) of the people with disability in verbal communication published in the past. Many of those studies employed analysis of N100 and P300 of the evoked potentials 1, 2, 3 which need to use signal averaging. In order to proceed with the signal averaging, large number of data is required. As the amount of data increased, it became practically difficult for the daily life.

C. Stephanidis (Ed.): HCII Posters 2018, CCIS 850, pp. 348–353, 2018.
https://doi.org/10.1007/978-3-319-92270-6_50

To solve that problem, EEG power spectrum obtained by fast Fourier transform (FFT) has been introduced. In the recent year, various kinds of Visual Evoked Potentials (VEP) are mainly used as the stimuli such as SSVEP and etc. 4, 5, 6. These stimuli are similar to the flashlight that may cause dizziness and vertigo. Therefore, checker board pattern stimuli with the two different frequencies were used in this experiment, aiming to derive the new non-invasive method of non-verbal communication for the disability people.

2 Experimental Methods

Nine healthy adults (seven male and two female) with the mean age of 22 years old volunteered to participate in the experiment. To record the EEG, the electrodes were placed on C3, C4, P3, P4, O1, O2 position and A1, A2 position as the references according to the 10–20 system.

The participant sat on a chair facing a personal computer display at the distance of about 60 cm so that both of the stimuli could be seen with the least eye movement. The experiment was carried out with 5 Hz and 15 Hz reversal checker board pattern stimuli (Fig. 1) in five different conditions as listed below.

1. 5 Hz reversal checker board pattern stimulus showed independently
2. 15 Hz reversal checker board pattern stimulus showed independently
3. Both 5 and 15 Hz reversal checker board pattern stimuli showed but pay attention to neither of them
4. Both 5 and 15 Hz reversal checker board pattern stimuli showed but pay attention only to the 5 Hz reversal checker board pattern stimulus
5. Both 5 and 15 Hz reversal checker board pattern stimuli showed but pay attention only to the 15 Hz reversal checker board pattern stimulus.

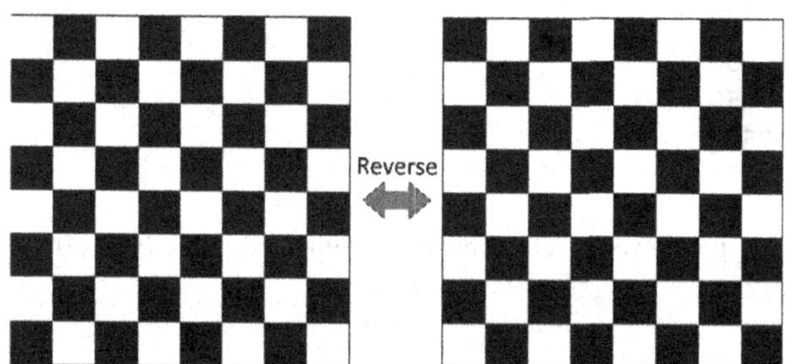

Fig. 1. Reversal checker board pattern stimulus

The EEG of each conditions was recorded for two minutes. Other than the above conditions, the EEG of the resting open eye was also recorded as a reference for investigating the spectral changes.

By using offline FFT analysis, the obtained data was processed and each conditions' power spectrum was calculated. As the attended stimulus changes, the peak near 5 Hz and 15 Hz of the EEG spectral peaks were investigated.

3 Results and Discussions

Results showed that the attended stimulus frequency generated the spectral peak at the corresponding frequency. The results of condition 1 and 2 are the example of the experimental result shown in the Fig. 2.

In condition 1, 5 Hz reversal checker board pattern stimulus was shown independently and all the volunteers were instructed to attend at it. As a result, the spectral peak near 5 Hz was obtained on the spectral change (← 1). In the same way, when the 15 Hz reversal checker board pattern stimulus was shown independently in the condition 2, the 15 Hz spectral peak appeared on the spectral change (← 2).

The average power spectral change of the condition 1 and 2 are presented on the Fig. 3. In comparison, the peak appeared at 5 Hz in condition 1 is very much larger than that of condition 2. On the other hand, the peak appeared at 15 Hz in condition two is bigger than that of the condition 1.

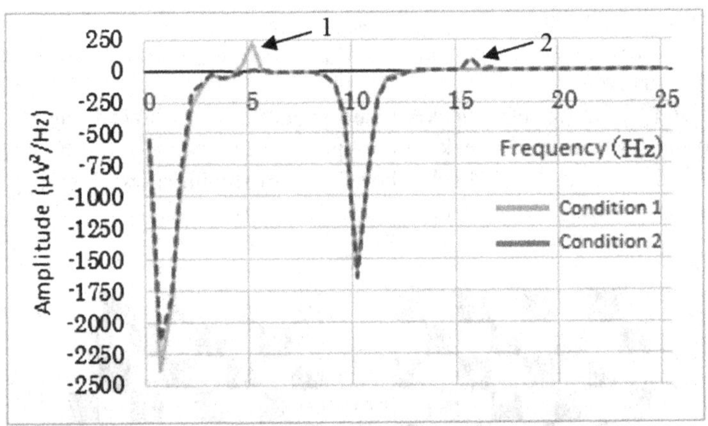

Fig. 2. Examples of the power spectral change as compared to the EEG power spectrum of the resting open eye.

In condition 3, 4, and 5, both 5 Hz and 15 Hz reversal checker board pattern were shown at the same time. The volunteers were instructed to just look at the screen without any attention in condition 3, attend only at 5 Hz stimulus in condition 4, and attend only at 15 Hz stimulus in condition 5.

In condition 3, for most of the volunteers, there was no peak appeared on the corresponding frequencies. However, two of the volunteers' spectral changes, the peaks with the same height appeared near 5 Hz and 15 Hz which can be considered that the volunteers attended at the stimuli unconsciously.

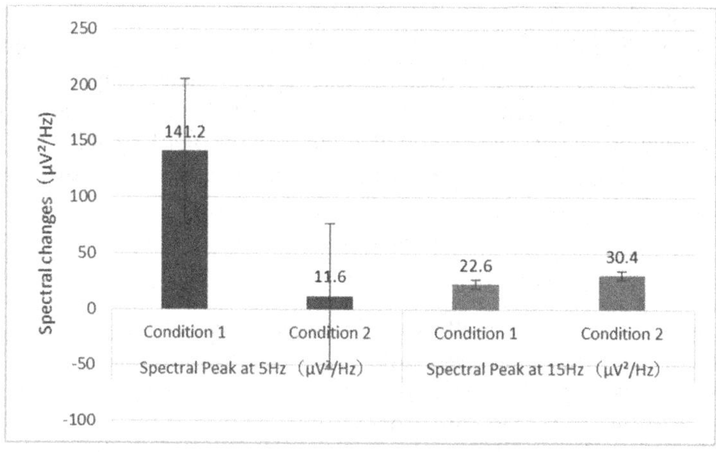

Fig. 3. Spectral changes (Condition 1 and 2)

In condition 4, the peak appeared at 5 Hz on the spectral change for all the volunteers and four out of nine volunteers' spectral change showed the peak at 15 Hz in condition 5. There was also a peak at 5 Hz appeared larger than 15 Hz peak for the rest of the volunteers in condition 5 too which means that these volunteers are more sensitive to the 5 Hz stimulus. However, in comparison to the EEG spectral change of the condition 3, the peak appeared at 15 Hz in condition 5 is much bigger than that in condition 4 for most of the volunteers.

Figure 4 represents the comparison of amplitude magnification of the spectral change in condition 4 and 5 as referred to condition 3. The amplitude magnification of the peak appeared at 5 Hz in the condition 4 is much larger than that of the condition 5 while the peak appeared at 15 Hz in condition 5 is bigger than condition 4.

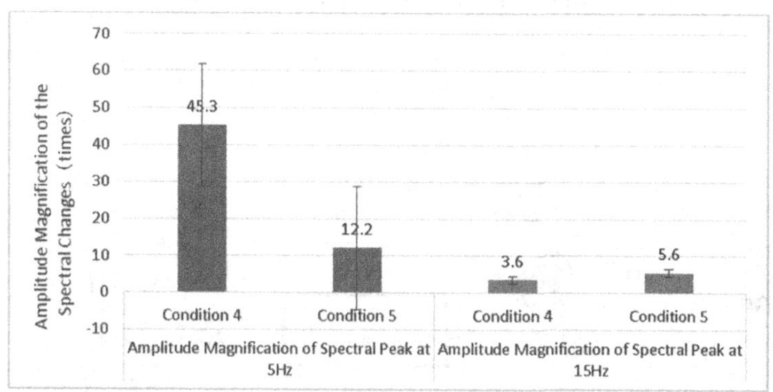

Fig. 4. Amplitude magnification of the spectral changes as compared to the EEG spectral change of the condition 3. (Condition 4 and 5)

The statistical significance was also calculated by using Wilcoxon's test. As a result, each conditions' P value are shown in the Table 1. All the conditions' result except condition 5 has statistically significant difference whereas the condition 5 does not. Therefore, the 15 Hz stimulus need to be reconsidered in order to acquire the most appropriate stimulus. By using this stimulus, EEG based BCI for subjective selection extraction can be constructed and the practical use in daily life for the disabled people is anticipated.

Table 1. Statistical test result (Wilcoxon's test)

Condition	P value	Significant difference
1	$P < 0.01$	Yes
2	$P < 0.03$	Yes
4	$P < 0.03$	Yes
5	$P > 0.05$	N.S

4 Conclusion

Using this binary selective method, the patient's desire could be derived from the EEG power spectrum (Fig. 5). It might start with a simple question, for example, yes or no question, till a little more complicated question by making multiple choices such as where the patient feel pain provided with the answer upper part or lower part of the body on the screen near each stimulus. However, before using this system, the patient need to be informed clearly that what frequency related to which answer so that more accuracy answer can be extracted.

However, to obtain the better result, the stimulus used in this experiment requires some further improvements to reduce the sensitivity difference between the two frequencies for each person such as the more appropriate frequencies, the numbers of the checker board pattern partition, and the contrast of the pattern.

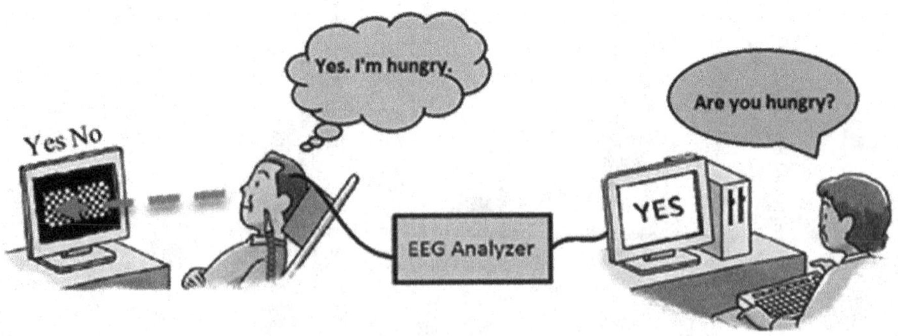

Fig. 5. Illustration of the purposed system

References

1. Hasegawa, R.P.: Development of a cognitive BMI "neurocommunicator" as a communication aid of patients with severe motor deficits. Clin. Neurol. **11**(53), 1402–1404 (2013). (in Japanese)
2. Dan, Z., et al.: Integrating the spatial profile of the N200 speller for asynchronous brain-computer interfaces. In: Annual International Conference of the IEEE in Medicine and Biology Society, EMBC (2011)
3. Sato, H., Washizawa, Y.: An N100-P300 spelling brain-computer interface with detection of intentional control, MDPI. Computers **4**, 31 (2016). https://doi.org/10.3390/computers5040031
4. Punsawad, Y., Wongsawat,Y.: Motion visual stimulus for SSVEP-based BCI system. In: 34th Annual International Conference of the IEEE EMBS, San Diego, California USA, 28 August–1 September 2012, pp. 3837–3840 (2016)
5. Nishifuji, S., Kuroda, T., Tanaka, S.: SSVEP-based BCI in Terms of EEG Change Associated with Mental Focusing to Photic Stimuli, ABML 2011, 2011/11/3–5, Tokyo, Shibaura Institute of Technology (2011). (in Japanese)
6. Kimura, T., Kumagai, Y., Hayasaka, Y., Ohshima, H., Kanai, N., Itoh, T., Tadokoro, H., Okamoto, K., Yamazaki, K.: A proposal for a new VEP based brain computer interface for disabled people – a fundamental study using an animal experimental model. In: IADIS International Conference Interfaces and Human Computer Interaction, pp. 319–321 (2012). (in Japanese)

A Consideration of Effects of Different Numbers of Seconds in Spontaneous Time Production with fMRI Analysis

Ryosuke Hayasaka(✉), Keita Mitani(✉), and Yukinobu Hoshino(✉)

Kochi University of Technology, 185 Miyanokuchi, Tosayamada, Kami City, Kochi 782-8502, Japan
{215046x, 196017w}@gs.kochi-tech.ac.jp,
hoshino.yukinobu@kochi-tech.ac.jp

Abstract. Time is a fundamental property of human perception and action. Previous studies on how time perception is related to the brain have been refined over the years. Cerebral activity areas relating to time are a basal ganglia, a cerebellum, an insula, a right inferior frontal gyrus (IFG) and a right inferior parietal lobule (IPL). In our previous study, a spontaneous time production task was conducted using the fMRI measurement. As the experimental conditions, the different number of seconds (5 s and 10 s) and the different situations were set. In brain analysis results by situation conditions, significant activities were obtained in the right IPL and the right IFG. Therefore, analysis results were considered to be brain activity related to time perception. In this paper, we describe analysis results by the difference in the number of seconds.

Keywords: Time perception · Time production · fMRI · BCI

1 Introduction

In recent years, numerous brain-computer interface (BCI) studies have been conducted. BCI is the external control system which interprets a subject's intentions by measuring brain activity. For example, it can be used for wheelchairs control [1] and character input support [2]. BCI is expected to support communication and comfort-able environment for quadriplegic patients, such as patients with Amyotrophic Lateral Sclerosis (ALS) or spinal cord injury. In previous BCI, there are many researches using motor area [3], visual cortex [4] or auditory cortex [5] located on the brain surface. And many of them use only one area. For the future development of BCI, it is expected to use the brain region which has not been used so far and to improve BCI function by combining many areas. In this research, we focus on using new brain regions.

In our lives, time is involved in every action, for example, when exercising, planning or sleeping. Time is a fundamental property of human perception and action. Research on time theory has started many years ago (as far back as 400) and research has been conducted in several fields such as psychology and medicine, physics, and engineering. Research on how time is related to the brain has been refined over the

C. Stephanidis (Ed.): HCII Posters 2018, CCIS 850, pp. 354–360, 2018.
https://doi.org/10.1007/978-3-319-92270-6_51

years [6–8]. Patients with Parkinson's disease, schizophrenia, attention-deficit/hyperactivity disorder, and autism were reported to have temporal perception modulation in the frontal cortex, basal ganglia, cerebellum, hippocampus, and parietal cortex [9]. In addition, it is revealed by magnetoencephalography using temporal shrinking illusion that temporal perception is controlled by the right hemisphere temporo-parietal junction and time judgment by the right hemispheric inferior frontal gyrus (IFG) [10]. It was reported that when the visual stimulus at the same time interval was repeatedly presented, the activation intensity of the right inferior parietal lobule (IPL) decreased as compared with the case where the time intervals of stimulation were different [11].

As a preliminary experiment for use in BCI, time guessing game was performed using fMRI measurement. Right Inferior Parietal Lobule (IPL) was obtained as a common area due to the difference in situations of the time guessing game [12]. Since it is reported that the right IPL is related to the time length [11], we consider that time-based brain activity was obtained from the time guessing game. In this paper, we analyze specific brain activity about the difference of situation by time guessing game.

2 Materials and Methods

This experiment was conducted on 21 participants. Fourteen participants had corrected eyesight, and seven people had no eyesight correction. The participants with eyesight corrections were asked to use nonmetallic eyeglasses. Two of the participants were left-handed and the rest were right-handed. The average age of the participants was 21.42 years, and the standard deviation was 1.99. We asked the examinees whether they had stopped the determined time like a time guessing task with a stopwatch, and as a result, all 21 participants that they had done so.

Two types of evaluation method are often used for the time perception experiment. One is the time production method. In the method, a participant performs to measure a predetermined period of time. At this time, he/she measures the time by the mind without measurement clues. The other one is the time re-production method. Firstly, a participant receives a certain time width stimulus such as a sound or a visual image. Then, he/she is asked to measure this period of certain time in the mind [13]. This experiment was conducted by using a time guessing game based on the time production method. In the time guessing game, participants are required to stop a watch by pressing a button after a specified number of seconds. In this experiment, two kinds of conditions were set, one condition used the 2 measurement times, and the other condition used the 3 situations. Conditions are as follows.

- Measurement times
  - 5 s counts
  - 10 s counts
- Situations
  - No animation + open eyes (a Open eyes)
  - No animation + close eyes (a Close eyes
  - Animation stopwatch + open eyes (a Stopwatch)

As the first condition, the 2 measurement times were set for a section to measure five seconds (a 5 s counts) and another section to measure ten seconds (a 10 s counts). The 2 measurement times were set to verify whether there is an effect on cerebral activation with the difference in the number of seconds. The second condition consisted of the 3 situations. In the Open eye measurement, participants were asked to count the number of seconds without displaying the screen with their eyes open. In the Close eye measurement, participants were asked to count the number of seconds without the screen display with their eyes closed. In the Stopwatch measurement, participants were asked to count the number of seconds using a stopwatch displayed on the screen with their eyes open. The 3 situations were set to verify the difference in cerebral activation depending on the opening and closing of the eyes, the presence or absence of a display on the screen. This experiment was carried out in a total of six ways with conditions being two (the 2 measurement times) times three (the 3 situations).

A block design was adopted for experimental design. A run is included in the 2 measurement times. The 2 measurement times were included in the 3 situations. The 3 situations were included in a task block and a rest block. In the task block, participants performed the time guessing game. In the case of the Open eyes measurement and 5 s counts, there are probably individual differences. We considered whether the button would be pressed in seven or eight seconds, thus we set it for ten seconds in one task block. Likewise, the 10 s counts were set for one task block in fifteen seconds. The rest block was set at fifteen seconds. The rest block was placed in the participant's gaze point and participants were instructed to look at it. In the rest block, participants were asked to look at a gaze point without any thinking. A task sequence example is shown in Fig. 1.

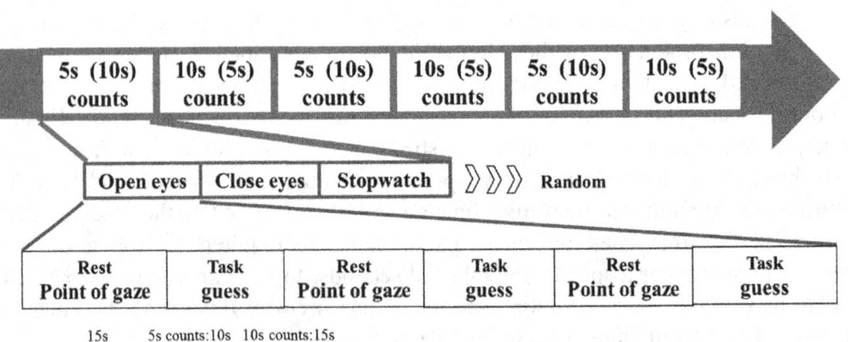

Fig. 1. Task sequence

The order of measurement times and situations was counterbalanced cross participants. The counterbalance is to counteract the effect of allowing the independent variable of the general linear model to equally influence the potential confounding factors. In this experiment, the counterbalance between participants became necessary because the grading improves gradually according to the order of experiments and the degree of concentration changes depending on fatigue and record. In order to the counterbalance between the conditions, we divided participants starting from the 5 s counts and participants starting from the 10 s counts. The task block of each section was also randomized in the 3 situations for each participant.

The flow of each section is shown in Fig. 2. First of all, the next task was introduced by the information screen. In the case of the Close eyed measurement, we instructed in advance to close their eyes when they saw the information screen. After the information screen disappeared, a start tone was played and the participants instructed to start counting numbers for Open eyes measurement and Close eyed measurement. The Stopwatch measurement was also used to check the 3 situations difference between tasks by playing the start sound. We instructed participants to push the button when they thought that the instructed time was reached. In Close eyed task, participants were taught to open their closed eyes when the last tone was heard. As a precaution to the examinees, we instructed them not to keep a timing with their body, such as with their hands or feet and not to count using their voice.

In this experiment, we tried to analyze the brain function map when fulfilling the time guessing task using the fMRI measurement. The fMRI captured the image using a MAGNETOM Verio 3T manufactured by SIEMENS. The imaging parameters were set with TR/TE = 2500/30 ms, FoV = 192 mm^2, Voxel size = $3.0 \times 3.0 \times 3.0$ mm, a slice thickness = 3.0 mm. the 5 s counts of the 2 measurement times were captured in 105 scans for one section and the 10 s counts of the 2 measurement times were captured in 123 scans for one section. Two scans from the start of the imaging process were excluded from the analysis because the longitudinal magnetization of the tissue was unsteady. Furthermore, in order to obtain the position information, an anatomical image with a resolution of $1.0 \times 1.0 \times 1.0$ mm was captured as a T1 weighted sequence. A presentation of the experimental tasks and the reaction acquisition were conducted by creating, executing and controlling the experimental programs using Matlab R2014a software manufactured by Math Works. Logs concerning time during the experiment were also recorded in Matlab.

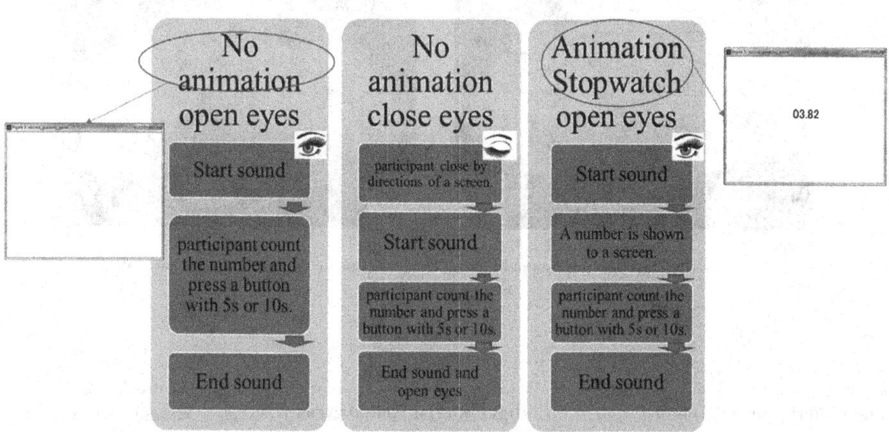

Fig. 2. Task blocks of 3 situations

3 Result and Discussion

Participant's experimental logs are used to confirm the difficulty level of the task. The purpose of this experiment was to compare the brain activities in the condition that the difficulty of the task condition is not different and to consider using the BCI. First, the number of samples of logs by each situation of 21 participants was 189 in total. Logs of the total participants were checked and there were participants who were not able to carry out the task or participants who made a mistake in the count time. In the fMRI analysis, it is necessary to make the number of data in the participant uniform, so the number of data was set for each participant in 3 situations. Six samples were excluded at 5 s counts and 30 samples were excluded at 10 s counts.

In this experiment, we consider brain areas related to time measurement. FMRI images were analyzed for SPM12 and the fMRI image data was been preprocessing. For example, standard time, spatial. To define specifically of 2 measurement times at the group level, one-sample t-test was conducted on the contrast images of specifically of 2 measurement times. The resulting set of voxel values for each contrast constituted the SPM{t}. The statistical height threshold was set at $p < 0.05$ corrected for multiple comparisons at the peak level over the whole brain (Family-Wise Error: FWE). Anatomic and Brodmann area labeling of activity clusters was performed using the Anatomy Toolbox [14]. In this paper, the analysis of 3 situations combined data are reported.

The analysis results of 2 measurement times are shown in Fig. 3. Both 5 s counts and 10 s counts showed the significant difference in brain activity in right inferior parietal lobule, right insula and right middle frontal gyrus. However, comparing these activities did not give a big difference. In this experiment, only two ways of difference in the number of seconds are done so it cannot be suggested accurately. Since the brain activity of the right insula has a larger brain activity amount compared with others, we considered that there is a possibility of seeing a difference when conducting an

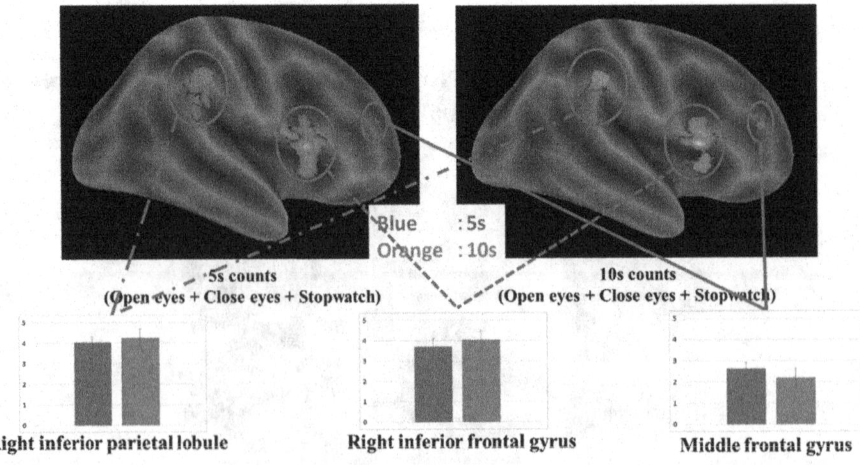

Fig. 3. The brain activity of 2 measurement times

experiment by adding a second number of seconds. If the change in brain activity appears in a specific area of the brain due to the difference in seconds, this feature is considered to be usable for brain-computer interface. In the future, we are planning to investigate the change in the amount of cerebral activity due to the difference in the number of seconds.

4 Conclusion

The time is a fundamental property of human perception and action. In this pa-per, we analyzed specific brain activity about the difference of situation by time guessing game. In this experimental result, there was no big difference in the number of seconds. From now on, we are going to experiment with increasing the number of seconds and we plan to make BCI using the time production.

References

1. Yu, Y., Zhou, Z., Liu, Y., Jiang, J., Yin, E., Zhang, N., Wang, Z., Liu, Y., Wu, X., Hu, D.: Self-paced operation of a wheelchair based on a hybrid brain-computer interface combining motor imagery and P300 potential. IEEE Trans. Neural Syst. Rehabil. Eng. **25**(12), 2516–2526 (2017)
2. Birbaumer, N., Ghanayim, N., Hinterberger, T., Iversen, I., Kotchoubey, B., Kubler, A., Perelmouter, J., Taub, E., Flor, H.: A spelling device for the paralyzed. Nature **398**(6725), 297 (1999)
3. Tanaka, K., Matsunaga, K., Wang, H.O.: Electroencephalogram-based control of an electric wheelchair. IEEE Trans. Rob. **21**(4), 762–766 (2005)
4. Kelly, S.P., Lalor, E.C., Finucane, C., McDarby, G., Reilly, R.B.: Visual spatial attention control in an independent brain-computer interface. IEEE Trans. Biomed. Eng. **52**(9), 1588–1596 (2005)
5. Gao, S., Wang, Y., Gao, X., Hong, B.: Visual and auditory brain-computer interfaces. IEEE Trans. Biomed. Eng. **61**(5), 1436–1447 (2014)
6. Espinosa-Fern, L., Mir, E., Cano, C.M., Buela-Casal, G.: Age-related changes and gender differences in time estimation. Acta Psychol. **112**(3), 221–232 (2003)
7. Bueti, D., Macaluso, E.: Auditory temporal expectations modulate activity in visual cortex. NeuroImage **51**(3), 1168–1183 (2010)
8. Ohmae, S., Uematsu, A., Tanaka, M.: Temporally specific sensory signals for the detection of stimulus omission in the primate deep cerebellar nuclei. J. Neurosci. **33**(39), 15432–15441 (2013)
9. Fontes, R., Ribeiro, J., Gupta, D.S., Machado, D., Lopes-Junior, F., Magalhaes, F., Bastos, V.H., Rocha, K., Marinho, V., Lima, G., Velasques, B., Ribeiro, P., Orsini, M., Pessoa, B., Leite, M.A., Teixeira, S.: Time perception mechanisms at central nervous system. Neurol. Int. **8**(1), 5939 (2016)
10. Hironaga, N., Mitsudo, T., Hayamizu, M., Nakajima, Y., Takeichi, H., Tobimatsu, S.: Spatiotemporal brain dynamics of auditory temporal assimilation. Sci. Reports **7**(1), 11400 (2017)

11. Hayashi, M.J., Ditye, T., Harada, T., Hashiguchi, M., Sadato, N., Carlson, S., Walsh, V., Kanai, R.: Time adaptation shows duration selectivity in the human parietal cortex. PLOS Biol. **13**(9), e1002262 (2015)
12. Hayasaka, R., Mitani, K., Hoshino, Y.: Basic verification of the brain areas related with the time measurement to use BCI. In: Joint 17th World Congress of International Fuzzy Systems Association (IFSA) and 9th International Conference on Soft Computing and Intelligent Systems (SCIS), pp. 1–6 (2017)
13. Kuriyama, K., Uchiyama, M., Suzuki, H., Tagaya, H., Ozaki, A., Aritake, S., Kamei, Y., Nishikawa, T., Yakahashi, K.: Circadian fluctuation of time perception in healthy human subjects. Neurosci. Res. **46**(1), 23–31 (2003)
14. Eickihoff, S.B., Stephan, K.E., Mohlberg, H., Grefkes, C., Fink, G.R., Amunts, K., Zilles, K.: A new SPM toolbox for combining probabilistic cytoarchitectonic maps and functional imaging data. Neuroimage **25**(4), 1325–1335 (2005)

Influence of User and Task Related Variables on Latency Perception

Nadine Rauh(✉), Miriam Gieselmann, and Josef F. Krems

Chemnitz University of Technology,
Wilhelm-Raabe-Str. 43, 09120 Chemnitz, Germany
Nadine.Rauh@psychologie.tu-chemnitz.de

Abstract. Nowadays, technical system latencies are nearly unavoidable in Human-Computer-Interaction. However, latencies, if detected by the user, were shown to have a negative influence on experience and satisfaction. Therefore, it is important to examine users' latency perception thresholds with respect to different influencing factors empirically.

In the present study the influence of movement type (circular vs. straight), motivation and visual processing speed were examined by using a mouse-based 2D-dragging-task. Thirty participants (67% female, M_{age} = 22.27) took part and had to move a cursor through a circular or straight tunnel by using a computer mouse.

Results showed that participants detected lower latencies when moving the cursor circular. An influence of the motivation on latency perception could not be found. Participants with higher visual processing speed detected lower latencies.

Future studies should explore further factors influencing latency perception. When designing Human-Computer-Interaction in matters of latency, the type of executed movement should be considered.

Keywords: Movement type · Motivation · Visual processing speed

1 Introduction

Nowadays, the interaction with a computer system is common for most people. Latencies, defined as time delays between user input and system output, due to hardware and software characteristics are nearly unavoidable in human-computer-interaction [1]. If the latency of a system exceeds a certain threshold, users might get aware of the latency [2], the user experience can be impaired [3] and the user satisfaction can be reduced [4]. Different system, task and user related characteristics can influence the detection of system latency [5], but more research is necessary in this regard [6]. In the present study user related (i.e., motivation and visual processing speed) and task related influencing factors (i.e., movement type) on latency perception were examined.

C. Stephanidis (Ed.): HCII Posters 2018, CCIS 850, pp. 361–369, 2018.
https://doi.org/10.1007/978-3-319-92270-6_52

1.1 Related Work

For the development of human-computer-systems it is important to know which latencies are perceivable by the user and impair the human-computer-interaction. Common design guidelines postulate a maximum latency of 100 ms to be sufficient to reach an optimal human-computer-interaction [7]. However, recent research could show that latencies considerably lower than 100 ms can be detected by the users (e.g., 64 ms; [2], 50 ms; [8], 60 ms; [6]). Results also indicate that the latency perception threshold differs dependent on several system related characteristics (e.g., input devices; [9]), task related characteristics (e.g., task complexity; [8]) or user related characteristics (e.g., experience with highly dynamic real-time computer games; [6]). There are some references in literature that also users' motivation to identify latencies as well as users' individual visual processing speed might be relevant user related characteristics [5].

In the present study the task related characteristic movement type representing one facet of task complexity and the two user related characteristics motivation and visual processing speed were examined.

Movement Type. Research could show that it is more difficult for users to identify latencies in more complex tasks (e.g., writing with a digital stylus) than in less complex tasks (e.g., simple dragging tasks) [8, 10]. The authors postulated that more complex movements during task processing leads to a higher cognitive load and, hence, to less available cognitive resources for recognizing the system latencies [10]. Movement complexity can be defined by the Index of Movement Difficulty (ID) which can be calculated by the Fitts' Law for straight movements [11] and by the Steering Law for circular movements [12]. Based on the research of [8, 10] it can be assumed that the latency perception is better for straight movement tasks (i.e., less complex movements) compared to circular movement tasks (i.e., more complex movements).

However, there is also research indicating that higher movement amplitudes (e.g., circular movements) could enhance the latency perception by providing more occasions to compare the input and the output signal [13] which should enhance the latency perception. One objective of the present research is to examine which task characteristic (i.e., movement difficulty or movement amplitude) are more prominent for latency perception in circular movement tasks compared to straight movement tasks.

Motivation. Participants of the present research revealed the information that their individual latency perception threshold will be examined representing a performance test situation. Motivation in such a context can be defined as the willingness to invest effort to solve the task as good as possible over the whole time [14]. Research could show that participants' motivation has an influence for instance on the performance in a simple detection task to examine participants' perception threshold [15].

It can be assumed that all participants of the present study had a certain level of intrinsic motivation because they took part voluntarily in the experiment. However, external incentives (e.g., positive materially incentives) can also influence the performance [16]. Hence, it is assumed that a financial incentive increases participants' external motivation to detect lower latencies and reduce the latency perception threshold.

Visual Processing Speed. The perception process includes the processing of information [17]. How long it takes to process all the relevant information depends on the individual processing speed [18]. The processing speed for visual tasks (i.e., visual processing speed] can be examined for instance by using the digit-symbol-test of the Wechsler-Adult-Intelligence-Scale III [19]. Several research could reveal that more economic tests like simple or choice reaction time tasks [20] show medium to strong correlations with the digit-symbol-test and, hence, can be used as indicators for visual processing speed. Moreover, it is assumed that there is a strong correlation between the visual processing speed and the inspection time, defined as the minimal duration of a visual stimulus that produces a certain amount of correct answers [21]. It is assumed that the visual processing speed influences the latency perception threshold.

1.2 Hypotheses

The hypotheses examined in the present research are the following:
H1: The latency perception threshold differs between the more complex circular movement task and the less complex straight movement task.
H2: The latency perception threshold of the experimental group who received further external motivation through financial incentives should be lower than the latency perception threshold of the control group.
H3: Higher visual processing speed (examined with simple and choice reaction time tasks and inspection time tasks) correlates with a lower latency perception threshold.

2 Method

The present study was a 4x2 mixed measures design with the independent variables movement type and visual procession speed as within subject factor and motivation as between subject factor. The dependent variable was the latency perception threshold.

2.1 Participants

30 participants (67% female, $M_{age} = 22.27$) took part in the experiment. At the beginning of the experiment all participants signed an informed consent, including all information about the experiment and the anonymization of collected data.

2.2 Material

Software. The experimental task was implemented in C++ by using the open source libraries of SFML [22] for 2D-displays in Code::Blocks (version 16.1.0). The technical system latency of the program was between 7.6 and 8.6 ms.

Hardware. A computer with a 6-core-processor and a basic clock frequency of 3.3 GHz was used. The input device was a gaming mouse (Logitech G303) with 800 dpi. The tasks were presented on an Acer XF240H monitor with an update rate of 144 Hz.

System. The mouse based 2D-dragging task included the navigation of a black square representing the mouse cursor through a white tunnel (straight or circular) as fast and accurate as possible (Fig. 1). Each trial consists of 2 sub trials with identical movement tasks but differing in the presented latencies. One sub trial had the technical system latency (i.e., no added latency) and the other sub trial has an added latency between one and 300 ms. After experiencing both sub trials in a randomized order the participants had to identify the sub trial in which the system reacts more instantly to the user input (i.e., the system without added latency).

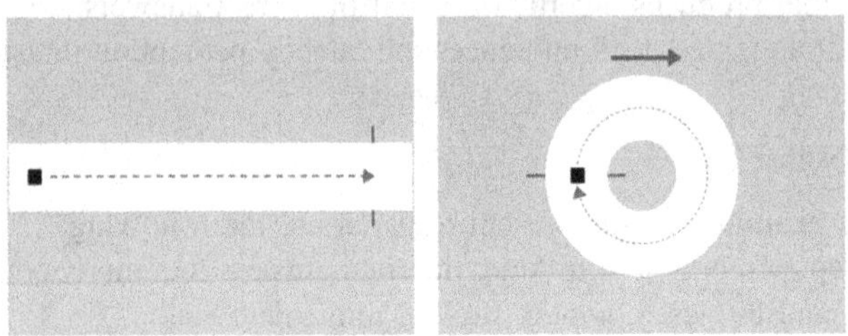

Fig. 1. Movement types – straight (left) and circular (right). The blue arrows represent the movement direction of the mouse cursor and were not visible for the participants. (Color figure online)

Examining the Latency Perception Threshold. In every dragging-task an adaptive threshold estimation method (ZEST, [23]) was used to estimate the latency perception threshold based on the participant's performance in the previous forced-choice-discrimination-task. With every correct (or false) answer of the participant the estimated perception threshold decreases (or increases) and, hence, the presented added latency of the next trial. The final latency perception threshold is defined as the added latency that can be correctly identified by the participant with a hit rate of 75% (see also [8]).

Movement Type. The straight movement task (left side of Fig. 1) had an ID of 6.76 and the circular movement task (right side of Fig. 1) had an ID of 8.97. Participants had to move the mouse cursor once per sub trial from the starting point to the target area (represented by the two grey bars).

Motivation. The experimental group received feedback regarding their latency perception threshold after the first part of the experiment. They were told that they will receive a financial incentive if they are able to improve their performance in the second part of the experiment. After each part of the experiment the participants filled out six items regarding their motivation on a 6-point-likert-scale (1 – fully disagree, 6 – fully agree).

Visual Processing Speed. The inspection time task as well as the simple and choice reaction time task were used [20]. The inspection time task was implemented in Presentation® (version 19.0, www.neurobs.com). The same stimulus (two lines with different length) was presented to the participants several times with different durations. The participants had to correctly identify the shorter line. During the simple reaction time task the participants' reaction time (button press) to a presented stimulus was examined. During the choice reaction time task participants, additionally, had to press one of four different buttons matching to the location on which the stimulus was presented.

2.3 Procedure

After a written instruction to the experiment as well as explanation of the term *latency* the participants started with a training in which they practiced the correct movement (i.e., straight and circular tunnel) as well as the latency perception task. After that, participants elaborated 30 trials for each movement type, followed by one test regarding participants' visual processing speed. After a short break the experimental group received the invention and all participants elaborated again 30 trials for each movement type, followed by the other test regarding participants' visual processing speed. After the experiment every participant was debriefed and received the financial incentive.

3 Results

Data analyses were done with *IBM SPSS Statistics* (Version 21.0) on a 5% significance level. Effect sizes were interpreted regarding [24].

3.1 Movement Type

Two outliers were identified regarding the conventions of [25] and were excluded from the analysis. Data revealed a difference between both movement types: Participants perceived lower latencies in the circular ($M = 62.04$ ms; $SD = 29.24$) compared to the straight movement task ($M = 94.71$ ms; $SD = 59.49$). A t-test for dependent samples revealed a medium effect: $t(27) = -3.79$, $p = .001$, $d = -.59$. Hence, H1 can be accepted.

3.2 Motivation

A repeated measures ANOVA revealed no differences between the experimental and the control group regarding the latency perception threshold ($F(1, 28) = 0.336$, $p = .567$). The manipulation check revealed, that both groups did not differ regarding their motivation after the intervention ($t(28) = -0.96$, $p = .346$, $d = -.35$), but were strongly motivated with $M = 5.32$ ($SD = .51$) for the experimental group and $M = 5.10$ ($SD = .71$) for the control group. Because the intervention regarding participants' external motivation did not work in the present study, a linear regression with motivation as predictor was calculated over all participants. Results indicated that motivation is no significant predictor ($\beta = -.099$, $t = -1.084$, $p = .281$). Hence, H2 has to be rejected.

3.3 Visual Processing Speed

A Pearson correlation was calculated and revealed significant correlations between the values of the simple and choice reaction time as well as the inspection time task with the lowest identified latency perception threshold. Additionally, a multiple regression analysis was calculated with the values of the three tests as predictors. 41,9% of the variance could be explained (R^2= .419, strong effect with f = .849). The choice reaction time task was the strongest predictor for the latency perception threshold and reached statistical significance (β = 393, p = .040). Hence, H3 is supported by the data.

4 Discussion

4.1 Movement Type

The results of the present study revealed that a slightly higher ID has no negative influence on latency perception opposed to the results of [8, 10]. Indeed, the more complex, circular movement leads to a lower latency perception threshold. These results are in line with the research of [13] and contribute to the assumption that higher movement amplitudes could enhance the latency perception by providing more occasions to compare the input and the output signal. Possibly, this effect overlapped the assumed negative impact of the slightly higher task complexity.

More research should be done with more complex movement types (e.g., several curves) to better understand the relationship of task complexity and movement amplitudes. Furthermore, in the present study movement type and ID were manipulated through the same variable (straight vs. circular tunnel). Hence, the results cannot clearly be related to one of these two factors. Hence, future research should focus on replicating the found effects when just one of factor (movement type or ID) is manipulated.

4.2 Motivation

In the present study, no correlation between participants' motivation and the latency perception threshold could be found. However, it should be considered that all participants were strongly motivated to solve the task as good as possible. One explanation for the high motivation might be the sample itself. All participants were students who voluntarily took part in the experiment. It can be assumed that all participants had an above average tendency to strive for success, because they chose a demanding study with situations in which the individual performance is tested. Furthermore, it was clear that the individual latency perception threshold was tested in the present experiment which might led to a further self-selection of the sample. Hence, it is possible that the intrinsic motivation to solve the task as good as possible was very high for all participants and couldn't be increased any further by the financial incentive [26].

Future research should focus on a more differentiated sample regarding the motivation to correctly identify the latencies to gather more insights to its role in this regard.

4.3 Visual Processing Speed

Results indicated that visual processing speed might be an important user characteristic with respect to latency perception. Nevertheless, it must be considered that the used tests examine the visual processing speed only indirectly.

Further tests should also directly measure the visual processing speed to replicate the found effects. A further research questions arises from the results that elderly people have more problems with latency perception [27] and that the processing speed decreases with higher age [28]. The questions arises, if the negative effects of age on latency perception are only caused by the reduced processing speed or if other variables (e.g., experience with computers) have an additional effect.

4.4 Conclusion

The present research found movement type and visual processing speed to be relevant influencing factors on latency perception in 2D-dragging tasks. The results should be considered in human-computer-design and provide implications to further research. Moreover, the identified latency perception thresholds in the present study were considerably under 100 ms (M = 49.63 ms; SD = 21.24), supporting the need for revised design guidelines regarding human-computer-interaction.

References

1. MacKenzie, I.S., Ware, C.: Lag as a determinant of human performance in interactive systems. In: Arnold, B., van der Veer, G., White, T. (eds.) Proceedings of the SIGCHI Conference on Human Factors in Computing Systems - CHI 1993, pp. 488–493. ACM Press, New York (1993). https://doi.org/10.1145/169059.169431
2. Jota, R., Ng, A., Dietz, P., Wigdor, D.: How fast is fast enough? In: Mackay, W.E., Brewster, S., Bødker, S. (eds.) Proceedings of the SIGCHI Conference on Human Factors in Computing Systems - CHI 2013, p. 2291. ACM Press, New York (2013). https://doi.org/10.1145/2470654.2481317
3. Zhou, R., Shao, S., Li, W., Zhou, L.: How to define the user's tolerance of response time in using mobile applications. In: 2016 IEEE International Conference on Industrial Engineering and Engineering Management (IEEM), pp. 281–285. IEEE (2016). https://doi.org/10.1109/IEEM.2016.7797881
4. Fischer, A.R.H., Blommaert, F.J.J., Midden, C.J.H.: Monitoring and evaluation of time delay. Int. J. Hum.-Comput. Interact. **19**(2), 163–180 (2005). https://doi.org/10.1207/s15327590ijhc1902_1
5. Attig, C., Rauh, N., Franke, T., Krems, J.F.: System latency guidelines then and now – is zero latency really considered necessary? In: Harris, D. (ed.) Engineering Psychology and Cognitive Ergonomics: Cognition and Design. EPCE 2017. LNCS, vol. 10276, pp. 3–14. Springer, Cham (2017). https://doi.org/10.1007/978-3-319-58475-1_1
6. Forch, V., Franke, T., Rauh, N., Krems, J.F.: Are 100 Milliseconds fast enough? characterizing latency perception thresholds in mouse-based interaction. Paper presented at the 19th International Conference on Human-Computer Interaction, Vancouver, Canada, pp. 9–14, July 2017

7. Miller, R.B.: Response time in man-computer conversational transactions. In: Proceedings of the December 9–11, Fall Joint Computer Conference, Part I, AFIPS 1968 (Fall, Part I), p. 267. ACM Press, New York (1968). https://doi.org/10.1145/1476589.1476628
8. Annett, M., Ng, A., Dietz, P., Bischof, W.F., Gupta, A.: How low should we go? understanding the perception of latency while inking. In: Kry, P.G. (ed.) Graphics interface 2014, Montreal, Quebec, Canada, 7–9 May 2014, Proceedings, [part of the 2014 AI/GI/CRV Conference; Including the Annual General Meeting of CHCCS/SCDHM held during the Graphics Interface Conference]. CRC Press, Boca Raton (2014)
9. Deber, J., Jota, R., Forlines, C., Wigdor, D.: How much faster is fast enough? In: Begole, B., Kim, J., Inkpen, K., Woo, W. (eds.) Proceedings of the 33rd Annual ACM Conference on Human Factors in Computing Systems - CHI 2015, pp. 1827–1836. ACM Press, New York (2015). https://doi.org/10.1145/2702123.2702300
10. Ng, A., Dietz, P.H.: The effects of latency and motion blur on touch screen user experience. J. Soc. Inform. Display **22**(9), 449–456 (2014). https://doi.org/10.1002/jsid.243
11. Fitts, P.M.: The information capacity of the human motor system in controlling the amplitude of movement. J. Exp. Psychol. **47**, 381–391 (1954)
12. Accot, J., Zhai, S.: Performance evaluation of input devices in trajectory-based tasks. In: Williams, M.G., Altom, M.W. (eds.) Proceedings of the SIGCHI Conference on Human Factors in Computing Systems the CHI is the Limit - CHI 1999, pp. 466–472. ACM Press, New York (1999). https://doi.org/10.1145/302979.303133
13. Rank, M., Shi, Z., Hirche, S.: Perception of delay in haptic telepresence systems. Presence Teleoperators Virtual Environ. **19**(5), 389–399 (2010). https://doi.org/10.1162/pres_a_00021
14. Baumert, J., Demmrich, A.: Test motivation in the assessment of student skills: the effects of incentives on motivation and performance. Eur. J. Psychol. Educ. **16**(3), 441–462 (2001). https://doi.org/10.1007/BF03173192
15. Chan, D., Schmitt, N., DeShon, R.P., Clause, C.S., Delbridge, K.: Reactions to cognitive ability tests: the relationships between race, test performance, face validity perceptions, and test-taking motivation. J. Appl. Psychol. **82**(2), 300–310 (1997). https://doi.org/10.1037/0021-9010.82.2.300
16. Wolf, L.F., Smith, J.K.: The consequence of consequence: motivation, anxiety, and test performance. Appl. Measur. Educ. **8**(3), 227–242 (1995). https://doi.org/10.1207/s15324818ame0803_3
17. Gerrig, R.J., Zimbardo, P.G.: Psychologie, 18th edn. Pearson Higher Education, München (2011)
18. Titz, C.: Informationsverarbeitungsgeschwindigkeit, altersbedingte. In: Wirtz, M.A. (ed.) Dorsch - Lexikon der Psychologie, 18th edn. Hogrefe, Bern (2014)
19. Wechsler, D.: WAIS-III: Administration and Scoring Manual: Wechsler Adult Intelligence Scale, 3rd edn. Psychological Corporation, San Antonio (1997)
20. Deary, I.J., Liewald, D., Nissan, J.: A free, easy-to-use, computer-based simple and four-choice reaction time programme: the Deary-Liewald reaction time task. Behav. Res. Methods **43**(1), 258–268 (2011). https://doi.org/10.3758/s13428-010-0024-1
21. Kreutzer, J.S., DeLuca, J., Caplan, B. (eds.): Encyclopedia of Clinical Neuropsychology. Springer, New York (2011). https://doi.org/10.1007/978-0-387-79948-3. p. 1323
22. Gomila, L.: Simple and Fast Multimedia Library. https://www.sfml-dev.org/. Accessed 15 Mar 2016
23. King-Smith, P.E., Grigsby, S.S., Vingrys, A.J., Benes, S.C., Supowit, A.: Efficient and unbiased modifications of the QUEST threshold method: theory, simulations, experimental evaluation and practical implementation. Vis. Res. **34**(7), 885–912 (1994). https://doi.org/10.1016/0042-6989(94)90039-6

24. Cohen, J.: A power primer. Psychol. Bull. **11**, 155–159 (1992). https://doi.org/10.1037/0033-2909.112.1.155
25. Field, A.: Discovering Statistics Using IBM SPSS Statistics: and Sex and Drugs and Rock 'n' Roll, 4th edn. SAGE, Los Angeles (2015)
26. Camerer, C.F., Hogarth, R.M., Budescu, D.V., Eckel, C.: The effects of financial incentives in experiments: a review and capital-labor-production framework. In: Fischhoff, B., Manski, C.F. (eds.) Elicitation of Preferences, pp. 7–48. Springer, Dordrecht (1999). https://doi.org/10.1007/978-94-017-1406-8_2
27. Mäki-Patola, T., Hämäläinen, P.: Latency tolerance for gesture controlled continuous sound instrument without tactile feedback. In: International Computer Music Conference Proceedings (2004)
28. Salthouse, T.A.: The processing-speed theory of adult age differences in cognition. Psychol. Rev. **103**(3), 403–428 (1996). https://doi.org/10.1037/0033-295X.103.3.403

Individual Differences in Trust in Code: The Moderating Effects of Personality on the Trustworthiness-Trust Relationship

Tyler J. Ryan[1], Charles Walter[2], Gene M. Alarcon[3(✉)], Rose F. Gamble[2], Sarah A. Jessup[3], and August A. Capiola[4]

[1] SRA International, Inc., A CSRA Company, Dayton, OH 45431, USA
tyler.ryan@csra.com
[2] University of Tulsa, Tulsa, OK 74104, USA
[3] U.S. Air Force Research Laboratory, 711th HPW RHXS, WPAFB, Dayton, OH, USA
gene.alarcon.1@us.af.mil
[4] Consortium Research Fellows Program, Lancaster, OH, USA

Abstract. The daily use of technology has made people ever more reliant on software. It is important these software systems are produced in a manner that is both efficient and secure. In this context, psychological trust of software is a pertinent aspect of research. The present study explored the relationship of trustworthiness ratings, propensity to trust, and trait suspicion on software reuse. In addition, we explored personality as a moderator of the trustworthiness-reuse relationship, as hypothesized in the interpersonal trust literature [1]. We recruited participants from Amazon's Mechanical Turk and requested they assess classes of Java code. Analyses revealed trait suspicion influenced decisions to reuse code and moderated the trustworthiness-trust relationship. A dual-process model of information processing was adopted for interpretation of these effects. Implications include contributions to research and theory on psychological trust, as well as practical implications for personnel selection with regard to software production.

Keywords: Trust · Suspicion · Software reuse

1 Introduction

The integration of software systems into nearly every aspect of modern life has increased productivity, but also vulnerability. Our reliance on these systems creates a need for safe and secure software produced in a timely manner. This, in turn, has led to a need for reusing software. However, little is known about how developers perceive and comprehend code. Designing software systems with the human user in mind requires an understanding of the factors involved in human decision-making. The human-computer interaction literature emphasizes that systems should not be relied upon beyond their capabilities [2]. Psychological theories of trust can help inform software development and reuse practices by understanding the antecedents to software reuse.

C. Stephanidis (Ed.): HCII Posters 2018, CCIS 850, pp. 370–376, 2018.
https://doi.org/10.1007/978-3-319-92270-6_53

1.1 Software Reuse and Review

Modern software production relies on source code reuse practices [3]. Frakes and Kang [3] defined software reuse as, "the use of existing software or software knowledge to construct new software," (p. 529). Reusing software increases productivity by reducing development time [4]. Systematic reuse practices can even lead to fewer software defects in the source code [5]. However, reuse practices can lead to decreased reliability and increased vulnerability if software is not properly vetted. Additionally, integrating components written by different developers into a single project requires some degree of trust in the software. Developers can choose to review code in great detail, but this is less time-efficient. Instead, developers may perform a cursory review of the code to make a decision.

1.2 Trust and Software Reuse

Trust is defined as the willingness to make oneself vulnerable to another [1]. Although this definition was created for describing the interpersonal trust process, the definition has also been applied to trust in automation contexts [2]. Recent research has investigated how software characteristics can influence psychological trust in software systems and source code [6–8]. In this context, trust is the willingness to reuse the code [6]. Reusing code makes one vulnerable, as the code may contain defects. A recent cognitive task analysis indicated that the software, the environment, and individual differences in the developer can influence user perceptions of software trustworthiness [6].

1.3 Heuristic Systematic Processing Model of Code

Researchers [7, 8] have developed a model of trust in software systems based on the heuristic-systematic model (HSM) of information processing [9, 10]. The HSM was originally developed as a model of psychological persuasion and presents two primary ways to process information in a message, namely heuristic and systematic processing [9]. Heuristic processing entails mental shortcuts that serve as sufficient justifications for accepting arguments [10]. In the programming context, coders may view easily identifiable code attributes (e.g., source of the code). These attributes serve as cues, which influence a developer's decision to reuse [7]. In turn, reuse can be attributed to heuristic processing of the source cue. Systematic processing involves a detailed analysis, requiring significantly more cognitive processing [9]. The sufficiency principle in the HSM states that perceivers attempt to strike a balance between conserving cognitive resources and obtaining sufficient confidence in their assessments [10]. The sufficiency threshold is the minimum level of desired confidence about one's judgements before making a decision. When the sufficiency threshold is low, little information is needed for a decision. When the sufficiency threshold is high, more information is needed and systematic processing is typically employed. Individual differences can influence one's sufficiency threshold [7]. Some developers may tend towards heuristic processing while others may tend towards systematic processing. Researchers [7, 8] have suggested personality may influence developer's information processing strategies, leading to different reuse outcomes.

1.4 Personality, Trust, and Software Review

Personality is the "characteristic patterns of thought, emotion, and behavior together with the psychological mechanisms – hidden or not – behind those patterns" [11] and is a topic of interest in the computer science literature [12]. Studies have focused on the influence of personality on pair programming [13], team climate, and performance [14]. Although research has explored the effects of personality on software development, no research has explored how personality affects psychological trust in software systems. Trust is based on the individual's perceptions of the referent from information in the environment (i.e., trustworthiness) [1, 15]. Trust can be based on one's general propensity to trust [1] or situation specific information (e.g., interacting with a referent) [15], such as aspects of the software [6]. According to Mayer et al. [1], perceptions of trustworthiness affect decisions to trust, and this in turn affects outcomes of trust (i.e., actual reuse of code). Therefore, we hypothesize that perceived trustworthiness positively relates to trust intentions (H_1).

Trust perceptions are not objective. Individual differences in the trustor can affect their willingness to trust the referent, as well as the relationship between perceived trustworthiness and trust [1]. In other words, individual differences have been hypothesized to have direct and moderating influences on trust intentions [1, 6]. However, no research to date has explored these effects on code reuse (i.e. trust intentions). We explored propensity to trust [1], or PT, and trait suspicion [16] as individual differences that would have direct and indirect effects on reuse. PT is the disposition to trust others across contexts [1]. In contrast, trait suspicion [16] is characterized by uncertainty, perceived mal-intent, and cognitive activity. Participants that have a tendency to trust others should have a higher likelihood of reusing code. We hypothesize that PT has a positive direct effect on trust intentions (H_2). In contrast, those who have a propensity to be suspicious of others will be less likely to reuse code, as they are inclined to seek information and be wary of potential harm. Therefore, we hypothesize that trait suspicion has a negative direct effect on trust intentions (H_3).

Trust perceptions can be influenced by individual differences [1]. Individuals high in PT may have lower sufficiency thresholds. PT may moderate the trustworthiness-trust relationship, as the information gained from the code should be relied on to a greater extent. We hypothesize that PT has a moderating effect on the relationship between trustworthiness perceptions and trust in code (H_4). In contrast, individuals higher on the cognitive activity dimension of suspicion should have a higher sufficiency threshold and require more information about the referent to make a decision. Trustworthiness ratings comprise perceptions of a referent. As such, the cognitive activity dimension of trait suspicion should affect how relevant trustworthiness perceptions are for informing trust. Therefore, we hypothesize that trait suspicion moderates the relationship between perceived trustworthiness and trust intentions (H_5).

2 Method

Subjects were recruited using Amazon's Mechanical Turk (Mturk). Participants were required to have at least 3 years of coding experience and have a working knowledge of Java. A total of 45 participants were recruited. The final sample consisted of 11 (24.4%)

females and 34 (75.5%) males, with a mean age of 29.13 years ($SD = 6.57$), and a mean of 6.69 ($SD = 4.99$) years of programming experience, respectively. Participants received 10.00 USD for participation in the study, which was paid through Mturk's worker payment system.

2.1 Measures

Trustworthiness and Trust Assessments
Perceived trustworthiness was measured with a single item asking participants, "How trustworthy is the code?" Participants responded using a 1 to 7 Likert-type scale (1 = strongly untrustworthy, 7 = strongly trustworthy). Trust in the code was measured with a single item asking participants whether they would use the code or not.

Personality Measures
Propensity to trust (PT) was measured with the eight item Propensity to Trust scale [17], which contains items measuring beliefs about everyday phenomena. Participants responded on a Likert-type scale (1 = strongly disagree, 5 = strongly agree), $\alpha = .66$. The Suspicion Propensity Index – I [16] was used to measure trait suspicion. Participants evaluate eleven fictional vignettes on four Likert-type sub-scales (1 = strongly disagree, 5 = strongly agree), two of which we implemented in the present study: (1) uncertainty and mal-intent, $\alpha = .78$, measuring one's propensity to view the motivations of others as malicious, and (2) uncertainty and cognitive activity, $\alpha = .73$, measuring one's propensity to seek out and reflect on information about a referent they are unsure about. Trait suspicion scores were calculated as the sum of the two facets, as recommended by Calhoun et al. [16].

2.2 Stimuli

Stimuli consisted of images of Java code artifacts which were taken from publically available open source Java code repositories on GitHub.com. Each artifact selected from the overall code. Artifacts were complex enough to require review to fully understand, but simple enough to be reviewed within approximately 10 min by an experienced reviewer. Artifacts had 4.4% to 78.3% of their lines commented. The commenting percentage range is reflective of the expectations Java programmers have when reviewing code samples. Some samples need very few comments for large, straight-forward sections, while other samples need long, multi-line comments for more complex, possibly smaller, code segments. The artifacts were cleaned by removing existing or references to authorship, which could influence participant trust. Cleaning resulted in the removal or rewriting of unusual comments, as well as adjusting the code in accordance with Java style guides [18]. This allowed us to separate the most common commenting errors into three categories: style, validity, and placement.

The artifacts were then reviewed by outside reviewers to ensure that no additional errors were present. The artifacts were separated such that there were two code samples, each with minimal or heavily degraded style, validity, and placement. Style degradations resulted in adding in old code which was commented out, commenting only some of the defined functions, or not using proper Java style for long comments.

Validity degradations included adding new or modifying existing comments to be incorrect (e.g., possibly indicating a code change or multiple editors), to lack useful information, to include information relating to code that needs to be added, and to be irrelevant. Placement degradations altered comments in ways that were against Java conventions and included comments which were overly verbose for simple concepts.

Each artifact was displayed to participants through an online portal that collected their responses to the trust and personality assessment questions. All stimuli were presented to the participants in the form of images of the code, with syntax highlighting consistent with the default highlighting of Eclipse, a widely used Java development program.

2.3 Procedure

Participants were administered the initial surveys and then provided written instructions for the upcoming task. Each participant was then given 18 different Java classes ranging between 29 and 390 lines of code. Participants were asked to evaluate their perceived trustworthiness of each Java class and then decide whether they would use the code. Upon completion of the code evaluation task, participants were provided remuneration for their time.

3 Analysis and Results

A generalized estimating equation approach was used for the primary analysis to account for the repeated measures design and model the binary outcomes [19]. A model building approach was used, successively adding and selecting those variables that improved model fit using Wald χ^2 tests and comparing Quasi-information criterion statistics (QIC) [20]. An exchangeable correlation structure was chosen to model the residual correlation between the repeated measures.

An initial null model was run with only an intercept as a predictor to compare successive models, QIC = 935.90. Model 1 consisted of the main effects of the four factors, style, validity, placement, and order of stimulus presentation. None of the main effects were significant, and the factors did not provide significant explanation of the variance in reuse over the null model, Wald χ^2 (4) = 3.24, p = .520, QIC = 941.00, and were excluded from further analyses. Model 2 regressed trust intentions onto perceived trustworthiness. Trustworthiness, Wald χ^2 (1) = 132, $p < .001$, QIC = 373.88 was a significant predictor of reuse intentions supporting H_1. Model 3 added PT as a covariate to the model. The addition of PT was only marginally significant, Wald χ^2 (1) = 2.81, p = .093, QIC = 373.64, failing to support H_2. PT was thus dropped from further analyses, and H_4 was not tested. Model 4 added trait suspicion as a main effect with trustworthiness. Trait suspicion significantly increased the amount of variance explained in use, Wald χ^2 (1) = 7.22, p = .007, QIC = 369.76, supporting H_3. Model 5 included the main effects of trustworthiness and trait suspicion, along with their interaction. The inclusion of the interaction term significantly changed the model, Wald χ^2 (1) = 6.50, p = .011, QIC = 366.12, supporting H_5. The intercept for the model was not significant, β = 1.75, χ^2 (1) = 0.31, p = .579. Trustworthiness as a main effect was also not significant, $\beta = 0.08$, χ^2 (1) = 0.01, $p = .912$. The main effect of trait suspicion had a significant negative influence on reuse intentions, $\beta = -1.79$, χ^2 (1) = 8.65, $p = .003$. The main effect was qualified with a two-way interaction. The interaction between trustworthiness and trait suspicion was positively significant, $\beta = 0.38$, χ^2 (1) = 6.50, $p = .011$.

4 Discussion and Conclusion

The current study explored trustworthiness perceptions, personality, and the interaction of the two as predictors of trust (i.e., code reuse). As expected, trustworthiness perceptions accounted for significant variance in code reuse. PT was not a significant predictor. These findings may be due to the scale focusing on the general beliefs about others trustworthiness, rather than computer mediated behaviors such as code review. Suspicion propensity had a significant negative effect on use intentions. When reviewing software, a developer may not yet understand the code, inducing uncertainty with regard to its trustworthiness and reliability. Developers that tend to address this uncertainty by seeking out and processing information about the code, while also perceiving the potential for malicious intentions in the code, will be less likely to reuse the code. The current study also found an interaction effect between trustworthiness perceptions and trait suspicion. The effect was positive, suggesting that trait suspicion strengthens the relationship between perceived trustworthiness and trust. From an information processing perspective, results indicate that trustworthiness perceptions are trust-relevant information about a referent that the trustee can use to inform their trust decisions. Those that are naturally higher in suspicion, and therefore cognitive activation, should have a higher propensity to systematically process information in the face of uncertainty. These results also support Mayer et al.'s [1] hypothesis that individual differences moderate the trustworthiness-trust relationship. The study contributes to the current literature by providing new insight for the trust process. The study also suggests that an understanding of a developer's personality may be useful for personnel selection for software development teams.

References

1. Mayer, R.C., Davis, J.H., Schoorman, F.D.: An integrative model of organizational trust. Acad. Manag. Rev. **20**, 709–734 (1995). https://doi.org/10.5465/AMR.1995.9508080335
2. Lee, J.D., See, K.A.: Trust in automation: designing for appropriate reliance. Hum. Factors **46**, 50–80 (2004). https://doi.org/10.1518/hfes.46.1.50_30392
3. Frakes, W.B., Kang, K.: Software reuse research: status and future. IEEE Trans. Softw. Eng. **31**, 529–536 (2005). https://doi.org/10.1109/TSE.2005.85
4. Banker, R.D., Kauffman, R.J.: Reuse and productivity in integrated computer-aided software engineering: an empirical study. MIS Q. **14**, 375–401 (1991). https://doi.org/10.2307/249649
5. Lim, W.C.: Effects of reuse on quality, productivity, and economics. IEEE Softw. **11**, 23–30 (1994). https://doi.org/10.1109/52.311048

6. Alarcon, G.M., Militello, L.G., Ryan, P., Jessup, S.A., Calhoun, C.S., Lyons, J.B.: A descriptive model of computer code trustworthiness. J. Cognit. Eng. Decis. Mak. **11**, 107–121 (2017). https://doi.org/10.1177/1555343416657236
7. Alarcon, G.M., Ryan, T.J.: Trustworthiness perceptions of computer code: a heuristic-systematic processing model. In: Proceedings of 51st Hawaii International Conference on System Sciences, pp. 5384–5393 (2018). http://hdl.handle.net/10125/50560
8. Alarcon, G.M., Gamble, R., Jessup, S.A., Walter, C., Ryan, T.J., Wood, D.W., Calhoun, C.: Application of the heuristic-systematic model to computer code trustworthiness: the influence of reputation and transparency. Cogent Psychol. **4**, 1389640 (2017). https://doi.org/10.1080/23311908.2017.1389640
9. Chaiken, S.: Heuristic versus systematic information processing and the use of source versus message cues in persuasion. J. Pers. Soc. Psychol. **39**, 752–766 (1980). https://doi.org/10.1037/0022-3514.39.5.752
10. Chen, S., Duckworth, K., Chaiken, S.: Motivated heuristic and systematic processing. Psychol. Inq. **10**, 44–49 (1999). https://doi.org/10.1207/s15327965pli1001_6
11. Funder, D.C.: The Personality Puzzle. WW Norton & Co, New York (1997)
12. Cruz, S., da Silva, F.Q., Capretz, L.F.: Forty years of research on personality in software engineering: a mapping study. Comput. Hum. Behav. **46**, 94–113 (2015). https://doi.org/10.1016/j.chb.2014.12.008
13. Sfetsos, P., Stamelos, I., Angelis, L., Deligiannis, I.: An experimental investigation of personality types impact on pair effectiveness in pair programming. Empirical Softw. Eng. **14**, 187–266 (2009). https://doi.org/10.1007/s10664-008-9093-5
14. Soomro, A.B., Salleh, N., Mendes, E., Grundy, J., Burch, G., Nordin, A.: The effect of software engineers' personality traits on team climate and performance: a systematic literature review. Inf. Softw. Technol. **73**, 52–65 (2016). https://doi.org/10.1016/j.infsof.2016.01.006
15. Jones, S.L., Shah, P.P.: Diagnosing the locus of trust: a temporal perspective for trustor, trustee, and dyadic influences on perceived trustworthiness. J. Appl. Psychol. **101**, 392–414 (2016). https://doi.org/10.1037/apl0000041
16. Calhoun, C., Bobko, P., Schuelke, M., Jessup, S., Ryan, T., Walter, C., Gamble, R.F., Hirshfield, L., Bowling, N., Bragg, C., Khazon, S.: Suspicion, Trust, and Automation (SRA International Inc. Publication No. AFRL-RH-WP-TR-2017-0002) (2017). https://pdfs.semanticscholar.org/de09/24c9e525b8003a28c75eec1554baacb6d15a.pdf
17. Mayer, R.C., Davis, J.H.: The effect of the performance appraisal system on trust for management: a field quasi-experiment. J. Appl. Psychol. **84**, 123–136 (1999). https://doi.org/10.1037/0021-9010.84.1.123
18. Google: Java Style Guidelines (2014). https://google.github.io/styleguide/javaguide.html
19. Zeger, S.L., Liang, K.Y., Albert, P.S.: Models for longitudinal data: a generalized estimating equation approach. Biometrics **44**, 1049–1060 (1988). https://doi.org/10.2307/2531734
20. Pan, W.: Akaike's information criterion in generalized estimating equations. Biometrics **57**, 120–125 (2001). https://doi.org/10.1111/j.0006-341X.2001.00120.x

Don't Lie to Me: Tracking Eye Movement and Mouse Trajectory to Detect Deception in Sharing Economy

Ping Wu[1], Jie Gu[2(✉)], and Tian Lu[1]

[1] Fudan University, Shanghai 200433, China
[2] Shanghai Academy of Social Sciences, Shanghai 200235, China
gujie@sass.org.cn

Abstract. As trust and security are key for the sustainability of sharing economy, it is important to detect deceptive information and screen out suspicious users. This study aims to design a new paradigm to identify deceptive information based on eye movement and mouse trajectory. A collaborative travelling experiment environment is developed to collect data. By tracking and analyzing abnormal user reactions and the consistency between eye movement and mouse trajectory, this research-in-progress work expects to distinguish lie-telling users from honest ones. Our design is expected to improve the efficiency to detect deceptive information and identify suspicious users.

Keywords: Nuanced behavioral cue · Eye movement · Mouse trajectory HCI · Deception detection

1 Research Background

Sharing economy is one of the most distinctive business phenomenon in the last few years [1]. Sharing economy, also known as collaborative consumption, depicts the economic model that consumers conduct sharing activities in various forms of renting, travelling or trading [2]. The concept of "sharing" originated from resource exchange in acquaintance community made up of family members or friends. However, the adherence to the offline acquaintance network constrains the flow of resources. In recent years, the advance of information technology, such as mobile Internet, social networking and digital payment, has given new impetus to sharing economy. On the one hand, the technology-supported sharing platforms enable resource sharing among online strangers, pushing the collaborative activities forward to a larger scale of user population. On the other hand, as collaborative activities (e.g. travelling or renting) often request offline face-to-face contact, interaction between strangers entail more risk than regular ecommerce [3].

As security are key for the sustainability of sharing economy, it is important to detect deceptive information and screen out suspicious users with malicious intention. Most of these sharing platforms request real-name registration and rely on information that is directly submitted by users. While the current information review system is necessary and helpful in detecting users who use faked identity, it still has some

C. Stephanidis (Ed.): HCII Posters 2018, CCIS 850, pp. 377–381, 2018.
https://doi.org/10.1007/978-3-319-92270-6_54

characteristics that limit its efficiency. First, the detection of faked identity demands external database that is reliable for information comparison. The richness and reliability of external information determines the accuracy of deception detection. Second, it takes manual effort for users to input information, and it also takes time for the review process. The manual effort and waiting time may result in the loss of some "inpatient" first-time users. Third, although the identity review process can screen out users who use faked personal information, it cannot be used to detect deceptive information or malicious intention dynamically for each single transaction. An alternative method is to ask users to display purpose for each sharing activity. However, judgements based on verbal answers and subjective commitments tend to be biased, because people can easily lie in their self-reported information [4].

Drawing on this background, an automated online detection system is therefore important to assure the security of sharing economy. The development of HCI research and the advance of nuanced behavioral analytics make it possible to track and analyze nuanced cues such as eye movement or mouse movement. Previous research suggested that these nuanced behavioral cues indicate concealed information about individuals' true purpose or intention [4]. To this end, this study developed an experiment environment in which peer-to-peer interview is designed and users' reaction including verbal answers and non-verbal nuanced HCI behaviors are collected. The collaborative travelling scenario is used in our experiment because traveling with strangers entail risks and thus it is important to detect faked information and lie-telling users. "WebGazer" and "MouseTracker" are embedded in the interactive experimental interface to collect users' eye movement data and mouse trajectory data. Basically, eye movement and mouse click represent input/output in information processing. This research-in-progress work expects that abnormal temporal reaction and mismatch between eye movement and mouse movement may indicate a suspicious and possibly deceptive response.

2 Experiment Design

Most of the user screening procedures are to manually vetting information that is directly submitted by users, but fail to account for nuanced cues that are spontaneously produced during human-computer interaction. As with the advancement of noninvasive sensors, it is possible and valuable to track and analyze nuanced behavioral cues without physical contact.

This study aims to design a new paradigm to identify deceptive information based on eye movement and mouse trajectory. Eye movement and mouse click represent input/output in information processing. We choose to use these two nuanced behavioral indicators because they appear consistently during HCI process and the nuanced movements are hard for people to purposely control. Since previous research suggested that no single behavioral or physiological variation correlates perfectly with deception [5], we combine the two indicators, rather than rely on single one, to improve the precision of "lie-spotting" in HCI process. Our basic idea is: abnormal temporal reaction and a mismatch between input and output may reflect a suspicious and possibly deceptive response. For the latter one, if a user looks at answer A but clicks at answer B, the answer should be treated with caution.

An interactive web-based interface is developed to simulate the HCI process between users on an online travelling platform. To catch eye movement on fine granularity level, we embedded "Webgazer" into the interactive web interface (https://webgazer.cs.brown.edu/#home). Webgazer uses webcams to infer the eye-gaze locations of web visitors on a page in real time. The eye tracking model it contains self-calibrates by watching web visitors interact with the web page and trains a mapping between the features of the eye and positions on the screen. To catch mouse dynamics, we embeded "MouseTracker" to collect data (http://www.mousetracker.org/). MouseTracker is a free software package that allows researchers to record and analyze hand movements traveling toward potential responses on the screen (via the x, y coordinates of the computer mouse).

A lab experiment is arranged to collect empirical data. College students will be recruited as experiment subjects. A sharing travel scenario is developed in which students are told that a platform user is inviting them to share a trip in order to reduce the economic cost. Before the formal experiment, all subjects will be asked to fill a questionnaire that contain questions about their personal information and their travel preference. Subjects will be asked to give honest answers. Their answers will used as a baseline for lie spotting.

Subjects will be randomly split into two groups. In the honest group, subjects will be told that they are invited by a goodwill traveler to join a trip in order to share and reduce the travel cost. Subjects will be presented a series of questions that the traveler care about and they will be asked to give honest answer. To motivate them to behave honest, they will be told that those who give inconsistent answer with the preliminary survey results will be deleted and only honest ones can be awarded (monetary: 30 RMB or non-monetary: A-score mark for subjects' lab work).

In the lie group, subjects will be given a plot that they should follow in the experiment. In the plot, subjects are told that they are employees for a travel agency, rather than a cooperative travel partner. They should do whatever possible to persuade the traveler to go to the named destination and buy travel products from the agency. Their task is to lie about their personal information and true intention. To motivate subjects to lie, they will be told that only successful role players would get award (monetary: 30 RMB or non-monetary: A-score mark for subjects' lab work). Those who tell the true answer or fail to conceal their identity will be removed from the experiment.

To control for external interference, the interface is designed as a question-answer system. All subjects will be told that the travelers will first ask them a series of questions to determine whether they are the appropriate one for the planned trip. Questions include their personal information, travel intention, travel preference and prior knowledge and experience about the alternative destinations. The question interface will be displayed as Fig. 1. All questions will appear from the central of the interface and four options will be located at the four corners. After the subject click on one option, the next question will immediately appear on the interface. 30 questions will be displayed one by one. Some questions may be repeatedly asked but alter the words usage or the order of options. The repetition is to check the consistency of one's answers.

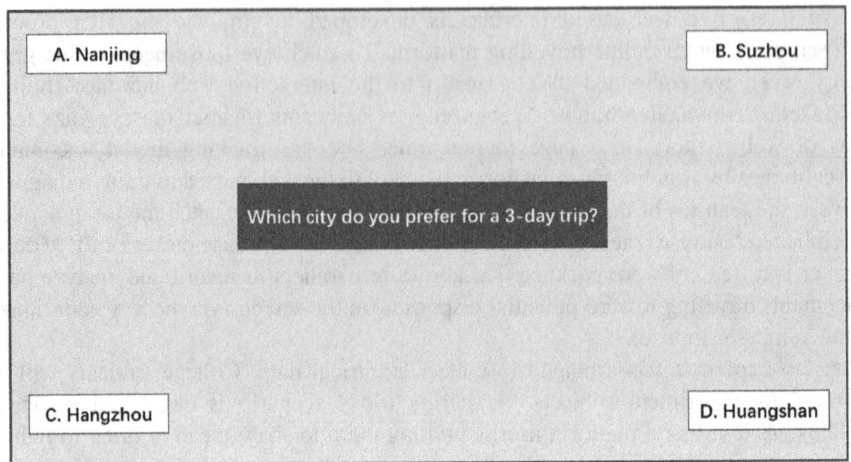

Fig. 1. Example for the interface

3 Expected Results

While the verbal answer cannot tell the two groups apart if we do not have the baseline answers, the nuanced behavioral cues may help in lie-spotting. For personal information questions, for example, past travel experience, honest subjects will react quicker than lie-telling subjects because they do not need extra time and effort to invoke the faked information. For the cognitive questions, for example, which city do you prefer for a 3-day trip, honest subjects will take time to think and compare alternative options. However, lie-telling subjects will respond quicker because the answer is pre-determined rather than from their own cognitive processing.

The above differences are expected to be reflected in the pattern of eye movement and mouse dynamics. A natural eye movement trajectory starts from the central question, then move from A to B to C to D. For personal information questions, honest subjects will (1) move their eye point smoothly; (2) move mouse consistently especially for complex questions with long answers; (3) stop at one answer and click it with no hesitation. In contrast, lie-telling subjects will (1) have small eye pause at the option that reflects their true information; (2) move their mouse directly to the faked answer but with a longer respond time. Therefore, the eye movements and mouse dynamics of lie-telling subjects will show a slightly inconsistence due to the nuanced stumbling action at the true answer. For the cognitive questions, honest subjects will (1) move their eye point around the alternative answers several times; (2) move mouse consistently to help them for information input; (3) have small hesitation among alternatives until click at the final one. However, lie-telling ones will (1) move eye point to detect the pre-determined answer; (2) quick click at the answer without taking a thinking time. A quicker respond time and still an inconsistent trajectory are expected for cognitive questions.

To quantitatively analyze the HCI data, two types of information will be coded and analyzed: pause time/response time, and movement trajectory. The latter one will be analyzed in a x- and y-coordinate system and geographic analysis will be use. Due to the limited lab resources, our formal experiment has not been conducted yet. However, the preparation work of development of the travel sharing interface and the subject recruitment have been completed. We expect to conduct the experiment in the coming semester.

4 Contribution

As trust and security are key for the sustainability of sharing economy, it is important to detect deceptive information and screen out suspicious users. However, judgements based on subjective commitments and answers tend to be biased, because people can easily lie in their self-reported information. This research-in-progress work is expected to improve the efficiency to detect deceptive information and identify suspicious users by integrating nuanced behavioral cues of eye movement and mouse movement. The lie-spotting work based on automated nuanced behavioral analytics reduces the time and cost associated with the screening process.

References

1. Zervas, G., Proserpio, D., Byers, J.W.: The rise of the sharing economy: estimating the impact of Airbnb on the hotel industry. J. Mark. Res. **54**(5), 687–705 (2017)
2. Tussyadiah, I.P.: An exploratory study on drivers and deterrents of collaborative consumption in travel. In: Tussyadiah, I., Inversini, A. (eds.) Information and Communication Technologies in Tourism 2015, pp. 817–830. Springer, Cham (2015). https://doi.org/10.1007/978-3-319-14343-9_59
3. Ert, E., Fleischer, A., Magen, N.: Trust and reputation in the sharing economy: the role of personal photos in Airbnb. Tour. Manag. **55**, 62–73 (2016)
4. Pentland, S.J., Twyman, N.W., Burgoon, J.K., Nunamaker, J.F., Diller, C.B.R.: A video-based screening system for automated risk assessment using nuanced facial features. J. Manag. Inf. Syst. **34**(4), 970–993 (2018)
5. DePaulo, B.M., Lindsay, J.J., Malone, B.E., Muhlenbruck, L., Charlton, K., Cooper, H.: Cues to deception. Psychol. Bull. **129**(1), 74 (2003)

Experimental Study Based on Impacts of Time Pressure on Human-Computer Interaction Performance

Yi-qian Zhao(✉), Tian-yu Wu, and Ya-jun Li

School of Design Art and Media, Nanjing University of Science and Technology, Nanjing, Jiangsu Province City, People's Republic of China
1355256445@qq.com

Abstract. According to studies, time pressure is a key factor impacting human-computer interaction performance. In an appointed task, the time pressure can be controlled by testing and designing a quota time length. In this paper, simulations and studies were conducted on the impact of time pressure on human-computer interaction performance through numerical calculation and input experiments. Through comparative analysis of experiment data, the impact of time pressure on numerical calculation and input performance, together with the changing pattern, was obtained. The human-computer interaction performance could be promoted if the pattern obtained from the experiment was applied to practical human-computer interactions and a reasonable time pressure was regulated and exerted by setting quota time lengths for specific interaction tasks.

Keywords: Time pressure · Quota time
Human-computer interaction performance · Numerical calculation and input
Interaction efficiency · Interaction accuracy rate

1 Study of Human-Computer Interaction Theory

With the study standard as a reference, the human-computer interaction process at the overall human-computer interaction logic level contains three links, namely information input, information processing, and information output [1]. At the level of human-computer interaction relations, there are many factors affecting human-computer interaction performance. According to analysis conducted by statistical software, time pressure has a great impact on human-computer interaction performance [2].

2 Study of Time Pressure Theory

For an assigned task in the human-computer interaction, if a quota time is set for this task, the person performing the task will feel pressure, that is, the time pressure, which can comprehensively reflect the adequacy and inadequacy of the quota time set for completing the task. With the time pressure evaluation standard as a reference, the intensity of time pressure in an assigned task can be measured according to the ratio of

C. Stephanidis (Ed.): HCII Posters 2018, CCIS 850, pp. 382–389, 2018.
https://doi.org/10.1007/978-3-319-92270-6_55

the actually available time to the time perceived to be needed [2]. The calculation formula is:

$$T_p = \frac{T_R}{T_C} \qquad T_R \neq 0,\ T_R \in (0,\ +\infty) \tag{1}$$

where TP represents time pressure, TR represents the actually available time for the completion of the assigned task, namely, the quota time, the length of which can be determined and set according to the assigned task. TC represents the time perceived to be needed for completing the task, which, according to the minimum output principle, is usually longer than the quota time [2]; The smaller the ratio of the two is, and thus the higher the TP (time pressure) is, and vice versa.

3 Experiment of the Impact of Time Pressure on Human-Computer Interaction Performance

3.1 Experiment Contents and Methods

The experiment design requirements include that: the experiment task should be well ordered and logic, contain input, processing and output links, and control the difficulty of the experiment task, so that the experiment can accurately reflect the information input, processing and output links in the practical human-computer interaction process and reduce the errors. Thus, this study used a numerical calculation and input experiment commonly used in human-computer ergonomical studies. So the performance of the experiment tasks included three processes, namely, numerical recognition, numerical calculation, and result output. Thus human-computer interaction process was simulated based on numerical calculation and input. In the experiment, the number and difficulty of tasks were controlled, different time pressures were reflected by the different lengths of quota time, and a study was conducted on the impacts of different time pressures on the performance of assigned experiment tasks.

In conclusion, with the standard for designing ergonomic experiments as a reference, the experiment samples were calculated and input through addition and subtraction of figures smaller than 10. The contents of the samples were 100 randomly generated calculation questions of addition and subtraction of figures smaller than 10. The test objects calculated and input the contents of the experiment samples respectively.

The experiment consisted of four stages, namely, preparatory experiment, validity experiment, formal experiment, and experiment result analysis. The preparatory experiment determined the average value and standard deviation of the time taken by the test objects to complete a numerical calculation and input task, and the corresponding quota time under no time pressure was determined based on the time pressure study standard. Then, the corresponding quota time under different time pressures was gotten one by one through calculation based on different pressure coefficients stated in the standard. Then, validation was conducted on the validity of quota time gotten from the preparatory experiment, so as to provide a basis for the setting of independent variables in the formal experiment. The contents and form of the tasks in the formal experiment took those of the preparatory experiment as references. The independent variables were different time pressures, the dependent variables were numerical calculation and input performances, and at last, through experiment result analysis, the results delivered by the formal experiment were summarized and analyzed.

3.2 Test Objects

To reduce experiment errors and raise the reliability of results, the conditions of screening people to be test objects were that: 50 people were randomly selected from 100 NUST students volunteering to participate in this experiment, including 25 male students and 25 female students at 20–25 years old, 22.8 years old on average, with a standard deviation of 0.91, and they were healthy undergraduate or graduate students with normal thoughts and logic and usually handling things with right hand.

3.3 Experiment Equipment and Software

The hardware equipment in this experiment was a laptop of Asus G60VW6700, with an operating hardware environment of Intel Core i7 CPU 3.6 Ghz. Its display part was 15.6" LED display screen of the laptop, with a resolution ratio of 1920*1080 and a refresh rate of 60 Hz. The experiment program was designed and programmed with Quiz Creator software. As a powerful test question producing tool, Quiz Creator can create and evaluate test questions as well as output and analyze test results accurately [3].

3.4 Preparatory Experiment

The fifty test objects conducted the experiment tasks as per the procedures of the preparatory experiment in turn. After every test object completed the task of the preparatory experiment correctly, the total time taken to perform the task was output. Through SPSS 23.0 was used to conduct descriptive statistics on the values of time taken by the fifty test objects to complete the task of the preparatory experiment, which is shown in Table 1:

Table 1. Descriptive statistics of values of time taken by the fifty test objects to complete the preparatory experiment task

Time taken to complete the experiment task (S)	Maximum	Minimum	Average value	Standard deviation	Number of valid test objects
	83.86	51.26	69.37	6.398	50

The standard for judging the intensity of time pressure was obtained from the study of Ordonez and Lehman and the study of Weening and Maarleveld, and this standard was widely accepted in studies [1]. In this study, with this standard as a reference, the average value of time taken to complete the experiment task was taken as the quota time under no time pressure. The value of time 50% lower than the average value was taken as the quota time under a high time pressure [1]. Then, the corresponding quota time under low, relatively low, medium, and relatively high time pressures was calculated according to different time pressure coefficients specified in the standard. The lower the time pressure coefficient was, the shorter the quota time was, and vice versa. Time pressure state, coefficient, and quota time are shown in the following Table 2 respectively:

Table 2. Setting of corresponding quota time under different time pressures

Time pressure state	No pressure	Low pressure	Relatively low pressure	Medium pressure	Relatively high pressure	High pressure
Time pressure coefficient	1	0.88	0.79	0.68	0.59	0.49
Quota time (S)	69.37	61.05	54.80	47.17	40.93	33.99

3.5 Validity Test

Validation was conducted on the validity of the quota time determined and set in the preparatory experiment. To conduct the validation, Likert scale was used in the form of questionnaire inquiries to quantitatively evaluate the pressure subjectively felt by the test objects conducting the experiment tasks under different time pressures, with the evaluated data being processed and analyzed. First, SPSS 23.0 was used to conduct descriptive statistics on quantitative data of the test objects' subjective feelings about pressure, and the statistical results showed that such feelings increased with the increase of time pressure. Then, the data of descriptive statistics was tested by testing F values in SPSS 23.0. The test results were that: F(no and low time pressure) = 55.69, P = 0.000; F(low and relatively low time pressure) = 69.36, P = 0.000; F(relatively low and medium time pressure) = 71.68, P = 0.000; F(medium and relatively high time pressure) = 78.87, P = 0.000; and F(relatively high and high time pressure) = 85.59, P = 0.000. It showed that there were significant differences in the pressure felt by the test objects conducting the experiment tasks under different time pressures. The quota time obtained from the preparatory test could be used for the setting of variables in the formal experiment.

3.6 Formal Experiment

In the formal experiment, fifty test objects performed the assigned experiment task under different time pressures respectively. During the experiment, when they completed the task in the quota time or the experiment time exceeded the quota time, the experiment would end, with experiment data being output. The procedures of the formal experiment are as shown in the following Fig. 1.

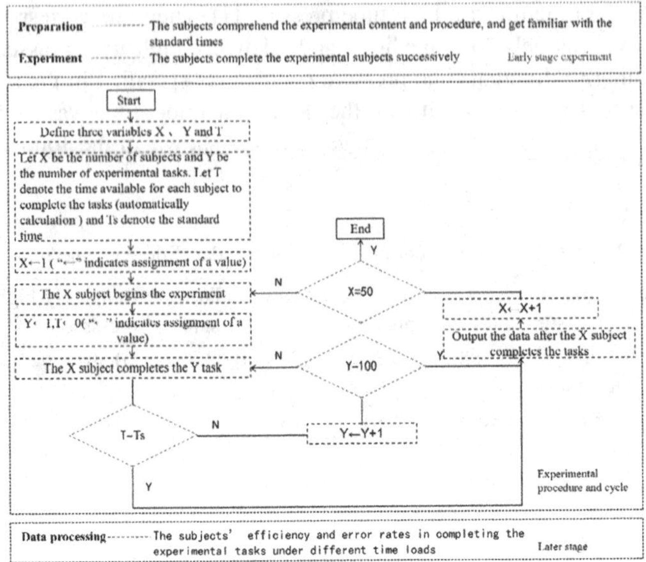

Fig. 1. Formal experiment procedures

3.7 Experiment Evaluation Index

With human-machine interaction performance evaluation standard as the reference, this experiment evaluated the task completion results based on numerical calculation and input performance. The performance consisted of two parts, namely, the efficiency and accuracy rate of numerical calculation and input [5].

The formula for calculating the numerical calculation and input efficiency is as follows:

$$C = \frac{N_X - F_X}{N_X} \times 100\% \qquad X \in [1, 50],\ N \in [1, 100], N^* = 100 \tag{2}$$

where E represents numerical calculation and input efficiency; NX represents the number N of tasks actually completed by the test object X within the quota time in the formal experiment; N*x represents the number N* of tasks required to be completed by the test object X within the quota time in the formal experiment [5].

The formula for calculating the numerical calculation and input accuracy rate is as follows:

$$E = \frac{N_X}{N_X^*} \times 100\% \qquad X \in [1, 50],\ \mathrm{F} \in [1, 100], N \in 100 \tag{3}$$

where C represents numerical calculation and input accuracy rate; FX represents the number F of mistakes among tasks actually completed by the test object X within the quota time in the formal experiment; NX represents the number N of tasks actually completed by the test object X within the quota time in the formal experiment [5].

The formula for calculating the numerical calculation and input performance is as follows:

$$Q = \frac{N_X}{N_X^*} \times \frac{N_X - F_X}{N_X} \times 100\% \quad (4)$$

where Q represents numerical calculation and input performance and it is the product of efficiency and accuracy rate [5]; the higher the efficiency and accuracy rate of numerical calculation and input are, the higher the performance is, and vice versa.

3.8 Discussion and Analysis of Experimental Results

According to deep comparative analysis of the performance of the test objects conducting assigned experiment tasks under different time pressures, a summary was made with respect to the pattern of how the time pressure impacted the performance of numerical calculation and input. Analysis was conducted on the impact of time pressure on numerical calculation and input performance. SPSS 23.0 was used to conduct descriptive statistics on the experiment results, which is shown in Fig. 2.

Time pressure state	Maximum(%)	Minimum (%)	Average(%)	Standard deviation	Number of valid test objects
No time pressure (pressure coefficient: 1)	98.00	76.00	88.16	5.571	50
Low time pressure (pressure coefficient: 0.88)	99.00	80.00	90.72	4.131	50
Relatively low time pressure (pressure coefficient: 0.79)	88.00	69.00	76.58	4.603	50
Medium time pressure (pressure coefficient: 0.68)	75.00	55.00	66.22	4.196	50
Relatively high time pressure (pressure coefficient: 0.59)	65.00	51.00	57.54	3.829	50
High time pressure (pressure coefficient: 0.49)	55.00	39.00	46.22	4.344	50

Fig. 2. Descriptive statistics of numerical calculation and input performance under different time pressures

According to the statistical indexes of the average value in the descriptive statistics, the performance of numerical calculation and input under low time pressure is the highest (90.72%); it is slightly higher than that under no time pressure (88.16%); and that under high time pressure is the lowest (46.22%).

Based on this, a further study was conducted on the pattern of how the numerical calculation and input performance changed with the time pressure, which was to conduct deep analysis on the average value, maximum, and minimum of the descriptive statistics about the performance by using the statistical diagram, which is shown in Fig. 3.

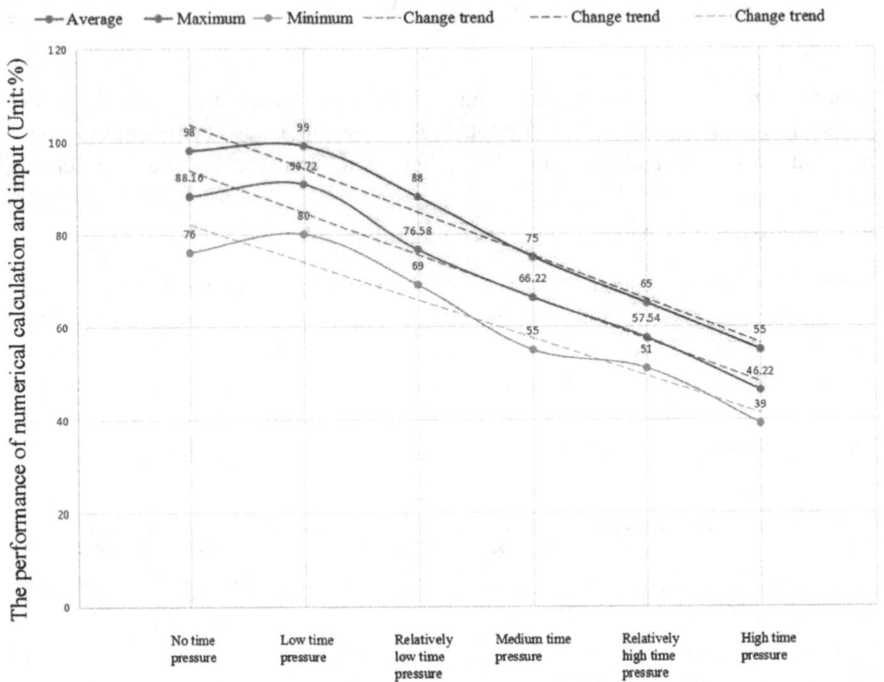

Fig. 3. Pattern of how the numerical calculation and input performance changed with the time pressure

As shown in the figure, the maximum, minimum, and average value of the numerical calculation and input performance of the test objects all show a trend of slightly increasing and then significantly decreasing under six different time pressures, namely, no time pressure, low time pressure, relatively low time pressure, medium time pressure, relatively high time pressure, and high time pressure. This means that, as the time pressure increases gradually, the performance of numerical calculation and input increases slightly first and then drops significantly. Among these pressures, the difference in performance under no time pressure and low time pressure is minor.

The judgment standard for the intensity of the time pressure was applied [5]. In the case of an assigned task, the coefficient of no time pressure, that is 1, was taken as a reference, and the length of the quota time was set as per a low time pressure coefficient of 0.88. The performance of numerical calculation and input were raised accordingly by selecting proper time pressure. With the time pressure coefficient being decreased further, that is, the shortening of the quota time, the time pressure increased gradually and exceeded the reasonable scope. The performance dropping correspondingly.

4 Conclusion

The following study conclusions were drawn by extending the study results and pattern of numerical calculation and input to the practical human-computer interaction occasions:

In the human-computer interaction process, its performance showed a changing pattern of increasing first and dropping then with the increase of time pressure. Compared with the occasions without any time pressure, a reasonable time pressure could make people in the interaction more focused and concentrated and thus deliver better human-computer interaction performance.

In practical human-computer interaction occasions, with the experiment study method being a reference, the time pressure was controlled by setting the quota time length of the assigned task. First, a preparatory experiment was conducted to obtain the time taken under no time pressure. Then, the corresponding quota time under a low time pressure was set by referring to the standard of time pressure coefficient. After that, a reasonable time pressure was given to improve the efficiency and accuracy rate of human-computer interaction so as to maximize the performance and reduce human errors effectively.

Acknowledgement. This study is supported by the Project supported by the National Social Science Foundation of China (Project No. 16BSH127).

References

1. Ordonez, L., Iii, L.B.: Decisions under time pressure: how time constraint affects risky decision making. Organ. Behav. Hum. Decis. Process. **71**(2), 121–140 (1997)
2. Baer, M., Oldham, G.R.: The curvilinear relation between experienced creative time pressure and creativity: moderating effects of openness to experience and support for creativity. J. Appl. Psychol. **91**(4), 963–970 (2006)
3. Walrath, L.C., Backs, R.W.: Time stress interacts with coding, density, and search type in visual display search. Hum. Factors Ergonomics Soc. Ann. Meeting Proc. **33**(20), 1496–1500 (1989)
4. Kawado, M., Hinotsu, S., Matsuyama, Y., et al.: A comparison of error detection rates between the reading aloud method and the double data entry method. Control. Clin. Trials **24** (5), 560 (2003)
5. Svenson, O., Edland, A.: Change of preferences under time pressure: choices and judgements. Scand. J. Psychol. **28**(4), 322–330 (1987)

Social Media and Analytics

Multi-dimensional Echo Chambers: Language and Sentiment Structure of Twitter Discussions on the *Charlie Hebdo* Case

Svetlana S. Bodrunova(✉), Ivan S. Blekanov, and Mikhail Kukarkin

St. Petersburg State University, St. Petersburg 199004, Russia
s.bodrunova@spbu.ru

Abstract. *Background.* Public discussions on social networks have trans-border and multilingual nature. This is especially true for conflictual discussions that reach global trending topics. Being part of the global public sphere, such discussions were expected by many observers to become horizontal, all-involving, and democratically efficient. But, with time, criticism towards the democratic quality of discussions in social media arose, with many works discovering the patterns of echo chambering in social networks. Even if so, there is still scarce knowledge on how affective hashtags work in terms of user clusterization, as well as on the differences between emotionally 'positive' and 'negative' hashtags. *Objectives.* We address this gap by analyzing the Twitter discussion on the *Charlie Hebdo* massacre of 2015. In this discussion, the Twittershpere has created #jesuischarlie and #jenesuispascharlie - two discussion clusters with, allegedly, opposite sentiments towards the journal's ethics and freedom of speech. *Research design.* We were interested in whether echo chambers formed both on the hashtag level (based on language use) and within a language (based on user sentiment of French-speaking users). For data collection, we used vocabulary-based Twitter crawling. For data analysis, we employed network analytics, manual coding, web graph reconstruction, and automated sentiment analysis. *Results.* Our results show that #jesuischarlie and #jenesuispascharlie are alike in language distribution, with French and English being the dominant languages and the discussions remaining within the Euro-Atlantic zone. The language-based echo chambers formed in both cases. But if #jesuiuscharlie was a clear sentiment crossroads, #jenesuispascharlie was a negative echo chamber, thus allowing us to draw conclusions about multi-layer echo chambering.

Keywords: Twitter · *Charlie Hebdo* · Sentiment analysis · Echo chambers

1 Introduction

Public discussions on social networks potentially have trans-border and multilingual nature. This comes true in heated conflictual discussions that reach global trending topics. Such discussions are expected to demonstrate 'civilizational clashes' [1].

Being part of the global public sphere, since the 1990s, such discussions were expected by many observers to be more horizontal, all-involving, and democratically

C. Stephanidis (Ed.): HCII Posters 2018, CCIS 850, pp. 393–400, 2018.
https://doi.org/10.1007/978-3-319-92270-6_56

efficient [2] than the traditional mass-mediated discussions [3]. But, with time, criticism towards the democratic quality of discussions in social media arose, with many works discovering the patterns of echo chambering and discourse polarization in social networks [4–9], which lowered the capacities of inter-group discussions and, thus, just formed an additional line of social segregation.

Object-oriented hashtagged discussions have been thoroughly studied in the 2010s, including those on political and social conflicts. But there is still scarce knowledge on whether affective hashtags [10] that convey emotions – either of solidarity with or of anger towards a particular social group – work in terms of user clusterization. Also, there is no clear understanding of comparative democratic quality of emotionally 'positive' and 'negative' hashtags in terms of echo chambering.

In this paper, we address these gaps by analyzing the Twitter discussion on the *Charlie Hebdo* massacre of 2015. In the discussion upon the mass killings, the Twittershpere has created #jesuischarlie and #jenesuispascharlie - two emotionally differing discussion clusters with, allegedly, opposite sentiments towards the journal's ethics and freedom of speech; the hashtags soon became 'role models' for online solidarity towards the victims of terrorist attacks and anthropogenic disasters.

To analyze the echo chambering patterns in the two discussions, we have focused upon two levels of echo chambers. We were wondering whether echo chambers formed on the level of a hashtag (based on language use) and within a particular language (based on user sentiment of French-speaking users).

The remainder of the paper is organized as follows. Section 2 reviews the literature on echo chambering in social media. Section 3 presents our methodology and the conduct of the research. Section 4 presents our results and discusses them.

2 User Groupings on Twitter and the Efficacy of Public Sphere

2.1 Social Media and the Public Sphere: Echo Chambers vs. Opinion Crossroads

Public sphere as a spatial metaphor for a complex of discussions and procedures with a public status and decision-making goals [11] has been amplified by the appearance of social media in the 2000s. By 1990s, it had been established in the academic literature that mediatized public sphere with traditional media playing the role of information hubs was uneven and hardly efficient in terms of access to opinion expression, as whole social groups remained under-represented, and newsmakers privileged in comparison to *vox populi*. With the appearance of social media, hopes arose that the new communicative milieus would foster horizontalization of communication and provide for democratization and higher political participation [2]. Also, hopes for better understanding and resolution of non-political inter-group conflicts existed.

But with time, these hopes fainted, as offline disparities seemed to reproduce online, including political interests, race, gender, and other inequalities [12]; emotion and affect proved to rule the discourse [10], with publics even in most democratically developed countries moving from diverse in opinion to dissonant and disconnected

[13]. With the development of social network analysis (SNA) and its application to social media research, the question of the efficacy of the public discussions in social media [14] became linked to network and structural features of the discussions, such as the influencer status [15, 16] and clusterization of users also known as user polarization [6, 7] and echo chambering [8, 9]. Some evidence was also gathered on discussion sphericules forming on the global scale just as well as nationally [17].

2.2 Why the Twitter Discussions Fragment: Linguistic Properties of Speech as Catalyzers of Echo Chambering

In early studies of social networks and its users, authors interested in testing the ability of networks to pull together users from distant locations and weak ties linked geographical distance with factors like residence of users and their language profile [18]. This is why Twitter that enabled the (arguably) quickest possible information spread across locations and languages became a major attractor of scholarly attention [19, 20]. But despite the global reach of the platform, several studies have found that people were still connected locally on Twitter [17, 21].

Along with locality and residence, linguistic factors, arguably, play a major role in user grouping on the global scale. Thus, the language(s) used by the discussion participants is the first natural barrier that is expected to make users group together and communicate within their language-based echo chambers [22], both on Twitter on the whole and within particular hashtags [23].

Other factors have also been discussed as the catalyzers of user grouping on Twitter. Among those, political attitudes lead the research agenda [6, 7]. Here, several ways to detect user clusterization exist. Of them, use of network or semantic proxies like friendship ties [24], patterns of following [25] and retweeting [26], content sharing [8, 27] etc. is till today the most prominent; another is automated analysis of user sentiment, either in general or toward an issue/actor in question (object-oriented) [28].

But all these studies depict user groupings within a single dimension; our idea is to try and trace user groupings multi-dimensionally – both on the level of a hashtag (based on language use) and within a language nebula (based on user sentiment).

2.3 The *Charlie Hebdo* Case: Emotional Hashtags and User Groupings

To search for multi-dimensional echo chambers, we have chosen the case of the *Charlie Hebdo* massacre of 2015. Here, we could hypothesize that the existence of emotionally opposite hashtags (#jesuischarlie and #jenesuispascharlie) already creates enclaves within the general discussion on the case. Then, within the hashtags, several clusters based on language structure may exist. Then, on the third level, we will look whether within the language clusters sub-clusters of sentiment form. In general, our idea is to see how exactly the language clusters correspond to the sentiment clusters in each language and whether 'positive' users within one language are linked to such in another language, while 'negative' users also group across languages in a similar way. But here we present only preliminary results that check if the user clusters may at all be detected based on language and on sentiment within a language.

2.4 Research Hypotheses

Thus, our hypotheses are the following:

H1a. Non-random user groups will be detected for both hashtags, as based on language use.

H1b. #jesuischarie will not differ from #jenesuispascharlie in their language structure, as both hashtags have reached global trending topics and are expected to show 'civilizational clashes'.

H2a. Non-random user groups will be detected within one language (French), as based on positive and negative sentiment.

H2b. #jesuischarlie will differ from #jenesuispascharlie in the grouping based on user sentiment, due to the emotional opposition of the hashtags themselves.

H3. Multi-layer echo chambering may be detected in trans-border hashtagged discussions of global reach.

3 Data Collection and Conduct of Research

3.1 Data Collection and the Datasets

Using a web crawler developed especially for the Twitter data collection, we gathered all the tweets published openly under the hashtags #jesuischarlie and #jenesuis-pascharlie (by separate crawls) within January 7 to 9, 2015, as these three days covered the active conflict (from the killings in the editorial office to the assailants' death) when the users provided virtually millions of tweets for collection.

The collected datasets included: for #jesuischarlie: 420,080 tweets; 266,904 tweeters; 719,503 users who interacted with the posted tweets (by likes, retweets, or comments); for #jenesuispascharlie: 7,698 tweets; 5,466 tweeters; 17,872 users who posted and interacted with the posted tweets (by likes, retweets, or comments).

These full datasets were later used to reconstruct the overall web graphs for the two hashtags. But the datasets were very different in size, and be able to color them with language markers, we needed to sample the users for coding having in mind the volume difference of the datasets.

3.2 Language Analysis: Sampling, Coding, and Graph Reconstruction

To answer H1a and H1b, we have coded the users for their language use and then applied these data to the datasets for web graph reconstruction.

After eliminating bots and bot-like users (those who posted over 60% of doubled tweets) as well as hashtag-only tweets, we have followed the strategy developed by the research group for previous Twitter studies [29–31], namely uniting random sampling with detection of influential users (influencers) for taking them into account. Then, we have coded all the influencers (disregarding the number of tweets they posted; for #jesuiuscharlie, 402 users, for #jenesuispascharlie, 85 users) and 'ordinary users' sampled in the feasible and comparable way. For #jenesuispascharlie that was substantially smaller, all the users with 3 and more tweets were coded (339 users); for

#jesuischarlie, the 'ordinary users' with 5 tweets or more were taken into account (9,090 users), and of them, each second was coded (4500 users).

All the sampled underwent expert reading and were coded manually marking the number of tweets in language 1, language 2, and other languages; thus, users posting on one, two, and three or more languages were defined. The languages were identified for each user; in case of rare languages, Yandex language identifier was employed.

To reconstruct the graphs, we use Gephi API algorithms openly available online. Of the available algorithms, two were chosen: Hu [32] and OpenOrd [33]; here, YifanHu-based graphs are presented, as the OpenOrd graphs require more space for presentation. We colored both the nodes (users) and the edges (connections between users). To prove that the visual nebulae are not artifacts of subjective viewership, we calculated the percentage of edges between and inside language groups, eliminating the 'loops' of self-commenting/liking by the users.

3.3 Sentiment Analysis: Sampling, Vocabulary Building, and Graph Reconstruction

After we have proved that the French-speaking users show non-random grouping in both cases (see below), we have taken them for sentiment analysis. The number of users for #jesuischarlie included 1291 user; for #jenesuispascharlie, 117 users.

Our strategy for French-language sentiment analysis was the following. We have united three sources in our vocabulary: the existing French dictionary with sentiment marking, machine translation from an additional Wordnet vocabulary, and the case-based vocabulary created from the collected tweets and manually marked for positive, negative, and neutral sentiment regardless of the case-specific meanings.

This vocabulary was applied to each tweet of the abovementioned French-speaking users; for each tweet, the sentiment was calculated. Then, the thresholds were defined: positive and negative were the users with positive(+neutral) and negative(+neutral) tweets, respectively; neutral were those with neutral tweets only; mixed were those with positive + negative(+neutral) tweets.

Then, we also checked the groupings with by calculating the percentage of edges both between and inside language groups, eliminating the 'loops' of self-commenting/liking by the users.

4 Results and Discussion

Our results are described below with regard to the hypotheses stated above.

H1a/H1b. To assess the user groupings in both hashtagged discussions, we have reconstructed the web graphs for the coded users (see Fig. 1a for #jesuischarlie and Fig. 1b for #jenesuispascharlie, respectively). What we see on the graphs are three nebulae for (a): French, English, and other European, and two for (b): French and Engish. But the results of calculations of percentage of edges between and inside groups tell that the actual grouping is slightly different from what we see with unaided eyes. For #jesuischarlie, the nebulae with density higher than the inter-group ones are French, English, and French/English (52.1%, 16.7%, and 16.9%, respectively, against

6.17% for inter-group edges) and not other European. For #jenesuispascharlie, the graph is much denser (26%), but still the same three clusters show up, with 26.2%, 22.4%, and 18.8%, respectively; in both cases, other language clusters are virtually non-existent and do not mount to 3%. As we stated in our earlier investigations [31], we have not seen a sign of 'civilizational clashes' in any of the hashtags.

Thus, H1a is proven; H1b is proven too but not due to 'civilizational clashes'.

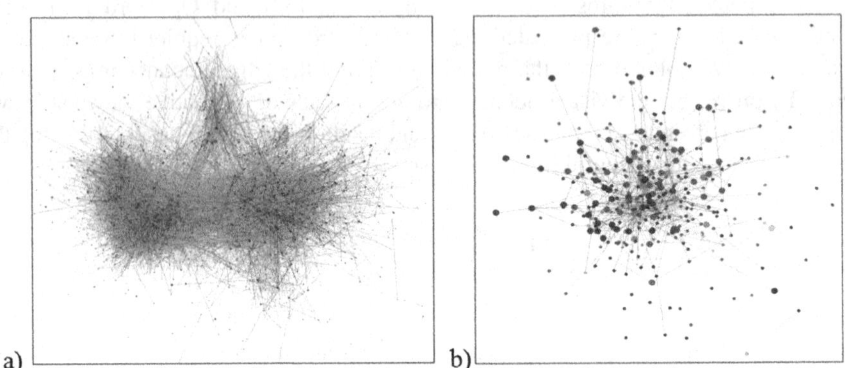

Fig. 1. The YifanHu graphs (fragments) for language distribution in (a) #jesuischarlie and (b) #jenesuispascharlie. Red: French; blue: English; lilac: French/English; green: other European. (Color figure online)

H2a/H2b. To see the user grouping and sentiment cleavages within the French-speaking parts of the discussions, we have reconstructed the web graphs for them (see Fig. 2a for #jesuischarlie and Fig. 2b for #jenesuispascharlie, respectively).

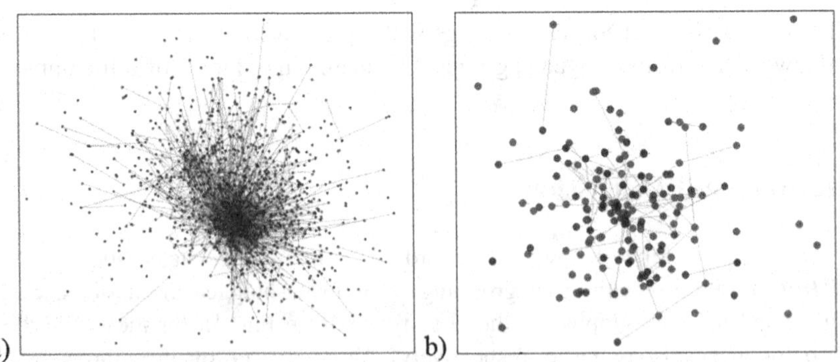

Fig. 2. The YifanHu graphs (fragments) for language distribution in (a) #jesuischarlie and (b) #jenesuispascharlie. Red: French; blue: English; lilac: French/English; green: other European. (Color figure online)

Here, H2a should be rejected for #jesuischarlie and partly supported for the second hashtag. Both in the graph and in the edge percentage calculations, it is only users with mixed sentiment who form a group (38.33% against 56.05% for the inter-group connections) in #jesuischarlie. But for #jenesuispascharlie, both mixed and negative user groups seem to have a potential for grouping (19.5% and 15% against 62.1% for inter-group connections). Thus, H2b is supported: the cases do differ.

Even with the cases of such different sizes, H3 is supported: thanks to the negative nebula in #jenesuispascharlie, we can state that echo chambers are able to form on at least two levels of the trans-border conflictual discussions of global (or, more precisely, macro-regional) reach. This adds to our understanding of the nature of public discussions in social media, even if lowers hopes for all-encompassing public spheres.

Acknowledgements. This research has been supported in full by Presidential Grants of the Russian Federation for young scholars with Doctoral degrees (grant МД-6259.2018.6).

References

1. An, J., Kwak, H., Mejova, Y., De Oger, S.A.S., Fortes, B.G.: Are you Charlie or Ahmed? Cultural pluralism in Charlie Hebdo response on Twitter. In: Proceedings of ICWSM, pp. 2–11 (2016)
2. Fuchs, C.: Social Media: A Critical Introduction. Sage, London (2017)
3. McQuail, D.: Media Performance. Sage, Thousand Oaks (1992)
4. Sunstein, C.: Republic.com. Princeton University Press, Princeton (2001)
5. Sunstein, C.: The law of group polarization. J. Polit. Philos. **10**(2), 175–195 (2002)
6. Barberá, P., Jost, J.T., Nagler, J., Tucker, J.A., Bonneau, R.: Tweeting from left to right: is online political communication more than an echo chamber? Psychol. Sci. **26**(10), 1531–1542 (2015)
7. Bastos, M.T., Mercea, D., Baronchelli, A.: The spatial dimension of online echo chambers. arXiv preprint arXiv:1709.05233 (2017)
8. Colleoni, E., Rozza, A., Arvidsson, A.: Echo chamber or public sphere? Predicting political orientation and measuring political homophily in Twitter using big data. J. Commun. **64**(2), 317–332 (2014)
9. Conover, M., Ratkiewicz, J., Francisco, M.R., Gonçalves, B., Menczer, F., Flammini, A.: Political polarization on Twitter. In: Proceedings of ICWSM, vol. 133, pp. 89–96 (2011)
10. Papacharissi, Z.: Affective Publics: Sentiment, Technology, and Politics. Oxford University Press, New York (2015)
11. Kleinstüber, H.J.: Habermas and the public sphere: from a german to a European perspective. Javnost Publ. **8**(1), 95–108 (2001)
12. Daniels, J.: Race and racism in Internet studies: a review and critique. New Med. Soc. **15**(5), 695–719 (2013)
13. Pfetsch, B.: Dissonant and disconnected public spheres as challenge for political communication research. Javnost Publ. **25**, 1–8 (2018)
14. Bruns, A., Highfield, T.: Social media and the public sphere. In: The Routledge Companion to Social Media and Politics, vol. 56 (2015)
15. Bodrunova, S.S., Blekanov, I.S., Maksimov, A.: Measuring influencers in Twitter ad-hoc discussions: active users vs. internal networks in the discourse on Biryuliovo bashings in 2013. In: Proceedings of AINL, pp. 1–10. IEEE (2016)

16. Bodrunova, S.S., Litvinenko, A.A., Blekanov, I.S.: Influencers on the Russian Twitter: institutions vs. people in the discussion on migrants. In: Proceedings of EGOSE, pp. 212–222. ACM (2016)
17. Cammaerts, B., Audenhove, L.V.: Online political debate, unbounded citizenship, and the problematic nature of a transnational public sphere. Polit. Commun. **22**(2), 179–196 (2005)
18. Takhteyev, Y., Gruzd, A., Wellman, B.: Geography of Twitter networks. Soc. Netw. **34**(1), 73–81 (2012)
19. Lotan, G., et al.: The revolutions were tweeted: information flows during the 2011 Tunisian and Egyptian revolutions. Int. J. Commun. **5**, 1375–1405 (2011)
20. Hong, L., Convertino, G., Chi, E.H.: Language matters in Twitter: a large-scale study. In: Proceedings of ICWSM, pp. 518–521 (2011)
21. Yardi, S., Boyd, D.: Dynamic debates: an analysis of group polarization over time on Twitter. Bullet. Sci. Technol. Soc. **30**(5), 316–327 (2010)
22. Chen, W., Tu, F., Zheng, P.: A transnational networked public sphere of air pollution: analysis of a Twitter network of PM2. 5 from the risk society perspective. Inf. Commun. Soc. **20**(7), 1005–1023 (2017)
23. Bastos, M.T., Puschmann, C., Travitzki, R.: Tweeting across hashtags: overlapping users and the importance of language, topics, and politics. In: Proceedings of the 24th ACM Conference on Hypertext and Social Media, pp. 164–168. ACM (2013)
24. Barberá, P., Rivero, G.: Understanding the political representativeness of Twitter users. Soc. Sci. Comput. Rev. **33**(6), 712–729 (2015)
25. Rivero, G.: Preaching to the choir: ideology and following behaviour in social media. Contemporary Soc. Sci. 1–17 (2017)
26. Calais Guerra, P.H., Meira-jr, W., Cardie, C., Kleinberg, R.: A measure of polarization on social media networks based on community boundaries. In: ICWSM Proceedings (2013)
27. Bakshy, E., Messing, S., Adamic, L.A.: Exposure to ideologically diverse news and opinion on Facebook. Science **348**(6239), 1130–1132 (2015)
28. Conover, M.D., Gonçalves, B., Ratkiewicz, J., Flammini, A., Menczer, F.: Predicting the political alignment of twitter users. In: Privacy, Security, Risk and Trust (PASSAT) and 2011 IEEE Third International Conference on Social Computing (SocialCom), pp. 192–199. IEEE (2011)
29. Authors, 2016a
30. Authors, 2016b
31. Authors, 2018
32. Hu, Y.F.: Efficient and high-quality force-directed graph drawing. Math. J. **10**, 37–71 (2005)
33. Martin, S., Brown, W.M., Klavans, R., Boyack, K.: OpenOrd: an open-source toolbox for large graph layout. In: Proceedings of the SPIE Conference on Visualization and Data Analysis (VDA), vol. 7868. https://www.researchgate.net/profile/Kevin_Boyack/publication/253087985_OpenOrd_An_Open-Source_Toolbox_for_Large_Graph_Layout/links/0deec5205279e8c66a000000.pdf

LineChange: An Analytic Framework for Automated Moderation of Crowdsourcing Systems

Brent D. Fegley(✉), Ryan Mullins, Ben Ford, and Chad Weiss

Aptima, Inc., Woburn, MA 01801, USA
bfegley@aptima.com

Abstract. If humans are more productive in collective problem-solving with a modicum of active help and guidance, then the potential of automated moderation of crowdsourcing systems has yet to be realized. Here, we present the conceptual design of an intelligent machine capable of (a) monitoring the temporal, structural, and emergent characteristics of participant behavior in a problem-solving process, and (b) modifying team structure and prompting participants for input at opportune or transitional moments in that process—by configuration, rule, or inference—to achieve collective goals and optimize output. The design is unique in treating teams as composable objects, in being scale-free, in relying on configuration and inference (not hard-coding), and in treating participant behaviors as sensory input.

Keywords: Crowdsourcing · Insourcing · Network generation Automated facilitation · Decision support

1 Overview

Despite reported successes of human collective intelligence in collaborative problem-solving and decision-making, the power and utility of crowdsourcing remains encumbered by the nature and facilitation of its tasking. Crowdsourcing continues to be explored in a variety of contexts where focus tends toward highly structured, relatively simplistic, and parallelizable tasks, including, but not limited to, text editing [3] and dataset development [14]. For example, the Good Judgment Project [11] excels in part because of the elegance of its methods for eliciting and scoring forecasts from participants who work in parallel, and largely independently, on tasks that require an assessment of event probability, for which participants are personally accountable. In contrast, research shows that complex problem-solving by groups achieves more effective outcomes (collectively and interpersonally), especially when actively facilitated. However, expert human facilitators are rare; and the resources and coordination necessary to engage them represent significant hurdles to their use. (Note [1,16], among others.) Opportunity exists to address problems of increased social and technical

C. Stephanidis (Ed.): HCII Posters 2018, CCIS 850, pp. 401–408, 2018.
https://doi.org/10.1007/978-3-319-92270-6_57

complexity—especially those involving defeasible and incendiary arguments—through automated facilitation of ideation, collaboration, and consensus.

Here, we present work-in-progress to design a framework for automated moderation, facilitation, and intervention of participant activities within a hypothetical crowdsourced problem-solving process. We call the underlying analytic framework *LineChange*. We hypothesize that in problem-solving, like hockey, better outcomes may be obtained by varying the lineup of participants throughout the endeavor.[1] In an idealized implementation of this process, an intelligent machine (i.e., background service) monitors the temporal, structural, and emergent characteristics of participant behavior and then, at opportune or transitional moments, by configuration, rule, or inference, prompts participants for input or modifies team structure.

2 Related Work

If a goal of crowdsourced problem-solving is enlightened decision-making, then brainstorming, debate, and consensus are surely corresponding high-level objectives. These objectives have been discussed variously and extensively in the context of non-cooperative game theory, political science, and economics, as well as IS (information system)-centric research on group decision support systems (GSS), electronic brainstorming (EBS), and computer-supported cooperative work (CSCW; e.g., [2,5,9,13]).

Brainstorming (ideation) provides a useful way to understand problem-solving. Problems cannot be solved without some amount of creative thinking; but *quality* does not necessarily follow *quantity* in idea creation. Briggs and Reinig [4] identify six factors ("boundaries") that affect the quality of ideation: *mental ability*, a "function of both intelligence and domain-relevant expertise"; *solution space*, a group-level effect, the continuum of which extends from closed-ended tasks that have a finite number of solutions to open-ended tasks that have an infinite number of solutions; *problem understanding*, or the extent to which participants have accurate information about the problem and understand their task; *attention*, which is analogous to cognitive load; *goal congruence*, or "the degree to which participants perceive that working toward a group goal will be instrumental to the attainment of their salient private goals"; and *exhaustion* in both mental and physical contexts. *Dissent* should be added to this list as well, having been found to encourage "creative and divergent thinking" [12]. Thus, the factors defined by [4] should have currency in debate as well as brainstorming.

3 Methodology

LineChange augments and facilitates complex, crowdsourced problem-solving, particularly efforts involving unstructured deliberation among participants,

[1] The National Hockey League formalized the term *line change* in its official rules; we co-opt the term here in name and spirit only. In our formulation, teams do not compete directly with one another but act independently, for collective benefit and in service of a single goal.

using parameterized rules based on a process model for problem-solving. One possible model is depicted in Fig. 1. This model is illustrative only; many different models are possible, including those that eschew debate or re-conceive problem-solving objectives entirely. Here, brainstorming and consensus bound a cycle of debate (i.e., argument) intended to help participants shrink the space of possible solutions. Arrows indicate control flow; activities with red backgrounds are participant-directed and time-limited, by configuration (not hard-coding). The model always produces a result, whether conclusive or not, and contains no short-circuits for "failure."

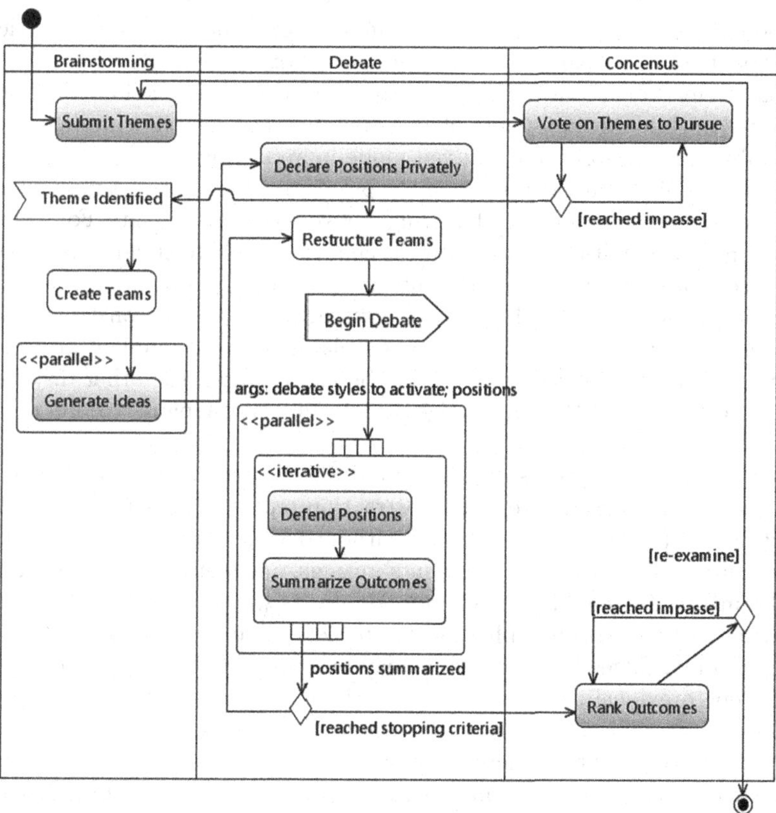

Fig. 1. Hypothetical process model for crowdsourced problem-solving. The process begins with brainstorming and ends with consensus but is facilitated by configurable rewiring of a supporting artificial network of participants.

LineChange is charged with (a) specifying how participants engaged in problem-solving should be organized at appropriate steps in the process, (b) monitoring participant use of computer input devices to trigger individual action or team progression from one activity to another, because events initiated by participant interaction with the system are the inputs of greatest interest, and (c) monitoring time bounds for participant-directed activities to signal delivery of messages or prompts to participants ahead of deadlines. In implementation, all of these responsibilities can be initialized by configuration and managed by inference. The first two may interact and deserve more explanation. The former is the subject of the wiring protocol; the latter, triggering mechanisms, which may be described and measured about the boundaries of Briggs and Reinig [4]. For reasons of space, only the wiring protocol will be discussed herein.

3.1 Wiring Protocol

A phase entails a period of activity about a single objective and a particular arrangement of participants, such as "Declare Positions Privately" or the combination "Defend Positions" and "Summarize Outcomes" in the foregoing figure. Additionally, while the anonymity of participants is assumed for simplicity, nothing prohibits identifiability or a mixed mode in application.

We hypothesize that each phase of the problem-solving process may be facilitated by a particular arrangement (wiring, network) of participants. For example, brainstorming is facilitated by isolates or cliques (complete subgraphs), consensus by a complete graph (all participants are connected to one another and have global knowledge; note [8]). This is one approach, not a hard constraint. When not otherwise arranged as a collection of isolates or as a complete graph, participants may be configured as a set in a bipartite graph, the other disjoint set representing teams. In this case, edges would link participants to one or more teams.

Each phase of the process is structured about who can see what when. A team, as the term is used here, is an abstraction representing a group of participants with a flat structure (a structure without formal roles or hierarchies) that share resources (such as posts, comments, ratings, and summaries). For example, while brainstorming could be done individually as well as in teams, the content of a particular brainstorming phase would be accessible to members of the immediate team only. Edges between teams may be created to grow a team, in which case content previously accessible to some is now accessible to all members of the larger team. Self-organization is possible within teams, depending on task (such as in debate), but not across teams.

The wiring protocol determines how the bipartite graph is initialized and (re)configured during activity transitions. A few considerations follow in how the protocol could be enacted. First, a team may be *non-persistent*, in which case, unlike participants, teams would exist only for the duration of the activity (task). The wiring protocol would need to define how teams are lumped or split from one activity to another. Alternatively, a team may be *persistent*, in which case teams would persist from one activity to another. Characterizing teams becomes possible only if at least one team member remains. Edges could be added or dropped between teams to preserve original team structures (simplifying post hoc analysis), thus expanding or restricting the collective team resources to which individual participants have access. Second, participants could be allowed to vary in number from one activity to another (such as by transitioning to/from active or inactive status) depending on metrics of their performance or level of engagement, however those metrics might be defined. Edges between participants (not just between participants and teams) could be established to influence whether the participants are likely to remain paired (i.e., on the same team). Rewiring may be necessary if participants drop out, either actively (e.g., by deactivating their account) or passively (e.g., by not using the system again).

The wiring protocol could be extended in several ways. For example, a non-uniform probability distribution could be created over teams to allow selection of teams with different sizes. Additional parameters could include (a) the propensity of a participant to work with a previous collaborator (a control for increasing or decreasing team degree or team member swapping; see [7]) and (b) the probability that a given participant will be chosen as a boundary spanner (i.e., linked to more than one group, in the spirit of [6]). The foregoing could be predetermined or adaptive per phase, informed by metrics of participant behavior, for example, the ratio of ostensibly positive interactions over all interactions with another participant.

Example rewiring protocol (simplistic instantiation)
Setup

- Participants remain active throughout the problem-solving process.
- Teams, as well as edges between teams and participants, persist from one phase to another.
- The process model has three objectives (brainstorming, debate, and consensus), each with associated activities and with parameters held constant.

Parameters
N: (integer) number of eligible participants; K: (integer) number of separate subgraphs (i.e., teams); D: (integer) number of debate cycles; Q: (ratio) proportion of actual to possible pairwise participant connections at D.

Initialization

1. Set $K, where\ 1 \leq K \leq N$.
2. Assign N participants to K teams uniformly at random so that each team has N/K members, adjusting when necessary to ensure that no participant is left behind (integers only). At this point, all participants belong to a team, each with equal weight; and each team constitutes a subgraph.

Phase Transition

- debate → consensus: Ensure that all teams are connected to one another, creating a complete graph of them. Implication: participants achieve global knowledge.

- brainstorming → debate: Drop all edges between teams; but retain the edges between teams and participants. Implication: participants now have local knowledge only.
- debate → debate: Add edges selectively between teams that have none otherwise—a function of D, Q, the number of non-existent edges, and the index of the current cycle. Implication: exposure to new or different ideas or perspectives is controlled to minimize cognitive load and help narrow focus towards convergence on problem solutions.

4 An Example

To illustrate how *LineChange* might facilitate problem-solving, we will now explore the organizational challenge of company reorganization due to an influx of new employees following merger or acquisition, with particular focus on roster selection following a decision about hierarchical structure.

The essential task is relatively straightforward: closed-category card sorting [15], where the categories are the leaves in the organizational chart (including an "I don't know" category) and where the cards are the personnel that need to be sorted. The challenges in this task are twofold: (a) coordinating the elicitation of solutions to mitigate groupthink (i.e., bias towards majority opinion); and (b) resolving conflicting sorts (e.g., one person is equally valued in two or more parts of the organization).

LineChange might be engaged as follows, given the workflow of Fig. 1. First, a few assumptions: a participant in the workflow is anonymous unless that participant explicitly chooses to reveal his or her identity; participants include the personnel being sorted; at least one "theme" (a concise statement of the problem to be solved) submitted by a participant would include a call for card-sorting with a recommendation to make card-sorting tractable by creating disjoint subsets of the personnel for sorting; participants use a voting system to select the foregoing submission; themes subsidiary to the one submitted are constructed, each containing a disjoint subset of personnel, each queued for submission to the brainstorming objective; and consensus is reached by majority vote using the Borda count method (see [10]).

For the brainstorming objective, by configuration, isolates (that is, participants working in virtual isolation of one another rather than teams) carry out idea generation. When the configured time limit for this activity has ended, the results of card-sorting efforts are fed to the debate objective where they become privately declared positions. Isolates are then organized into teams.

Debate begins (a) with the anonymized exposure of team members' private positions to the rest of their team, not to all teams, and (b) using one or more of several possible debate interfaces (again, by configuration; pro vs. con debate, threaded discussion, argument mapping) to compare and narrow down the set of possibilities. *LineChange* prompts all teams to begin summarizing positions in anticipation of the time-bound set for a round of debate. At the end of a round, the summarized positions of all teams are gathered and, if stopping criteria have not been met, another round of debate commences with a team rewiring. For simplicity, we imagine that *LineChange* is configured to rewire teams by connecting nodes representing teams in the bipartite graph. By this method, team size increases with each round of debate, thus limiting participant exposure to too many new positions at once.

Criteria that stop debate for all teams could entail an overall time-bound for debate or a target mixing rate. Once such criteria have been met, the problem-solving process ends with all participants ranking the summarized positions of the last teams engaged in debate. This process continues to iterate until all cards have been sorted into agreement.

Consensus is determined by voting using the Borda count method. Conceivably, the workflow just described may end in stalemate, where agreement about categorization cannot be reached. In such cases, a preferential method of voting could be used, such as that used by the Australian electoral system; voting recurs after the least popular choice is dropped. Regardless, a call can be made for re-examination in the form of a new theme submission.

5 Epilogue

LineChange is an analytic framework that makes active moderation, facilitation, and intervention part of the problem-solving process. In practice, it could function as an automated service, listening to events representing participant interaction with a crowdsourcing system and triggering actions intended to elicit different behaviors as a process unfolds.

LineChange distinguishes itself from other approaches, in part, because (a) it treats teams as composable objects (they may vary in size or number or cease to exist from one phase of a problem-solving process to the next, depending on the wiring protocol); (b) the framework is scale-free in being unaffected by time (process duration), space (proximity of participants to one another), and size (of the participant pool); (c) the framework is configurable in depending on a parameterized set of rules; and (d) participants provide first-order input as sensors.

Acknowledgements. This research was performed in connection with contract N68335-18-C-0040 with the U.S. Office of Naval Research. We would like to thank Dr. Yiling Chen and Dr. Predrag Neskovic for their contributions to this work as thought partners.

References

1. Anson, R., Bostrom, R., Wynne, B.: An experiment assessing group support system and facilitator effects on meeting outcomes. Manag. Sci. **41**(2), 189–208 (1995). https://doi.org/10.1287/mnsc.41.2.189
2. Austen-Smith, D., Feddersen, T.: Deliberation and voting rules. In: Austen-Smith, D., Duggan, J. (eds.) Social Choice and Strategic Decisions: Essays in Honor of Jeffrey S. Banks. Studies in Choice and Welfare, pp. 269–316. Springer, Heidelberg (2005). https://doi.org/10.1007/3-540-27295-X_11

3. Bernstein, M.S., Little, G., Miller, R.C., Hartmann, B., Ackerman, M.S., Karger, D.R., Crowell, D., Panovich, K.: Soylent: a word processor with a crowd inside. Commun. ACM **58**(8), 85–94 (2015). https://doi.org/10.1145/2791285
4. Briggs, R.O., Reinig, B.A.: Bounded ideation theory. J. Manag. Inf. Syst. **27**(1), 123–144 (2010). https://doi.org/10.2753/MIS0742-1222270106
5. Dennis, A.R., Williams, M.L.: Electronic brainstorming: theory, research, and future directions. In: Paulus, P.B., Nijstad, B.A. (eds.) Group Creativity: Innovation Through Collaboration, pp. 160–180. Oxford University Press, Oxford (2003). https://doi.org/10.1093/acprof:oso/9780195147308.003.0008
6. Granovetter, M.: The strength of weak ties: a network theory revisited. Sociol. Theory **1**, 201–233 (1983). http://www.jstor.org/stable/202051
7. Guimer, R., Uzzi, B., Spiro, J., Amaral, L.A.N.: Team assembly mechanisms determine collaboration network structure and team performance. Science **308**(5722), 697–702 (2005). http://science.sciencemag.org/content/308/5722/697
8. Judd, S., Kearns, M., Vorobeychik, Y.: Behavioral dynamics and influence in networked coloring and consensus. Proc. Nat. Acad. Sci. **107**(34), 14978–14982 (2010). http://www.pnas.org/content/107/34/14978.abstract
9. Kim, T., Chang, A., Holland, L., Pentland, A.S.: Meeting mediator: enhancing group collaboration using sociometric feedback. In: Proceedings of the 2008 ACM Conference on Computer Supported Cooperative Work, CSCW 2008, pp. 457–466. ACM (2008). https://doi.org/10.1145/1460563.1460636
10. Mao, A., Procaccia, A.D., Chen, Y.: Better human computation through principled voting. In: AAAI (2013)
11. Mellers, B., Stone, E., Murray, T., Minster, A., Rohrbaugh, N., Bishop, M., Chen, E., Baker, J., Hou, Y., Horowitz, M., Ungar, L., Tetlock, P.: Identifying and cultivating superforecasters as a method of improving probabilistic predictions. Perspect. Psychol. Sci. **10**(3), 267–281 (2015). https://doi.org/10.1177/1745691615577794
12. Nemeth, C.J., Nemeth-Brown, B.: Better than individuals? The potential benefits of dissent and diversity for group creativity. In: Paulus, P.B., Nijstad, B.A. (eds.) Group Creativity: Innovation Through Collaboration, pp. 63–84. Oxford University Press, Oxford (2003). https://doi.org/10.1093/acprof:oso/9780195147308.003.0004
13. Ottaviani, M., Srensen, P.: Information aggregation in debate: who should speak first? J. Public Econ. **81**(3), 393–421 (2001). https://doi.org/10.1016/S0047-2727(00)00119-5
14. Post, M., Callison-Burch, C., Osborne, M.: Constructing parallel corpora for six Indian languages via crowdsourcing. In: Proceedings of the Seventh Workshop on Statistical Machine Translation, pp. 401–409. Association for Computational Linguistics, Montréal, June 2012. http://www.aclweb.org/anthology/W12-3152
15. Spencer, D.: Card Sorting: Designing Usable Categories. Rosenfeld Media, New York (2009)
16. Wong, Z., Aiken, M.: Automated facilitation of electronic meetings. Inf. Manag. **41**(2), 125–134 (2003). https://doi.org/10.1016/S0378-7206(03)00042-9

The Digital Evolution of Gender

A Visual Analysis of Women's Representation Through Emoji Communication

Raquel Forma Klafke(✉) and Daniela Kutschat Hanns

University of São Paulo, São Paulo, Brazil
{raquel.klafke, dk.hanns}@usp.br

Abstract. For the past 20 years, the Unicode Consortium put efforts to implement a consistent pictorial alphabet across multiple systems and platforms: the emoji. This long term, continuous initiative intended to narrow the gap between face-to-face and digital communication, adding subjective cues – such as emotions – and synthesizing textual content into smaller information units to optimize interactions through computers and mobile devices. As the graphical technology gained complexity, the emoji's aesthetic developed as well, embracing new symbolic possibilities regarding user experience. This short paper aims to develop a qualitative visual analysis within a range of 20 years – from 2000 to 2017 – to better understand how one particular symbolic feature, the gender, was addressed in digital communication. The work will be organized as a comparative visual timeline, showing how the study object gained complexity, new attributions and purposes. The historical progression will be based on notable examples of interface history, especially ICQ and Apple, with its correspondent emoji set decomposed within a design perspective – colors, textures and forms. The gendered dimension was chosen due its contemporary importance in community discussion, political measures and mediatic repercussion. As a result, the poster will demonstrate how the language influence (and can be influenced) by technology and cultural demands, growing as an emergent, complex and vivid system.

Keywords: Emoji · Digital language · Gender · Visual design

1 Introduction

For the past 20 years, the Unicode Consortium put efforts to implement a consistent pictorial alphabet across multiple systems and platforms: the emoji, visual icons which represents a broad spectrum of concepts (places, objects, emotions, and more). This long term, continuous initiative intended to narrow the gap between face-to-face and digital communication, adding subjective cues and synthetizing textual content into smaller information units to optimize interactions through computers and mobile devices. As the graphical technology gained complexity, the emoji's aesthetic developed as well, embracing new symbolic possibilities regarding user experience.

As emoji gain more importance to mediate digital communication processes, several political discussions arise over its development, such as sexual, ethnical and gender

C. Stephanidis (Ed.): HCII Posters 2018, CCIS 850, pp. 409–414, 2018.
https://doi.org/10.1007/978-3-319-92270-6_58

diversity. The objective of debate is the possibility to create consciously a diverse pictorial alphabet, helping to integrate a bigger inclusive agenda. As a result, the poster will demonstrate how the language influence (and can be influenced) by technology and cultural demands, growing as an emergent, complex and vivid system.

2 Objectives

This short paper aims to develop a qualitative visual analysis within a range of 20 years – from 2000 to 2017 – to better understand how one particular symbolic feature, the gender, was addressed in digital communication. The work will be organized as a comparative visual timeline, showing how the study object gained complexity, new attributions and purposes.

3 Method

This research was organized in two parts. The first one was an exploratory look into the emoji history through the perspective of official sets launched by companies such as ICQ and Apple. The sets were chosen according to their recurrence in the desktop research. This was crucial to understand how the visual language was being designed and used in a large-scale basis. The main consulted authors include Gülşen [1] and Oliveira e Paiva [2], both based on linguistic and cultural approaches, and Davis and Edberg [3], from a technical background. Since the emoji history is still recent and yet to be academically compiled, web articles from reliable resources, such as *Wired* magazine, were consulted to complement the historical and theoretical framework. It is important to observe that, for the matters of this short paper, the emoji's predecessors (emoticons, smileys, and other minimalistic or pictographic signs) won't be taken into consideration.

The second part is the construction of the visual timeline, composed of two dimensions: chronological perspective and design perspective. The temporal sections were based on *Wired*'s "Guide to emoji", which take into consideration gender, diversity and other criteria that match the objective of this paper. The design criteria were based on Lupton [4] and Royo [5] works, and consist in form, color and texture. Those criteria combined result in more complex concepts, such as detail and symbolical values. Lastly, the emoji from each group were compared against each other from a single and collective perspective, resulting in a conclusion about the evolution of gender in this scope of digital language.

4 The Digital Evolution of Gender

4.1 A Brief Emoji History

According to Oliveira e Paiva [6], language is a complex adaptive system, since it's expression is based on people's past experiences which feeds actual interactions. The speaker's behavior can be influenced by several motives, from perceptual restrictions to social motivations. As result, the language structures emerge from interrelated patterns of experience, social interaction and cognitive mechanisms.

Oliveira [7] splits the cognitive dimension in two categories: verbal and non-verbal. The difference between them is the way the brain reads and interprets information, in a linear or non-linear way, and both of them are equally important for the communication process. Visual cues and voice tones, among other signs, helps to convey messages [8] in this multimodal system, and the technological development changed how those pieces of information are delivered – especially subjective concepts such as pain, excitement, anger, fear or happiness. Gülşen [9] states that "[…] When verbal language is inadequate in explaining reality that requires paralinguistic elements to be expressed, users replaced such elements of language systems with digital iconic or pictorial elements in order to construct meaning." This is an effort to fill the gap between face-to-face and remote social interactions, deeply changed after the mass use of digital technology [10].

In the 90's, the emoticon, typographical signs used to express feelings and disambiguities in digital channels, were transformed into design objects: the emoji, pictograms with aesthetic, functional and commercial concerns to deliver better messages across digital devices [11]. The first emoji set, projected by Japanese designer Shigetaka Kurita, from the company DOCOMO, counted with 176 original icons, from human expressions to objects and abstract symbols. The idea quickly spread among the market, and as soon as cellphones developed to smartphones in the 2000's, emoji had been accepted as a complementary alphabet to text-based messages (Fig. 1).

Fig. 1. Original emoji set by Shigetaka Kurita. (Source: Wired. https://www.wired.com/story/guide-emoji/)

In the 2000's, emoji got even more complex. With the development of computer graphics, those symbols got more definition, colors and textures, reaching greater detail levels. Finally, in 2010, the Unicode Consortium, international organization responsible for developing encoding standards across multiple platforms, accepted to index emoji because of their high usage. In other words: emoji was officially accepted as a legit form of communication.

The complexity of emoji development resulted in Unicode creating the Unicode Emoji Subcommittee, a group dedicated to deliberate and coordinate the emoji creative guidelines for companies as Google (directly involved in Unicode's emoji history [12]), Microsoft, Facebook, Apple, and others. The Consortium, with non-profiting objectives, organized a top-down submission process which included the user's preferences and proposals for new symbols. From 2010 to 2017, it is observed an intense debate regarding how emoji was and could represent better people's subjectivity and social inclusion, arising a strong political potential. In 2015, Unicode included the Fitzpatrick scale to represent different ethnicities and a set of same-sex couples to represent sexual diversity. Later on, a project led by Been [13] included woman representation in the labor market, which was reflected in creating male and female emojis for every type of symbol (Figs. 2 and 3).

Fig. 2. Contrast between two ICQ's emoji sets: ICQ 2000 a, from 2000, and ICQ 5.0, from 2005. (Source: M-GAMES, http://www.m-games.iplace.cz/menu/smajlici-na-icq)

4.2 The Visual Evolution of Gender in Emoji

Emoji and gender came stronger in the 2010's. Although the main conceptual change was the inclusion of male/female facial icons with skin variations, increasing considerably the number of emoji in the set, few was done regarding a broader discussion about gender. In 2017, Hunt [14] goes further and questions the current binary gender model, proposing neutral gender emoji. He argues that "[…] In terms of emoji reflecting our emerging understanding of gender, the addition of three gender inclusive people emoji is only a first step."

Until then, gendered emoji went through several design modifications. This short paper will analyze a specific case, the "open mouth smile", one of the oldest emoji to date. This emoji will be compared with its correspondent version from 2000 to 2017, including its gendered approximate version. The visual analysis will take three aspects into consideration: form, color and texture, as specified in Method.

In a general sense, it is possible to observe that the improvement of computer graphics made an increase of the number of colors and the complexity of textures possible, giving more details to emoji. Emoji got more resolution, smoother aspects and volume. With higher resolution, female and male emoji got details to differentiate visually them even more, with distinct eyes, eyebrows and noses.

Fig. 3. Contrast between Apple's emoji set. To the left, emoji from the iOS 6.0, 2012. To the right, emoji from the iOS 11.2, 2017. (Source: Emojipedia. https://emojipedia.org/)

The cultural symbols of femininity and masculinity, however, still remain. The hair length, the face format and the difference between bigger lips and moustache. As Hunt indirectly pointed, the gender discussion in emoji won't remain in the increasing number of details and features to tell male and female apart, as the timeline suggests. Rather it involves a whole new symbolic discussion, in which not only the aesthetic perfection is sought, but also *what is represented* is subject of discussion (Fig. 4).

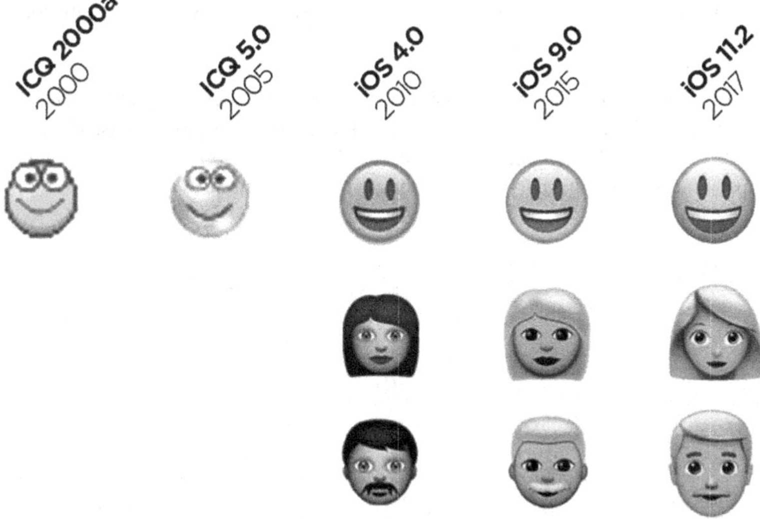

Fig. 4. Timeline with one of the oldest emoji and its evolution through 17 years. (Source: Emojipedia and M-GAMES. Organized by the authors)

5 Conclusion

The technological development, which brought deep changes in how people think and create their personal narratives and discourses, lead the transformation of the emoji concept. If the first version, back in 1999, was meant to be simple, beautiful and commercially competitive, the emoji set shared among companies such as Google, Apple and Microsoft, are meant to bring meaning and personal touch to their users. In this sense, the gender dimension represents not only physical traits or individual characteristics, but also an urge to introduce a broader political discussion within the creation of language.

References

1. Gülşen, T.T.: You tell me in emojis. In: Computational and Cognitive Approaches to Narratology, pp. 57–65 (2016)
2. Oliveira, E., Paiva, V.L.M.: A linguagem dos emojis. Trabalhos em Linguística Aplicada **55** (2), 379–399 (2016). https://doi.org/10.1590/010318134955176321. Campinas, Maio/Agosto
3. Davis, M., Edberg, P.: Unicode Technical Standard #51: Unicode Emoji. The Unicode Consortium (2017). http://unicode.org/reports/tr51/
4. Lupton, E.: Novos Fundamentos do Design. Cosac Naify, São Paulo (2008)
5. Royo, J.: Design Digital. Edições Rosari, São Paulo (2008)
6. Oliveira e Paiva, V.L.M.: (2016)
7. Oliveira, M.K.: O verbal e o não-verbal. In: Revista USP, São Paulo, no. 16, pp. 52–61 (1992)
8. Pentland, A.S.: Honest Signals: How They Shape Our World. MIT Press, Cambridge (2010)
9. Gülşen, T.T.: (2016)
10. Crystal, D.: A revolução da linguagem. Jorge Zahar, Rio de Janeiro (2005)
11. Pardes, A.: The Wired Guide to Emoji. Wired (2018). https://www.wired.com/story/guide-emoji/
12. Pardes, A.: (2018)
13. Been, R.: Expanding Emoji Professions: Reducing Gender Inequality. The Unicode Consortium (2016). https://unicode.org/L2/L2016/16160-emoji-professions.pdf
14. Hunt, P.: What is Gender and Why Does it Matter to Emoji? Emojipedia. https://blog.emojipedia.org/what-is-gender-and-why-does-it-matter-to-emoji/

Design Social Media Interface to Better Support Collaborative Travel Planning

Jie Gu[1], Xinlin Yao[2(✉)], and Anan Hu[3]

[1] Shanghai Academy of Social Sciences, Shanghai, People's Republic of China
[2] Nanjing University of Science and Technology, Nanjing, People's Republic of China
hsinlinyao90@gmail.com
[3] Fudan University, Shanghai, People's Republic of China

Abstract. Social media, which facilitate online interaction among travelers, have significantly impacted the travel industry. While prior literatures have addressed the "information media" feature of social media in travel planning, the effect of social media as a collaborative communication tool has been largely ignored. The purpose of this working paper is to design various social media interfaces to assist collaborative travel planning process. Four interfaces (dialogue-flow interface, user-centric interface, wiki-mode interface and integrated interface) emphasizing different aspects of collaborative communication were developed. The interface prototype forms the experimental foundation for our future research.

Keywords: Social media · Interface design · Travel plan
Collaborative decision-making

1 Introduction

The travel industry becomes increasingly digitized accompanied by the fusion of offline experience and online decision-making [1]. Industry report showed that the scale of China's online travel transaction has reached 593 billion RMB [2]. It was reported that a majority of travelers relied on information technology and digital applications to collect destination information and arrange travel planning [3]. Because of the relatively high costs (both monetary and non-monetary) and information-intensive nature, travel decisions are complex and highly involving [4]. These features of travel decisions make the industry highly reliant on technology [5].

The proliferation of social media has further strengthened the connection between tourism and technology [3, 6, 7]. Social media refer to "a group of Internet-based applications that build on the ideological and technological foundations of Web 2.0, and that allow the creation and exchange of user-generated content" [8]. Two basic features of social media, i.e. information exchanging and social interaction, have transformed the nature of travel decision-making. On one hand, the information

C. Stephanidis (Ed.): HCII Posters 2018, CCIS 850, pp. 415–422, 2018.
https://doi.org/10.1007/978-3-319-92270-6_59

exchanging via social media enables travelers to gather the first-hand destination information from others who share but not for monetary rewards [6, 9]. On the other hand, the social characteristics of social media allows travel stakeholders[1] to make decisions collaboratively. As travel stakeholders may disperse geographically, social media become a necessity to communicate and make traveling plans.

Although several studies have explored the role of social media in tourism, two gaps still exist. First, while many studies have examined the information feature of social media [6, 9], few concerned the social feature in collaborative travel planning. Tourism literatures have proposed personal features and travel characteristics would shape individuals' travel decision-making [10]. However, travel decision makers should be addressed as groups and not only as individuals because (a) mostly, travel decision-making is a social process, and (b) social interaction is also a major motive for traveling [11]. Collaborative travel planning is more complex than individual decision-making because of diverse preferences and interpersonal conflicts. Therefore, conclusions drawn from individual decision-making cannot be simply applied in the context of collaborative travel planning.

Second, few studies took a technological perspective in understanding how to facilitate collaborative travel planning via social media. Prior studies on group decision support system (GDSS) have found that merely introducing media led low-quality group performance [12]. Therefore, technological features of social media, interfaces in particular, call for further investigation for collaborative travel planning.

To fill the two gaps, this working paper developed the system prototype to assist collaborative travel planning. Drawing on media synchronicity theory, we considered four interfaces: (1) the basic dialog-flow interface, which is widely used in popular instant messaging tools; (2) the user-centered interface, which adds a user-centered window next to the dialog-flow window; (3) the wiki-mode interface, which adds a wiki-mode board next to the dialog-flow window; (4) and the integrated interface which incorporates both user-centered and wiki-mode windows. And a lab experiment is designed to test the effectiveness of the four interfaces. This study aims to contribute to the literature on group decision in the context of traveling and provide implications for the tourism industry.

The rest of this study proceeds as follows. We first reviewed prior research of social media in tourism. Then we reviewed literature on media synchronicity theory, which guide our design logic for this study. Interface design was presented, followed by our experiment design. We finally listed future research plan.

2 Literature Review

2.1 Social Media in Tourism

The research on the influence of social media on tourism consumption behavior are concentrated in three areas. First, the role and mechanism of social media in the tourism

[1] To distinguish between general travelers and those who decide to travel together for a trip, the latter is noted as travel stakeholders.

marketing process [13, 14]; second, incentives for tourists to share information to their social media accounts [15]; third, motivation for potential tourists to utilize social media information in destination information collection [6, 7]. However, several gaps still exist and call for further research.

First, for potential tourism consumers, the "social" role of social media needs to be further analyzed [16]. The common "read-comment-respond" practice of social media in tourism is a semi-duplex process, i.e., an interactive mode in which one party shares information, other user reviews, and one party responds again, which leads various problems such as time lag and information asymmetry. The social feature may better facilitate the synchronous process in interpersonal information cooperation and collaborative decision making, while limited studies concerned this.

Second, what kinds of social media interfaces are more conducive to support travel planning are worthy of experimental research. Given the technological interfaces impacted the process of collaborative decision-making, it is necessary to combine the characteristics of tourism decision-making and social media interactive communication to design interface to better support collaborative travel planning.

2.2 Media Synchronicity Theory

Media synchronicity theory (MST) predicts that effectiveness of communication and task performance are related to the capabilities of a medium. MST proposes that all task performing is composed of two fundamental communication processes: conveyance and convergence [17]. Conveyance processes and convergence processes differ in the need of information exchanging and processing. Specifically, conveyance focuses on the transmission of a variety of new and relevant information, while convergence focuses on developing mutual understanding for exchanged information [17, 18]. Therefore, the effectiveness of communication and task performance would be enhanced when the capabilities of a medium meet the requirements of communication processes. In general, convergence benefits from media that support a high level of synchronicity, while conveyance benefits from media with less synchronicity [18].

Synchronicity refers to "a shared pattern of coordinated synchronous behavior with a common focus" [17] (p. 581), could be support given the capabilities of a medium, which includes transmission velocity, parallelism, symbol variety, rehearsability, and reprocessability [17, 19]. MST has been widely applied to investigate the role of media capabilities in team communication and collaboration [20], conflict management [21], and e-learning [22]. Unlike previous theory, MST argues that no one medium outperforms under any circumstances or is best for both conveyance and convergence. Thus, MST particularly suits the social media context because it often contains multiple media that are used in combination by users [23].

3 Interface Design

Communication in a collaborative group is reflected as user-generated content that is organized interactively and in real time. According to this identification, collaborative communication can be decomposed along three dimensions.

1. **Time dimension.** Social media facilitate synchronous, dialogue-flow communication among group members. In our context, travel stakeholders interactively provide information, give travel proposals, discuss and comment on others' proposals. The existing interface of social media communication is organized along time dimension, that is, user-generated information is presented as dialogue flow in real time. The dialogue-flow interface constitutes the basic design in this study.
2. **User dimension.** Group members, or in our context, travel stakeholders, are the basic units in collaborative travel planning. Individual travel stakeholder may have their own preference and constraint (budget and time). The diversity may bring innovative ideas to the final travel plan, but also make it difficult to reach a convergent plan. An interface that explicates individual opinion may overcome the flaw of the existing dialogue design that real-time dialogue information is fragmented and it is difficult to trace back to early personal opinions.
3. **Content dimension.** User-generated content is the core of collaborative communication. The key of travel planning is information sharing and collaborative decision-making. To update with newly input information and present temporal agreements, a wiki-mode content model flushes into our mind. Wiki model is also known as commons-based peer production, by which individuals provide small fragments of content that gradually add up to a common decision [24].

This study developed four interfaces that address either one aspect of the three dimensions, or an integration of more than one dimension.

1. **The basic dialog-flow interface**, which addresses the time dimension discussed above. The dialog-flow design is widely used in popular instant messaging tools.
2. **The user-centered interface**, which adds a user-centered window next to the dialog-flow window. This interface emphasizes the feature of user dimension.
3. **The wiki-mode interface**, which adds a wiki-mode board next to the dialog-flow window.
4. **The integrated interface**, which incorporates both user-centered and wiki-mode windows.

In the user-centered interface, each user can establish his/her own information book, in which he/she can add, delete or update travel information. Users' information is split but visible to all others. In the wiki-mode interface, content is organized just as Wikipedia: travel information is structured to different parts (destination, travel time, transportation, travel fee and detailed plan). Each user can edit travel information in different parts, and all modifications are all recorded and can be reviewed by others. Through the above discussion, we can easily detect that the dialog-flow interface is the basic design and advanced functions are added to it to improve the assistance to collaborative decision-making.

We only display the integrated interface to illustrate our design in Fig. 1 because it contains all elements of other interfaces.

Drawing on media synchronicity theory, we expect that integrating the user-centered interface and the wiki-mode interface to the basic dialogue-flow interface will afford information conveyance and decision convergence, respectively. The user-centered interface allows the messaged to be organized based on the sender (tagged as 2 in Fig. 1). Organizing information through a personal space will be quite helpful to conveyance processes because of the need of exchanging large amount of new and raw information [17]. However, the user-centered interface has negative effects on developing a common focus during the communication because the independent space for each participant could distract attention, thus lowering the level of synchronicity. Therefore, we expect that conveyance processes will benefit from the user-centered interface but convergence processes do not.

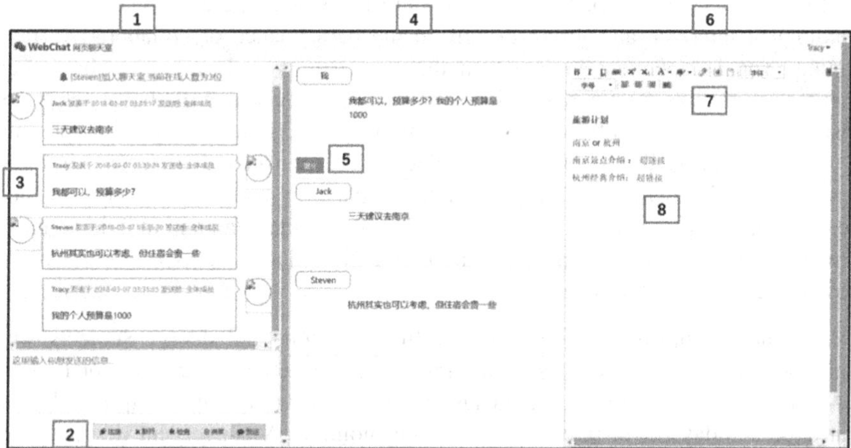

Fig. 1. The integrated interface. 1-dialogure-flow interface. 2-dialogue functions (connect; disconnect; check; full screen; send). 3-dialogure content. 4-user-centered interface. 5-Update. 6-wiki-mode. 7-edit functions. 8-Collaborative content in wiki-mode.

The wiki-mode interface reflects fundamental characteristics of the real-world Wikis, such as open, universal, unified, observable, and convergent [25]. The universal and convergent nature of wikis allows participants to understand "what we have known" or "what we have done" based on mutual agreements, even temporarily. From this perspective, the wiki-mode interface will be helpful on developing common understanding which is the focus in convergence processes. However, the unified and convergent nature wikis will exert deindividualization during communication, which might produce conflicts and undermine conveyance processes. Thus, we expect that convergence processes will benefit from the wiki-mode interface but conveyance processes do not.

In this study, three indicators of collaborative travel planning outcome will be considered: time to reach convergent plan, group satisfaction of the final plan and individual user's perceived degree of compromises for the convergent plan. Based on our statements, we develop several basic propositions.

Proposition 1. Participants will use the least time to reach convergent plan when using the integrated interface, and participants will use the most time to reach convergent plan when using the basic dialog-flow interface.

Proposition 2. Participants will have the highest level of satisfaction of the final plan when using the integrated interface, and participants will have the lowest level of satisfaction of the final plan when using the basic dialog-flow interface.

Proposition 3. Participants will have the highest level of perceived degree of compromises when using the wiki-mode interface, and participants will have the lowest level of perceived degree of compromises when using the user-centered interface.

4 Experiment Design

The developed interfaces form the experimental foundation for future research. We intend to conduct a series of lab experiments to investigate the combinatory effect of technological interface and group design on the performance of collaborative travel planning. The independent variables in the experiments will include technological interfaces, group size, group type (friends or strangers), existence of choice set or not, decision-making stages (information cooperation and decision-making), time pressure and so on. Additional independent variables will be considered to serve our future research. Three indicators of collaborative travel planning outcome will be evaluated: time to reach convergent plan, group satisfaction of the final plan and individual user's perceived degree of compromises for the convergent plan. The experimental procedures are designed as followings.

5. Experiment subjects will be recruited from a China university. Subjects were grouped according to group size and group type, in terms of strangers or friends.
6. All subjects will be told that their task is to discuss with other group members to arrange a 3-day travel plan for the coming holiday. A convergent decision with detailed plan (including accommodation, transportation, schedule, activity and so on) is demanded. As incentives, their completed travel plan could possibly be supported by monetary award. Therefore, the task and award are closely associated with subjects' real travel decision.
7. Subjects will discuss and make decisions in the collaborative travel planning system (Fig. 2). All collaborative groups will be randomly assigned to one of the four interfaces. Group members will have 5 min to get familiar with each other, the interface and the function of the system. After the 5 min, a specific instruction about the task will be given. 30 min will be left to them for travel planning.

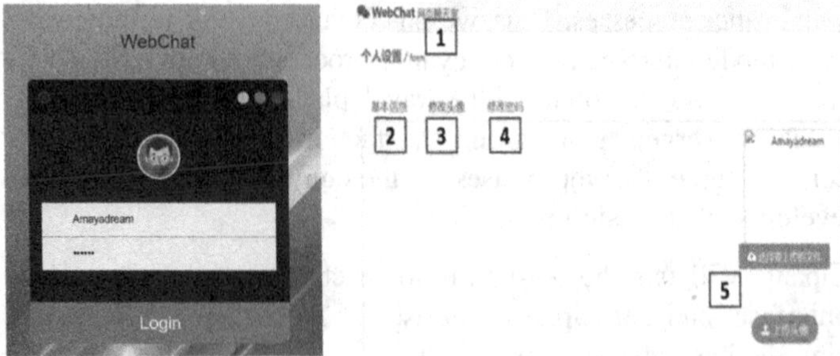

Fig. 2. log interface and personal setting interface. (1-setting; 2-basic information; 3-change head portrait; 4-change code; 5-update head portrait)

5 Implication and Future Research Plan

This study will contribute to literate in two main aspects. First, our exploration of collaborative travel planning addresses the social affordance of social media. While prior research has emphasized the importance of social media in providing user-generated travel information, we noticed the gap that few have direct the value of social media towards real decision-making process, that is, travel planning. As travel is a highly social event and travel decision is mostly made by groups, it is important to introduce the idea of collaborative decision-making into travel planning. Second, this study has both theoretical and practical implications through introducing new collaborative interfaces. Noticing that barely relying on social tools for collaborative decision may result in low-quality group performance, this study aims to develop and test different interfaces in facilitating collaborative travel planning.

Our future research will focus on the effectiveness of different interfaces in assisting different-stage cooperation and collaboration. The experiment we have depicted in this study will be conducted to collect first-hand data.

Acknowledgement. This work was supported by the National Natural Science Foundation of China (Grant #71702103 and #71531006).

References

1. Nezakati, H., Amidi, A., Jusoh, Y.Y., Moghadas, S., Aziz, Y.A., Sohrabinezhadtalemi, R.: Review of social media potential on knowledge sharing and collaboration in tourism industry. Procedia Soc. Behav. Sci. **172**, 120–125 (2015)
2. IResearch: 2017 Annual Report of China's Online Tourism. http://www.199it.com/archives/615171.html. Accessed 06 Mar 2018
3. Bizirgianni, I., Dionysopoulou, P.: The influence of tourist trends of youth tourism through social media (SM) & information and communication technologies (ICTs). Procedia Soc. Behav Sci. **73**, 652–660 (2013)
4. Sirakaya, E., Woodside, A.G.: Building and testing theories of decision making by travellers. Tour. Manag. **26**(6), 815–832 (2005)
5. Kiráľová, A., Pavlíčeka, A.: Development of social media strategies in tourism destination. Procedia Soc. Behav. Sci. **175**, 358–366 (2015)
6. Xiang, Z., Gretzel, U.: Role of social media in online travel information search. Tour. Manag. **31**(2), 179–188 (2010)
7. Nezakati, H., Amidi, A., Jusoh, Y.Y., Moghadas, S., Aziz, Y.A., Sohrabinezhadtalemi, R.: Review of social media potential on knowledge sharing and collaboration in tourism industry. Procedia Soc. Behav. Sci. **172**, 120–125 (2015)
8. Kaplan, A.M., Haenlein, M.: Users of the world, unite! The challenges and opportunities of Social Media. Bus. Horiz. **53**(1), 59–68 (2010)
9. Zeng, B., Gerritsen, R.: What do we know about social media in tourism? A review. Tour. Manag. Perspect. **10**, 27–36 (2014)
10. Ricci, F., Del Missier, F.: Supporting travel decision making through personalized recommendation. In: Karat, C.M., Blom, J.O., Karat, J. (eds.) Designing Personalized User Experiences in eCommerce. Human-Computer Interaction Series, vol. 5, pp. 231–251. Springer, Dordrecht (2004). https://doi.org/10.1007/1-4020-2148-8_13

11. Decrop, A.: Group processes in vacation decision-making. J. Travel Tour. Mark. **18**(3), 23–36 (2005)
12. Baltes, B.B., Dickson, M.W., Sherman, M.P., Bauer, C.C., LaGanke, J.S.: Computer-mediated communication and group decision making: a meta-analysis. Organ. Behav. Hum. Decis. Process. **87**(1), 156–179 (2002)
13. Buhalis, D., Law, R.: Progress in information technology and tourism management: 20 years on and 10 years after the Internet—The state of eTourism research. Tour. Manag. **29**(4), 609–623 (2008)
14. Richard, D., Do Twitter and Facebook matter? Examining the economic impact of social media marketing in tourism websites of Atlantic Canada. J. Tour. Res. Hospitality (2012)
15. Gretzel, U., Fesenmaier, D.R., O'Leary, J.T.: The transformation of consumer behaviour. In: Tourism Business Frontiers: Consumers, Products and Industry, pp. 9–18 (2006)
16. Schultz, D.E., Peltier, J.: Social media's slippery slope: challenges, opportunities and future research directions. J. Res. Interact. Mark. **7**(2), 86–99 (2013)
17. Dennis, A.R., Fuller, R.M., Valacich, J.S.: Media, tasks, and communication processes: a theory of media synchronicity. MIS Q. **32**(3), 575–600 (2008)
18. Weick, K.E., Meader, D.K.: Sensemaking and group support systems. In: Group Support Systems: New perspectives, pp. 230–252. MacMillan, New York (1993)
19. Dennis, A.R., Valacich, J.S.: Rethinking media richness: towards a theory of media synchronicity. In: Proceedings of the 32nd Annual Hawaii International Conference on Systems Sciences, HICSS-32. IEEE (1999)
20. Espinosa, J.A., Nan, N., Carmel, E.: Temporal distance, communication patterns, and task performance in teams. J. Manag. Inf. Syst. **32**(1), 151–191 (2015)
21. Maruping, L.M., Agarwal, R.: Managing team interpersonal processes through technology: a task-technology fit perspective. J. Appl. Psychol. **89**(6), 975 (2004)
22. Sun, J., Wang, Y.: Tool choice for e-learning: task-technology fit through media synchronicity. Inf. Syst. Educ. J. **12**(4), 17 (2014)
23. Cao, X., Vogel, D.R., Guo, X., Liu, H., Gu, J.: Understanding the influence of social media in the workplace: an integration of media synchronicity and social capital theories. In: 2012 45th Hawaii International Conference on System Science (HICSS). IEEE (2012)
24. Aaltonen, A., Seiler, S.: Cumulative growth in user-generated content production: evidence from Wikipedia. Manage. Sci. **62**(7), 2054–2069 (2015)
25. Wagner, C.: Wiki: a technology for conversational knowledge management and group collaboration. Commun. Assoc. Inf. Syst. **13**(1), 58 (2004)

Text Mining Analysis of Online Consumer Reviews on Home IoT Services

Jihyung Hong, Jaehye Suk, Hyesun Hwang(✉), Dongmin Kim, Kee Ok Kim, and Yunjik Jeong

Sungkyunkwan University, Seoul, South Korea
h.hwang@skku.edu

Abstract. This study explores the context of use, functions, and benefits of home Internet of Things (IoT) services through a text mining analysis of online consumer reviews. Data were collected from online text reviews that are open to the public and analyzed with R.3.3.3 and Ucinet6. The results were as follows. First, the CONvergence of iterated CORrelations analysis showed four clusters: control for convenience, safety from intruders, safety from users' carelessness, and saving. Second, the results of a cross-analysis of the 20 most frequently used keywords in the 3 service categories were as follows. In the context of use, in reviews about control and safety services, the frequently used terms included "go out," "going to work," "outside," and "forgetfulness." Reviews about safety services mentioned protection concerns, such as "children," "pets," "parents," and "alone." Further, some reviews about saving services used keywords related to seasonal cycles, such as "summer," "air conditioner," and "cumulative tax." Regarding functions, "check" was a frequently used keyword for all three service categories. Specific actions such as "turn off," "setting," and "control" were frequently present in reviews about control and saving services. Regarding benefits, the most frequently used keywords were "convenience" and "saving" in reviews about control services; "relief," "convenience," and "safety" in reviews about safety services; and "saving" and "convenience" in reviews about saving services. These results demonstrate that many consumers who use home IoT services positively experience a more convenient, safe, and economical life by using check and control functions in various situations.

Keywords: Home IoT services · Text mining · Online consumer reviews

1 Introduction

In recent years, the Internet of Things (IoT) service market has expanded in South Korea. According to the Ministry of Science and ICT in South Korea, the total number of IoT subscribers (vehicle control, remote control, wireless payment, tablet PC, and wearable devices among others) exceeded six million as of December 2017 [1]. The number of home IoT service subscribers of the telecommunication company with has the largest market share in South Korea, crossed one million in December 2017 [2].

C. Stephanidis (Ed.): HCII Posters 2018, CCIS 850, pp. 423–428, 2018.
https://doi.org/10.1007/978-3-319-92270-6_60

It is important to understand the present state of IoT services and obtain consumer opinions on home IoT. Therefore, by using text mining analysis, this study explores the context of use, functions, and benefits of home IoT services by analyzing online consumer reviews on a leading Korean telecommunication company.

2 Method

Data were collected from publicly available online text reviews posted from June 23, 2016 to November 7, 2017 by using R.3.3.3. The cleaned dataset consisted of 4,932 reviews from which the words with the highest frequency and matrix data were extracted using R and the CONvergence of iterated CORrelations (CONCOR) analysis, which was conducted using the NetDraw packages of the Ucinet6 program. This was done to investigate the connection between similar keywords and clusters. Data were then analyzed to extract the top 20 keywords and the connection to clusters subsequently established after they were categorized into three main service categories: control, safety, and saving (Table 1) with R.

Table 1. Number of consumer reviews by home IoT service categories

	Service	F (%)	N (%)
Control	Electric power controller	1,879 (38.1)	2,414 (48.9)
	Electric light controller	443 (9.0)	
	Temperature controller	92 (1.9)	
Safety	Monitoring home situations with cameras and smartphones	948 (19.3)	2,303 (46.7)
	Remote control of gas valves (locking)	688 (14.0)	
	Alerting when door or window is opened	437 (8.9)	
	Monitoring automatic door lock system	230 (4.7)	
Saving	Checking power consumption	215 (4.4)	215 (4.4)
Total			4,932 (100)

3 Results

First, the CONCOR analysis revealed four clusters based on attributes of the 100 most frequently used keywords (Fig. 1). The first cluster was named "control for convenience" and included "power supply," "smart phones," "remote," "operation," "setting," "control," "automatic," "reservation," "simple," "convenience," and "surprising." The second was "safety from intruders" and included "going to work," "dual-income households," "office," "alone," "children," "pets," "inside of house," "guard," "check," "observation," "vacation," and "long-term." The third group of attributes was "safety from user's carelessness" and included "gas," "lock," "electric light," "danger," "forgetfulness," "remember," and "mind." The fourth was "energy and cost saving" and included "prevention," "electric charge," "effect," "helpful," "attention," "habit," "saving," and "reduction."

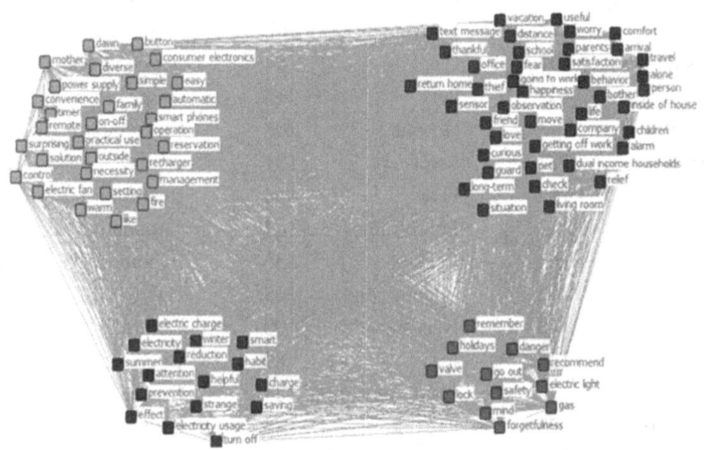

Fig. 1. Results of CONCOR analysis and visualization

Second, the cross-analysis of the 20 most frequently used keywords in each service category can be summarized in terms of three features of home IoT: context of use, functions, and benefits (see Table 2 and Figs. 2, 3 and 4).

Context of Use. Frequently used words in reviews about control and safety services were "go out," "going to work," "outside," and "forgetfulness." Reviews about safety services mentioned protection concerns, such as "children," "pets," "parents," and "alone." Furthermore, some reviews about saving services used keywords related to the seasonal cycles, such as "summer," "air conditioner," and "cumulative tax."

Functions. "Check" was a frequently used keyword for all three service categories. Specific actions such as "turn off," "setting," and "control" were recurrent in reviews about control and saving services.

Benefits. The most frequently used keywords in reviews about control services were "convenience" and "saving"; those about safety services were "relief," "convenience," and "safety"; and those about saving services were "saving" and "convenience."

Table 2. Top 20 keywords in consumer reviews

Rank	Control		Safety		Saving	
	Keyword	Frequency	Keyword	Frequency	Keyword	Frequency
1	Convenience	545	Relief	475	Electric charge	112
2	Electricity	515	Check	365	Electricity	73
3	Saving	337	Worry	315	Saving	53
4	Power supply	322	Children	286	Check	47
5	Check	212	Convenience	267	Summer	37
6	Outside	201	Gas	254	Air conditioner	36
7	Worry	193	Pets	219	Usage	30
8	Go out	193	Go out	208	Convenience	25
9	Forgetfulness	192	Safety	181	Worry	23
10	Children	189	Fear	154	Real time	23
11	Turn off	183	Forgetfulness	144	Cumulative tax	16
12	Electric charge	160	Parents	136	A bomb like	12
13	Setting	152	Recommend	105	Habit	11
14	Timer	140	Necessity	90	Control	11
15	Going to work	135	Life	89	Life	9
16	Relief	125	Inside of house	87	Recommend	9
17	Necessity	123	Outside	86	Estimate	8
18	Automatic	117	Going to work	80	Useful	7
19	Electric light	115	Alone (single)	76	Winter	7
20	Electric fan	106	Behavior	70	Achieve	7

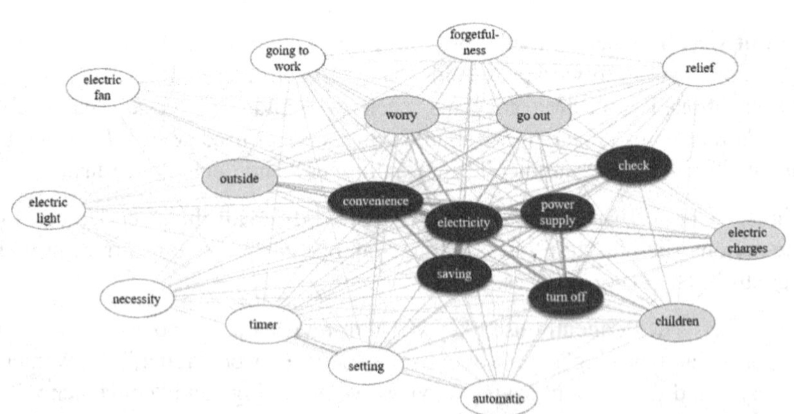

Fig. 2. Top 20 keywords in reviews about control services

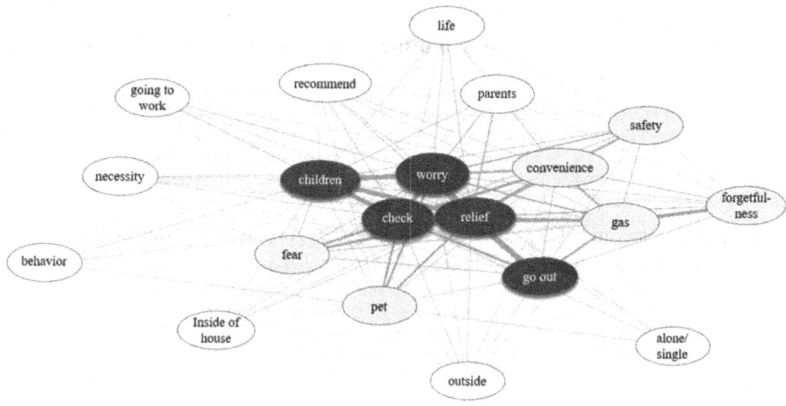

Fig. 3. Top 20 keywords in reviews about safety services

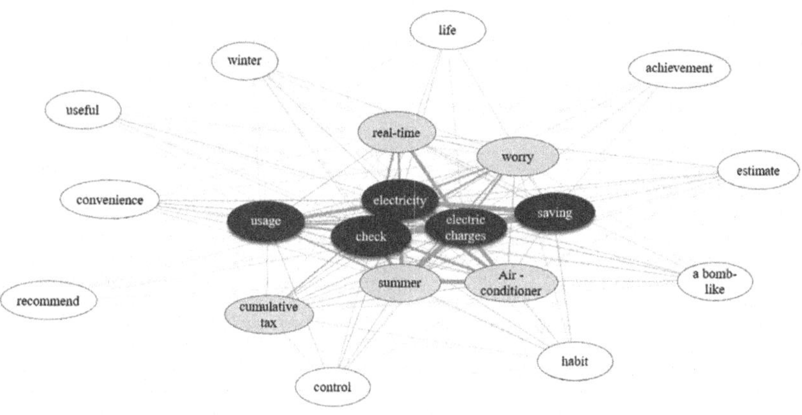

Fig. 4. Top 20 keywords in reviews about saving services

4 Conclusions

These results demonstrate that many consumers who use home IoT services positively experience a more convenient, safe, and economical life by using check and control functions in various situations. In particular, the frequency of the keyword "recommend" was relatively high in reviews about safety and saving services that contribute to the mitigation of risks and prevention of losses. Despite the growth of the home IoT market, consumers found themselves experiencing only convenience, savings, and safety offered by the service. Accordingly, in designing these home IoT services, it is necessary to maximize the emotional satisfaction of consumers, rather than provide them with a simple functional benefit. Further research should therefore be conducted to maximize consumer satisfaction.

References

1. Ministry and Science and ICT. http://www.msit.go.kr. Accessed 11 Mar 2018
2. LG Uplus. http://www.uplus.co.kr. Accessed 11 Mar 2018

Text Mining of Online News and Social Data About Chatbot Service

Yunjik Jeong, Jaehye Suk, Jihyung Hong, Dongmin Kim, Kee Ok Kim, and Hyesun Hwang(✉)

Sungkyunkwan University, Seoul, South Korea
h.hwang@skku.edu

Abstract. The growth in World Wide Web (WWW) has made it difficult for any user to access the information they require, quickly and simply. With such demands and artificial intelligence technology advances, many companies have recently launched chatbot services. A chatbot can be considered a question–answer system in which experts provide knowledge on users' behest. It often acts as a personal assistant also. Collaboration between artificial and human intelligence is necessary to increase and improve the ease of user interactions with systems. If it does, the chatbot may progress to a real virtual human over time. This study has tried to investigate the issue of and consumers' reactions to chatbot services through online news and social media data. Through text mining, this study analyzes the positive and negative expressions about chatbot services. Ultimately, this study will be useful for future research on consumer satisfaction with chatbots. This paper can also possibly analyze and seek implications of the online news and social media perspective.

Keywords: Chatbot service · Text mining · Online news media
Social media

1 Introduction

A chatbot is a software designed to simulate an intelligent conversation with a human partner [1]. With improvement in data mining and machine learning techniques, better decision-making capabilities, availability of corpora, and robust linguistic annotation/processing tool standards such as XML and its applications, chatbots have become more practical and gained many commercial applications. Many companies are integrating chatbots into their websites to provide a better user experience. In South Korea, many companies have recently launched chatbot services in various industries such as finance, airlines, manufacturing, and food industries. Consumers have shown interest in launch of chatbot services, and the mention of chatbots has also increased in various articles and on social media.

This study investigated how people feel about chatbot services, inquired the buzz volume of chatbot services on online news and social media in South Korea, and compared positive and negative keywords revealed in each media. Analyzing the chatbot services online text data enabled the investigation of the emerging attributes and factors that must be considered in its future service development.

C. Stephanidis (Ed.): HCII Posters 2018, CCIS 850, pp. 429–434, 2018.
https://doi.org/10.1007/978-3-319-92270-6_61

2 Method

This study classified as positive or negative the top 10 keywords collected from online news and social media data through text mining, also known as text data mining [2] or knowledge discovery from textual databases [3]. It generally refers to the process of extracting interesting and non-trivial patterns or knowledge from unstructured text documents and can be viewed as an extension of data mining or knowledge discovery from (structured) databases [4].

Text data were collected from three online news media and four social media using Trendup 3.0, which is a big online data collection engine. From January 1, 2016 to December 31, 2017, 1,438 news articles and 15,687 social media mentions were collected; R 3.4.1 was used to analyze.

3 Results

The results were as follows:

First, we extracted the most frequently mentioned industries regarding chatbot services in South Korea. The result shows that financial businesses were mentioned most, followed by communication businesses, as shown in Fig. 1.

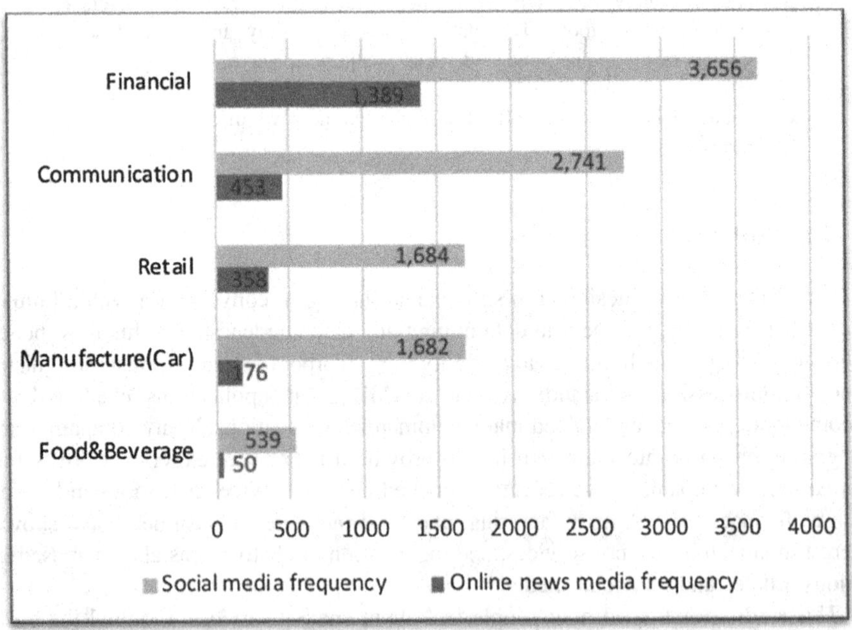

Fig. 1. Top five online text data frequencies of chatbot service industries in Korea

Second, the number of online texts has been gradually increasing since 2016, as shown in Fig. 2. In particular, there was a sharp increase during the third quarter of 2016 when there was the major issue of Microsoft's Tay chatbot making racist and misogynistic comments.

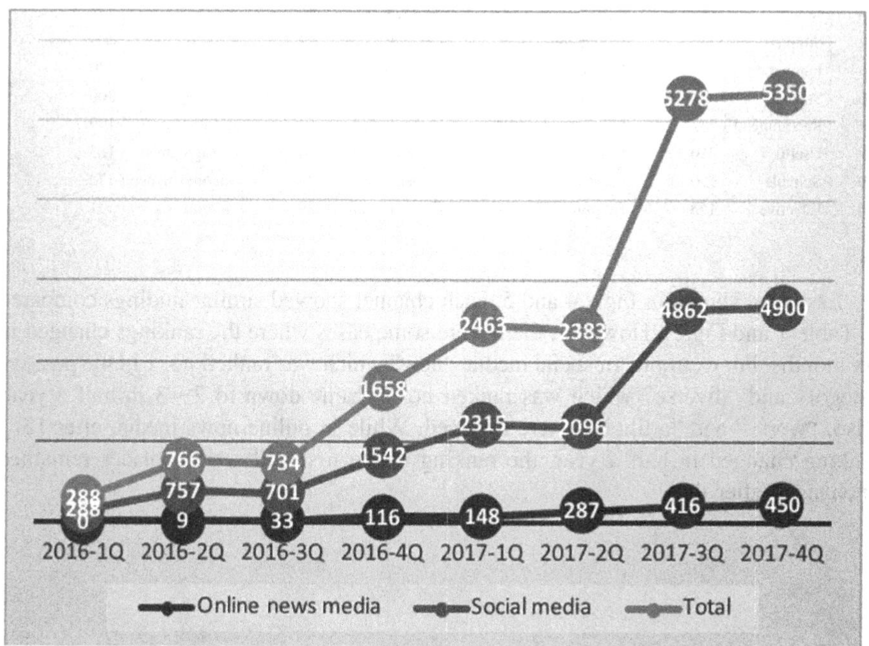

Fig. 2. Online text data volume of chatbot services

Third, as shown in Table 1 and Fig. 3, the most frequently mentioned words on online news media and social media were compared. In positive words, "convenient" was the most frequently mentioned followed by "fast" in online news media, whereas on social media "new" was the most frequently mentioned feature followed by "diverse." The positive words in the two sources were almost similar and most of the extracted words related to functional terms. In negative words, "dry" was the most frequently mentioned word in online news, whereas on social media, it was "worry." In both sources of online text, the artificial features of chatbot services was in second place by frequency of use. The negative words in online news such as "difficulty" and "rude talk" revealed inconvenience and dissatisfaction with functional aspect of chatbot, while the negative words in social media such as "worry" and "doubt" revealed distrust of the chatbot.

Table 1. Word frequency

Rank	Positive word				Negative word			
	Online news media		Social media		Online news media		Social media	
	Word	Frequency	Word	Frequency	Word	Frequency	Word	Frequency
1	Convenient	979	New	3407	Dry	164	Worry	940
2	Fast	680	Diverse	3162	Artificial	103	Artificial	860
3	New	558	Fast	2700	Inconvenience	86	Impossible	441
4	Simple	530	Innovation	1685	Difficult	79	Complicated	403
5	Innovation	501	Necessary	1636	Childish	72	Illegality	220
6	Smart	381	Simple	609	Expensive	70	Lacking	200
7	Recommend	357	Suitable	519	Bad influence	64	Doubt	199
8	Useful	310	Easy	447	Rude talk	54	Disappointed	183
9	Suitable	190	Close	444	Unnecessary	49	Inconvenience	172
10	Effective	155	Helpful	420	Complicated	39	Wrong	131

Lastly, as shown in Figs. 4 and 5, each channel showed similar findings compared to Table 1 and Fig. 3. However, there were some cases where the rankings changed in six months. For example, in social media, "new" which was ranked no. 1 in the positive category and "diverse" which was ranked no. 2, came down to 2~3 in half a year. Also, "worry" and "artificial" were reversed. While in online news media, after 1~2 ranking changed in half a year, the ranking in the first and second places remained unchanged after that.

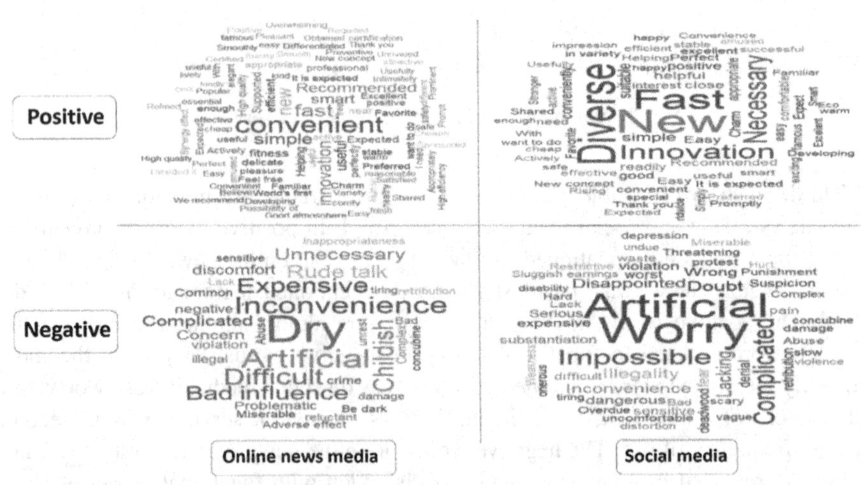

Fig. 3. Word frequency cloud

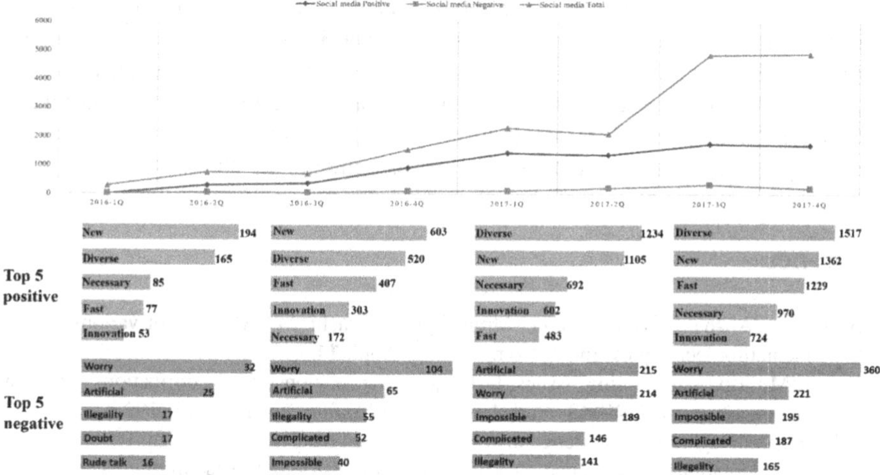

Fig. 4. Half yearly top 5 positive and negative words in social media

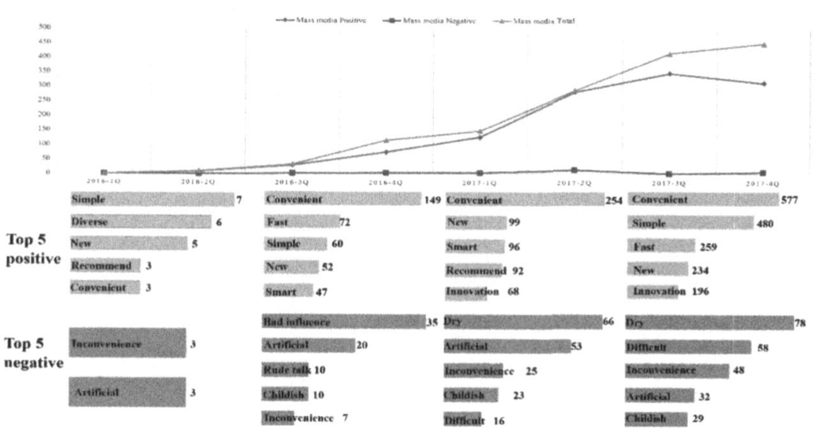

Fig. 5. Half yearly top 5 positive and negative words in online news media

4 Conclusion

These results demonstrate that the number of comments on chatbots has continuously increased over time and revealed a lot of words that were overwhelmingly positive about chatbots. Chatbot services mentioned in online news and social media had the merit of being convenient, fast, smart, useful, and helpful for consumers. Negative words, on the other hand, took up only a small percentage. But the keyword "dry" is what we should pay attention to. Consumers who mentioned chatbot services negatively hope chatbot will be more like humans. In this regard, chatbot services need to be designed to provide not only functional benefits but also emotional and more humanlike values to consumers. Even though chatbot services deliver great values to consumers that are basically based on technological attributes, these functional benefits, on the other hand, may increase consumer resistance to adopt these new technological services. Therefore, service designers should be aware of the fact that consumers' perceptions on these services are shaped by their cumulative experiences that are affected by not only instrumental aspects but also emotional values.

References

1. Aditya, D., Alisha, S., Darshana, G., Mrunmayi, D., Prachi, M.: A survey of various chatbot implementation techniques. Int. J. Comput. Eng. Appl. **11**, 1–7 (2016)
2. Hearst, M.: Text data mining: issues, techniques, the relationship to information access. In: Presentation Notes for UW/MS Workshop on Data Mining, pp. 112–117 (1997)
3. Feldman, R., Dagan, I.: Knowledge discovery in textual databases (KDT). In: Proceedings of the First International Conference on Knowledge Discovery and Data Mining (KDD 1995), Montreal, pp. 112–117 (1995)
4. Fayyad, U., Shapiro, G., Smyth, P.: From data mining to knowledge discovery: an overview. In: Advances in Knowledge Discovery and Data Mining, pp. 1–36. MIT Press, Cambridge (1996)

Facilitating Analysis of Mass Media Influence Through Content Analysis and Emotional Computing

Stefanie Niklander(✉)

Universidad Autónoma de Chile, Av. Pedro de Valdivia, Santiago, Chile
stefanie.niklander@uautonoma.cl

Abstract. During the last years, different HCI applications have successfully employed sentimental, emotional, and affective computing algorithms for solving various recognition, interpretation and simulations tasks related to the study of human affects. In this paper, we combine content and sentimental analysis to facilitate the understanding of how mass media may influence and/or control a given information context. We employ as case study the army and police corruption information. We analyze the speeches constructed by the press and the comments that users post on the mass medias web sites. Interesting results are obtained where all topics that readers visibilize and/or invisibilize when constructing their representations about the study cases are precisely detected.

Keywords: Sentimental analysis · Content analysis · Social networks

1 Introduction

During the last years, different HCI applications have successfully employed sentimental, emotional, and affective computing algorithms for solving various recognition, interpretation and simulations tasks related to the study of human affects. However, the interpretation of emotions is particularly hard as the many variables involved in the process. For instance, emotions are widely present in the discourse of mass media, which is a key actor in the influence of people opinions and as a consequence in the configuration of universes. This paper focuses on combining content and sentimental analysis to facilitate the understanding of how mass media may influence and/or control a given information context.

Content analysis is a quantitative technique that allows one to reveal the hidden meaning of what is reported by the media; while sentimental analysis –also known as opinion mining– uses techniques from computational linguistics, text analysis and natural language processing to interpret emotions, affects on given corpus. By combining both techniques we are able to study the degree of appropriation by readers of the representations and emotions communicated by the mass media. We employ as case study a large corpus related to the most important corruption cases occurred during the last 3 years in Chile. This kind of case study is relevant as the many emotions involved in. From this corpus, we do not only analyze the speeches constructed by the press, but

C. Stephanidis (Ed.): HCII Posters 2018, CCIS 850, pp. 435–438, 2018.
https://doi.org/10.1007/978-3-319-92270-6_62

also the comments that users post on the mass medias web sites. Interesting results are obtained where all topics that readers visibilize and/or invisibilize when constructing their representations about the study cases are precisely detected. The remainder of this paper is organized as follows: Next section provides the discussion and results followed by conclusions and some directions of future work.

2 Discussion and Results

Corruption scandals have become a new scenario where political actors use these spaces to publicize and make visible their political thinking [1]. However, not only politicians take advantage of these situations, the media also use scandals to increase their sales as some past investigations have pointed out [2]. The economic logic behind these publications leaves very far that vision that conceptualized the media as vigilantes of the public sphere [3]. In this way, whether by economic logic or surveillance, the media have the power to define the agenda. According to the Agenda Setting, the media influence public opinion and the attitude that these have in relation to certain issues [4]. Its authors affirm that the Theory of the Agenda Setting covers more than the well-known affirmation: “the media tell us what to think”.

The Agenda Setting is framed in how the media exert influence on their audiences through a choice of topics that are considered relevant to them [5]. Also part of this theory is the frame or framing attributed to the news. This dimension focuses more on “how to think”, leaving behind “what to do”. Therefore, the framing that has a discursive construction will deliver the guidelines with which the citizen will interpret the information communicated [6]. What is tried with the framing is to prioritize some elements over others, making them easy for citizens to remember. The information consumed by the citizen/user is charged with the framing of the producer of that discursive work; however, the reader will accept that information as a “real fact” [7]. This way in which the media communicate information will have an important weight in society, in the sense that the frames influence the opinions of the recipients, emphasizing values or events that give more importance to certain positions than to others.

Likewise, we maintain that in the production of the news text there would be no random selection. This implies that the producer of the discursive work will always be framing a piece of news according to its computer principles, constructing it with a certain informative bias. The cases that will be analyzed are the following: Milicogate and Pacogate. The first one is a corruption case that was unveiled in 2015. Milico is the colloquial name for military in Chile. Pacogate, is the largest fraud in the history of the country and was unveiled in March 2017. Paco is the colloquial name for the Police in Chile. The latest published news of each of the corruption scandals was analyzed in the portal of the digital newspaper El Mercurio on line (EMOL), for being one of the 3 most read in the country.

When analyzing the news through the Content Analysis, we could see that Emol constantly doubts that the Police officers have committed fraud. We can observe this situation through the constant use of conditional verbs to refer to these issues. In addition, the sources used in the news do not have a critical position against the institution, so we believe that these elections are made according to the editorial line of the media that tends to protect the Armed Forces. Unlike what happens with the police, when analyzing the news of the corruption scandal in the Army, we could confirm that the media is much more critical of the Army. Moreover the media does not incur information hiding techniques at the moment of reporting on this news. Next, we apply emotional computing (via SentiStrength [8]) to the news comments. In the Pacogate corruption scandal, although the media tries to soften the issue, users who comment are very critical of the information disseminated (Table 1).

Table 1. Polarity statistics in Pacogate news-comments

Positive	29.73%
Negative	51.33%
Neutral	18.92%

When analyzing Milicogate's comments, users were even more critical than with the Pacogate case. The difference between valuations can be due to two reasons. One of them is that the Police was the institution most valued by Chileans and the comments may have been influenced by this situation. Another possible explanation is in the media coverage of the case (Table 2).

Table 2. Polarity statistics in Milicogate news-comments

Positive	11.54%
Negative	75%
Neutral	11.46%

The negative comments in Milicogate news have two possible explanations: (1) The Army has been a very questioned institution since the military coup of 1973. (2) The construction of the digital mass media about militaries has been quite critical.

3 Conclusion

In this paper we have studied the combination of sentimental and content analysis, in order to include more topics and enrich the research. We may conclude that sentimental analysis tool is of great help to compare the influence of the digital media information in the social network users. However, to enrich the research, we believe it is necessary to enlarge the corpus in order to obtain definitive results.

References

1. Thompson, J.B.: El escándalo político. Poder y visibilidad en la era de los medios de comunicación. Paidós, Barcelona (2001)
2. Lawrence, R.G., Bennett, W.L.: Rethinking media and public opinion: reactions to the Clinton-Lewinsky scandal. Political Sci. Q. **116**(3), 425–446 (2001)
3. Lasswell, H.: The structure and function of communication in society. In: Bryson, L. (ed.) The Communication of Ideas. Harper, New York (1948)
4. McCombs, M., Shaw, D.L.: The agenda-setting function of the mass media. Publ. Opin. Q. **36**, 176–187 (1972)
5. Rodriguez, R.: Teoría de la Agenda-Setting aplicación a la enseñanza universitaria. Observatorio Europeo de Tendencias Sociales, Madrid (2004)
6. Eyal, C.H., Winter, J.P., Degeorge, W.F.: The concept of time frame in agenda-setting. In: Wilhoit, G.C., DeBock, H. (eds.) Mass Communication Review Yearbook, vol. 2, pp. 212–218. Sage, Beverly Hills (1981)
7. Entman, R.: Framing: toward clarification of a fractured paradigm. J. Commun. **43**(4), 51–58 (1993)
8. Thelwall, M., Buckley, K., Paltoglou, G.: Sentiment strength detection for the social web. J. Am. Soc. Inform. Sci. Technol. **63**(1), 163–173 (2012)

A Tale of Two Earthquakes: Analyzing Social Media Responses in Natural Disasters

Cuauhtémoc Rivera-Loaiza(✉), Francisco J. Domínguez-Mota, María Isabel López-Huerta, and Daniel Santana-Quintero

Facultad de Ciencias Físico-Matemáticas, Universidad Michoacana de San Nicolás de Hidalgo, Ciudad Universitaria, Morelia, Mexico
criveramx@gmail.com, motahoo@gmail.com, i.lopez.huerta.96@gmail.com, dasaqui@gmail.com

Abstract. Social media can be of uttermost importance in providing relief to areas affected by natural disasters. Thanks to the wide availability of mobile devices and the resilience of communication networks, people more than ever use internet-based systems to reach out to people in distress, express sympathy and create ad-hoc emergency lines. In 2017, two major earthquakes affected Mexico in a span of a month: one happened in the southern region of the country, and the second one in the central highlands. Although the response was massive, their economic and social differences were also reflected on social media. This empirical study compares the social media response to these events.

Keywords: Social networks · Twitter · Mexico · Emergency response

1 Introduction

On September 2017, two major earthquakes hit Mexico: one on the 7th with an epicenter close to the southern state of Chiapas (marked with number one in Fig. 1 and the other on the 19th (number 2) in the central plateau of the country, which includes Mexico City and other densely populated centers[1]. The epicenters were located approximately 800 km apart from each other with very strong seismic forces: 8.2 Mw the first one, and 7.1 Mw the latter. Despite the very high intensity of these earthquakes, casualties remained under 320 persons [5,6], although there were severe damages in buildings and roads on those areas.

Mexico is geographically located in one of the most active seismic zones in the world. Particularly on its western side, the country rests over the Cocos, Pacific, Rivera and North American plates [9] which are in constant motion. The aforementioned tectonic plates are regularly causing earthquakes, most of negligible effect, almost every day of the year.

[1] Sistema Sismológico Nacional, http://www2.ssn.unam.mx:8080/sismos-fuertes/.

C. Stephanidis (Ed.): HCII Posters 2018, CCIS 850, pp. 439–443, 2018.
https://doi.org/10.1007/978-3-319-92270-6_63

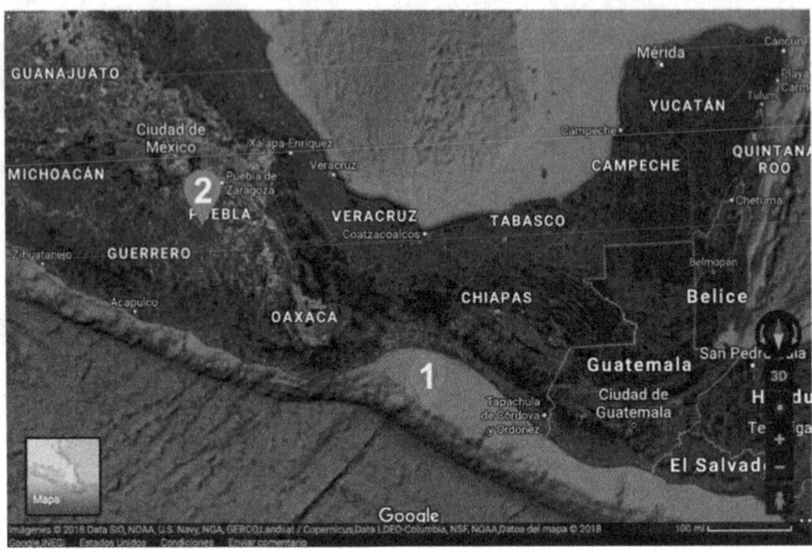

Fig. 1. September 7th, 2017 earthquake (1) and September 19th, 2017 earthquake (2).

In contemporary Mexico, there have been massive affections caused by earthquakes. Coincidentally, also on September 19th, 1985 there was an earthquake that has the record of the most destructive in the history of Mexico, with a magnitude of 8.1 Mw and which caused more than 9,000 deaths and major infrastructure affectations, particularly n Mexico City [8].

2 Social Media Activity During the September 7th and 19th Earthquakes

According to [3], in 2016 47% of Mexican homes had an internet connection and 73.6% of people over 6 years old in the country had a smartphone. However, the states where the September 7th earthquake occurred (Oaxaca and Chiapas) are the ones with the least internet access in the country, whilst two of the states most affected by the September 19th earthquake (Mexico City and Morelos) are above the national average (Fig. 2). It must also be noted that both Oaxaca and Chiapas are at the bottom of GDP distribution in Mexico [1].

As expected, social media activity was very intense in the aftermath of those events and was vital in disseminating very important information for everyone involved. Social networks such as Facebook, Twitter and WhatsApp were flooded with posts regarding the earthquakes. They were particularly useful for the coordination of all the support networks and on a personal level to keep track of friends and family living in the affected areas. For our research purposes, we focused in analyzing the information generated on Twitter. As of 2017, Twitter is one of the most prominent social network in the country [7] with more than

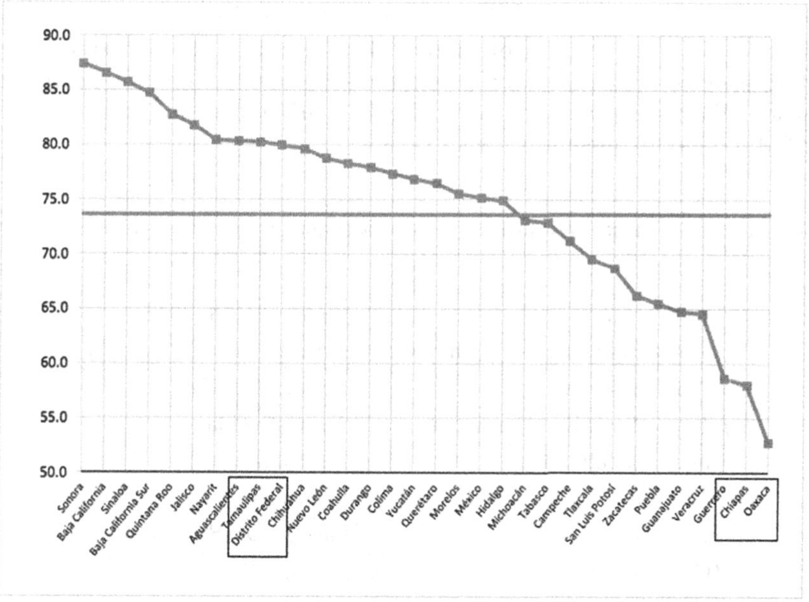

Fig. 2. Percentage of mobile internet access by state in Mexico

nine million active users in Mexico alone, and was extensively used during the earthquakes.

However, as in other regions of the world that have experienced natural events as these ones there are several problems attached to all this flow of data coming from social networks, such as information overload, questionable speed of information delivery, difficulties of processing information in a non-standard format from different sources and in various languages, the complexity of managing volunteer communities and the very limited value of using information at the street level [2].

3 Tweets Filtering

Immediately after the September 7th earthquake we began collecting tweets that were pertinent to this event. We used a linux machine to constantly monitor tweet activity originated in Mexico. As [4] mentions, when a disaster occurs, time is limited and safety is in ques- tion, so people need to act quickly with as much knowledge of the situation as possible. It is becoming more common for affected populations and other stakeholders to turn to Twitter to gather information about a crisis when decisions need to be made, and action taken.

The trending topic for these tweets were by far related to the seismic phenomenon. Those tweets were clustered based on their hashtags[2], and after that

[2] A hashtag is a keyword or a phrase used to describe a topic or a theme in Twitter.

we ordered them based on their frequency. We decided to let the computer gather tweets during the rest of the month to check on the persistence of the hashtags selected. Unfortunately, during the same month the second earthquake happened. We then proceeded to apply the same procedure to this event to identify the most frequent hashtags (Table 1).

Table 1. Hashtags most used during the two earthquakes in Mexico during September 2017.

September 7th, 2017	September 19th, 2017
Oaxaca and Chiapas Earthquake	Central Mexico Earthquake
#PrayForMexico	# AyudaCDMX
#TacolaArepaEstaContigo	# SomosPuebla
#Porculpadeltemblor	# revisamigrieta
#Juchitan	#Rebsamen
#Oaxacatenecesita	#PartidosDenSuDinero
#Centrosdeacopio	#verificado19s
#earthquake	#HoyporMorelos
#Temblor	#jojutla
#Hoypido	#tuiterosunidos

During the first event, most tweets were sent to express solidarity (like those with the *#PrayforMexico* or *#TacoLaArepaEstaContigo* hashtags. Tweets coming from the affected areas were less prominent and sparse. Reports on telecommunication disruptions suggest that most inhabitants with mobile or wired internet access before the earthquake could not immediately communicate their well being or current needs.

Even when the state of emergency in southern Mexico was still active, the focus on Twitter turned completely to the event in Central Mexico on September 19th. Right after the event the tweets began to be sent, overwhelmingly coming from Mexico City, and the states of Puebla and Morelos (the states more affected during this event). The hashtags associated with those tweets were noticeably different in the sense that they served as the basis for the creation of a support network for people in distress (*#AyudaCDMX*). There was also an immediate call for government accountability (*#revisa mi grieta, #PartidosDenSuDinero*) through the tweets.

4 Future Work

The first phase of our work consisted in gathering tweets that would be filtered to search for those related to earthquakes in Mexico. Our server has been retrieving tweets ever since the September 7th earthquake, and during the course of our research another major seismic event hit Mexico: on February 13th a 7.2 Mw earthquake with an epicenter close to the Oaxaca coast, affecting the same zones as the September 7th one. We applied the same heuristics to the new bank of data, identifying hashtags and ordering based on their frequency. The next phase in our research aims to automatize this process and embed sentiment and trend analysis for tweet classification, which we hope will help for better decision making in the event of an emergency.

References

1. Consejo Nacional de Evaluación de la Política de Desarrollo Social: Medición de pobreza en méxico (2016). https://www.coneval.org.mx/SalaPrensa/Comunicadosprensa/Documents/Comunicado-09-Medicion-pobreza-2016.pdf
2. Dugdale, J., Van de Walle, B., Koeppinghoff, C.: Social media and SMS in the Haiti earthquake. In: Proceedings of the 21st International Conference on World Wide Web, WWW 2012 Companion, pp. 713–714. ACM, New York (2012). https://doi.org/10.1145/2187980.2188189
3. Instituto Nacional de Estadística y Geografía: Estadísticas a propósito del día mundial de internet (17 de mayo) (2017). http://www.inegi.org.mx/saladeprensa/aproposito/2017/internet2017_Nal.pdf
4. Olteanu, A., Vieweg, S., Castillo, C.: What to expect when the unexpected happens: social media communications across crises. In: Proceedings of the 18th ACM Conference on Computer Supported Cooperative Work & #38; Social Computing, CSCW 2015, pp. 994–1009. ACM, New York (2015). https://doi.org/10.1145/2675133.2675242
5. Secretaría de Gobernación.: Reporte preliminar por sismo magnitud 7.1 (2017). https://www.gob.mx/segob/prensa/reporte-preliminar-por-sismo-magnitud-7-1?idiom=es
6. Secretaría de Gobernación: Sesiona comité nacional de emergencias y presenta balance preliminar tras sismo de 8.2 (2017). https://www.gob.mx/segob/prensa/continuan-los-trabajos-de-ayuda-a-la-poblacion-tras-sismo-de-8-2
7. Statista: Reach of leading social networks in Mexico as of April 2017 (2017). https://www.statista.com/statistics/449869/mexico-social-network-penetration/
8. Universidad Nacional Autónoma de Mexico: El sismo del 19 de septiembre de 1985 (1985). https://web.archive.org/web/20120605040701/http://secre.ssn.unam.mx/SSN/Doc/Sismo85/sismo85inf.htm
9. Zúñiga, F.R., Suárez, G., Figueroa-Soto, Á., Mendoza, A.: A first-order seismotectonic regionalization of Mexico for seismic hazard and risk estimation. J. Seismol. **21**(6), 1295–1322 (2017). https://doi.org/10.1007/s10950-017-9666-0

Facebook Reactions: Impact of Introducing New Features of SNS on Social Capital

Rama Adithya Varanasi[1(✉)], Elaine Dicicco[2], and Andrew Gambino[3]

[1] Department of Information Science, Cornell University, Ithaca, USA
rv288@cornell.edu
[2] Department of Psychology, Pennsylvania State University, State College, USA
[3] College of Communications, Pennsylvania State University, State College, USA

Abstract. Receiving feedback from connections is an important aspect of Social Network Sites (SNS). 'Likes' in Facebook (FB) is one such feature which allows users to receive feedback for their posts. However, due to likes restrictive ability in expressing feedback, FB released a new feature called 'Reactions'. In this paper, we conducted a between-subjects experimental study (N = 44) that compares the effects of Facebook likes and reactions on perceived social capital. The results suggest that users who received reactions on their posts perceived higher levels of bridging and bonding social capital. Additionally, the effect of novelty was shown to be a mediator of these effects on social capital. These results help us understand the relationship maintenance, group cohesions, and user benefits of introducing a new feature into an SNS ecosystem.

Keywords: Social networking sites · Facebook groups
Reactions and likes · Social capital · Novelty

1 Introduction

The Social Networking Sites (SNS) arms race has seen constant evolution, with individual features being consistently introduced that engage users and aid them in maintaining online relationships. SNS is a homogeneous system composed of many features which allow users to interact with each other. One such feature is FB 'likes' which allow users to express and receive positive feedback on their content. Recently, Facebook has released a new feature in Facebook called 'reactions.' The reactions feature affords a more varied reaction to posts than likes-users can select "love", "haha", "wow", "sad", and"angry" in addition to the like in response to another user's post. Previous studies have shown that receiving likes leads to positive relational outcomes [1]. In this paper, we build upon those studies by exploring the effects of FB reactions. In a between-subjects experiment, we show that users who received feedback in the form of reactions (as opposed to likes) showed a significant difference in their perceived bridging and bonding social capital. Furthermore, we find that novelty is a key mediator in the relationship between feedback and perceived social capital.

C. Stephanidis (Ed.): HCII Posters 2018, CCIS 850, pp. 444–451, 2018.
https://doi.org/10.1007/978-3-319-92270-6_64

2 Background

2.1 Facebook Likes and Reactions

SNS use has been extensively studied to understand how users in the online ecosystem maintain relationships. However, studying use or a cluster of variables together makes it difficult to discern individual effects of specific technological features. Recently, research in the SNS domain has shifted to effects of more specific features like comments, likes and wall posts [9]. As [9] noted, studying SNS at the feature level allows researchers to capture granular diversity among users which is obscured at the SNS level. The feature of Facebook likes has been studied prevalently in the context of providing support and increasing online relationship maintenance. For example, [1] found that receiving direct communication such as FB likes increases user's perceived bridging social capital, thereby improving relationship maintenance. Additionally, [4] argued that engaging with one's Facebook connections using activities such as 'likes' builds trust among relationships and hence social capital [4]. Facebook reactions, on the other hand, are new Facebook features which can be used to provide more diverse emotional feedback towards the posts. They provide users with an opportunity to leave the additional feedback of love', 'haha', wow', 'angry' and 'sad'. Given this added functionality, it behooves researchers to study the independent effect that Facebook reactions may have on users.

2.2 Novelty

Considering the dynamic nature of current information systems, the effects of the general newness of features is a bit understudied. As [12] noted, a perception that a feature is novel can in and of itself have effects on user experience. Given that this study took place very soon after the introduction of Facebook reactions (introduced February 24th, data collected April 12th 2016), it allowed us to capture the effects of a novel feature, which is assumed to decrease over time [7]. Given the sparse amount of research on novelty, we are left to wonder about their effects and direction. However, given user's propensity for new products, we do posit perceived novelty as a mediating link between the technological feature and the perceived effects [12,13].

2.3 Social Capital

Social capital can be defined as benefits derived and accumulated from relationship existing between different people in various social scenarios [2]. In the context of social networks, social capital is considered a process of forming positive bonds and trust in relationships amongst people in online spaces [3]. Social capital generally takes two forms, bridging and bonding. Bridging social capital refers to external relations formed between individual of different backgrounds, whereas bonding social capital refers to close relations and usually exist between strongly knit communities [15]. Additionally, bridging social capital help users in feeling part of bigger community while bonding social capital involves strong ties and emotional support. SNSs also afford users the opportunity to expand and improve their social networks, by enabling socially relevant interactions. Thus, the study of social capital in SNS is quite prevalent and extends to a diverse range of topics [10]. Facebook usage, cultural background, and various affordance provided by Facebook [11] have been found to be related to bridging social capital. First, very few studies have found a positive relationship between an SNS variable and bonding social capital [8]. Second, there is a need for additional research on the individual features of SNS like Facebook reactions and their associated effect on social capital. This study reveals the specific impact of likes and reactions on a user's perceived social capital. Based on the literature reviewed above, we present two research questions for our study.

RQ1 - *What are the effects of FB reactions on the perceived bonding and bridging social capital?*

RQ2 - *Does novelty mediate the relationship between Facebook reactions and bridging & bonding social capital?*

3 Methods

To answer the aforementioned research questions, we conducted a between-subjects experiment. Exposure to feedback in the form of likes and reactions came within a controlled Facebook group. A total of 44 participants were recruited from a large east-coast university for this study. The participants constituted both undergraduate and graduate students from two separate classes. The average age of the participants was 26.5 years old. Participants identified as 71% White, 14% Asian or Asian American, 9% Latino, 4.5% Black, and 2.3% Middle Eastern. Additionally, a group of students (13) was recruited to serve as 'confederates' in the study. Confederate students were recruited from a different department to reduce the chance of prior interaction or familiarity with the experimental participants. All participants were given extra credit for their participation. In addition, they were also provided with a 50$ gift card in the form of lucky draw.

3.1 Procedure

Two FB groups were created called Social Proceedings for (a) Likes and (b) Reactions respectively. The 44 participants were randomly assigned to either the 'likes' group or 'reactions' group regardless of the class from which they were recruited. From here on we refer to these groups as likes/reaction group. The participants in the likes group received only likes whereas the participants in the reaction group only received reactions (wow, love and sad). Each Facebook group was strictly visible to only participants assigned to that respective group. Participants were tasked with posting status updates three times per day in their respective Facebook groups. Their interaction with other group members was structured and controlled by fixing the amount of posting they could do in one day and interacting with other group members by observing how many likes/reaction they got in their posts. Aside from these instructions, participants were free to use Facebook functionalities such as notifications, chat etc.

The following rules were given to participants regarding their individual posts:

1. The post must be about one of the following topics - Music, Movies or Politics.
2. The post needs to contain a personal opinion and be longer than nine words.
3. The post could also be a shared link as long as it satisfied condition number.

Specific topics mentioned in point 1 were chosen as they are topics which students are interested in and post about frequently. The confederate teams used the whole day to like or react to the posts. Confederates had the strict instructions to not to communicate with participants in their group in any form apart from liking or reacting. Confederates were provided with the actual motivation of the study to make the idea more concrete. The amount of feedback given to each post was controlled and documented (Refer to appendix). As a participant posted, the confederates gave a specific amount of predetermined feedback. The amount of feedback given was randomly determined. This process of experiment participants posting in their appropriate groups and confederate group responding with likes or reactions to the posts lasted for two days. The study spanned across two days. At the end of each day the participants were tasked with observing the Facebook group.

As instructed, participants interacted with the others posts by the notifications they received (a) when other participants posted on the group or (b) when they received likes/reactions. The participants were told that the study's goal was to understand how new users of Facebook interact with the posts in a Facebook group. At the end of the second day the participants completed a post study questionnaire, which lasted approximately 15 min.

3.2 Social Capital

Social capital was measured using an adapted version of Williams's Internet social capital scale. The instrument is a 10-item, five-point, likert-type scale that measures (a) bridging and (b) bonding social capital. The items were slightly altered, by adding words such as "in the FB group" to correctly identify the network. Bridging social capital example items include: Interacting in FB group...made me want to try new things. Participants were asked to rate their agreement with the statement from 1 (strongly disagree) to 5 (strongly agree). The bridging sub-scale showed high reliability ($\alpha = 0.86$). Example items for the bonding social capital include: When I feel lonely, there are several people on the Facebook group that I could talk to; The people I interacted within the Facebook group would put their reputation on the line for me. The bonding social capital sub-scale showed high reliability ($\alpha = 0.91$).

3.3 Novelty

Novelty was measured using a 10-item, five point, adjective based, and semantic-differential measure adapted from [12]. The instrument contains questions such as: Facebook reactions/Facebook likes are distinct; Facebook reactions/Facebook likes are unique; Facebook reactions/Facebook likes are new. The reliability for this instrument was high ($\alpha = 0.90$).

3.4 FB Use, FB Friends, and FB Attitudes

Prior to participation in the experiment, a pre-test questionnaire was distributed to measure Facebook use, Facebook friends, and Facebook attitude. FB use was measured with the question: In the past week, on average, approximately how many minutes per day have you spent on Facebook? Number of Facebook friends was measured as: How many total Facebook friends do you currently have? The participants were allowed to check Facebook if they wanted to in order to get the details. The FB attitudes measure contained 11 five-point, likert-type scale questions. The scale was adapted from the standardized questions provided by [8]. It included questions such as: I feel I am part of Facebook and I feel out of touch when I haven't logged into Facebook for a while. The users could answer on a five point scale from 1 (strongly disagree) to 5 (strongly agree).

4 Results

In order to test RQ1, a series of ANCOVAs were conducted, controlling for FB use, FB friends, and FB attitudes, on the dependent variables of bridging and bonding social capital. The ANCOVA for bridging social capital showed that participants in the reactions condition (M = 3.18, SD = 0.56) showed significantly higher bridging social capital than those in the like condition (M = 2.71, SD = 0.74), $F(1, 39) = 7.72$, $p = .008$, $\eta p2 = .17$. Additionally, participants in the reaction group (M = 2.06, SD = 0.76) perceived higher bonding social capital as well (Likes, M = 1.56, SD = 0.65), $F(1, 39) = 4.27$, $p = .045$, $\eta p2 = .10$. Overall, we can conclude that receiving Facebook reactions engendered higher levels of both bridging and bonding social capital.

In order to test RQ2, a product of coefficients approach to mediation was adopted [6]. Using model 4 of Hayes PROCESS Macros in SPSS, two models were tested with novelty as the mediating variable between (1) bridging and (2) bonding social capital. For bridging social capital, the indirect effect (reactions novelty bridging) was found to be significant at the 95% CI level (5,000 bootstrapped samples) b = .22, SE = .12, 95% CI = .030, .514. For the relationship between reactions and bonding social capital (reactions novelty bonding), we found the indirect effect to be not significant, 95% CI = −.289, .747. Therefore, the effect of novelty mediates the relationship between reactions and bridging social capital, but not bonding social capital. In summary, we found that the Facebook reactions had positive effects on both bridging and bonding social capital, and furthermore, it appears that feature novelty is a key mediator of the relationship to bridging social capital.

5 Discussion

The present study focused on the affordances of FB reactions compared to those of FB likes. In particular, we examined how the reception of different feedback variants influences social capital in the Facebook group settings. Based on our results it may be said that FB reactions provide a wider set of affordance due to the presence of options like 'wow', 'sad', etc. as well as their novelty. We also found that receiving FB reactions resulted in greater bridging social capital than FB likes, which was mediated by perceptions of the feature as new. Interestingly, we found that FB reactions even led to greater bonding social capital compared to FB likes. This finding is significant because little existing literature on SNS has found a relationship between features/uses and bonding social capital. Furthermore, our work shows that merely receiving reactions can increase feelings of connection with others (i.e., social capital), and that the effect of novelty may lead to feelings of connection.

5.1 Theoretical Implications

The existing literature has established a strong relationship between FB features (e.g., likes, messages) to bridging social capital, but less of a connection has been made to bonding social capital [1,3]. This may be because most FB users' friends consist of more weak ties (friends of friends) than strong ties (family and close friends). Given that the participants in the present study were not likely to be close friends with the confederates, they were likely interacting with weak ties. Weak ties are typically associated with providing new information to others and as sources of bridging social capital [5]. However, [14], suggest that weak ties may provide more support than solely new information - for instance, comments on a post from weak ties provided support to FB users interviewed in Vitak and Ellison's study. They argued that FB lowers barriers to showing support. Given that content posted in the present study was not personal and did not appear to differ between FB reactions or likes groups, we conclude that it is the FB reaction feature itself that allowed users to feel increased trust and support from those who left reactions to their posts. This supports the idea that weak ties can also be sources of bonding social capital, particularly when these weak ties use a new feature to respond to a post. Because novelty did not mediate the relationship between receiving reactions and bonding social capital, there are likely other unmeasured variables that account for this relationship. [4] argued that likes can be thought of as a social grooming activity in that it is a metric of a user's attention to another's post, and that these signals of attention communicate trust. FB reactions appear to be a social grooming practice that can be distinguished from FB likes in the effects they produce for receivers of the reactions or likes. Perhaps positive feelings about users who reacted to participants' posts created perceptions of trust and social support and therefore explain the increased reported bonding social capital of those in the reactions group. Additionally, positive feelings about the self, or feeling validated that the content of their posts garnered a more varied response than a like may also be a potential mediator for bonding social capital. [4] suggested that likes signal the norm of reciprocity. Users may feel more reciprocal attention when they receive reactions compared to receiving likes. Thus, positive feelings about the other users reacting to their posts, positive feelings about the self, or increased attention may be mediators that could explain the relationship between receiving reactions and bonding social capital.

6 Limitations and Future Directions

There were numerous limitations within this study. First, we could not control for any pre-existing relationships that participants may have had with one another before the experiment took place. All participants were from two classes. Although the reactions and likes were from strangers, it is possible that the extent to which participants felt connected to others in the group (bridging social capital) or felt they could trust others in the group (bonding social capital) was affected by their pre-existing relationship that had been created in the classroom context. However, the fact that participants felt any increase in social capital when given reactions compared to likes suggests that the social capital effects with users that participants do know may have been even stronger. One possible explanation could be content of the posts. If the effects of novelty wear down as the time progresses, it is unclear how for long a period of time a feature such as FB reactions would be perceived as novel. A longitudinal study would increase this study's ecological validity as well as further explicate the effect of novelty (and its likely dissipation). However, the benefit of an experimental study is that it provides a stronger case for the reactions feature as causing increases in social capital compared to the likes feature.

7 Conclusion

This study is one of the first to understand the effects of receiving an SNS feature, particularly the FB reactions feature, on the social psychological elements of users. Our study revealed that a novel feature introduced in SNS had a direct effect on bridging and bonding social capital. We also showed that the effects of novelty significantly mediated the relationship between receiving reactions on bridging social capital.

References

1. Burke, M., Kraut, R., Marlow, C.: Social capital on Facebook: differentiating uses and users. In: Proceedings of the SIGCHI Conference on Human Factors in Computing Systems, pp. 571–580. ACM (2011). http://dl.acm.org/citation.cfm?id=1979023
2. Coleman, J.S.: Social capital in the creation of human capital. Am. J. Sociol. **94**, S95–S120 (1988). http://www.jstor.org/stable/2780243

3. Ellison, N.B., Steinfield, C., Lampe, C.: The benefits of Facebook friends: social capital and college students use of online social network sites. J. Comput.-Mediat. Commun. **12**(4), 1143–1168 (2007). https://doi.org/10.1111/j.1083-6101.2007.00367.x
4. Ellison, N.B., Vitak, J.: Social network site affordances and their relationship to social capital processes. Handb. Psychol. Commun. Technol. **32**, 205 (2015)
5. Granovetter, M.S.: The strength of weak ties. In: Leinhardt, S. (ed.) Social Networks, pp. 347–367. Academic Press (1977). https://doi.org/10.1016/B978-0-12-442450-0.50025-0. ISBN 978-0-12-442450-0
6. Hayes, A.F.: Introduction to Mediation, Moderation, and Conditional Process Analysis: A Regression-based Approach. Methodology in the Social Sciences. The Guilford Press, New York (2013)
7. Karapanos, E.: User experience over time. In: Karapanos, E. (ed.) Modeling Users' Experiences with Interactive Systems, vol. 436, pp. 57–83. Springer, Heidelberg (2013). https://doi.org/10.1007/978-3-642-31000-3_4
8. Lampe, C., Ellison, N.B., Steinfield, C.: Changes in use and perception of Facebook. In: Proceedings of the 2008 ACM Conference on Computer Supported Cooperative Work, pp. 721–730. ACM (2008). http://dl.acm.org/citation.cfm?id=1460675
9. Smock, A.D., Ellison, N.B., Lampe, C., Wohn, D.Y.: Facebook as a toolkit: a uses and gratification approach to unbundling feature use. Comput. Hum. Behav. **27**(6), 2322–2329 (2011). https://doi.org/10.1016/j.chb.2011.07.011. http://linkinghub.elsevier.com/retrieve/pii/S074756321100149X
10. Steinfield, C., DiMicco, J.M., Ellison, N.B., Lampe, C.: Bowling online: social networking and social capital within the organization. In: Proceedings of the Fourth International Conference on Communities and Technologies, pp. 245–254. ACM (2009). http://dl.acm.org/citation.cfm?id=1556496
11. Steinfield, C., Ellison, N.B., Lampe, C.: Social capital, self-esteem, and use of online social network sites: a longitudinal analysis. J. Appl. Dev. Psychol. **29**(6), 434–445 (2008). https://doi.org/10.1016/j.appdev.2008.07.002. http://linkinghub.elsevier.com/retrieve/pii/S0193397308000701
12. Sundar, S.S., Tamul, D.J., Wu, M.: Capturing: measures for assessing coolness of technological products. Int. J. Hum.-Comput. Stud. **72**(2), 169–180 (2014). https://doi.org/10.1016/j.ijhcs.2013.09.008. http://linkinghub.elsevier.com/retrieve/pii/S1071581913001328
13. Tokunaga, R.S.: Engagement with novel virtual environments: the role of perceived novelty and flow in the development of the deficient self-regulation of internet use and media habits: novel virtual environments. Hum. Commun. Res. **39**(3), 365–393 (2013). https://doi.org/10.1111/hcre.12008
14. Vitak, J., Ellison, N.B.: 'There's a network out there you might as well tap': exploring the benefits of and barriers to exchanging informational and support-based resources on Facebook. New Media Soc. **15**(2), 243–259 (2013). https://doi.org/10.1177/1461444812451566
15. Williams, D.: On and off the 'net: scales for social capital in an online era. J. Comput.-Mediat. Commun. **11**(2), 593–628 (2006). https://doi.org/10.1111/j.1083-6101.2006.00029.x

An Intelligent and Context-Aware Touring System Based on Ontology

Chian Wang(✉)

National Changhua University of Education,
No. 1, Jin-de Rd., Changhua 500, Taiwan
cwang@cc.ncue.edu.tw

Abstract. With the explosive development of mobile applications, users can find a tremendous amount of travel information with just a few phone taps. However, from the perspective of information quality, most applications lack a well-organized structure that can fit various user needs. On the other hand, it is also important to consider the cultural and historical characteristics of the visited sites, in addition to focusing on sightseeing. The reason is that there are often some specific relationships among the sites. For example, many temples in Taiwan are branched from a root temple. Thus, the presented information should not be limited to a single site at a single time point. A mechanism that can help users to get the desired information more effectively and efficiently is preferred. In this paper, we are going to present an intelligent and context-aware touring system by developing an active recommendation mechanism and application. We will adopt ontology to construct the temporal, spatial, and causality relationships among the tourist attractions. Then, a personalized recommendation mechanism will be developed by integrating context-aware and data mining techniques to make recommendation decisions and "push" the information to the user's mobile devices. In this way, users can get the most appropriate information while sightseeing.

Keywords: Intelligent touring system · Context-aware · Ontology

1 Introduction

In general, tourism not only focuses on the combination of local natural environment and cultural attractions, but also expects users to conduct field visits and learning through live interaction through personal experience and feelings. However, we should not focus solely on collecting information on the current status of attractions during the site visit. We must also consider the connection with the surrounding environment. The implication of the so-called cultural pulse is that the historic and scenic spots between the time and space relations in series to allow users to conduct integrated and comprehensive learning. In terms of timeliness, each historical site has its own story behind the evolution of different ages. In spatiality, there are often some relations between attractions in different geographical locations. Only by introducing the concept of history and literature into the study of tourism can we allow users to understand the past, present and future of the historical sites from a macroscopic perspective, not just

C. Stephanidis (Ed.): HCII Posters 2018, CCIS 850, pp. 452–457, 2018.
https://doi.org/10.1007/978-3-319-92270-6_65

the observation of the scene because the formation of any attraction is by no means. It will not be formed on its own, but accumulated through the evolution of many literary genres. In fact, the pulse of literature and history is based on tourism to carry out a comprehensive extension of time and space, tourism focuses on first-hand information collection, and literature and history pulse is added to the human and cultural evolution of time and space factors.

As mentioned earlier, tourism is a kind of "out of the classroom" practical learning mode. The location, time and route are often not fixed. Therefore, the combination of action learning is an inevitable trend. With the advancement of network technologies and the popularization of mobile devices, the touring environment has also undergone tremendous changes. Through different types of mobile devices such as tablets, smartphones and laptops, users can access information anytime, anywhere, and also have access to instant information services through a guided system or location-based services. In order to resolve these difficulties in order to improve the effectiveness of touring, we will propose a recommendation mechanism in this paper to avoid allowing users to directly face the huge amount of touring information. It will be more friendly by a variety of considerations such as location, environmental sensing information, visiting history, etc. And to obtain more timely and appropriate information so as to enhance the user experiences.

2 Literature Review

At present, ontology has been widely used in many fields such as water exploration [1], social security [2], semantic web [3, 4], and recommendation system [5, 6]. At the same time, ontology can also be inferred between different semantic meaning. For example, through ontological inference, it is known that there is a high degree of relevance between "mobile phone" and "cellular telephones". Ontology is characterized by multiple words to build relationships to show its connotation. While ontology is the concept of a number of different concepts in combination. In general, ontology consists of the following five parts:

(1) Concepts: describe things in specific areas, also known as categories (classes) or entity (entities), such as sports include badminton, running, swimming, and badminton, running, and swimming is a sub-concept of sport. Sub-concepts can be used to define and describe the concept of the higher level in more detail.
(2) Example (instances): all the attributes and relationships concept known as specific thing (particular things), i.e., for the particular example of the concepts, specific examples of the concept may be expressed.
(3) Characteristics (attributes): also known properties or property values, and to the concept described, such as color, weight and the like.
(4) Association (relations): for explaining the relationship between the rules and examples with occasional instance concept.
(5) Constraints: used to describe the main characteristics of the constraints and rules.

In short, ontology is the use of hierarchical tree structure diagram to describe the relationship and associated projects in the field of knowledge and information between them. The purpose of which will be conceptualized its domain knowledge. Ontology is like vocabulary, used to describe domain-specific knowledge, through conceptualization, even if the language or words are different, the knowledge concept is still the same. Therefore, the system will use ontology to construct the temporal and spatial relationship between cultural and historical sites, and then use the preferences of users and situational awareness data to make recommendations.

3 Ontology Inference Mechanism

In terms of temporal and spatial relationship between the cultural and historical attractions, we will adopt ontology architecture and inference. The term ontology derives from philosophy and was applied to the field of artificial intelligence from about the 1980s to the 1990s. Neches and others have argued that "ontology defines the basic vocabulary and relationships that make up a thematic area, as well as the rules for combining words and relationships" [7]. In other words, ontology conceptualizes domain knowledge and classifies data items into attributes or eigenvalues to analyze the similarity and relevance of data items [8, 9]. W3C (World Wide Web Consortium) in Web-Ontology Working Group also noted that the ontology can be used to describe a variety of different fields of knowledge, and then to compare the results through the conceptualization, consolidation, or correction, so that the semantic. Based on available conceptualization characteristic of ontology, the system will use ontology to construct literature and history relational structure recommendation system, and then use ontology-matching techniques to compare between individuals of the recommended conditions, in order to produce adaptive recommended results. Our idea is to use ontology structure to carry out ontology comparison in order to find out the differences between the sites. We will design the structural similarity matching rules to carry out this part of the work. We can directly use the already defined ontological structure quickly and efficiently to identify the association among the sites, and thus more suitable for real-time travel environment.

According to the functional architecture planning, this system is expected to be divided into five stages, of which the first four stages of the build and associated algorithms focus on the various functional elements of deduction. The final stage will be the actual user experiment and evaluation.

(1) The objectives of the first stage of research are to establish the user's personal information and situational information on the location of the user in order to analyze the characteristics of the user for subsequent recommendations. This stage will combine browsing history, information retrieval, and environmental sensing, in order to establish user profile information.
(2) The second stage is the construction of ontology structure of scenic spot materials as well as the discussion of comparative rules in order to concatenate the relationship between the history of literature of the sites. The result of ontology comparison can be used as one of the bases for the recommendation.
(3) Third stage of focusing on content-oriented build mechanisms of recommendation. At this stage, the system will make use of web mining and data capture

techniques to deal with information in the user profile then the results of the first stage of the building of information similarity comparison, in order to initially determine the recommended content.

(4) The fourth stage builds collaborative filtering recommendation mechanism. The focus at this stage is to make recommendations to integrate the user evaluation.
(5) At this stage we will use practical experience by the user to analyze the effectiveness of the system, and to investigate their acceptance and satisfaction with the results of the recommendation.

4 Ontology Structure Construction and Comparison

The system uses ontology techniques to describe the temporal and spatial relationship between cultural and historical sites, and to deduce the rule of comparison in order to generate recommendations. First of all, the following tasks must be completed in ontology construction of cultural and historical sites.

(1) List important lexical knowledge areas.
(2) Define field category and class relations.
(3) Define attributes and restrictions.
(4) Join the instance.

The reason we use ontology technology is that when a user enters a keyword, it can be through semantic and ontological knowledge of the scope and architecture represented in detail the concept of deduction to avoid inaccuracies in the results due to unclear semantic. In this way, the recommendation can be made according to the real needs of the user and the recommendation can be promoted quality. Another focus of this stage is structural similarity ratio for the purpose of accuracy to strengthen the semantic properties similar alignments, and to explore the potential of semantic ontological structure. We will divide the following steps into structural similarity alignment.

(1) Calculate the similarity between the semantic meaning and the type of the entity according to the constructed ontology structure.
(2) Use of RDF (resource description framework) to compare, as shown in Fig. 1.
(3) Build the matching tree, to record the value of the ratio of the state and structure similarity calculation.
(4) Decompose RDF into the semantic set to establish the aligned index structure.

After constructing the tree structure of RDF, the structural similarity can be calculated by the following formula:

$$\begin{aligned}\mathrm{Sim}_{structure}\left(e_{i1}, e_{j2}\right) &= w_1\mathrm{Sim}_{\mathrm{element}}\left(e_{i1}, e_{j2}\right) + w_2\mathrm{Sim}_{element}\left(F\left(e_{i1}, e_{j2}\right)\right)\\ &+ w_3\frac{\sum_{i=1}^{n}\mathrm{Sim}_{selement}\left(S\left(e_{i1}, e_{j2}\right)\right)}{n}\end{aligned}$$

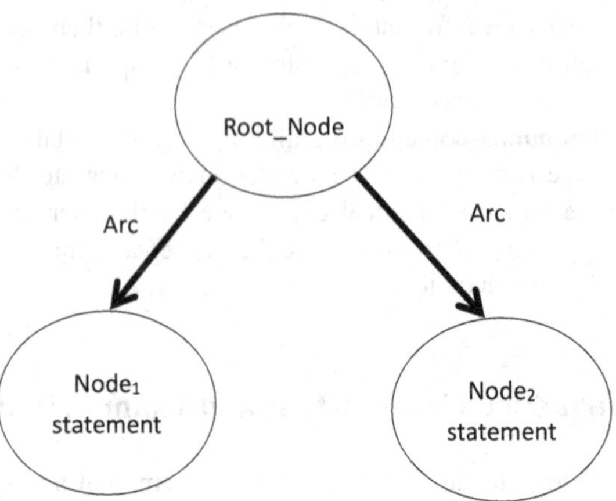

Fig. 1. The resource description framework.

5 Conclusion

The reason we use the aforementioned structural similarity is in accordance with the characteristics of the data item or property to be divided for other classes to build on the structure of the body. The similarities between different ontological structures have the advantage that the similarities and dissimilarities between other ontological structures can be found quickly and effectively by using the already defined ontology structure.

We also conduct a systematic benefit assessment based on the acceptance rate of recommended sites and recommended strength and the user ratings on the recommended materials, which can be obtained from the system record is the most direct and error-free basis to measure the effectiveness of the recommendation mechanism. In addition, we will also use questionnaires to investigate the practicality, ease of use and willingness of users to perceive recommended systems so as to understand whether the recommendation mechanism with situational awareness can really help users to grasp the resources.

References

1. Islam, A.S., Piasecki, M.: Ontology based web simulation system for hydrodynamic modeling. Simul. Model. Pract. Theor **16**(7), 754–767 (2008)
2. Kaza, S., Chen, H.: Evaluating ontology mapping techniques-an experiment in public safety information sharing. Decis. Support Syst. **45**(4), 714–728 (2008)
3. Wang, J., Ding, Z., Jiang, C.: GAOM: genetic algorithm based ontology matching. In: Proceedings of the 2006 IEEE Asia-Pacific Conference on Services Computing (APSCC 2006), pp. 617–620 2006
4. Blanco Fernández, Y., Pazos Arias, J.J., Gil Solla, A., Ramos Cabrer, M., López Nores, M., García Duque, J., Fernández Vilas, A., Díaz Redondo, R.P., Bermejo Muñoz, J.: A flexible semantic inference methodology to reason about user preferences in knowledge-based recommender systems. Knowl. - Based Syst. **21**(4), 305–320 (2008)

5. Li, L.H., Lee, F.M., Chan, S.C.: The blog-article recommendation system(BARS). In: Proceedings of the 2008 IAENG International Conference on Internet Computing and Web Services (ICWS), pp. 771−776 (2008)
6. Yuan, S.T., Cheng, C.: Ontology-based personalized couple clustering for heterogeneous product recommendation in mobile marketing. Expert Syst. Appl. **26**(4), 461–476 (2004)
7. Neches, R., Fikes, R., Finin, T., Gruber, T., Patil, R., Senator, T., Swartout, W.: Enabling technology for knowledge sharing. AI Mag. **12**(3), 36–56 (1991)
8. Guarino, N., Giaretta, P.: Ontologies and knowledge bases, towards a terminological clarification. In: Knowledge Building and Knowledge Sharing, pp. 25−32 1995
9. Weng, S.S., Chang, H.L.: Using ontology network analysis for research document recommendation. Expert Syst. Appl. **34**(3), 1857–1869 (2008)

Author Index

Printed in the United States
By Bookmasters

Printed in the United States
By Bookmasters